KU-821-291

Also by Arnold Schwarzenegger

Arnold: The Education of a Bodybuilder
Arnold's Bodybuilding for Men (with Bill Dobbins)

Also by Bill Dobbins

The Women: Photographs of the Top Female Bodybuilders

THE NEW ENCYCLOPEDIA OF MODERN BODYBUILDING

Arnold Schwarzenegger

WITH BILL DOBBINS

SIMON & SCHUSTER PAPERBACKS

New York London Toronto Sydney

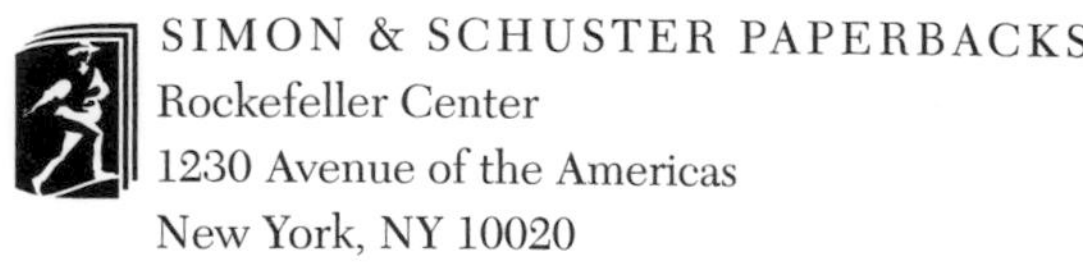
SIMON & SCHUSTER PAPERBACKS
Rockefeller Center
1230 Avenue of the Americas
New York, NY 10020

For information about special discounts for bulk purchases, please contact Simon & Schuster Special Sales: 1-800-456-6798 or business@simonandschuster.com.

Designed by Pagesetters, Inc.

Manufactured in the United States of America

40 39 38 37 36 35 34

The Library of Congress has cataloged the hardcover edition as follows:

Schwarzenegger, Arnold.
The new encyclopedia of modern bodybuilding / Arnold Schwarzenegger with Bill Dobbins.
p. cm.
Rev. ed. of: Encyclopedia of modern bodybuilding, c1985.
Includes index.
1. Bodybuilding. 2. Exercise. 3. Weight training. I. Dobbins, Bill, date. II. Schwarzenegger, Arnold. Encyclopedia of modern bodybuilding. III. Title.
GV546.5.S383 1998
646.7'5—dc21 98-44469
CIP

ISBN-13: 978-0-684-84374-2
ISBN-10: 0-684-84374-9
ISBN-13: 978-0-684-85721-3 (Pbk.)
ISBN-10: 0-684-85721-9 (Pbk.)

ACKNOWLEDGMENTS

I would like to express my great appreciation to all of the bodybuilders in this book, who I think are the greatest bodybuilders in history, and whose cooperation helped to make this book a reality.

Also, my gratitude to all the highly talented and hardworking photographers whose photographs you will find in these pages.

Special thanks to the folks at Simon & Schuster for all their hard work on the new edition; Albert Busek for his unfailing support and encourgement; to Joe Weider for opening his archives to me and providing valuable research material; to Franco Columbu, a true friend and great training partner; to Jim Lorimer for consistently providing great advice; and to Jerzy W. Meduski, M.D., Ph.D., for his nutritional advice.

Thanks to Ronda Columb, Lynn Marks, David Beck, and my assistant Beth Eckstein. And last but not least, thanks to all the people at Weider Publications—Jim Chada, Lisa Clark, Eric Donald, Jeff Feliciano, Bill Geiger, and Peter McGough—for all their hard work on the book.

To my parents,
Aurelia and Gustav,
and my family,
Maria, Katherine, Christina,
Patrick, and Christopher

C O N T E N T S

BOOK FOUR COMPETITION

BOOK FIVE HEALTH, NUTRITION, AND DIET

FOREWORD TO THE 2ND EDITION

Who would have thought that anyone could compile an encyclopedia on bodybuilding and resistance training, let alone one more than eight hundred pages long? After all, how much is there to say about hoisting heavy metal plates? Bodybuilding isn't, as they say, rocket science.

Well, many people take exactly that approach when they begin a bodybuilding program; I know because they're easy to spot at the gym. Such individuals generally load excessively heavy weights on a bar, heave the iron with whatever form it takes to get the weight up (with an extra thrust from the lower back for good measure), and then let the bar come crashing down. That's not bodybuilding! Strong on desire but short on smarts, these folks are either sidelined by an injury or often will give up quickly because they aren't seeing any significant results from all the work they're doing.

The truth is, it doesn't take a Ph.D. to learn the complexities of bodybuilding, but neither does it come as naturally as, say, riding a bike. Heck, the bodybuilding vocabulary is like a foreign language: pyramid training, gastrocnemius, negatives, periodization, instinctive training, spotting. Learning the many distinct elements of resistance training, from the hundreds of unique exercises and variations to understanding how to put together a results-producing workout, all take time and practice. To make progress at the fastest rate possible, you've simply got to know what you're doing.

If you're rich enough to afford $50 (or more) an hour for a personal trainer you might be able to get away with being a bodybuilding dumbbell. Or, for about the price of a single session, you can invest in this encyclopedia and reap a lifetime of gains that'll start with your very next workout.

Many people forget that I, like you, was once a beginner, and started building my body and my career standing in exactly the same position you are right now. If you find that difficult to believe, there's a selection of photos from my teenage years that will show how far I had to come, how much work I had to do. What made me stand apart from my peers, though, was a deep, deep desire to build muscle and the intense commitment to let nothing stop me. Along the way I made countless mistakes because the only guidebooks I had were a couple of Joe Weider's English-language muscle magazines, and I didn't even speak the language! The magazines inspired me to learn English so I could follow my early idol Reg Park's routine. Still, the magazine could teach me only some rudimentary concepts; everything else was done by trial and error.

Experience, however, is the best teacher as long as you learn from your mistakes. When I began, I trained biceps far more intently than I did triceps, a larger muscle group. I pretty much skipped ab training altogether because that era's conventional wisdom dictated that the abdominals received enough stimulation during many heavy compound movements. I put so little effort into calf training in those early years that when I finally came to America, I was forced to redouble my efforts. I even went so far as to cut off the pant legs on my training sweats so that my calves were constantly visible and under scrutiny—a constant reminder to me that my weaknesses deserved greater attention. Nor did we have many machines available; I never used a leg curl or leg extension during my first years as a bodybuilder. Most of all, though, I was handicapped by my lack of knowledge; my catalog of exercises to shape the total body consisted of just a few movements. Fortunately, with this book, you don't have to make the same mistakes I did.

You'll find, as I did, that building muscle builds you up in every part of your life. What you learn here will affect everything else that you do in your life. As you witness the fruits of your labor, your self-worth and self-confidence improve, and these traits will color your work and interpersonal relationships long past your competitive days. I credit bodybuilding with giving me not just physical attributes but also with laying the foundation for everything else I've accomplished—in business, acting, even family. I know I can succeed in anything I choose, and I know this because I understand what it takes to sacrifice, struggle, persist, and eventually overcome an obstacle.

Even today, many of the people I work with comment upon my commitment; when I'm making a movie, I'm ready to do a difficult scene over and over again until we get it right. Why? It all comes back to discipline. If you make a commitment to better your physical health, you'll find the same self-discipline, focus, and drive for success carries through into the rest of your life's activities. Though you may not realize it now, you'll eventually recognize it when you take the same disciplined approach in tackling a particular challenge. That's another reason I'm so enthusiastic about what bodybuilding can do.

This book is not a biography, not the story of my life as a seven-time Mr. Olympia winner or even a history of my life as an actor. (If you're interested, you can find all that elsewhere.) Though I'm known mainly as a bodybuilder-turned-actor and businessman, on various occasions I've been able to take on another role, one that brings me the greatest amount of personal pride, and that's the role of teacher. That's why I published the original encyclopedia in 1985 and have continued my close association with the sport. In the years since that first publication I've been collecting, studying, and revising information for this expanded and updated reference. That I can say I was able to inspire a generation of men and women of all ages to take charge of their health and fitness is truly gratifying. From the couple of dozen students of bodybuilding who heard me give a seminar in the mid-1970s at a Santa Monica gym, to the elementary and high schoolers I tried to empower to exercise when I traveled to all fifty states as chairman of the President's Council on Physical Fitness and Sports, to the less fortunate who compete in the Inner City Games throughout the year and the developmentally challenged who participate in the Special Olympics, to the readers of my weekly syndicated newspaper column and the ones I write in the muscle magazines, to you the reader of this encyclopedia, you are all very much the reason I've undertaken this gargantuan effort. I am indeed grateful that you've chosen me as your teacher.

That I can share with you my greatest passion in the world, which is truly the only real secret to health, longevity, and a better quality of life, has made this book an endeavor of absolute necessity—and joy! Bodybuilding is my roots, and I will continue to promote the sport and spread the word through my work.

I've accumulated more than thirty-five years of bodybuilding experience, including tens of thousands of hours training with the world's top bodybuilders from yesterday, like Bill Pearl, Reg Park, Dave Draper, Frank Zane, Sergio Oliva, and Franco Columbu, to the champions of today, including Flex Wheeler, Shawn Ray, and eight-time Mr. Olympia, Lee Haney. I've studied the writings of the predecessors to modern-day bodybuilding, some of which date back more than a century, including Eugen Sandow's *System of Physical Training* (1894), the United States Army's *Manual of Physical Training* (1914), and Earle Liederman's *Muscle Building* (1924). I've interrogated the world's pre-eminent exercise scientists, researched questions from students at seminars I've given on all the major continents from Africa to Asia to South America to more recent ones I hold each year in Columbus, Ohio—and poured every ounce of that knowledge into this encyclopedia. With this reference book, which is designed for students ranging from rank beginners to competition-level bodybuilders to athletes looking to improve their performance to those who simply want to look better and be healthier, readers are free to pick through the expansive knowledge it's taken me so many years to accumulate.

In one sense, I feel like a doctor on call who is continually asked for expert advice. A skier in Sun Valley asked me recently how to build quad strength and muscular endurance to improve his performance; at a health convention, several people inquired about the latest on the muscle-building properties of creatine; at Wimbledon, a top tennis champion wanted some advice on building his forearm strength; on vacation in Hawaii, a woman came up to me and asked what she could do to lose a hundred pounds of body fat and keep it off; at seminars, young bodybuilders want to know how to put a peak on their biceps and improve their outer-thigh sweep; when speaking to military personnel, I'm commonly asked how to get more out of training with just very basic equipment. Every day I'm asked questions on topics ranging from vitamins A to zinc, to the need for rest and recuperation, to the false promises of performance-enhancing substances. This is why I decided long ago that if I was going to spread the gospel on the benefits of bodybuilding I'd absolutely have to stay current with the material.

That's been no easy chore. Evolution in bodybuilding has occurred at the speed of light, both at the competitive level and among recreational athletes. Those who simply write that off as due to a greater use of anabolic drugs fail to see what's taken place in the industry. Muscle-building exercise, long scoffed at by coaches who claimed it made you muscle-bound and inflexible, has come under intense scrutiny by researchers. In fact, the science of resistance training is really becoming a science as exercise scientists verify what we bodybuilders have been working out by trial and error for years. That's not to say we didn't know what we were doing; on the contrary, early physique champions were pioneers in the health and fitness field, planting the seeds of development for each generation that followed. We coined such phrases as "No pain, no gain," words that every bodybuilder today knows and understands.

Though science is showing us how best to manipulate the variables that make up your training, you cannot discount the importance of environmental factors. I grew up in a poor family in post–World War II Austria, yet those conditions gave me a greater drive to succeed. Developing an instinctive sense about your training is another intangible factor that many top bodybuilders develop. Desire, discipline, and drive all play a role. Science has a hard time quantifying these factors, but their importance is certainly profound. So, too, are your genetics: Some individuals have the bone structure and muscle-fiber makeup to succeed at the competitive level in power sports or bodybuilding. The bottom line is that with bodybuilding, anyone can make improvements and achieve 100 percent of his or her potential, even without the potential to become a world-class athlete.

Still, exercise scientists and medical experts studying the body, as well as researchers in the fields of diet and sports nutrition, are applying the lessons of yesterday to tweak and refine training techniques. If not set in stone, many of the ideas may best be characterized as principles. Ultimately, however, any finding presented by the scientific community must be useful to students of the sport and bodybuilding champions themselves, who are the ultimate test of the validity of such ideas. Applying these truths to achieve results is the practical basis of this encyclopedia. The information that I present on these pages is proved, of practical value, and will also work for you!

Since I last published the encyclopedia, the nature of bodybuilding has undergone an evolution of sorts in a number of ways. A bench press is still a bench press, and a squat a squat. In fact, the execution of various exercises has changed very little, but I've witnessed a number of other very important factors that have. Let me briefly review not just these developments, but how they can be applied to your workout. You'll learn:

- how to structure your workout, whether your goal is to become a physique champion or simply to firm and tighten your body, and how you can effectively target lagging areas;
- how power athletes can adjust repetition speed to build explosive strength;
- which exercises to include for the greatest muscular benefits, and which ones are best left to advanced-level trainees;
- how to put together a workout that emphasizes body-fat control vs. one that maximizes strength, and even how to cycle them to get the best of both worlds;
- how to not only reduce your risk of injury but actually lift more weight by adding a 5- or 10-minute warm-up and light stretching;
- how to get the most out of each rep and each set, taking your muscles to total failure and reaping the greatest benefits in the pain zone;
- how to mix up the training variables when you hit a training plateau;
- when too much enthusiasm will start reversing your muscle and strength gains.

As I mentioned, few exercises are done any differently now than they were twenty years ago. Exceptions: Science has weighed in with a differing opinion on how you should do abdominal movements. The crunch movement, which features a shortened range of motion whereby the pelvis and ribcage are drawn together, is a safer exercise than the common full-range sit-up. The best bodybuilders of my competitive era did have outstanding abdominals from doing sit-ups, but their strong midsections probably saved them from incurring spinal problems. Because lower-back pain afflicts more than three-quarters of all Americans at some point, the sit-up is fairly universally contraindicated. So, I've completely overhauled the abdominal training section to meet current scientific opinion. I've also expanded the list of exercises to include the wide variety of crunch variations.

The basic raw materials of weight training—barbells, dumbbells, and bodyweight exercises—haven't changed much either, but we can't say the same about resistance-training machines, which have traditionally been favored by some users because of the safety factor. Today, dozens of manufacturers vigorously compete with one another, which is radically changing the face of the industry and the sport. Each year new versions of old favorites are becoming increasingly sophisticated and smooth to operate, now closer than ever to mimicking free-weight movements. Some allow you to alter the angle of resistance from one set to the next; others increase resistance on the negative; still others use a computer to vary the resistance. I would expect we'll see even more radical developments over the next couple of decades.

Commercial gyms aren't the only ones to benefit; home gym use has skyrocketed as large, clunky machines have given way to smaller, safer models that don't take a big bite out of the wallet and still fit nicely into a spare bedroom. That's an ideal choice for individuals too busy to make it into the gym.

In terms of nutrition, the raw concept "You are what you eat" still rings true, but don't discount the dramatic changes that have occurred in sports nutrition, either. Sure, science has engineered some super-foods, like firmer tomatoes, and we're now raising fish in so-called farms and leaner meats from ostrich and beefalo, for example. Today, we also know more about the dietary needs of the hard-training athlete and have seen the introduction of some important supplements that aid sports performance.

Let's start with the basic bodybuilding diet. I've seen a thousand and one fad diets come and go, but nearly every bodybuilder I know follows the same basic guidelines that I present in this book. More often than not, a lack of progress in your muscle-building efforts can be linked to nutritional shortcomings in your diet. If I can hijack a phrase from computer technicians, if you put in garbage, you'll very likely get garbage out. I present several commonsense strategies that can work for you. Among the macronutrients, I'm often asked about the role of protein and the key amino acids that support tissue growth, how much you should be consuming in a given day, and how to time your meals for optimal absorption. Fats, mistakenly thought of as an enemy to bodybuilders, who may avoid them at all costs, play an important role in synthesizing key muscle-building hormones and maintaining health.

No discussion on nutrition would be complete without mentioning the most important supplements, some of which have dramatically changed the face of sports nutrition. Creatine is a proven performance enhancer, but a number of other products, including the amino acid glutamine, branched-chain amino acids, and antioxidants, are important to athletes as well.

We also know more about the ways in which nutrients are absorbed into the bloodstream; since not all foods are absorbed at the same rate, the glycemic index was created to measure insulin response, a key anabolic process. Given that a hard workout depletes your muscles of their glycogen stores (basically stored energy), the post-workout meal is especially crucial. Research now tells us what it should contain and how soon you should be refueling after your training session. And who better than top-ranked bodybuilders themselves, who've endured innumerable contest-preparation cycles, to explain the tricks that even the noncompetitive bodybuilder can use to reduce his body fat, even if it's just to look great at the beach.

The field of sports psychology is thriving along with the payroll of milion-dollar athletes. New theories and techniques demonstrate the importance of the mind in training and competition, how to spur motivation and stay focused, and how to set achievable short- and long-range goals. If you have a goal of becoming Mr. Olympia, you'd better start by having a clear vision of your ultimate physique, then follow it up with a plan on how you'll create it. Nothing happens by accident. You won't, for example, become a respected doctor by happenstance; you'll need to plan on years of intensive studies to reach your goal. The same goes with your training.

Once you have your goals clearly in mind, I'll show you how to create your own personal workout routine, but the role of the mind doesn't end there. As it did for me, that vision will inspire you on each burning rep of every set and successively take you one step closer to your goal. But there's more to it than just what goes on in the gym: Dietary and lifestyle considerations will also move you either closer to your desired destination or further away. That's why the mind is so crucial in all sports, including bodybuilding. Your mind must first create the picture, and your training must be in sync with that visualization. As you begin to see changes, you start to feel better about yourself. The result is a self-perpetuating process: You focus your mind to train your body, and the changes that begin to take place impact your mind as well. Dream it, believe it, and you can achieve it!

The exponential growth of bodybuilding has spawned a billion-dollar industry with unlimited career opportunities in health clubs, apparel, equipment, nutritional products, publications and media, physical therapy, personal training and coaching, and other areas. Can you imagine making a living every day from an activity you freely choose to do as a hobby? If that's where you'd like to be, learning all you can about the body and how it works is a great place to start.

Paralleling the changes made in the study of bodybuilding are the ones in society at large. Today, weight training is one of the most popular recreational fitness activities in America, but it certainly wasn't that way some twenty-five years ago. I can remember hearing various coaches and athletes bash muscle-building, claiming it would hinder sports performance. (Gee, I wonder where those guys are now!) Resistance training is being used by all kinds of people today.

From the high schools to colleges and professional sports teams, weight training is helping to create better, stronger, even faster athletes. Sure it takes incredible natural ability to rise to the top of your sport, but without question resistance training provides the winning edge. Baseball slugger Mark McGwire hits the iron regularly even during the season, as does just about every position player in the National Football League. I've even seen members of the NBA's World Champion Chicago Bulls over at Gold's Gym working out while they were in Los Angeles. You can bet they weren't there taking pictures like tourists!

You can strengthen your backhand for tennis, build up your quads for skiing, add valuable height to your vertical leap in volleyball, improve your ability to withstand a hit in soccer, power your stroke and kick in swimming, and improve your strength and stride in sprinting, all with resistance training. What's more, you'll be more injury-resistant should a mishap occur.

Of course, you wouldn't expect a long-distance runner to train like a football player. Choice of exercises and manipulation of the training variables allow each athlete to tailor the activity to individual needs and goals. For some, like boxers and wrestlers who compete in weight classes, or gymnasts who can't afford to significantly increase their bodyweight, strength is critical, but a different type of training is required from traditional bodybuilding. A football lineman, shot-putter, or discus thrower each has his own specific training requirements for his activity. If you play a sport, you'll learn how to customize your workout to meet your sport-specific (and even position-specific) requirements. Still, in the end, no matter whether the athlete is 150 or 250 pounds, strength training is the common thread.

Some occupations demand that personnel pass strenuous physical conditioning that mimics on-the-job conditions. Entrance requirements into the military, fire, and police academies require exacting levels of fitness—in terms of strength, muscular endurance, and aerobic fitness—to ensure everyone's safety and mission effectiveness. This is especially demanding (but by no means impossible) for women, who must train perhaps more vigorously than their male counterparts. Once you're selected for admission doesn't mean you no longer have to stay in shape, either; to that end, police and fire departments are installing weight rooms in their facilities and encouraging their veterans to maintain peak levels of physical conditioning.

Just a few years back during the Gulf war, the *Washington Post* reported that the number one request of servicemen in the Middle East was to have weights sent over so they could keep up their training. To that point, they had been lifting pails full of sand. At that time I was serving as chairman of the President's Council on Physical Fitness and Sports, and I approached a number of large equipment companies seeking donations. In all, we amassed more than four hundred tons of equipment, which General Colin Powell insisted be *airlifted* to the troops. That's how important physical fitness is to some of these guys!

Resistance training is even being used by the elderly. After about age twenty-five you lose about a half pound of muscle for every year of life. Without an appropriate training stimulus, your muscles will eventually decrease in size and strength. Regular exercise will help to hold back this aging process, which is really nothing more than a result of disuse. For many seniors, greater strength leads to independence and improved quality of life.

Now before you visualize Granny under the squat rack, realize that even just basic movements can strengthen your muscles and bones and improve flexibility, but must be tailored to the user. Today, exercising against the resistance of water in a pool is a popular activity among many seniors.

New research shows that exercise can aid in the disease-fighting process, too. Don't just take my word for it; this is confirmed fact. Just recently I read a report in the *Journal of Strength and Conditioning Research* that weight training is aiding cancer patients. Numerous other studies have linked resistance training to improvements in individuals with diabetes, hypertension, heart disease, arthritis, asthma, and AIDS. Exercise can boost the immune system, allowing you to better fight off minor ailments, even mild depression. Again, the weight-training program must be customized to meet the individual's particular needs.

What about younger people? Yes, they, too, can enjoy some of the benefits of a resistance-training program by making a few modifications, such as using a high-rep protocol and bodyweight exercises that will both strengthen and build bones and muscle.

One of the most remarkable recent fitness trends has been the doubling in popularity of strength training among women between 1987 and 1996. At the competitive level, the sport now offers contests for both bodybuilders and fitness competitors. At the noncompetitive level, most women prefer a workout that simply tightens and reshapes the body and works particular problem areas like the glutes, hips, and triceps. Most often, women have different goals than men, who are generally more interested in bulking up and significantly increasing their strength. Though the goals of men and women may differ, which is reflected in program setup and choice of exercises, the execution of the movements is identical. The female body also differs physiologically from a male's: smaller skeletal structure, less upper-body mass in relation to the legs, more body fat and fat cells located in the hip, thigh, and glute areas compared to the waist. But given these facts, muscle fiber is muscle fiber and, whether on a male or female, responds to the same type of exercises and training techniques. For many women, then, following the strength-training guidelines put forth with some modifications is the answer.

Does that mean you'll grow bigger muscles if you train like a man? Certainly not: Women produce so little testosterone, the anabolic hormone largely responsible for muscle growth, that the training effect is far less pronounced. The bottom line here is that this book addresses various goals for just about every body type, age, and gender; a woman can make an equally impressive physique transformation even if her goal is not traditional bodybuilding per se.

Ever broken a bone and later visited a physical therapist to begin rehab? Strength training is useful here, too. Not only does it lower your risk of soft-tissue and joint injuries, but it's your best tool for full recuperation and a speedy return to your activity. Whether it be temporary muscle soreness, lower-back pain, tight joints, or returning to action after you break a bone, resistance training will allow you to more quickly regain your former levels of strength.

From the days when Charles Atlas offered help to pencilnecks who had sand kicked in their face, bodybuilding has come a long way. Resistance training is now practiced worldwide. No doubt, it's far more than building big arms and looking great at the beach (but those aren't bad goals, mind you); weight training can reshape and tone your body, improve your health as well as your game, keep you injury-free, and ensure a long, active future. Whether you're a beginner looking for the nuts and bolts of training, an intermediate seeking to split your workout and bring up a lagging body part, or an advanced trainee looking to refine your physique and incorporate advanced training techniques, you'll find the answers in these pages.

Obviously, then, the scale of changes that have occurred in the scope of bodybuilding and among its participants since I first published the encyclopedia are far greater than merely evolutionary—they approach revolutionary. Besides those just mentioned, we have a greater understanding of the benefits of resistance training, which accounts in part for its tremendous popularity.

Every person who enters a gym or health club brings a personal motivation as to why he or she has chosen resistance training to accomplish certain goals. Sure, the aim of bodybuilding is to develop greater muscle size and improve physical appearance, but they are by no means the only reasons individuals train with weights. Consider also the effects on strength: You have the capacity to do greater work, both in terms of being able to lift a heavier weight one time (muscle strength) and to lift a lighter weight more times (muscle endurance). Some types of bodybuilding, like circuit training, are a good choice to build heart health and improve the functioning of your lungs and respiratory system as well. Traditional bodybuilding combined with some type of aerobic training will promote even greater health benefits.

In an increasingly technology-driven society that sits for long periods in front of computers and televisions and eats too many calories from fat, obesity—and several major health consequences—is the result. Bodybuilding plays a major role in building lean muscle tissue and reducing body fat. Unlike adipose (fat) tissue, muscle tissue is metabolically active and has a high energy requirement for maintenance and rebuilding. An increase in muscle tissue corresponds to an increase in your metabolic rate. Bodybuilding allows you to literally redesign your body and lose as much as two pounds of fat per week—without risking your health with diet pills or fad diets! One of life's curious ironies is that individuals who are overweight also have a tendency to be tired, while those who expend a lot of energy exercising seem to have more.

Other healthful effects can be measured as well. Research shows that resistance training done correctly makes you more flexible, not muscle-bound. That's because when one muscle flexes during a movement, the antagonist muscle is stretched. Many top athletes who've spent years in the weight room, like muscular gymnasts and track sprinters, must have tremendous flexibility to excel at their respective sports. I've even seen top pro bodybuilders like Flex Wheeler do the full splits onstage! Movement maintains flexibility, and I encourage you to work all body parts over their normal ranges of motion.

As you age, especially if you're a woman, your bones lose strength and size. Resistance training can prevent and even reverse osteoporosis. That holds true for tendons and ligaments, too. Stronger muscles, bones, and connective tissue reduce your risk of injury. Skeletal muscle serves as a kind of shock absorber that helps dissipate force from a repetitive activity like running to a simple fall onto a hard floor.

As I mentioned, the importance of the psychological component in bodybuilding can't be understated. Mental health professionals today agree that nothing beats exercise for defusing anxiety. In terms of self-respect, you can get this from a job well done, and physical fitness is no exception. You work to achieve your goals and can rightfully feel proud once you have achieved them, gaining respect from others in the process. Let me finally add that training regularly can dramatically boost your sex life by giving you more energy, increasing testosterone levels, decreasing anxiety, and improving self-esteem.

The summation of all this makes a remarkable and compelling case for bodybuilding. No wonder working out with weights became the most popular fitness activity in America in 1995 as measured by the Fitness Products Council and has remained on top ever since. Even *USA Today* reported that "significant improvements in muscle strength and tone by lifting weights only two times a week for 20 to 30 minutes" are possible, despite the myth that bodybuilders spend countless hours in the gym each day. So, are you going to be a part of this revolution in fitness or among the ever-expanding ranks of the nation's obese?

Here's what I can offer you. It's taken a book the size of this encyclopedia to put down in writing my vast experiences, ranging from training with yesterday's champions to conversations with today's top-ranked bodybuilders, from consultations with exercise scientists, nutritionists, and researchers worldwide to investigating questions from readers like yourself who have asked me about training. As knowledge is never finite, I've endeavored to remain on top of the sport even as a retired competitor, studying the winning formulas of the past as well as today's most current theories. In reality, that still makes me a student of the sport, but because I still very much love bodybuilding, it's something I plan on continuing for a very long time. At the same time, by sharing the wealth of knowledge, I can serve as teacher as well. If it suits you, think of me as your private personal trainer.

Here's what you must do for me. It's pretty simple, really, but I didn't say easy—after all, as I said, the slogan "No pain, no gain" originated in bodybuilding circles. It's what sets those who succeed apart from those who don't: You must have a sincere and burning desire to achieve what you dream, dedicate yourself to making progress, and take control of your circumstances to change your body. You must realize that such shortcuts as using anabolic/androgenic steroids lead only to short-term progress and potentially some very serious long-term health problems. Understand that bodybuilding isn't an overnight process, but rather a lifelong one. Personal factors like your attitude, commitment, and desire to improve your appearance play an important role in your ultimate success. Endeavor to learn all you can, train smart, listen to your body, and combine it with a good diet. But don't get too caught up in trying to understand all the training ideas and myriad principles at once. You most likely don't have the experience to properly interpret all the information anyway.

If you're with me so far, you're miles ahead of everybody else and are destined for greatness.

I've tried to make this book as honest, accurate, and practical as possible. Study it, reviewing the material over and over, constantly referring to it when you have questions, need motivation for your next training session, or are just looking for ways to make changes in your workout. You hold the answers right here in your hands.

Ready to get started? I thought so. Let's do it!

Arnold Schwarzenegger
November 1998

B O O K   O N E

Introduction to Bodybuilding

CHAPTER 1

Evolution and History

AT THE END of the nineteenth century a new interest in muscle-building arose, not muscle just as a means of survival or of defending oneself; there was a return to the Greek ideal—muscular development as a celebration of the human body.

This was the era when the ancient tradition of stone-lifting evolved into the modern sport of weightlifting. As the sport developed, it took on different aspects in different cultures. In Europe, weightlifting was a form of entertainment from which professional strongmen emerged—men who made their living by how much weight they could lift or support. How their physiques looked didn't matter to them or to their audience. The result was that they tended to develop beefy, ponderous bodies.

In America at this time, a considerable interest in strength in relation to its effect on health developed. The adherents of physical culture stressed the need for eating natural, unprocessed foods—an idea that took root in response to the increasing use of new food-processing techniques. Americans were beginning to move from farms and small towns to the cities; the automobile provided a new mobility. But at the same time, life was becoming increasingly sedentary, and the health problems that arise when a population eats too much of the wrong food, doesn't get enough exercise, and exists in constant conditions of stress were just becoming apparent.

The physical culturists were battling this trend with a belief in overall health and physical conditioning, advocating moderation and balance in all aspects of life. The beer-drinking, pot-bellied strongmen of Europe were certainly not their ideal. What they needed was a model whose physique embodied the ideas they were trying to disseminate, someone who more closely resembled the idealized statues of ancient Greek athletes than the Bavarian beer hall bulls of Europe. They found such a man

Eugen Sandow

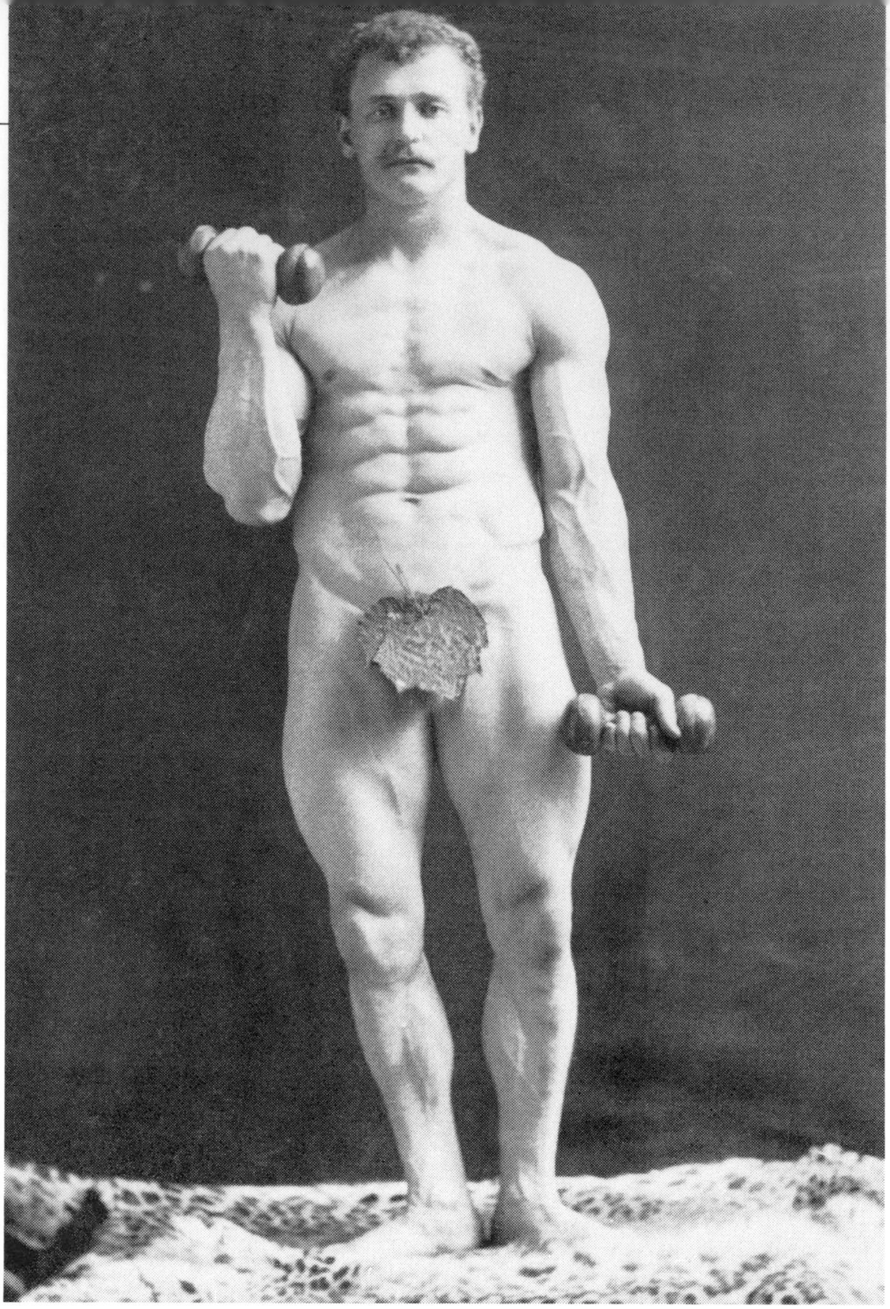

in the person of Eugen Sandow, a turn-of-the-century physical culture superstar.

Sandow made his reputation in Europe as a professional strongman, successfully challenging other strongmen and outdoing them at their own stunts. He came to America in the 1890s and was promoted by Florenz Ziegfeld, who billed him as "The World's Strongest Man" and put him on tour. But what really set Sandow apart was the aesthetic quality of his physique.

Sandow was beautiful, no doubt about it. He was an exhibitionist and enjoyed having people look at his body as well as admire his strongman stunts. He would step into a glass case and pose, wearing nothing but a fig leaf, while the audience stared and the women oohed and aahed at the beauty and symmetry of his muscular development. This celebration of the aesthetic qualities of the male physique was something very new. During the Victorian age men had covered themselves in confining clothing, and very few artists used the male nude as a subject for their paintings. This is what made Sandow's appeal so amazing.

Due largely to Sandow's popularity, sales of barbells and dumbbells skyrocketed. Sandow earned thousands of dollars a week and created a whole industry around himself through the sale of books and magazines. Contests were held in which the physical measurements of the competitors were compared, then Sandow awarded a gold-plated statue of himself to the winners. But, ultimately, he fell victim to his own macho mystique. It is said that one day his car ran off the road and he felt compelled to demonstrate his strength by single-handedly hauling it out of a ditch. As a result the man whom King George of England had appointed "Professor of Scientific Physical Culture to His Majesty" suffered a brain hemorrhage that ended his life.

Around the same time George Hackenschmidt earned the title "The

Eugen Sandow

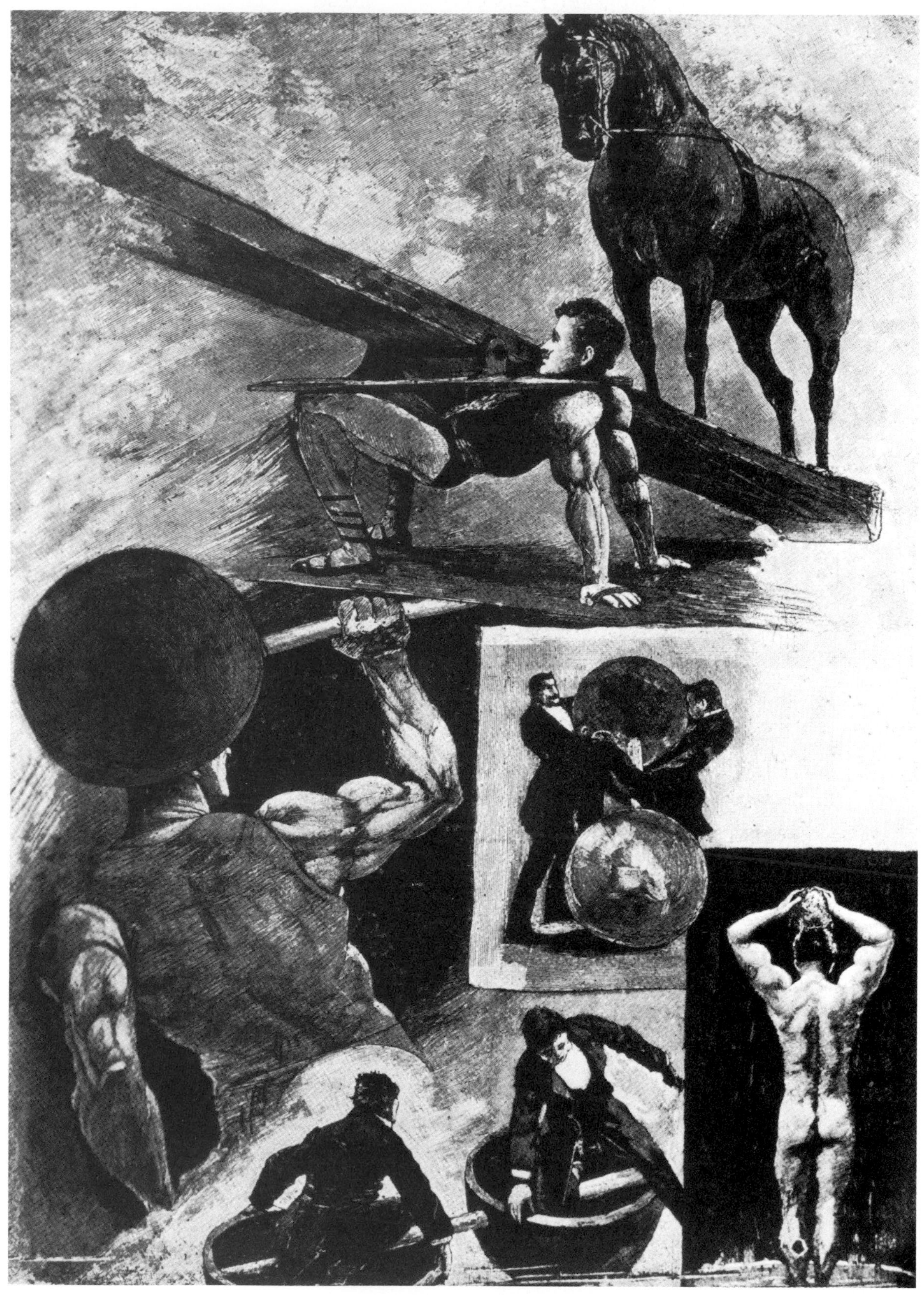

Feats of strength popularized by The Great Sandow

George Hackenschmidt

Russian Lion" for his performance when he won the Russian weightlifting championship in 1898 as well as various world wrestling championships. After immigrating to Great Britain, he eventually made a fortune. He was also a fluent orator and a prolific writer who turned out philosophical books such as *The Origins of Life,* debated intellectuals like George Bernard Shaw, and even challenged Albert Einstein to an exchange of ideas.

And there were many more—Professor Louis Attila, Arthur Saxon, Hermann Goerner, Oscar Hilgenfeldt, and W. A. Pullum. They created an illustrious tradition of men of strength that continues right up through Paul Anderson and Vasily Alexeev and other weightlifters of our day.

One of those for whom the pursuit of physical culture became practically a religion was the publisher-businessman Bernarr Macfadden, a man who could serve as the prototype health nut of all time. To promote the idea that physical weakness was actually immoral, he founded the magazine *Physical Culture.* Later he went on to publish the *New York Evening Graphic,* a newspaper aimed at an uneducated, unsophisticated audience.

Macfadden was a master promoter and, starting in 1903, he presented a series of contests at Madison Square Garden in New York to select the "Most Perfectly Developed Man in the World." At that first contest, he

Arthur Saxon

Hermann Goerner

offered a prize of $1,000—a small fortune in those days—along with the title. Both the contests and the magazine were successful for decades. And Macfadden practiced what he preached, walking barefoot every morning from his home on Riverside Drive in New York City to his office in midtown and appearing bare-chested in his own magazine. He was an example of health and fitness until well into his seventies.

Macfadden probably would not have approved of modern bodybuilding, with its emphasis on the visual development of the body rather than athletic skill. However, he and other physical culturists played a big part in the evolution of bodybuilding. His contests helped to promote interest in how the body looked rather than simply how strong the muscles were, and there emerged from these contests a superstar who was to become one of the most famous men in America for decades to come.

The winner of Macfadden's contest in 1921 was Angelo Siciliano. To capitalize on his growing fame, this magnificently developed man changed his name to Charles Atlas and acquired the rights to a mail-order physical fitness course called dynamic tension. For more than fifty years boys have grown up seeing the ads for this course in magazines and comic books, including the one where the scrawny kid gets sand kicked in his face, sends

Charles Atlas

away for a muscle-building course, then goes back to beat up the bully and reclaim his girl. "Hey skinny, your ribs are showing!" became the most memorable slogan of one of what author Charles Gaines calls the most successful advertising campaign in history.

THE TRANSITION TO BODYBUILDING

By the 1920s and 1930s, it had become evident that health and the development of the physique were closely connected, and that weight training was the best way to produce the greatest degree of muscular development in the shortest possible time. Despite his advertisements even Charles Atlas used weights rather than the dynamic tension of isometrics to produce his outstanding body. Training knowledge was limited, but bodybuilders of that day were learning a great deal simply by comparing their physiques with those of the stars of the previous generation.

For example, one of the most famous turn-of-the-century strongmen was Louis Cyr, 300 massive pounds, thick, chubby, huge around the middle and every inch the barrel-shaped strongman. But by the twenties there appeared men like Sigmund Klein, who exhibited a physique with beautiful muscular shape, balance, and proportion, as well as low body fat and extreme definition. Klein became very influential as a gym owner and writer on training and nutrition. His physique, compared to Cyr's, was as day to night. Klein, along with Sandow and influential physical culturists like Macfadden, gradually began to convince people that the look of a man's physique—not just his ability to perform feats of strength—was worthy of attention because the kind of training that produced the aesthetically muscular body also contributed to overall health. But the era in which the male physique would be judged purely on an aesthetic basis was still a few years away.

Louis Cyr

Strength developed by weight training was still somewhat suspect in the 1930s, as if weightlifters were not truly worthy to be called athletes. It was almost considered cheating to build up your body by training in a gym instead of participating in a variety of sports. In his earliest writing, the late John Grimek, an Olympic weightlifter who served as the model for so many aspiring bodybuilders, volunteered the information that his magnificent muscles were created by weightlifting, although you'd think that anyone seeing that physique on a beach would have realized that no amount of hand-balancing or water polo could have led to such development.

However, the tradition of physique competition continued, and by the late thirties occasional shows brought together boxers, gymnasts, swimmers, weightlifters, and other athletes. These contestants had to perform some sort of athletic feat as well as display their physiques, so it was common for weightlifters of the day to be able to do hand-balancing and other gymnastic moves.

In 1939 things started to change. The Amateur Athletic Union (AAU) stepped in and created a Mr. America contest of its own in Chicago on July 4. The winner was Roland Essmaker. The participants were still not full-fledged bodybuilders, but came from all sorts of athletic backgrounds and posed in everything from boxer shorts to jock straps.

But as more and more emphasis was put on how the physique looked, the weightlifters began to enjoy a distinct advantage. Weightlifting changed the contours of the body more than any other kind of training, so they were able to make a very strong and increasingly favorable impression on the judges.

Sigmund Klein

John Grimek

In 1940 the AAU produced the first real modern bodybuilding event. Mr. America that year and the next was John Grimek, who trained primarily by lifting weights in a gym. This served notice to anyone who wanted to compete against him that they would have to follow a similar training program. Grimek also put the lie to the idea that men who trained with weights were muscle-bound and unable to perform well athletically. During exhibitions, he was able to stay on the stage doing lifting and posing that involved an extraordinary degree of strength, flexibility, and coordination.

BODYBUILDING IN THE FORTIES AND FIFTIES

The winner of the Mr. America title in 1945 was a man whom many believe to be the first truly modern bodybuilder. Clarence “Clancy” Ross's physique would not look out of place on any stage today—wide shoulders, flaring lats, narrow waist, good calves and abs. By this time the distinction between lifting weights purely for strength and training with weights to shape and proportion the body had been clearly made. The bodybuilder's physique, as opposed to other types of muscular development, was now recognized as something unique.

However, bodybuilding still remained an obscure sport. No champion was known to the general public until Steve Reeves came along. Reeves was the right man in the right place at the right time. He was handsome, personable, and had a magnificent physique. Veterans of the Muscle Beach era (Muscle Beach, now located in Venice, California, was that area of Santa Monica Beach where bodybuilders congregated in the late 1940s and early 1950s) recall how crowds used to follow Reeves when he walked along the beach, and how people who knew nothing about him would simply stop and stare, awestruck.

Clarence (Clancy) Ross

Steve Reeves

After winning Mr. America and Mr. Universe, Reeves made movies and became an international star with his portrayal of the title roles in *Hercules* (the role that both Reg Park and I were later to undertake for the movies), *Morgan the Pirate,* and *The Thief of Baghdad.* As far as the general public was concerned, in the 1950s—except for the perennial Charles Atlas—there was only one famous bodybuilder: Steve Reeves.

Up to this point, it's likely that no human being in the history of the

Reg Park in his early twenties

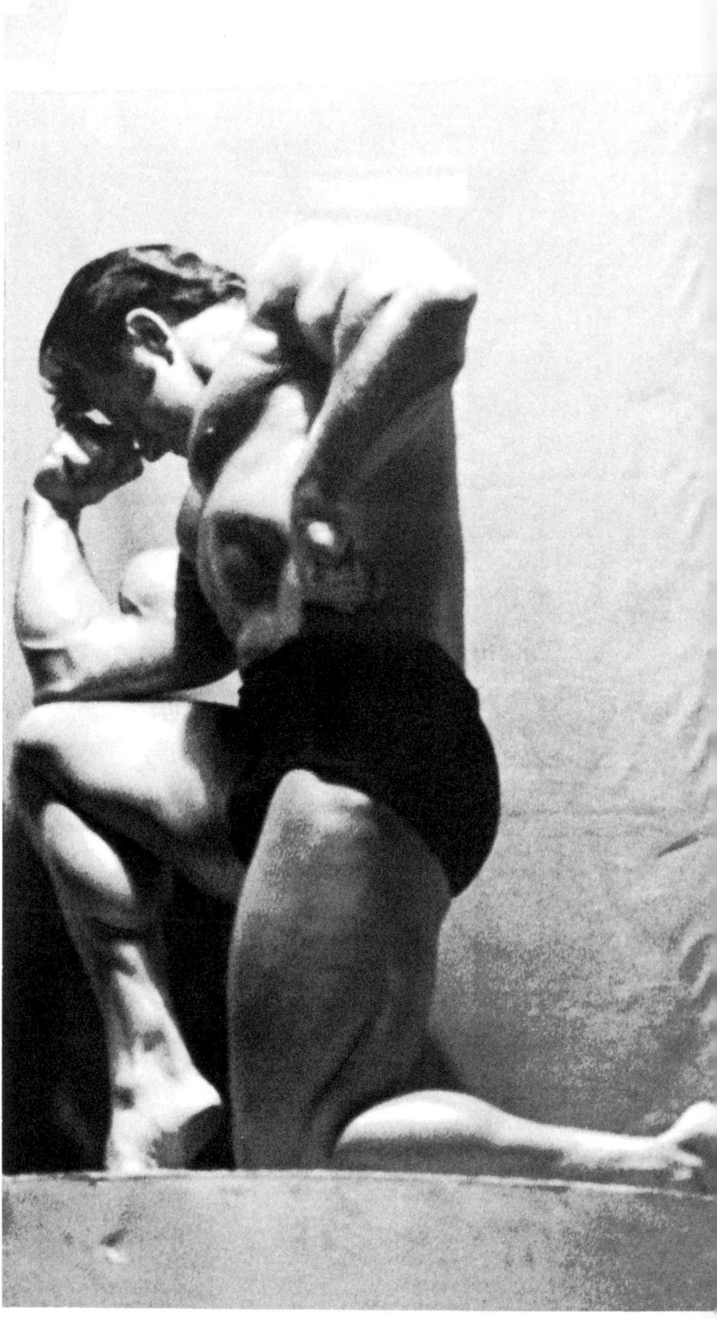

Reg Park at forty

planet had ever achieved the level of development of men like Grimek, Ross, and Reeves. Because they were training harder and more methodically than anyone else ever had, bodybuilders began to learn things about the physical potential of the body that even medical scientists could not have predicted. The word spread and soon there were more and more great bodybuilders coming along every year—Bill Pearl, Chuck Sipes, Jack Delinger, George Eiferman, and one of my great idols, Reg Park.

I remember how incredible it seemed when I met Reg Park in 1967. I was almost speechless with awe. One reason I have always admired him is that he is a big man, very strong, with a powerful-looking physique. When I was just getting started I knew I wanted to build the kind of mass and density that I had seen in his photos—big, rough, and Herculean. Reg was the next major champion to emerge when Reeves left competition for his movie career. He became Mr. Universe in 1951 and became Professional Mr. Universe in 1958 and in 1965. At this point, everyone recognized that Reg was far above all other leading bodybuilders. He dominated the bodybuilding scene for two decades.

BODYBUILDING IN THE SIXTIES

I first came on the international bodybuilding scene in 1966. At that time most of the top bodybuilders I read about in magazines lived and trained in California.

Beating Dennis Tinerino in 1967—Mr. America of that year—in the National Amateur Body Builders' Association (NABBA) Mr. Universe contest was my first big international victory, but that meant I would now have to go against the other champions of the day. There was certainly some fierce competition around—Frank Zane, a man who prepares as thoroughly for a contest as anyone else in bodybuilding; my good friend Franco Columbu, who went from being a great powerlifter to a Mr. Olympia practically by sheer determination of will; and, of course, Sergio Oliva.

Anytime people discuss who might be the best bodybuilder of all time, the name Sergio Oliva inevitably comes up. He and I had some unbelievable confrontations onstage. The only way I could beat him was to be in absolutely perfect shape—massive, dense, and cut—and then not make any mistakes. Sergio was so good he could beat you in the dressing room if you weren't careful. His shirt would come off, and there would be that incredible mass. He would transfix you with a look, exhale with a kind of animal grunt, and suddenly the lats would begin to flare . . . and just when you thought they were the most unbelievable lats you ever saw, BOOM—out they would come, more and more, until you began to doubt that this was a human being you were looking at.

In 1967 Bill Pearl won the pro Mr. Universe title and I won amateur Mr. Universe.

Joe Weider and Sergio Oliva—1967 Olympia

While I was battling for titles in Europe, I was very much aware of the competitions in the United States. Larry Scott had won the first two Mr. Olympia contests, and I knew I would eventually have to beat Larry and other top stars like Chuck Sipes. But one bodybuilder I was also impressed with, not just because of his outstanding physique but also because of the image he was able to create, was Dave Draper.

Draper represented the epitome of California bodybuilders—big, blond, and sun-tanned, with a personable manner and winning smile. Surrounded as I was by three feet of snow in the middle of an Austrian winter, the image of Dave Draper on a California beach was a very attractive one indeed. And Dave's roles in movies like *Don't Make Waves* with Tony Curtis and his appearances on television shows made me aware of the possibilities of bodybuilding beyond the competition arena.

In the 1960s there were two distinct worlds in bodybuilding: Europe and America. My Universe titles in '67 and '68 established me as the preeminent bodybuilder in Europe (Ricky Wayne wrote in an article, "If Hercules were to be born today his name would be Arnold Schwarzenegger"), but the question still remained as to how well I would do against the American champions.

I looked across the ocean and saw Dave Draper, Sergio Oliva, Chet Yorton, Frank Zane, Bill Pearl, Freddy Ortiz, Harold Poole, Ricky Wayne, and others. My challenge was to compete against these great bodybuilders and defeat them.

My awareness of the world had expanded tremendously in just a few years. While training in Austria, I had considered winning the Mr. Universe contest in London to be the highest achievement I could aspire to. Now I found that taking that title was only the beginning! I still had a long journey ahead of me and many bodybuilders to defeat before I could con-

Larry Scott

Dave Draper

Freddy Ortiz

Harold Poole

Rick Wayne

With Dennis Tinerino at the 1968 Mr. Universe contest

sider myself the best. And that meant confronting the top American bodybuilders. So after winning my second NABBA Mr. Universe title in 1968, I set off for the States.

In 1969, I devised a plan that involved winning three top titles in one year, the championships of all the important federations. I competed in the International Federation of Bodybuilders' Mr. Universe

With Roy Velasco at the 1968 Mr. International in Mexico

1968 NABBA Mr. Universe

contest in New York and then went immediately to London for the NABBA Universe—which gave me two titles in one week! But even with these victories I had not beaten everyone, so I planned to do even more the next year.

As the sixties drew to a close, six names emerged as dominant among the ranks of those who had been competing in the championship events: Dave Draper, Sergio Oliva, Bill Pearl, Franco Columbu, Frank Zane, and me.

1969 Mr. Universe

BODYBUILDING IN THE SEVENTIES

In 1970, I went all out—I won the Pro AAU Mr. World, the NABBA Mr. Universe, and the IFBB Mr. Olympia titles. Finally, I had defeated everybody, and now felt I could justifiably call myself world champion. The year 1971 marked the high point of the remarkable career of Bill Pearl. Pearl first won Mr. America in 1953, then went on to victories in the Universe in 1953, 1961, and 1967. At the 1971 Mr. Universe, eighteen years after his Mr. America title, he came back to defeat the awesome Sergio Oliva and prove, once more, that he was one of the greatest bodybuilders of all time. Unfortunately, he did not continue on and enter the Mr. Olympia that year, so I never had a chance to compete against him, which prevented us from seeing who would come out as the top champion.

I won six Olympia titles between 1970 and 1975, but it was not without considerable opposition. In 1972, for example, the formidable Sergio gave me a battle that is still talked about today. Serge Nubret emerged as

1970 Mr. Universe posedown with Dave Draper and Reg Park

a potent force during this period, and at the 1973 Olympia he was amazing in his ability to create such size and definition on what was essentially a small frame.

In 1973 a new monster came on the scene. Lou Ferrigno won the IFFB Mr. Universe title and gave notice that a new force in bodybuilding was on the horizon. Lou went on to win the IFFB Universe title again the next year and then entered the Olympia. He may have admitted he had always idolized me, but that did not keep him from doing his best to take the Olympia title away from me.

The 1975 Mr. Olympia was something of a high point in the history of this great event. Ferrigno returned, determined to achieve victory; Serge Nubret was also back and in top shape. For the first time, there were six or seven absolutely first-rate champions contending for the title, and I was especially proud of this victory, after which I retired from competition.

The next year saw a truly earthshaking event in the history of bodybuilding: Franco Columbu won the 1976 Mr. Olympia title, the first small

Bill Pearl

In 1970 Frank Zane won the amateur Mr. Universe and I won the pro Mr. Universe. Christine Zane won Ms. Bikini.

1970 Mr. Olympia posedown with Sergio Oliva

1970 Mr. World

With Serge Nubret and Joe Weider at the 1971 Olympia

Sergio Oliva

Posedown at the 1972 Olympia with Serge Nubret and Sergio Oliva

Joe Weider handing out trophies to the 1973 winners—Ken Waller, Mr. World; Lou Ferrigno, Mr. America; and me, Mr. Olympia

1973 Olympia posedown with Serge Nubret and Franco Columbu

The 1974 Olympia with Lou Ferrigno and Joe Weider

The 1975 Olympia with Serge Nubret, Ben Weider, and Lou Ferrigno

1975 Olympia with Franco Columbu

Franco Columbu

man to do so. Until this time, the big man always won, but from '76 on the small man came into his own. Muscularity and extremely low body fat became the winning factor, and this required an almost scientific approach to training and diet to achieve. The late seventies saw Frank Zane hit his prime, winning three consecutive Olympia titles with his aesthetic physique. Robby Robinson also achieved world-class status and displayed both highly aesthetic and muscular qualities. In contrast, when Kal Szkalak won the 1977 World Amateur Bodybuilding Championship, it was more by virtue of an incredible development of mass than a Zane-like symmetry.

In 1980, I came out of retirement to win the Mr. Olympia contest in Sydney, Australia. I could hardly believe how competitive the sport had become by then, or that I would be pushed so hard by a bodybuilder as small as Chris Dickerson. All around me I saw examples of once unthinkable development, from Tom Platz's legs to Roy Callender's lats, unbelievable thickness, incredible density. My career has lasted longer than most (due in part, I believe, to the fact that I started competing so young), but in the 1970s the growing popularity of the sport meant that many of the stars of the sixties could stay active in competition to contend against the rising champions of the seventies.

The 1970s also saw the rise of the International Federation of Bodybuilders as the dominant bodybuilding organization. Under the guidance of its president, Ben Weider, the IFBB consisted of more than a hundred member countries and had become the sixth largest sports federation in the world. In addition, the Mr. Olympia title was now recognized as the top professional championship in bodybuilding, comparable to Wimbledon in tennis and the U.S. Open in golf.

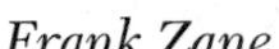

Frank Zane

Robby Robinson

PUMPING IRON

One of the greatest influences on bodybuilding in the seventies was the book, and later the movie, *Pumping Iron.* Charles Gaines and George Butler took a subject most people knew virtually nothing about and made it one of the hot topics of the decade. It was the first time that anyone had given the general public insight into what bodybuilding was all about and what bodybuilders were really like. Gaines and Butler were able to attract the public to a sport that had long been neglected and misunderstood, and the success of *Pumping Iron* set the stage for two decades of explosive growth in the popularity of bodybuilding. The success of the book not only gave my career a big boost and helped bodybuilding find its way into network sports broadcasts and big-budget movies, but it was also influential in taking bodybuilding from the local high school gym to culture palaces like the Sydney Opera House and New York's Whitney Museum. Bodybuilders have been featured on countless magazine covers and bodybuilding is the subject of numerous best-selling books.

BODYBUILDING IN THE EIGHTIES AND NINETIES

Once, I could stand on the Olympia stage and be challenged by one or two other competitors. In 1980 the Olympia stage included Frank Zane, Chris Dickerson, Boyer Coe, Ken Waller, Mike Mentzer, Roger Walker, Tom Platz, Samir Bannout, and Roy Callender, among others. That lineup of talent would have been unthinkable in 1967, although a Sergio Oliva, Larry Scott, Reg Park, or Harold Poole in top shape would have been as impressive as ever in the 1980 Olympia. It isn't that the best are better, but that there are so many more top contenders than ever before.

As the eighties got fully under way, it was clear that this breadth of competition was here to stay. The 1981 and 1982 Olympia winners were experienced competitors—Franco Columbu and Chris Dickerson, respectively—but within a few years these champions had retired and we entered an era in which massive physiques would dominate the Mr. Olympia. Until this time the smaller man had had just as good a shot at winning the Mr. Olympia as the bigger competitor. At the beginning of the 1980s there had been more Mr. Olympias won by under-200-pound bodybuilders (Scott, Zane, Columbu, Dickerson) than by competitors bigger than 200 pounds (Oliva, Bannout, and me)—and Samir weighed just slightly over 200 pounds at that.

Then Lee Haney came along and was able to make use of his massive and aesthetically well-proportioned physique to win eight Mr. Olympia titles, breaking my record of seven wins. After Lee came Dorian Yates,

1980 Olympia posedown with Boyer Coe and Frank Zane

1981 Olympia—Franco Columbu

England's answer to Mount Rushmore, who was able to win his multiple Mr. Olympia titles by dominating his competition with a Herculean physique of 265 pounds or more of hard, ripped muscle. Any bodybuilding fan journeying by time machine from the mid-1960s to the mid-1990s and looking at the modern Mr. Olympia lineup might well have thought we had been invaded by an alien species, so huge were the competitors. Alongside Dorian he would see Nasser El Sonbaty, almost the same size, along with Paul Dillett, Jean-Pierre Fux, and Kevin Levrone—all so massive that only near-perfect development allowed smaller bodybuilders like Shawn Ray (an Arnold Classic champion) and Lee Priest to hold their own onstage. A sign of the times in the 1990s has been that aesthetically awesome Flex Wheeler, weighing about what I did in my final Mr. Olympia victories, has never been one of the biggest competitors onstage.

Obviously, this represented a trend that could not go on indefinitely. A 270-pound Mr. Olympia, yes, but the competitive physique is getting to the point where the necessity of maintaining symmetry, proportion, and detail will not allow much more increase in size. It's just physically impossible for a 320-pound bodybuilder to have the same aesthetic quality of one weighing 220 pounds. Not only that, but as the 1990s progressed the bodybuilding audience itself showed increasing dissatisfaction with the judges' choice of sheer mass over traditional ideals of aesthetics and

1982 Olympia—Chris Dickerson

symmetry. But bodybuilding goes in cycles as do most other things, so a pendulum that swings one way will inevitably swing back to center and then to the other extreme.

THE EXPLOSIVE GROWTH OF BODYBUILDING

The 1980s witnessed explosive growth in bodybuilding, not just as a competitive sport, but in terms of its effect on our culture and the public in general. When the decade began, the International Federation of Bodybuilders was already a successful organization, boasting more than one hundred member nations. By the 1990s the IFBB included 160 countries and, according to IFBB president Ben Weider, had become the fourth-largest sports federation in the world.

The Soviet Union became an IFBB member in the mid-1980s, and after the breakup of the Soviet Union the various countries that had made it up also petitioned for IFBB membership, which also helped to swell the ranks of the organization. In 1990, China joined the IFBB as well and

Competitors in the '90s have become massive.

They still must maintain symmetry, proportion, and detail, as shown in this Mr. Olympia posedown.

began hosting competitions, not just for men but for women bodybuilders as well.

The culmination of this success came when bodybuilding received official recognition from the International Olympic Committee in 1997, making the sport of physique competition a full member in the international amateur sports community.

The impact of bodybuilding on modern culture also became apparent as we began to see more and more muscular physiques represented in both print and television advertising. One bank trumpeted its strength as a financial organization by including a muscular arm curled in a biceps shot. Viewers were encouraged to use a particular collect-call service in an ad featuring Arnold Schwarzenegger look-alike, sound-alike bodybuilder Roland Kickinger. Bodybuilding has certainly changed the physiques of movie action heroes. Once the public got used to seeing the kinds of bodies featured in films like *Conan, Rambo,* and Jean-Claude Van Damme martial arts movies, young movie and television actors, print and runway models all got the message that you'd better be in shape if you want to impress the public.

Of course, all this growth presented problems of its own. The bigger you get, the more attention you draw—both positive and negative. While President Bush was pushing the idea of bodybuilding training through the vehicle of the President's Council on Physical Fitness, and publications like *USA Today* published articles praising the benefits to be gained from training with weights as the bodybuilders do, bodybuilding's detractors devoted increasing energy to attacking the sport.

The worst beating bodybuilding had to take was over the issue of the use of anabolic steroids and other performance-enhancing drugs. There is certainly no doubt that drug abuse exists in the sport of bodybuilding, but too often it was overlooked that these same problems also exist in a wide variety of other sports. At one point *Sports Illustrated* published what many felt was a highly irresponsible article holding up the misdeeds of a former bodybuilder, who had not competed in some fifteen years, as somehow representative of behavior to be expected from physique competitors because of their penchant for drug use.

However, in response to both public pressure and the requirements set forth by the IOC, the IFBB announced the federation would be instituting an ambitious drug-testing program, expanding upon the testing already being performed regularly at the IFFB World Amateur Bodybuilding Championships (formerly Mr. Universe). I hope this program will not only help to educate young bodybuilders about the dangers of using proscribed substances and dissuade them from experimenting with these drugs, but will also help persuade the public that bodybuilding is indeed a legitimate, exciting sport and its champions legitimate, admirable athletes.

THE ARNOLD CLASSIC WEEKEND

One innovation in competitive bodybuilding, beginning in 1994, has been the series of events I have promoted with my longtime associate Jim Lorimer in Columbus, Ohio. As I moved from the world of bodybuilding into the movie industry, I became more and more aware of how little bodybuilding has been treated as the exciting spectacle it could be. So Jim and I developed a whole package of events that included the Arnold Classic for men, the Ms. International for women bodybuilders, a fitness competition for women, a major fitness industry trade show, and exciting martial arts competition and exhibitions.

This full weekend of excitement has attracted so many physique fans to the city that Jim Lorimer has informed me that it is the third-highest attended annual event in Columbus, with only a national and international horse show drawing larger attendance. "It's no wonder they attract more of a crowd," I told Jim. "They have bigger competitors than we do."

THE PROFESSION OF BODYBUILDING

The success of the Arnold Classic is only one indication of the degree to which bodybuilding has grown into a major professional sport. As bodybuilding has gained in popularity, the money to be made from the sport has also increased. Some bodybuilders have always been able to make money from their physiques—for example, John Grimek, Bill Pearl, and Reg Park were in demand for seminars and exhibitions back in the 1950s—but very few physique stars were able to make a full-time living from the sport. Even as late as the mid-seventies I think the only two bodybuilders making a full-time living from bodybuilding were Franco and me. You have to remember that in 1965 the prize awarded at the first Mr. Olympia was only a crown. In 1998, a top pro winner could expect to walk away with $110,000, and the total prize money available in a Mr. Olympia or Arnold Classic has climbed to six figures.

Of course, whenever a lot of money suddenly becomes involved, everything starts to change and success breeds even more opportunities. Many physique stars have opened gyms, begun manufacturing equipment, or created clothing or supplement lines. Most have augmented their incomes through mail-order sales of all these products and, of course, seminars and exhibitions.

The growth of bodybuilding has paralleled the increased awareness of fitness in the mainstream culture. Interest in fitness has expanded explosively in the last few years, as indicated by the tremendous increase in the number of gyms and gym members around the country and in the remarkable increase we have seen in the sales of workout clothing, exercise equipment, and diet supplements.

Throughout the 1980s bodybuilding became more and more visible on television, covered by all three major networks as well as ESPN and other cable sports outlets. Unfortunately, this interest on the part of the media did not continue to expand as the 1990s progressed. The reason was the drug controversy. Although many other sports are also plagued by problems with anabolic steroids and other performance-enhancing drugs, the attention of the public has tended to focus disproportionately on the world of physique competition. Obviously, both the problem itself and the public perception of bodybuilding will have to be dealt with in the future if bodybuilding is to achieve the success it is capable of.

JOE WEIDER

Any discussion of bodybuilding would be incomplete without mention of the contribution of Joe Weider and his magazines *Muscle & Fitness* and *Flex*. Since the early 1940s, Joe has done more than simply provide good articles and photos detailing bodybuilding competitions, how-to training articles, and personality profiles of the top physique stars. He has also managed to gather and preserve enormous amounts of valuable training information and to use his magazines, books, and videotapes to make this information available to one new generation of young bodybuilders after another.

Joe has spent an enormous amount of time over the years going into gyms around the country and observing how the stars trained. For instance, back in the 1960s he noticed that Larry Scott used a preacher bench to do Curls, and that the super-strong Chuck Sipes continued to do set after set with great intensity by quickly taking weight off the bar between sets. He took note of these methods, wrote them down, then gave them names. Scott didn't call his technique Scott Curls, and Sipes didn't realize he was using the Stripping Method. But, through Joe, soon everyone had access to these valuable training techniques.

In Austria, I trained in the morning and again in the evening because that's what my daily schedule demanded. Now, this is known as the Weider Double-Split System, and is being used by bodybuilders all over the world. The Weider Training Principles are a collection of the best bodybuilding techniques ever created. Joe Weider recognized these principles, tagged them with his own name (the Weider Instinctive Principle, the Weider Priority Principle, the Weider Peak-Contraction Principle, and so on), and promoted them in his magazine. It would be impossible to count the number of bodybuilders who have benefited from Joe's ideas on training, nutrition, diet, and everything else it takes to make oneself a success in bodybuilding.

Joe Weider with bodybuilders

THE EVOLUTION OF MODERN TRAINING

One reason that bodybuilders have continued to get bigger, harder, and more cut over the decades is that they have figured out over time, largely by trial and error, better ways of training and more effective methods of dieting. *Every* sport has improved during the past five decades and bodybuilding is no exception. In fact, some would argue that the level of fitness in *every* sport has improved as bodybuilding techniques have become more widely known and adopted.

In the days of John Grimek, bodybuilders still trained largely like weightlifters and tended to work the whole body three times a week. Bodybuilding training is much more sophisticated than that today. Bodybuilders train each body part more intensely, hit all the muscles from different angles, use a wider variety of exercises and equipment, and are much more aware of the need to train hard in relatively short bursts and then allow the body to rest, recuperate, and grow. Where once just getting "big" was the main goal, now bodybuilders try to achieve "quality"—creating a physique with spectacular shape and symmetry, with every muscle defined and separated—a level of definition that makes today's top competitors look like walking anatomy charts.

As bodybuilders developed new techniques, the tools used to shape their bodies also changed. Gyms in the thirties and forties were primitive places by today's standards. Gym owners like the late Vic Tanny, one of the creators of the modern health club, experimented with various types of cable and pulley devices to give their patrons a wider choice of exercises, but the barbell and dumbbell still dominated the gym. In the early sixties, the introduction of exercise machines made a greater variety of exercises possible. Today Cybex, Hammer Strength, Body Masters, Paramount, Universal, Nautilus, and many other manufacturers produce training equipment that is essential to supplementing a bodybuilder's free-weight training. At World Gym, Joe Gold (founder of Gold's Gym as well) designed and built equipment so successfully that his designs have been widely copied and imitated around the world.

Bodybuilders have also learned to master the principles of diet and nutrition. Lean muscularity was not always the important factor in bodybuilding competition that it is today; pure muscle mass was considered more important. But bodybuilders realized along the way that the bulk produced by body fat had no place in a quality physique, and that it was necessary to get rid of as much fat as possible in order to fully reveal their muscular development.

So bodybuilders stopped bulking up. They learned to follow strict diets while still training very hard, and to take vitamin, mineral, and protein supplements to enhance their progress. They investigated the effect on the body of steroids, thyroid, and a whole range of biochemical agents.

And they began using motivational techniques and even hypnosis to harness the power of the mind to force the body's development beyond previous limits. And in doing so, bodybuilders began attracting the attention of doctors and medical scientists, who came to realize that the ability of these athletes to develop the human body represented a major breakthrough in our understanding of exercise and its effect on the body. This led to a revolution in exercise and fitness techniques available to the general public.

A clear sign of the growth of the popularity of weight training in the United States and around the world is the proliferation of serious gyms. When I was a young bodybuilder traveling around it was frequently all I could do to find one local gym in which I could do a real workout. Now no matter where I go there is a World Gym, a Powerhouse Gym, a Gold's Gym, a Bally's, a Family Fitness Center, or some other well-equipped local training facility. There is no longer much difference in the equipment available in a hardcore bodybuilding gym or a so-called health spa. People have learned that muscle is muscle and you need the same range of exercise equipment whether you are training to stay fit and healthy or to win the Mr. Universe or Mr. Olympia contest.

THE FUTURE OF BODYBUILDING

As I travel across the country and around the world, seeing more and more good bodybuilders develop in the United States and an increasing number of competitors from Europe winning international contests, I have great hope for the future of the sport. Bodybuilding is so specialized and so difficult that only a small percentage of people will ever want to do what it takes to become an international champion, but athletes who once would have been drawn to other sports are now beginning to consider a career in bodybuilding. This is one of the things that will ensure that the sport will continue to grow, that the level of competition will remain high, and that the public's interest will continue to increase.

There is no doubt that the top competitors will tend to be much bigger in the future than they were in the past. I like to use boxing as an analogy. Years ago, heavyweight champions frequently weighed under 200 pounds—look at Joe Louis and Rocky Marciano as cases in point. Today the smallest heavyweight contenders weigh more than 200 pounds, and 230-pound heavyweights like, say, Riddick Bowe are becoming more common. But despite the huge size being attained by football players, weightlifters, and other athletes, there are no 260-pound heavyweight contenders—and there may never be. At a certain point, gaining more size detracts from rather than increases your ability to perform in a given sport. That is true in boxing, tennis, and soccer, to name a few examples, and it is probably true in bodybuilding as well.

Bodybuilding means so much more today than it did when I first fell in love with it. Then, there was only competition, but now it has developed a recreational side—bodybuilding for physical fitness, health, and as a means for developing confidence and a better self-image. Orthopedists are beginning to use it as a means of rehabilitation for patients with certain types of physical problems. It is being used by the elderly as a means of combating many of the debilitating effects of aging. It is also becoming more important in sports training as many athletes find that bodybuilding can greatly enhance their performance. Women, children, and even whole families are becoming involved in bodybuilding programs. This is not a fad; it is obviously here to stay.

But as the ranks of professional bodybuilders increase, and bigger cash prizes become available, it should not be forgotten that the primary reason for bodybuilding is a fundamental love for the sport. Without this love, the camaraderie between bodybuilders is lost and the athletes compete without joy or satisfaction. If you consider only the financial side, then when another bodybuilder beats you, he has not just bested you in a contest, he has taken away part of your living, and it is difficult for anyone in this position to have anything but negative feelings for other competitors, and eventually for bodybuilding itself.

But I would like to see bodybuilding introduced to many more people than just those who are considering competition. Bodybuilding training is one of the best methods of achieving physical fitness, and the more people who understand this and benefit from it the better. Organizations like the IFBB often forget there is a world out there beyond organized bodybuilding, and put restrictions on bodybuilders as to where, when, and for whom they can give bodybuilding seminars. My view is that bodybuilding should be energetically encouraged on any occasion and for any audience. Enhancing all aspects of life through better physical fitness is a need that takes priority over any jurisdictional considerations.

One relatively new development in bodybuilding is that of the bodybuilder as personal trainer. While many people look at a bodybuilder and say, "I don't want to look like that," they also seem to realize that these individuals would not look as they do unless they knew something very special about how to train the body. And so bodybuilders are increasingly in demand as personal trainers, a trend that began in California and has now spread across the country and around the world. The techniques of bodybuilding apply to every body and can be adapted for every purpose. And who could be more capable of teaching you the best and most efficient way to train than a dedicated bodybuilder? So although I never expect bodybuilding to be a mass sport (although in the future, who can tell?), I am confident that the real impact of bodybuilders on the culture as a whole will be in the role of personal trainers.

WOMEN'S BODYBUILDING

One major development in bodybuilding has been the advent of bodybuilding competition for women, as well as the increasing number of women using bodybuilding training for the development of fitness, health, and strength.

Modern bodybuilding competition for women had its tentative beginnings in the late 1970s, with George Synder's "The Best in the World" contests perhaps the most successful (despite the fact that women still appeared onstage in high heels). In 1980 the National Physique Committee held its first National Championships for women, and the International Federation of Bodybuilders sanctioned the first Ms. Olympia contest. Bodybuilding for women as a recognized national and international sport for both amateurs and professionals was officially on its way.

The first well publicized female bodybuilder was Lisa Lyon, who essentially invented the kind of combination muscle-posing and dancelike movements that characterizes presentation in women's contests to this day. Lisa also sought out top-name photographers like Helmut Newton and Robert Mapplethorpe, and their photos of her were the introduction many people had to the aesthetically developed muscular female body. Bodybuilding was extremely fortunate when Rachel McLish became the first Ms. Olympia. Rachel's combination of sleek, sexy looks, muscularity, and personality set a standard of excellence that female bodybuilders have used as a benchmark ever since. Cory Everson and Lenda Murray dominated the 1980s and 1990s, winning six Ms. Olympia titles apiece. They were followed by Kim Chizevsky, three-time winner of the Ms. Olympia crown. Kim's incredible levels of hardness and muscularity immediately began generating the same sorts of controversy regarding muscle vs. aesthetics as we saw during the course of Dorian Yates's dominance of the Mr. Olympia.

Bodybuilding for women is such a new idea that it is no wonder there is controversy surrounding it. Never before in history have women developed their muscles for aesthetic purposes. *Pumping Iron* author Charles Gaines calls this look a "new archetype." Many don't approve of this activity for women and don't like how it looks. Everyone is entitled to an opinion, but in my view women have the same skeletal muscles as men and should be free to develop them as they wish. Bodybuilding is a sport both men and women participate in it. This is why I hold both the Arnold Classic and the Ms. International in Columbus each year. We live in a time in which women are becoming involved in all manner of activities and professions that were once denied to them. As the father of two daughters, I couldn't be more pleased that this is happening. I am happy to see women increasingly overcoming the artificial barriers that have limited them in the past. Bodybuilding for women is just one more example of this cultural transformation.

But as far as I'm concerned, the most significant aspect of bodybuilding for women is its impact on health and fitness. Women in our society too often suffer from loss of strength, lean body mass, and physical ability, especially as they grow older, because they don't exercise their muscles properly. Too many women concentrate on aerobic exercise at the expense of resistance training because they have been convinced that working their muscles will make them look unfeminine. Additionally, they often go on extreme and unhealthy diets that cause a loss of both bone and muscle mass. I have great hopes that the example of female bodybuilders will help to teach women the benefits of bodybuilding workout and diet programs so that as many women as possible can enjoy the benefits to their health and well-being of a fit, strong, and shapely body.

Why, then, it might be asked, aren't there any programs developed specifically for women in this encyclopedia? The primary reason is that the fundamentals of muscle training and diet programs are essentially the same for both sexes. Though women may have different goals from men—to tone up rather than build maximum muscle size—this is reflected not in how they execute particular exercises but in sets and reps, combinations, and choices of some exercises that target a woman's particular problem areas. Diet is a matter of the appropriate intake of the various necessary nutrients and the correct number of calories. True, it's a fact that the female body responds somewhat differently, but *every* individual is going to find the need to adjust training and diet programs to suit his or her personal needs. So my advice to women is to learn the bodybuilding techniques in this book and put them into practice to the best of your ability and, once you've been on these programs long enough to see results, just stand in front of your mirror and admire what you've achieved!

CHAPTER 2

The ABCs of Bodybuilding

SPORT VS. EXERCISE SYSTEM

Bodybuilding as a system of exercise is the most effective and efficient way to strengthen and develop the muscles of the body. Some think bodybuilding is only an intense form of competition but not a sport. However, I think bodybuilding qualifies as a sport for a number of reasons. One is the incredible amount of athletic effort involved in training, in developing the physique to prepare it for competition. Another is the high level of athletic demand involved in the performance part of bodybuilding—that is, posing and flexing onstage. As we'll go into in more detail later, to be able to pose during a contest, to squeeze and flex your muscles, be able to hold poses for as much as an hour or more at a time—and to do it really well, with high energy levels and full control of your entire body the whole time—is an athletic feat comparable to a boxer going twelve rounds for the heavyweight championship of the world.

One reason people have trouble understanding the nature of bodybuilding is that there are two basic kinds of sports—those judged by measurement (how far, how fast, how high, and so forth) and those judged by form (diving, gymnastics, ice skating). *Bodybuilding is a sport of form,* but instead of movement the form involved is that of the body itself—the size, shape, proportion, detail, and aesthetic quality of the physique as developed in the gym, prepared by dieting, and displayed by performing bodybuilding poses.

In any event, although bodybuilding has not yet become an Olympic sport, it has been accepted by the international amateur sports community and been included in such events as the Asian Games and Pan American Games. So I am not alone in my opinion that bodybuilding is a sport.

PROGRESSIVE-RESISTANCE TRAINING

Of course, the majority of people who train with weights are never going to compete (just as most people who play tennis or golf don't expect to enter Wimbledon or the Masters Invitational). But whether you bodybuild with the aim of sculpting a competition physique or are training to improve your performance at sports, to be healthy and fit, to look and feel better, or to rehabilitate an injury, all muscle-building done correctly depends for its results on the same basic exercise principle, that of progressive-resistance training.

Progressive-resistance training works because the body is designed to adapt and grow stronger in response to greater amounts of stress than it is used to. If you are used to running two miles a day, then running five miles puts more demand on your muscles and the ability of your cardiovascular system to supply enough oxygen and nutrients to keep the muscles functioning under the stress of this greater demand. You may be in shape to run two miles, but you have to get in better shape to run five miles. Improving your conditioning in this case is a matter of increasing how far you run and giving the body time to change and adapt to this increase.

When it comes to muscle-building the same principle applies. The muscles are adapted to dealing with a certain level of demand, specifically to a certain amount of weight in your exercises lifted with a certain degree of intensity. When you increase the amount of weight and/or intensity, your muscles have to become bigger and stronger to deal with it. Once they have adapted to the new level of demand, you increase the amount of weight and/or intensity in your workouts so that they will *continue* to get bigger and stronger. In other words, you progressively increase the demands you make on your muscles over time.

Dr. Lawrence Golding of the University of Nevada explains it this way: "If you have a 10-horsepower motor and you subject it to a 12-horsepower load, it will burn out. But when you have a human body that is the equivalent of a 10-horsepower motor and you subject it to a 12-horsepower load, it eventually becomes a 12-horsepower motor."

But not every kind of training you do with weights is going to end up creating a bodybuilding physique. You have to do the right kind of exercises, using the right techniques, so that you send a *specific message* to the nervous system that tells the body what kind of adaptation you wish to achieve. This is called specificity of training and it is why learning how to train the right way is so important. I like to compare this with working on a computer. Anyone who has used a computer for any length of time has probably had the experience of the machine not doing what you wanted or expected it to. You try over and over and the same thing happens. You figure there is something wrong with the machine or the software. Then you realize you made some very small mistake, maybe just putting in a period where you should have put a semicolon. But the computer can't think; it just follows your instructions. So if you aren't very specific in what you tell it to do, you're in trouble. The computer doesn't know what you *think* you're telling it to do, only what you are actually telling it to do.

Bodybuilding is based on that same principle. The body doesn't know what you *think* you are telling it to do; it only registers and adapts to the specific instructions you are giving it by the way you are working out. You may feel you are building muscle, you can be working hard, sweating, getting tired and sore, but unless you are sending the right code to the body, you are going to be disappointed in your results. And the code in this case is a correct understanding of the principles of progressive-resistance bodybuilding training.

WEIGHTLIFTING, RESISTANCE TRAINING, AND BODYBUILDING

I have been asked many times whether bodybuilders are really strong or whether their big muscles are just for show. The answer is that some bodybuilders are indeed strong but that strength for physique competitors is a means to an end rather than the ultimate goal. The athletes who are most concerned with ultimate strength are weightlifters.

Weightlifting is a sport which is judged by the amount of weight a competitor can handle for any given type of lift. Over the course of history there have been many types of strength-testing and weightlifting competition. Today there are two basic types of recognized competition weightlifting: Olympic lifting (involving the snatch and clean and jerk) and powerlifting (with three events—the deadlift, bench press, and squat).

Nowadays, weightlifters do a lot of bodybuilding training—that is, they work on balanced development of all the muscle groups—but their primary goal is *strength training.* This is even more true of powerlifters than Olympic weightlifters because their lifts involve a lot less technique, timing, and coordination, and are designed to be a more specific test of strength and power.

The major difference in programs between a weightlifter's strength training and bodybuilding is that the lifter works in a much lower rep range. That is, while bodybuilders (as we shall see in the sections of this encyclopedia on how to train) use less weight and do higher repetition sets, weightlifters are training to do *one maximum rep* in competition, so they frequently pile on the weight in their workouts and do triples (three reps), doubles (two reps), or singles (one rep) to prepare them for handling huge poundages in a meet.

The Bodybuilding Physique

There are other sports in which athletes develop big muscles, but bodybuilding is about the *maximum aesthetic development of the entire physique.* The ideal bodybuilding physique would look something like this: Wide shoulders and back tapering down to a tight waist; legs in proper proportion to the torso. Big, shapely, and proportionate muscular development, with full muscles tapering down to small joints. Every body part developed, including such areas as rear delts, lower back, abdominals, forearms, and calves. Good muscular definition and muscle separation.

Of course, there is no such thing as a perfect athlete in any sport. Athletes always have strengths and weaknesses. In bodybuilding, all of us who have competed in the sport have had weak points that we strove to overcome by specific types of training and posing techniques. Nature makes some physiques better than others, more ideally proportioned, more responsive to training.

In past years, there have been champions like Frank Zane, who had beautiful aesthetics and was a master poser, but who many thought lacked the mass and density they would like to see in a champion. Franco Columbu won two Mr. Olympias in spite of being much shorter than you'd think would be possible in a champion competing at that level. Dorian Yates won many Mr. Olympias, deservingly, but he has also been continually criticized by some for being much too thick and blocky and lacking the overall aesthetic and athletic look they feel bodybuilding ought to be about.

It may seem strange that having too much muscle can be a drawback, but although bodybuilding is about big muscles, it can be a disadvantage to be too mesomorphic, with thick slabs of muscle rather than aesthetic tapering ones. Many seemingly massive bodybuilders actually have fairly small skeletons and joints, which help to give muscles that more aesthetic shape. Most people are surprised that, even at my heaviest competition weight, the average individual could still nearly close his fingers around my wrist. I had big muscles, not big bones, which is one reason I was so successful in my competition career. Lee Haney, who dominated the Mr. Olympia in the 1980s, got into bodybuilding after twice breaking his leg playing football. Again, he has huge, powerful muscles, but a lighter and more aesthetic skeletal structure.

In any sport—in fact, in any area of life—it's a fact that some people have more talent in specific areas than do others. In the same way, bodybuilding champions are made, but also born. You have to have the right kind of genetics. You can't train to change your skeletal type or proportions (although you build bone strength and size when you do muscle training). Keep in mind, however, that what kind of genetic potential you have is not always obvious. Sometimes you need to train for a few years to see what kind of potential you may ultimately have.

And it's also a fact that the "race doesn't always go to the swift." Sometimes you need to overcome obstacles to develop to your full potential and it is often the case that the most gifted athlete does not always learn to work hard enough to rise to the top in a sport. Olympic decathlon champion Bruce Jenner told me that when he was in high school he wasn't the best in any sport in which he participated. But by hard work over the years and learning all of the skills involved in the decathlon's ten events he was ultimately able to win the coveted title of "Best Athlete in the World." Sometimes, it pays to remember the story of the tortoise and the hare.

But whatever your genetics, the kind of training you do is what influences the type of muscular development you achieve. To be a really good bodybuilder, you need to create muscle shape, and this happens when you train every part of a muscle or muscle group, at every angle possible, so that the entire muscle is stimulated and every possible bit of fiber is involved. Muscles are really aggregates of many smaller units—bundles and bundles of fiber—and every time you use the muscle in a slightly different way you stimulate different combinations of these bundles and activate additional fibers. The bodybuilder attempts to achieve total development of every muscle in the body, to create the fullest possible shape in each muscle, to have the muscles proportionate to one another, and to achieve an overall symmetry that is as aesthetically pleasing as possible.

Developing the body this way requires a complete knowledge of technique. You may want to change the shape of your pectoral muscles, peak the biceps more fully, or achieve a better balance between upper and lower body development, but these results do not come about by accident. So the best bodybuilders are those who understand how muscle tissue works, how training actually affects the body, and what sort of techniques lead to specific results.

How Bodybuilding Training Works

Imagine you have a barbell in your hands and you press it up over your head. Several things happen at once: First, the muscles of the shoulder (the deltoids) lift your arms upward; then the muscles at the back of the upper arm (the triceps) contract and cause the arms to straighten. Any movement you make, whether pressing a weight overhead, walking, or simply breathing, is the result of any number of complex combinations of muscle contractions.

The action of individual muscle fibers, on the other hand, is quite simple—a fiber contracts when stimulated and relaxes when the stimulation ceases. Contraction of an entire muscle is the result of the contraction of many tiny, individual muscle fibers. Fibers contract on an all-or-nothing basis. That is, they always contract as hard as they can, or they don't contract at all. However, after a series of contractions a fiber begins to get tired and the amount of effort it can generate diminishes. When you lift a maximum amount of weight one time, you use only a fraction of the total amount of fiber in the muscle. The amount of weight you can lift is determined by three things: (1) how much fiber you are able to recruit; (2) how strong the individual fibers are; and (3) your lifting technique.

When you do only one or two repetitions of a lift, your body never gets a chance to recruit fresh fiber to replace what is getting weak and tired. Weightlifters learn to recruit an unusually large number of fibers in one maximal lift. But they put such an immense strain on those fibers that the body adapts and protects itself by making those fibers bigger and thicker. This is called fiber *hypertrophy*.

No matter how many fibers the weightlifter involves in one maximal lift, he still uses fewer than he would if he used less weight and did more repetitions. Therefore, he trains and strengthens only part of the muscle structure. Also, the weightlifter does a limited number of different kinds of lifts, so there are many angles at which the muscle is never trained at all.

Bodybuilders have learned that you can create greater visual change in the body by a different kind of training. Instead of one maximal lift, a bodybuilder uses less weight and does more repetitions, and does each set to failure—until the muscles are unable to do even one more repetition. Then he rests briefly and continues on to do more sets, perhaps as many as 15 to 20 sets of various exercises for any given body part.

How did bodybuilders arrive at this knowledge of how much weight to lift, and how many sets and reps to do? After all, the legendary Eugen Sandow, who pioneered weight training in the nineteenth century, used to do hundreds of reps! The basic answer is that bodybuilders discovered this training system by trial and error. No expert in the early years of bodybuilding told them to do this; they invented it on their own.

The proof they were on the right track was the bodybuilding physique itself. Could anyone look at the physiques of Steve Reeves, Bill Pearl, Reg Park, Sergio Oliva, Lee Haney, or me and claim we didn't know something pretty special about building muscle? More recently, exercise physiology has confirmed the bodybuilding method. As a general rule, the best way to get maximum development of muscle volume is by lifting about 75 percent of your one-rep capacity—that is, the maximum amount you could lift for one repetition. It should come as no surprise that, for most people, using a weight that is 75 percent of your one-rep maximum allows you to do—that's right—about 8 to 12 reps for the upper body and 12 to 15 reps for the legs.

Of course, stimulating growth isn't enough. To grow, a muscle also needs to rest and to absorb sufficient nutrients for it to recover and recuperate. That's why learning how to do specific exercises and how to put them together in sets is only part of the information you'll find in this encyclopedia. We will also talk about your overall training program, how much to do in a training session, how often to schedule training sessions, and what kind of diet provides the raw materials your body needs to grow in response to your workouts.

Bodybuilding and Aerobic Endurance

There are two fundamentally different kinds of endurance: muscular and cardiovascular.

- Muscular endurance is the ability of the muscle to contract over and over during exercise and to recruit the maximum number of fibers to perform that exercise. For example, while doing heavy Squats, you fatigue muscle fibers in the leg so quickly that if you want to get through an entire set you need muscle fibers that recuperate quickly and you need to be able to bring many additional fibers into play during the course of the set.
- Cardiovascular endurance is the ability of the heart, lungs, and circulatory system to deliver oxygen to the muscles to fuel further exercise and to carry away waste products (lactic acid).

While these two aspects of endurance are distinct, they are also connected. What good is having a well-developed cardiovascular capacity if the muscles you are using in some effort can't keep up the pace and give out? And how well can you perform if your muscles have tremendous endurance ability but your circulatory system can't deliver the oxygen they need?

Just about everyone understands that you increase cardiovascular capacity by doing high volumes of aerobic exercise—exercise that makes you breathe hard, causes your heart to race, and that you can keep up for long periods of time. When you do this you:

- increase the ability of your lungs to take oxygen from the air and transfer it to the bloodstream;
- increase the capacity of your heart to pump large volumes of blood through the circulatory system and to the muscles;
- increase the number and size of the capillaries that bring blood to specific muscles;
- increase the capacity of the cardiovascular system to flush lactic acid (which causes the feeling of burning in the muscles during intense exercise) out of the muscles.

You increase muscular endurance by performing a relatively high volume of muscular contractions. When you do this you:

Frank and Christine Zane

- increase the size and number of capillaries to the specific muscles being exercised;
- increase the ability of the muscles to store glycogen (carbohydrate), which is needed to create energy for muscular contractions;
- increase the mass of the muscle mitochondria (energy factories) that create substances like ATP out of glycogen which are used to fuel muscular contraction;
- increase the development of the type of muscle fiber mostly involved in endurance exercise.

As a reminder, there are basically two types of muscle fiber (as well as a lot of intermediate, in-between fiber types):

1. White, fast-twitch fiber is nonaerobic power fiber that contracts very hard for short periods but has little endurance and a relatively long recovery period.
2. Red, slow-twitch fiber is 20 percent smaller than and not as powerful as white fiber, but is aerobic and can continue to contract for long periods as long as sufficient oxygen is available.

Because bodybuilding training relies on a higher volume (sets and reps) of effort than, say, weightlifting, it has some cardiovascular benefit and also leads to an increase in muscular endurance. Bodybuilders tend to train at a pace which is just below the threshold of cardiovascular failure—that is, they train as fast as they can without overwhelming the ability of the body to provide oxygen to the muscles. This doesn't automatically make them good at endurance activities, such as running or riding a bicycle, but it keeps them in pretty good cardiovascular shape. When it comes to those other types of activity, you are dealing with *both specificity of training and specificity of physical adaptation*. You have to train on a bicycle to be good on one. You have to work at running to improve your ability as a runner. However, a well-trained bodybuilder will usually be in good enough shape to do well at these kinds of exercises and to show considerable improvement very rapidly, providing his size and bodyweight are not too much of a negative factor.

I have always believed that cardiovascular endurance is almost as important to a bodybuilder as muscular endurance. Hard training results in a buildup of lactic acid in the muscles being used—a waste product of the process that produces the energy for muscular contraction. If the heart, lungs, and circulatory system have been able to provide enough oxygen to the area, the lactic acid will be reprocessed by the body into a new source of energy; if not, the buildup will eventually prevent further contraction, leading to total muscular failure.

I have always liked to run several miles a day to develop my aerobic capacity. Some bodybuilders, however, find that running does not suit them or causes them to have problems with their legs and ankles, so they seek other ways of developing cardiovascular conditioning—using Lifecycles, treadmills, steppers, and other types of aerobic equipment. The fact is, the better conditioned your heart, lungs, and circulatory system, the more intense training you will be able to do in the gym and the more progress you will make as a bodybuilder.

AEROBICS AND MUSCULAR DEFINITION

In addition to helping them to stay in top aerobic shape, bodybuilders use aerobic exercise as a way of burning up extra calories in order to achieve the ripped, contest definition they desire while still being able to take in the extra calories necessary to sustain their nutritional needs. So every serious bodybuilder interested in being both massive and lean—that is, developing muscularity as well as size—should do a sufficient amount of aerobic training to help burn off unwanted calories. I remember that Tom Platz, whose leg development was legendary, would work his legs to exhaustion in the gym, then get on a bicycle and ride for twenty miles. In spite of this high volume of training, his legs remained incredibly huge, and his quad definition and muscular separation were awesome.

Using aerobic activity to help you get cut up makes sense. If you metabolize an extra hundred calories doing cardiovascular exercise, that is another hundred calories contributing toward reducing the body's fat stores, or another hundred calories of, say, valuable protein you can eat while continuing to lose weight on your contest preparation diet.

However, the body's ability to tolerate the stresses of aerobic exercise is not unlimited. As we will discuss later, too much cardiovascular exercise can end up being detrimental. *Excessive* aerobics (and there are those who have tried doing endless hours prior to a contest, to their later regret!) can cut into the recuperative ability of the muscles involved and the physical system as a whole, leading to the scavenging of muscle tissue for energy (using the larger white fiber as fuel for the smaller red fiber), and resulting in inducing a state of *overtraining*.

"Overtraining" doesn't mean simply being tired from too much training. It is a condition you get into from too much exercise over too much time in which certain mechanisms in the body that supply you with energy and allow your body to recuperate are depressed or shut down. Overtraining is a chronic state in which you just can't perform no matter how hard you try. If you find yourself overtrained, the only good remedy is rest, sometimes weeks of it. But you can avoid the overtraining syndrome by properly scheduling your training, making sure you get enough rest and enough nutrients in your food. Instructions on how to do all this will be offered in Book 5.

But one good way of preventing overtraining is not to go overboard on the cardiovascular training. Remember, to look like a bodybuilder you need to train like one. To benefit from the concept of specificity of adaptation, you need to make sure that the main influence shaping and developing your body is progressive-resistance weight training—pumping that iron, not aerobics.

BODYBUILDING FOR ATHLETES

Athletes are bigger, stronger, and faster than ever before, and records continue to be broken or even smashed to bits. In my opinion, one cause of this overall improvement in athletic performance is that it's hard to find serious athletes in any sport who don't do at least some kind of resistance training.

But it wasn't very long ago that coaches not only discouraged but pretty much *forbade* athletes to do any kind of training with weights. Iron pumping, it was thought, made athletes "muscle-bound," interfering with their agility and flexibility. It was considered somehow "unnatural," whereas building up your body by straightforward hard work—on a farm or ranch, logging, something outdoors and "manly"—was encouraged. Think of Sylvester Stallone training for the fight with Dolph Lundgren in *Rocky IV*, scrambling through the snow dragging a heavy log, chopping wood in subzero weather, and you've got the picture.

"The belief that weight training would slow you down," explains Frederick C. Hatfield, Ph.D., and Fellow of the International Sports Sciences Association (ISSA), "make you muscle-bound, ruin your touch and coordination, was the prevailing view for decades. This stemmed from associating weight training with weightlifting—that is, increasing your limit strength, your ability to do a one-rep, maximum lift. This kind of weightlifting or powerlifting training is inappropriate for most athletes, who rely much more on speed for increasing performance rather than on absolute strength."

The role of weight training in sports today, Dr. Hatfield says, is to develop the strength of the various muscles to a basic, minimum level that allows the athlete to perform at optimum levels. But this "optimal" strength training should not focus on creating muscle mass or limit strength for their own sakes unless they are specifically required for success in a specific athletic activity. "If you worship strength for its own sake," he adds, "then you can indeed run into problems with speed, mobility, flexibility, agility, coordination, and so forth."

Some sports have been faster to accept the benefits of "optimal" weight training than others. Fred Dryer, actor and former NFL football player, recalls that virtually nobody was training with weights when he began his pro football career in the 1960s, but by the time he retired in the late 1970s *everyone* on the team was spending at least some time in the weight room.

Bruce Jenner, 1976 Olympic decathlon champion, realized in the early 1970s that achieving optimum performance in such a wide variety of different athletic events would require his using weights to substantially increase both his strength and his muscle mass. "The decathlon is designed to test all-around athletic ability," Jenner points out, "with a variety of running, jumping, and throwing events. Starting out, I was very lean and strong for my size, but I realized I would have to be bigger and stronger to score the kind of point totals I would need—yet developing size and strength past a certain point would be detrimental to my overall performance." In those days, track-and-field athletes were only beginning to rely on weight training to build up their bodies, so Jenner tried to be very careful in what kind of program he followed and how much effort he put in with the weights. "Actually," he recalls, "because a lot less was understood about training back then, I did a lot of exercises that were more like weightlifting than weight training, they felt much more 'athletic' to me. But however inefficient some of what I did might have been, my strength did improve, I was able to gain enough solid muscle mass so I was successful in the 1976 Olympic Games in Montreal."

There tends to be an ideal type of body for any sport (although, as we've seen, we can sometimes be surprised by what kinds of bodies succeed in various sports), and any kind of training you do should develop the body in the direction of this ideal rather than away from it. "Body composition assessment has revealed that athletes generally have physique characteristics unique to their specific sport," report physiology experts William McArdle and Frank and Victor Katch in their 1994 book *Exercise Physiology: Energy, Nutrition and Human Performance,* 4th ed. (Williams & Wilkins). "For example, field-event athletes have relatively large quantities of lean tissue and a high percent body fat, whereas long-distance runners have the least amount of lean body weight and fat weight. . . . Physique characteristics blended with highly developed physiologic support systems provide important ingredients for a champion performance."

Although getting "too big" can be a problem in many sports, in some instances, athletes need to pack on a substantial amount of muscle mass in order to be successful. For example, if you compare the average size of football linemen in the 1960s with the size of football players today the difference is amazing, not only in size, but also in body composition. A 300-pound football player thirty years ago might well have had a body composition that was 15 to 25 percent body fat. Today, any number of powerful, 300-pound players measure in at under 12 percent body fat, and a few are much leaner than that.

Boxing as well as wrestling is a sport which has traditionally shied away from training with weights. One reason is that building up your muscle mass puts you in a heavier weight division, which means you may be in combat against opponents who are naturally bigger and stronger. Another is that too many young boxers who have worked with weights tend to try to "muscle" their punches, rather than relying as they should on speed, timing, and coordination. But the world of boxing was astonished when Evander Holyfield, originally fighting at the cruiserweight/light-heavyweight level, gained something like thirty pounds of solid muscle and became

Heavyweight Champion of the World—with the help, to a large extent, of Lee Haney, Mr. Olympia.

"Most boxers rely almost entirely on traditional approaches to training and nutrition," says Haney. "But Evander was very open to new ideas. To become a real heavyweight, he had no choice but to get bigger, and he saw that bodybuilders are the best athletes when it comes to packing on substantial amounts of lean body mass. So he adopted a lot of bodybuilding techniques, as well as a variety of scientific approaches to such things as diet, cardiovascular fitness, and agility."

Holyfield was successful in part because he never forgot that boxing is a speed sport, as well as one that depends a great deal on muscular and cardiovascular endurance. He recognizes the importance of bodybuilding: "Part of my success comes from maintaining a consistent weight program, which gives me confidence and enables me to be both mentally and physically fit." So, for Holyfield, building his body up with weights and proper nutrition was simply the first necessary step; then he concentrated on maximizing his boxing skills.

Magic Johnson came to the NBA in an era in which young basketball players were already fully aware of the benefits of strength training to their performance on the court. But interestingly enough, Magic has explained in a number of interviews that exercising and staying in shape have become even more important to him since his retirement as a means of

Evander Holyfield defends his title against Michael Moorer.

keeping in peak health in his battle to stave off the potential debilitating effects of his illness. I thought I had an active life, but Magic describes a daily regimen that makes even me tired—aerobics classes, weight training, pickup basketball games with an intensity just shy of the NBA, even as he maintains a killer pace in his other business and media activities.

There was an L.A. Lakers coach who for years brought players into World Gym in order to work on their strength and muscular development, Magic Johnson among them. When I worked with Wilt Chamberlain on the sequel to *Conan,* I learned he had started training with weights long before it was generally accepted, when coaches were still warning players to stay out of the weight room. I believe that's one reason why he was such a dominant player during his career.

Even before that, golfer Frank Stranahan was known in the 1950s for using weight training to build up his body and improve his game. Nowadays, a lot of golfers do resistance training as part of their overall conditioning program, although weight training for golf is not yet as accepted as it is in many other sports. So Stranahan was a good thirty years or more ahead of his time when it came to understanding the benefits of training with weights to improve athletic performance.

Another sport which traditionally resisted weight training is baseball. Not very long ago, most baseball players tended to be small and wiry, fast and coordinated, and there weren't many big guys over 200 pounds to be found in the upper ranks of the sport. Today, baseball is full of 230-pound home run hitters who can also run and field their positions. Just look at Mark McGwire, a player so strong that he turns what would have been pop flies into four-baggers. The difference, of course, is the prevalence of weight training, to which athletes are now frequently introduced at the high school or junior high levels, as well as advanced knowledge of how to eat to maximize performance—the science of diet and nutrition.

Traditionally, football teams' weight rooms have been filled with linemen and linebackers who depend on muscle to give them the bulk they need to play their positions. But Dallas Cowboys quarterback Troy Aikman also depends on weight training as part of his conditioning program. Aikman does weight training to increase his upper body strength, including arms and shoulders, but as he explained in *Men's Journal* (September 1998), he also works his legs and hips, since that is where much of the power required to throw the "long bomb" comes from. Aikman wisely does a wide range of exercises for all of the major body parts, which not only strengthens the muscles involved in throwing hard but also creates a better balanced, all around physique that has no areas of weakness that could be overwhelmed and produce injury.

Another believer in the benefits of weight training is the legendary wide receiver for the San Francisco 49ers Jerry Rice. After undergoing knee surgery, Rice dedicated himself to a program of fitness designed to

Mark McGwire hits his record-tying sixty-first home run.

allow him to come back to football better than ever. His six-day-a-week program includes two hours of cardio work in the morning and three *hours* of weight training in the afternoon.

Weight training for sports is on its way to becoming universal. Michael Schumacher, Formula 1 racing phenomenon, pursues a very disciplined conditioning program that includes training with weights. Soccer great Diego Maradona discovered the possibilities of increased athletic performance through weight training late in his career. Tennis players, swimmers, pole vaulters, and even jockeys are turning to training with weights to improve their chances of athletic success.

Weight training and other conditioning programs are valuable to elite athletes in particular because there is frequently little they can do to further hone their specific abilities in their chosen sports. For example, during the latter part of his competitive career, Dwight Stones, one of the great high jumpers of all time, devoted several days a week to a training program which included training with weights and only short periods to practicing his sport. Why? Because, after all the years of effort he had put into perfecting his jumping technique, he reached a point of diminishing returns. He was so close to his absolute potential in terms of technique and neuromuscular coordination that he couldn't expect much improvement no matter how hard he tried. Instead, what he needed was a better "instrument" through which to express his ability and technique. And that's why he devoted a lot of time to pumping iron.

In addition to making muscles strong, weight training is particularly beneficial in building up areas sufficiently weak that the resulting imbalance could be detrimental to execution of various sports movements. As

Dr. Laurence Morehouse observed in his 1974 book *Maximum Performance* (Simon & Schuster), "The nervous system uses the path of least resistance. If you try to execute a motion with weak muscles, your nerves will tend to enlist stronger ones to take over if possible. . . . The result: muscle imbalance, less than ideal movement—and possible deformity."

When you learn, practice, and play a sport, the muscles involved develop up to the level required, but no more. The muscles not involved, or less involved, tend to *deteriorate* over time, leading to even more muscular imbalance. As a result, after years of playing a particular sport, athletes develop a level of imbalance which makes injury extremely likely. Moreover, performing a sport over time at an intense level tends to wear the body down, and unless some kind of exercise program is used to counteract this, you increase your risk of injury as well as a deterioration in your athletic performance.

For example, runners often tear hamstrings because their quadriceps become too powerful in comparison to the leg biceps. Golf does little to build a lot of muscular strength, and because of the powerful twisting motion of the golf swing golfers often experience back problems, especially as they grow older. Sprinters find their performance is improved when their upper bodies are somewhat more muscular, but sprinting by itself won't give them this kind of development. Tennis tends to develop one side of the body much more than the other—notice how tennis pros have one arm obviously larger than the other—and this kind of imbalance in strength can easily cause physical difficulties and performance problems over time.

Doing generalized weight training—that is, following a basic program of exercises, techniques, sets, reps, and workout schedules outlined in this book—builds up the body, gives the athlete a *better overall physique* to work with, and in doing so tends to even out the imbalances caused by the specific demands and stresses of individual sports. Iron pumping allows you to create, shape, and sculpt the kind of body *best suited to your sport*—mass, strength, overall body weight—as is possible with no other exercise program.

"Making the body stronger," says Mark Verstegen, director of the National Performance Institute, located in Bradenton, Florida, "not only increases performance in sports—in terms of strength, speed, and endurance—but also decreases the chances of injury. It allows the athlete to change his body composition to better suit the demands of his sport—that is, to become bigger and stronger if that's what is called for, or to maintain or reduce body weight but create the maximum amount of strength for any given body size." Verstegen creates individual programs for the pro athletes he trains, programs that can include everything from calisthenics to agility drills to the medicine ball to resistance training with free weights and exercise machines.

Verstegen's clients include NCAA basketball top scorers, an American League rookie of the year, NFL football players, and Los Angeles

Lakers phenom Kobe Bryant. "Once you've fully developed your skills," Verstegen adds, "all you can do is improve your physical ability. You want increased power output for both endurance and explosive sports, core strength so you have better posture, and joint stability to reduce injury."

But knowing exactly what kind of weight-training program to follow for any particular sport is not that simple. As exercise physiologists George Brooks and Thomas Fahey explain it, "The intensity and duration of tension are the most important factors eliciting strength increases. The strength requirements of each sport must be assessed in order to develop an appropriate, specific program. In general, sports requiring muscular endurance employ strength-training schedules involving a great number of repetitions, while those requiring strength use fewer repetitions."[1] Therefore, serious athletes need to work under the direction of strength-training coaches who have the knowledge and experience to create the kinds of programs appropriate to any given sport. However, whatever sport you may be training for, there are a few general ideas that I think will apply:

1. Generalized, bodybuilding-type weight training is the ideal system for controlling your body composition—getting bigger and more massive, getting stronger without gaining mass, or losing excess body fat to get lean and hard. This training should be tailored to create the kind of body best suited to your sport. Being "too big" or "too massive" for your sport can be as bad as not being big or strong enough.
2. Diet and nutrition are as important to controlling your body composition as is weight training. You have to eat right to gain, eat right to lose, and eat right to get strong.
3. The basic purpose of weight training for an athlete is to create a better body, a better instrument, to build strength to appropriate levels and to build up weak areas. Weight training done to improve specific sports movements should be done under the direction of a qualified coach.
4. Since the benefit of bodybuilding-type weight training to athletes is due to its "nonspecific" nature, keep in mind that training with free weights produces a much more general adaptive response than does working out with machines.
5. Remember that weightlifting is a specific sport, involving specific techniques and the development of maximal one-rep strength. The purpose of weight training for athletes, on the other hand, is to develop optimal rather than maximum strength, and to bring up weak areas and achieve a better balance of strength among the various muscle groups.

[1] George A. Brooks and Thomas D. Fahey, *Fundamentals of Human Performance* (New York: Macmillan, 1987).

Weight Training and Fitness

Did you realize that, according to *Time* magazine, training with weights has become the number-one athletic activity in the United States? The most popular form of exercise in the whole country?

In the years since this encyclopedia was first published I have seen more and more people making use of weight training who are not competition bodybuilders or professional athletes, but simply want to get fit, to look good and feel better, and to keep their bodies as young and strong as possible as they get older.

Doing bodybuilding to get in great shape and to keep your body fit and strong makes sense. After all, if this method can produce Mr. Olympia winners, it can certainly do wonders for the majority of people whose goals are so much more modest. And if you're going to do something, why not do it the best way possible. To people who say to me, "I want to get fit and firm up, but don't want to get too big," I say in reply, "Do you go to your tennis pro and say you want to learn tennis but don't want to play well enough to qualify for Wimbledon?" Would you tell a golf pro, "Teach me golf, but don't make me as good as Tiger Woods?"

The fact is, most people don't have the genetics, the time, or the energy to create really massive, bodybuilding-type physiques. So if you are bringing less to the table, isn't it important to use the most efficient and effective means of developing your body possible? After all, who wants to waste time and effort exercising without results?

Why is muscular fitness so important? Well, as we have seen, muscles are adaptive; they change according to what and how much they are asked to do. Throughout most of human history, labor was done primarily by the human body. People didn't need exercise; they needed a rest! A hundred years ago the physical exertion of even a relatively sedentary individual would exhaust most people today. In the 1950s and 1960s when I was a kid, we used to run around, climb hills, and engage in all kinds of sports, not sit around and watch television or type on a computer.

So what happens to muscle in our modern, sit-all-day-behind-a-desk world? Our why-should-I-walk-300-yards-when-I-have-a-car culture? Our hand-me-the-remote-control-so-I-don't-have-to-get-up-and-change-channels universe? Simple—when we don't use our muscles they atrophy and shrink. We don't use them, we lose them. This happens slowly in our twenties, more quickly in our thirties, and accelerates after that. "The average man," explained the late Dr. Ernst Jokl, "loses fifty percent of his muscle mass between the ages of eighteen and sixty-five." But the body doesn't have to deteriorate in this fashion. We can do something about it. And the specific program that best counteracts this deterioration of youthful muscle mass is bodybuilding.

Don't worry about "getting big." Concern yourself instead with keeping what you already have. As Alice found in *Alice in Wonderland,* sometimes you have to run faster and faster to stay in the same place.

Having strong and fit muscles keeps you looking and feeling good. It increases your ability to play sports, even if you are only a weekend athlete. Bodybuilding training also tends to stabilize or lower blood pressure over a period of time (using sustained, high-volume training rather than heavy weightlifting), to strengthen the back and so reduce the chances of back problems, and to increase the flow of blood to the skin, keeping it younger-looking and more flexible. Exercise is a stress reducer, and the benefits of lower stress can range from better functioning of the immune system to lowering your risk for cancer or heart disease.

It is a fact that the number of calories you burn up during the day is not just a function of how much exercise you do, but how much muscle you have as well. Muscle burns calories. That's what "burn" means—the oxidation process in the cells that creates energy for exercise. So the more muscle you have, the easier it is to get and stay lean.

Obviously, there are dangers associated with the lifting of excessively heavy weights, and serious weightlifters are prone to any number of more or less serious physical problems due to the demands of their sport. But bodybuilding involves the *controlled* use of weight training, with submaximum levels of resistance and a relatively high volume of training. Therefore, if done properly, with sufficient attention to technique, there is no reason a bodybuilder should ever suffer a training-related injury beyond common muscle soreness or the occasional minor strain or sprain that any athlete comes to expect.

Finally, I'd like to point out that bodybuilding training is also a very good way of introducing more discipline and control in the rest of your life. When you develop your body with training you tend to pay much more attention to your diet and eating habits. After all, why cover up all that nice muscle with unsightly fat? You have to take control of your schedule to make sure you get your workouts in, and that means organizing your time better the rest of the day as well. Bad habits? Smoking, drinking too much, things like that, also tend to interfere with your training discipline and physical progress. Got an early morning workout tomorrow? Don't stay up and waste so much time watching late-night television. If you use bodybuilding as an organizing principle in your life, it can change not only your body and your energy levels, but what you do and whom you do it with as well.

CHAPTER 3

The Training Experience

EVERY BODYBUILDER GETS tremendous satisfaction from looking in the mirror, hitting some poses, and watching his developing muscles pop out all over his body. Or using a measuring tape to calculate exactly how many inches he has put on in each body part. But for me, the training experience itself was always very rewarding and pleasurable. The hours I spent in the gym were the high point of my day. I liked the way training felt, the pump I would get during my workout, and the relaxed sensation of near exhaustion that came afterward. I not only enjoyed *being* a bodybuilder, I really got off on actually *doing* bodybuilding.

Training with this kind of enthusiasm is vital. Going into the gym every day and subjecting yourself to workouts that would fell an elephant is too difficult unless you really love it. Bodybuilders who have to force themselves to go to the gym and work out will never achieve the kind of success possible for those who can't wait to hit the gym and start pumping iron. Some athletes need to be encouraged to train more intensely and others have to be cautioned not to do too much. As far as I'm concerned, the athlete who has to be held back is going to come out on top every time.

WHAT YOU THINK IS WHAT YOU GET

When it comes to bodybuilding, the mind is almost as important as the body. The champion bodybuilders I have known have been so motivated that they practically *willed* their muscles to grow. But the mind is important for another reason. To succeed in bodybuilding or in any other sport, you need to learn to think. You have to understand what you're doing. You have to master training techniques. You have to go beyond the basic principles of bodybuilding and find out what really works for *you*. You must develop your own instincts just as you develop your muscles and learn to listen to them. Sure, you have to train hard, but it won't do that much good unless you also train smart.

Of course, that all comes with time. In the beginning, every bodybuilder should stick pretty much to the basics. When you are starting, you can't train according to "how you feel" because you have no idea what correct training feels like. That takes experience. The trick is to master the correct training techniques, get used to how working out this way feels, and then you can begin to rely on "feel" or "instinct" to guide you.

Like other bodybuilders, I started out doing the basic exercises. Over time, experimenting in my own workouts, thinking about what I was doing, I found that I could do many sets for chest or for lats, train these muscles with as much intensity as possible, but I still didn't get as good a result as when I supersetted the back and chest—combined a pulling movement with a pressing movement. But this same technique does not necessarily apply to every muscle, nor will every bodybuilder get the same good results training like this that I did. You must learn all of the relevant techniques, and then study how each technique affects you as an individual. *This is the true art of bodybuilding.*

The first step in this process is to understand exactly what you are doing in the gym, and to learn to interpret the feelings you experience from day to day as you go through your training routine. Remember, if you contemplate ever becoming a competitive bodybuilder, your opponents will probably know just as much about technique as you. What will make the difference is the degree to which you have been able to utilize your own instincts and feelings.

No matter how advanced a bodybuilder gets, there are still questions that arise, which is another reason you have to use your mind—to analyze what you're doing and evaluate your progress. Even a Mr. Olympia can find himself unhappy with his progress in the gym and begin to experiment with various training principles to find something that works better. This is all the more reason to learn as much as possible about different principles and ways of training, so you will understand what alternatives are available to you.

All of this is the reason I have created an *encyclopedia* of bodybuilding rather than just another book on how to exercise. I describe how to do a Bench Press or a Barbell Curl, how to choose which exercises to do, and how to put them together in a program. I deal with basic training and then go on to give you the information you need to move on to advanced training and, if that's your goal, to competition. You'll also find instruction on how to eat to gain muscle, how to diet to lose fat, how to pose, to tan, and everything else involved in the sport and exercise activity of bodybuilding. But, as I've said, this isn't just a matter of hard work, although that's necessary. It also involves thinking and learning—training smart, using the mind and acquiring the knowledge you need to achieve your personal bodybuilding goals.

But before you go on to begin learning the basic principles of exercise, I think it's important that you understand some of the *specific* experiences you will be going through in your workouts, things like the "pump," the nature of training intensity, muscular soreness and muscular pain (and how to tell the difference), and the huge benefits you can get from having the help of a good training partner—all of which I will deal with in the rest of this chapter.

The Pump

One of the first things you will experience when you start training is the pump. Your muscles swell up well beyond their normal size, your veins stand out, you feel huge, powerful, and full of energy. The pump is usually felt after about 4 or 5 sets. Often you can keep this sensation throughout your workout, feeling an increased pump over time as more and more blood is forced into the area being exercised, bringing in fresh oxygen and nutrients for continued intense, muscular contraction.

What causes the pump is that blood is forced *into* the area by the action of the muscles and the pressure of the cardiovascular system, but there is no comparable force drawing the blood *out* of the muscle. Therefore, this extra blood stays in the muscle for some period of time, swelling it up to a much bigger size. The fact that your muscles get bigger and more impressive when you have a pump is why bodybuilders like to pump up before they pose. When you're in a tough competition, every little bit of advantage helps.

Getting a great pump is one of the best feelings in the world. It's so good that it's been compared to sex—by me, now that I come to think of it, in the movie *Pumping Iron*. According to Dr. Fred Hatfield ("Dr. Squat" to his fans), champion powerlifter and exercise physiology expert, "Quantities of blood flooding a muscle stimulate any number of proprioceptive sensors. Exercise and the resulting pump create a whole cascade of hormonal responses, including the release of endorphins and enkephalins, which are nature's painkillers." This is the bodybuilder's version of the runner's high, which also occurs due to the release of hormones such as endorphins. In addition, an association develops over time, Dr. Hatfield explains, between the exercise and the positive feeling you get from it, so your pleasure centers are stimulated even more as your body relates the sensation of exercise with the good outcome.

This combination of the physical and the psychological can have a tremendous effect on how you feel and how hard you can train. When you are pumped up, you feel better and stronger, and it is easier to motivate yourself to train hard, to achieve a high level of intensity. Sometimes, you think you're King Kong walking around the gym! Of course, this feeling may differ from day to day. From time to time you will walk into the gym feeling tired and lazy, but when you get a fantastic pump after a few minutes of work suddenly you feel big, strong, energetic, and ready to lift every weight in sight.

However, there are days when you don't feel very energetic, when the pump just doesn't happen no matter what you do. Sometimes there's a physical reason for this. You haven't gotten enough sleep, you've done too many workouts in a row, or you are dieting and your body simply lacks the nutrients it needs to get a good pump easily. But in most cases, I have found that a lack of pump indicates a lack of full concentration. Sure, it's better to get enough rest, not to overtrain, and to eat well enough to fuel your workouts, but no matter how bad you feel or how much energy you lack I have found you can still get the pump to come if you focus and concentrate hard enough.

Training Intensity

I consider myself a bottom-line kind of guy. What I'm interested in when I undertake something is *results.* In that regard I figured out very early in my bodybuilding career that, as with most things, what you get out of training depends on what you put into it. The harder you work, the more results you will see, *assuming that your training methods are as effective as possible.*

But at a certain point it becomes very difficult to get more out of your workouts. You're working as heavy as you can, so you can't add more weight. You're already doing as many sets as possible and training as often as you can without overtraining. So what do you do now?

Getting better results at this point is a matter of increasing your training intensity. What do I mean by that? Simple. *Intensity is a measure of what you get out of your training, not what you put into it.* What kinds of techniques can you use to increase intensity? For example, you can:

- add weight to your exercises;
- increase the number of reps in your sets;
- cut down on your rest period between sets;
- do two or more in a row of an exercise without resting (supersets).

There are also a number of special-intensity training techniques, many depending on the participation of your workout partner. They include forced reps, burns, forced negatives, supersets, giant sets, partial reps, and rest/pause. They will all be described in detail when we look at how to do bodybuilding exercises in Book 2.

Cardiovascular endurance is one limiting factor in increasing intensity. If you outrun your ability to supply oxygen to the muscles, they will fail prematurely and you will not fully stimulate them. However, if you cut down on rest periods and speed up your training on a gradual basis, you will give your body time to adapt and your ability to train both hard and for longer periods will increase.

It is also a fact that, as you increase your training intensity, you tend to tire more quickly. That is, when you train very hard it's difficult to train very long, even when you are in great condition. This is why modern bodybuilders split up their body part workouts, hitting only a few muscles in each workout rather than trying to train the entire body in a single session. A further increase in intensity occurs when you do a double-split workout, dividing up your day's training into two different sessions, giving yourself plenty of time to rest in between. When I was competing and wanted to train with even *more* intensity I always liked to schedule my heaviest training in the morning, when I felt strongest, rather than trying to handle huge poundages later on in the day. (All the different ways of organizing your workouts will be dealt with in detail in Book 2.)

Of course, there is a big difference in the level of intensity that beginning, intermediate, or competition bodybuilders need—or, in fact, can achieve. When you are starting out, just getting through your workouts can be such a shock to the body that additional intensity is not required. Intermediate bodybuilders, however, may find that they have to give some thought about how to shock the body into further growth. And competition bodybuilders, who are striving for the ultimate in physical development, must generate an unbelievable amount of intensity.

The more advanced you become, the harder it is to continue developing and the harder you have to train. This is known as *the law of diminishing returns*. In 1971, when I was doing thirty sets for shoulders and wanted to shock them into even more development, my training partner, a professional wrestler, told me I didn't have to add more reps, but just to follow him. We started with 100-pound Dumbbell Presses, then went on down to 90-pound, 80-pound, and 40-pound weights—and then without resting we started doing Lateral Raises. After a one-minute rest we went back and did the whole thing over again. In one hour I did so many more repetitions and sets than normal that my shoulders felt as if they had been tortured! But the bottom line was that it worked.

Pain vs. Muscle Soreness

Every bodybuilder has heard the phrase "No pain, no gain," but it is important to be able to differentiate the (almost) enjoyable pain of an intense workout from pain resulting from actual physical injury.

Muscle soreness following a heavy workout is common among bodybuilders. This soreness is the result of microdamage to muscles, ligaments, or tendons—nothing that really constitutes an injury, but is often painful nonetheless. A certain amount of soreness is inevitable, a sign that you have really trained intensely.

Another common cause of soreness is the buildup of lactic acid in the muscle, which tends to accumulate in the area being exercised when muscular activity produces it faster than the circulatory system can take it away. The presence of an excessive amount of lactic acid is what gives you the burn when you do a lot of hard repetitions, and it also tends to produce a certain amount of post-workout soreness.

Soreness is not a bad thing and, in fact, can be taken as a good sign, an indication that you have trained intensely enough to produce results. However, should you get so sore that it interferes with your training or other areas of your life, you should ease up for a while. Being a little bit sore does indicate you've had a good, hard workout; being very, very sore simply means you've abused your body and should take things a little easier.

Of course, I haven't always followed my own advice. When I was sixteen years old I was such a fanatic about training that no amount of soreness could possibly have deterred me. In fact, after my very first workout in a gym, after blasting my body as hard as I was able, I actually fell off my bicycle riding home because I was so numb with fatigue. The next day I was so sore I could hardly lift a coffee cup or comb my hair. But I took pleasure in this feeling because it meant I had really gotten something out of my training. Many times since I have deliberately bombed a certain body part—done Chin-Ups all day or countless sets of Squats—and ended up sore for a week! I never minded the inconvenience if it meant I had shocked my muscles into growth.

Surprisingly, soreness seems to result more from "negative" repetitions—that is, when you are lowering a weight—than from positive repetitions, lifting the weight. The reason for this is that eccentric contraction of muscle—lowering a weight—puts a disproportionate amount of stress on the supporting tendons and ligaments, and this is what seems to cause the damage.

In general, you can train despite soreness. In fact, you will start to feel better when you begin working out because you pump more blood into the painful area. Saunas, massage, and other treatments can also make you feel better, but ultimately you will have to wait several days for the overstressed tissue to heal before you fully recover.

But pain can also signal injury, which is much different from simple soreness. It can be a warning that you have damaged yourself in some fairly serious way. The very real pain of a strain, sprain, or other stress-related injury is telling you to STOP—immediately! There is no working through this kind of pain. Anything you do that causes you to feel the pain is just going to make the injury worse. Your only recourse is to rest the area in question, and to seek medical help if the injury is serious or if it persists.

(For more information on injuries, how to recognize them and what to do about them, see Injuries and How to Treat Them, page 774.)

Eventually, you have to learn to tell the difference between "good" pain and the pain of injury if you want to succeed in bodybuilding. Trying to train through a real injury can put you out of action for a considerable time or can even cause an acute injury to become a chronic one that you have to battle against for years.

But some kinds of pain are not only inevitable in bodybuilding, they are practically essential. After all, it is those last few reps that you perform after your muscles are burning and telling you to stop that often mean the difference between progress and the lack of it. The tenth or eleventh repetition of Barbell Curls, while your biceps are screaming in agony, may be the only way to develop championship arms. This phenomenon of working until your muscles are burning with pain isn't something that happens just in bodybuilding. When the legendary Muhammad Ali was asked how many Sit-Ups he did in preparing for a championship fight he replied that he didn't know. "I don't start counting till it starts to hurt," he explained.

Obstacles and Setbacks

Progress in bodybuilding usually does not come about in a smooth, upward curve. But when it does, the results can be very gratifying. I remember a time when I could count on seeing a one-inch increase in the size of my arms every couple of months, regular as clockwork; those were the days I could count on putting on more than twenty pounds of muscle every year no matter what.

But events can conspire to put obstacles in the way of your training progress. There is getting sick, for example. When most people get the flu it is a matter of inconvenience. But for a bodybuilder with eight weeks left to go to a contest it can be a disaster. You can't just lie in bed and throw away months of effort, but you don't feel well enough to train. The solution in this case, at least in part, is finding a sports medicine–oriented doctor who understands your situation and will do what he can to help you get well while you continue trying to get in the best shape you can under the circumstances. There can be worse obstacles. I've known bodybuilders with severe juvenile diabetes who nonetheless managed to train and diet hard enough to win amateur bodybuilding titles. And there is the case of Dennis Newman, the USA Bodybuilding Champion, who battled successfully with leukemia and was eventually able to resume his career in the professional division of the IFBB.

Overcoming obstacles is often a matter of being able to make adjustments. I remember being in New York in the dead of winter and not being able to go out and run to get in my cardiovascular training. What did I do? I ran up and down the fire stairs of the Park Lane Hotel, and the amount of soreness I felt the next day showed me what a terrific type of exercise this really was. Nowadays, most good hotels have at least some kind of training facility, and it's a lot easier to find gyms in cities all over the world than it used to be, so getting in a workout when you're traveling is not as difficult as it used to be. But as much as I recommend training in a gym with good equipment, if you are really pressed for time or somewhere no gym is available, taking along some kind of exercise device with rubber bands or springs or whatever is a lot better than doing nothing. Again, bottom line, if you don't do the work, you don't get the results, no matter what your excuse is.

There are environmental factors you will sometimes be faced with, too. For example, I remember being in Denver on a book promotion tour and going into the gym with a television crew. With the lights and camera on, I got all psyched up and did lots of Bench Presses and other exercises, but at the end of twenty minutes I was so out of breath I could hardly stand up. The television producer told me, "Okay, we have enough," and all I could think of was, I've had enough too! I realized that my difficulty came from being over a mile above sea level and not being able to get enough oxygen. I knew I would have to pace myself carefully if I ever tried to really work out at that altitude before becoming fully adapted to the thinner air.

High humidity is another difficult environmental condition. Try training in Florida or Hawaii in the summer with no air-conditioning and you will find you cannot hit your workouts nearly as hard as normal. I once went to South Africa to train with Reg Park—it was the middle of winter in Austria and the middle of a very hot and humid summer below the equator—and I found myself using thirty pounds less on most exercises, fifty pounds less on others, until I had been there for a week or two and my body became acclimatized to those very different conditions.

Cold does the same thing. During a break in the filming of *Conan* I flew from Spain to Austria at Christmastime, accompanied by Franco Columbu, and we trained every day in freezing weather in an unheated garage with one door open to the outside environment. That was the coldest I have ever been working out and I learned that training when it is very cold requires very specific kinds of adaptation—you have to warm up more thoroughly and keep your warm clothes on even after you start to sweat. You also have to be careful because it can get so cold that your hands will literally stick to the metal dumbbells and barbells. I adapted fairly quickly to this environment because I had trained in fairly cold conditions before, but it still required an effort to get a good workout without the sunny California climate helping me along.

Another obstacle that can produce severe setbacks is injury. Many bodybuilders never experience a serious injury, but you have to consider the possibility. My worst injury did not happen while training, but occurred when a posing platform slipped out from under me during a competition in South Africa. My knee was so badly injured that it was feared for a while that my bodybuilding career was over. The first doctor I saw advised me not to continue training, but I soon realized that he did not understand athletes and sports injuries, so I simply went and found another doctor.

This was a very discouraging period. I had worked for five years to build my thighs up from twenty-three to twenty-eight inches, but two months after the accident my thighs measured twenty-three inches again! I felt as if five years of sweat and sacrifice had been thrown out the window.

Luckily, I found a specialist, Dr. Vincent Carter, who was able to help me. He told me, "Don't you know that the body is stronger after an injury than before? That a broken bone heals stronger than before the break? We'll whip you into shape in no time!" That positive attitude cheered me up right away. I had an operation, but when the cast came off I still had that twenty-three-inch thigh.

Now I had to not only rehabilitate the injured knee but deal with the psychological setback as well. I found a physical therapist, Dave Berg, who put me on a serious exercise program and wouldn't let me baby myself. In only three weeks I gained 1½ inches on my thigh and soon was starting to do Squats again. When I went back to Dr. Carter, he asked me how much I was squatting with, and I told him 135 pounds. "Why?" he said. "What's wrong with you? The injury is healed, it's all finished with. You told me you could squat with four hundred pounds, so it's time to get back into it."

My injury and operation had taken place in November 1971, and by March 1973, I was healed and ready to train seriously again. It was seven months until the Mr. Olympia contest, so I decided to forget about the injury and train for the competition, and this led to another Olympia title. However, if I had not kept a positive attitude, sought out the medical help I needed to completely recover, and fought against the discouragement that comes with any serious setback, my career might really have ended right then.

Your Training Partner

Throughout my bodybuilding career, having the right training partner was essential to my success. Franco Columbu is one of the best training partners I ever had. In the years Franco and I trained together, I know I made much more progress than I would have training alone.

What are the necessary qualities of a good training partner? For one thing, he has to be giving. He has to care about your success as well as his own. He can't just do his set and walk away while you do yours. He has to be there with you. "Okay, yesterday you did eight reps, today let's go for nine!" A good training partner wants to train at the same time you do—not at six if you want to train at five. A good training partner calls you and asks, "How are you feeling today?" He not only shows up on time for your

Dave Draper was the original "golden boy" of the sport. To Europeans he represented the classic California-type bodybuilder.

My training was always first-rate when I had training partners like Franco Columbu and Ken Waller to push me.

Casey Viator was one of the most powerful training partners I've ever had.

workout but also suggests, "Hey, let's get together and do some posing practice." Ideally, he should have the same goals as you. If you're training for competition, if you're trying to build up to a 400-pound Bench Press, if you're on a strict diet and trying to lose a lot of body fat, it all goes much easier if your training partner is focused on achieving the same kinds of things.

A training partner should bring a lot of energy to your workouts. Nobody is at 100 percent every time he walks into a gym, and if you're having a low-energy day your training partner should be there to kick you into gear and get you going, and you should do the same thing when you're the one with the most energy. It's also a great advantage to have somebody waiting in the gym expecting you to show up no matter what the weather is like, how much sleep you got the night before, or how you happen to be feeling.

Franco and I used to compete constantly, each trying to lift more weight than the other and do more sets and reps. But we weren't competing in order to defeat each other. We simply used competition to create an atmosphere in which any incredible effort seemed possible.

I have relied on different training partners for different results, depending on their individual characteristics. I trained with Franco in the morning, since he trained only once a day, and we did mostly power training. I trained with Dave Draper for lats because I wanted extra sets for

Training with Ed Corney got me in my best possible shape for the 1975 Mr. Olympia in South Africa.

Franco Columbu, Jusup Wilkosz, and I all started out as weightlifters, which gave us a muscle density that bodybuilders who have not done power training lack.

One of the biggest thrills of my life was when I actually got to train with and compete against my bodybuilding hero, Reg Park.

these muscles; Dave just loved working in the gym and would train for hours doing endless sets. Frank Zane was a good training partner for isolating specific muscle groups. Each training partner has his own particular value, so you may want to train with more than one person in order to get a whole range of benefits.

Choosing a training partner is a lot like a marriage, and you want to marry somebody who is an addition to your life, who makes it better, not somebody who causes you to say, "Whew, this marriage stuff. What did I get myself into?" This is not just a matter for competition bodybuilders. A beginning bodybuilder might want to train with someone more advanced, but that advanced bodybuilder may be working on refining his physique rather than creating a basic, powerful muscle structure, and the beginner would not profit much from that kind of workout. A businessman who wants to train to stay in shape might find himself overtaxed trying to train with a full-time bodybuilder. It's all very simple: A training partner who helps you make faster and better progress is a good one; a partner who holds you back in any way is a poor one.

Scheduling Training

If you are motivated enough, you will find a way to make sure you get in your training sessions, no matter what.

One of the most common complaints I hear is from people who say they just can't find the time to get in their workouts. Some are young bodybuilders who are in school or have jobs that make scheduling workouts difficult. "I envy the pro bodybuilders," they say, "who have nothing to do all day but train, eat, and sleep." When I hear that I remember Sergio Oliva working all night as a butcher and then going to the gym for killer workouts. Or what Franco and I had to deal with when we were first in this country and trying to maintain our training schedules while working during the day laying bricks.

I made much of my best early progress when I was in the Austrian Army and had a lot of other demands on my time. When out on maneuvers for six weeks along the Czechoslovakian border and driving tanks fifteen hours a day, I had to pump in fuel with a hand pump, wrestle with huge fuel drums, change wheels, and do maintenance. We slept in

Bill Pearl never talked me into becoming a vegetarian, but he did convince me that a vegetarian could become a champion bodybuilder.

trenches under the tanks until we were awakened each morning at six. But I had another idea: My buddy and I would get up at five, open the tool compartment of the tanks where we had stored our barbells, and exercise for an hour before everybody else woke up. After we finished maneuvers for the day, we would train for another hour. I can't imagine any more difficult circumstances in which to train, so I submit that finding the time and energy for your workouts is simply a matter of motivation plus imagination. Each bodybuilder has to find a time to train that suits his particular situation.

Even today I still have to deal with the same scheduling problems. For example, when I was filming *Batman and Robin,* I had to begin makeup at 5 A.M., which took three hours and there was no time to train in the morning. But during the day when there was a change of setup I would ask how much time it would take. "An hour and a half," I was told. So I would take the time to get out of all my "Mr. Freeze" armor, go to the exercise trailer and do light exercises, enough to give me a pump, but nothing that would make me sweat too much and ruin all that makeup. Filming other movies, where we got an hour for lunch, I figured that it doesn't take an hour to eat. So I would go and work out for half an hour, spend fifteen minutes eating, and then the final quarter hour have my makeup fixed for the next take.

All the actors I work with in the movies know I work out early in the morning or during the course of the day, and that I will always try to get them to come along and do some exercising with me. On talk shows, when they are asked about the difficulty of filming, they always say things like, "Making the movie was easy. What was hard was having to work out every day with Arnold!"

So I am fully aware that scheduling workouts can also be a problem for those not dedicated to pursuing a competitive bodybuilding career. Busy with jobs, careers, family, or raising kids, people think, There is not a single hour in the day I can put aside for working out. But the bottom line is this: If you don't find the time, if you don't do the work, you don't get the results. Are you sure there's no time to spare? For example, I've read reports that said the time most wasted during the day is the period between 10 P.M. and midnight. Is your favorite late-night television program more important to you than building a great body? Why not go to bed and get up an hour early? I've trained a lot at 5 A.M., and while it takes some getting used to, I've had some of my best workouts at that time of the morning.

When my wife, Maria, and I had an audience with the Pope in the 1980s, he told me that *he* worked out every morning at five. Ronald Reagan and George Bush both managed an hour workout a day when they were in office. Most of the most successful men in business and the movie industry tell me that they do their best never to go a day without exercising. These are the busiest men in the world! How do they manage? They are good at organizing their time and they recognize the importance of including training in their lives.

Sometimes it's hard to keep on a schedule because people around you, sometimes with good intentions and sometimes not, seem to do everything they can to dissuade you from attaining your goals. For example, how supportive of your training ambitions are your family, friends, or spouse? Negative vibes from the people in your life can be difficult to handle. It takes extra effort to retain your confidence and stick to your routine when those close to you don't accept your chosen goals. "Why can't you come out for beer and pizza?" they may ask. And the answer that you are on a diet and have to get up early may not meet with a positive reception. You can end up being called egotistic or self-centered by those who don't realize that *they* are the ones being self-centered by not appreciating how important training is to you and what it costs to pursue this kind of effort. And I am sure I am not the only one who has had his girlfriend complain about his getting up at five o'clock in the morning to go to the gym.

Your diet regimen can create problems, too. Eating with friends is a very pleasant social ritual, but one you will have to forgo much of the time. When somebody who should know you are in training keeps offering you food that is not on your diet, you know they don't understand or, worse, don't have your best interests at heart.

Many serious bodybuilders who work take food with them to the job, or even keep a hot plate at the workplace so they can make meals during the day. Having a supportive boss who understands what you are trying to do can be very helpful. If you don't, then you will simply have to make whatever adjustment is necessary.

TRAINING FOR WOMEN

How different is bodybuilding training for women than it is for men? In my opinion, not very—which is why I am not devoting space in this book to dealing with training for women separately.

Some people have trouble grasping this concept. Women are smaller. They have different hormones. They aren't as strong. Sure, but muscle is muscle and a Bench Press is a Bench Press. Women have less upper-body muscle than men do, so it generally takes them longer to develop this area than it does the legs. They usually can't handle the same poundages as men (although plenty of women in the world can bench over 300 pounds!). But what differentiates a woman's training are her goals: She's probably more interested in shaping and tightening her body than in building big muscles. So, even though she'll commonly do the same exercises as a man (with additional exercises thrown in to target problem areas like hips, thighs, and triceps), her program setup will probably differ rather dramatically from a man's. The most likely difference will be that her workout consists of fewer sets per muscle group but more reps per set. This builds muscle endurance while sacrificing maximum muscle size. The *execution* of those exercises, though, remains exactly the same. We all need to develop programs that suit our own individual needs, our strengths and weaknesses. The goal for men and women is the same: to create the maximum possible *aesthetic* development of the physique.

Women can benefit from training partners, need to deal with soreness and setbacks, should avoid overtraining, can feel a great pump, have to cope with injury—just as men do. In fact, I often trained with female training partners, which I found both motivating and challenging. So my advice to women interested in serious training is simple: Your muscle cells don't know you are a female. They will respond to progressive-resistance weight training as does a man's. If you admire physiques such as those of Rachel McLish, Cory Everson, Anja Langer, or Lenda Murray, don't forget that they worked long and hard to develop those bodies. They sweated in gyms right alongside men. Bodybuilding is a sport, and both men and women do it, just as both men and women play tennis, basketball, and volleyball. And as far as the training experience is concerned, all that counts is getting through the next rep, the next set, the next workout. The correct approach to training is what produces the best results.

CHAPTER 4

The Gym

WHEN YOU ARE a bodybuilder, the gym is your office. It's where you take care of business. You can easily end up spending three or four hours in a gym, which means it should have the kind of equipment you need, the kind of people training around you that add energy to your workouts, and an overall atmosphere that will motivate you to achieve your personal goals.

THE GYM EXPLOSION

When I began serious bodybuilding training it was hard to find adequate training facilities. Good gyms were few and far between. For example, when I was working out in Austria as a young man we had no standard incline bench, the kind you lie back on. Instead, there was a *standing* incline bench, which was quite a different piece of equipment. In order to do incline barbell presses, rather than being able to lift the bar off a rack we had to pick it up off the floor, clean it up to shoulder height, and then fall back against the bench before being able to do a set. That, I can tell you, is doing it the hard way.

When I later went to live in Munich, I had the advantage of being able to train at my good friend Albert Busek's gym, which was very advanced for the time and provided all the equipment I needed to train to become Mr. Universe and Mr. Olympia. In California, I trained at Joe Gold's gym, which had equipment like no other because most of it was designed and fabricated by Joe himself.

Today, it is relatively easy to find a well-equipped gym. World Gym, for example, has franchises all over the United States and the world. Gold's Gym and Powerhouse both have numerous franchises as well.

Bally's, Family Fitness Centers, and many other excellent gyms are located both in big cities and smaller towns. Of course, most health clubs and spas are not oriented toward serious bodybuilding, but they generally provide at least some free-weight facilities in addition to their inventory of machines, cables, and other workout equipment. There are also training facilities in schools and universities, military bases, YMCAs, hotels, corporate office buildings, and upscale apartment complexes.

Gym memberships are generally available by the day, week, month, and year. When you join a gym that is part of a chain, you frequently get reciprocal training privileges, which means you can train at other gyms that are part of the chain at no additional cost or for a small fee.

WHAT TO LOOK FOR IN A GYM

The first thing to consider in choosing a gym is ascertaining what kind of equipment and facilities it provides:

1. A gym should not be too big or too small. If it is too small, you constantly have to wait for equipment and you can't keep up the rhythm of your training. But if it is huge, you can feel dwarfed by too much space, which makes it hard to keep up your concentration.
2. If you want to make the best progress, the gym you train in has to have a full complement of free weights and benches. It should have sets of dumbbells heavy enough for most intense lifts. There should be exercise machines and cable setups that allow you to work all the major body parts.
3. There should be equipment for doing your cardiovascular training—treadmills, exercise bicycles, steppers, aerobic classes, whatever you need for your individual aerobic workouts.
4. Some gyms and health clubs have other facilities like saunas, steam rooms, staff massage therapists, swimming pools, and even indoor running tracks, so if any of these things is important to you check what's available before you sign up for a membership.

ENVIRONMENT AND ATMOSPHERE

Along with the "hardware" a gym has to offer, you need to consider whether it provides the kind of environment that will help to energize and motivate your workouts, whether the atmosphere of the gym makes you comfortable or ill at ease.

Bodybuilders for the most part are not interested in training in a gym they feel is too "fancy." Training, after all, is tough and sweaty, not refined like an afternoon tea party. After winning my second NABBA Universe in 1968, I trained for a while in a health spa in London—very elegant and posh—and I found I couldn't get a pump no matter how hard I tried. It felt like a living room, nice carpeting, chrome equipment, as antiseptic as a doctor's office. I was concentrating on training while trying to block out conversations going on around me about the stock market or what kind of car somebody was thinking of buying. I can accept that a spa with that kind of atmosphere is probably perfect for most of the people who work out there, who merely wanted to shape up their bodies and maybe lose a few inches around the waist. But it is not appropriate for those with serious bodybuilding ambitions.

Of course, even for the hard-core competition bodybuilder, it is no fun training in a smelly dungeon either, so don't be afraid to call a dump a dump, although I have had some very good workouts in some very definite dumps! Again, what counts is not aesthetics but how the gym makes you feel. Also, there is the matter of music. I like to train to really loud rock 'n' roll, but others prefer different music or none at all. Check to see what kind of music is played in any gym you intend to train in.

Personally, I could never be comfortable in a gym in a basement, someplace you have to go *downstairs* to get to. I also preferred gyms at street level or on an upper floor. Atmosphere is important. You are going to be spending as much as three or four hours in a gym and you don't want to be looking around and asking yourself, What am I doing in this place? I always liked a serious, industrial kind of look, something that made me feel "I'm here to work."

Being in the right environment is very important in many areas of life. Why do people prefer to go to certain restaurants or bars than others? The food isn't that different from one good restaurant to the other and the drinks are the same. It's the atmosphere, how the overall environment makes you feel, what kind of mood it puts you in. You furnish and decorate your home to create a certain environment. Great museums like the Getty Center in Los Angeles create a special atmosphere which makes viewing the art they contain that much more rewarding. Restaurants, clothing stores, your home, a gym—you get certain vibes that you often can't explain but that can make a very big difference in the experience of being there.

At the Arnold Seminar held as part of the weekend of events in Columbus each year including the Arnold Classic, I frequently make a comparison between how environment affects the development of a child and how the gym environment can affect the development of a bodybuilder. If you grow up among successful, motivated people, you yourself will tend to be successful and highly motivated; growing up in an impoverished environment, among people with little hope and little motivation, you are going to have to fight that influence all your life.

WHO ELSE IS TRAINING IN THE GYM?

I remember coming to California in 1968 and training at Joe Gold's gym in Venice. I was already a two-time NABBA Mr. Universe, but training every day among bodybuilders like Frank Zane and Dave Draper—Mr. Americas and Mr. Universes all over the place—and bodybuilders like Sergio Oliva showing up from time to time, I practically had no choice but to become better.

The kind of people who train alongside you in a gym makes a difference. If you are surrounded by people who are serious and train with a lot of intensity, it's easier for you to do the same thing. But it can be pretty hard to really blast your muscles while the people around you are just going through the motions. That is why good bodybuilders tend to congregate in certain gyms. By having the example of other serious bodybuilders constantly in front of you, you will train that much harder.

That is what made Joe Gold's original gym in Venice, California, such a great place—a small gym with just enough equipment, but where you would constantly be rubbing shoulders with the great bodybuilders against whom I had the privilege of competing—like Franco Columbu, Ed Corney, Dave Draper, Robby Robinson, Frank Zane, Sergio Oliva, and Ken Waller. Nowadays, it's rare to find that many champions in the same place, but if you aren't sharing the gym floor with great bodybuilders like Flex Wheeler, Shawn Ray, Nasser El Sonbaty, or Dorian Yates, it can be very motivating if there are pictures or posters of these individuals on the walls or championship trophies displayed.

In 1980, training at World Gym for my final Mr. Olympia competition, I showed up at the gym at seven o'clock one morning to work out and stepped out on the sundeck for a moment. Suddenly the sun came through the clouds. It was so beautiful I lost all my motivation to train. I thought maybe I would go to the beach instead. I came up with every excuse in the book—the most persuasive being that I had trained hard the day before with the powerful German bodybuilder Jusup Wilkosz, so I could lay back today—but then I heard weights being clanged together inside the gym and I saw Wilkosz working his abs, Ken Waller doing shoulders, veins standing out all over his upper body, Franco Columbu blasting away, benching more than 400 pounds, Samir Bannout punishing his biceps with heavy Curls.

Everywhere I looked there was some kind of hard, sweaty training going on, and I knew that I couldn't afford not to train if I was going to compete against these champions. Their example sucked me in, and now I was looking forward to working, anticipating the pleasure of pitting my muscles against heavy iron. By the end of that session I had the best pump I could imagine, and an almost wasted morning had turned into one of the best workouts of my life. If I hadn't been there at World Gym, with these other bodybuilders to inspire and motivate me, I doubt that day would have ended up being so productive.

Even today, when I'm training for other reasons, such as getting into top shape for a movie role, or just trying to stay in shape, I absorb energy from people working out around me. That's why I still like to go to gyms where bodybuilders are training for competition. Even today, after all this time, it still inspires me.

YOU DON'T HAVE TO TRAIN IN LOS ANGELES

I've been asked many times whether young bodybuilders need to come to California in order to become champion bodybuilders or whether a young physique competitor can create a great physique working out in Des Moines, Pittsburgh, Seattle, or elsewhere. My response is simple: If you are motivated, train hard, have adequate workout facilities available, and learn the fundamentals of training detailed in this encyclopedia, you can build your body to its genetic potential almost anywhere in the world.

In the early days of my career it was somewhat different. There weren't as many bodybuilders, bodybuilding media, or great places to work out, so there were good reasons for a lot of top champions to gather in Venice, California. There was also tradition. The famous Muscle Beach of the late 1940s was located right next to Venice in Santa Monica. The physique stars of that era created a whole new kind of lifestyle based on bodybuilding, sun, and fun. I can remember some fifteen years after that seeing photographs of "golden boy" Dave Draper on the beach in the pages of Joe Weider's magazines (often with Joe's lovely wife, Betty) and I became determined to go to Los Angeles someday to live and to train.

Nowadays, there are still a lot of champions in the Venice area, but most of them developed their physiques elsewhere and came to California to promote their careers—to live in a nice, warm climate, of course, but also to have access to both the bodybuilding and the mainstream media.

A lot of young bodybuilders come out to train in places like World Gym or Gold's Gym for short periods and then go back home, inspired by having worked out shoulder to shoulder with a Mr. Universe or Arnold Classic champion, and I think that's great. But I don't recommend that young would-be champions come out to Los Angeles to live at early points in their careers. While working out next to the top professionals is exciting, it can also be discouraging since most of them are likely to be years ahead of a young bodybuilder in development. For most young hopefuls, it makes more sense to train in your hometown, begin by entering local and regional contests and working your way up, and scheduling occasional visits to California just to "dip your toe in the water," get your dose of motivation, and then return home.

GYMS FOR NONCOMPETITORS

A major difference in bodybuilding between now and when I started training is the number of people training like serious bodybuilders—that is, following a hard-core, muscle-building program—who have no intention of getting into competition. This category includes everyone from doctors and lawyers to accountants, teachers, businessmen, military personnel, and a lot of actors I've worked with in the movie business. The question is whether these individuals, since they have no ambition to be Mr. or Ms. Olympia, need the same sort of serious training facilities as do would-be physique champions.

The answer, of course, is not absolutely, but it really helps. After all, if you have a good swing you can play a decent round of golf with almost any clubs, but if your equipment is modern and state of the art you are going to get better results, no matter what your level of expertise might be.

The point of bodybuilding training is to develop every body part in a proportionate, balanced way. It takes a certain amount of different kinds of equipment to do that, no matter who you are or what your training goals might be. Sure, you may not need a gym with sets of dumbbells going up to 150 pounds or more. But there should be an adequate amount of free weights and benches for you to do the basic exercises. A certain gym may not have a great number of choices of machines for particular exercises, but you have to have a certain minimum or you can't do what you're trying to do. So if you're using a gym that doesn't meet these standards, by all means try to find one that does.

Remember, muscle is muscle, and *your* muscles respond to the same training techniques and require the same exercise equipment to do a full workout as anyone else's. So if you are serious about the results you want to obtain, find a gym with the right equipment, an atmosphere that suits you, and people training around you that will inspire and motivate you to do your best.

TRAINING AT HOME

I have some rudimentary training facilities at home. Joe Weider has a fully equipped gym in his garage. So does Lou Ferrigno. A few years ago Hugh Hefner built a nice little gym in the basement of the Playboy Mansion. Although there is really no substitute for training at a good gym, some training at home can be useful. You can do extra ab work, for example, with just an abdominal board. With a simple bench and a basic set of weights, you can do reps and sets whenever you feel like it. This can be very valuable if you occasionally have trouble getting to the gym or if you run out of time in the gym and can't get a full workout. And, of course, aerobic work on a treadmill, stepper, or stationary bicycle can be done at home as well as anywhere else.

For those with more money to invest, there is quite a bit of good equipment available for the home. Most sporting goods stores carry benches and weight sets starting at a few hundred dollars. Stores like Sears, Montgomery Ward, and JC Penney sell weight-training equipment as well. Also, nowadays specialty stores in most cities sell everything from dumbbells and barbells to complex multi-station machines costing thousands of dollars; they usually advertise in the Yellow Pages. Walk into a store like this and you'll see brand names like Para-Body, Pacific Fitness, Vectra, Hoist, and Ivanko. Equipment is also available by mail order through the various physique magazines.

But training at home vs. the gym is a little like working on a car in your backyard compared to a fully equipped automotive garage. Sure, you can repair simple car problems under a shade tree, but more demanding and complex repairs are much more difficult, if not impossible. In the same sense, a home gym is not going to provide you with the same training facilities as a fully equipped facility—unless, of course, your home gym *is* as well equipped as a World Gym, which is something that is not very common.

Most people with equipment at home do *some* training, supplementing their gym training rather than trying to duplicate a full gym-oriented workout. If you are planning to do some training at home, the questions to consider are what areas of the body you plan to train at home. Major muscles, or just things like abs? Do you want a set of free weights, or are you more interested in machines? Individual machines or a single machine that allows you to do a lot of different exercises? How much space do you have? If you plan to do cardiovascular training, what kind—treadmill, exercise bike, stepper? And, of course, how much do you want to spend? Remember, the equipment you are used to in a gym generally costs thousands of dollars for each piece. You may not need an "industrial-strength" piece of equipment, but some of the cheaper stuff doesn't give you a very good "feel" compared to the state-of-the-art equipment you find in good gyms. Make sure you try a piece of equipment before you buy it to make sure it feels right to you.

Also, the least expensive pieces, such as treadmills, for example, tend to break down more easily than you might want. If you buy a top-notch treadmill by a company like Trotter or a stationary bike by Lifecycle you can be assured of getting good quality. But if you buy a lesser brand at more of a bargain price, be sure you know where to go to get it repaired if you run into problems. Of course some inexpensive pieces of equipment work just fine. I use a simple ab-training device at home that I take with me on my airplane and do two hundred reps before I eat dinner.

Very few bodybuilders have been able to boast of making much progress training at home. And if top champions, who have better genetics, energy, and motivation than almost anyone else, have not benefited much from home training, this fact should give pause to others considering going that route. There are some exceptions, of course. Frank Zane, for example, had some success training at home during his career. Franco Columbu and I used to use his home gym for training specific body parts. But I have always preferred the energy level of the gym, the excitement and interaction with the rest of the bodybuilders. In any event, even if you've made good progress by training at home, I recommend that you get thoroughly familiar with a gym and be able to make full use of the facilities you find there. To my knowledge there has never been a champion bodybuilder who developed his physique anyplace other than in a good gym, and I recommend that you find one to train in if you have any serious aspirations.

CHAPTER 5

Getting Started

TO A DEDICATED bodybuilder, the time spent training in the gym is the high point of his day. He's always thinking about his next workout, planning what he is going to do. As soon as he finishes one training session he is immediately looking forward to the next. So while I am a great believer in learning all you can about bodybuilding programs and technique, at a certain point you just have to get into the gym and get started. As the famous ad slogan says, "Just do it."

If you are just getting started in bodybuilding, remember the old saying, "The longest journey begins with a single step." The more you know the better, but you don't have to master every bit of information in this encyclopedia before you begin your own workouts. What counts most when you're getting started is energy and enthusiasm. A student in medical school is not expected to perform open-heart surgery on her first day and a beginning pilot is not required to fly combat missions in an F-14 Tomcat like an experienced "Top Gun." When you climb Mount Everest you start at the bottom, not the top. Life is a process that involves continual learning and bodybuilding is no exception.

Most young bodybuilders have no trouble motivating themselves to start. They are like I was—so anxious to get going that they'll stand outside the door almost before the sun comes up waiting for the gym to open. But being enthusiastic doesn't mean you begin training without a plan. The thing to do right at the start is to set a clear goal for yourself. Why do you want to train with weights? When I was a beginner, the only reason anyone worked out in the gym was for bodybuilding, powerlifting, or Olympic weightlifting. These are still important reasons to pump iron, but nowadays people train for all sorts of other reasons as well:

- to improve their ability at a variety of sports;
- to become stronger for physically demanding jobs;
- to better overall health and fitness;
- to help gain or lose weight;
- to create a harder, more attractive body;
- to follow a physical rehabilitation program.

Setting these kinds of goals helps to determine where you should train, how often and how hard, what kind of training partner to have, and what famous bodybuilders to use as models. Remember, you can always alter your training goals later on. Many champion bodybuilders began working out with weights without any intention of becoming physique stars—to gain size and strength for sports like football, for example, or because they got out of school, were no longer playing sports, and just wanted a way to stay in good shape.

I recommend that before you begin, have photographs taken that show your physique from all four sides. Write down all your important measurements—neck, chest, biceps, forearms, wrists, waist, thighs, and calves—as well as your weight. This way you can always check back to find out what kind of progress you have made. Incidentally, if you are embarrassed to have body photos taken because you don't like your body very much, that is all the more indication of how much bodybuilding can do for you. We all want to look good on the beach, to stand naked in front of a mirror and be pleased with what we see—and, of course, have others be pleased with what they see when they look at us! Why not look good out of clothes as well as in them? You certainly don't want to take off your clothes and, as my friends "Hans and Franz" would say, set off a "flabberlanch."

As we discussed, you need to find a place to train that suits your goals. Additionally, you have to master the basic bodybuilding exercises in this book. Keep in mind that your first task is to create a solid, quality muscle structure. Advanced bodybuilders are concerned with improving muscle shape, achieving separation, and tying in various muscle groups—none of which need concern the beginner.

When I was starting out, I found it very important to find somebody on whom to model myself. A businessman training for fitness would be wasting his time trying to create a physique to rival Shawn Ray's; a serious bodybuilder with a frame and proportions like Dorian Yates's shouldn't spend his time studying physique photos of Flex Wheeler, and a bodybuilder six feet tall or more should probably not use a shorter competitor like Lee Priest as a role model. And if you are training to create a lean, muscular physique of the type you see so often nowadays with young actors or male fashion models, it wouldn't be very appropriate to tape a photo of a "no-neck" super-heavyweight powerlifter to your refrigerator door, would it?

In my case, it was Reg Park, with his great size and muscularity. I would put up photos of Reg all over the walls, then study them endlessly, picturing in my mind how that kind of development would look on my own frame. So much of bodybuilding is mental that you have to have a clear idea of what you want to be and where you are going if you want to achieve extraordinary results.

Too many young bodybuilders try to run before they learn to walk. They copy my routine or pattern their workout on some other champion's example, and end up doing exercises that are inappropriate to their stage of development. However, if after six months or so of training the idea of competing begins to appeal to you, start to work toward that goal: Learn your body, what makes it grow, its strengths and weaknesses; create a picture in your mind of what you eventually want to look like.

When I talk about sticking to the fundamentals, I don't mean doing anything less than a real bodybuilding program—whether you are training for competition or not. Remember, the exercise programs in this book are for *every body*. I only mean that you should limit your training to those exercises and methods that build the most mass in the shortest time, and then go on later, after you have achieved a certain degree of basic development, to carefully sculpt and shape that mass into championship quality. Again, even if you have no intention of becoming a competition bodybuilder, if you are only training for health and fitness, there is never any reason to waste time by training in any but the most effective and efficient way possible.

You build a basic structure, learn how to train correctly, acquire a knowledge of diet and nutrition, and then just give the body time to grow. In a year, maybe a little less or a little more, you will begin to see radical changes in your physique and will have enough experience to begin to develop an individualized training program based on your own instincts of what is right or wrong for your particular body.

And just as you write down your physical measurements and keep track of your development with photos, I would recommend that you keep a *training diary*. Write out a training program that is appropriate to your goals, noting how many sets of each movement you do and with how much weight, so that anytime in the future you can check back to find out how much you have really done and compare that with the actual progress you have made.

You should also learn to keep track of your eating habits, how many protein drinks you had during any given week, how long you dieted, and what kind of diet you followed. All of this will allow you, perhaps five years down the line, when memory no longer recalls these facts, to be certain exactly what you did or did not do in pursuing your bodybuilding development.

FAST AND SLOW DEVELOPERS

Some people believe that developing muscle happens slowly but surely over time, so the longer you train, the bigger you get. That's why they will frequently ask a bodybuilder, "How long have you been training?" Or, "How long will it take me to get that big?" The way they see it, one bodybuilder is bigger than another simply because he or she has been training longer. But the reality is that not everybody gains muscle at the same rate and not everyone has the talent to create the same level of development.

Your individual genetics have a lot to do with how your body will respond to training. For example, I started training at fifteen, and photos taken after only a year reveal the beginnings of the physique that won me

Me at sixteen

seven Mr. Olympia titles. Every month or two I gained ½ inch on my arms, so people told me right away, "You should be a bodybuilder." Casey Viator turned from powerlifting to bodybuilding at an early age and at nineteen became the first and only teenage Mr. America. Look at photos of Mr. Olympia Lee Haney at nineteen or twenty years of age and he already had a mature physique. Texas police officer and bodybuilder Ronnie Coleman won the World Amateur Bodybuilding Championships title only two years after he began serious physique training.

But not all successful bodybuilders were early bloomers. Frank Zane was good enough to win his share of victories in the sixties, but it wasn't until the seventies that he achieved the perfection of development that allowed him to be victorious in three Mr. Olympia competitions. Female bodybuilder Yolanda Hughes broke through and won her first pro show—the Ms. International that I promote every year in Columbus—after twelve years of amateur and pro competition. The problem for slow developers like this is that they don't get the immediate success, the positive feedback, that helps so much to keep you motivated. But bodybuilding is like the race between the hare and the tortoise: Ultimately, determination and endurance over a long period of time can win out over a quick start and headlong sprint for the finish line.

You should also be careful about being discouraged by comparing yourself to somebody who is a so-called overnight success. Nowadays, when you see a great young bodybuilder of, say, twenty-four or twenty-five, it is quite probable that he has been training since the age of twelve or thirteen, and if he started entering contests as a teenager could be the veteran of eight or nine years of competition. In golf, when Tiger Woods broke through and won the Masters tournament in his early twenties, a lot of people talked about how quickly he became a champion, forgetting that he had been practicing golf since he was a preschooler, and by the time he became a teenager had already hit hundreds of thousands of practice shots.

But I also remember seeing Tiger Woods *lose* a play-off to a golfer who was a late bloomer and had never won a pro tournament until his thirties. Winning that event was a matter of who shot the lowest score, not which golfer was the youngest or had had the earliest success. Victory was a matter of who put the ball in the hole with the fewest strokes, not who was the most famous or had the biggest reputation.

Remember, it is not how quickly you develop that will finally make the difference, but *how far you are able to go*. The judges don't look at competitors onstage and say, "That contestant has been training for eight years but the other one is better because he's only been training for three!" No, all that counts is how good you get, and you can't make your body develop any faster than your own biological makeup will allow.

But it is possible to develop *more slowly* than your biology would allow, simply by not believing that rapid gains are possible and not training to develop as far and as fast as you can. I remember watching Franco Columbu train for two years with only moderate gains. Then he saw me win the NABBA Mr. Universe and he suddenly decided that he too wanted to win that title. After that, he trained really hard for two or three hours a day and began to make unbelievable gains in a very short time. His mind believed he could develop a fantastic physique, create gigantic muscles, and be up onstage holding the championship trophy in his hands, so his body responded.

FREE WEIGHTS VS. MACHINES—A MATTER OF GRAVITY

For a beginning bodybuilder, the majority of training should be done with free weights. We live in a technological age, and the exercise machines being designed and manufactured today are better than ever. But your muscles were designed by evolution to overcome the pull of gravity rather than to work against machine resistance, so the biggest gains you will make in building size and strength will come from pumping iron—using a barbell and dumbbells—rather than by exercising on machines.

Moreover, most of the really good bodybuilders I know have also been powerlifters—a subject I will explore in more detail later. Forcing the body to lift against gravity, to coordinate and balance masses of iron, gives it a structure and quality that high-repetition, relatively light training alone does not provide. Additionally, a report in the *Journal of Strength and Conditioning Research* indicates that testosterone production is increased when you do large-muscle-group, free-weight exercises in which you use and coordinate a number of major muscle groups at the same time, like the Squat, Deadlift, and exercises you see performed less often today like the Power Clean. Testosterone production is not similarly increased by isolation free-weight exercises—or training on machines. Testosterone is anabolic, and with more testosterone in your system you get stronger and can build larger muscles more easily.

But bodybuilding is about sculpting the muscles as well as making them big and strong. Free weights give the experienced bodybuilder the freedom to isolate certain muscles and to work the body in any number of creative ways. They also enable people of different heights, weights, and physical proportions—long-armed, short-armed, long-legged, short-legged, etc.—to get a complete workout, while many machines seem to be designed only to satisfy those who represent the "average" customer of a commercial health spa.

Again, let me emphasize that I am not against machines. Joe Gold, who is a master craftsman when it comes to building exercise equipment, has filled World Gym with many useful machines and devices. Nowadays, when I go to different gyms and use a variety of different machines I find them to be marvels of technology. We've been through air- and water-resistance machines, and are now back to a more basic design, but a hundred times better than ever before. The people at companies like Cybex and Hammerstrength, as well as the other top manufacturers, work extremely hard to create machines that work well and feel good to use. Gone are the days when somebody would just weld some pieces of metal together and expect people to use a machine that didn't operate smoothly, that hit the end stops before moving through a full range of motion, was awkward to use, and always had something wrong.

I use a lot of machines in my own workouts. It is obviously impossible to get full thigh development, for example, without a Leg Extension or Leg Curl machine or to fully isolate the inner chest without using a pec deck or cables. And it is possible to shock the body into accelerated growth if you occasionally use a machine or circuit of machines you are not used to in place of your normal free-weight exercise for that body part. But I believe that a good bodybuilding program should include no more than 30 to 40 percent training (at most!) with machines. Certainly, a Curl gets better results done with dumbbells or a barbell because of the way you can isolate and stimulate the biceps, but it would be hard to really work the lats without a Lat Pulldown machine or to do Triceps Pressdowns without cables.

Also, when you think about it, machines keep the resistance working along one plane only, meaning that the muscle has to do things the machine's way or not at all. With no need to balance and control the resistance, you end up with less muscle. But the whole idea of bodybuilding and strength training is to use *as much* muscle as possible, so this is no real advantage at all! It is true that a muscle doesn't "know" what kind of resistance it is working to overcome. In that sense resistance is resistance. But the muscle does indeed react differently if it is constantly subjected to resistance that comes from varying angles and different directions as opposed to resistance that is always along a predictable line. And Franco tells me that in his chiropractic practice most of the muscle strains and joint injuries he sees come about as the result of using machines that put unnatural stresses on the body, that lock you into too rigid a position.

Muscle was developed to work against the pull of gravity. If we lived on the moon, we'd need only one-sixth the amount of muscle we need on earth, with its greater gravity. On Jupiter, we'd have to be built like elephants to move at all! Lifting something gives us the experience of "heavy." Pushing a weight along a track is not the same thing. Neither is pressing against a stationary wall—you're encountering a lot of resistance, but it isn't "heavy." And that means your muscles are not responding as fully as they are capable of doing.

If you are training somewhere that does not have the free weights you need for your workout, and there is nothing you can do about it, use whatever you have in order to accomplish your training! The bottom line is to get that workout, no matter how you have to do it. Whatever works, works—and, as a bodybuilder, that's all you need to worry about.

SHOES

The importance of shoes in training is simply to stabilize your feet and improve your balance. In that regard, all shoes are not created equal. Many running shoes are made so soft and light—great if you plan to run ten miles or so—that they don't give you much support. But support is not always what you want. Competitive powerlifters doing Deadlifts generally wear very thin slippers because being even a fraction of an inch lower can make the difference between success and failure lifting a huge poundage off the ground.

You can also find athletic shoes that are thick-soled, solid, and with good arch support. I've seen bodybuilders work out wearing hiking boots, combat boots, and a wide variety of other footwear. Remember how much pressure is borne by the feet when you are doing exercises like heavy Squats, and how hard that can be on the arches. So choose the appropriate shoe for whatever kind of workout you have planned.

GLOVES

Many good bodybuilders wear gloves while training to protect their hands. Others use pieces of rubber cut from inner tubes to improve their grip. This is okay, but I have always trained barehanded and used chalk whenever my grip felt too slippery. Powerlifters work with enormous amounts of weight and don't use any of these aids. If you have particularly sensitive skin, or if you are a chiropractor, concert pianist, or in some other profession which requires that you take special care of your hands, by all means wear gloves. However, I recommend most bodybuilders simply grip the weights with bare hands and let them toughen up and develop calluses. Don't worry about sponges, gloves, and other aids.

STRAPS

Straps are fastened around your wrist and then twisted around a bar to effectively strengthen your grip, although my personal feeling is that using aids like these keep hand strength from fully developing naturally. Straps are used because with bare hands it is often difficult to hold on to a weight that will really challenge your back in a heavy workout. However, champion powerlifters don't use straps, and they lift enormous amounts. Franco and I have always lifted heavy weights without the use of straps. If you lift without straps, your grip will gradually strengthen. If you continually use straps, you may never develop this kind of strength. However,

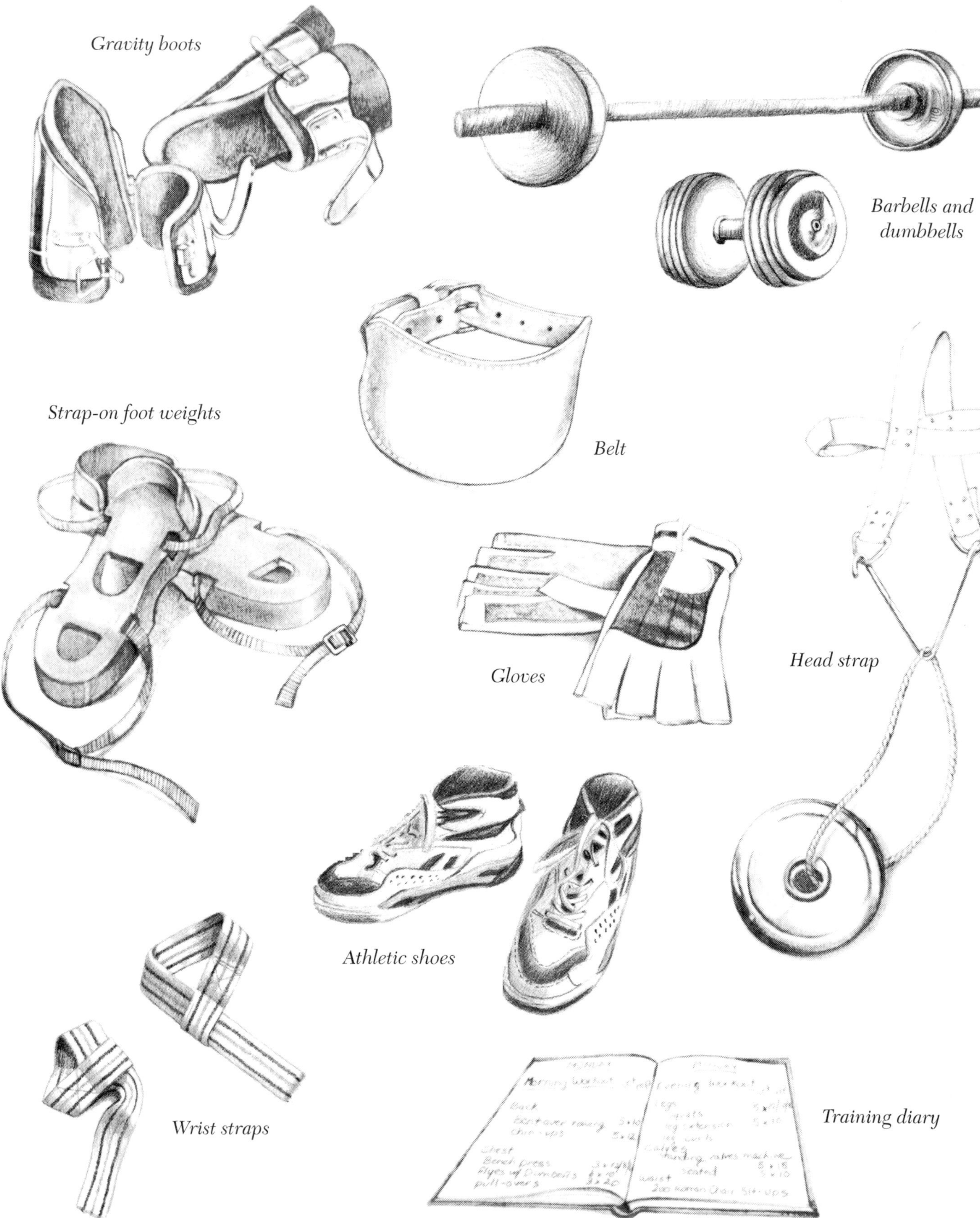
Gravity boots
Barbells and dumbbells
Strap-on foot weights
Belt
Gloves
Head strap
Athletic shoes
Wrist straps
Training diary

whether or not to use straps in your workouts is mostly a matter of personal preference.

BELTS

The purpose of wearing a heavy belt is supposed to be to support the muscles of the lower back when you are lifting very heavy weights. The waist belt was originally used by weightlifters doing heavy Overhead Presses. However, belts are often considered necessary by those doing heavy Squats, pressing heavy weight, or doing heavy standing Calf Raises.

Research in the past few years has indicated that weight belts may not protect the spine to the degree it was once thought, although they probably help stabilize the upper body by increasing pressure in the abdominal cavity. However, in my opinion too many bodybuilders wear belts too much of the time they are in the gym, which has the effect of binding the lower back muscles and preventing them from developing the strength they ought to have. This is a high price to pay for an illusory feeling of security. So I recommend you use a belt only when you feel you really need one, for very heavy lifts, and not as a kind of bodybuilding fashion accessory.

WRAPS

Wraps are used to support weak or injured joints and muscles. You will occasionally see a bodybuilder who has wrapped one or both elbows due to some physical problem. More commonly, wraps are used around the knees when doing very heavy Squats, or around the elbows when doing heavy Bench Presses. But wraps aren't something you need to use every day. Unless you have an injury or joint problem (for which you should seek medical attention), you will not need to wrap your knees until you have progressed to the point where you are using very heavy weights. Ace bandages are most frequently used, wrapped firmly, but not too tightly, around the area. Remember that whenever you wrap an area tight enough to give it additional support, you are also limiting its flexibility of movement.

HEAD STRAPS

A few years ago it was common for bodybuilders to use a kind of harness that fits around the head to which you can attach a dumbbell or weight plate so you can do progressive-resistance exercises for the neck. The "Barbarian Twins," David and Peter Paul, used to amaze people at Gold's Gym with the enormous amount of weight they could train their necks with—and sometimes they even attached the head strap to a car and pulled the vehicle across the parking lot.

This type of exercise seems to have fallen out of fashion, but maybe that's a mistake. If you feel your neck is too small, by all means find a way to train it. Indeed, some companies now make machines for this purpose. However, a complete workout routine tends to build the neck muscles along with everything else, so don't waste your time with these exercises unless you really see a need for them. In other words, if it ain't broke, don't fix it.

GRAVITY BOOTS

Here's another piece of equipment that used to be common but is seen much less often these days. Gravity boots enable you to hang upside down and stretch out the spine. Those who advocate using this device point to the fact that our bodies are constantly being compressed by the force of gravity—the spine is compressed, the internal organs are pulled earthward. As a result, over a lifetime, most of us are an inch or two shorter at age sixty than at age twenty-five. Stretching out the spine by hanging upside down and taking the strain off the internal organs is supposed to help counteract this process, and I can tell you that it feels very relaxing.

However, hanging upside down has no direct effect on building up your body, and it does tend to put a lot of strain on the lower back, so this remains an adjunct to training rather than a fundamental part of bodybuilding. If you use gravity boots, start out by hanging for only short periods—no more than a minute or so—until you get used to the unusual sensation of being upside down. Then gradually increase your suspension periods a little at a time as you feel necessary. Better, check out one of the bench-type gravity devices that let you keep your knees bent and take some of the strain off the lower back.

RUBBER SUITS

The primary use a competition bodybuilder would have for these suits would be to help lose water weight just before a contest. However, wearing a suit like this on a hot day when you are training hard could lead to hyperthermia, a dangerous increase in body temperature, and bodybuilders have ended up in the hospital or worse due to dehydration, so I don't really recommend this type of device. Keep in mind that any water loss due to the use of a rubber suit is only temporary.

TRAINING DIARY

Explorers use maps, sea captains rely on charts, astronauts navigate by the stars, and bodybuilders keep track of where they are and where they are going by keeping a training diary.

When I began to train, I wrote everything down—training routines, sets and reps, diet, everything. And I kept this up right through my 1980 Mr. Olympia victory. I would come into the gym and put a line on the wall in chalk for every set I intended to do. I would always do five sets of each movement. So, for example, the marks ////////// on my chest day would stand for five sets of Bench Presses and five sets of Dumbbell Flys. I would reach up and cross each line as I did the set. So when I finished Benches the marks would look like XXXXX/////, and I would never think to myself, Should I do three sets today, or four? I always knew it was five and just went ahead and did them. Watching those marks march across the wall as I did my workout gave me a tremendous sense of satisfaction and accomplishment. They were like an invading army crushing all opposition in its path. This visual feedback helped me to keep my training goals clearly in mind, and reinforced my determination to push myself to the limit in every workout.

Totally by instinct, I stumbled onto a concept widely accepted by educators and psychologists: Human beings work best and learn best when they are given the right kind of feedback. Knowing that you have accomplished something is one thing; seeing what you have accomplished is another. It makes your accomplishment all the more real and exciting, and therefore motivates you to try even harder the next time.

Feedback also lets you know when you are not on the right track. Memory can play tricks on you, but the information in the pages of a training diary is right there for you to see. If you are suddenly getting good results, you can look back to see what kind of exercise program and diet regimen helped you. If you begin to develop problems—your progress slows or you seem to be losing strength—you can check your records to try to determine where you might be making your mistake.

Continuing to keep a training diary over long periods helped my development tremendously. I would sit down at the beginning of the month and outline my program for the next thirty days—what days I would work out, what body parts I would train, and what exercises I would do. After a while, if a body part was lagging behind somewhat in development or I decided that certain muscles needed more training than I had been giving them, I would make an adjustment in my thirty-day plan and add the necessary exercises.

I would try various supplements to see what seemed to make a difference to how I looked and felt, and I would write all this down. Was I feeling full of energy or tired and fatigued? I would make note of this and then later go back through my diary to see how I could account for the differences in how I felt between one day and the next. I kept track of the days I canceled a training session, or when I had a particularly good workout.

I also kept a careful record of my body weight and would take measurements every month—neck, shoulder width, biceps (hanging and flexed), forearms, waist (standing relaxed and hitting a vacuum), and so forth—so that I could make comparisons of how much I had progressed from one period to another.

So be sure to keep a training diary. Write down your entire program; make note of sets, reps, and weights; record your physical measurements, and take periodic photographs of your physique to keep track of your development. This way you will always know what your training program is supposed to be, and can always look back and check to see how you were training in the past and what kind of success that program brought you.

BODYBUILDING AND THE VERY YOUNG

I don't like to see very young children lifting weights. Their bodies are too unformed, their bones still too soft, to stand up to the stresses of weight training. I have seen boys five to nine years of age, pushed into working with weights too young by their parents, profiled on television as supposed bodybuilders. And a very young girl of about sixty pounds who "lifted" (that is, barely moved) some 400 pounds on a Hack Squat machine. I hope none of these children were injured by these activities because I don't believe this kind of exercise or physical stress is appropriate for the very young with their immature, vulnerable bodies.

Preteen training, in my opinion, should rely on lots of athletic activities to develop all of the body's physical potentials, with the emphasis on calisthenics or gymnastic exercises rather than weight training—exercises that use body-weight resistance such as Push-Ups instead of Bench Presses, Knee Bends instead of Squats, and so on.

Once the body begins to mature, weight training can begin. I began at fifteen, but this doesn't mean that every fifteen- or sixteen-year-old has to decide whether he wants to pursue competition bodybuilding right from the start. It takes a few months, maybe a year, simply to learn the exercises and begin to understand the experience of training. Still, it is important during this phase to use light weights and keep reps relatively high. The sooner you make up your mind to pursue serious training, the better chance you have of going all the way.

STARTING LATE

"Am I too old to begin bodybuilding?" I am frequently asked. "You are too old not to!" is usually my reply. As we get older the muscle structure tends to atrophy at a faster and faster rate. The ideal remedy for this is bodybuilding.

But when it comes to competition, there are obviously disadvantages to starting very late. Certainly, there have been bodybuilders who started much later in life and gone on to become great competitors—Ed Corney, the master poser of my day, for example. But, generally, your chances of becoming a Mr. Universe or a pro champion diminish with a late start. But starting late in bodybuilding is not the same as in other sports. Many champions didn't begin training until their early twenties and went on to become amateur and professional champions within the next ten years. However, these successful late starters are usually already competitive athletes who are simply switching sports. Their bodies are pretrained by years and years of other types of sports training. World Amateur Champion Ronnie Coleman is an example of this. And Franco Columbu, who started out as a boxer and then a powerlifter, didn't switch to training for bodybuilding until he was well into his twenties.

Not only can you start relatively late in bodybuilding, but you can continue to compete long past the point where most athletes (golfers being the most obvious exception) have retired. Of course, a bodybuilder in his forties is not going to be able to get the kind of shape he could a few years earlier. There is wear and tear on the muscles, a gradual hormonal change, shortening of the muscles—and the fact that an older competitor generally has more in his life to deal with, distractions and responsibilities (family, children, business interests) than does a younger man just starting out, so it is much harder to dedicate himself 100 percent to his training and diet programs.

Masters bodybuilding competitions are now widely available to competitors in their forties, fifties, and up. Former top professionals are even vying for titles at the Arnold Classic and Masters Mr. Olympia. And it's amazing how hard, muscular, and in-shape many of the champions of the past are able to look.

BODYBUILDING AND THE ELDERLY

As I said earlier, one of the primary manifestations of aging is the gradual deterioration of muscle mass. But recent research has proved that muscle doesn't have to atrophy with age to the degree we always believed. In fact, muscle mass can be *increased* to a surprising degree with proper training even in those of advanced age. In short, recent scientific studies indicate that bodybuilding can be a fountain of youth.

Of course, the older you are the more careful you have to be when you start bodybuilding. "Consult a doctor" is not just a pro forma disclaimer when it comes to somebody in her sixties or seventies. Consult a doctor, find a good trainer, take every precaution. Learn proper technique. Get into training slowly. When you're older, injuries take longer to heal, so do everything you can to avoid any problems.

But the results can be spectacular. A return to more youthful levels of strength. A more youthful body. Energy, mobility, and an increased quality of life. Confidence and independence. Remember, much of what we consider to be inevitable aspects of aging are really just signs of underuse and neglect. You don't have to lose muscle or bone mass as you grow older; you can keep what you have and even build more of it.

MAKING THE TRANSITION

Making the transition from training for health and fitness to training for competition is largely an evolution of consciousness: You begin to appreciate certain potentials of your body that you were not previously aware of and slowly your attitude toward training begins to change and you have to make a decision—which way are you going to go? Are you going to keep this just a small part of your life, or will it gradually become the centerpiece of your existence?

I decided almost immediately that I wanted to be Mr. Universe. Franco competed for a while as a powerlifter before making that decision. Mike Katz was a professional football player, the late Carlos Rodriguez a rodeo rider. You can decide early or late, but if you find yourself caught up in training, looking forward almost obsessively to your workouts in the gym, relishing every new plane and angle revealed as your physique grows and develops, this may be a decision that you, too, will have to make. To get your feet wet, there are many local amateur contests to enter. There you can try competition and decide whether or not the rigors involved are to your liking.

There is so much more money in professional bodybuilding now than when I started that many athletes who might have concentrated on sports are deciding on a career in bodybuilding. But there are more and more opportunities on the amateur level as well, and many bodybuilders continue to train and compete while pursuing careers as doctors, lawyers, chiropractors, or businessmen.

Most bodybuilders are highly competitive individuals, but others are in the sport primarily for the meaning it gives their lives, regardless of whether or not they ever achieve a victory. Bodybuilding is more than a sport, it is also a way of life. It is an entire philosophy of how to live, a value system that gives specific answers to questions that concern so many of us these days—questions of what is worth doing and what value to give to excellence and achievement. It is a way of pursuing self-worth and personal validation, of finding satisfaction in your ability to set goals for yourself and working to reach them.

Of course, not everyone who takes up bodybuilding on a competitive level has the same experience, but no one goes very far in this sport without realizing the deeper meaning of physique.

COMPETITION

I always intended to do many things with my life besides compete in bodybuilding contests, but there is no aspect of my life that will not be influenced by or will not benefit from my having had the heady experience of competition. Bodybuilding *training*, I believe, is for everyone, but few are suited for the demands of competition. If the idea appeals to you even in the slightest, I urge you to give it some consideration. If you can share even a small part of what bodybuilding has given me, I know you will never regret your decision to try competition.

Just remember one thing—if you really take it seriously, bodybuilding competition will take over your life. It will determine where and how you live, what you eat, who your friends are, the course of your marriage. Sure, you can compete on a local level without giving yourself over totally to the demands of the competition lifestyle—still live somewhat of a "normal" life—but the further you go in bodybuilding the more it will consume you.

This is not so unusual. Think of the commitment it takes to train for the Olympics. The practice and dedication it takes to become a champion in tennis or golf. The demands of training to run a marathon. Success in any of these sports takes a degree of focus and concentration most people can hardly imagine. It takes sacrifice to get to the top. And bodybuilding is no exception.

Bodybuilding Hall of Fame

John Grimek

Steve Reeves

Reg Park

Bill Pearl

Larry Scott

Dave Draper

Sergio Oliva

Arnold Schwarzenegger

Franco Columbu

Frank Zane

Robby Robinson

Albert Beckles

Lou Ferrigno

Tom Platz

Chris Dickerson

Samir Bannout

Lee Haney

Shawn Ray

Vince Taylor

Dorian Yates

Kevin Levrone

Flex Wheeler

Nasser El Sonbaty

BOOK TWO

Training Programs

CHAPTER 1

Basic Training Principles

To LOOK LIKE a bodybuilder you need to train like one. Athletes like football players, wrestlers, and weightlifters have a lot of muscle; but only bodybuilders have the shapely, proportioned, completely developed muscular bodies we associate with physique competition. If you want to look like a bodybuilder—or even simply want to look more like a bodybuilder than you do now—you need to learn and master the training techniques that bodybuilders have developed on a trial-and-error basis over the past fifty years or so. Just as there is a specific technique involved in hitting a tennis ball or swinging a golf club, there is also a way of doing bodybuilding training that is the most efficient and effective means of muscular training possible.

It takes hard, dedicated work to build a great physique, but hard work alone is not enough. In addition to training hard, you need to train smart, which means mastering the fundamental principles of bodybuilding. These principles should be learned and practiced right from the beginning. It is much easier to learn the proper way to do something than it is to unlearn the wrong way and have to start over. As you continue to progress, you will be introduced to more and more complex approaches to training, but there is no need to worry about this at the beginning. The encyclopedia is organized to introduce you to these more advanced training ideas on a step-by-step basis so that you will have a chance to master one level of complexity at a time.

INDIVIDUAL NEEDS

Of course, different people have many different reasons for doing bodybuilding training. Some want to build their bodies just to look and feel better. Others want to improve their performance in a variety of sports. And many are interested in developing a dramatic, high-muscular and well-proportioned physique with the goal of competing in bodybuilding contests.

When it comes to learning how to do bodybuilding properly, some basic techniques and principles will apply to *everyone;* others must be tailored to the needs of the individual, often on a trial-and-error basis over a period of time. Everyone, regardless of why they are doing bodybuilding, needs to master the fundamentals and understand what is involved in putting a training program together. Most important, everybody needs to learn the basic exercises because they continue to be important no matter how advanced you become.

But I recognize that everyone is not the same. Body type, how fast or slow a person gains muscle, metabolic rate, weak points, and recuperation time are just a few of the things that can vary from one individual to another. I have tried to cover all the significant variables in this encyclopedia so that everyone will find the information they need to create the kind of body they want.

In golf, many champions don't swing like Tiger Woods, but every first-rate swing has to bring the club face into contact with the ball in just the right alignment. Not every skier uses exactly the same style as Olympic gold medalist Hermann "The Hermannator" Maier, but certain fundamentals have to be executed or you will never make it to the bottom of the run. When you walk into a gym full of competition bodybuilders, it is apparent that many of them are using very different approaches to their training. In the gym I hear the phrase "Every body is different" all the time, and that's true. But every body is much the same as well, so set your sights on mastering the basic guidelines *and let your body tell you* over time what individual variations and techniques are required for you to realize your potential.

PROGRESSIVE RESISTANCE

Your muscles will grow only when they are subjected to an *overload.* They will not respond to anything less. Muscles will not grow bigger or stronger unless you force them to. Making your muscles contract against a level of resistance they are not used to will eventually cause them to adapt and grow stronger. But once they have adapted sufficiently, this progress will stop. When this happens, the only way to make your muscles continue to grow is by further increasing the amount of overload to which you subject them. And the primary way of doing this is to add weight to your exercises.

Of course, this increase in resistance has to be done gradually. Using too much weight too soon usually makes it impossible for you to perform your sets using the proper technique, and can often increase your risk of injury as well.

REPS

A rep is one complete cycle of an exercise movement—a contraction of the muscle followed by an extension—that is, lifting a weight and lowering it again. A set is a group of these repetitions. How many reps you include in a set depends a great deal on what kind of set you are doing. For example, both research and experience have shown that bodybuilders get the most results using a weight in each exercise that represents about 70 to 75 percent of their *one-rep maximum*—that is, the amount of weight they could use doing one full-out repetition of that particular exercise. If you use this amount of weight you will generally find you can do sets of:

8 to 12 repetitions for upper-body muscles;
12 to 16 repetitions for the major leg muscles.

These figures are just approximations, but they work well as general guidelines.

Why can you do more repetitions for the legs than the upper body? Simply because the falloff in strength over the course of a set is slower in the legs than in the upper body—upper-body muscles just don't have the same kind of endurance as leg muscles. But in both cases the amount of weight used represents the same 70 to 75 percent of the one-rep maximum ability of the muscles involved.

Occasionally, there are reasons for using less weight than this (and therefore doing more reps) and some very useful types of sets which involve heavier weight (and fewer reps), such as low-rep sets for maximum strength and power. But these guidelines represent the majority of training bodybuilders do—and this is especially true for beginners.

TRAINING TO FAILURE

"Training to failure" in bodybuilding doesn't mean training to a point of complete exhaustion. It simply means continuing a set until you can't do any more repetitions with that weight without stopping to rest. What causes this failure? Basically it results from the gradual fatiguing of the muscle fibers involved and the inability of the muscle to recruit any more fibers to take their place. The process of contracting a muscle involves the process of oxidation—in effect, a form of burning, which is why we say you burn calories (create heat by the release of energy) when you exercise. Oxidation requires both a source of fuel (in the muscle, this is ATP) and oxygen. Whenever fuel or oxygen is in too short supply, the muscle fibers can't contract until they are replenished as you rest and recuperate.

Another limiting factor is the buildup of waste products that result from the release of energy due to muscular contraction. That burning sensation you feel in a muscle as you continue to pump out reps is due to the accumulation of lactic acid in the area. When you stop to rest, the body removes the lactic acid from the area and you are able to do more reps.

Aerobic exercise (which means "with oxygen") involves high-repetition effort at sufficiently low intensity so that the body can pump enough blood and oxygen to the area to keep the muscle supplied—running a marathon, for example. Or an aerobics class. Weight training is anaerobic ("without oxygen") and the muscular contraction involved is just too intense for the oxygen supply to keep pace. So your muscles run out of oxygen, you fatigue, and have to rest while the body pumps more blood and oxygen to the fatigued area.

Why is training to failure important? When you are doing reps with a weight less than your one-rep maximum, all the muscle fibers available don't come into play all at once. You use some, they become fatigued, and the body recruits others to take their place. Continuing a set to failure is a way of demanding that *all* the available fibers are recruited. At what point failure occurs depends on the weight you use in a particular exercise. If you are doing an upper-body exercise and want the muscles to fail at, say, 8 to 12 repetitions, you pick a weight that causes this to happen. If you find you are able to do 15 reps in that movement, you add weight to the next set to bring the failure point into the desired range. If you can do only 5 reps, you know you need to lighten the weight slightly so you can do a few more reps before your muscles fail. But you never just stop a set because you've counted off a certain number of reps.

One of the ways you gauge your bodybuilding progress is the change in where failure occurs during your training. As your individual muscle fibers get stronger, you are able to recruit more of them and your body increases its ability to deliver oxygen to the muscles during exercise (all components of the overall training effect). As a result you will find you can do many more reps with the same weight before hitting the failure point. This is a sign you need to use more weight.

Of course, you aren't a machine, so the way you actually do your sets is not that mechanical. Some sets need to be more demanding and more intense than others. Here, for example, is a typical upper-body set for an experienced bodybuilder:

First set: a warm-up set with a lighter weight; 15 repetitions or slightly more.

Second set: Add weight so that the muscles fail at about 10 to 12 repetitions.

Third set: Add more weight to bring the failure point down to 8 to 10 repetitions.

Fourth set: For maximum strength, add enough weight so your muscles fail after only 6 repetitions (power set).

Optional fifth set: Use the same weight, try to get another 6 reps; get some help from a training partner if necessary to complete the set (forced reps).

Training this way gives you the best of all possible worlds: You start out relatively light, which gives your muscles time to fully warm up for that particular exercise; you go on to do slightly fewer reps with a heavier weight, which forces lots of blood into your muscles and gives you a great pump; and finally, you add more weight so that you are training relatively heavy for power and strength.

SETS

Generally in the Basic Training Program I recommend doing 4 sets of each bodybuilding exercise, except where otherwise specified. I believe this is the best system for several reasons:

1. You need to do at least 4 sets in order to have the volume of training necessary to fully stimulate all the available muscle fiber. If you do more sets per exercise, your total training volume will be so great that you risk overtraining.

2. Doing 4 sets per exercise, for a total of 12 sets per body part (for the larger muscle groups) in the Basic Training Program and 20 sets in Advanced Training, enables you to do a sufficient variety of exercises to work all the areas of a body part—upper and lower back, for example, the outside sweep of the lats, and the inner back.

3. The experience of five decades of bodybuilders has proved that the maximum amount of weight you can handle that allows you to just make it through 4 sets of an exercise will stimulate the muscles and make them grow.

There is a difference in how much training small muscles require compared to large muscles or muscle groups. For example, if I'm training my back, that doesn't involve just one muscle—there are many different muscles in the back—such as lats, rhomboids, traps, spinal erectors of the lower back—and each of these areas has to be trained specifically. The same is true for the thighs. The thighs consist of four powerful quadriceps muscles, as well as the adductors at the inside of the upper leg. To fully train this area, you need both power and isolation movements, you have to hit the different heads at different angles, and you aren't going to accomplish this with just a few sets.

In training smaller muscles like the biceps and triceps, on the other hand, fewer total sets are needed because those muscles are just not that complex. You can get a complete biceps workout doing a total of about 9 to 12 sets, for example, whereas most bodybuilders would do 16 to 20 total sets to work the thighs. The rear deltoid is an even smaller muscle, and generally 4 to 5 sets for the posterior deltoid head is enough. However, muscle physiology also comes into play. The biceps are the fastest recuperating muscles, so if you feel like training them using higher sets (as I always did) they are still able to recover. And the calf muscles, which are relatively small, are designed to do virtually endless repetitions when you walk or run, so you can get great results training them with a relatively high number of sets.

But don't worry about trying to remember exactly which muscle should be trained with how many sets right off the bat. I've taken all of this into consideration in the exercise program recommendations coming up in later chapters.

FULL RANGE OF MOTION

For most purposes, bodybuilding exercises should take any muscle through its longest possible range of motion. (There are some specific exceptions which I'll talk about later.) You should take care to stretch out to full extension, and then come all the way back to a position of complete contraction. This is the only way to stimulate the entire muscle and every possible muscle fiber. So when I'm suggesting you do 8 reps, or 10 reps or more, in each case I am assuming you are going to be doing full-range-of-motion repetitions.

THE QUALITY OF CONTRACTION

Bodybuilding is about training muscles, not lifting weights. You use the weights and proper technique in order to target certain muscles or muscle groups. Weights are just a means to an end. In order to do this effectively, you have to isolate the muscles you are targeting. Remember how often you have been told to lift something with your legs and not your back? This technique deliberately brings as many muscles into play as possible to protect you from injury. This makes sense if you are a piano mover or a construction worker. But the task of the bodybuilder is very different. You don't want to make the lift easier, you want to make it harder! You want the target muscles to do all the work, with little or no help from other muscle groups.

Good technique helps you to do this. So does choosing the right amount of weight. Once you are using a weight that is too heavy for your target muscles to handle, your body will automatically call other muscles into play. That's the way your nervous system is designed. So the fact that you can lift a weight doesn't mean you are doing the exercise correctly. You also need to choose a weight that ensures that the target muscles alone are responsible for lifting that weight.

How do you do this? One way is to start out lifting very light and concentrate on how the muscles feel during the movement. Gradually increase the weight. But if and when you get to a point where you can no longer feel the muscles working as they did when the weight was lighter, chances are you are working too heavy and need to back down a few pounds until that "feel" is reestablished.

WARMING UP

Often when people talk about warming up, they don't understand how literally that should be taken. Remember, oxidation in the muscle is actually a form of burning. Because of this, when you use a muscle, the temperature in the area rises and the ability of the muscle to contract forcefully becomes greater.

Warming up also pumps fresh, oxygenated blood to the area, raises the blood pressure, and increases the heart rate. This provides a maximum oxygen supply to the body and helps to eliminate the waste products of exercise from the working muscles.

Finally, warming up properly helps to protect the body from becoming overstressed, prepares it for the demands of heavy training, and reduces the chance of injury, such as a sprain or strain.

There are lots of ways to warm up. Some do a short session of cardiovascular training prior to their workout (treadmill, exercise bicycle, running, etc.), enough to get the heart going but not enough to deplete the body of energy. Calisthenics and other light exercises also give you a warm-up without putting any great stress on the body. But the most popular method of warming up is with the weights themselves. First, spend some time stretching and then do some moderately light movements with a barbell or dumbbells, hitting each body part in turn until the body is ready for something more strenuous.

Then, for each different exercise during your workout you begin with one light warm-up set in order to get those specific muscles ready to do that specific movement. When you do a set or two with higher reps and less than maximum weight, your muscles are then prepared to deal with the greater intensity generated by heavier weights and 6-rep sets.

Warming up is even more important before heavy training sessions because you are about to subject the body to still greater stress. The best idea is not to do really heavy movements until your body gets into gear by doing the less stressful bodybuilding sets first.

The time of day is also a factor in determining how much warming up you need. If you are training at eight o'clock in the morning you are likely to be tighter and more in need of stretching and warming up than at eight at night, so adjust your preliminaries accordingly.

Always take care that you warm up thoroughly. If you are about to do heavy shoulder presses, for example, remember that you are going to involve more than the deltoids and triceps. The muscles of the neck and the trapezius will also contract intensely during the movement, and they should be given time to get ready as well.

Injuries in the gym generally happen for two primary reasons: Either the person used sloppy technique (used too much weight or failed to keep the weight totally under control) or didn't stretch and warm up properly.

I should also point out the effect of age on the physique and athletic ability. It is commonly known that the older you are, the more important protecting your body with warm-ups and stretching becomes. Young athletes can get away with things that older competitors can't. Nonetheless, learning proper technique, stretching, and warming up are good for *all* bodybuilders, regardless of age, and the sooner you make this a lifelong habit the better off you will be in the long run.

POWER TRAINING

There are various ways of assessing strength. If I can lift 300 pounds and you can lift only 250, I am stronger than you in one-rep strength. However, if you can lift 250 pounds ten times and I can lift it only eight times, that is a different kind of strength; you would be surpassing me in muscular endurance—the ability to continue to be strong over a series of movements.

To shape and develop the body, it is necessary to do a lot of endurance training—that is, the appropriate number of sets and reps. But I also believe that, unless you include low-rep strength training, you will never achieve the hardness and density necessary to create a truly first-class physique.

In the days of John Grimek, Clancy Ross, and Reg Park virtually all bodybuilders trained for power. Being strong was considered as important

Franco Columbu deadlifting 730 pounds

as having a physique that looked good. But keep in mind that there were then and are now different kinds of strength. The legendary Jack La Lanne could never compete with a Reg Park in a one-rep strength contest, but Jack could continue Chin-Ups and Dips, back and forth without stopping, long past the point where the bigger guys at Muscle Beach had collapsed with fatigue.

Although the bodybuilders of the 1940s and 1950s generally lacked the total refinement that top bodybuilders have today, they were extremely strong, hard, and impressive physical specimens. In the 1980s it seemed to me that the pendulum had swung too far and bodybuilders were overlooking the benefits of including traditional power moves in their overall programs. Nowadays, with so many competitors coming into pro shows weighing a solid 230, 240 pounds or more, there seems to have been a rediscovery of heavy power training. Certainly, you don't get to be as dense and massive as Dorian Yates without working with a lot of mind-bendingly heavy poundages.

"If you don't do heavy lifts," my friend Dr. Franco Columbu explains, "it shows immediately onstage. There is a soft look that shows itself clearly." There is abundant scientific and physiological evidence for why this is so. Power training puts tremendous strain on relatively few fibers at a time, causing them to become bigger and thicker (hypertrophy), and they also become packed much tighter together. This contributes enormously to that hard, dense look of the early champions.

Including some power sets in your program also helps to make you stronger for the rest of your training. You will move up to using heavier weights more quickly, so your muscles will grow that much faster. It also toughens and strengthens your tendons as well as your muscles, so you will be much less likely to strain them while doing higher-repetition training with less weight, even if you should lose concentration at some point and handle the weights with less than perfect technique.

Heavy training strengthens the attachment of the tendon to bone. Separating the tendon from the bone is called an avulsion fracture (see Injuries, page 775), and the right kind of power training minimizes the possibility of this occurring.

Muscle size and density created by a program that includes heavy training are easier to maintain for long periods of time, even with a minimum of maintenance training. With high-rep training only, much of the growth is the result of transient factors such as fluid retention and glycogen storage, but muscle made as hard as a granite wall through power training comes as a result of an actual increase in muscle fiber size. Also, as Franco tells me, the muscle cell walls themselves grow thicker and tougher, so they tend to resist shrinking.

Besides all this, when you do power training, you find out what the body can really do, how much weight you can really move, and this gives you a mental edge over someone who never does power training.

Chris Cormier's arms are so powerful he is able to do Triceps Extensions as a power exercise.

With my long arms, bench-pressing 400-plus pounds eight times takes a lot of effort and concentration.

Heavy T-Bar Rows is one of the best power exercises for the back.

Modern bodybuilders need to master many sophisticated techniques, but you can't forget that the basis of bodybuilding is developing muscle mass by lifting heavy weights. This does not mean that I believe bodybuilders should train like weightlifters. I recommend a program of total development that includes a certain number of power moves to give you the advantage of both kinds of training.

HEAVY DAYS

When I was a young bodybuilder just starting out, I used to do a lot of powerlifting (powerlifting is a form of weightlifting which involves three specific lifts: Bench Presses, Squats, and Deadlifts). As I progressed in the sport, winning competitions on higher and higher levels, I had to concentrate more and more on sculpting a complete, balanced, quality physique because the further you go in bodybuilding the higher the quality of your competition. Remember, at the top levels in *any* sport, everybody has a lot of talent. That's what got them there. So relying on talent or raw genetics will not work at the elite levels of competition. For example, when you get to the Mr. Universe or Mr. Olympia level, judges are looking more at what you *don't* have than what you do, focusing on your weak points, so having as complete a physique as possible becomes essential.

In my case, this meant doing a greater proportion of higher-rep isolation training, making sure I sculpted each muscle and achieved the greatest amount of definition and separation possible. But I never wanted to lose the basic thickness, density, and hardness that my early powerlifting training had created. That is why I always scheduled "heavy days" in my training routine. Once a week or so I would pick one body part and go to the maximum with strength moves that worked that area. When training legs, for instance, I would try for a maximum Squat; for chest, a maximum-strength Bench Press; and so on. By training this way I would not tax my body to such an extent that it could not recuperate before my next workout. But by going to the maximum on a regular basis, I gained a very accurate perception of just how much progress I was making in developing my strength, and by forcing myself to go to the limit every so often, I counterbalanced the lighter-weight, higher-rep training that made up the majority of my workouts.

I recommend you try the same thing. Once or twice a week pick one body part and test out your maximum strength. Have your training partner standing by to spot you so that you have no anxieties about handling a heavy weight. Stretch and warm up first to prepare your body for the effort. Keep track of your poundages in your training diary. You will feel a great deal of satisfaction watching the numbers climb as you grow stronger. Your ability to handle heavy weight will also contribute tremendously to increasing your confidence and mental commitment to your training.

OVERTRAINING AND RECUPERATION

The harder you work your body, the more time it takes to recover and recuperate from that training. Rest and recuperation are very important because, although you stimulate growth by training, it is during the subsequent period of recuperation that actual growth and adaptation take place. That's why bodybuilders frequently overcome sticking points by resting more rather than training harder or more often.

Overtraining occurs when you work a muscle too often to allow it to fully recuperate. You hear bodybuilders talk about tearing the muscle down and then letting it rebuild itself, but this is not really physiologically accurate. There can be small amounts of tissue damage during heavy exercise, and it is this damage that is associated with residual muscular soreness. But the soreness is a side effect and not the primary reason the muscles need time to recuperate after heavy exercise.

A number of complex biochemical processes accompany strenuous muscular contraction. The process of fueling muscular contraction results in the buildup of toxic waste products such as lactic acid. And during exercise the energy stored in the muscle in the form of glycogen is used up.

The body requires time to restore the chemical balance of the muscle cells, clear out the residual waste products, and restock the depleted stores of glycogen. But another factor is even more important: Time is needed for the cells themselves to adapt to the stimulus of the exercise and to grow. After all, bodybuilding is all about making muscles grow. So if you overtrain a muscle, forcing it to work too hard too quickly after the preceding exercise session, you will not give it a chance to grow and your progress will slow down.

Different muscles recover from exercise at different rates. As I mentioned, the biceps recover the fastest. The lower back muscles recover the slowest, taking about a hundred hours to completely recuperate from a heavy workout. However, in most cases, giving a body part 48 hours' rest is sufficient, which means skipping a day after training a muscle before training it again.

Basic training involves only medium levels of intensity, so the time necessary for recuperation is shorter. Once you move on to more advanced training, higher levels of intensity will be needed in order to overcome the greater resistance of the body to change and growth. There is one other important factor, however: Trained muscles recover from fatigue faster than untrained muscles. So the better you get at bodybuilding, the faster your recovery rate will be and the more intense your training program can become.

RESTING BETWEEN SETS

It is important to pace yourself properly through a workout. If you try to train too fast, you risk cardiovascular failure before you have worked the muscles enough. Also, you may have a tendency to get sloppy and start throwing the weights around instead of executing each movement correctly.

However, training too slowly is also bad. If you take 5 minutes between each set, your heart rate slows down, you lose your pump, the muscles get cold, and your level of intensity drops down to nothing.

Try to keep your rest periods between sets down to a minute or less. In the first minute after a weight-training exercise you recover 72 percent of your strength, and by 3 minutes you have recovered all you are going to recover without extended rest. But remember that the point of this training is to stimulate and fatigue the maximum amount of muscle fiber possible, and this happens only when the body is forced to recruit additional muscle fiber to replace what is already fatigued. So you don't want to allow your muscles to recover too much between sets—just enough to be able to continue your workout and to keep forcing the body to recruit more and more muscle tissue.

There is one other factor to consider: Physiologists have long noted the link between maximal muscle strength and muscular endurance. The stronger you are, the more times you can lift a submaximal amount of weight. This means that the more you push yourself to develop muscular (as opposed to cardiovascular) endurance, the stronger you become. So maintaining a regular pace in your training actually leads to an increase in overall strength.

BREATHING

I am surprised how often I am asked how you should breathe during an exercise. This has always seemed automatic to me, and I am often tempted to say, "Just relax and let it happen. Don't think about it."

But now I know that for some people this doesn't work very well, and for them I have a simple rule: Breathe out with effort. For example, if you are doing a Squat, take in a breath as you stand with the weight on your shoulders and squat down, and expel your breath as you push yourself back up. As you breathe out, don't hold your breath.

There is a good reason for this. Very hard contractions of the muscles usually involve a contraction of the diaphragm as well, especially when you are doing any kind of Leg Press or Squat movement. This increases the pressure in your thoracic cavity (the space in which the lungs fit). If you try to hold your breath, you could injure yourself. For example, you could hurt your epiglottis, blocking the passage of air through your throat. Breathing out as you perform a maximal effort protects you from this and, some people think, it actually makes you a little stronger.

STRETCHING

Stretching is one of the most neglected areas of the workout. If you watch a lion as he wakes from a nap and gets to his feet, you will see he immediately stretches his whole body to its full length, readying every muscle, tendon, and ligament for instant and brutal action. The lion knows instinctively that stretching primes his strength.

Muscle, tendon, ligament, and joint structures are flexible. They can stiffen, limiting your range of motion, or they can stretch, giving you a longer range of motion and the ability to contract additional muscle fiber. That's why stretching before you train allows you to train harder.

Stretching also makes your training safer. As you extend your muscles fully under the pull of a weight, they can easily be pulled too far if your range of motion is limited. Overextension of a tendon or ligament can result in a strain or sprain and seriously interfere with your workout schedule. But if you stretch the areas involved first, the body will adjust as heavy resistance pulls on the structures involved.

Flexibility will also increase if the various exercises are done properly. A muscle can contract, but it cannot stretch itself. It has to be stretched by the pull of an opposing muscle. When you train through a full range of motion, the muscle that is contracting automatically stretches its opposite. For example, when you do Curls, your biceps contract and your triceps stretch. When you do Triceps Extensions, the opposite happens. By using techniques that engage the full range of motion, you will increase your flexibility.

But that isn't enough. Muscles contracted against heavy resistance tend to shorten with the effort. Therefore, I recommend stretching before you train—to allow you to train harder and more safely—and stretching after you train as well—to stretch out those tight and tired muscles.

You can prepare for your workout by doing any number of the standard stretching exercises which follow. You might also consider taking a yoga or stretching class. Many bodybuilders feel that this extra effort devoted to flexibility is not necessary, but others, like Tom Platz, rely heavily on stretching to enhance their workouts. When Tom is limbering up for a workout, with those gargantuan legs of his twisted like pretzels beneath him, it is almost unbelievable to watch. He spends the first part of his calf workout stretching his calves as far as possible, often using very heavy weights, because he realizes that the more they stretch, the more fiber becomes involved in the contraction.

But as important as stretching before and after the workout may be, I believe it is also essential to do certain kinds of stretching during your training. Just as I recommend flexing and posing the muscles between sets, I also believe in stretching certain muscles between one set and the next. The lats, for example, benefit from careful stretching interspersed with various Chin-Up and Pulldown movements. You will find I have included stretches in various exercises where I feel stretching to be particularly beneficial.

It is, after all, details like these that set champions apart, and the difference will be immediately visible when you pose onstage in competition. The difference will be not only in how you look—the utmost in separation and definition—but will also show in the grace and sureness of your presentation. Bodybuilders like Ed Corney, known as perhaps the best poser in modern bodybuilding, could never move with such beauty if their muscles, tendons, and ligaments were tight and constricted.

I don't recommend spending too much time and energy stretching unless you have a severe flexibility problem or are trying to rehabilitate an injured area. For most purposes, I think spending about 10 minutes doing 10 basic stretching exercises for the bigger muscles before and after you work out is enough.

Stretching requires slow, gentle movements rather than quick, bouncing ones. When you put sudden stress on a muscle or tendon, it contracts to protect itself, thereby defeating your purpose. On the other hand, if you stretch it out carefully and hold that position for 30 seconds or more, the tendon will gradually relax and you will gain flexibility.

I recommend spending about one minute on each of the following exercises. However, this should be considered the bare minimum. The more time you spend stretching, the more flexible you will become.

Stretching Exercises

SIDE BENDS

Purpose of Exercise: To stretch the obliques and other muscles at the side of the torso.

Execution: Stand upright, feet slightly more than shoulder width apart, arms at sides. Raise your right arm over your head and bend slowly to the left, letting your left hand slide down your thigh. Bend as far as you can and hold this position for about 30 seconds. Return to starting position, then repeat to opposite side.

Frank Sepe

FORWARD BENDS

PURPOSE OF EXERCISE: To stretch the hamstrings and lower back.

EXECUTION: Stand upright, feet together. Bend forward and take hold of the back of your legs as far down as possible—knees, calves, or ankles. Pull gently with your arms, bringing your head as close as possible to your legs in order to stretch the lower back and hamstrings to their limit. Hold this position for 30 to 60 seconds, then relax.

HAMSTRING STRETCHES

PURPOSE OF EXERCISE: To stretch the hamstrings and lower back.

EXECUTION: Place one foot or ankle on a support. Keeping your other leg straight, bend forward along the raised leg and take hold of it as far down as possible—knee, calf, ankle, or foot. Pull gently to get the maximum stretch in the hamstrings. Hold for about 30 seconds, relax, then repeat the movement using the other leg.

LUNGES

Purpose of Exercise: To stretch the inner thighs, hamstrings, and glutes.

Execution: (1) Stand upright, move one leg forward, then bend that knee, coming down so that the knee of your trailing leg touches the floor. Place your hands on either side of your front foot and lean forward to get the maximum possible stretch in the inner thighs. (2) From this position, straighten your forward leg and lock your knee, stretching the hamstrings at the back of the leg. Bend your forward knee and lower yourself to the floor again. Repeat this movement, first straightening the leg, then coming down to the floor again. Stand upright once more, step forward with opposite foot, and repeat the stretching procedure.

FEET APART SEATED FORWARD BENDS

PURPOSE OF EXERCISE: To stretch the hamstrings and lower back.

EXECUTION: (1) Sit on the floor, legs straight and wide apart. Bend forward and touch the floor with your hands as far in front of you as possible. (2) Hold this position for a few seconds, then "walk" your hands over to one leg and grasp it as far down as possible—knee, calf, ankle, or foot. Pull gently on your leg to get the maximum stretch in the hamstrings and lower back. Hold this position for about 30 seconds, then walk your hands over to the other leg and repeat.

T. J. Hoban

INNER THIGH STRETCHES

PURPOSE OF EXERCISE: To stretch the inner thighs.

EXECUTION: Sit on the floor and draw your feet up toward you so that the soles are touching. Take hold of your feet and pull them as close to the groin as possible. Relax your legs and drop your knees toward the floor, stretching the inner thighs. Press down on your knees with your elbows to get a more complete stretch. Hold for 30 to 60 seconds, then relax.

QUADRICEPS STRETCHES

Purpose of Exercise: To stretch the front of the thighs.

Execution: Kneel on the floor. Separate your feet enough so that you can sit between them. Put your hands on the floor behind you and lean back as far as possible, feeling the stretch in the quadriceps. (Those who are less flexible will only be able to lean back a little; those who are very flexible will be able to lie back on the floor.) Hold this position for 30 to 60 seconds, then relax.

HURDLER'S STRETCHES

PURPOSE OF EXERCISE: To stretch the hamstrings and inner thighs.

EXECUTION: Sit on the floor, extend one leg in front of you, and curl the other back beside you. Bend forward along the extended leg and take hold of it as far down as possible—knee, calf, ankle, or foot. Pull slightly to get the maximum stretch and hold for 30 seconds. Reverse the position of your legs and repeat the movement. Do not overstress your bent knee.

SPINAL TWISTS

PURPOSE OF EXERCISE: To increase the rotational range of motion of the torso and stretch the outer thigh.

EXECUTION: Sit on the floor, legs extended in front of you. Bring your right knee up and twist around so that your left elbow rests on the outside of the upraised knee. Place your right hand on the floor behind you and continue to twist to the right as far as possible. Twist to the extreme of your range of motion and hold for 30 seconds. Lower your right knee, bring up your left, and repeat the motion to the other side.

HANGING STRETCHES

Purpose of Exercise: To stretch the spine and upper body.

Execution: Take hold of a chinning bar and let your body hang beneath it. Hold for at least 30 seconds so your spine and upper body have a chance to let go and stretch. If you have gravity boots or some other appropriate piece of equipment available, try hanging upside down to increase the amount of spinal stretch.

C H A P T E R 2

Learning Your Body Type

ANYONE WHO HAS spent time at a beach, swimming pool, or gym locker room can attest to the fact that human beings are born with a variety of different physical characteristics. Some are taller or shorter, lighter or darker, wider or narrower in the shoulders, longer and shorter in the leg; they have higher or lower natural levels of endurance, differing types of muscle cells, more or fewer muscle and fat cells.

One popular method of categorizing all these various body types recognizes three fundamentally different physical types, called somatotypes:

The *ectomorph:* characterized by a short upper body, long arms and legs, long and narrow feet and hands, and very little fat storage; narrowness in the chest and shoulders, with generally long, thin muscles.

The *mesomorph:* large chest, long torso, solid muscle structure, and great strength.

The *endomorph:* soft musculature, round face, short neck, wide hips, and heavy fat storage.

Of course, no one is entirely one type but rather a combination of all three types. This system of classification recognizes a total of eighty-eight subcategories, which are arrived at by examining the level of dominance of each basic category on a scale of 1 to 7. For example, someone whose body characteristics were scored as ectomorphic (2), mesomorphic (6), and endomorphic (5) would be an endo-mesomorph, basically a well-muscled jock type but inclined to carry a lot of fat.

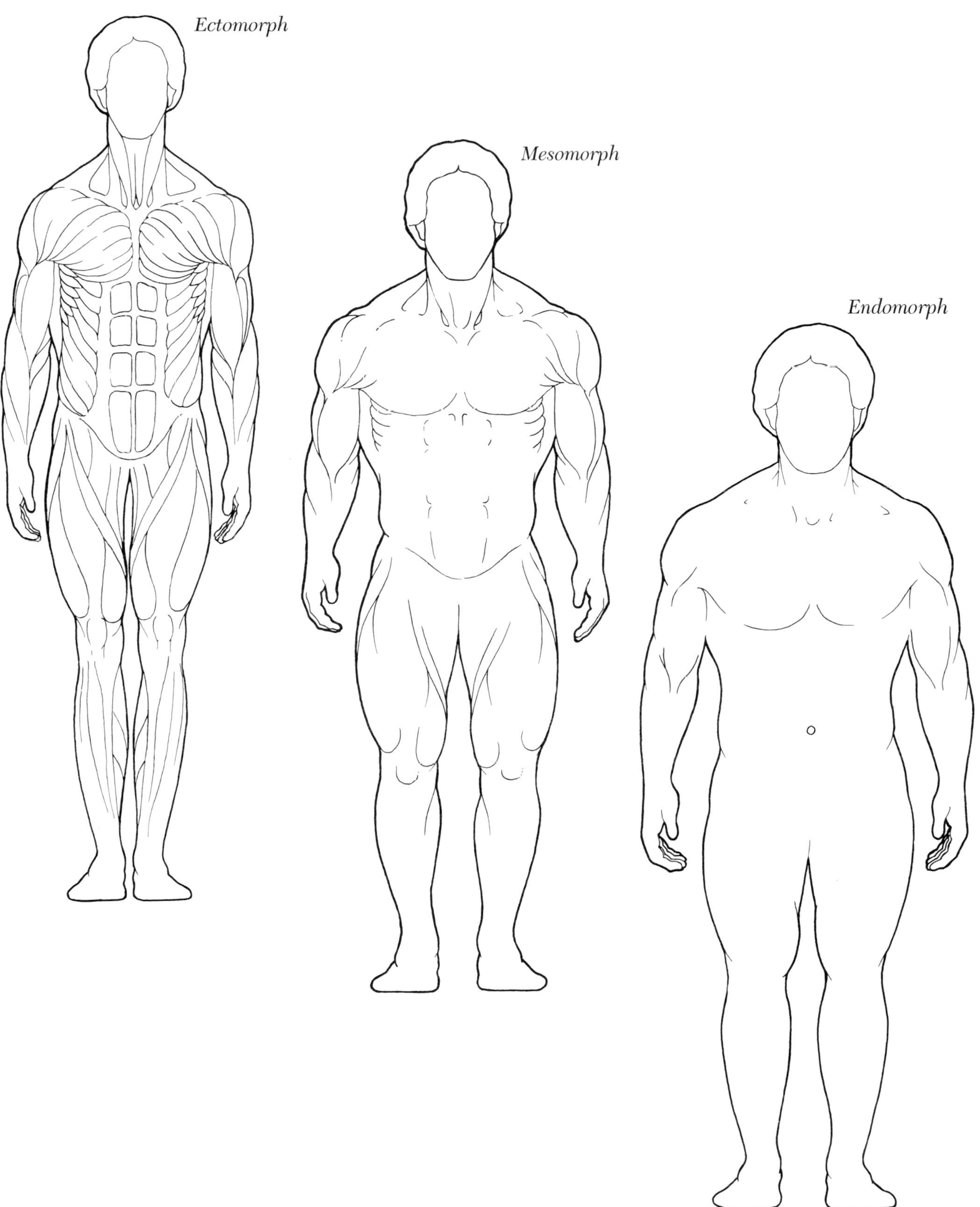
Ectomorph
Mesomorph
Endomorph

Although the fundamentals of bodybuilding training apply to all the somatotypes, individuals with different body types often respond very differently to training, and what works for one type may not necessarily work for another. Any body type can be developed by proper training and nutrition, but individuals with different body types will find it necessary to initially approach their training with different objectives, even though they may share the same long-term goals.

UNDERSTANDING YOUR BODY TYPE

There have been champions with every kind of body type. Steve Davis, a well-known competitor in the 1970s, once weighed in at around 270 pounds, which meant he tended heavily toward the endomorphic. It was necessary for Steve to lose a lot of fat while maintaining muscle mass in order to win bodybuilding titles. Mr. Olympia Dorian Yates is one of

Here is a good example of how bodybuilding can change your body. Steve Davis before, looking very endomorphic . . .

. . . and after, looking very mesomorphic

Nasser El Sonbaty, an endo-mesomorph

Frank Zane, an ecto-mesomorph

Dave Draper—classic endo-mesomorph

Chris Dickerson—endo-mesomorph

Flex Wheeler—ecto-mesomorph

Ken Waller—endo-mesomorph

Lee Priest—endo-mesomorph

Dorian Yates—mesomorph

Tom Platz—another classic mesomorph

the biggest champions of all time; in contest shape he weighs in at close to 270 pounds. However, during the off-season Dorian gets up to well over 300 pounds, which indicates his body type tends toward the endo-mesomorphic. The legendary Dave Draper was another endo-mesomorph (although, having less muscle, he'd be classified as more endomorphic than Dorian), tending to get heavy and smooth easily, but able to stay lean and hard for competition by hard training and strict diet.

Frank Zane, on the other hand, is much more ectomorphic. Muscle-mass gains have always taken Frank a long time to achieve, but this did not keep him from becoming Mr. Olympia three times. Bodybuilders like Frank and Shawn Ray, who at 200 pounds have managed to defeat most of the more massive competitors, are not naturally powerful, muscular individuals. Their muscular development and bodybuilding excellence have come about mostly by a lot of hard, dedicated work. "Muscle did not come to me naturally," says Larry Scott, the first Mr. Olympia and another bodybuilder tending toward the ectomorphic. "I was one of those 98-pound weaklings who was motivated to use bodybuilding training to get bigger."

In my own case, I am mesomorphic enough to be able to build muscle mass relatively easily, and at one point bulked up to a solid 240 pounds, but my natural physique has always tended to be lean, which makes me more an ecto-mesomorph than pure mesomorph or an endo-mesomorph.

Flex Wheeler, who is so renowned for his shape and proportion, is yet another ecto-mesomorph. Look at Flex and you'll see how relatively small his bones and joints are, despite his muscle size, especially compared to a powerfully built competitor like Dorian. In bodybuilding terms, Flex, Frank Zane, and I would be characterized as having Apollonian physiques (muscular, but tending toward the ectomorphic, more aesthetic than brute powerful), while thicker bodybuilders like Dorian, Nasser El Sonbaty, Tom Platz, Casey Viator, and Mike Mentzer would be classified as Herculean (very mesomorphic or endo-mesomorphic). Both Apollonian and Herculean physiques can have outstanding aesthetics, but the look is very different. Nowadays, the Apollonian physique is generally considered more artistic or beautiful because of its lines and proportion, but if you look back at classic art you frequently find the Herculean physique to be the more admired.

Of course, the top pro bodybuilders nowadays are so massive and well developed that it's sometimes hard to separate them into different body-type categories. But go to almost any amateur contest and the difference between the various body types will be much more apparent.

Really, though, no top bodybuilder can be *too much* an ectomorph or an endomorph. His body would lack proper proportion, symmetry, muscle mass, and definition. Remember, bodybuilding is not just about building muscle; it involves the maximum *aesthetic* development of muscle. Lifeguard-type physiques (lean and defined) can be very pleasing to look at, but lack the mass necessary to compete at the top levels in bodybuilding. Thick, massive, super-mesomorphic bodies are great for weightlifters, shot-putters, and football linemen, but the aesthetics of this kind of physique don't make it on the bodybuilding stage.

Understanding your own body type can save you a lot of time and frustration. An ectomorph who trains like an endomorph is likely to overtrain and not grow. The endomorph who thinks he is more mesomorphic will grow, but will always have trouble keeping his body fat down. Certain principles of training are the same for everybody. But how you organize your training and how you integrate it with diet and nutrition can be profoundly different depending on what kind of body type nature has given you.

METABOLISM AND MUSCLE-BUILDING

One of the factors that helps create different body types is metabolism. Some people naturally burn more calories than others. Some bodies seem naturally designed to turn food energy into muscle or fat while others turn this energy into fuel for exercise. However, as your body changes, so does your metabolism. Muscle burns calories, so a naturally heavy endomorph will find it easier to get lean as he builds more and more muscle mass. Also, the body is very adaptable, and the literally thousands of various metabolic processes that are going on all the time tend to alter in response to the demands you put on them—turning protein intake into muscle, for example, or increasing your ability to metabolize body fat for energy.

If you are extremely lean or extremely heavy, you should take the precaution of having your thyroid function checked by a physician. The thyroid gland plays a major role in regulating metabolism. When it is underactive (hypothyroid) it is very difficult to burn off excess body fat, and when it is overactive (hyperthyroid) putting on any additional body weight becomes almost impossible. However, I am strongly *against* using thyroid as a means of increasing your metabolism and "cutting up" (achieving a state of high definition) when your own thyroid levels are within normal limits. This is dangerous in a number of ways, including the risk that you will permanently damage your natural thyroid function.

ECTOMORPH TRAINING

The extreme ectomorph's first objective is gaining weight, preferably in the form of quality muscle mass. He will not have the strength and endurance for marathon training sessions, will find that muscle mass develops very slowly, and will often have to force himself to eat enough to ensure continued growth. Therefore, for the ectomorph I recommend:

1. Include plenty of power moves for a program that builds maximum mass. Your program should tend toward heavy weight and low reps (in the 6- to 8-rep range after proper warm-up).

2. Learn to train intensely and make every set count. That way you can keep your workouts relatively short and still make substantial gains (perhaps 14 to 16 sets per major body part rather than 16 to 20). Make sure to get enough rest between sets and give yourself enough time to recuperate between workouts.

3. Pay careful attention to nutrition; take in more calories than you are accustomed to, and if necessary, use weight-gain and protein drinks to supplement your food intake.

4. Remember, you are trying to turn food energy into mass, so be careful not to burn up too much energy with *excessive* amounts of other activities such as aerobics, running, swimming, and other sports. Some cardio exercise is both desirable and necessary for good health, but anyone who spends hours a day expending large amounts of physical energy outside the gym will have a lot more trouble building muscle while in the gym.

MESOMORPH TRAINING

The mesomorph will find it relatively easy to build muscle mass, but will have to be certain to include a sufficient variety of exercises in his program so that the muscles develop proportionately and well shaped rather than just thick and bulky. Therefore, for the mesomorph I recommend:

1. An emphasis on quality, detail, and isolation training, along with the basic mass and power exercises. You build muscle easily, so you can begin working on shape and separation right from the beginning.

2. Mesomorphs gain so easily that they don't have to worry much about conserving energy or overtraining. A standard workout of 16 to 20 sets per body part is fine, and you can train with as much or little rest between sets as suits you.

3. A balanced diet with plenty of protein which maintains a calorie level that keeps the physique within 10 to 15 pounds of contest weight all year long. No bulking up 30 to 40 pounds and then having to drop all of that useless weight for competition.

ENDOMORPH TRAINING

Generally, the endomorph will not have too much difficulty building muscle, but will have to be concerned with losing fat weight and then being very careful with diet so as not to gain that weight back. Therefore, for the endomorph I recommend:

1. A higher proportion of high-set, high-repetition training (no lower than the 10- to 12-rep range), with very short rest periods so as to burn off as much fat as possible. Doing a few extra sets of a few extra exercises while you are trying to get lean is a good idea.

2. Additional aerobic exercise such as bicycle riding, running, or some other calorie-consuming activity. Training in the gym burns calories, but not as much as cardio exercise done on a continuous basis for 30 to 45 minutes or more at a time.

3. A low-calorie diet that contains the necessary nutritional balance (see page 703). Not zero anything, but the minimum amount of protein, carbohydrates, and fats, with vitamin and mineral supplements to be certain the body is not being deprived of any essential nutrients.

BODY COMPOSITION TESTING

Even though nature has given you a particular body type, when you add lean body mass and cut down on fat weight you are actually changing the composition of your body. It is often difficult to keep track of these developments because your training is creating more muscle mass, so your body composition can change quite a lot without your realizing it. The mirror, the scale, and the tape measure are always useful, but sometimes they don't tell you enough.

In addition to simply studying yourself in the mirror, the best way to keep track of these physical changes is by some form of body composition testing. This testing gives you an indication of the percentage of muscle your body has compared to the amount of fat. So the test will help track your progress as you gain muscle and lose fat. The most common types of body composition testing are:

- skin-fold testing. Calipers are used to pinch folds of skin at various parts of your body, which indicates how much fat is under the skin, and this is used to calculate body composition.
- water-emersion testing. The subject is weighed out of the water, then in the water, and certain measurements such as the residual capacity of the lungs are taken. The numbers are applied to a formula to determine the ratio of fat to lean body mass—which is composed of muscle, bone, and internal organs.
- electrical impedance testing. A low-voltage current is passed through the body. Since fat, muscle, and water create different amounts of resistance to electrical current, the amount of resistance encountered allows for calculation of body composition.

However, while measuring body composition is useful in ascertaining the results of a diet or what changes training is creating in your physique, be aware that the *direction of change* from one test to another is more significant than the specific results you get in any one test. The reason is that all the test numbers are run through formulas that make certain assumptions about the body that don't necessarily apply very well to the extreme development of serious bodybuilders. So if you are tested as 12 percent body fat in one session and 9 percent two weeks later, you can be pretty sure you're headed in the right direction—assuming you are taking the same type of test administered in the same way, so that the retest accuracy is high.

I have heard some ridiculous claims made for body fat testing, such as by athletes asserting they have as little as 3 percent body fat. Any doctor will tell you that 3 percent might be the fat level of a *cadaver,* but not a strong, healthy athlete. In tests conducted at IFBB and NPC contests, using a variety of methods, it was shown that the bigger the bodybuilder the higher the fat percentage when the competitor is really ripped. So a massive bodybuilder might be ripped at 12 percent body fat measurement, while a lightweight amateur might look great at 7 or 8 percent.

Why is this? Because what we traditionally think of as fat is not the only fat in your body. There is also intramuscular fat, which is the fat in the muscle itself. So if a really big bodybuilder continues to diet past a certain point he is likely to just *shrink* rather than getting more cut-up. So while body composition testing is useful, don't forget to use the mirror or photographs to keep track of how you look. Remember, the judges don't take body fat tests into consideration during a contest. They go only by what they see. And you need to do the same thing.

CHAPTER 3

The Basic Training Program

THE FIRST TASK facing the beginning bodybuilder is to build up a solid foundation of muscle mass—genuine muscular weight, not bulky fat. Later, you will try to shape this muscle into a balanced, quality physique.

You do this by basic, hard training using heavy weights—grinding it out week after week until your body begins to respond. And what I mean by basic training is not just a few exercises like Bench Presses, Bent-Over Rows, and Squats, but 30 or 40 exercises all designed to stimulate and develop the major muscle groups of the body.

At the end of this period what you want is size, the raw material of a great physique. In my own case, or in the case of other bodybuilders like Dave Draper or Lee Haney, we had pretty much achieved this in our early twenties. I was huge, 240 pounds, but unfinished—like an enormous, gangling puppy who has not yet grown up to match the size of his feet. Although I had won major championships, I was like an uncut diamond. But I had plenty of mass and at that point I set out to create the kind of finished, polished look I needed to become the best I could be.

This initial period may last two, three, or even as long as five years. The length of the process depends on a number of factors such as genetics, body type, and how much energy and motivation you are able to put into your training. Whether a bodybuilder develops faster or slower is no particular guarantee of ultimate quality. What counts is how far you are able to go, not how fast. Dorian Yates, for example, who is incredibly massive, didn't even begin serious bodybuilding until his late teens and early twenties. So no matter when you start, how old you are, or what kind of body type you have, the process is the same—heavy, consistent, dedicated training over an extended period of time.

SPLIT SYSTEM TRAINING

Split System Training involves dividing up your training so that you work only some of your muscles in each session, not the whole body all at one time.

Me at nineteen with four year's training

In the early days when champions like John Grimek and Clancy Ross reigned, bodybuilders usually attempted to train the entire body three times a week. They could train the entire body in one exercise session because they usually performed only 3 or 4 sets per body part. But as bodybuilding evolved it became evident that more precise training was needed to totally shape and develop the body. Different kinds of exercises were required so that the muscles could be worked from a variety of angles, and more sets of each exercise were necessary to stimulate the maximum amount of muscle fiber. But this meant that it was no longer possible to train the entire body in one workout. Too much effort was involved, so the Split System of training was developed.

The simplest type of Split System Training is just to divide the body into two parts: upper-body muscles and lower-body muscles. To hit each of the muscles even harder, you can further divide the muscles so that you take three training sessions to work the entire body—an example of this being training all the "pushing" muscles in one session (chest, shoulders, triceps), the "pulling" muscles the next (back, biceps), and the legs in the third. And various bodybuilders over the years have developed variations of the Split System that they felt best suited their individual needs.

In the exercise programs that follow, I will give you specific recommendations for how to best do Split System Training.

Dave Draper at nineteen

THE BASIC MUSCLE GROUPS

The human body has more than six hundred separate muscles, but in learning the fundamentals of bodybuilding we need concern ourselves with only a few of these.

Usually bodybuilders divide the body up into the following basic categories or muscle groups:

- back
- shoulders
- chest
- arms
- forearms
- thighs and glutes
- waist
- calves

But to really sculpt and develop each important area of the body, you need to subdivide the muscle groups even further:

- *back*—both the width and length of the latissimus dorsi (the lats), back thickness, middle back muscularity, development of the spinal erectors of the lower back
- *shoulders*—size and fullness, development of each of the three heads of the deltoids (front, rear, and side), the trapezius
- *chest*—upper and lower pectorals, middle chest thickness, fullness

of the rib cage, detail muscles at the side of the torso, the serratus and intercostals

- *biceps*—upper and lower biceps, overall length, thickness
- *triceps*—development of all three triceps heads, detail and separation, mass and thickness
- *forearms*—extensor and contractor development, brachialis tie-in to the elbow
- *quadriceps, and glutes*—development of all four quadriceps heads, separation of the quad muscles, sweep of the outer thigh, the adductors of the inner thigh
- *hamstrings*—fullness and sweep of the leg biceps, separation between the hamstrings and the quads
- *abdominals*—upper and lower abs, external obliques at the side of the waist
- *calves*—the upper calf muscle (gastrocnemius) and the underlying calf muscle (soleus)

There are many exercises for each individual muscle. As you go from basic to advanced training, you'll find that the programs I recommend begin to include more and more specific movements for each of the important muscle subdivisions.

ORGANIZING YOUR TRAINING

For the Basic Training Program, I recommend the following split:

Level I: *each body part 2 times a week*—using a 3-day split (taking 3 days to train the entire body)
Level II: *each body part 3 times a week*—using a 2-day split (taking 2 days to train the entire body)
Abdominals: every workout, both levels

I always liked to train 6 days a week, taking Sunday off as a rest day. This made it easy for me to keep track of my workouts—Monday, a certain group of body parts; Tuesday, a different group, etc. If you're on a different schedule you can do each of your workouts on whatever days they fall—just think of it as Workout #1 instead of Monday, Workout #2 instead of Tuesday, and so on through your entire training program.

REST AND RECUPERATION

When you plan a workout program, you have to be sure to include rest days. Remember, when you train intensely you have to get enough rest to

Front View

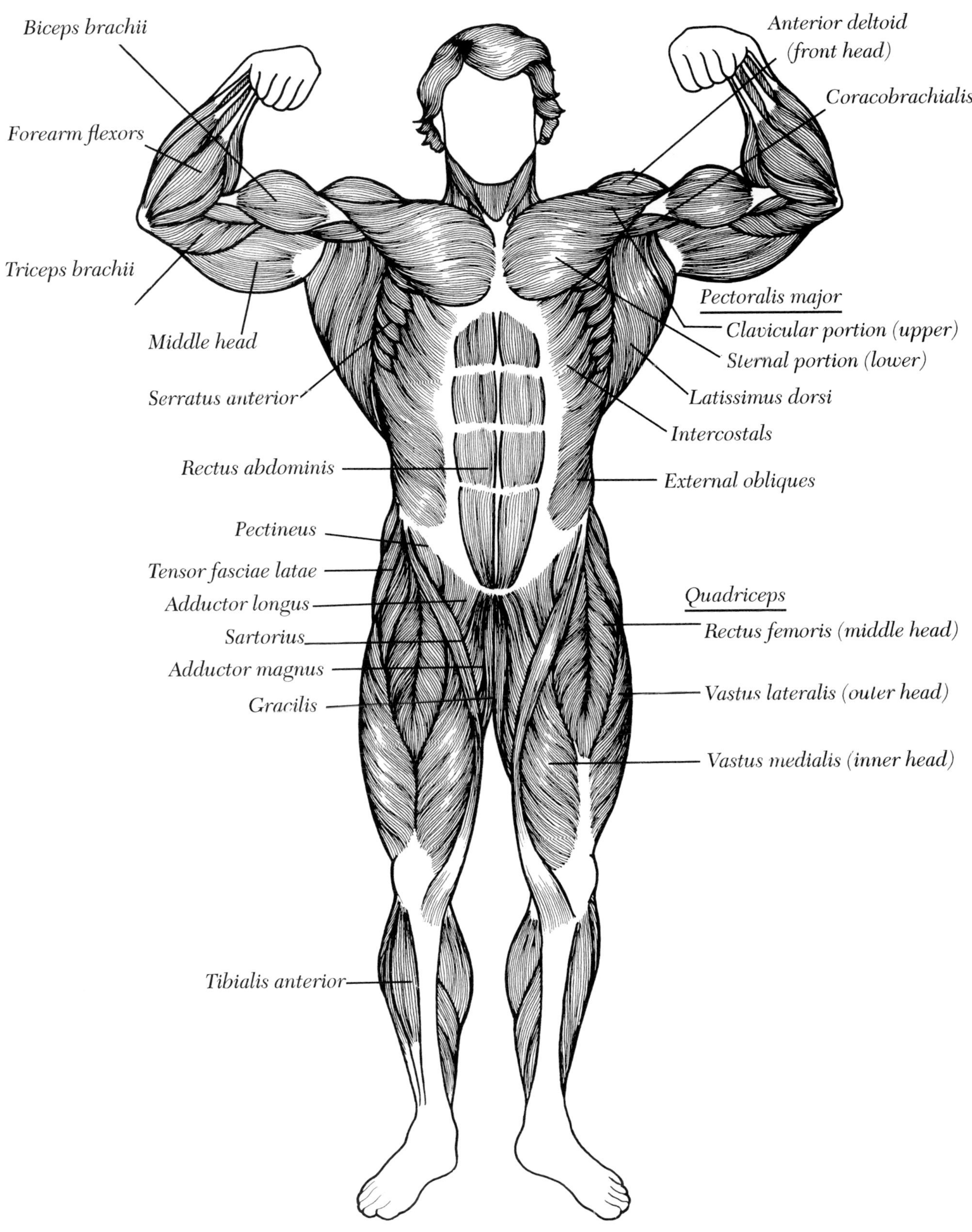
Biceps brachii
Forearm flexors
Triceps brachii
Middle head
Serratus anterior
Rectus abdominis
Pectineus
Tensor fasciae latae
Adductor longus
Sartorius
Adductor magnus
Gracilis
Tibialis anterior
Anterior deltoid
(front head)
Coracobrachialis
Pectoralis major
Clavicular portion (upper)
Sternal portion (lower)
Latissimus dorsi
Intercostals
External obliques
Quadriceps
Rectus femoris (middle head)
Vastus lateralis (outer head)
Vastus medialis (inner head)

Back View

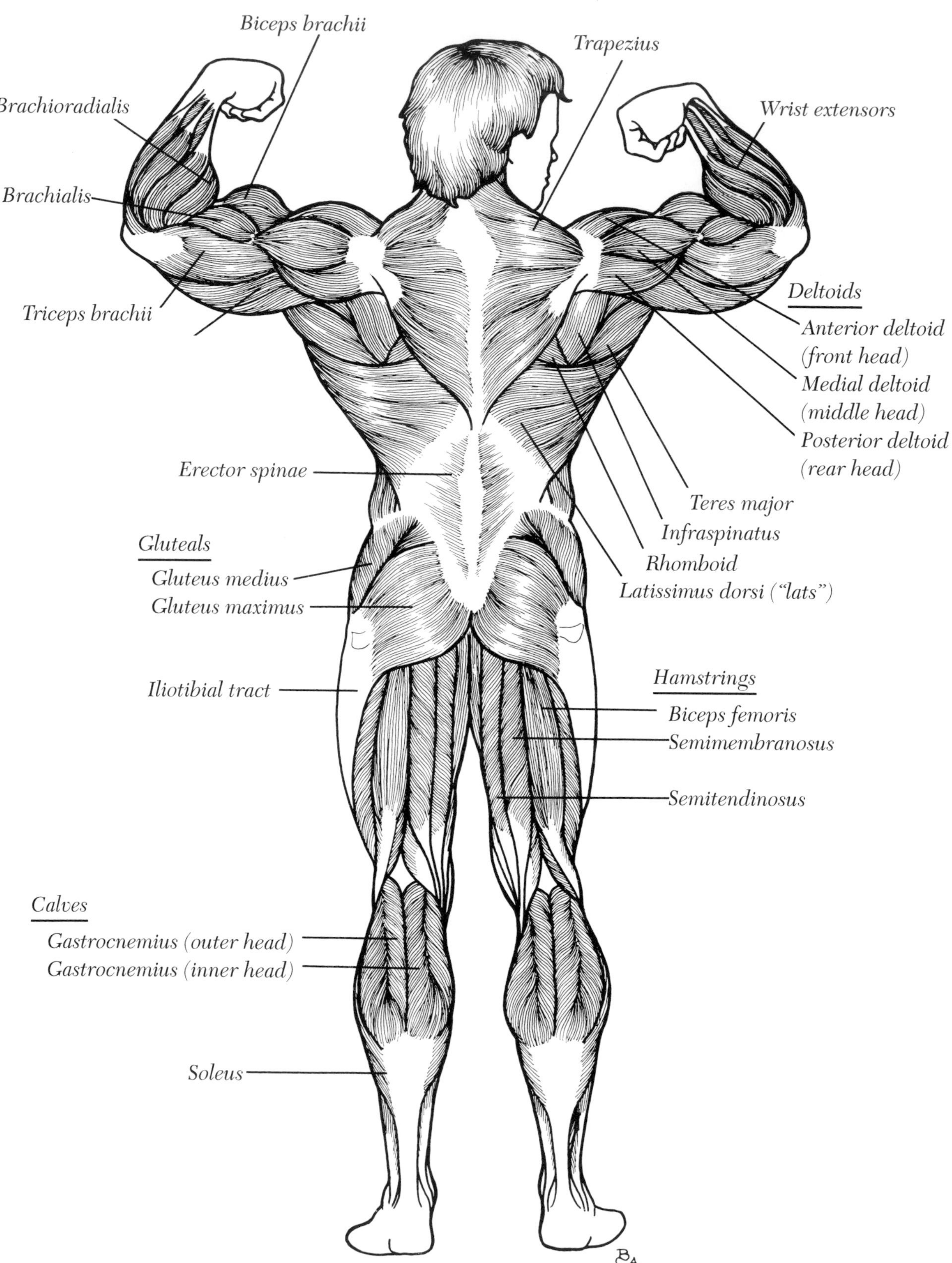
Biceps brachii
Trapezius
Brachioradialis
Wrist extensors
Brachialis
Deltoids
Anterior deltoid (front head)
Medial deltoid (middle head)
Posterior deltoid (rear head)
Triceps brachii
Erector spinae
Teres major
Infraspinatus
Rhomboid
Latissimus dorsi ("lats")
Gluteals
Gluteus medius
Gluteus maximus
Iliotibial tract
Hamstrings
Biceps femoris
Semimembranosus
Semitendinosus
Calves
Gastrocnemius (outer head)
Gastrocnemius (inner head)
Soleus
BA

allow the body to recuperate and build both strength and mass. This means getting plenty of sleep (8 hours is best). It also means you need to pay attention to priorities. If building maximum muscle is your goal, you will need to be careful not to exhaust yourself doing too many other sports or physical activities—just as you would have to be careful to save on a regular basis if you wanted to put money aside to buy a house or a car.

You also need to rest on your off days. This doesn't mean you can't engage in any physical activities on that day—you don't have to stay in bed or anything—but if you are running marathons or involved in Hawaiian canoe racing on Sunday you are probably not going to have much energy when you go back to the gym and work out on Monday.

WHEN TO TRAIN

My best workouts were always in the morning, when I was rested and fresh. Some bodybuilders prefer to train later in the day, but the majority of the competitors I've been around also liked to train first thing in the day. To this day, Bill Pearl gets his workout in at 5 A.M. and then has the rest of the day to pursue his other interests. If you work regular hours at a job, this means getting up very early to get your training in. When Franco and I got to the gym at 7 A.M. we would frequently see lawyers, accountants, teachers, and others with a full work schedule just finishing their training and hitting the showers before going to their jobs. This showed a lot of dedication on their part, but it's this kind of dedication that yields the best results.

If you absolutely have to train in the evening, or if that's your personal preference, of course you can get results with that schedule as well. Just ask yourself whether you think you are achieving the *maximum* possible from your workouts this way and whether you are training late because it's best for you or because you don't have the motivation to get up as early as necessary for regular morning workouts.

Level I Exercise Program

LEVEL I BASIC TRAINING

WORKOUT #1 MON	WORKOUT #2 TUE	WORKOUT #3 WED	WORKOUT #1 THUR	WORKOUT #2 FRI	WORKOUT #3 SAT
Chest Back	Shoulders Upper arms Forearms	Thighs Calves Lower back	Chest Back	Shoulders Upper arms Forearms	Thighs Calves Lower back

Abdominals every day

WORKOUT #1

Monday and Thursday

CHEST

Bench Press
Incline Press
Pullovers

BACK

Chin-Ups (do as many as you can at a time until you reach a total of 50 reps)
Bent-Over Rows

Power Training
Deadlifts, 3 sets of 10, 6, 4 reps to failure

ABDOMINALS

Crunches, 5 sets of 25 reps

WORKOUT #2

Tuesday and Friday

SHOULDERS

Barbell Clean and Press
Dumbbell Lateral Raises

Power Training
Heavy Upright Rows, 3 sets of 10, 6, 4 reps to failure
Push Presses, 3 sets of 6, 4, 2 reps to failure

Upper Arms

Standing Barbell Curls
Seated Dumbbell Curls
Close-Grip Press
Standing Triceps Extensions with Barbell

Forearms

Wrist Curls
Reverse Wrist Curls

Abdominals

Reverse Crunches, 5 sets of 25 reps

WORKOUT #3

Wednesday and Saturday

Thighs

Squats
Lunges
Leg Curls

Calves

Standing Calf Raises, 5 sets of 15 reps each

Lower Back

Power Training
Straight-Leg Deadlifts, 3 sets of 10, 6, 4 reps to failure
Good Mornings, 3 sets of 10, 6, 4 reps to failure

Note: Although these power movements work the lower back directly, they also involve the trapezius and the leg biceps, and help to develop overall strength.

Abdominals

Crunches, 5 sets of 25 reps

Level II Exercise Program

LEVEL II BASIC TRAINING

WORKOUT #1 MON	WORKOUT #2 TUE	WORKOUT #1 WED	WORKOUT #2 THUR	WORKOUT #1 FRI	WORKOUT #2 SAT
Chest	Shoulders	Chest	Shoulders	Chest	Shoulders
Back	Lower back	Back	Lower back	Back	Lower back
Thighs	Upper arms	Thighs	Upper arms	Thighs	Upper arms
Calves	Forearms	Calves	Forearms	Calves	Forearms

Abdominals every day

WORKOUT #1

Monday / Wednesday / Friday

CHEST

Bench Press
Incline Press
Pullovers

BACK

Chin-Ups (do as many as you can at a time until you reach a total of 50 reps)
Bent-Over Rows

Power Training
Deadlifts, 3 sets of 10, 6, 4 reps to failure

THIGHS

Squats
Lunges
Leg Curls

CALVES

Standing Calf Raises, 5 sets of 15 reps each

ABDOMINALS

Crunches, 5 sets of 25 reps

WORKOUT #2

Tuesday/Thursday/Saturday

SHOULDERS

Barbell Clean and Press
Dumbbell Lateral Raises

Power Training
Heavy Upright Rows, 3 sets of 10, 6, 4 reps to failure
Push Presses, 3 sets of 6, 4, 2 reps to failure

LOWER BACK

Power Training
Straight-Leg Deadlifts, 3 sets of 10, 6, 4 reps to failure
Good Mornings, 3 sets of 10, 6, 4 reps to failure

Note: Although these power movements work the lower back directly, they also involve the trapezius and the leg biceps, and help to develop overall strength.

UPPER ARMS

Standing Barbell Curls
Seated Dumbbell Curls
Close-Grip Press
Standing Triceps Extensions with Barbell

FOREARMS

Wrist Curls
Reverse Wrist Curls

ABDOMINALS

Reverse Crunches, 5 sets of 25 reps

Until the emergence of modern bodybuilders, this kind of muscular detail was never seen outside of an anatomy chart: the powerful forearms; full, striated triceps; an incredible biceps peak; all three heads of the deltoid; the trapezius muscles below the neck; the wide and powerful latissimus dorsi muscles at the side of the back; the spinal erectors. (Ronnie Coleman)

The overall shape and proportion of a bodybuilding physique is extremely important, but the whole is also the sum of its parts. Building a complete physique means developing each and every detail of every one of the major body parts.

A six-pack extraordinare. Abs like a bronze statue and well-developed, clearly defined intercostal muscles. (Shawn Ray)

The quality of a bodybuilding physique is in the details: the deltoids, triceps, both heads of the biceps, upper and lower pecs, abdominals, and all the smaller muscles at the side of the torso are totally developed. (Ronnie Coleman)

A top competition physique needs detailed "tie-ins" between the muscles and muscle groups. Muscles don't just sit next to each other but are tied together and interconnected. Notice the well-defined split between upper and lower pectorals. (Ronnie Coleman)

The upper and lower legs need to balance each other. In this case, the powerful development and sweep of the quadriceps and adductors would make less of an impression if the calf muscles below them weren't also so huge and detailed. (Nasser El Sonbaty)

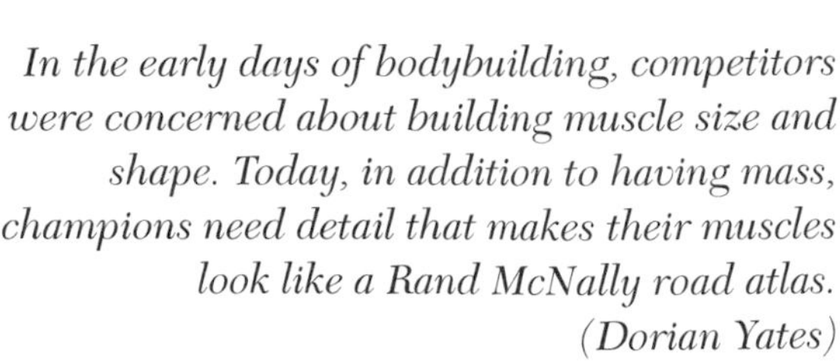

In the early days of bodybuilding, competitors were concerned about building muscle size and shape. Today, in addition to having mass, champions need detail that makes their muscles look like a Rand McNally road atlas. (Dorian Yates)

Ideally, the size of your calves should be about the same as your upper arms. (Dorian Yates)

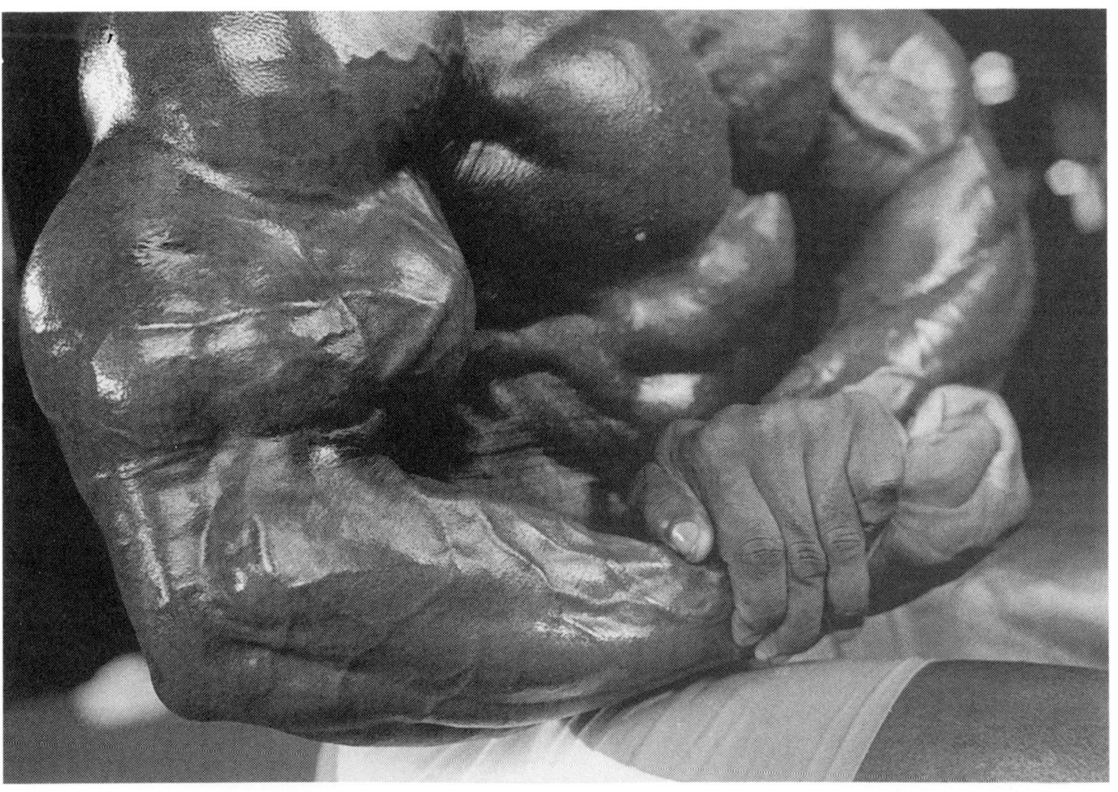

An example of a terrific biceps peak. Notice how the development of the arm is made that much more impressive by the overall muscularity of the rest of the upper body. (Ernie Taylor)

CHAPTER 4

Advanced Training Principles

INTENSITY IS THE key to making progressive-resistance training work for you. What is intensity? One kind involves how hard you feel yourself trying. That is intensity of effort. Another is the amount of stimulation you are able to deliver to the muscles, causing them to respond and develop. This is intensity of effect. It is important to realize the difference between these two types of intensity, otherwise you are likely to just keep trying harder (often to the point of injury) rather than mastering the type of intensity techniques described in this chapter that produce maximum training progress.

INCREASING TRAINING INTENSITY

Increasing intensity in the beginning is not that difficult. You learn to do more exercises and how to do them correctly; you get stronger and in better condition so you can work harder and longer and put more stress on your muscles. Once your body gets used to this effort, however, it becomes more difficult to continue to escalate intensity at the same rate.

Obviously, if you take long rest periods and train very slowly, so it takes you half the day to get through your workout, the actual intensity of your efforts will be minimal. Time, therefore, is an important factor in increasing training intensity. By manipulating time, you can increase intensity in two basic ways: (1) by doing the same amount of work in less time; and (2) by doing an increased amount of work in the same time.

But the most obvious way to increase workload is simply to train with more weight. Another valuable method is to cut down on rest periods between sets and try doing two or three exercises in a row without stopping.

This puts greater demand on your powers of endurance. Endurance, like strength, is something that can be developed in a progressive manner, a little at a time. You should also work at the fastest pace you are capable of without getting sloppy in your technique. This will help you to do the maximum amount of work in the minimum amount of time.

Beyond increasing intensity by manipulating time or adding weight, there are a number of special training techniques that can help ensure your progress in the Advanced Training and Competition Training Programs. These all involve methods of putting extra, unusual, or unexpected stress on the muscles, thereby forcing them to adapt to the increased demand.

Intensity Techniques

The Shocking Principle

The Shocking Principle involves literally shocking the body, catching it by surprise by changing various aspects of your workout. The body is amazingly adaptable and can accustom itself to workloads that would fell a horse. However, if you always put the same kind of stress on the body, in the same way, it gets used to this, and even very intense training will yield less response than you expected. You can shock it by training with more weight than usual; doing more reps and/or sets; speeding up your training; cutting down your rest time between sets; doing unfamiliar exercises; doing your exercises in an unfamiliar order; or using any or all of the Intensity Techniques listed here.

Change by itself tends to shock the body, even if the unfamiliar workout is no more demanding than the one you are used to. But you'll get to a point where you'll find it difficult to make additional progress without shocking your muscles into getting bigger and stronger, fuller, harder, and more defined. One way I introduced radical change into my workout was by training superheavy one day each week, typically on Friday. We'd overload the weights on a couple of sets of each exercise to really train for power, then take Saturday off to recover from the soreness. Check out the power training photos of Behind-the-Neck Presses (page 273), Dumbbell Presses (page 274), and Incline Dumbbell Presses (page 329) for some good examples.

Forced Reps

One method of forcing out extra reps is to have your workout partner supply a little extra lift to help you keep going. However, I have never liked this method because your partner has no real way of knowing how much lift to supply, what you are really capable of doing on your own, and how much help you actually need. I prefer a kind of forced reps which is sometimes called Rest/Pause Training. You use a fairly heavy weight and go to failure in the set. Then you stop, let the weight hang for just a few seconds, and then force out an extra rep. Again, rest only a few seconds before forcing out another. This method depends on the fast initial recovery that muscles make from exercise, and you can use this recovery to force out several extra reps. If you rest too long, however, too many of the tired fibers recover and you end up using them again instead of stimulating new fiber. For ultimate rest/pause forced reps, you can put the weight down for a moment, pick it up again, and force out additional reps. For exercises like Chin-Ups, you can do your reps, let go of the bar, rest momentarily, and then attempt to force out some more.

Partial Reps

Continuing to do partial reps when you are too tired to complete full-range-of-motion repetitions is a shock method I have always used for almost any muscle in the body, and it is a particular favorite of Dorian Yates. Dorian has done a lot of training where he forced his muscles past the point of momentary failure to almost total exhaustion, using techniques like forced reps and partial reps. Partial reps are most effective at the end of a set, when you are almost exhausted. For example, if you were doing Preacher Curls, you would have your workout partner help you lift the weight and then you would lower it a few degrees and then lift it as much as possible, even if only a few inches; then lower it some more and do some partial reps from that position, repeating this on the way down until your muscles are burning and exhausted.

Isolation Training

Isolation training involves focusing your efforts on a specific muscle or muscle group or even part of a muscle in isolation from other muscles. Here is an example of how specific isolation training can get: When you do compound exercises like a Bench Press, the muscles involved are the pectorals, the triceps, and the front delts. An exercise like Dumbbell Flys, on the other hand, works the pecs in isolation and lets you hit them with maximum intensity. As a further step, you can do Incline Dumbbell Flys as a way of isolating just the upper pecs. Carrying this to an even further extreme, you can perform Incline Cable Crossovers, making a special effort to cross your hands and get the maximum Peak Contraction of the test. This would isolate and develop the inner area of the upper pecs.

Isolation training can allow you to develop every part of your physique completely, bringing up any weak areas and helping to achieve the degree of muscle separation and definition necessary for that sculpted, champion look.

Negative Repetitions

Whenever you lift a weight using the contractile force of your muscles you perform what is defined as a positive movement; when you lower the weight, extending the working muscle, you perform negative movement. Negative repetitions actually put more stress on the tendons and supportive structures than on the muscles themselves. This is beneficial because you want tendon strength to increase along with muscular strength. To get the full benefit of negatives in your normal workouts, always lower the weights slowly and under control, rather than letting them drop. To work harder at negatives, first try cheating a weight up that would otherwise be too heavy to lift strictly and then lower it slowly and deliberately (see The Cheating Method, below). Your muscles can lower a weight under control that they could not actually lift in the first place. At the end of a set, when your muscles are very tired, you can have your workout partner give you a little assistance in lifting the weight, and then do strict negatives on your own.

Forced Negatives

To develop even more intensity in negative repetitions, have your workout partner press down on the weight as you lower it, forcing you to cope with greater resistance. This should always be done carefully and smoothly so that the muscles and tendons are not subjected to any sudden jerks. Forced negatives are more easily done with machines or cables than with free weights.

The Cheating Method

The Cheating Method is an exception to the general rule that strict technique is necessary in bodybuilding. This kind of cheating doesn't involve using sloppy training technique. It is a method in which you deliberately use other muscles or muscle groups to work in cooperation with the target muscles. This is not something you should do all the time, but it is very useful for achieving certain specific goals.

Say you are doing a heavy Barbell Curl. You curl the weight up five or six times, and then find you are too tired to continue to do strict reps. At this point you begin to use your shoulders and back to help in the lift slightly so that you can do another 4 or 5 reps. But you cheat *just enough* so that you can continue the set, and your biceps continue to work as hard as they can. By cheating, you have forced the biceps to do more reps than they could have done without the help from the other muscles, so you have put more stress on them, not less.

Cheating is used to make the exercise harder, not easier. It is also a way of doing forced reps without the help of a training partner. But to make cheat reps work, you have to concentrate on making sure that the extra effort being applied by the other muscles *is just enough* and not too much, so that the target muscles are still being forced to contract to the max.

Heavy-Duty Method

Heavy-Duty Training is a name applied to different approaches to working out. For some, it involves a lot of extended sets—that is, following your regular repetitions with forced reps, negatives, forced negatives, and partial reps to exhaustion. I always used the term to mean going right to the heaviest weight you can handle (after warming up) rather than pyramiding up—that is, gradually increasing weight and decreasing reps. So if I could do strict Dumbbell Curls with, say, 65 pounds, rather than slowly working up to that weight I would do two light warm-up sets and then *immediately* pick up the 65-pound dumbbells and do my normal amount of reps and sets with that heavy poundage, forcing my biceps to work to their maximum from beginning to end. The key to this kind of training is not to use a weight too heavy for you to do your normal amount of sets and reps—say 5 sets of 8 to 12 reps. If you can do only 6 or 7 reps, the weight is *too* heavy.

POWER-TRAINING PRINCIPLE

Power sets are the kind a competitive weightlifter would do, training for maximum strength and power. You do a couple of warm-up sets and then choose a heavy weight that lets you do only about 8 reps. Keep adding weight so that your sets become 6, 4, and 3 reps, and do a couple of sets of only one rep. This kind of training teaches your muscles to deal with maximum poundages, in comparison to lighter weights for more reps. Power Training works best for exercises that use a lot of muscles at the same time, such as Bench Presses, Squats, and Deadlifts (see page 142 for more on Power Training).

Staggered Sets

Staggered Sets involve doing a number of sets of a body part you want to train with increased intensity in between other exercises throughout your workout. For example, when I decided I need extra effort on my calf training, I would come into the gym, do a few sets of calves, then go do Bench

Presses, then a few more sets of calves, then Incline Dumbbell Presses, back to calves for a few sets, and by the end of the workout I had done 25 sets or more for calves—really giving them a workout. The next few days I would do my normal calf workout and then train with Staggered Sets again to really bomb and blast them.

The Priority Principle

The Priority Principle involves giving any area of your physique that is weak or lagging behind the others special priority in your workout schedule. This is necessary because every bodybuilder has weak points. No champion, no matter how many titles he has won, has a perfect physique. Some body parts always develop better and faster than others no matter who you are or how good your genetics may be. There are a number of ways of doing this:

- You can schedule a specific body part so that you train it immediately after a rest day, when you are fresh, recuperated, and strong.
- You can schedule a body part workout at the beginning of your training session rather than later, when you are more fatigued.
- You can choose exercise specifically designed to achieve the kind of development you are looking for (size, shape, definition, separation, etc.).
- You can work on improving your basic training technique to increase the efficiency and effectiveness of your workouts.
- You can change your training program so that you include extra intensity training for any lagging body part, such as making use of a variety of Intensity Techniques.

You can use Priority Training to enhance the size and the sweep of your quadriceps, to make your arms bigger, biceps peak higher, deltoids more pronounced and separated, or to improve any weak area of your physique. When I was a young bodybuilder, I knew I would need better calves to become the kind of champion I wanted to be, so I would always train my calves first, before any other body part, would subject them to any number of intensity techniques to force them to grow—often doing Staggered Sets throughout my entire workout. Since my triceps were never as overwhelming as my biceps, and I was going up against the likes of Sergio Oliva, who had absolutely phenomenal arms, I would give my triceps priority treatment in precontest workouts to give me the arms I needed to defeat Sergio "The Myth." In more recent times, when I was getting ready to film the second *Conan* movie, although I was in good shape, I wasn't happy with how tight my waistline looked. So I began giving abdominal training priority in my daily workouts, piling set upon set and eventually brought my waist measurement down two inches before filming started.

Shawn Ray is another example of what Priority Training can do for you. He was able to stay competitive against the big guys by working his back on a priority basis over a period of years, coming into the Mr. Olympia each time with his back a little wider and a little thicker. Nasser El Sonbaty also improved his back muscularity in an effort to defeat Dorian Yates, but in addition he reduced his waistline, which gave him a much better V taper. I could go on with examples forever, but the point to remember is that nobody has a perfect physique and if a body part is not responding, don't just accept that as a fact, but do something about it—and one primary remedy for such a problem is the employment of the Priority Principle.

Supersets

Supersets are two exercises performed in a row without stopping. For extra intensity, you can even do three sets in a row without stopping (trisets). It takes a while to build up the endurance necessary to do a lot of supersets, but this kind of conditioning develops in time if you keep working on it.

Actually, there are two ways you can use supersets: (1) You can do two exercises in a row for the same body part (such as Cable Rowing and Cable Pulldowns); or (2) you can train two different body parts (Bench Presses followed by Chins, for example). Supersetting within the same muscle group allows you to hammer away at that area and give it an ultimate pounding. You will be surprised how a muscle that seems to be totally fatigued will still have a lot of strength remaining if you demand that it perform a slightly different movement. To do this, however, you need to start with the most difficult movement and then go to one that is less demanding—Bent-Over Rows followed by Seated Cable Rows, for example.

Supersetting two different body parts, such as chest and back (one of my favorites) or biceps and triceps, allows one muscle group to rest while you are working the other, allowing you to exercise on a continuous basis, which is great for cardiovascular conditioning. Personally, I have always liked to use supersets to train opposing muscle groups because of the tremendous pump you get, which can make you feel you have the body of King Kong.

The Stripping Method

The Stripping Method means you reduce the weight you are using as you begin to fail at the end of a set so that you can continue on and do more repetitions. When I was first learning about bodybuilding training it was obvious to me that when you come to the end of a set and seemingly cannot do another repetition, that doesn't mean all the muscles are totally fatigued. It only means that they are too tired to lift that amount of weight. If a plate or two is removed, you can do more repetitions. Take another plate off, and you can keep going even longer. Each time you do this, you are forcing the muscles to recruit more muscle fiber. (Actually, unknown to me, this same discovery was made in 1947 by Henry Atkins, editor of *Vigor* and *Body Culture* magazines. He called it the multi-poundage system.) You should never use the Stripping Method at the beginning of an exercise when you are fresh and strong, but only for your last set.

Since the changes in weight must be made quickly so that the muscles don't have time to recuperate, it helps to have a workout partner ready to slip plates off the bar or move the pin in a machine weight stack. For example, you might do Bench Presses with the heaviest weight on the bar you can handle for 6 reps. Say that weight is 300 pounds. After you have failed, your partner would quickly strip off weight so that you could do more reps with 250 pounds. I don't recommend going too low, however, unless you are training for maximum definition, because you won't grow by handling weights that are too light. Many bodybuilders use this principle in a different way by working their way down a dumbbell rack as they do more sets of an exercise and get more and more tired.

A variation of this method is called Running the Rack, in which you do your set with one weight, go to failure, put the weight down and go to the next lightest in line, go to failure, and continue this process to exhaustion.

The Isotension Principle

During your one-minute rest period between sets, don't just sit around watching your training partner do his set. Continue to flex and contract the muscles you are training. This not only keeps them pumped and ready for more action, but is in itself a very beneficial kind of exercise as well. Flexing is a form of isometric exercise, and isometrics (although they do not usually apply to bodybuilding because they do not work your muscles through their entire range of motion) involve very intense muscle contractions. A bodybuilder who poses and flexes in the gym, watching himself in the mirror, is engaged in a very important part of his workout.

In fact, I don't think you can win a major championship without practicing Isotension between your sets. It isn't enough to have big muscles; you have to be able to control them as well, and that's something you have to learn. You get the same kind of benefits from really hard sessions of posing practice, too, as we will discuss later (see Posing, page 565).

The Instinctive Principle

When you begin bodybuilding training and are attempting to master the fundamental exercises and create a basically sound muscle structure, it pays to follow a set program. But after you have been training for a longer period, you will find that your progress will increase if you learn to perceive and understand your body's individual responses to training and vary your workouts accordingly. In my early years I tended to go through my workouts in a rigid, set pattern, the same way every time. Then I started training with Dave Draper and he taught me another approach. Dave would come into the gym knowing which body parts he was going to train and which exercises he was going to do, but he would change the order of those exercises depending on how he felt on that particular day. If he usually began a back workout with Wide-Grip Chins, he might decide instead to begin with Bent-Over Rows and finish off with Chins. He had learned to trust his instincts to help guide him through his workouts. Occasionally, he would abandon his normal workout and do something entirely different: 15 sets of Bench Presses, for example; fewer, very heavy sets or a lot of sets done rapidly. I learned from Dave that the body has its own rhythms, that it is different from day to day and that the more advanced you become, the more you need to be aware of these variations and cycles. Let me caution you, however, that this awareness does not come overnight; a year or more of training is usually needed before you can begin to profit from making these occasional instinctive adjustments in your program.

Pre-exhaust Principle

The total bodybuilding effect comes about when you fully stimulate and innervate as many fibers in the muscle as possible. But some muscles are bigger than others and, when used in combination with smaller ones, will still have unused fiber available when the smaller muscles are totally exhausted. But you can plan your training so that you isolate and fatigue the big muscle first, before you train it in combination with smaller ones. When you do a Bench Press, for example, you are using your pectorals, front delts, and triceps in combination. The pectorals are by far the strongest of these muscles, and normally, when you press the weight up, the smaller delts and triceps fail long before the pectorals. To compensate for this, you can do Dumbbell Flys first, which isolate and pre-exhaust the pectorals. Then if you go on to do Bench Presses, the pectorals, which are already tired, will go to total fatigue at about the same time as the other muscles. Other pre-fatigue routines could involve doing Leg Extensions before Squats (pre-fatiguing the quadriceps), Dumbbell Laterals before Shoulder Presses (pre-fatiguing the deltoids), or fatiguing the lats in isolation on a Nautilus Pullback machine before doing Seated Rows, T-Bar Rows, or another rowing exercise involving the biceps.

I Go/You Go

In this method for increasing your training intensity and shocking your muscles, you and your training partner finish a set and immediately hand over the weight to the other, never putting the weight down, each one going in turn. I can remember doing Barbell Curls, handing the bar off to Franco and going back and forth, not really counting reps, just going to failure. After a while I was screaming and hoping Franco would take his time because my biceps were burning so bad. You stay in pain, your partner hands you back the weight again, and the number of reps you can do gets shorter and shorter. But the point of this technique is that you go when it's your turn, ready or not, no matter how tired you are getting. The degree of intensity you can develop using this method is fantastic. Talk about shocking the body! The only problem is the soreness you feel the next day.

The I Go/You Go Method is more useful for training smaller muscles like the biceps or calves than it is for the big thigh and back muscles. Exercises like Squats and Bent-Over Rows demand so much energy that you run out of steam in a hurry even without this intensive kind of training.

The Flushing Method

The Flushing Method involves holding a (relatively light) weight steady at various points along the path of the exercise, forcing the muscle to maintain a constant contraction for extended periods. For example, after I have done as many Dumbbell Laterals as possible I hold my arms locked out by my sides and then lift them about 5 inches away from my thighs, feeling the deltoids tense and flex. I hold this position for about 10 seconds as the burn accompanying the buildup of lactic acid gets stronger and stronger. This tension applied at the end of an exercise causes an enormous increase in muscle separation, and can be done for many muscles in the body: for lats, hanging from the chinning bar and lifting the body only a few inches; doing Cable Crossovers, holding your hands crossed with chest fully contracted, flushing blood into the pectorals; holding a Curl steady, at various angles of the total arc; or locking your legs out in a Leg Extension and holding as long as you can.

Multi-exercise Sets

To shock the body, instead of doing 5 or 6 sets of a specific exercise for a body part, you do your sets using a different exercise for that body part each time. Multi-exercise sets are not done as supersets; you do them one at a time and rest in between, but you do only one set of each exercise and then go on to another. For example, you might do one set of Barbell Curls, rest for a minute, then do a set of Dumbbell Curls, Cable Curls, Incline Curls, and so on down the line until you have fully exhausted the biceps. The idea here is to make the stress of each set slightly different, attacking the body part from every possible angle to ensure that the entire muscle is trained and providing a shock that will force the maximum amount of response from the body.

The "One-and-a-Half" Method

Another way to vary the stress you put on your muscles in any set is to do a complete rep of a movement, followed by a half rep and then alternating full and half reps until the set is finished. When you do this, make sure that the half rep is very slow and very strict. Hold the weight momentarily at the extreme point of the movement, then lower it slowly, totally under control.

The Platoon System (21s)

This system is more elaborate than one-and-a-halves because you do a series of half reps in the lower range of motion, a series of half reps in the upper range of motion, and then a series of full reps. You can use any number of reps—I always did 10-10-10—as long as you do the same number for each of your half reps and full reps. Traditionally, many bodybuilders have used 7 reps—hence the name 21s: 3 × 7. The extra stress generated by this kind of training comes about because you have to stop the movement right in the middle, and this forces the muscles to exert themselves in ways they are not used to.

Progressive Workload

Nobody can go all out every workout. Using this training system, you plan your three-times-a-week body part sessions so that the first is intense, with relatively high reps and sets, but you don't use the heaviest weights possible. You increase the weight for the second session, but still stay short of going all out. For your third workout, however, you go very heavy, keeping your reps down to 4 to 6 maximum per set. By gradually building up each workout during the week, you prepare your body to handle the shock of very heavy weight.

Ballistic Training

Ballistic Training refers to a technique in which you drive a weight up, or explode it (but in a smooth and controlled manner), rather than lifting it at a constant speed. This is done with relatively heavy poundages, so the weight doesn't really move all that fast. But the attempt to force the weight to go faster accomplishes a number of things:

1. It creates variable resistance. Why? Because you are stronger in one part of a lift than in another, due to the difference in mechanical leverage advantage. When you are stronger, the weight accelerates a little more. And an accelerated weight is heavier than one that is not accelerated or not accelerated as much. Therefore, the weight is heavier when you are stronger and not as heavy when you are weaker—which is variable resistance.

2. It recruits a maximum amount of white, fast-twitch power fibers, which are bigger (by about 22 percent) and stronger than red, slow-twitch endurance fibers.

3. It creates constant failure. The muscles grow when they are given a task that is just beyond their capabilities. When you are trying to accelerate a weight, there is always a limit to the amount of acceleration you can achieve. Your muscles are failing to move it any faster. Therefore, rather than failing only at the end of your set, you are actually experiencing a degree of failure during each rep of the set.

Ballistic Training should be done primarily with exercises that use a lot of big muscles—for example, Bench Presses, Shoulder Presses, and Squats. You should use a weight you can normally do about 10 reps with. Since an accelerated weight is heavier, you'll find you can do only about 7 reps with the same weight when using the ballistic method. Also, ballistic reps require a slightly different type of technique than do normal, constant-speed repetitions:

1. Lower the weight normally, using constant speed. Pause at the bottom, then drive the weight up, accelerating it smoothly throughout the range of motion.

2. Continue the set not to the point of absolute failure, but to failure of power. That is, when you can't accelerate the weight anymore, and can only lift it slowly, you have finished the set. When doing ballistic reps, there is no point in going past this point.

3. Get plenty of rest between sets, from one to 2 minutes. White, fast-twitch fiber takes longer to recuperate than does red fiber and this is the type of muscle you are focusing on with ballistic sets.

LEARNING TO USE ADVANCED TRAINING PRINCIPLES

Rome wasn't built in a day and neither is a first-class bodybuilding physique. Creating a highly developed muscular body means starting out using the basics, learning the necessary skills, developing strength and conditioning over time, and then gradually raising the level of training intensity, in part by learning to use Advanced Training Principles.

To be effective, your training should be goal oriented, and your goals may change over the course of time. In the beginning, your goal is to just get started, learn basic techniques, and condition your body to the point where you have the strength and conditioning you need to make the most of your workouts. For some people, who are interested mostly in training for overall health and fitness and who aren't able or willing to devote more than a couple of hours a week to working out, this is the most they will ever want to achieve.

But for those who look to a higher goal, the development of a superior, muscular body or who are training for the purpose of entering a competition, the next step is to increase intensity, both by lifting heavier weights and by using the appropriate intensity techniques.

My best recommendation is to master the intensity techniques listed above one at a time. Try a particular technique, get familiar with it, and observe how it feels and how it affects your body. When you feel totally comfortable using that intensity technique, go on and do the same thing with another. Not every bodybuilder uses or wants to use every intensity technique. But getting familiar with them, learning how they work and what they feel like, will enable you to incorporate the ones that best suit you into your future workout programs.

CHAPTER 5

Building a Quality Physique: The Advanced Training Program

THE ADVANCED TRAINING Program is for people who want to challenge themselves more, who are not content with simply being fit but want to develop a powerful, impressive physique. For these individuals, it is not enough to just gain a few pounds of muscle. Instead, they want not only serious gains in strength and muscle mass, but to sculpt the body as well—to achieve muscle shape and separation, to balance the proportions of the various muscle groups, and to create impressive muscular definition.

But wanting to achieve it is not enough; you also have to learn how to do it. Nobody would expect to become a surgeon without learning everything about the body—how it is constructed, how it is put together, what all the parts are. To become a great bodybuilder you must learn all about the body—what the body parts and muscles are, the different areas of the body, how they tie together, and how the body responds to various programs of exercise. If you don't know these things, you won't be able to develop your body to its full potential no matter how intense your motivation may be. And these are the subjects I will be dealing with in this and subsequent chapters of this encyclopedia.

The bodybuilder's physique is a carefully balanced combination of many factors, including shape, proportion, and symmetry. Bodybuilding has been compared to sculpture, with the bodybuilder creating and shaping a physique the way the artist sculpts a statue from marble or granite. For the bodybuilder, the only material he has to work with is muscle.

The exercises and training principles you learned in the Basic Training Program are not enough to give you the total control over your body that is needed to develop a sculpted, championship physique. You need more and different kinds of exercises, a knowledge of how to design your workouts to get very specific results, and an ability to generate sufficient intensity so your body will continue to grow and change. You can't leave any muscle groups out. You must include everything—the forearms, the two major calf muscles, the lower back, the rear delts, the serratus, and the intercostals. And it isn't enough to have big muscles. For the chest, for example, you need upper, lower, and middle pecs, inner and outer fullness and development. There are three heads of the deltoids to be developed and separated. You need traps, middle back, lats, and lower back in order to be complete. In addition to developing the quadriceps and the hamstrings you have to create a distinct line between them. Biceps require length, thickness, and peak—not just size.

Development on this level is absolutely crucial when you finally enter a competition, but waiting until you are training for competition to start detail and Weak Point Training is too late. The time to start is when you begin serious, advanced training and then you can *further* refine your training program when you go on later to Competition Training.

Of course, setting these higher goals for yourself in Advanced Training will demand more time, energy, dedication, and, therefore, commitment. And it will be much more demanding mentally, requiring a steadfast awareness of purpose. Purpose doesn't come from just an act of will. It has to involve a real and joyful degree of motivation; you have to be *hungry* to achieve your goals; the necessary effort shouldn't be seen as a burden but an opportunity. Not, "Damn, I have to go work out today," but "Wow, I can't wait to get to the gym and work out." The additional workload is nothing if you are hungry enough.

One way to achieve this state of mind is by having a *vision*—a clear idea in your mind of where you are going and what you want to become. I'll deal with this subject in detail in Chapter 7. As a young bodybuilder I remember looking at a lot of photos of Reg Park hitting the major poses. When I saw his Herculean but highly detailed physique—his abdominal development, lower back, and calves in particular—that gave me the vision of what I needed to become a Mr. Universe. I could close my eyes and *see* clearly in my mind what a championship physique should look like, and that vision guided me in my training, diet, posing, and everything else I did in bodybuilding.

Summing up, the specific goals you will be working toward in Advanced Training workouts include:

1. developing extra mass and, eventually, muscle shape;
2. focusing not just on muscle mass but on the details of each muscle group as well;
3. creating a physique with the aesthetic qualities of balance, proportion, and symmetry;
4. working on the separation between muscles and the major muscle groups;
5. learning to totally control your physical development so that you are able to correct imbalances, weak points, and problem areas.

WHEN TO MOVE ON TO ADVANCED TRAINING

Once you have gained 15 pounds or more of muscle mass, put about 3 inches on your arms, 5 inches on your chest and shoulders, 4 inches on your thighs, and 3 inches on your calves, you are then ready to begin adding a greater variety of exercises to your routine, to train for shape as well as size, for balance as well as mass.

But this is not accomplished in one sudden jump. You need time to learn new exercises, to begin to understand how specific exercises affect the body in different ways, and to learn to use these exercises and a wide range of new training principles to accelerate the response of your body to your workouts.

Since you gradually increase your workload, your transition from Basic to Advanced Training does not happen all at once. The point is that if you want a championship body, you have to train with championship intensity, technique, and knowledge. It is a difficult task, but it can be one of the most rewarding challenges of your life.

"HIGH-SET" TRAINING

Some training systems claim you can make great progress by training with only a few sets per body part. Actually, this idea is not new; that was the way bodybuilders trained in the early days of the sport.

When Reg Park began serious training, many bodybuilders still used the old-fashioned, low-set approach to working out. "Training strictly for power like a weightlifter," Reg says, "gave us certain advantages in the old days, a really solid foundation of muscle. But it wasn't until I learned to do fifteen or twenty sets per body part that I felt I was getting enough shape and definition in my physique. I'm sure that a lot of the bodybuilders from the very early days would have improved a lot if they had understood the need for high-set workouts the way we do today."

True, but it's also true that the more advanced you become as a bodybuilder, the more the body tends to resist further development. That means you have to work harder to create the necessary intensity in your workouts and be certain that you are training in the most efficient manner possible. To ensure that this continued development takes place, the Advanced Training Program requires performing a relatively high number of sets. This is not arbitrary or just a matter of personal preference; it is designed with specific physiological purposes in mind: (1) to recruit and innervate all the fiber available to each muscle, then work the muscle to exhaustion in any particular exercise; and (2) to do enough different exercises for every single body part so that each individual muscle is worked from every angle to create the fullest possible shape and development—and to be sure that no major muscle of the body escapes this complete stimulation.

Some training systems advocate as many as 75 sets per workout, but this is not what I mean by high sets. As far as I'm concerned, the ideal training program involves *doing 4 sets per exercise.* The fact that you can keep going for 4 sets, resting very little in between, proves that there is still fresh and unrecruited fiber available after the first few sets. The second task is sheer necessity, since no one exercise is enough to fully develop even the simplest muscle. Take, for example, a relatively small muscle like the biceps: You can train to develop the upper area (point of origin), the lower area (point of insertion), the thickness of the muscle, the inner and outer areas, or to create a really high peak. Once you start dealing with the larger and more complex muscle groups, the number of different ways you can train and shape them becomes really immense.

You don't have to be a mathematician to realize that a task this size cannot be accomplished by doing 3 or 5 total sets per body part. The physiques of those modern bodybuilders who are seduced into following an old-fashioned theory of training masquerading under the guise of a new scientific approach to bodybuilding will surely be lacking. It takes a minimum of 4 or 5 exercises to train each major body part, at least 3 for the smaller ones, and this can add up to a total of 20 sets.

With the right combination of exercises, you not only develop each individual muscle fully, but also build definition, striations, and a full separation between one muscle group and another.

DOUBLE-SPLIT TRAINING

One way to deal with the demands of Advanced Training is by following a program of Double-Split Training, which simply means breaking up each day's workout into two different training sessions.

I discovered Double-Split Training on my own, strictly as a matter of necessity. After a year of training I really began trying to push my body to its ultimate limits. I wanted to train each body part as hard as possible and then come back the next time and train it even harder. One day I came into the gym and had a really dynamite chest and back workout. I felt great. Then I went on to do legs, but I noticed I was not training with the same intensity and enthusiasm as I had felt during my upper-body workout. Looking in the mirror at my developing teenage physique, I had to admit that my legs were not progressing as rapidly as my upper body. The next day, after training shoulders, biceps, triceps, forearms, and calves, I again took stock and realized that those last three muscle groups were also somewhat weak. They obviously were lagging behind.

As I thought about it, it didn't seem to me that I lacked real potential to develop those weaker areas, *so it had to be some fault in my approach to training.* I experimented with nutrition, being much more careful of what I ate, trying to keep my blood sugar level up, but though this helped, it was not enough.

As I analyzed my training further, it became obvious that each of these body parts came toward the end of my workouts, when I was tired from doing numerous sets. Training my chest, back, and legs in one day was very demanding, and it occurred to me that I could train each body part with more intensity if I trained my chest and back in the morning, and then came back late in the afternoon, fresh and rested, to give my legs a really hard workout. Without knowing that any other bodybuilders trained this way and never having heard the name, I found myself doing Double-Split Training as the only means possible for training the entire body with the kind of intensity I knew had to be generated if I were to become Mr. Universe.

Advanced Training can often involve 75 total sets—15 to 20 sets for each of four body parts, or three body parts plus calves and abdominal training. Trying to do all of this work in one workout would be a killer, especially since some of the same muscles are involved in training different body parts, and if these muscles get too tired and don't have a chance to recuperate, your training can be severely hindered.

A 75-set session takes something like 3 hours to accomplish, and nobody can train straight through for this long without running out of energy. Many bodybuilders try to cope with this workload by pacing themselves, not training as hard as possible the first and second hours, knowing that they could never make it if they did. But this lack of intensity means the body will not be forced to respond and grow. You have to go all out if you want maximum results.

With the Double-Split System, you train full out in the morning, recuperate during the day, and come back to the gym rested and ready to go the limit again. I've always preferred a good 8 to 10 hours between workouts to ensure full recovery. And that means making sure you actually get some rest. If you are too active during the day, that 10-hour rest period won't be enough.

Of course, scheduling a second training session in the late afternoon or evening creates yet another demand on your time, and you will have to make further adjustments in your schedule. An added advantage to this system is that you burn up a lot of additional calories in the course of your two workouts, which means you do not have to subject yourself to quite so demanding a diet as you would training only once a day.

Advanced Training Program

THE TWO-LEVEL ADVANCED PROGRAM

Just as in the Basic Training Program, I have created two levels for Advanced Training to provide a ready means of increasing workload and generating greater intensity on a progressive basis.

Both Level I and Level II in this program require that you train each body part three times a week. Level II, however, is a more demanding program, including a lot of supersets and a number of extra exercises.

Begin your training with Level I, and take the time to learn each new exercise thoroughly (or twice if you need extra recuperation time). Once you have been working at this level for 6 weeks or longer and feel your conditioning and recuperative powers will allow you to work even harder, go ahead and begin to add new exercises to your routine until you have made the full transition to Level II. One final note: If you are sore from a previous workout, take an additional day off. Work up to the suggested workload.

ADVANCED TRAINING SPLIT

WORKOUT #1 MON	WORKOUT #2 TUE	WORKOUT #1 WED	WORKOUT #2 THUR	WORKOUT #1 FRI	WORKOUT #2 SAT
		MORNING			
Chest Back	Shoulders Upper arms Forearms Calves	Chest Back	Shoulders Upper arms Forearms Calves	Chest Back	Shoulders Upper arms Forearms Calves
		EVENING			
Thighs Calves		Thighs Calves		Thighs Calves	

Abdominals every day

Level I Exercise Program

WORKOUT #1

Monday/Wednesday/Friday

CHEST

Barbell Bench Presses	4 sets: 1 set of 15 rep warm-up; sets of 10, 8, 6, 4 reps—stripping last two sets
Barbell Incline Bench Press	4 sets: same formula as Bench Presses Every third workout, substitute Dumbbell Presses and Incline Dumbbell Presses for barbell exercises.
Dumbbell Flys	3 sets of 10, 8, 6 reps
Parallel Bar Dips	3 sets of 15, 10, 8 reps
Pullovers	3 sets of 15 reps each

BACK

Chin-Ups	4 sets: 10 reps minimum each set Use a dumbbell fastened around your waist for greater resistance; do chins to the rear one workout, to the front the next.
Close-Grip Chins	4 sets of 10 reps each
T-Bar Rows	4 sets of 15, 12, 8, 6 reps
Bent-Over Barbell Rows	4 sets of 8 to 12 reps

THIGHS

Squats	5 sets of 20 rep warm-up; 10, 8, 6, 4 reps
Front Squats	4 sets of 10, 8, 8, 6 reps
Hack Squats	3 sets of 10 reps each
Leg Curls	4 sets of 20, 10, 8, 6 reps
Standing Leg Curls	4 sets of 10 reps each
Straight-Leg Deadlifts	3 sets of 10 reps each

CALVES

Donkey Calf Raises	4 sets of 10 reps each
Standing Calf Raises	4 sets of 15, 10, 8, 8 reps

ABDOMINALS

Crunches	3 sets of 25 reps
Bent-Over Twists	100 reps each side
Machine Crunches	3 sets of 25 reps
Crunches	50 reps

WORKOUT #2

Tuesday/Thursday/Saturday

SHOULDERS

Behind-the-Neck Barbell Presses	5 sets of 15 rep warm-up; 10, 8, 8, 6 reps
Lateral Raises	4 sets of 8 reps each
Bent-Over Dumbbell Laterals	4 sets of 8 reps each
Dumbbell Shrugs	3 sets of 10 reps each

UPPER ARMS

Standing Barbell Curls	5 sets of 15, 10, 8, 6, 4 reps
Incline Dumbbell Curls	4 sets of 8 reps each
Concentration Curls	3 sets of 8 reps each
Lying Triceps Extensions	4 sets of 15, 10, 8, 6 reps
Triceps Cable Pressdowns	3 sets of 8 reps each
One-Arm Triceps Extensions	3 sets of 10 reps each

FOREARMS

Barbell Wrist Curls	4 sets of 10 reps each
Reverse Wrist Curls	3 sets of 10 reps each

CALVES

Seated Calf Raises	4 sets of 10 reps each

ABDOMINALS

Reverse Crunches	4 sets of 25 reps
Seated Twists	100 reps each side
Vertical Bench Crunches	4 sets of 25 reps

Level II Exercise Program

WORKOUT #1

Monday / Wednesday / Friday

ABDOMINALS Begin workout with 5 minutes of Roman Chairs.

CHEST AND BACK

Superset:	Bench Presses	1 set of 15 rep warm-up; 5 sets of 10, 8, 8, 6, 4 reps
	Wide-Grip Chins (to back)	5 sets of 10 reps
Superset:	Incline Dumbbell Presses	4 sets of 10, 8, 8, 6 reps
	Close-Grip Chins	4 sets of 10 reps
Dumbbell Flys		4 sets of 10, 8, 8, 6 reps
Parallel Bar Dips		4 sets of 15, 10, 8, 8 reps
T-Bar Rows		4 sets of 15, 10, 8, 8 reps
Bent-Over Rows		4 sets of 10 reps
Superset:	Seated Cable Rows	4 sets of 10 reps
	Straight-Arm Pullovers	4 sets of 15 reps

THIGHS

Squats		6 sets of 15, 10, 8, 8, 6, 4 reps
Front Squats		4 sets of 10, 8, 8, 6 reps
Superset:	Hack Squats	1 set of 15 rep warm-up; 4 sets of 10, 8, 8, 8 reps
	Lying Leg Curls	1 set of 15 rep warm-up; 4 sets of 10, 8, 8, 8 reps
Superset:	Standing Leg Curls	4 sets of 10 reps
	Straight-Leg Deadlifts	4 sets of 10 reps

CALVES

Donkey Calf Raises	4 sets of 10 reps
Standing Calf Raises	4 sets of 10 reps
Seated Calf Raises	4 sets of 10 reps

ABDOMINALS

Hanging Reverse Crunches	4 sets of 25 reps
Seated Leg Tucks	4 sets of 25 reps
Bent-Over Twists	100 reps each side

WORKOUT #2

Tuesday/Thursday/Saturday

ABDOMINALS Begin workout with 5 minutes of Roman Chairs.

SHOULDERS

Superset:	Behind-the-Neck	1 set of 15 rep warm-up;
	Barbell Presses	4 sets of 10, 8, 8, 6 reps
	Dumbbell Laterals	4 sets of 8 reps
Superset:	Machine Front Presses	4 sets of 8 reps
	Bent-Over Laterals	4 sets of 8 reps
Superset:	Upright Rows	4 sets of 10 reps
	Seated One-Arm Cable Laterals	4 sets of 10 reps each

UPPER ARMS

Superset:	Standing Barbell Curls	4 sets of 15, 10, 6, 4 reps
	Lying Triceps Extensions	4 sets of 15, 10, 6, 4 reps
Superset:	Alternate Dumbbell Curls	4 sets of 8 reps
	Triceps Cable Pressdowns	4 sets of 8 reps
Superset:	Concentration Curls	4 sets of 8 reps
	One-Arm Triceps Extensions	4 sets of 12 reps
Reverse Push-Ups		4 sets of 15 reps

FOREARMS

Triset:	Wrist Curls	4 sets of 10 reps
	Reverse Curls	4 sets of 10 reps
	One-Arm Wrist Curls	4 sets of 10 reps

CALVES

Standing Calf Raises	4 sets of 15, 10, 8, 8 reps
Calf Raises on Leg Press Machine	4 sets of 10 reps

ABDOMINALS

Vertical Bench Crunches	4 sets of 25 reps
Seated Twists	100 reps each side
Cable Crunches	4 sets of 25 reps
Hyperextensions (lowerback)	3 sets of 10 reps

GOING TO THE LIMIT

In Basic Training, we talked about the necessity of occasionally having "heavy days"—trying to go to your maximum on certain lifts. Heavy days are even more important when you get to Advanced Training.

I recommend that every so often you forget about your regular program and do an entire workout consisting of only power exercises or just heavy ballistic training. Remember that no amount of refinement, balance, and proportion looks exactly right unless it coexists with the kind of hard and dense muscle structure that comes from occasionally challenging your body to the maximum with heavy weights.

VARYING YOUR PROGRAM

Advanced Training requires that you change your exercise program every three to six months, dropping certain exercises in favor of others. This is necessary in order to: (1) provide the variety of movements to develop every area of every single muscle and muscle group; (2) force the body to do new and unexpected movements to help shock it into further growth; and (3) help keep you from getting bored.

Exercises that seem fairly similar can feel very different. For example, if you are used to pressing a barbell over your head, doing the exercise with dumbbells instead feels totally different, although both are for the front deltoids. Having to balance and coordinate two weights instead of one puts very different demands on your muscles. Therefore, after a couple of months of an exercise like Behind-the-Neck Barbell Presses, it makes a lot of sense to switch to Dumbbell Presses for a while.

Certain basic exercises are so fundamental that they have to be included in any complete exercise program. However, exploring a whole range of different exercises like this gives you a much better idea as to which exercises work best for you and which don't really suit you. This will lead eventually to a much better understanding of your own body and of how to get the best results.

A Sample Alternate Workout

ABDOMINALS Begin workout with 5 minutes of Roman Chairs.

CHEST AND BACK

Superset:	Bench Presses (on machine)	5 sets of 12, 10, 8, 8, 8 reps
	Wide-Grip Pulldowns	5 sets of 12, 10, 8, 8, 8 reps
Superset:	Incline Presses (on machine)	4 sets of 12, 10, 8, 8 reps
	Close-Grip Pulldowns	4 sets of 12, 10, 8, 8 reps
Dumbbell Flys		4 sets of 8 reps
Decline Dumbbell Presses		4 sets of 12, 10, 8, 8 reps
Bent-Over Rows		4 sets of 8 reps
One-Arm Dumbbell Rows		4 sets of 10 reps each arm
Superset:	Seated Cable Rows	4 sets of 10 reps
	Machine Pullovers	4 sets of 10 reps

Thighs

Squats		6 sets of 15, 10, 8, 8, 6, 4 reps
Machine Front Squats		4 sets of 8 reps
Superset:	Vertical Leg Presses	4 sets of 8 reps
	Lying Leg Curls	4 sets of 10 reps
Superset:	Standing Leg Curls	4 sets of 10 reps
	Good Mornings	4 sets of 10 reps

Calves

Donkey Calf Raises, Standing Calf Raises, Seated Calf Raises as in regular workout

Abdominals

Crunches	30 reps
Seated Leg Tucks	30 reps
Hanging Reverse Crunches	30 reps
Seated Twists	50 reps each side
Stomach Vacuums	5 minutes

Shoulders

Superset:	Dumbbell Presses	5 sets of 10, 8, 8, 8, 6 reps
	One-Arm Cross Cable Laterals	5 sets of 10 reps each arm
Superset:	Front Dumbbell Raises	4 sets of 8 reps
	Bent-Over Cable Laterals	4 sets of 8 reps
Superset:	Wide-Grip Upright Rows	4 sets of 8 reps (each side)
	Lying Side Laterals	4 sets of 10 reps (each side)

Upper Arms

Superset:	Standing Dumbbell Curls	5 sets of 8 reps
	Lying Dumbbell Extensions	5 sets of 10 reps
Superset:	Incline Curls	4 sets of 8 reps
	Standing Barbell Triceps Extensions	4 sets of 10 reps
Triset:	Preacher Curls	4 sets of 8 reps
	Dips	4 sets of 10 reps
	One-Arm Cable Reverse Pressdowns	5 sets of 10 reps each arm
Dumbbell Kickbacks		5 sets of 12 reps

Forearms

Preacher Bench Reverse Curls	4 sets of 8 reps
Behind-the-Back Wrist Curls	4 sets of 10 reps
One-Arm Wrist Curls	4 sets of 10 reps

WEAK POINT TRAINING

Once you have developed the necessary mass, you must then begin to concentrate on quality. To do this, you need to study your body in the mirror or in photos and try to discover your weak points (although your friends at the gym will probably be all too happy to tell you exactly what they are). For me, my initial weak points were the thighs and calves, so I adjusted my training to put more emphasis on the legs, to bring them up and improve my lower body in proportion to my upper body.

A year later when I was ready to compete in the Mr. Europe and the NABBA Mr. Universe contests, my thighs and calves had improved—they weren't perfect, but they certainly were a lot better. Now the criticism was that my muscle separation and definition weren't as good as they could be. So I had to add more exercises to my routine. For example, I started doing a lot of Front Lateral Raises to separate the pectoral muscles from the deltoids, and a lot of Pullovers to separate the serratus from the lats.

But even this wasn't enough. People told me, "The center of your back isn't cut enough," so I started doing more Bent-Over and Cable Rows. "Your leg biceps aren't as good as your quadriceps," "You could use some more rear deltoid development," and so on—and each time, when I realized where I needed improvement, I changed my program to try to overcome the deficiency.

Too many bodybuilders train to improve their strong points at the expense of their weak points. One bodybuilder who is famous for his tremendous arm development and equally infamous for his lack of leg development comes into the gym day after day and trains—arms! Endless repetitions of biceps and triceps work, set after set, yet anyone looking at him can tell that he should do nothing but basic maintenance training on his arms for the next year while he bombs and blasts his thighs and calves to bring them up to championship level. But he seems to lack that "sense of perfection," and it is doubtful he will ever learn to balance his physique.

Many bodybuilders do not start out with a sense of perfection, but acquire it later on. The truth is, it is possible to go quite far in competition—winning the Mr. Universe title, for example—with glaring weaknesses in your physique. But all too often a Mr. Universe winner will go straight from the amateur championship to a professional contest and finish very poorly or even dead last!

Stepping up from one level of competition to another—from state contests to the National Championship, from the Nationals to the Universe, from amateur bodybuilding to the pros and on to the Mr. Olympia—you will find that weak points in your physique become increasingly detrimental. Bodybuilders often find themselves unable to make the effort needed to correct them because it means, in a sense, starting over. After years of successful competition, you have to admit that you have a weakness that might take one or two years to totally correct. Making the decision to overcome a weak point, once you are advanced in a bodybuilding career, can take a great deal of moral courage.

When I came to the United States I was criticized for my poor calf development, so I cut off the bottoms of my sweatpants to make sure my calves were visible at all times. That not only reminded me to train them harder, but let everyone else see how they looked—which doubly motivated me to train them even harder.

As another example, my left arm used to be slightly smaller than my right arm. I noticed that whenever I was asked to show my biceps, I would automatically flex the right arm. So I consciously made an effort to flex my left arm as much or more than my right, to work on that weak point instead of simply ignoring it, and eventually I was able to make my left biceps the equal of my right.

Actually, this stage of training, this pursuit of perfection, never really ends because there is no such thing as a perfect body and you can always improve your physique. Every year, as you train and compete, you learn more about your body and what kinds of diet and exercise programs benefit it the most. You never really stop doing the basics, you just add new ways of doing things.

TRAINING WEAK AREAS

Bodybuilding is as much an art as a science, so you can't always be governed by a rigid and unchanging program. From the first day you walk into a gym it may be apparent to you that one body part or another is much weaker than all the rest. One basic method of correcting such imbalances is by using the Priority Principle—work your weak areas first, when you are fresh and capable of generating the greatest amount of intensity. Or arrange your Double-Split schedule so that you are training only the weak body part in one of the sessions.

Another remedy is to increase the number of sets you do for the weaker area from 5 to 7 sets. Continue doing this for as long as necessary, until you see an improvement, and then go back to a more balanced routine. This is a good time to use the Staggered System. Every third or fourth set, throw in one set of an exercise for the weak area in addition to the normal sets you do for that body part.

There will also be times when a body part lags behind because you are *overtraining* it, hitting it so hard, so often, and so intensely that it never has a chance to rest, recuperate, and grow. The answer to this problem is simply to give the muscles involved a chance to rest and recover, and then to adjust your training schedule so that you don't overtrain it again. Remember, too much can be as bad as too little when it comes to bodybuilding training.

But how do you tell the difference between slow growth due to not enough training and lack of development because of overtraining? To a degree, this is something you need to learn to tell instinctively as you get more experience, but here is a good rule of thumb:

1. The remedy for understimulation is most often learning to train harder, more intensely, using additional Intensity Techniques, than it is increasing sets to any great degree.

2. Overtraining is almost always the result of training with too many sets, too often, with too little time to rest for a body part between workout sessions. (One sign of possible overtraining is a lack of a pump during your workouts.) Remember, one of the reasons there are so many good bodybuilders nowadays is that they have learned to *train extremely intensely in short bursts*, while giving their muscles plenty of time to rest and recuperate between workouts. Always keep in mind that training stimulates growth, but that actual growth takes place while you are resting.

Of course, sometimes your weakness is in just one area of a body part—your biceps may have a great peak, but not enough width; your lats may be wide and sweeping enough, but you might lack density and mass in the middle back. The answer is to choose the particular exercises that work that specific area and arrange your training program to give those exercises special priority.

In the exercise section (beginning on page 247) you will find a full analysis of each body part designed to help you spot your weak points and specific instructions as to which exercises or specific training techniques you can use to correct any weaknesses.

C H A P T E R 6

Competition Training Program

TODAY AN ENORMOUS number of bodybuilders are working out for two or three hours a day and dedicating themselves to building a bigger and better physique. Yet only a small percentage of these obviously motivated bodybuilders ever go on and take the next step—to Competition Training.

The barrier that has to be overcome in order to work toward competition is more mental than physical: You have to make up your mind that what you really want is to join the ranks of the competitive bodybuilders, pitting yourself against bodybuilders whom you have probably admired in the past and whose images have helped to inspire and motivate you to continue training.

BUILDING A COMPETITION PHYSIQUE

Competition is a whole other ball game. You suddenly become concerned with things like skin tone, presentation, posing routines, and, above all, learning to deal with a kind of pressure that simply does not exist in the gym and against which you may have developed no defenses.

Physically, you are not just trying to develop a massive, balanced, and defined physique. Now you must reach for total perfection, every muscle and muscle group sculpted and chiseled into its ultimate form and a body fat percentage so low that every striation and muscle separation shows itself clearly. In Advanced Training we talked about developing each area of each body part. When you get to Competition Training this becomes even more complex and you need to consider such details as:

Chest—upper, lower, and middle pecs, the split between the upper and lower pecs, the inner pecs along the sternum, the outer pecs where they insert under the deltoids, chest striations, separation between the pecs and front deltoids, serratus definition.

Back—width and thickness of the latissimus dorsi, length of the lats where they insert above the waist; rhomboid and middle back detail and muscularity; the spinal erectors of the lower back; intercostal definition.

Shoulders—development and separation of all three heads of the deltoids: anterior, side, and posterior delts; mass and thickness of the trapezius muscles; separation of the traps from the back and rear delts.

Biceps—upper and lower biceps, width, length, and peak.

Triceps—development of all three heads of the triceps, thickness and length.

Forearms—development of both extensors and contractors; brachialis development at the elbow.

Waist—upper and lower ab development and definition; development of external obliques and separation between abs and obliques.

Quadriceps—mass and separation of all four heads of the quads, outer sweep, lower quad insertion at the knee; development of the adductors at the inside of the thigh.

Hamstrings—development of both heads of the leg biceps, separation between the hamstrings and quadriceps; development and striations of the glutes and separation between hamstrings and glutes.

Calves—development of the underlying soleus muscle and the gastrocnemius muscle that lies on top; calf size, length, and peak.

Think about what you need so that *you're* the one with all of this development and your competitors are trying to keep up with *you.* This involves learning what exercises work each of these areas and incorporating them into your workouts, figuring out at what angles you need to train each muscle and what intensity techniques are needed to get the development you're after. Of course, as you progress, you include more exercises as you go along and therefore more total sets, and that requires higher levels of conditioning and endurance.

You can be quite advanced in your training and not have a complete grasp of what you need to create a complete physique. I was winning the NABBA Mr. Universe title in Europe and didn't realize I needed additional calf development. I didn't know that my calves should have been the same size as my arms. When I came to America people like Joe Weider told me, "Your waist ought to be smaller. You need more serratus. Your calves should be bigger. You need to work on developing more muscularity and definition." That's when I started to get down to serious detail and weak point training, but if I had understood this earlier I wouldn't have wasted that much time, and I wouldn't have lost against Chet Yorton and Frank Zane and, who knows, I might not have lost against Sergio Oliva.

Competition Training involves more sets, more reps, an across-the-board increase in volume of training—both in terms of what you do inside the gym with weights and the additional aerobic training outside the gym that helps supplement your overall program. This is all accomplished while you are cutting down your intake of food to the bare minimum in order to strip away as much body fat as possible. As a result, it is almost impossible to make a lot of gains in mass and strength on this kind of program, which is designed for *refinement* of the physique, not for building fundamental size and strength.

Competition Training, along with strict diet, can often result in losing hard-won mass if you aren't careful. It is very probable that many of the top champions have actually slowed their progress in the last few years simply because of the opportunities that the rise in popularity of bodybuilding has afforded them. They participate in so many contests, exhibitions, and seminars that they spend most of their time in or close to competition shape. But, ideally, Competition Training should be a concentrated program you use for a short period in order to get ready for a specific contest, not one you stay on for extended periods or try to do too often. In the days when bodybuilders entered only a few contests a year—which tended to be clustered together at a certain time of the year—there was plenty of time for off-season training for more mass and growth. So a bodybuilder would spend much of the year doing a lot of power training and eating as much as necessary, then shift gears into a competition mode of training in order to attain the quality and refinement necessary to be competitive onstage.

But today's top amateur and pro bodybuilders have had to alter their training methods drastically, picking their contests carefully and trying never to get too much out of shape between events. I, of course, have always been a believer in choosing particular contests rather than entering everything that came along, but many professional bodybuilders exhaust themselves entering one Grand Prix after another. This strategy has its price, since staying in shape too long results in your not being able to get in super-shape at all and in its general debilitating effect on your muscle mass and strength. Instead of this approach, I recommend competing only in contests that are really important to your individual competition career. It's better to compete only once a year and win than it is to compete too often and not do that well. Still, with so many more contests being held, deciding where and when to compete is more difficult than it used to be.

But if you are a beginner or early intermediate at bodybuilding competition, you probably won't face that sort of problem until later in your career. For now, it is important simply to realize what Competition Training does and doesn't do: It does not build mass, it is not intended to make you bigger and stronger, and, in fact, can sometimes do the opposite; but what it does do is bring out the quality in the development you have created, strip away the nonessentials, and reveal the diamond-like brilliance of each facet of your musculature.

THE FEAR OF SMALLNESS

One psychological block that many bodybuilders face when they attempt Competition Training has to do with their perception of their physical size. Whatever other motive bodybuilders may have for getting into training in the first place, part of it is always the desire to get big and strong. Therefore, anything which makes them feel smaller becomes a threat. That is why many bodybuilders are made very anxious by the effects of Competition Training.

The competition physique should be as much pure lean mass as possible, with any excess body fat stripped away. As the saying goes, "You can't flex fat." But fat on your body makes you feel bigger than you actually are, and this sense of being bigger is psychologically satisfying to most bodybuilders.

A person who weighs 240 pounds with 16 percent body fat would be lean for an average man, but not for a competition bodybuilder. When he starts to train and diet for competition he alters his body composition so that ultimately he gets down to 9 percent body fat. What does this change mean in practical terms?

At 240 pounds, he was originally carrying almost 38 pounds of fat. His lean body mass was therefore around 202 pounds. At 9 percent body fat he will find himself weighing about 222 pounds, assuming he has not lost any muscle mass. So, in terms of muscle he will be the same size, but he will feel a lot smaller. And this sense of smallness affects some individuals to the extent that they find themselves psychologically unable to keep to their program.

I have been through this experience myself. When I came to America in 1968 for the IFBB Mr. Universe contest, I weighed 245 pounds. I thought I had it made. Joe Weider took one look at me and declared me the biggest bodybuilder there was. Here I was in America to show everybody how great I was—and I lost! Frank Zane took the title with his smaller but cut-to-ribbons quality physique. And that taught me a valuable lesson.

A year later, at 230 pounds, I completely dominated my competitors, winning both the NABBA and IFBB Universe contests. I had realized that sheer bulk alone was not the stuff of top champions. I didn't take off the extra fat weight in two months; it took a full year. Because I took this amount of time, I was able to get used to my new proportions, to realize that the lighter weight did not really make me smaller—my arms were still huge and so were my thighs. But all my clothes were loose around the waist, indicating a real loss of unwanted bulk. The result? By changing my body composition, I won every contest I entered.

Mass is vital to a bodybuilder's physique. But it is the shape and the quality of this mass that win contests. Seeing big numbers on a tape measure or scale, or striving for the feeling of your clothes being tight all over your body, and not paying enough attention to stripping away fat, achieving ultimate definition and contest quality, will give you one inevitable result—you'll lose. And that I can tell you from experience.

THE ELEMENTS OF COMPETITION TRAINING

There are a number of special goals you need to set for yourself when training for competition:

1. You need to focus with even greater concentration on isolating each area of every single muscle.
2. You need to use an additional number of intensity training principles and a wider variety of exercises.
3. You need to increase the total number of sets and weights in your workout sessions.
4. You need to vary your workout pace, doing a number of supersets and trisets that drastically reduce your rest time between sets.
5. You have to make significant changes in diet. (See Contest Diet Strategies, page 748.)
6. You need to be *constantly* flexing and posing in the gym between sets.
7. You need to consider the benefits of having a training partner to help focus your energies on creating super-intense workouts. (See below.)

Analyzing and correcting your weak points becomes even more important when you are training for competition. Whereas you might previously have given weaker areas priority, now you must become a fanatic about correcting these imbalances. Of course, you have to realize that only so much can be done in a few weeks or months of training—totally correcting every weak area may take a year or two—but there are changes that can be made (bringing up the rear delts, for example, further developing the split in the leg biceps) even in such a short time that will increase your chances of doing well in competition.

DEPENDING ON YOUR TRAINING PARTNER

At no time is having a dependable training partner more important than when you are preparing to compete. As the contest approaches, every workout counts and there is no time for any letdown in training intensity. Your training partner helps to provide the extra motivation you need to diet and train hard at the same time. Of course, this relationship is a two-way street: You have the same responsibility when it comes to helping your training partner.

If you are a beginner at competition, you would do well to train with somebody who has more experience than you do. A knowledgeable training partner, who has been through it all before, can show you a lot of shortcuts and make your contest preparation that much easier and more effective.

When I was training at World Gym for the 1980 Olympia, I trained some days with two young bodybuilders getting ready for their first competition. They were both young and extremely strong, and they were able to push me hard in our workouts. On the other hand, because of my greater experience, I was able to show them training techniques they hadn't seen before and help them with their dieting and posing. We made a really fair trade: their energy and my knowledge. And we all got better because of it.

TRAINING VOLUME

Training for competition, you need to do more sets and use more different exercises. But, as we've discussed, overtraining can be as detrimental as not training hard enough. So here is a volume of training I recommend:

Chest, Back, Thighs, Shoulders	low volume—16 to 20 sets
	high volume—20 to 26 sets
Biceps, Triceps, Hamstrings	low volume—12 to 16 sets
	high volume—16 to 20 sets
Calves	low volume—10 sets
	high volume—15 sets
Abdominals	low volume—3 exercises
	high volume—4 to 6 exercises

CHOOSING EXERCISES

In the Competition Training Program, I recommend specific exercises, as I did in the previous training program. As you will see, the number of exercises listed in the competition program far exceeds what you can or should do in any one workout. By the time you get to the competition level *you should be experienced enough to make some decisions for yourself.* But these are some of the criteria you should use in putting together an individual workout:

1. Make sure you include both mass building, power or ballistic exercises, plus isolation exercises to create quality in each body part.
2. Concentrate on using free weights for mass and strength, and use cables and machines more for isolation exercises.
3. Include exercises to hit every part of each muscle. For example:

THE TRAINING SPLIT

There are two common ways of dividing up your competition training:

2-day split

the whole body in 2 days, each body part 3 times a week

3-day split

the whole body in 3 days, each body part 2 times a week

Again, I always trained 6 days a week, Monday through Saturday, as did most of my contemporaries. If the demands of your life or your job require you to train on a different schedule, you can also keep track of your workouts as Workout #1, Workout #2, and so forth, rather than in terms of days of the week.

A *2-day double-split* would look like this:

WORKOUT #1 MON	WORKOUT #2 TUE	WORKOUT #1 WED	WORKOUT #2 THUR	WORKOUT #1 FRI	WORKOUT #2 SAT
			MORNING		
Chest Back	Shoulders Upper arms Forearms	Chest Back	Shoulders Upper arms Forearms	Chest Back	Shoulders Upper arms Forearms
			EVENING		
Legs		Legs		Legs	

Calves and Abdominals in every evening workout

A *3-day double-split* would look like this:

WORKOUT #1 MON	WORKOUT #2 TUE	WORKOUT #3 WED	WORKOUT #1 THUR	WORKOUT #2 FRI	WORKOUT #3 SAT
			MORNING		
Chest Back	Shoulders Traps	Thighs	Chest Back	Shoulders Traps	Thighs
			EVENING		
Forearms	Upper arms	Hamstrings	Forearms	Upper arms	Hamstrings

Calves and Abdominals in every evening workout

Competition Exercise Program

Select the desired number of the appropriate exercises for each body part.

ABDOMINALS Begin workout with 10 minutes of Roman Chairs.

CHEST AND BACK

Deadlifts		3 sets of 10, 8, 6 reps
Superset:	Weighted Chin-Ups —behind neck	4 sets of 10 reps
	Incline Barbell Presses	4 sets of 15, 12, 8, 6 reps
Superset:	Bench Presses	4 sets of 15, 12, 8, 6 reps
	Chin-Ups—to front	4 sets of 15 reps
Superset:	Dumbbell Flys	4 sets of 10 reps
	Wide-Grip Bent-Over Barbell Rows	4 sets of 12 reps, using Stripping Method
Triset:	Machine Pullovers	4 sets of 15 reps, using Stripping Method
	Dips	4 sets, each to failure
	Cable Flys	4 sets of 12 to 15 reps
Triset:	Seated Cable Rows	4 sets of 10 reps, using Stripping Method
	One-Arm Cable Rows	4 sets of 12 to 15 reps
	Dumbbell Pullovers	4 sets of 15 reps

SHOULDERS

Triset:	Front Machine Presses	4 sets of 10 reps
	Dumbbell Lateral Raises	4 sets of 10 reps
	Bent-Over Lateral Raises	4 sets of 10 reps
Triset:	Barbell Presses, alternating front and back	4 sets of 12 reps
	Cable Side Laterals	4 sets of 10 reps
	Lying Incline Laterals	4 sets of 10 reps
Triset:	Front Barbell Raises	4 sets of 10 reps
	Seated Cable Rear Laterals	4 sets of 10 reps
	Shrugs	4 sets of 10 reps

THIGHS

Superset:	Leg Extensions	5 sets of 12 reps
	Squats	5 sets of 15 to 20 reps
Superset:	Front Squats	5 sets of 12 to 15 reps
	Leg Curls	5 sets of 12 reps
Superset:	Hack Squats	5 sets of 15 reps
	Leg Curls	the Stripping Method
Straight-Leg Deadlifts		3 sets of 6 reps, standing on block or bench

Upper Arms

Superset:	Barbell Curls	4 sets, the Stripping Method
	Standing Close-Grip Triceps Extensions with bar	4 sets of 10 reps
Triset:	Barbell Preacher Bench Curls	4 sets of 10 reps
	Lying Barbell Triceps Extensions	4 sets of 10 reps
	Barbell Preacher Bench Reverse Curls	4 sets of 10 reps
Triset:	Lying Dumbbell Extensions	4 sets of 10 reps
	Incline Curls (increase incline each set)	4 sets of 10 reps
	Lying Reverse-Grip Barbell Extensions	4 sets of 10 reps
Superset:	Concentration Curls	4 sets of 15 reps, using "One-and-a-Half" Method
	Standing One-Arm Triceps Extensions	4 sets of 12 reps
Superset:	Kneeling Cable Triceps Extensions	4 sets of 12 reps
	Kneeling Cable Triceps Extensions with rope	4 sets of 12 reps

Forearms

Triset:	Barbell Reverse Wrist Curls	4 sets of 10 reps
	Barbell Wrist Curls	4 sets of 10 reps
	One-Arm Dumbbell Wrist Curls	4 sets of 10 reps

Calves

(Alternate foot position: toes in, toes forward, toes out)

Donkey Calf Raises	5 sets of 15 reps
Standing Calf Raises	5 sets of 10 reps, as heavy as possible
Seated Calf Raises	5 sets of 15 reps
Front Calf Raises	5 sets of 15 reps
Leg Press Calf Raises	4 sets of 12 reps
Standing One-Leg Calf Raises	4 sets of 12 reps
Donkey Calf Raises	4 sets of 12 reps

Abdominals

(One cycle is 4 to 6 exercises, no rest between exercises)

Crunches	30 reps
Reverse Crunches	30 reps
Twists	50 reps each side
Seated Leg Tucks	30 reps
Vertical Bench Crunches	30 reps
Hyperextensions (lower back)	15 reps
Twisting Crunches	30 reps
Hanging Reverse Crunches	15 reps
Bent-Over Twists	50 reps each side
Machine Crunches	15 reps

INDIVIDUALIZING THE TRAINING PROGRAM

Once you get to the competition level, you have to put together a workout program that is suited to you as an individual. Because each individual has different strengths and weaknesses, there is no way I can give one routine that is perfect for everyone. I can outline general approaches, show you how to change your program so that you burn more calories, create more muscularity and definition—but it is you who must look in the mirror and determine where your weakness lies, whether it be in upper, lower, or middle pec development, biceps, triceps, or lat width.

Suppose your lower lats are not developing quite the way you want them to. It would make sense for you to add about 4 extra sets for lower lats. But 4 sets in addition to everything else you are doing would probably be too much, so you could eliminate one set each of exercises like Close-Grip and Wide-Grip Chin-Ups, Seated Rows, and T-Bar Rows. You would still do these exercises, but with fewer sets of each, so the overall demand of your total workout would remain about the same.

The program outlined here lists specific exercises, but if you are more experienced and have a clear perception of your weaker areas, then you should consult the exercise sections to find which movements are best for correcting the problems and make whatever alterations in your training routine you feel necessary.

All the top bodybuilders go through this process. I know when Franco and I used to train together I would do extra sets for certain areas and Franco would do extra for others. For instance, Franco had trouble getting his thighs really ripped, so he would do additional sets of an exercise like Front Squats on a Smith machine to help define his quadriceps. I didn't have this problem, so I would work harder on shoulders, triceps, abs, or whatever else I felt needed it the most. You can be sure that the bodybuilders who followed us in competition, such as Lee Haney, Dorian Yates, Shawn Ray, and Flex Wheeler, go through the same process.

As you make adjustments in your training, just be certain that you don't create new weaknesses trying to correct old ones. You must continue to give the rest of your body sufficient attention even while you work to correct problem areas.

MUSCLE SEPARATION

I talked earlier about the need for quality, and one aspect of physical development that is most important to achieving quality is muscle separation. Muscle separation is a level of muscularity that goes far beyond simple definition. Training and diet can give you good definition, but it takes something more to become the walking anatomy chart that will win competitions.

The quality physique must show clear separation between each muscle group. For example, when you do a rear double-biceps shot, the borders between the biceps and triceps, shoulder, traps, and upper and lower back should leap out at the judges. Each individual muscle group itself should show clear internal distinctions: the two heads of the biceps, the three heads of the triceps. And each head should be further patterned with visible striations of individual bundles of muscle fiber.

Total muscle separation is the result of training each muscle so thoroughly that every plane, contour, and aspect is brought out and fully revealed once you have lowered your body fat sufficiently. To achieve this requires many different exercises for each muscle and a lot of sets and reps. But it takes specific technique as well:

1. It is necessary to totally isolate each muscle and then each specific area of every muscle in order to engage every fiber possible, thereby creating clear separation between each muscle and major body part. This is done by knowing exactly how each exercise affects the muscles and putting together a program that sculpts the body exactly as you intend.

2. The utmost muscle separation cannot be achieved without strictness of movement involving concentrated effort through the entire range of motion of the exercise, so that every engaged fiber is subjected to the maximum amount of stress. Any sloppiness of execution will defeat your purpose.

Unless you perform an isolation exercise in a totally strict manner, you will not be working the narrow and specific area for which the exercise was designed. When doing a Front Dumbbell Raise to get deltoid-pectoral separation, for example, if you swing the weight up instead of making the muscle do all the work you will not bring out the full shape of the muscles, nor will you get the kind of separation you are after. If you want to work a certain area, you have to do the movement strictly enough so that you feel the effort exactly where you want it.

3. Obviously, whatever separation you achieve will not show if the muscle is covered with body fat. So proper diet resulting in low body fat is also an important factor in achieving spectacular muscle separation.

MUSCULARITY AND DEFINITION: ANALYZING YOUR PROGRESS

Ultimately, you are judged in bodybuilding competition based on how you look—a combination of what your physique looks like and how you present it. As we've discussed, there are other ways you can keep track of your progress, but these can be problematical. For example, at the 1980 (AAU)

Mr. America contest Ray Mentzer showed up to compete for a spot on the American team going to the World Amateur Bodybuilding Championships. For several months prior to the contest he had been going for body composition testing every three weeks. He came into the competition seemingly confident of victory because his last test had indicated that his body fat was below 4 percent.

Despite the results of the testing procedure, he failed in his bid to win a place on the Universe team because—in my opinion—he looked smooth onstage. He lacked cuts and muscularity. He had failed to realize that how much he weighed, what his physical measurements were, or what his body composition testing had revealed had nothing directly to do with what bodybuilding competition is all about.

The only real way to know whether or not you are in shape is by how you look. After all, the judges are not going to use underwater weighing, a tape measure, or any other device to make their decision. They are going to go by what they see. And you have to do the same thing.

Of course, it helps to have some basis for comparison. It is easier to measure the difference between two things than it is to analyze a thing by itself. One good way to do this is to take photos periodically and compare how you look now with how you looked then. Another way is to stand alongside another bodybuilder in the gym, hit some poses, and see exactly how you stack up.

But the ultimate test is when you are actually onstage and either win or lose. That is why it is sometimes necessary to enter several contests before you can really judge your progress. How well you do from one contest to another can tell you very clearly whether or not your training methods are working.

In the short term, though, it is your mirror that will be your most honest critic—if you allow it to be. Body composition testing doesn't tell you anything about your muscle separation; the tape measure cannot analyze your muscularity and definition; and you cannot judge the proportion and balance of your physique by stepping on a scale. But looking into a mirror and seeing only what you want to see is not the way to become a champion. You have to see things as they are, no better and no worse.

Also remember to keep your training diary so you will have an accurate record of your progress. When I was training for the 1980 Olympia, I had Franco shoot photos of me every week, which I studied very carefully to see how hard, defined, and muscular I was becoming. Between the photos, my own ability to look at myself in the mirror, and Franco's insightful comments, I knew all the time just how fast I was making progress and was able to arrive in Australia in shape to win my seventh Olympia title.

Franco and me on Venice Beach

OUTDOOR TRAINING

I have always enjoyed training outdoors in good weather. Training in the sun helps to give you a healthy look, tighter skin, and a good tan. Since the early Muscle Beach days, bodybuilders have taken advantage of sunny weather and trained outdoors.

You can certainly begin exercising outdoors right from the first day you start Basic Training, but outdoor training is most valuable prior to competition because of the finished look it helps to give the physique. When Franco and I trained on Venice Beach, we would work out, go lie on the beach for a while, and then return to the weight pit for more lifting. My tan became much deeper this way, and I benefited from training before an audience because it helped to get me ready for the pressures of appearing onstage in a hall full of people.

When you train outdoors I advocate a slower workout, but with very heavy weights. This can give you a nice break from your normal competition training and is another way of surprising and shocking the body.

Not everybody has a California beach right down the street, but when I lived in Austria and then later in Munich, my friends and I would often go out to a local lake and spend the entire day training outdoors. You can go to a park, a recreation area, or even somebody's backyard and enjoy outdoor training yourself.

CHAPTER 7

Mind over Matter: Mind, the Most Powerful Tool

THE BODY WILL never fully respond to your workouts until you understand how to train the mind as well. The mind is a dynamo, a source of vital energy. That energy can be negative and work against you, or you can harness it to give yourself unbelievable workouts and build a physique that lives up to your wildest expectations. Whenever you hear about anyone performing unbelievable physical feats—Tiger Woods in golf, Michael Jordan in basketball, Michael Johnson in track, Hermann Maier in skiing, and so many more athletes—it is because of the power of their minds, not just technical, mechanical skill. And you can be sure you will never perform at that level unless you can match their inner drive as well as their physical abilities.

People can walk on coals when they are sufficiently motivated. They can endure the rigors of Navy Seal training. They can cross vast deserts, dogsled across arctic wastes, climb Mount Everest, swim the English Channel, bicycle around the world, lift incredible amounts of weight. They perform in spite of terrible pain, despite being ill, no matter the odds or the obstacles.

There are a number of specific ways in which the power of the mind can be harnessed to help you achieve your goals:

1. *Vision.* As I alluded to in Chapter 5, the first step is to have a clear vision of where you want to go, what you want to achieve. "Where the mind goes, the body will follow" is a saying I have always believed in. If you want to be Mr. America or Mr. Universe, you have to have a clear vision of yourself achieving these goals. When your vision is powerful enough, everything else falls into place: how you live your life, your workouts, what friends you choose to hang out with, how you eat, what you do for fun. Vision is purpose, and when your purpose is clear so are your life choices. Vision creates faith and faith creates willpower. With faith there is no anxiety, no doubt—just absolute confidence.

2. *Visualization.* It is not enough to just want to "get big." Bodybuilding is more than that. It is about mass and shape and symmetry and definition. It is a kind of sculpture. It is almost like an art form. You have to have a picture in your mind of the kind of physique you need to build in order to achieve your goals. When you look in the mirror, you have to see yourself as you are—and as you want to be as well. You have to see in your mind's eye the masses of muscle you will be creating, the powerful physique that is in your future. Focusing on such images gives your mind and body a clear-cut task, a well-defined goal to strive for.

3. *Role models.* I talked in Chapter 5 about how I used to study photos of Reg Park because he had the kind of Herculean physique that I wanted someday to emulate. I remember as I traveled in the 1970s with Franco Columbu how many shorter bodybuilders used to come up to and thank him for inspiring them to train for competition. A medium-size, aesthetic type could choose Frank Zane or Shawn Ray. Really thick, slab-muscled competitors can turn to Dorian Yates or Nasser El Sonbaty for inspiration. When you find somebody who represents your ideal physique, study as many photos of him as you can, tear them out of magazines and put them up on the wall, tape them to the refrigerator—whatever it takes to help keep your mind focused on the task at hand.

4. *Motivation.* Motivation is the driving force that allows you to develop a single-mindedness of purpose that ultimately gives you the will to go into the gym for two to four hours a day and put yourself through the most punishing workouts possible. It makes the difference between just going through five sets of this and four sets of that and really pushing your body to the limit. Motivation creates discipline. Discipline comes from the joy of looking forward to achieving the goal you have learned to picture so clearly in your mind and consistently hammering away, rep by rep, set by set, workout by workout.

5. *Training strategy.* Beyond the act of visualizing the end product of your training, you should decide exactly what kind of development you need in each of the major muscle groups and what specific exercises and exercise techniques will achieve this. You've decided where you're going, now you need to map out how to get there. This is the point where you learn to truly individualize your workouts, find out how your body responds to specific movements and Intensity Techniques, and decide exactly what strategy you are going to employ to create the kind of body you

A little help from my friend—Franco Columbu was always my best training partner.

You and your training partner can feed off each other's energy, creating the kind of intensity that will push you beyond your limits.

are striving for. In addition to this, you have to consider factors we have discussed, such as what gym to train in and what kind of workout partner will help you to succeed, as well as any other factors that can help you to have great workouts or can get in the way.

6. *Mind in the muscle.* The key to success in your workouts is to get the mind into the muscle, rather than thinking about the weight itself. When you think about the weight instead of the muscle, you can't really feel what the muscle is doing. You lose control. Instead of stretching and contracting the muscle with deep concentration, you are simply exerting brute strength. So you end up not working to the limits of your range of motion, not contracting and extending the muscle in a smooth, intense, controlled manner. For example, when I am doing Barbell Curls, I am visualizing my biceps as mountains—not just big, but huge. And because I am thinking of the muscle, I can feel everything that is happening to it. I know whether or not I have fully stretched it at the bottom of the movement and whether I am getting a full, complete contraction on top.

BIG GOALS AND LITTLE GOALS

Along with the big goals you set for yourself—the kind of physique you hope ultimately to create, the competitions you want to win—you also have to learn to set smaller goals—day-to-day challenges, short-term achievements. Before you can develop 19-inch arms, you first have to build them up to 16 inches, 17 inches, and 18 inches. Before you can do a 400-pound bench press, you have to be able to press 250 pounds, 300 pounds, and 350 pounds.

Sometimes focusing only on long-term goals can be discouraging. But as the old saying goes, a journey of a thousand miles begins with a single step. I always had plans that covered different periods of time. My plan for the whole year dictated what I wanted to achieve in order to win another Mr. Olympia title. But I would also make plans that covered only a month at a time, and at the end of that period I would look back, evaluate my progress, and make whatever changes I felt were necessary for the next 30-day period. Maybe I wanted to pump up my triceps an inch or so, or take a little off my waist.

I do the same thing today when I have a movie scheduled. "Oh, two months to go before filming, I'd better hit the gym a little harder, increase my cardio." So I recommend, instead of always concentrating on the far horizon of your ambitions, try to take your long-term goals and break them down into smaller, incremental, and more manageable segments.

LEARNING FROM FAILURE

Anytime you undertake any difficult task, you have to face the possibility of short-term failure, obstacles that block your path and have to be overcome. Failure doesn't have to discourage you. It can be a great training tool. It defines limits for you, it instructs you as to which parts of your program are working and which aren't. It tells you what step of the staircase you are on and helps to motivate you to climb higher. Failure is not what hurts the aware; it is *fear of failure* that most often gets in the way. This prevents you from really trying hard, from releasing all of your energies, from summoning up total motivation. In fact, it often helps to seek out failure! Train as hard as possible, find out what your strength and endurance limitations really are. Push yourself until you run into a wall and can go no further. "You don't know how much enough is until you know how much too much is" is a phrase I have often heard. Once you experi-

Jeff Bridges and me in Stay Hungry

Carl Weathers and I battle an alien in Predator.

Conan the Barbarian

The Terminator

Commando

James Belushi watches me pump iron in Red Heat.

Terminator 2

Danny Devito and I played hardly identical twins in Twins.

I've always been proud to be involved with The Special Olympics. They are what sports are really all about—not competing against the other guy, but competing against yourself, concentrating your energies on achieving the highest standard of excellence you are capable of.

President Reagan believed in weightlifting. He said, "This is real power."

Even before I was involved with the President's Council on Physical Fitness, I spent time working with the armed forces. Here, I was working with the crew of a Navy carrier.

Governor Pete Wilson and I do push-ups during the Great California Workout.

President George Bush and I at the Great American Workout, an event held at the White House to help promote the health and fitness of all Americans.

ence failure—failure to lift a weight, to get through a workout, to place well in a contest—you will know much more about yourself and can plan the next stage of your training more intelligently. Learn from it, benefit by it, but don't be intimidated and fail to dare. You may attempt a lift you are certain you cannot make, but make it anyway! The satisfaction and confidence that come from stepping over your supposed limit is enormous, but it never comes to those who fear to test their limits.

MUSCULAR INHIBITION

When you contract a muscle, the brain not only sends out signals that stimulate fiber contraction, but inhibitory signals that limit it as well. This protects you from overcontraction, which could cause injury, but limits the amount of muscle being stimulated. Whenever you experience a muscle spasm or cramp, you are getting a taste of what would happen if these inhibitory signals did not exist.

Training progress happens in part because you are making your muscle fibers bigger and stronger, and in part because you gradually reeducate your nervous system so that it will decrease the inhibitory signals involved and allow for a stronger contraction. It takes energy to overcome this inhibition, to overwhelm the protective mechanisms. The more intense the imagery you use, the harder you concentrate and focus the mind into the muscle, the more you break through these inhibitory limitations your brain is creating and the more rapid your progress.

MAXIMIZING YOUR MOTIVATION

All of us have certain body parts that feel good to train and respond easily, and others that we have to force ourselves to train and that respond reluctantly. In my case, training biceps has always been a piece of cake, while I never had the same great feel doing triceps movements. But a bodybuilder with competition ambitions can't afford to let this situation stand.

Joe Weider and I present Flex Wheeler with a trophy at the Arnold Classic.

He has to concentrate on putting the mind into the muscle and establishing precise control of every muscle of every body part.

But there is only so much mental energy we can summon up on our own. Good bodybuilders have to be intelligent, but training is not an intellectual exercise. The training movements are sensual, and the deep motivation that excites you and keeps you going is *emotional*. You can't just sit down and feel those things any more than you can deliberately feel that you are in love. In both cases, something outside yourself has to inspire you.

I remember working out with Ed Corney before the 1975 Mr. Olympia and on one particular day I just couldn't get myself into training my back. Ed saw this and said to me, "Remember, you are going to be going up against Lou Ferrigno in South Africa, and his lats are so huge that if you stand behind him onstage the audience won't even be able to see you!"

Needless to say, when I started to think about competing against Lou, and how good his back was, I couldn't wait to do my Chins, Bent-Over Rows, and the rest of my back exercises. Corney's remark had inspired me, given me an energy I couldn't create all by myself.

BREAKING BARRIERS

When the going gets tough, it is always the mind that fails first, not the body. The best example of this I can think of occurred one day when Franco and I were doing Squats in the old Gold's Gym. Franco got under 500 pounds, squatted down, and couldn't get back up. We grabbed the bar and helped him get it back on the rack. Five hundred pounds for even one rep was apparently just too much for him that day.

Just then four or five Italian-American kids from New York came in. "Wow," they said, "there's Franco! Hey, Franco!" They were great fans, and were looking forward to watching him work out—only Franco had just failed in a lift and it seemed probable that he would miss it again on the next try.

I took Franco aside and told him, "Franco, these guys think you're the king. You can't get under five hundred pounds again and fail." All of a sudden his face changed. He looked at me with big eyes, realizing he was on the spot. Then he went out onto the street and spent a while psyching himself up, taking deep breaths and concentrating on the lift.

He stalked back into the gym, grabbed the bar, and, instead of the six reps he was supposed to do with 500 pounds, he did eight! Then he walked away coolly, as if it were nothing.

Obviously Franco's muscles didn't get any stronger in those few minutes between sets, his tendons didn't get bigger; what did change was his mind, his drive and motivation, his desire for the goal. It was impossible to overlook how important the mind was in making the body do what he wanted.

HOW BODYBUILDING AFFECTS THE MIND

We have been talking about the effect the mind has on the body. But the effect that bodybuilding has on the mind is also significant. Hard training causes the body to release endorphins (naturally occurring morphine-like substances), which lead to a mood elevation. There are many beneficial effects from the highly oxygenated blood that is pumped through your system. But bodybuilding can also have a profound effect on personality, lifestyle, and success in dealing with the demands of the modern environment.

Discipline is all-important to success in bodybuilding. So is the ability to concentrate, to set yourself a goal and not let anything stand in your way. But as much as bodybuilding demands, it gives back a great deal more.

I have worked with thousands of youngsters who wanted to become bodybuilders. I have taught weight training to Special Olympics kids and to prison inmates, and discussed the role of weight training with physical therapists, medical scientists, and the experts at NASA. And in all my experience I have never seen a case in which an individual made progress in bodybuilding without experiencing an accompanying boost in self-esteem, self-confidence, and enjoyment of life.

I had the same thing in mind when I helped form the Inner-City Games Foundation in Los Angeles in 1995. The mission of the Inner-City Games is to provide opportunities for inner-city youths to participate in sports, educational, cultural, and community enrichment programs; to build confidence and self-esteem; to encourage youths to say no to gangs, drugs, and violence and yes to hope, learning, and life.

Programs like the Special Olympics and the Inner-City Games work so well because a sense of self-worth should be based as much as possible on *reality;* you shouldn't just "believe" in yourself, but be able to point to real achievement. For these youngsters, and for everyone else as well, educating your mind, sharpening your talents, and creating a physically superior body are all ways of realistically enhancing your self-esteem. When you have a superior body, it is not egotism to take pride in it; egotism is when you attempt to take credit for qualities you don't really have.

Bodybuilding changes you. It makes you feel better about yourself, and it changes the way people treat you. It is an avenue open to anybody. Man, woman, or child, you can improve your body through proper training and your self-confidence along with it. Bob Wieland, for example, is a

Vietnam veteran who lost both legs in combat. Rather than treat himself as a cripple, he began training seriously in a gym and has since entered numerous powerlifting contests, breaking the world record for Bench Press in his weight class. Bob does not have to think of himself as handicapped; thanks to the benefits of training, he can rightfully claim the accolade of champion.

It has always seemed to me that bodybuilding is a good way to get in touch with reality. When you're working out, there is the reality of that cold iron in your hands . . . you can lift it, or you can't. That's reality. And then there is the progress you make. If you train correctly, you get results. Train incorrectly, or don't put enough intensity into your efforts, and you get little or nothing. You can't fake it. You have to face the facts.

The human body was never designed for a sedentary lifestyle. It was created to hunt saber-toothed tigers and walk forty miles a day. When we have no physical outlet, tensions build up within us. The body reacts to minor frustrations, such as somebody cutting us off in traffic, as life-and-death situations. The "fight or flight" mechanism is tripped, adrenaline floods our system, our blood pressure skyrockets. Exercise in general and bodybuilding in particular give us an outlet for these tensions and satisfy the body's need for strenuous activity.

If this is true for most of us, it is particularly evident when you are dealing with people in extreme circumstances—for example, prisoners serving time in penitentiaries, the Special Olympians, or kids forced to walk the streets of gang- and drug-ridden inner-city neighborhoods.

In my work teaching bodybuilding to prisoners around the country I have been struck by what an effective system of rehabilitation training with weights can be. Many men in prison suffer from a poor self-image, have found themselves ignored and overlooked in life, and felt trapped behind the bars of economic and social exclusion long before they found themselves behind real bars.

Many of these men have spent their lives blaming others for their own mistakes, rationalizing the behavior that has continually gotten them in trouble, failing to take responsibility for their own actions. All of this can change when they begin seriously pumping iron. The eventual achievement of getting through the set, building up the strength of the muscles, and learning the discipline necessary to continue making progress has its effect on the mind and spirit of the individual. Whereas many of these men had sought attention through antisocial means, now they attract admiring attention from people who respect their achievements. With this attention come pride and self-confidence, and this is one reason weight training has become so popular in prisons around the country. With the Special Olympians, the benefits are even more obvious. I remember working with some kids in Washington, D.C. One youngster was lying on a bench ready to do a bench press, while a line of others waited their turn. I handed him just the bar with no plates on it, and he freaked out—this kind of effort was more than he was used to or mentally prepared for. I didn't pressure him, but let him move off while I worked with the other boys. After a few minutes I saw him edging nearer, watching the others closely. Finally, he indicated he wanted to try, and I helped him press the bar three or four times, but he was still afraid and quickly got off the bench. But it wasn't long before he was back, this time with more confidence, and now he managed to do ten repetitions with very little help.

From that moment on, he was hooked. Not only did he join in the line of those waiting to try the exercise, he tried to push others out of the way so that he could have his turn sooner. In a world that contained so many frustrations and disappointments for him, this boy had found something to test his strength against, a physical barrier that could be approached and overcome, giving him a self-confidence usually denied him.

We are all a little bit like that youngster, only we possess enough ability and competence so our needs are not always so obvious. But they are there. All of us run into limitations, have to deal with frustrations and disappointments, and most of us realize that few individuals ever really live up to the physical potential that evolution has built into the human body. But mind and body are interconnected, two facets of the same thing. As the body's health improves, so do the health and strength of the mind, and bodybuilding is the ideal vehicle for achieving this necessary balance.

BOOK THREE

Body Part Exercises

As SUCCESSFUL AS I may have been in winning bodybuilding competitions, I would be the first to admit that nobody has a completely perfect physique. Certainly, when it came to body parts like the chest and biceps, I felt I could stand up to a direct comparison with anyone. But what bodybuilder could say with confidence that he would be willing to compare lats with Franco Columbu or legs with Tom Platz? It takes a great set of triceps to compare favorably with the huge arms of Jusup Wilkosz and a fantastic midsection to bear comparison with the washboard abdominals of Dennis Tinerino.

For this reason, and to make certain this book represented the absolute best in bodybuilding, I have selected a number of the top champions, known for their outstanding body part development, to help me illustrate the many different exercises in this section of the book. Pay particular attention to all the details in the photos, including head, torso, hand, and foot position to ensure maximal effectiveness and safety. After you start to get the hang of each movement, go back and check the photos again to guarantee that slight form deviations haven't crept in. By using strict exercise technique, you'll hasten muscular gains.

For the photos of myself used as illustrations, I have selected from my files and the photo library of Joe Weider a variety of pictures dating from my earliest competitions right up through the present. This range of photographs shows my physique at every stage of its mature development, creating a picture album of my personal history as well as technically correct bodybuilding illustrations.

The Shoulders

THE MUSCLES OF THE SHOULDERS

The **deltoid** is a large, three-headed, thick, triangular muscle which originates from the clavicle and the scapula at the rear of the shoulder and extends down to its insertion in the upper arm.

Basic function: To rotate and lift the arm. The anterior deltoid lifts the arm to the front; the medial deltoid lifts the arm to the side; the posterior deltoid lifts the arm to the rear.

The **trapezius,** is the flat, triangular muscle that extends out and down from the neck and then down between the shoulder blades.

Basic function: To lift the entire shoulder girdle, draw the scapula up, down, and to either side, and help turn the head.

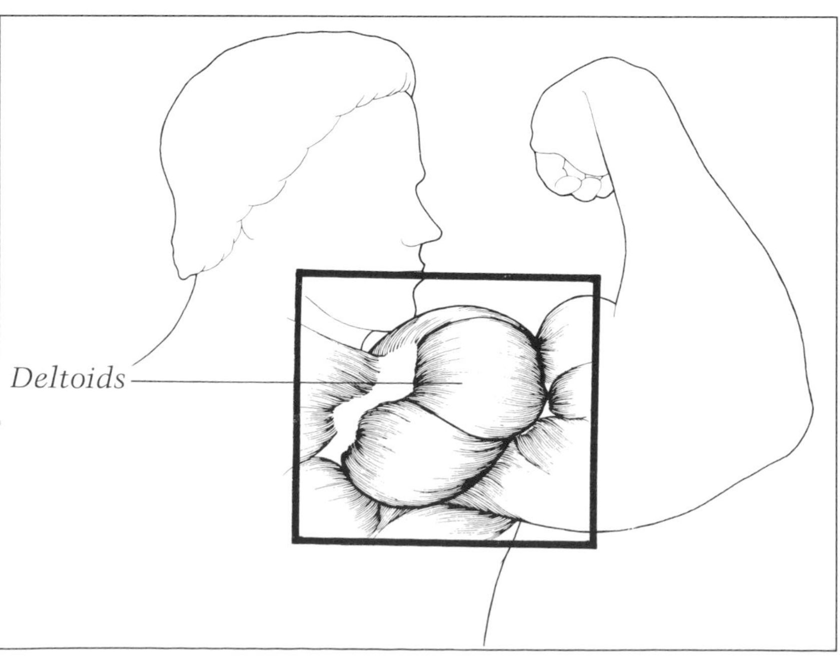

LOOKING AT THE SHOULDERS

In the 1940s men wore coats with huge, padded shoulders and pinched waists, giving them an exaggerated V shape (a style that seems to have come back into fashion recently). Coincidentally, that is the shape that bodybuilders work very hard to develop, and a significant part of this look is wide, fully developed shoulders.

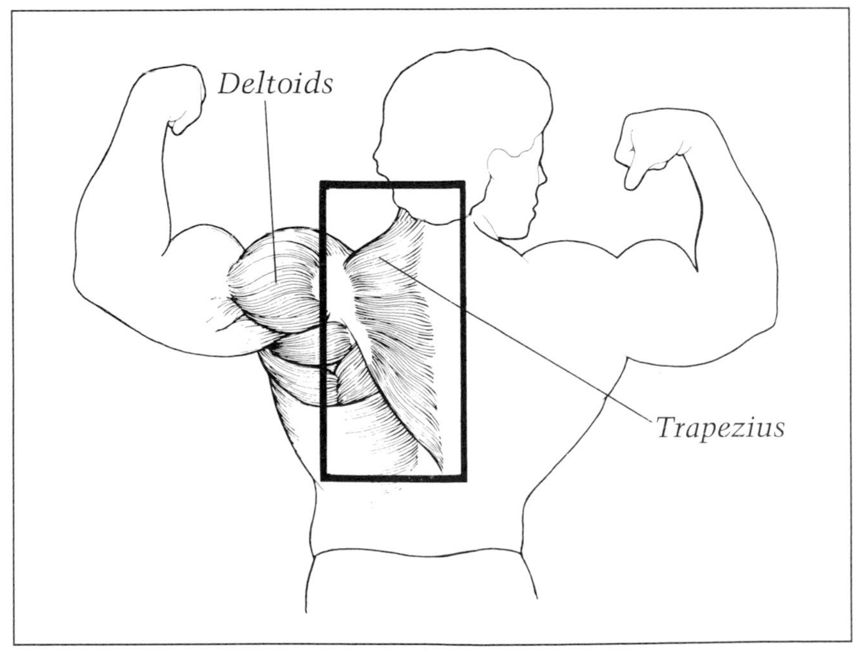

Flex Wheeler

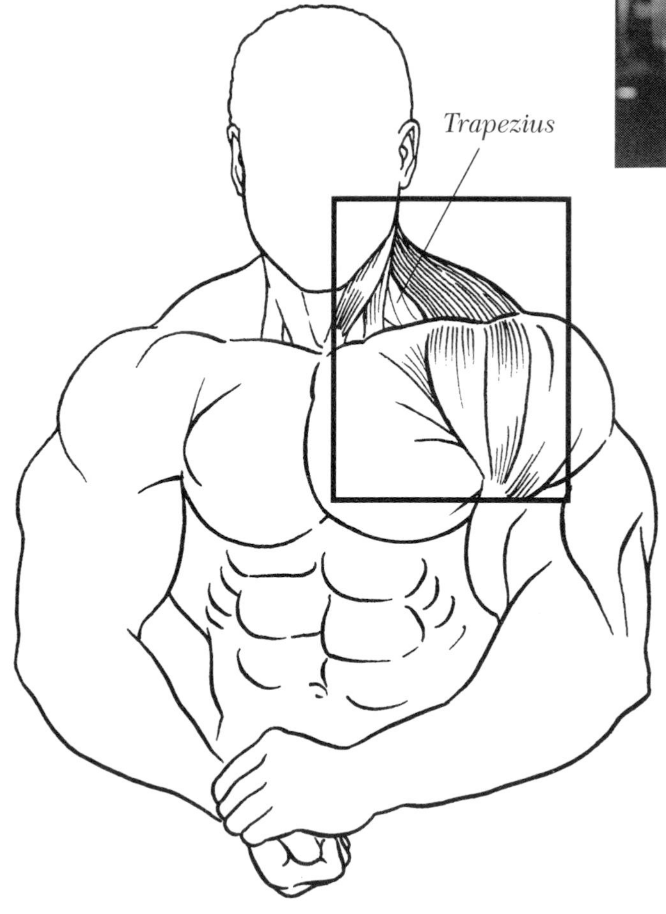

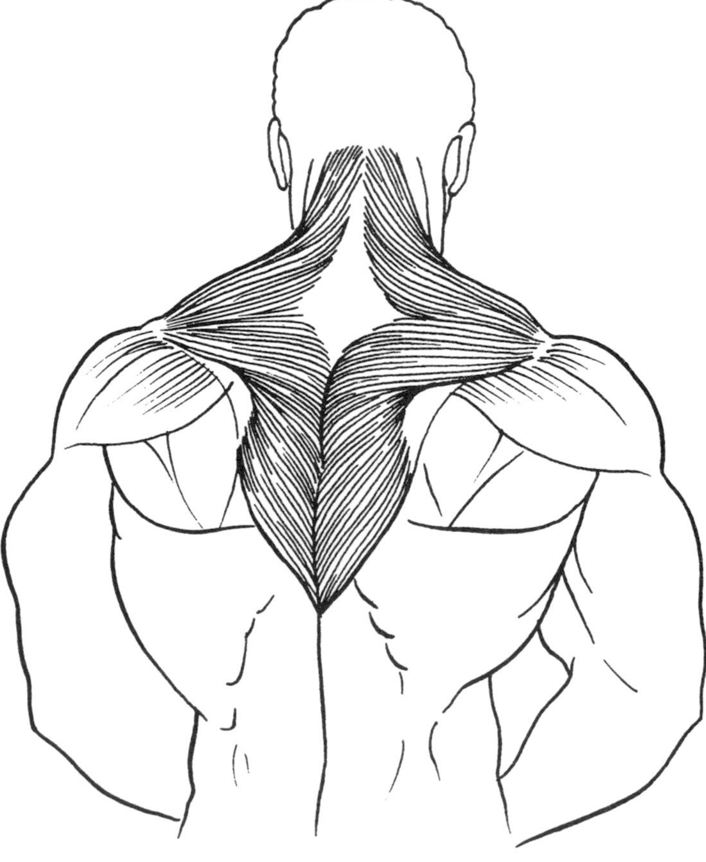

Steve Reeves

Steve Reeves was one of the first bodybuilders to develop the classic V shape. He was able to achieve this look because he had naturally wide shoulders and a small waist. Proportions like these help create the most aesthetic physiques in bodybuilding.

Shoulder width is, to a great extent, determined by skeletal structure. That is something you are born with. A bodybuilder like Reeves, with his very wide shoulder structure, has an enormous advantage, especially when he is standing relaxed. Don Howarth, Dave Draper, and Frank Zane, all champions who began training around the time I did, are other good examples of this wide, square-shouldered look. Kevin Levrone and Nasser El Sonbaty also possess wide shoulders.

There is another type of physique which is characterized not by narrowness through the shoulders, but by a "hanging" look. Reg Park was not narrow, but his traps and shoulders sloped downward. My own shoulders have this same sort of hanging look, so they look much narrower when I stand relaxed than when executing a pose like a lat spread, where the real width becomes apparent. Watch Paul Dillett onstage and you'll see somewhat of the same structure.

The other factor involved in a wide-shouldered look is the development of the side deltoids. When these muscles are fully developed, you get a very impressive display when they are flexed. Sergio Oliva and Tom Platz, for example, have tremendous shoulder development, yet do not look particularly wide and square when they are standing relaxed onstage. The ideal look for the competition bodybuilder is to have both a square bone structure and great side deltoid development. Look at Dorian Yates's shoulder development and you'll understand how valuable a structure like this can be.

Incidentally, bodybuilders noted for fantastic deltoid development are usually also known for enormous shoulder strength—Behind-the-Neck Presses with 225 pounds and up; Front Presses with 315, as both Sergio and Franco used to do; Ken Waller, with his powerful front deltoids, did Dumbbell Presses with 140-pound dumbbells.

But width—and the development of the side head of the deltoid—is only one aspect of the total development of the deltoid muscles. Shoulders also need to be thick, to show development in the front and the rear, to tie in properly to the pectorals and the biceps as well as to the traps and the rest of the back.

The deltoids are extremely versatile. In order to move the arm forward, back, side-to-side, up and around, the deltoids have three distinct lobes of muscle called heads: the anterior (front) head, the medial (side) head, and the posterior (rear) head.

The deltoids play a prominent part in virtually every bodybuilding pose. They add to your width and size in a front double-biceps pose; to your muscularity in a most-muscular pose. The thickness and development of all three heads play an important part in poses seen from the side,

Dave Draper

such as the side chest shot or a triceps pose. From the rear, the effect of a pose like the rear double-biceps is highly dependent on how much shape, separation, and definition you have achieved in the rear delts.

Your deltoid development should show definition and striations no matter what movement you make, while hitting all of the poses just cited as well as when you are moving in transition from one to another. There has to be an interconnection so that the three heads work together with all the adjacent muscles, thereby giving you a hard, muscular look.

But having complete deltoid development is also important while standing relaxed. From the front and from the back, good side deltoid development makes you look wider. In front, you should have complete separation of the deltoids and pectorals. For some people, this separation is natural; for others, it requires a lot of specialized weak point training. From the side, rear delt development gives you that "bump" in the back of the shoulders you see so clearly in great champions like Flex Wheeler or Dorian Yates, and both the rear deltoids and traps are extremely important when viewed from the back.

Here is Lee Haney displaying a lat spread pose. His square shoulders combined with great deltoid development turn a simple pose into an awesome look.

The square-shouldered look is also a matter of posing. When I was competing, standing relaxed, I had a hanging-shoulder look . . .

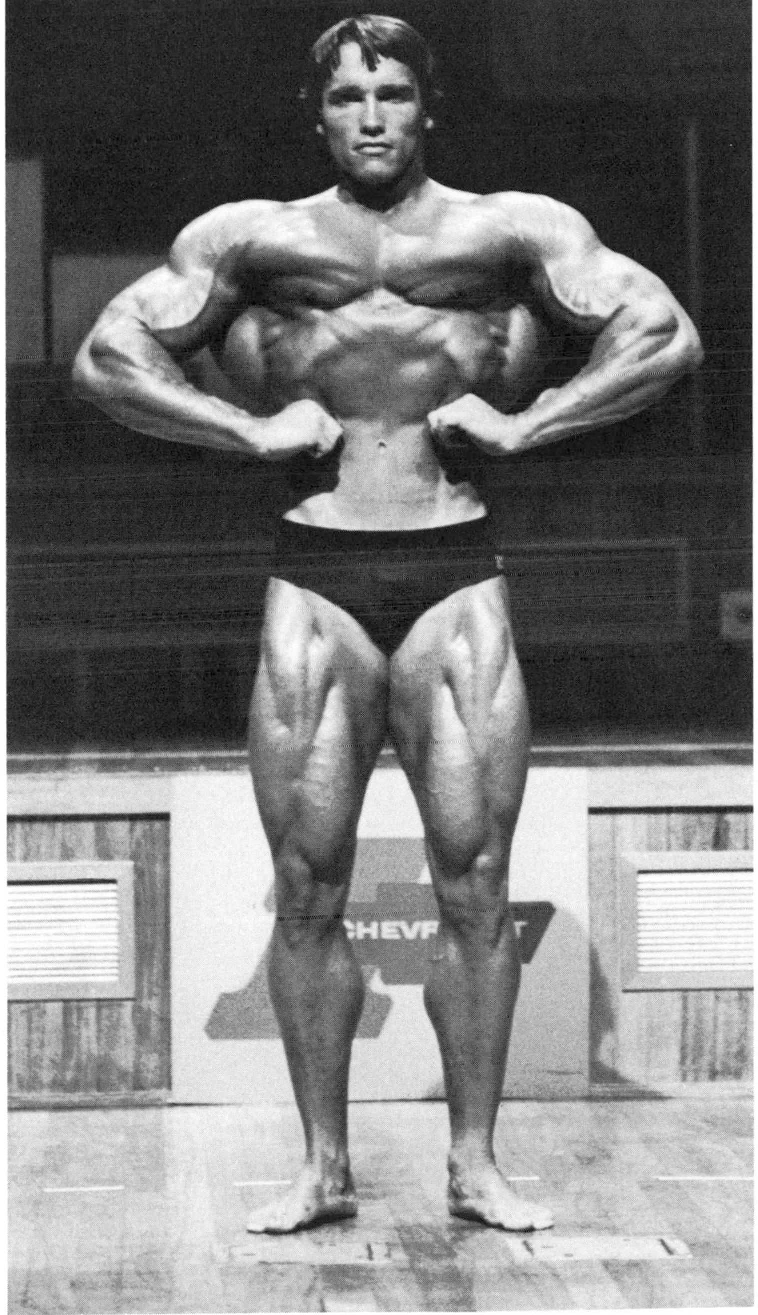

. . . but when I did a front lat spread, you can see how much wider my shoulders appeared.

Samir Bannout

Shawn Ray

. . . me executing a biceps pose . . .

. . . a most-muscular pose by Franco Columbu . . .

. . . and a fantastic back double-biceps pose by Ronnie Coleman.

Of course, shoulder width and deltoid development are actually two different things. Steve Reeves, for example, was not particularly thick and massive through the delts, in spite of his great width. Conversely, Larry Scott, who in the 1960s won the first Mr. Olympia competition, exhibited thick, muscular deltoids whose massive development offset his natural rather narrow proportions. Shawn Ray's shoulder width is not exceptional, but you don't notice because his deltoids are so thick and fully developed.

Many bodybuilders with comparatively narrow proportions have been saved by great deltoid development. My favorite example of this is Reg

Franco Columbu

Park. Reg worked very hard to compensate for relatively narrow skeletal proportions, and he ended up with enormous shoulder development. He was the first bodybuilder to bench-press 500 pounds, and this was possible only because of the size and strength of his front deltoids, which along with the chest and triceps work very hard in that lift.

One additional point worth making is that all of these champions trained very differently. Franco developed enormous front deltoids from all the pressing he did, so he had to add a lot of rear deltoid training to his workouts to achieve the correct balance. Larry Scott got his best results in shoulder training using the Stripping Method, starting with heavy weights and going lighter set after set to really burn the deltoids—90-pound dumbbells on down to 30-pound dumbbells. Dorian Yates spent a number of years doing a kind of high-intensity training that stressed relatively few sets but all kinds of intensity techniques like negatives, forced reps, forced negatives, and partial reps.

My point here is that no two individuals have bodies that are exactly alike or will end up training any body part exactly the same. There is not a bodybuilder alive who has never had to adjust his training to overcome weak points in order to create a well-proportioned and balanced physique.

Larry Scott

TRAINING THE DELTOIDS

There are two basic kinds of exercises for the shoulders—Straight Arm Raises and Presses.

Raises involve lifting your extended arm upward in a wide arc, which better isolates the heads. You need to do Raises to the front, to the side, and to the rear. When you do Raises, you do not involve the triceps, but almost completely isolate the various heads of the deltoids. However, because you are isolating the deltoids, you cannot lift as much weight as with pressing movements, because you keep your arm virtually straight throughout.

In Shoulder Presses, you begin with your arms bent, the weight about shoulder height, and lift the barbell or dumbbells straight up over your head. Because you are straightening your arms as well as lifting upward, Presses involve both the deltoids and the triceps. You can vary the stress on your shoulders to a slight degree to direct it toward the different deltoid heads by doing different kinds of Presses—to the front or rear, using a barbell, dumbbells, or various machines.

BASIC TRAINING

I believe in doing a lot of power training to develop shoulders no matter how advanced you are. But power training is perhaps most valuable when you are beginning. The deltoids respond well to working with heavy weights. This helps your overall development because so many other power exercises—from Bench Presses to Deadlifts to Bent-Over Rows—require a lot of shoulder strength.

Therefore, right from the beginning I recommend that you do movements like the Clean and Press, Heavy Upright Rows, and Push Presses in addition to Dumbbell Laterals. This kind of program will build up the shoulder mass and strength you need to enable you to go on to Advanced Training. Why I prefer to start beginners out with the Clean and Press exercise rather than just Shoulder Presses is that the extra movement—lifting the barbell off the floor, bringing it up to shoulder height, and tucking the arms in underneath to support it—works so many additional muscles besides the deltoids, specifically the back, traps, and triceps.

ADVANCED TRAINING

When you get to the level of Advanced Training, you need more than just mass and strength. At this point, you have to work toward overall shoulder development—all three heads of the deltoids as well as the trapezius muscles. Therefore, in addition to exercises like Dumbbell Laterals, designed specifically for the side deltoids, I have included Behind-the-Neck Presses for the front and side delts, Bent-Over Laterals for the rear delts, and Shrugs for the traps. Incidentally, for those who believe that the trapezius muscles are more associated with the back than the shoulders, just remember that once you have lifted your arm higher than the level of your head in any Lateral or Press movement the traps come heavily into play, pulling the shoulder up and in and allowing you to complete the full range of motion.

You will also find a number of supersets in this part of the program, to further stress and shock the shoulders, including exercises like Upright Rows (for the front delts and the traps), Machine Presses (to work the front delts and allow you to lower the weight farther than with a barbell), One-Arm Cable Laterals (which isolate the side deltoids), and Bent-Over Cable Laterals (for the rear deltoids).

THE COMPETITION PROGRAM

The function of the deltoids is very complex, enabling your arm to move in virtually a 360-degree circle—and this means that there are many angles at which you can train your shoulders to bring out their full shape and development.

In this pose you can see how the front deltoids are clearly separat from the pectorals, a quality you can develop with specific exercis such as Front Dumbbell Raises and Barbell Upright Row

The Competition Program, therefore, introduces a few extra movements such as Lying Incline Laterals and Seated Cable Rear Laterals. There is also a great increase in time intensity, with every exercise done as part of a superset or triset. This intense work is very effective in sculpting and defining the deltoid muscles, bringing in all the tie-ins and creating unbelievable muscular striations.

When training for competition, you have to pay close attention to detail. Not only must each head be developed in proportion, but each must be totally separated from the others, with all three heads clearly defined and visible. Additionally, the deltoid structure must be totally separated from the muscles of the upper arm as well as from the trapezius and upper back muscles. The front delts also must be clear and distinct from the sweep of the pectoral muscles.

On top of all of this, you need the striations and cross striations that give you the kind of quality that makes you competitive at the highest levels. Certainly, none of this comes easily. You can't just take any shoulder routine and expect to develop championship deltoids. It takes continually increasing intensity using techniques like supersets, trisets, the Stripping Method, and as many of the Shocking Principles as possible. If you find that despite your efforts you still have weak points in your deltoid development, intensive training is the only solution; you need to carefully study the weak point options (see page 265) and decide how to reorganize your workouts to deal with these problems.

In 1971, when I trained with Franco, we did Dumbbell Presses down the rack starting with 100 pounds, then immediately went and punished our delts with Lateral Raises until we were unable to lift our arms. Or sometimes we would do trisets: first a front delt exercise, then one for side delts, and finally a set for rear delts. Believe me, after a couple of these our shoulders felt as if they were on fire, with every fiber screaming for mercy.

TRAINING THE TRAPEZIUS MUSCLES

The trapezius muscles are the visual center of the upper back, the trapezoidal structure that ties together the neck, deltoid, and latissimus muscles. The traps play an important part in both front and rear poses. In shots like the back double-biceps, the traps help produce that fantastic effect where your muscles ripple from elbow to elbow clear across the top of your back. In a rear lat pose, as your lats come forward and sweep out, the traps form a clear triangle of muscle in the middle of your back. Trap development also helps to separate the rear delts from the upper back. And in most front poses, the line of the traps, from neck to deltoids, is extremely important, especially if you want to be able to do an impressive most-muscular shot.

The traps are important to both front and back poses. For example, see how they help tie the back together in a back double-biceps shot.

Flex Wheeler

But the traps have to be developed in proportion to the rest of your body. If they stick up too high and slope down too abruptly, your deltoids will appear too small.

The traps work in opposition to the pulldown function of the lats—they raise the entire shoulder girdle. In the Basic Training Program, I included Heavy Upright Rows as part of your power training so that your traps will build mass and strength right from the start. But the traps also benefit from the Barbell Clean and Press and from heavy Deadlifts, which are also included in the Basic Program.

Incidentally, you will get some trap development from Dumbbell Laterals, provided you do them the way I have described in the exercise section, starting with the dumbbells in front of the thighs rather than hanging down by your sides.

In the Advanced Program, I have included Dumbbell Shrugs as part of your trapezius training. These work the traps directly, and you can build up to a tremendous amount of weight in this exercise. You will also find in the Advanced and Competition Programs a number of exercises that train the traps, though they are not specifically designed to do so: Almost any rowing exercise (Bent-Over Barbell Rows, for example) or Shoulder Press (barbell or dumbbell) involves a lifting motion of the traps as well as other muscle functions. And strong traps help you use heavier weight in all of these other movements.

WEAK POINT TRAINING

If shoulders are a weak point in your physique, adjust your training so that you do more sets and more exercises for shoulders, and use as many of the Shocking Principles as possible to work that area with maximum intensity.

I like to use the Stripping Method for shoulders. With dumbbells, you start with heavy weights and move on down the rack; with Machine Presses or Cable Laterals, you just keep moving the pin one plate lighter each set.

Another way of accelerating deltoid development is by supersetting Presses and Raises—for example, a Barbell Press followed by Front Dumbbell Raises (or Upright Rows) in order to completely blitz the front delts. For a really intense delt workout, try doing a 3-Pump Set: Presses, Front Dumbbell Raises, and Upright Rows. But be prepared to bear the pain.

To get the best results from Raises, remember two things:

1. Keep your palm turned downward throughout the movement; or, even better, turn the hand a little farther so that the little finger is higher than the thumb (like pouring water out of a pitcher). This helps isolate the deltoids and make them fully contract during the movement.

2. Be as strict as possible. Raise the weight without any cheating, and lower it fully under control. The stricter you are, the more intense the effect on the deltoids.

Another way of increasing the intensity of your deltoid training is, after each set of Dumbbell Raises, go over to the rack, take a heavier set of weights, and just lift them out to the side as far as possible and hold them there as long as you can. This "isometric lateral" will help fully exhaust the deltoids and bring out maximum striations.

As a way of getting extra development in the rear deltoids, I used to leave a light dumbbell—usually 20 pounds—under my bed and, first thing in the morning, would do 5 sets of Lying Side Laterals with each hand without stopping. However, I never counted this as part of my regular shoulder workout. I also did a 2-Pump Set, starting with facedown Incline

Lateral Raises and, when I was too tired to continue the set, changing to a kind of Dumbbell Rowing motion to fully exhaust the rear delts.

Following are extra exercises and techniques you can use to develop a specific area that you have identified as a weak point.

Front Deltoids

Machine Presses, because you can lower the weight farther with machines than with barbells or dumbbells, thereby stretching the front deltoids to the maximum and getting a longer range of motion

Do not lock out on top in any press movement.

Use dumbbells whenever possible to better stress the deltoid heads.

Arnold Presses—my favorite front delt exercise—especially using techniques like Running the Rack or the Stripping Method (page 193)

Front Dumbbell Raises for maximum front deltoid and pectoral separation

Front Barbell Presses

Upright Rows

Incline Barbell and Dumbbell Presses

Incline Dumbbell Flys (see Chest Exercises)

Many bodybuilders forget that front deltoids are also important to back poses. Franco Columbu demonstrates how the front deltoids are visible in a back double-biceps shot.

You can see in this semi-relaxed pose how the front deltoids, besides having mass and separation, can also be defined and striated.

In all Presses, the forearms should be held straight, not in toward the center, which overinvolves the triceps.

The side deltoids help to create a very wide look, even in this pose by Serge Nubret that is basically an abdominal pose.

Side Deltoids

Dumbbell Laterals, beginning with the dumbbells held beside the thighs instead of in front while standing straight or sitting on a bench with your back straight

Cable Laterals, raising your arm from the side of the body, not across the front

Do super-strict Laterals (not letting the weight rise about your head, to ensure that the delts do the work instead of the trapezius).

Do burns after your Lateral Raises (taking very heavy dumbbells and holding them out with totally straight arms about 10 inches from your thighs for as long as possible—but at least 30 seconds).

Seen from the side, the development of the side deltoid creates separation from the trapezius above and from the triceps and biceps below.

Shoulder width from good side deltoid development increases the effectiveness of a front lat spread.

This three-quarter back pose by Franco Columbu demonstrates the necessity of having good rear deltoid development.

Rear Deltoids

Use the Priority Principle (page 192), beginning your deltoid training with rear delt movements.

Add extra rear delt sets: Bent-Over Laterals, Bent-Over Cable Laterals, Bent-Over Barbell Rows, Seated Cable Rear Laterals, Incline Bench Lateral Raises (facedown), or Lying Side Laterals—try 10 sets for each arm done continuously without stopping (I used to do this every day, whether it was a shoulder day or not).

Take extra care to work the rear delts with the strictest technique possible, since any cheating will allow other muscle groups to do too much of the work.

In all Rear Laterals, twist the wrist as if pouring water from a pitcher in order to increase rear delt development.

Total shoulder development—the traps, the front, side, and rear deltoids, and the separation and definition of all the muscles involved—is extremely important in a most-muscular shot.

Trapezius

Shrugs
Upright Rows
Deadlifts
Clean and Press
Reverse Laterals (very popular with British bodybuilders, these work the traps from an unusual angle as well as hitting the front delts)
Rowing exercises, such as T-Bar Rows and Cable Rows
Cable and Dumbbell Laterals

The twisting back pose is one that does not work at all unless you have well-developed rear deltoids along with all the other important back muscles.

Shoulder Exercises

ARNOLD PRESSES

PURPOSE OF EXERCISE: To develop the front and side heads of the deltoids. This is the very best deltoid exercise I know, and I always include it in my shoulder routine. By using dumbbells in this manner—lowering them well down in front—you get a tremendous range of motion.

EXECUTION: (1) In a standing position, elbows at sides, grasp one dumbbell in each hand and raise the weights to your shoulders, palms turned toward you. (2) In one smooth motion, press the weights up overhead—not quite to the point where they are locked out—and at the same time rotate your hands, thumbs turning inward, so that your palms face forward at the top of the movement. (3) Hold here for a moment, then reverse the movement, lowering the weights and rotating your hands back to the starting position. Don't get so concerned with pressing the weight overhead that you begin to sway and cheat; this movement should be done strictly, keeping the dumbbells fully under control. By not locking the arms out when you press the weight overhead, you keep the stress on the deltoids the whole time. This exercise is half Lateral Raise and half Dumbbell Press, and works both the anterior and medial heads of the deltoids thoroughly.

Nasser El Sonbaty

BEHIND-THE-NECK PRESSES

Purpose of Exercise: To train the front and side deltoids. Any pressing movement involves the triceps as well.

Execution: You can do these Presses standing, but I prefer doing them sitting, since it makes the movement stricter. (1) Either lift the barbell overhead and set it down on your shoulders behind your head or lift it off the rack of a seated press bench. (I personally prefer to hold the bar with a thumbless grip.) (2) Press the weight straight up and then lower it again, keeping it under control and your elbows as far back as possible during the movement.

Flex Wheeler

DUMBBELL PRESSES

Purpose of Exercise: To train the front and side deltoids. This exercise may seem to be similar to Barbell Presses of various kinds, but there are important differences, the most significant being the greater range of motion you get using the dumbbells.

Execution: (1) Hold one dumbbell in each hand at shoulder height, elbows out to the sides, palms facing forward. (2) Lift the dumbbells straight up until they touch at the top, then lower them again as far as possible. You will find that you are able to both raise and lower the dumbbells farther than you can a barbell, although the need to control two weights independently means that you are lifting slightly less poundage.

Flex Wheeler

Kevin Levrone

MILITARY PRESS

Purpose of Exercise: To train the front and side deltoids. This is the granddaddy of shoulder exercises. When done from a seated position the movement will be stricter than when standing.

Execution: (1) From a sitting or standing position, grasp a barbell with an overhand grip and hold it at shoulder level, palms underneath for support, hands outside your shoulders, elbows tucked in and under. (2) From a position about even with the collarbone, lift the bar straight up overhead until your arms are locked out, being careful to keep the weight balanced and under control. Lower the weight back to the starting position.

CLEAN AND PRESS

PURPOSE OF EXERCISE: To train the front and side deltoids and build total body density and power.

Cleaning a weight is a method of lifting a barbell from the floor to the starting position of the Military Press. The Clean and Press is an important exercise that starts off with a lot of leg movement to get the weight moving, then involves the traps, arms, and back as well as the shoulders to help you develop a truly Herculean look.

EXECUTION: (1) Squat down, lean forward, and take hold of the bar with an overhand grip, hands about shoulder width apart. (2) Driving with the legs, lift the bar straight up to about shoulder height, then tuck the elbows in and under to support the weight in the starting position of the Military Press. (3) Then, using your shoulders and arms, press the weight up overhead, bring it back down to shoulder height, then reverse the cleaning motion by bending your knees and setting the weight back onto the floor.

Lee Haney

STANDARD
45
GYM

MACHINE PRESSES

Purpose of Exercise: To train front and side deltoids. Doing Presses on a machine helps you do the movements very strictly, and allows you to avoid cleaning a weight if you have some sort of physical problem. Also, you can let the weight come down much lower, which gives you extra stretch in your front delts. There are any number of machines on which you can do a Shoulder Press movement—Cybex, Nautilus, Hammer Strength, or Universal, to name a few—but the principle remains the same.

Execution: (1) Grasp the bar or handles at shoulder level and (2) press upward until your arms are locked out, then come back down slowly to the starting position, going through the longest range of motion possible. You can also use machines to do Front Presses or Behind-the-Neck Presses; both will work the front and side deltoids.

PUSH PRESSES

Purpose of Exercise: To use a heavier than normal weight, or to continue to do repetitions of shoulder presses after reaching a point of failure; to develop additional deltoid strength.

This is a Cheating Principle exercise. You can use it in power training to lift a barbell that you would normally find too heavy to use for strict Shoulder Presses. You can also use the Push Press to do forced reps at the end of a set, when you are too tired to continue to do strict Shoulder Press reps.

Execution: (1) Taking hold of a barbell with an overhand grip, hands slightly wider than shoulder width apart, clean the weight up to shoulder height. (2) Bend your knees slightly and then press up with your legs to get the bar moving. Use this additional impetus to press the bar up overhead. Lock it out, then slowly lower once more to shoulder position.

David Dearth

Eddie Robinson

STANDING LATERAL RAISES

PURPOSE OF EXERCISE: To develop the outside head of the deltoid, with secondary benefit to the front and rear heads.

EXECUTION: (1) Take a dumbbell in each hand, bend forward slightly, and bring the weights together in front of you at arm's length. Start each repetition from a dead stop to keep yourself from swinging the weight up. (2) Lift the weights out and up to either side, turning your wrists slightly (as if pouring water out of a pitcher) so that the rear of the dumbbell is higher than the front. (3) Lift the weights to a point slightly higher than your shoulders, then lower them slowly, resisting all the way down. (A common mistake with this movement is to rock back and forth and swing the weights up instead of lifting them with the deltoids. Doing this cuts down on the effectiveness of the movement and should be avoided.)

VARIATION: You may have a tendency to cheat a little when doing Standing Lateral Raises—this can be avoided if the same exercise is done in a seated position.

Seated Lateral Raises

ONE-ARM CROSS CABLE LATERALS

PURPOSE OF EXERCISE: To work the outside head of the deltoid and, to a lesser degree, benefit the front and rear heads. Doing One-Arm Laterals with a cable and floor pulley gives you two advantages: It allows you to isolate first one side of the body, then the other; and the cable provides constant tension unaffected by your motion relative to the pull of gravity.

Dorian Yates

EXECUTION: (1) Grab the handle and stand with your arm down and across your body, your free hand on your hip. (2) With a steady motion, pull outward and upward, keeping the angle in your elbow constant throughout the movement, until your hand is just slightly higher than your shoulder. Twist your wrist as you raise your arm as if you were pouring a pitcher of water. Do your reps with one hand, then an equal number with the other. Don't lift the weight by raising up with your body—use the deltoids.

VARIATION: Try doing the movement with the cable running behind your back instead of in front.

Porter Cottrell

If you have a weak point in the rear delts, bending your torso forward slightly while doing Cable Laterals works this area in addition to the side delts.

ONE-ARM SIDE CABLE LATERALS

Purpose of Exercise: To focus the work on the side delt head. This movement, which was a favorite of Sergio Oliva's, helps bring out definition in the shoulders, and works the rear and front heads as well.

Execution: (1) Stand upright, with your arm down beside you, holding on to a handle attached to a floor-level pulley. Place your other hand on your hip. (2) Keeping your arm straight, lift it up in an arc in one smooth motion until it is higher than your head. Lower your arm back to your thigh. Finish your repetitions, then repeat using the other arm.

SEATED ONE-ARM CROSS CABLE LATERALS

PURPOSE OF EXERCISE: To develop the rear deltoids by isolating and flexing the rear deltoid when reaching the top position of the Cable Lateral movement.

EXECUTION: (1) Sitting on a stool or low bench, take hold of a handle attached to a floor-level pulley in such a way that your arm is fully extended across the front of your body. (2) Keeping your body as still as possible, pull the handle across and up until your arm is fully extended to the side at about shoulder height. (3) At the top of the movement flex your rear deltoid to get a really full contraction. Lower the weight back to the starting position. Finish your repetitions, then repeat with the other arm.

Isolating and flexing the rear deltoid when reaching the top position of the Cable Lateral

Aaron Maddron

REVERSE OVERHEAD DUMBBELL LATERALS

Purpose of Exercise: To develop the side and rear deltoids. This exercise, a favorite of British bodybuilders, also helps develop the traps.

Execution: (1) Take a dumbbell in each hand, then extend your arms straight out to either side, palms turned up. (2) Slowly lift your arms up and bring them together over your head. Your arms do not have to be locked out on top. Keep your body steady during the entire movement. From the top, lower the dumbbells slowly down to the starting position.

MACHINE LATERALS

Various machines have been developed that attempt to duplicate the lateral movement of the deltoids yet do not put any appreciable stress on the wrists, elbows, or upper arms. When using these machines, either with one arm at a time or both together, concentrate on feeling the deltoids lift the arm from a position at your side all the way up through the entire range of motion of the machine and then back down again under control, resisting the pull of gravity from the weight stack at all times.

FRONT DUMBBELL RAISES

PURPOSE OF EXERCISE: To develop the front head of the deltoids.

This exercise not only works the front head of the deltoids through its entire range of motion, but also involves the traps during the top of the movement. It can be done either standing or sitting.

EXECUTION: Stand with a dumbbell in each hand. (1) Lift one weight out and up in a wide arc until it is higher than the top of your head. (2) Lower the weight under control while simultaneously lifting the other weight, so that both arms are in motion at the same time and the dumbbells pass each other at a point in front of your face. In order to work the front head of the deltoids directly, make certain that the dumbbells pass in front of your face rather than out to the side. To do this same movement with a barbell, grasp the bar with an overhand grip, let it hang down at arm's length in front of you, and with arms kept locked, lift it to a point just higher than your head, staying as strict as possible, then lower it again under control.

VARIATION: Do Front Raises in a seated position for a stricter movement, since you can't use your body to cheat on the lifts.

Seated Front Dumbbell Raises

SEATED BENT-OVER DUMBBELL LATERALS

Purpose of Exercise: To isolate and work the rear head of the deltoids.

By bending over while executing a Lateral, you force the posterior head of the deltoids to work more directly. Doing them seated allows you to do a stricter movement than when standing.

Execution: (1) Sit on the end of a bench, knees together, and take a dumbbell in each hand. Bend forward from the waist and bring the dumbbells together behind your calves. Turn your hands so that your palms face one another. (2) Keeping your body steady, lift the weights out to either side, turning your wrists so that the thumbs are lower than the little fingers. Be careful not to lift up your body as you lift the weights. With your arms just slightly bent, lift the dumbbells to a point just higher than your head, then, keeping your knees together, lower them again slowly to behind your calves, resisting all the way down. Try not to cheat doing this exercise. And be sure you are lifting straight out to either side; the tendency doing this exercise is to let the weights drift back behind your shoulders.

STANDING BENT-OVER DUMBBELL LATERALS

PURPOSE OF EXERCISE: To develop the rear deltoids.

EXECUTION: (1) Stand with a dumbbell in each hand. Bend forward from the waist 45 degrees or more, letting the dumbbells hang at arm's length below you, palms facing each other. (2) Without raising your body, lift the weights out to either side of your head, turning your wrists so that the thumb ends up lower than the little finger. (Don't allow your arms to drift back behind your shoulders.) Lower the weights again under control, resisting all the way down.

Lee Priest

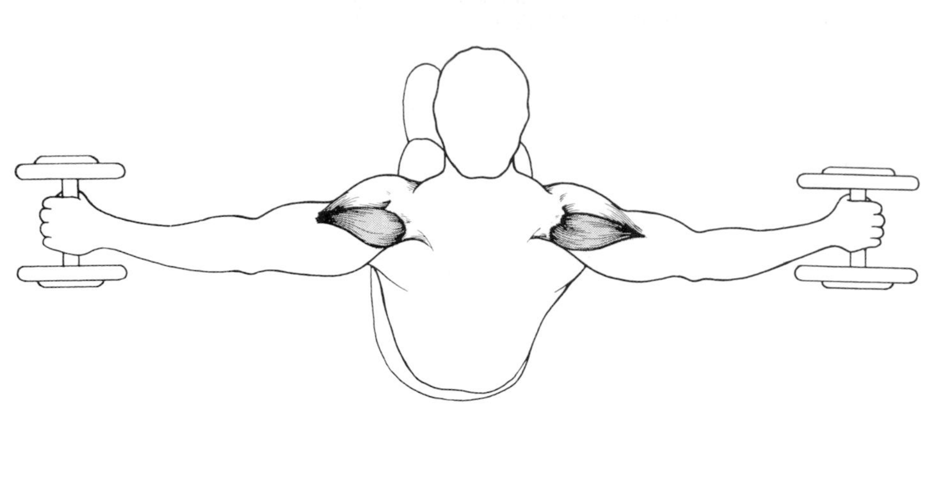

The proper angle for working the rear deltoids—the dumbbells and the shoulders are in a straight line. Notice also that the dumbbells are kept horizontal, with the palms facing the floor.

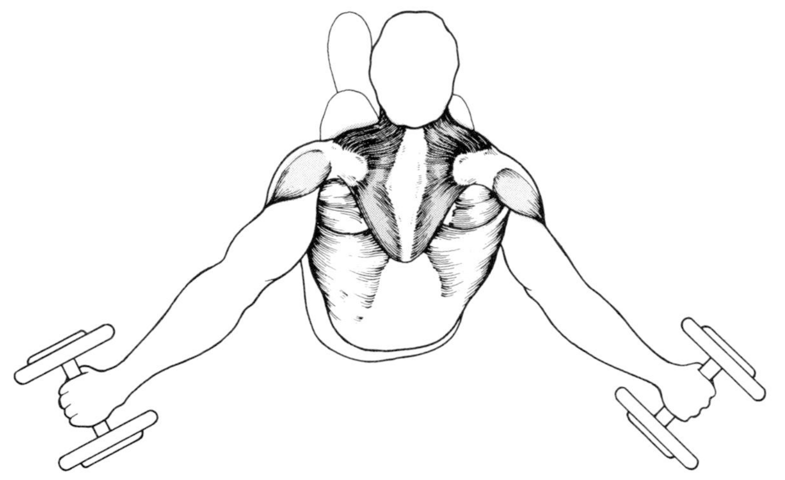

Lifting the dumbbells too far to the rear involves the traps and lats, diminishing the effect of the exercise on the rear deltoids.

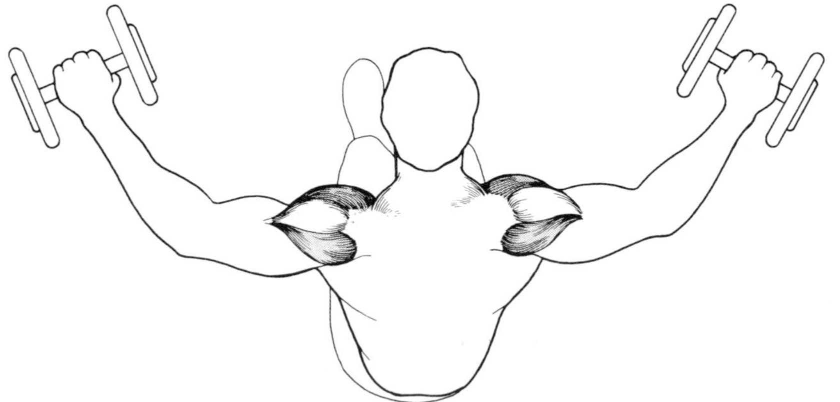

Lifting the dumbbells too far to the front works the front part of the deltoids instead of the rear.

BENT-OVER CABLE LATERALS

Purpose of Exercise: To work the rear head of the deltoids.

By using cables, you get a slightly longer range of motion with continuous resistance throughout the movement. This is one of Franco Columbu's favorite rear deltoid exercises, and his rear delts are fantastic.

Execution: (1) Using two floor-level pulleys, take a handle in each hand with your arms crossed in front of your body (left hand holding right-side cable, right hand the left-side cable). Keeping your back straight, bend over until your torso is about parallel to the floor. (2) With a smooth pull, and arms nearly straight, draw the handles across your body and extend your arms straight out to either side, turning your wrists slightly, thumbs down, as if pouring a pitcher of water. Stretch as far as possible, then release and let your arms come back slowly across your body as far as they can.

Rich Gaspari

LYING SIDE LATERALS

Purpose of Exercise: To work the rear and side deltoids.

This exercise was often recommended by France's Serge Nubret, and will work wonders for both your rear and side deltoids. It should be done only with a moderate weight and performed very strictly.

Execution: Preferably, you should use an abdominal board set at an angle. You can do the movement without a board, but it shortens the range of motion. (1) Lie on your side, with your head raised. Holding a dumbbell in one hand, lower it almost to the floor. (2) Then raise it up all the way over your head, keeping your arm straight. Remember to twist your hand slightly while lifting, turning the thumb down, to further contract the rear deltoid. When you have done the reps with one arm, turn over and do an equal number for the other side.

Trapezius Exercises

UPRIGHT ROWS

Purpose of Exercise: To develop the trapezius and the front deltoids and create separation between deltoids and pectorals.

Execution: (1) Stand grasping a barbell with an overhand grip, hands 8 to 10 inches apart. Let the bar hang straight down in front of you. (2) Lift it straight up, keeping it close to your body, until the bar just about touches your chin. Keep your back straight and feel the traps contract as you do the movement. Your whole shoulder girdle should rise as you lift the weight. From the top, lower it once more under control to the starting position.

This is an exercise that you should do strictly, not cheating or swinging the weight up, keeping your body still, and making sure that you feel the traps working as well as the biceps and front delts. (You can substitute a short bar and cable for the barbell and use Cable Upright Rows as a variation. The constant resistance of the cable helps you do the movement as strictly as possible.)

Shawn Ray

HEAVY UPRIGHT ROWS

Purpose of Exercise: A heavy cheating movement for advanced bodybuilders to strengthen the entire shoulder girdle and upper back.

Execution: (1) Choose a heavy barbell and grasp it with an overhand grip, hands about 12 inches apart. Let the bar hang down at arm's length in front of you. (2) Lift the bar straight up to a point just below your chin, allowing yourself to cheat by swaying with the back, pushing with the legs, and even helping with the calves. As you lift, keep your elbows out and up higher than the bar. Then lower the bar back to the starting position. Remember, this is a power movement in which cheating plays a vital part. This makes Heavy Upright Rows quite a different exercise from standard Upright Rows, which must be done very strictly.

Rich Gaspari

DUMBBELL SHRUGS

Purpose of Exercise: To develop the trapezius muscles.

This exercise can be done extremely heavy to thicken the traps, which really helps you in doing back poses.

Execution: Stand upright, arms at sides, a heavy dumbbell in each hand. Raise your shoulders up as high as you can, as if trying to touch them to your ears. Hold at the top for a moment, then release and return to the starting position. Try not to move anything but your shoulders.

BARBELL SHRUGS

PURPOSE OF EXERCISE: To develop the trapezius muscles.

EXECUTION: Stand upright, holding a barbell at arm's length in front of you, using an overhand grip. Raise your shoulders as high as you can, as if trying to touch them to your ears. Hold in this position for a moment, then lower the bar, under control, back to the starting position.

You can sometimes find Shrug machines in a gym and can also use a variety of Bench Press machines to do Shrugs as well. To get really heavy, try to position a barbell on a low support using a Squat rack, which lets you handle very heavy poundages without having to expend energy lifting the bar off the floor.

The Chest

THE MUSCLES OF THE CHEST

The **pectorals** consist of two parts, the clavicular (upper) portion and the sternal (lower) portion. The upper part is attached to the clavicle (collarbone). Along the mid-body line, it attaches to the sternum (breastbone) and the cartilage of several ribs. The largest mass of the pectorals starts at the upper arm bone (humerus), fastened at a point under and just above where the deltoids attach to the humerus. The pectorals spread out like a fan and cover the rib cage like armor plates. Attached to the rib cage in the center and across to the shoulder, this muscle lets you perform such motions as pitching a ball underhanded, doing a wide-arm Bench Press, twisting a cap off a bottle, swimming the crawl stroke, and doing parallel bar Dips. In addition, because of its attachment to the humerus, it plays a large role in movements like Chinning. There is, in fact, a prominent interdependence between chest and back muscles. The chest will not reach its full potential size unless the latissimus dorsi muscles of the upper back are fully developed.

Basic function: To pull the arm and shoulder across the front of the body

The **subclavius,** a small cylindrical muscle between the clavicle and the first rib

Basic function: To draw the shoulder forward

The **serratus anterior,** a thin muscular sheet between the ribs and the scapula

Basic function: To rotate the scapula, raising the point of the shoulder and drawing the scapular forward and downward

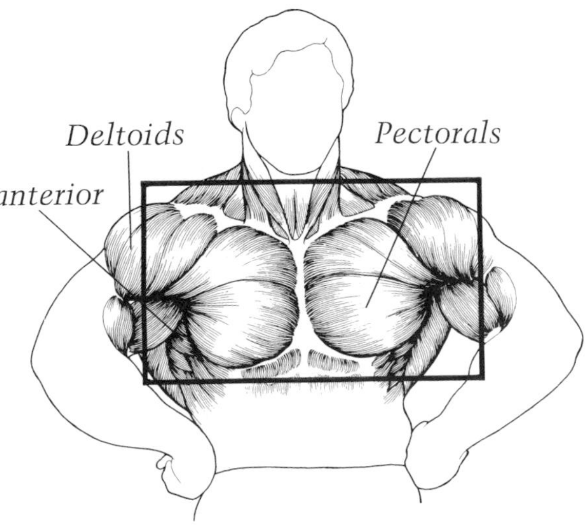

TOTAL CHEST DEVELOPMENT

A really deep, well-shaped chest is one of the most important qualities in a bodybuilding physique. To achieve this requires training with a variety of exercises—to develop the upper and lower pectorals, the inside and outside pectorals, and the tie-ins to the deltoids, and to expand the entire rib cage to show off the pectoral muscles to their best advantage.

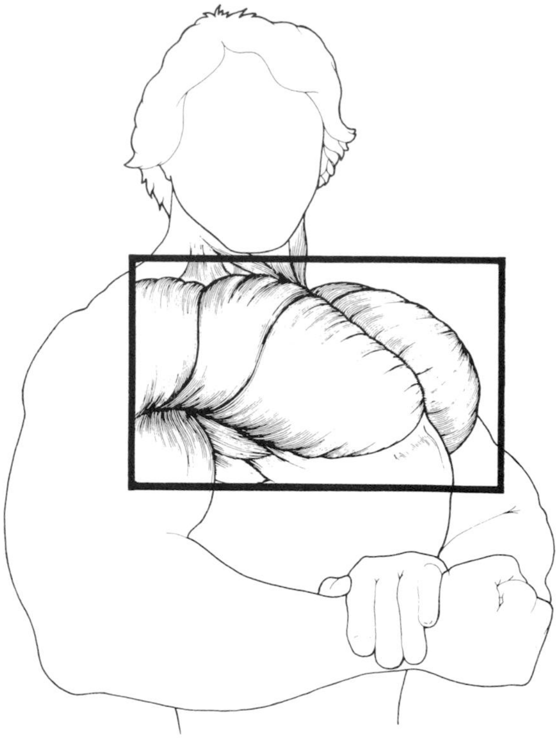

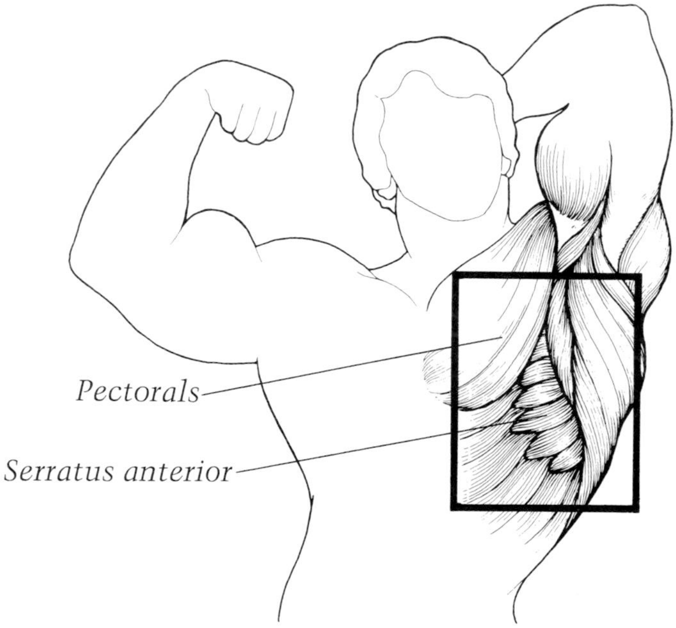

Pectorals

Serratus anterior

But perfecting the chest is more difficult than many bodybuilders believe. You can have a huge rib cage and huge, thick pectoral muscles, but this will not guarantee a perfect chest. Chest perfection, especially if you are interested in competition, involves all of the following:

1. A great rib cage
2. Thick pectoral muscles
3. Development of the inside, outside, upper, and lower areas of the pectorals

This is what you need to make a side chest pose really effective: a great rib cage under big, fully developed pectoral muscles.

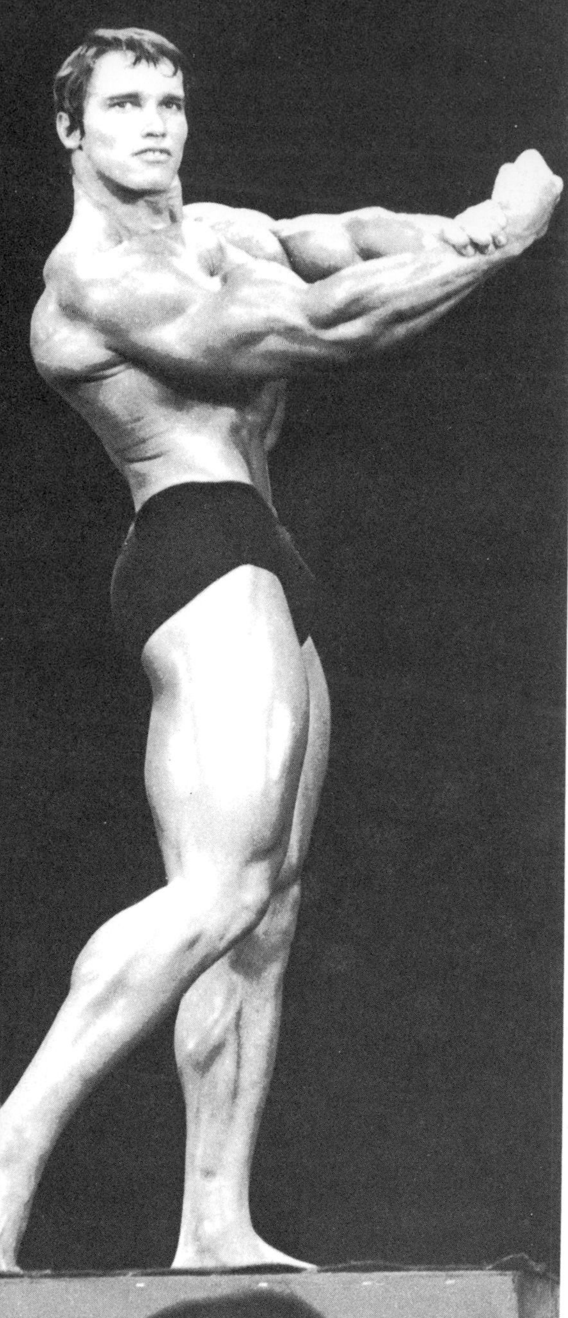

Thick pectoral muscles complement deltoid and upper-arm muscularity in a straight-arm side pose.

4. Visible striations when the pectorals are flexed, such as in a most-muscular shot, with the striations showing from the middle of the rib cage all the way across and from top to bottom
5. A clear separation of upper and lower pectorals
6. A shape that gives a nice square look, achieved by a lot of upper pectoral development, rather than one in which the muscle seems simply to be hanging down
7. Sufficient development so that the pectorals don't totally disappear when you lift your arms over your head or do a front double-biceps shot

The chest program included here is specifically designed to help you achieve complete pectoral development as just outlined. Of course, some bodybuilders are extremely lucky in their genetic potential for chest development. Sergio Oliva used to do only one kind of exercise for the chest—Bench Presses—and his chest muscles would rise like a loaf of bread. Reg Park is gifted with an enormous rib cage, making his pectoral development all the more impressive. John Grimek also displayed a wonderful rib cage that made his chest poses look terrific. As a former

When Franco Columbu hit a chest pose, you could see every area of the chest clearly delineated—the upper and lower chest, the separation of upper chest from deltoids, the inner pectorals, and the tie-in of the chest to the serratus.

The chest is the centerpiece of the most-muscular pose. Notice how the striations of the pectorals hold together all the other elements: the traps, front delts, arms, and abdominals.

Franco Columbu probably has the most separation of upper and lower chest of anyone in bodybuilding.

Serge Nubret's chest development is complete, including upper and lower, inner and outer pectorals. That's what gives him the desired square shape in this picture.

powerlifter, Franco Columbu has developed his chest so that the split between upper and lower pecs is awesome. Sometimes we used to jokingly refer to this vast chasm as the "Grand Canyon."

But genetically gifted or not, if you want to be a complete bodybuilder you need to develop your chest properly, and this means making up with skill, effort, and technique for what nature may have neglected to hand you on a silver platter.

As Steve Reeves demonstrates, with proper chest development your pectorals will not disappear when you lift your arms above your head.

Really thick pectorals allow a bodybuilder to hit a lot of very powerful poses, and when it comes to Herculean chest development, Casey Viator and Dorian Yates have always been among the most impressive.

TRAINING THE CHEST

There are two basic kinds of exercises for the chest: *Flys,* in which the extended arms are drawn together across the chest in a kind of hugging motion; and *Presses,* in which the weight is pressed upward off the chest with the involvement of the front deltoids and triceps in addition to a primary effort from the pectorals. The basic Bench Press is done with a barbell on a flat bench and is an all-time favorite exercise of bodybuilders as well as one of the three movements used in powerlifting competition. If you do Bench Presses correctly—using the proper grip and getting the fullest range of motion possible—you will be able to develop the overall mass of the chest.

However, changing the angle of the Bench Press—by doing it on an incline, for example—you transfer more of the effort from the middle pectorals to the upper pectorals and front deltoids. I believe in including Incline Presses in your program right from the beginning so that you don't find your upper pecs are underdeveloped relative to the middle and lower portions of your chest. Also, doing a lot of Incline Presses will help you create that split between upper and lower chest that is so impressive in most-muscular poses.

As with training other muscles, the greater the range of motion you get in chest exercises, the more intense the muscle contraction you achieve—which ultimately leads to the maximum amount of muscle growth. Therefore, especially when you are doing Flys, it is very important to stretch the pectorals as much as you can. This helps develop maximum flexibility, and increased flexibility results in more development. This is why so many of the top bodybuilders, as massive as you can imagine, are also flexible enough to twist themselves into pretzels.

But simply having large pectoral muscles is not enough if they are hung on a small, unimpressive rib cage. Though it's subject to controversy, I am convinced that I could effectively expand the rib cage by performing Dumbbell Pullovers. Be aware, however, that Pullovers performed on machines do not have the same effect. When you are locked into a machine the latissimus muscles bear most of the stress, so you do not get as much expansion of the rib cage.

As you progress in your training, you need to build on the basics and pay more attention to details. So that every area is reached for complete pectoral development I recommend including in your program a lot of Dumbbell Flys, Cable Crossovers, Dips, and other pectoral exercises.

Also, as you become more advanced, the program is designed so that you superset chest training with back movements. I believe that the pectorals, like the lats, need to be stretched as much as possible as well as developed by resistance exercise. Therefore, after you do an exercise like a Bench Press, you should immediately go to something like Chins, which stretch the pecs to the fullest. This is also a highly time-efficient way to train, since you can work a different set of muscles while the first group is recuperating, making your workouts go much faster and burning off extra calories.

In the Advanced Program you also need to concern yourself with the serratus muscles, which are just below and to the side of the chest. The serratus will be dealt with in a special section, along with the intercostals. Development of these muscles shows the judges that you have achieved a high degree of quality as well as mass.

BEGINNING AND ADVANCED PROGRAMS

In my own early training, I practiced what I am now preaching: I started with the basics—Bench and Incline Presses, Dumbbell Flys, Dips, and Pullovers. After three years I was still doing only these five basic chest exercises.

When I moved to Munich after having been training for about four years, my pectorals were huge and I had certain weaknesses—upper pecs, for example. There I began training with my friend Reinhard Smolana, who showed me a very different kind of pectoral training. We would begin by doing Incline Presses standing and leaning back against a bench—which meant we had to clean the weight, fall back against the bench, do the set, then manage to stand upright again and put the weight back down. Only after we finished our Incline Press sets would we go on and do Bench Presses and Flys.

This emphasis on Incline Presses had its effect—after a while my upper pecs grew enormously until I could literally stand a glass of water on the upper part of my chest when I hit a side chest shot. Seeing how a change in one's training program can overcome a weak point was an important lesson for me.

Incidentally, this particular way of doing Incline Presses, having to clean the weight and handle the bar as I was falling back against the bench, gave me a secondary benefit—it enabled me to develop enormous strength, and with that strength came the added thickness and density that results from power training with heavy weights.

Dorian Yates has great upper chest development

By increasing the development of my upper pecs, I was learning two important lessons about how to sculpt the body and train for physical perfection: (1) It pays to put special emphasis on weak areas, especially to train them first when you are strong and fresh (Priority Principle); and (2) changing your training routine so that the body has to perform in unexpected ways accelerates development (Shocking Principle).

I also discovered how much the training ideas in any gym affect those who train there: In Austria, where the first exercise bodybuilders wanted to do was Curls, everyone had great biceps; in Munich, where we all used the same chest routine, everyone had good upper pecs; in Reg Park's gym, everyone had terrific calves and deltoids, just like Reg, but relatively less developed pecs because Reg himself believed excessive pec development interfered with the impressiveness of shoulder width.

It was also in the early days that I discovered the advantages of stretching the pectoral muscles while training them. Doing Dumbbell Flys or cable exercises, I would always stretch the chest muscles to their limit and then frequently include some back movements to further stretch the pecs.

One's particular anatomy can make certain exercises more or less effective. Bodybuilders like Nasser El Sonbaty, with huge, barrel-like chests and short arms, get very little out of doing regular Bench Presses unless they use an extraordinary amount of weight. When Nasser lowers the bar down to his massive chest and then lifts the bar back up, because of his relatively short arms he has more limited range of motion than somebody with a different structure, so the pectorals never get the kind of workout they need. People with this body type usually need to include more Incline Presses in their workouts or do Presses with dumbbells instead of a barbell so that they can lower the weights down past the top of the chest. This doesn't mean they shouldn't do Barbell Bench Presses at all, just that they must also include exercises with a greater range of motion. (I have also seen a bar used that has a curve in the middle, allowing you to drop your hands much lower when doing a Bench Press and thereby extending the range of motion considerably.)

Ken Waller (featured in both *Pumping Iron* and *Stay Hungry*) had enormously strong front deltoids. When he did a Bench Press, his delts got a tremendous pump and his pectorals seemed to work hardly at all. So Ken always relied a lot on Decline Dumbbell Presses instead.

In all matters involving your genetic inheritance and your natural leverage advantages and disadvantages, you are going to have to learn to adjust your training accordingly.

COMPETITION PROGRAM

When I first came to the United States, I already had plenty of size so I began to concentrate on detail training. I developed a more sophisticated program with additional exercises which included a lot of isolation movements for each of the important pectoral areas. Experts like the late Vince Gironda gave me a lot of ideas, so I went from simply having huge pecs to having first-rate chest development.

Each time I competed I learned something more. Gradually, I mastered all of the training principles outlined in this book from the Stripping Method to forced reps, and so on. And I learned from competitors like Serge Nubret, Frank Zane, and Franco Columbu that it takes a lot of dieting and, especially, endless hours of posing to give the chest the totally finished, muscular and defined look.

I have always gotten good results finishing off my chest workout with a triset—for example, a set of Dumbell Flys, then Dips, followed by Cable Crossovers. This pumps an enormous amount of blood into the area and forces you to go all out at the end, rather than pacing yourself and taking it easy—to make you hard, defined, and competition-ready.

As you prepare for competition, you need to concern yourself with even more specific details—things that you would hardly notice at other times suddenly become major weak points. For example, I have seen bodybuilders hitting a side chest pose and showing striations in the inner pecs, but not farther up on the chest. This kind of detail can make a big difference in a close contest. Therefore, I would advise these bodybuilders to superset Incline Presses (with a barbell or dumbbells) with Cable Crossovers to rectify this weakness. Sergio Oliva used to force his muscles to work in harder and unexpected ways by doing only three-quarter movements, lifting the bar off his chest in a Bench Press, for example, but not going all the way up, so that the triceps never came into play in the movement and his chest never got any rest at all. After using this method of training for just a few months, I found my chest became much harder-looking and more defined—which shows you how relatively small alterations in your training technique can make very substantial differences in your physique.

The Competition Program for the chest is designed on a push-pull basis, combining movements for chest and back done as supersets and trisets. Combining these exercises gives you a tremendous pump, and will really blast your chest muscles and give them the size, shape, definition, and tie-ins you need for successful competition.

Supersets like Weighted Chins plus Incline Bench Presses, Flat Bench Presses plus Wide-Grip Chins, and Dumbbell Flys plus Bent-Over Barbell Rows keep the back and chest pumped at the same time and allow you to train pectorals and lats each in turn—muscles which work in opposition to each other—so that one has a chance to rest while the other does a set. And since you are dealing with opposing muscles, every set for the back helps stretch the pectorals while they are recuperating for the next chest set.

WEAK POINT TRAINING

As with any other body part, once you have been training for a while you are likely to notice that some areas of the chest are developing better and more rapidly than others. To correct this imbalance, you will have to alter your program and include more exercises to stimulate the areas that are lagging behind. Following is a list of exercises for improving each area of the chest, though no exercise works in complete isolation.

Serge Nubret has developed one of the most balanced chests in the world, with every one of the pectoral areas in complete proportion to the rest.

Upper Pectorals

Incline Presses with a barbell or dumbbells or Smith machine
Incline Flys

Lower Pectorals

Decline Presses with a barbell or dumbbells or machines
Dips
Decline Flys
Cable Flys

Inner Chest

Cable Crossovers
Presses or Flys holding the contraction at top for several seconds
Bench Presses done with narrow grip

Outer Chest

Dumbbell Flys concentrating on full stretch and lower range of motion
Dips
Incline Presses and Bench Presses done with a wide grip and lower three-quarter movement
Dumbbell Flys
Dumbbell Bench Presses stretching at bottom, coming up only three-quarters of the way and not letting dumbbells touch
Incline Presses with bar

Rib Cage

Dumbbell and Barbell Pullovers

When you have a weak point in chest development, train your pectorals according to the Priority Principle, doing the exercise for that weak area first, when you are fresh and at your strongest. In the early stages of my career, I always felt I suffered from a comparative lack of upper pectoral development. So I would begin my chest training with Barbell Incline Presses followed by Dumbbell Incline Presses to really hit this area. Only then would I go on to regular Bench Presses and the rest of my chest routine.

But there are times when this kind of specialized weak point training is not justified. For example, if you have problems with the inner chest, I would not recommend starting out your routine with an exercise like Cable Crossovers. Instead, try to work on this area as you are doing the rest

This is the proper way to do Narrow-Grip Bench Presses: Keeping the elbows out and away from the body at the bottom of the movement . . .

. . . allows a full contraction of the pectorals at the top, which helps to develop the inner part of the chest.

This shot of Hamdullah Aykutlu shows clearly the sharp and defined development of his inner chest.

Taking a wide grip on the bar . . .

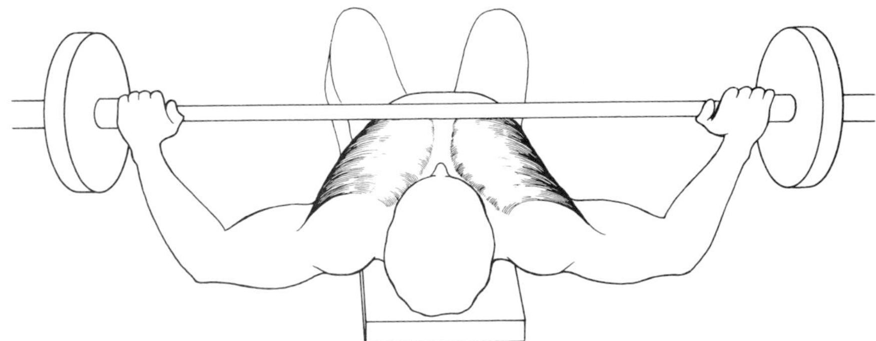

. . . allows you to get a tremendous stretch in the pectoral muscles as you lower the weight. This is very effective in developing the outer pectorals.

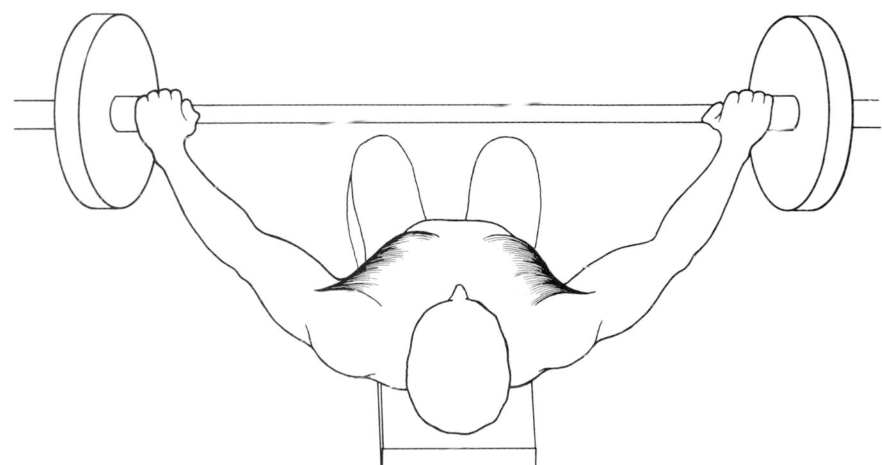

The development of the outer chest is what gives the pectorals a really full look when seen from the front. In this photo I am standing relaxed, but my outer pecs and biceps are almost touching.

This picture of Dorian Yates shows how important a good rib cage is for executing a side chest pose.

of your chest workout—perhaps locking out all of your pressing movements, and really tensing and contracting the inner pecs. Then, at the end of your workout, you could add on some extra Cable Crossovers or other exercises specifically designed to hit the inner chest.

The same thing can be done for outer chest development. You can emphasize this area during your routine by lowering the weights a few inches farther when doing Dumbbell Flys and by getting the fullest possible stretch with other pectoral exercises. You don't have to schedule specific outer pec movements at the top of your routine in order to deal with this weak point the way you would if your problem was the upper, lower, or middle chest. The most adjustment I would recommend for pectoral weak points would be to widen your grip while doing Bench Presses in order to hit the outer pecs or use a narrow grip to work the inside pecs harder.

When doing Presses the area of the pecs you work hardest is determined by the angle at which you do the exercise. For example, in training the upper chest I used to start out doing 3 sets of Dumbbell Incline Presses at an angle of only 15 degrees. I would go to 25, 35, 50 degrees, and so on, doing 3 sets at each angle. At the end of a workout like that, I could feel I had really blasted the entire upper chest and that no part of that area had escaped attention.

Barbell exercises normally allow you to use more weight, so you develop maximum mass and strength. Dumbbell exercises give you a longer range of motion, so you get more extension and contraction. Cables allow you to work at a variety of angles, so you get more shaping for a better finished look. A disadvantage of machine training for the chest is that the apparatus only lets you work at very specific angles, but you can turn that to an advantage if you want to work the muscle at that angle to develop a weak area.

Dumbbell Flys are ideal for developing the outer pecs, but you need to employ a particular technique to get the most out of this movement. Lie on a bench and let the dumbbells down just as far as you can. Then when you come up, stop about three-quarters of the way. This technique puts all the effort on the outer pecs and never lets them disengage from the exercise.

But you can use Dumbbell Flys to work the inner pectorals as well, by bringing the weights all the way up, squeezing the muscles together at the top, and even crossing the dumbbells over slightly to get a full contraction of the inner pectorals.

Inner pectoral development in general comes about by working the top range of pectoral movements—a Bench Press with a narrower grip, for example, with the bar pushed all the way up; or Cable Crossovers, letting the arms cross over each other, which really contracts the inner pecs.

Decline exercises work the lower pec region more intensely. These include Decline Presses, Decline Flys, Decline Cable movements, and Dips. I like Dips because, by bending farther forward or holding yourself straighter, you can change the way the stress hits the muscle even right in the middle of a set.

If your pectorals just seem to disappear when you raise your arms over your head, I recommend doing a series of Incline Dumbbell Presses at a variety of angles, starting out almost flat and going up until you are almost doing a Shoulder Press. This will produce the kind of total development that gives you impressive pecs even when your arms are raised or when doing a front double-biceps shot.

There are exercises you might do for weak point training that you would never do in a normal workout if you weren't trying to overcome a problem. This is why I caution young bodybuilders against simply copying what they see a champion doing in the gym. He may be doing some sort of One-Arm Cable Lateral motion at a special angle in order to deal with a weak point. If you assume that exercise is a standard one and include it in your regular routine, you might end up wasting a lot of time and energy and holding back your overall progress.

Remember, even when doing weak point training, don't totally neglect any area of the muscle group. However, you can cut down on the number of exercises that work a strong area while adding extra movements to work a weak point.

Some experts say that you can't develop the size of your rib cage once you reach a certain age—about the early twenties. It is certainly true that the cartilage binding the rib cage stretches more easily at a younger age, but I have seen too many older bodybuilders improve their rib cage size to believe that this cannot be done. It is just a matter of time, effort, and patience—like so much else in the discipline of bodybuilding.

Finally, remember that the best way to force a weak body part to develop is by using a variety of Shocking Principles to increase training intensity. Chuck Sipes always liked to do Bench Presses using the Stripping Method. He would start off pressing around 400 pounds, do as many reps as he could, and then have his training partner strip plates off the bar so that he could keep going and really blast his pectorals. You can also use techniques like forced reps, Rest/Pause, three-quarter movements, Staggered Sets, or anything else that will force the kind of development you need.

I especially like the idea of heavy days for maximum chest development. Once a week I usually trained my chest with extra heavy weight: 5 or 6 reps at the most, 100-pound Flys, Incline Presses using 365 pounds for 6 to 8 reps, super-heavy (450-pound) Bench Presses to produce the maximum pectoral mass and thickness.

POWER TRAINING

To develop maximum power, mass, and strength in the chest, I recommend a program in which you:

1. Begin with Bench Presses. Do 20 reps the first set, then 10 reps. At this point, raise the weight so you go immediately down to 5 reps, 3 reps, and 1 rep.

2. Continue doing as many sets as you can (at least 5) with a weight that allows you only 1 or 2 repetitions.

3. Perform the last set with a lighter weight that allows you to go back up to high repetitions.

4. Go on to Incline Presses and do them the same way. Afterward, follow the same program with Dumbbell Flys.

POSING AND FLEXING

On heavy days especially, I always include a great deal of posing and flexing along with heavy weight training. Hitting a lot of side chest shots and most-muscular poses along with intense training is the best way I know to bring out pectoral striations. I've seen a lot of bodybuilders try to create these striations by artificial means—dehydrating themselves with diuretics, for example—but it just never looks as good as the results you get from hard training, posing, and flexing.

Learning to pose the chest properly takes a lot of practice. When you do a side chest shot, a front double-biceps, a most-muscular, or a front lat shot, in each shot the chest is posed differently and you need to practice each of these poses separately to get the effect you want. For a front double-biceps, you need to pose with your shoulders forward to create that sweeping line of the chest from sternum to deltoid; in the side chest shot, you need to keep the shoulder down and lift the chest to make it look high and full. Flexing the chest as you train it is the only way to create maximum pectoral definition—and endless hours of posing practice is the only method that will give you total control of your physique for presentation.

Not only do you constantly need to pose and flex your pectoral muscles, you also need to practice a variety of ways of showing off the chest. Here, I am doing a side chest shot.

Franco Columbu checks out his inner pectoral development.

The front double-biceps shot is one of the most difficult in bodybuilding. Any faults you have become immediately visible, especially if your chest tends to disappear when you lift your arms.

Sometimes you don't need to pose at all—just flex your pecs as hard as possible, hold it, and see what happens.

When you hit a most-muscular pose, the chest should look like an anatomy chart—every area developed, defined, separated, and striated.

Upper and outer pec development is particularly important when you hit a front lat spread.

THE SERRATUS MUSCLES

The serratus muscles lie parallel to the ribs, coming out from under the lats and forward to tie into the pectorals and the intercostals and downward to the external obliques. When they are properly developed, these muscles look like fingers, with each digitation clearly defined and separated from the others. The serratus muscles are not like other muscles in that you don't measure their level of development with a tape measure; it is their visual impact that makes the difference.

Complete serratus development is important for a variety of reasons: For one, it announces clearly that this bodybuilder has achieved real quality detail training; for another, the serratus helps separate the lats from the chest and the obliques, and aids in making them appear much larger when seen from the front. Good serratus development also helps make you more symmetrical and athletic.

Steve Reeves at fifteen

Some people are naturally gifted with great serratus development. There is a photo of Steve Reeves doing a front lat spread when he was fifteen years old and had been training for only a year—and sure enough, you can see the serratus already several fingers deep. Later, when he went on to win the NABBA Mr. Universe contest, his serratus development was really spectacular.

Bill Pearl was able to combine impressive size with aesthetic qualities like highly defined serratus muscles, proving that you can achieve both mass and quality without compromising either. Pearl was able to hit a variety of overhead and front poses because of his outstanding serratus development, and this made him a much more formidable opponent on the competition stage.

However, if you weren't born with great serratus development you can train for it by making a conscious effort to bring out these muscles. Frank Zane worked very hard at serratus training, and this helped establish him as a model for the complete bodybuilder and win three Mr. Olympia titles. Like Bill Pearl, Zane has found that his superior serratus development allows him to do a greater number of poses effectively, especially the aesthetic hands-over-the-head shots. (I recall standing onstage next to Zane in 1968, outweighing him by fifty pounds, and discovering that his lat spread was more effective than mine because of the tremendous lat separation his serratus development gave him. You can bet I started training the serratus extra hard after that!)

Reeves, Zane, and Pearl were my inspiration for developing the serratus. When they hit poses, especially ones in which the arms are raised, they demonstrated to me exactly what the serratus should look like.

Steve Reeves at twenty-four as Mr. Universe

TRAINING THE SERRATUS

Since a basic function of the serratus is to pull the shoulder forward and down, you train these muscles whenever you do movements like Chins, Close-Grip Pulldowns, various kinds of Dumbbell and Barbell Pullovers, and when you use the Nautilus Pullover machine. (When I do Dumbbell Pullovers, the structure of my body is such that this exercise becomes a rib cage expander. For others with different proportions—like Frank Zane and Bill Pearl—Dumbbell Pullovers tend to hit them more in the serratus.) There are, however, two exercises that work those muscles more specifically and that you can use if you have a weak point in this area: Rope Pulls and One-Arm Cable Pulls. In both cases, you have to do the movement as strictly as possible to get the maximum effect.

Working the chest and back with Chins and Pullovers, you will have already done some serratus work. This is the time to consciously isolate the serratus, to concentrate on making these muscles burn. It is not enough just to throw in a few sets for the serratus, any more than for abs, calves, or intercostals. You need to train each muscle with maximum intensity if you want a complete and quality physique.

The combination of outstanding serratus development and an impressive vacuum make this hands-over-the-head pose one of Frank Zane's best.

Chest Exercises

BARBELL FLAT BENCH PRESSES

Purpose of Exercise: To build mass and strength in the pectorals, front delts, and triceps.

The Bench Press is a fundamental compound exercise for the upper body. It produces growth, strength, and muscle density, not only for the chest muscles but for the front deltoids and triceps as well.

Execution: (1) Lie on a flat bench, your feet on the floor for balance. Your grip should be medium-wide (which means that as you lower the bar to your chest, your hands should be wide enough apart so that your forearms point straight up, perpendicular to the floor). Lift the bar off the rack and hold it at arm's length above you. (2) Lower the bar slowly and under control until it touches just below the pectoral muscles. Keep the elbows pointed outward in order to fully involve the chest. The bar should come to a complete stop at this point. Press the bar upward once more until your arms are fully locked out. Always go through a full range of motion unless instructed specifically to do otherwise.

The classic Bench Press starting position: The hands are positioned on the bar slightly wider than shoulder width. This distributes the stress so that the pectorals do a major part of the work, with minimal front deltoid and triceps involvement.

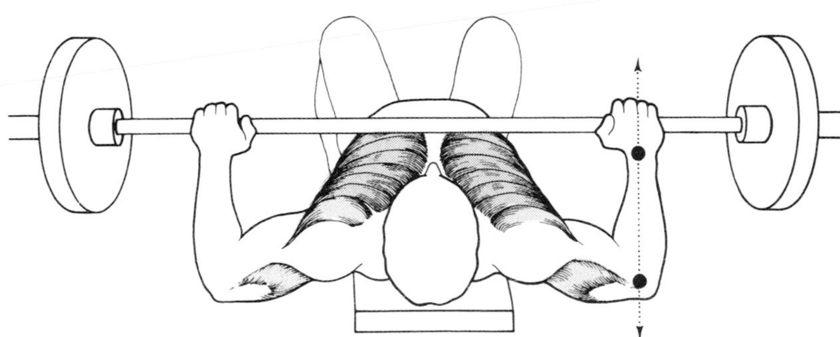

Notice that as the weight is lowered to the chest, the hand position is such that the forearms end up perpendicular to the floor. This hand position gives the best overall results, developing the complete pectoral muscle—inner, outer, and through the middle.

I frequently did my heavy chest training on Sundays at Venice Beach. I got extra motivation for doing reps with 450 pounds because so many people were standing around watching me.

BARBELL INCLINE BENCH PRESSES

Purpose of Exercise: To develop the mass and strength of the pectoral muscles (middle and upper regions) and front deltoids.

Changing the angle of the movement so you are pressing at an incline tends to put extra stress on the upper chest muscles and make the deltoids work harder. But you will find you can't lift as much weight as you can when doing a Flat Bench Press.

Execution: (1) Lie back on an incline bench. Reach up and grasp the bar with a medium-wide grip. Lift the bar off the rack and hold it straight up overhead, arms locked. (2) Lower the weight down to the upper chest, stop for a moment, then press it back up to the starting position. When working at an incline, it is extremely important to find the right "groove" or you are likely to find the bar drifting too far forward. It is useful to have a training partner to spot you while you are getting used to this movement.

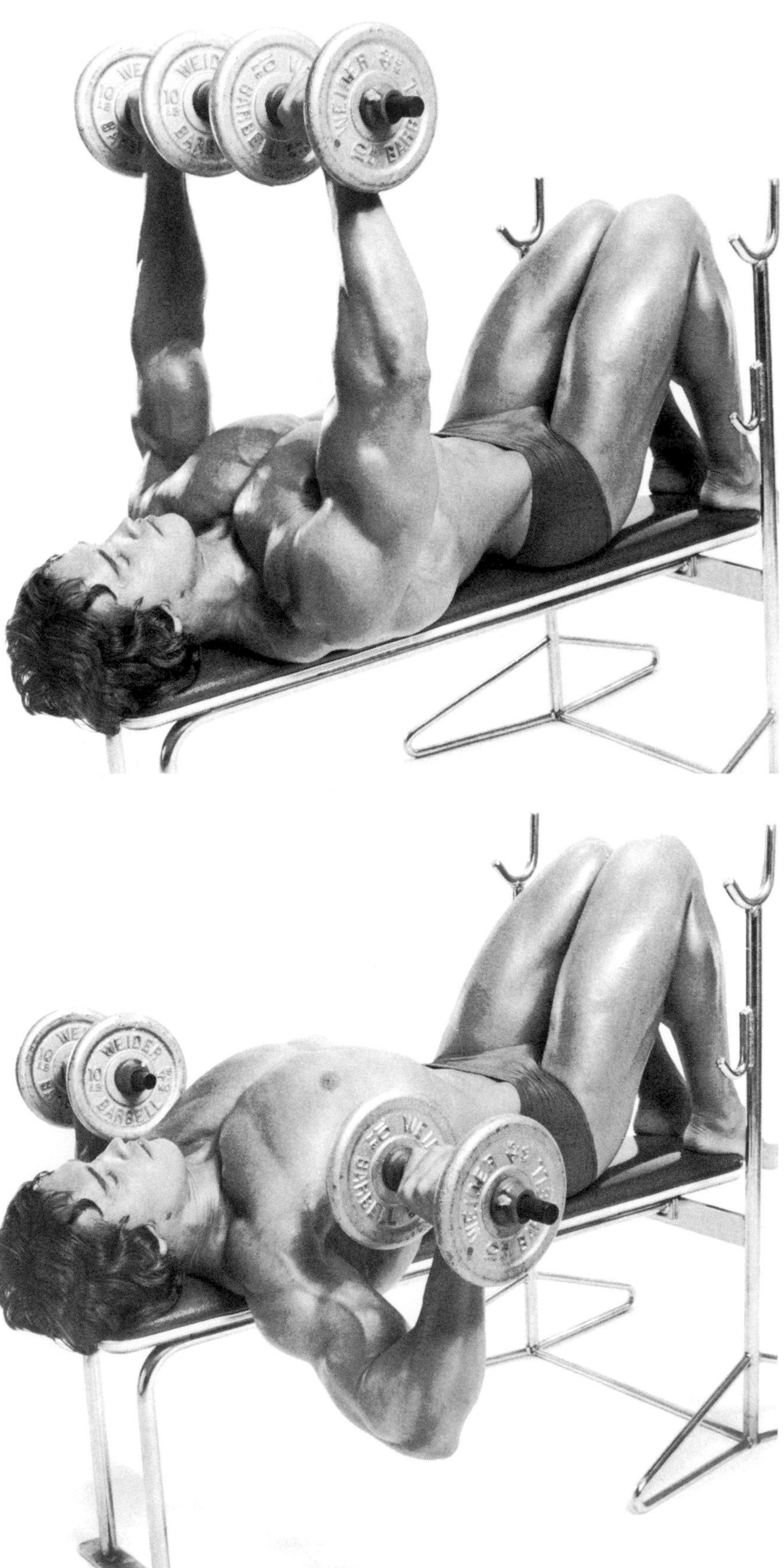

DUMBBELL FLAT BENCH PRESSES

PURPOSE OF EXERCISE: To develop the mass and strength of the middle and outer pectoral muscles. By using dumbbells rather than barbells, you can work the chest muscles through a greater range of motion, and the need to balance and coordinate two separate weights forces stabilizer muscles to assist as well.

EXECUTION: (1) Lie on a flat bench, knees bent, feet flat on the bench or floor. Take a dumbbell in each hand and hold the weights straight up overhead. Turn the dumbbells so that your palms face forward. (2) Lower the weights toward your outer chest, concentrating on keeping them fully balanced and under control. Lower them as far as you can, feeling a complete stretch in the pectoral muscles. Press the weights back up and lock your arms straight overhead.

Lee Priest

INCLINE DUMBBELL PRESSES

PURPOSE OF EXERCISE: To develop the middle and upper pectoral muscles. You can vary the angle of the incline bench from almost flat to almost upright; the more upright the bench, the more you work the delts.

EXECUTION: (1) Take a dumbbell in each hand and lie back on an incline bench. Clean the dumbbells and hold them at shoulder height, palms facing forward. (2) Lift them simultaneously straight up overhead, then lower them back to the starting position. As a variation, you can begin with palms facing each other and twist your wrists as you lift so that the palms face forward at the top, then twist them back to the starting position as you lower the dumbbells. You can vary the angle at which you train from workout to workout, or from set to set in the same workout. If you do the latter, begin at a steep incline and work downward toward a flatter angle or increase the angle set to set.

DECLINE DUMBBELL PRESSES

PURPOSE OF EXERCISE: To develop the middle and lower pectoral muscles.

EXECUTION: (1) Take a dumbbell in each hand and lie back on a decline bench. Hold the weights at shoulder height, palms facing forward. (2) Lift the dumbbells simultaneously straight up overhead, then lower them slowly back to the starting position.

Kevin Levrone

PARALLEL BAR DIPS

Purpose of Exercise: To develop the pectoral muscles, triceps secondarily.

Dips are a chest and triceps exercise that have a similar effect on the body as Decline Presses. However, with Dips you begin training with your own body weight, but can continue to progressively increase the resistance by holding a dumbbell between your legs or hooking a weight to the appropriate kind of belt. You can get a very long range of motion with this exercise.

Execution: (1) Hold yourself at arm's length above the bars, (2) then lower yourself slowly as far as you can. From the bottom, press back up to the starting position, tensing the pectorals at the top. In this movement, the farther forward you lean, the more chest you involve, so try crossing your feet behind your glutes, which will shift your center of gravity forward and hit the pectorals harder.

Porter Cottrell

MACHINE PRESSES

PURPOSE OF EXERCISE: To work the pectoral muscles. One of the advantages of doing Presses on a machine is that the machine stays in a certain groove, precluding any need for spending energy on balance and coordination. This is especially beneficial for people rehabbing a shoulder injury. Also, using a machine, your workout partner can push down on the mechanism to allow you to do heavy forced negative repetitions. However, being forced to stay in that groove somewhat limits the stimulation to the muscles.

Flat Bench Machine Presses. The pectoral station of most machines is constructed to give you a flat Bench Press movement.

Incline Machine Presses. Using an incline bench and a Smith machine, you can mimic certain angles of the free-weight movement in a very strict manner.

Decline Machine Presses. A decline bench on a Smith machine effectively allows you to press at a decline angle.

DUMBBELL FLYS

PURPOSE OF EXERCISE: To develop the mass of the pectorals.

The function of the pectorals is basically to pull the arms and shoulders inward across the body, and this is exactly what you do using a Dumbbell Fly movement.

EXECUTION: (1) Lie on a bench holding dumbbells at arm's length above you, palms facing each other. (2) Lower the weights out and down to either side in a wide arc as far as you can, feeling the pectoral muscles stretch to their maximum. The palms should remain facing each other throughout the movement. Bend the arms slightly as you do the movement to reduce the stress on the elbows. Bring the weights to a complete stop at a point in line with the bench, your pectorals stretched as much as possible, then lift them back up along the same wide arc, as if giving somebody a big bear hug, rather than coming in and pressing the weights up. Bring the weights back up to the starting position and then contract the pectorals further, giving a little extra flex to make the muscle work that much harder.

INCLINE DUMBBELL FLYS

PURPOSE OF EXERCISE: To build the mass of the upper pectorals.

EXECUTION: These Flys are done like normal Dumbbell Flys, except you lie on an incline bench, with your head higher than your hips. (1) Lie on the bench with the dumbbells held straight overhead, palms facing each other. (2) Lower them out and down to either side in a wide, sweeping arc, keeping the palms facing each other and bending the elbows slightly. Lower the weights until your pectorals are fully stretched. Come back up through that same wide arc, as if giving a big hug. Avoid bringing the weights in and pressing them straight up. At the top, flex the pectoral muscles to ensure a full contraction.

Shawn Ray

STANDING CABLE CROSSOVERS

Purpose of Exercise: To develop the inside of the pectoral muscle.

Doing a flying motion using cables to provide resistance is a specialized exercise that works the center of the pecs and brings out those impressive cross striations, as well as develops the middle and lower pectoral region.

Execution: (1) To do this movement from a standing position, take hold of handles attached by cables to overhead pulleys, step slightly forward of the line directly between the pulleys, and extend your arms almost straight out to either side. (2) Bend forward slightly from the waist, then bring your hands around and forward in a big hugging motion, elbows slightly bent, feeling the pectoral muscles contracting. When your hands come together in the center don't stop—cross one hand over the other and contract your chest muscles as much as you can. On each repetition of this movement, alternate which hand crosses over the other.

Paul Dillett

BENT-FORWARD CABLE CROSSOVERS

PURPOSE OF EXERCISE: To work the inside of the middle and lower pectoral muscles.

EXECUTION: (1) Using two floor-level pulleys, grasp a handle in each hand and bend forward, extending your arms out to either side. (2) Draw your hands toward each other, allow them to cross, and continue pulling until you feel your pectorals contract to the maximum. Hold for a moment and flex for extra contraction, then release and let your arms be pulled back to the starting position.

Porter Cottrell

FLAT BENCH CABLE CROSSOVERS

Purpose of Exercise: To develop and define the middle and inner pectoral muscles.

Execution: (1) Lie on a flat bench between two floor-level pulleys. Take a handle in each hand and bring your hands together at arm's length above you, palms facing each other.
(2) With your elbows slightly bent, lower your hands out to either side in a wide arc until your pectorals are fully stretched. Bring your arms back toward the starting position, passing through the same sweeping arc as if giving a big hug. You can stop at the top or continue on and cross your arms over slightly to create the fullest possible contraction of the pectorals.

Lee Labrada

MACHINE FLYS

PURPOSE OF EXERCISE: To build middle chest size and definition and striations in the pectoral muscles.

Fly machines are not your best choice for building mass, but are very useful in creating definition.

EXECUTION: Many gyms are equipped with a variety of "pec decks" that approximate the flying motion. When using these in your training, work toward getting the fullest possible range of motion, stretching the pectorals to the maximum at full extension, then giving the muscles an extra, isometric contraction once you've brought your arms as close together as possible.

Sonny Schmidt

STRAIGHT-ARM PULLOVERS

Purpose of Exercise: To develop the pectorals and expand the rib cage.

This is the best movement for expanding the thorax as well as working the pectorals and building up the serratus anterior muscles.

Execution: (1) Place a dumbbell on a bench, then turn and lie across the bench with only your shoulders on its surface, your feet flat on the floor. Grasp the dumbbell with both hands and hold it straight up over your chest, with both palms pressing against the underside of the top plate.
(2) Keeping your arms straight, lower the weight slowly down in an arc behind your head, feeling the chest and rib cage stretch. Drop the hips toward the floor at the same time to increase this stretch. When you have lowered the dumbbell as far as possible, raise it back to the starting position through the same arc. Don't let your hips come back up as you lift the weight. Keep them low throughout the movement to ensure the maximum possible stretch and therefore the greatest expansion of the rib cage.

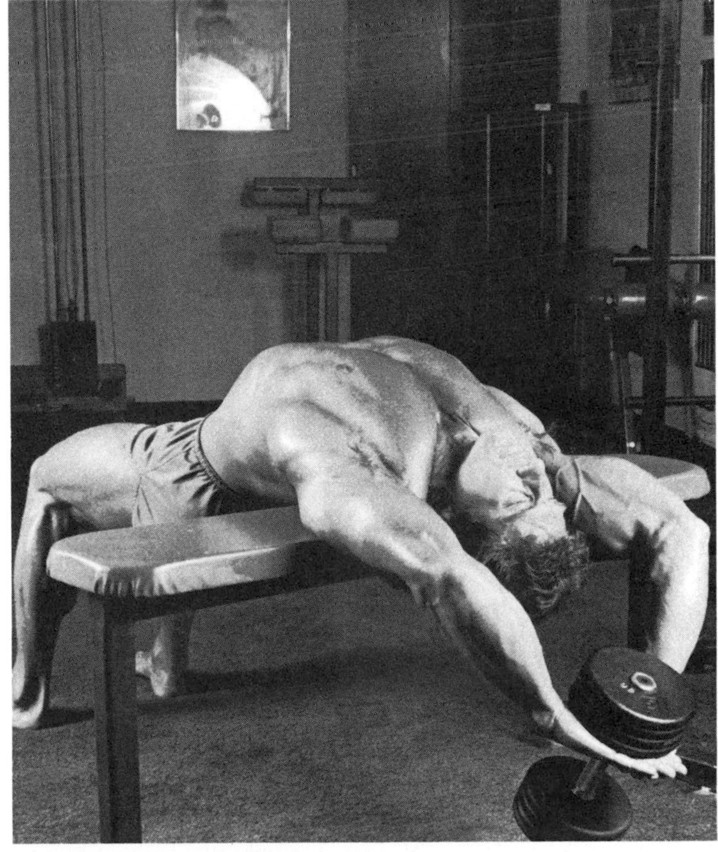

Pullovers can be used to develop the serratus as well as the pectorals. For serratus, do the regular pullover movement, but concentrate on making the serratus muscles do a maximum amount of the pulling.

ROPE PULLS

Purpose of Exercise: To develop the serratus muscles.

Execution: (1) Kneel on the floor holding on to ropes attached to a cable and overhead pulley. (2) Keeping your arms extended above you, curl your body forward and down, pulling with the lats. Continue this motion until your head is almost touching your thighs. Bring your elbows down to the floor, pulling with the elbows. Release, uncurl, and come back up to the starting position, straightening your arms and feeling the stretch in your lats. You need to be very strict with Rope Pulls, not try for maximum weight. Try to make the serratus really burn by the end of the set—and you'll be feeling it in your abdominals as well.

ONE-ARM CABLE PULLS

Purpose of Exercise: To work the serratus muscles.

Execution: (1) Kneeling on the floor, grasp a handle attached to a cable and overhead pulley with an underhand grip. (2) Pulling with the lats, bring your elbow down to your knee. Consciously crunch the serratus and lats, getting a full contraction. Release and come slowly back to the starting position. The key to this exercise is absolute strictness. Do the movement slowly and under control, concentrating on feeling the contraction in the lats and serratus. Repeat using the other arm.

Lee Apperson

MACHINE PULLOVERS

(See page 379.)
Machine Pullovers can be used to develop the serratus as well as the lats. Learn to feel when the serratus muscles are working the hardest, and adjust the position of your body and the movement of your elbows until you feel them contracting to the maximum.

CLOSE-GRIP CHINS

(See page 367.)
By concentrating on contracting the serratus during this movement, you can change it from a lat exercise to one that also involves the serratus to a great degree.

HANGING SERRATUS CRUNCHES

Purpose of Exercise: To isolate and develop the serratus.

Execution: (1) Hold on to a chinning bar with a palms-forward grip. (Using lifting straps will take some of the strain off your hands and wrists.) (2) Slowly swing your legs up and to one side, feeling the serratus muscles stretch fully on one side and contract to the maximum on the other. Slowly came back to the center, then repeat the movement to the other side. Concentrate on trying to get the maximum stretch possible and on executing the movement just with the serratus, isolating these muscles as much as possible. This exercise calls for complete control and strict technique. Bring your legs deliberately to each side; do not swing them back and forth like a pendulum.

HANGING DUMBBELL ROWS

PURPOSE OF EXERCISE: An advanced exercise to develop the serratus.

EXECUTION: (1) Using a pair of gravity boots, hang upside down from a chinning bar. Take a dumbbell in each hand and let the weights hang down below you, feeling the serratus muscles stretch to their maximum. (2) Concentrating on using the serratus in isolation as much as possible, lift the dumbbells up in front of you. As you lift, your elbows come toward the front, not out to the side. Hold at the point of maximum serratus contraction, then lower the dumbbells slowly back to the starting position, feeling the serratus stretch once more. During the movement, be sure to keep your elbows and the dumbbells as close to your body as possible.

The Back

THE MUSCLES OF THE BACK

The **latissimus dorsi,** the large triangular muscles that extend from under the shoulders down to the small of the back on both sides. These are the largest muscles of the upper body.

BASIC FUNCTION: To pull the shoulders downward and to the back

The **spinal erectors,** several muscles in the lower back that guard the nerve channels and help keep the spine erect. They are also the slowest muscles in the body to recuperate from heavy exercise.

BASIC FUNCTION: To hold the spine erect

Note: The **trapezius,** the flat, triangular muscle that extends out and down from the neck and down between the shoulder blades, is included in the shoulder section.

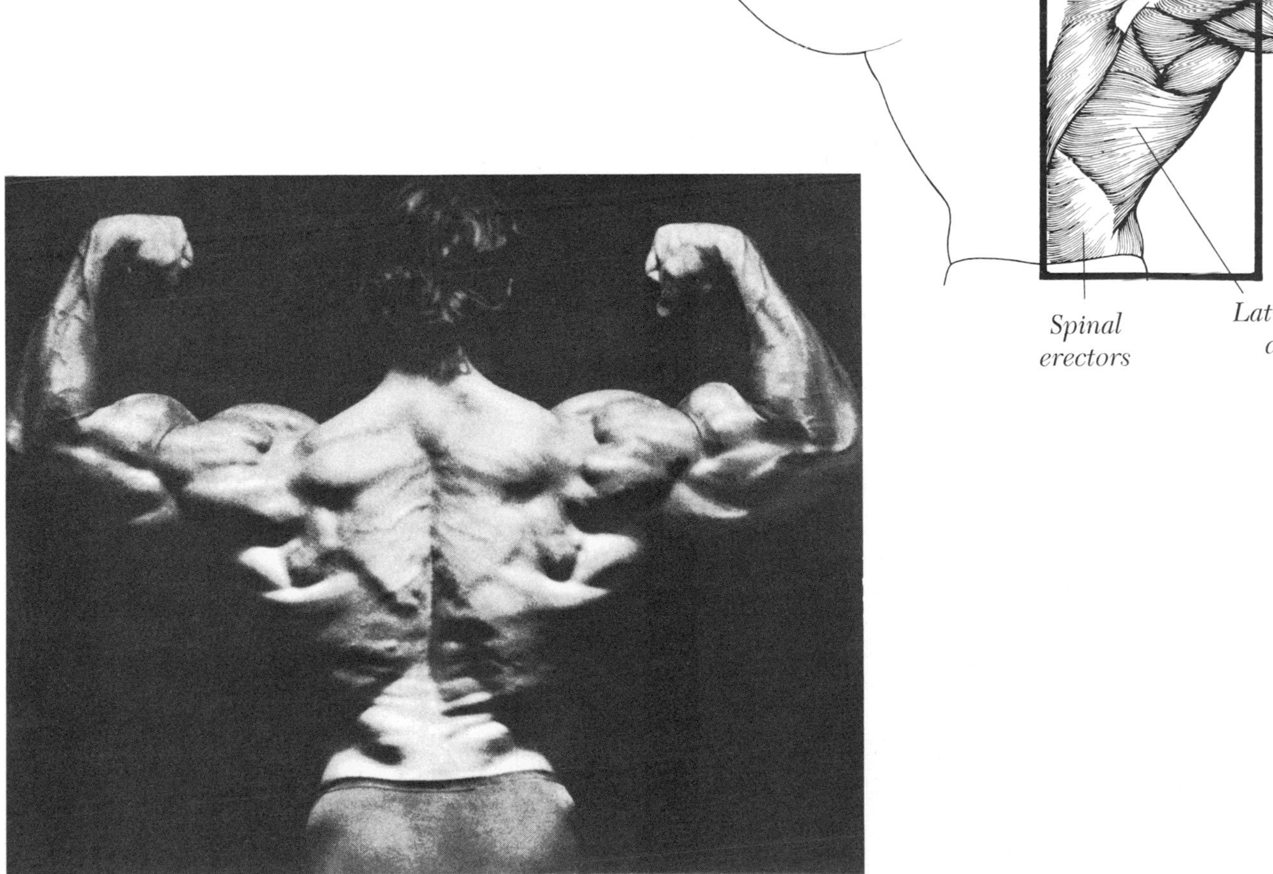

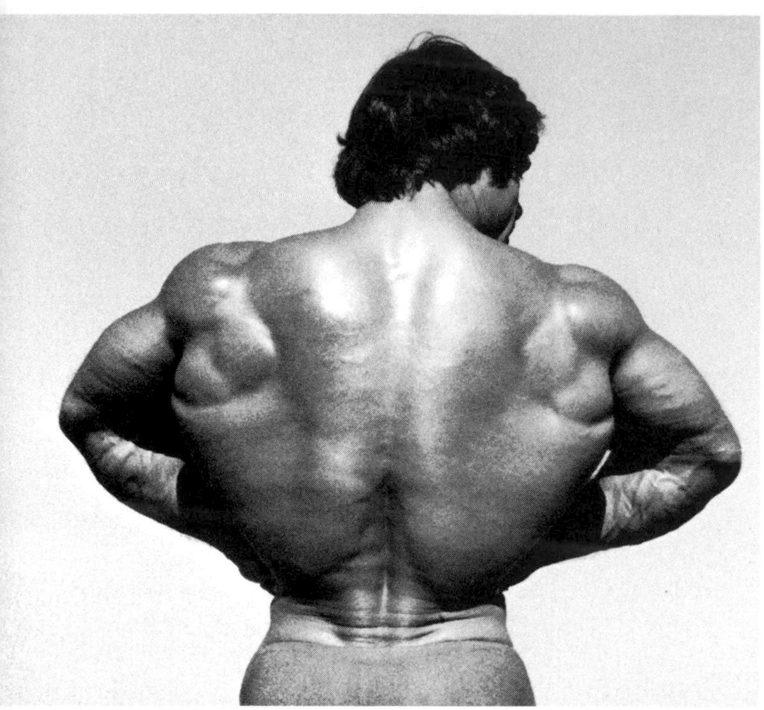

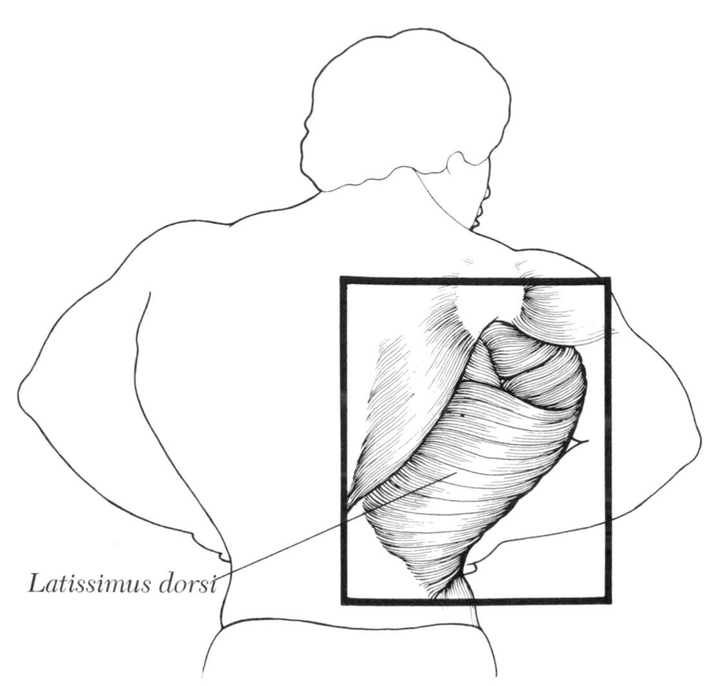

TRAINING THE BACK

Developing a broad, thick, and massive back is absolutely necessary in the creation of a quality bodybuilding physique. Strong back muscles are essential for lifting and carrying heavy weight, and a highly muscular back has always been considered the measure of a man's strength.

"My back is a weapon I use to destroy my opponents," says two-time Mr. Olympia winner Franco Columbu. "I place my thumbs in the small of my back and begin to spread my lats. It doesn't all come on at once. First I flex them a few times and then begin to let them extend their widest. Each time the audience and the judges think that is all, I flex harder and they come out farther. And just when everyone is gasping with surprise that a human being could achieve such development, I lift my arms into a powerful double-biceps shot, displaying enormous muscularity, thickness, and separation. Only the very best of bodybuilders can stand beside me when I do this without being blown offstage by the shock wave."

When a bodybuilding judge looks at a competitor's back, there are three things he is especially interested in: (1) the thickness and muscularity of the upper back; (2) the sweep and width of the lats; and (3) the definition and development of the lower back and lower lats.

THE UPPER BACK

Upper back development involves more than just the back muscles themselves. When you hit a rear double-biceps pose, the traps and the muscles of the upper and middle back are dominant, but all the muscles from elbow to elbow play their part, including the biceps and the rear delts.

The central muscle of the upper back is the trapezius, an angular muscle that extends down to the shoulders from either side of the neck, then comes together over the spine about halfway down the back. In a highly developed back the traps will be full and massive, balancing off the lats on either side and clearly separated from them in back poses. Exercises that specifically work the traps include anything which involves lifting the shoulders—Shrugs and Upright Rows, primarily, but also Rowing in certain positions and some kinds of Presses—and are covered in the Trapezius training program (beginning on page 295).

In a twisting back shot, you need a thick and muscular upper back to balance off the development of the shoulders, biceps, triceps, and forearms.

Sergio Oliva is a perfect example of how impressive a thick upper back can be.

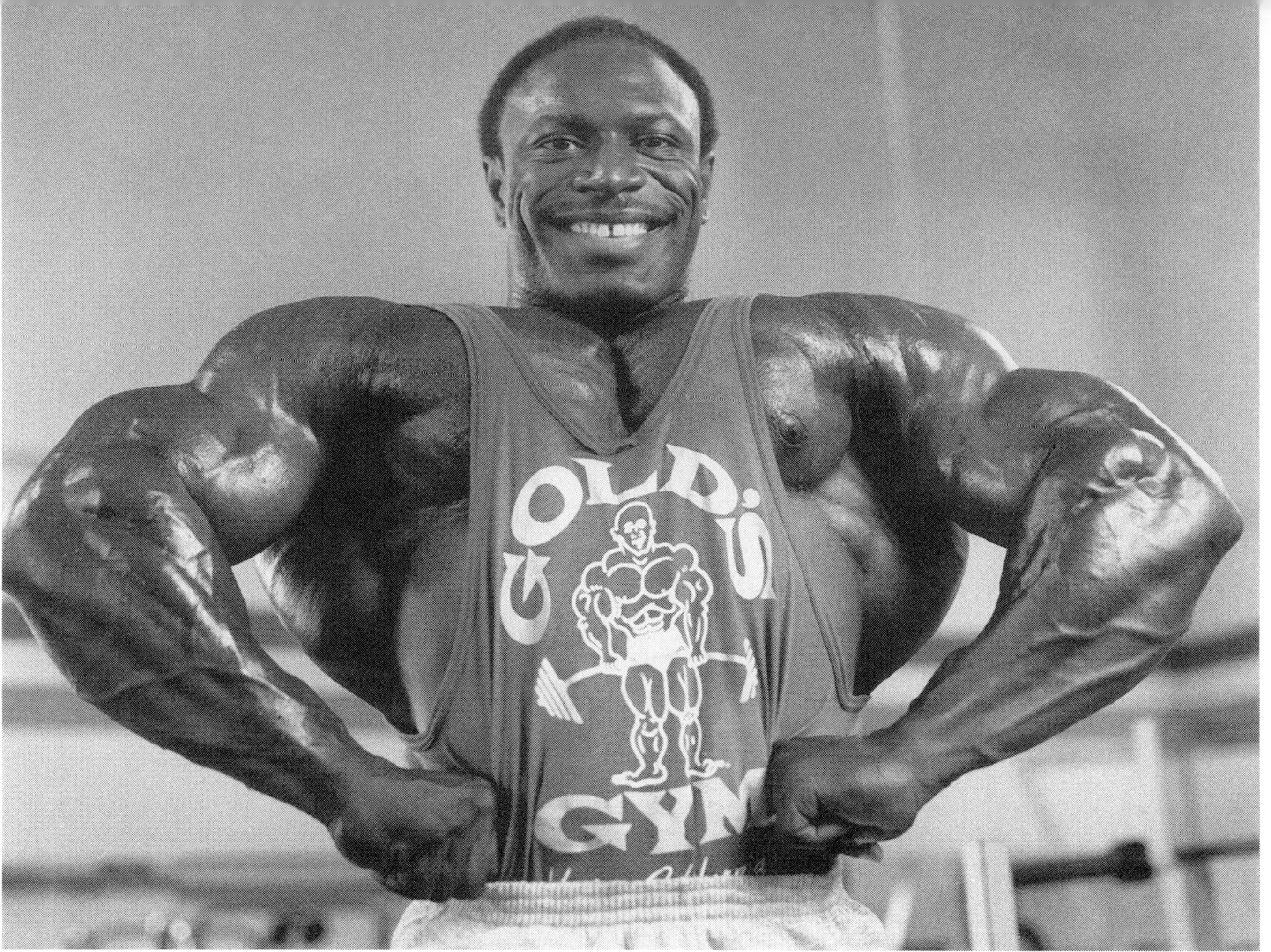

Lee Haney

THE LATS

The most impressive area of a fully developed back is the sweep of the lats. It is this muscular width that declares to the world that you are really a bodybuilder. And it is the lats that are likely to first attract the judges' attention, even when standing relaxed in the first round. The traditional V shape of the bodybuilder—wide shoulders descending to a firm, tight waistline—is dependent on the right kind of lat development. A friend of mine once told me that when he did a lat shot onstage, he imagined his lats were so wide that the audience would think the curtains were closing!

The width of the lats is developed by any kind of pulldown movement, such as Cable Pulldowns or Chins. The precise way that the pulldown movement affects the lats is determined by the angle you are working at, how wide apart your arms are, and whether you are pulling down in front or to the rear. So I have included a variety of close-grip and wide-grip movements as well as front and rear Chins and Pulldowns in the back program to encourage total lat development.

The lats are also evident from the front view, complementing the chest by widening the torso, with the line of the back muscles acting as a frame for the pectorals. The lats contribute to any number of poses, including front and rear double-biceps and a variety of twisting shots.

Lee Haney, Ronnie Coleman, and Robby Robinson are three great bodybuilders known for the V shape of their torsos—from the back and from the front—which is the result of outstanding lat development.

Ronnie Coleman

Robby Robinson

Franco Columbu

LOWER LATS

When you see a Franco Columbu or a Frank Zane do a twisting back shot you can't help being impressed by the way their lower lats sweep all the way down and insert into the waistline. This gives the lats a terrifically aesthetic look.

To develop the lower lats, you need to do your back exercises with a very narrow grip—Close-Grip Chins and Close-Grip Pulldowns, for example—as well as One-Arm Cable Rows and One-Arm Dumbbell Rows. It is also important to do stretches between sets, grabbing hold of something with one hand at a time and really pulling until you can feel the lower lat almost down to the hip.

Well-developed lower lats will also help you in rear back poses because they come down at an angle and form a kind of frame that shows off a well-striated lower back.

Frank Zane

MIDDLE BACK THICKNESS

Not only should the lats be wide and sweeping, but they should also look thick and powerful where they come together in the middle back. Many bodybuilders have wide backs with sweeping lats but fail to look their best in back poses because the center of the back lacks that strong, thick look that a really great bodybuilder has to have. When you look at Dorian Yates, for example, you are immediately struck by the solid thickness of his back muscles. Dorian's back shows thickness even when he is standing relaxed.

Chris Cormier

Flex Wheeler is credited with having incredibly good genetics, but the thickness and muscularity of his back indicate just how hard he has trained to realize his potential.

Thickness in the back is achieved primarily by doing rowing exercises—Barbell Rows, Cable Rows, T-Bar Rows, and so forth. However, if you want to target the middle back, do rowing that gives you a longer range of motion so that you can fully contract that area—Cable Rows with separate cables or a wide grip, One-Arm Rows, or Barbell Rows with a wider grip.

The back can be posed in a number of different ways, but as you can see, total back development is necessary to make each one effective. Serge Nubret, Franco, and I all show thick upper and lower back development, lots of lat width, and good muscularity.

LOWER BACK

Many top bodybuilders have a great upper back but have never developed the lower back to the degree that they should. A really great lower back has two columns of muscle that stand out on either side of the spine, an indication of years of heavy Deadlifts, Bent-Over Rows, and other power exercises. When you see Boyer Coe onstage you notice the tremendous sweep of his lats, but when he stands next to someone like Danny Padilla, with his thick and powerful lower back, you can see he is weak in this particular area.

A truly Herculean physique needs that lower back development and thickness. Look at a Sergio Oliva, Franco Columbu, Dorian Yates, or Nasser El Sonbaty and you will see magnificent lower back development. Frank Zane at one time was very weak in the lower back. I recommended to him that he begin doing Bent-Over Rows, starting out with a relatively low weight and gradually increasing his poundages as his back developed. Zane is such a dedicated bodybuilder that within a relatively short time his lower back development increased enormously, and within a year you could see striations across the lower back.

Shawn Ray, although he had already won pro titles, eventually found himself threatened by the extreme back development of a number of the increasingly bigger bodybuilders against whom he was competing. Instead of giving up, or mindlessly just trying to gain additional overall mass, Shawn instead concentrated on back development, particularly on back width, to the point where competitors who were often fifty pounds bigger than he was couldn't blow him off the stage in rear lat spread comparisons.

Because we tend to store a disproportionate amount of fat around the waistline, leanness and definition in the lower back are visible proof that a bodybuilder has worked hard to get in shape. When he hits a back double-biceps shot and the judges see a clearly defined, sculpted lower back they know instantly that he has done an enormous amount of work, not just for the lats but for the entire back.

I have included exercises for the lower back right from the beginning so that bodybuilders following my training program will not find themselves with a weak lower back a year or so down the line. Heavy power exercises like Deadlifts are ideal because they not only develop the lower back but also strengthen it; you are able to do a variety of other exercises like Bent-Over Rows without having your lower back give out before your upper back.

Three of the top bodybuilders, Chris Cormier, Dorian Yates, and Flex Wheeler, demonstrate three different ways to display the muscularity of the back. Note the "Christmas tree" that can be created by the striations and muscularity along the center of the back.

BACK MUSCLE FUNCTIONS

The lats have two basic functions as far as bodybuilding is concerned: They pull the shoulder back (a rowing motion) and pull the shoulders down (a pulldown or chinning motion). A common mistake when doing these movements is to use too much biceps effort and not enough back, or to involve the muscles of the lower back in a swaying motion instead of making the lats do most of the work. You have to make an effort when training lats to isolate them so that only these muscles are involved in the movement.

The lower back muscles function differently from most other muscles in the body. They are stabilizers, holding the body steady rather than constantly contracting and relaxing through a full range of motion like, say, the biceps. Therefore, when you do full-range exercises like Hyperextensions or Straight-Leg Deadlifts you put so much strain on the lower back that it can take up to a week to fully recuperate. This means that total-effort lower back training using power exercises and maximum weights is necessary only once a week. On the other days, do your sets with nonpower exercises and less than maximum poundages.

DESIGNING A BACK PROGRAM

To plan a comprehensive program of back training you need to consider how each of the important back muscles functions so that you include exercises for each vital area. If you don't properly appreciate the complexity of the back and how many different movements it takes to get full back development, you will end up with serious weak points in this part of your physique.

For example, it doesn't do any good to do 5 sets of Chins to the front, 5 sets to the back, 5 sets of Wide-Grip Pulldowns, and 5 sets of Close-Grip Pulldowns and then figure you have worked your back adequately. Every one of those exercises works the pulldown function of the back, which develops the width of the lats, but a complete back program also has to develop the thickness of the back, the lower lats, and the strength and definition of the lower back.

The Basic Training Program starts out with simple exercises like Deadlifts and Chins. Later, to Deadlifts you'll add other back exercises such as Hyperextensions and Good Mornings. Similarly, chinning movements can be supplemented by various kinds of pulldown exercises, two-handed rowing exercises can be replaced occasionally by One-Arm Rows, and so forth. In the Advanced and Competition Training Programs, I have included an even greater variety of back exercises, so that by the time you are ready to compete you will be doing several movements for each of the important areas of the back.

WEAK POINT TRAINING

The most common problem of today's competition bodybuilders is incomplete back development. One reason for this may simply be that they do not get to study their backs as clearly as they can a front view, and so are not as motivated to train their backs as diligently as their chests or arms. One other reason, however, is poor back training technique. Back training is more subtle and more difficult than most people realize. For one thing, the basic function of the lats and other back muscles is to pull the shoulder girdle down and back. Many bodybuilders don't understand this and get confused as to which muscles they are supposed to be using. If they lurch back during the exercises and use the lower back or shoulders themselves, then the back muscles never get to work through a full range of motion.

Early in life you learned to coordinate your muscular efforts to make lifting easier. You learned to bend your knees when lifting something, to take as much strain as possible off the back muscles and distribute it more evenly to allow adjacent muscles to help. This is the opposite of what you try to accomplish as a bodybuilder. The trick to effective back training is to learn to isolate the various areas of the back, then make it harder on each individual area of the back instead of easier.

I have watched bodybuilders do Bent-Over Rows with an impossible amount of weight, so that they had to heave the bar into the air using every muscle in the body. This kind of cheating will never build a quality back. When doing Seated Rows, many bodybuilders add weight to the stack, as if lifting heavy weights is all that matters and then sway way back, using too much lower back, in an effort to finish off the movement.

Also, many bodybuilders allow the biceps to do too much pulling when they are doing pulldown or rowing exercises, which results in some powerful arm development but doesn't do much for the back. They need to concentrate on using the arms simply as a link between the back and the bar or handle, and not as a primary means of lifting the weight.

But even if you learn absolutely correct back training technique, the back consists of a number of complex and interrelated muscles and they do not necessarily all develop at the same rate in all individuals. As you become more advanced in bodybuilding and you begin to see which areas of the back have responded more quickly than others, you will want to alter your program to include more work for the muscles that are lagging behind.

Outer Back Development

The outer back responds to Rows done with a narrow grip because with a narrow grip the handles or bar allows you to go back no farther than the front of the torso and shortens the range of motion. One of my favorite outer back exercises is T-Bar Rows, done as strictly as possible.

Upper Back Development

The primary exercise I recommend for developing the upper back is heavy Bent-Over Barbell Rows. Additionally, you can do Seated Wide-Grip Rows, using a long bar instead of handles. If one side of the upper back is more developed than the other, try doing One-Arm Dumbbell Rows to work each side in isolation.

What a difference three years can make! At age eighteen, I realized I needed more upper back thickness . . .

. . . by age twenty-one, after concentrated weak point training, this area had become my strong point.

Lat Width

The lats are extremely important for both front and back poses. Dorian Yates and Kevin Levrone have truly Olympian lats, and they look good no matter what pose they hit or what angle they are viewed from. The sweep and width of the lats is accentuated by doing exercises that pull the lats out to the side as far as possible. Wide-Grip Chins and Wide-Grip Pulldowns are the primary exercises for achieving this.

Dorian Yates

Kevin Levrone

Lower Lat Development

The sweep of the lats is less effective if the lats do not extend all the way down to the waistline. Exercises to help you train the lower lats include One-Arm Cable Rows and close-grip movements such as Close-Grip Chins and Close-Grip Pulldowns.

Middle Back Thickness

The middle back receives the greatest amount of work when you extend the range of motion as far as possible. Therefore, Seated Rows done with separate handles, allowing you to bring your elbows farther back, put more stress on the middle back. Rows done with a fairly wide grip or T-Bar Rows done on a machine allowing a wider grip create the same effect.

Lower Back Development

Many bodybuilders forget that the lower back is an essential element in making any back shot really effective. Heavy Deadlifts force the lower back to work to the maximum. But you can also use exercises like Good Mornings and Hyperextensions to isolate and develop this area.

Overall Back Development

Remember that other muscle groups contribute to your back poses, especially straight-on back shots like the rear double-biceps and rear lat spread. Therefore, you need to be concerned with muscles like the rear deltoids, the trapezius, and even the biceps and triceps. Everything ties in with everything else, and judges may watch you pose and give you low marks for the back when in reality it was some other aspect of your development that was at fault.

Sergio Oliva displays perfect middle and lower back thickness.

STRETCHING AND FLEXING

I am a firm believer in flexing and posing the muscles between each set. This is especially true for the back. You have to keep posing and flexing your back in order to gain full control over the muscles needed to show it off effectively in competition. Continually stretching the lats also helps achieve that long sweep and low tie-in at the waistline that make the champions' backs so impressive.

Flex the back or hit poses like a back double-biceps shot between sets of Rows and Pullovers. If you pose while your training partner is doing his set, you will keep the muscles pumped and warm and ready to really hit the next set.

When you are training lats with Chins and Pulldowns, between sets grab hold of something solid and really stretch them out one at a time as pictured here, or both at once. Also, all the serratus exercises (beginning on page 340) can be used to stretch the lats. This lengthens the muscles, helps you get a fuller range of motion and a deeper contraction, and develops the lower area of the lats as they extend down to the waist.

Ken Waller

Shawn Ray

Dorian Yates

This series of poses demonstrates the number of different ways the complex muscle system of the back can be presented, and why it is necessary for the aspiring bodybuilder to achieve total back development in order to ensure success.

Franco Columbu

Back Exercises

WIDE-GRIP CHINS BEHIND THE NECK

PURPOSE OF EXERCISE: To widen the upper back and create a full sweep in the lats.

Wide-Grip Chins widen the lats and develop the entire shoulder girdle. This exercise is primarily for the upper and outer regions of the lats and also spreads the scapula, making it easier to flare the lats.

EXECUTION: (1) Take hold of the chinning bar with an overhand grip, hands as wide apart as practicable. (2) Hang from the bar, then pull yourself up so that the back of your neck touches the bar. This is a strict exercise, so try not to help your back by kicking up with the legs. At the top of the movement hold for a brief moment, then lower yourself slowly back to the starting position. Chins involve your entire body weight, so some beginners may not be able to do the requisite number of repetitions for each set. I recommend they do what I used to do: Instead of trying to do 5 sets of 10 reps each, do as many reps as possible at a time—maybe only 3 or 4 until a total of 50 reps is achieved. The stronger you get, the fewer sets it will take to get to 50 reps and the shorter the time it will take to do it.

WIDE-GRIP CHINS TO THE FRONT (OPTIONAL)

PURPOSE OF EXERCISE: To widen the upper back and create a full sweep in the lats.

Chinning yourself so that you touch your chest to the bar rather than the back of the neck gives you a slightly longer range of motion and is less strict, allowing you to cheat slightly so you can continue your reps even after you are tired.

EXECUTION: (1) Take hold of the chinning bar with an overhand grip, hands as wide apart as practicable. (2) Hang from the bar, then pull yourself up, trying to touch the top of your chest to the bar. At the top of the movement, hold for a brief moment, then lower yourself back to the starting position.

CLOSE-GRIP CHINS

Purpose of Exercise: To work the back muscles, widen the lower lats, and develop the serratus.

This exercise is great for widening and lengthening the appearance of the lats. It also develops the serratus anterior, those little fingers of muscle that lie under the outside of the pecs, which add so much to front poses such as double-biceps or any other overhead pose.

Execution: (1) Take hold of the chinning bar (or close-grip triangle device found in many gyms) with your hands close together, one hand on either side of the bar. Hang below the bar. (2) Then pull yourself up while leaning your head back slightly so that the chest touches (or nearly touches) your hands; lower the body slowly for a full stretch of the lats. Work for the fullest range of motion.

You can also do Close-Grip Chins by pulling on a straight bar instead of a double handle.

LAT MACHINE PULLDOWNS

PURPOSE OF EXERCISE: To widen the upper lats.

This exercise allows you to do Chins with less than your total body weight, so you can do a lot of extra reps for the upper back if you feel you need more work in that area (but it should not replace Chins as the standard exercise for widening the upper lats).

EXECUTION: (1) Using a long bar, grasp it with a wide, overhand grip and sit on the seat with your knees hooked under the support. (2) Pull the bar down smoothly until it touches the top of your chest, making the upper back do the work and not swaying back to involve the lower back. Release, extend the arms again, and feel the lats fully stretch.

VARIATION: Try doing Lat Pulldowns behind the neck instead of in front.

CLOSE- OR MEDIUM-GRIP PULLDOWNS

Purpose of Exercise: To work the lats, especially the lower lat area.

Again, working with an overhead cable and weight stack allows you to do the chinning movement with less than body weight.

Execution: (1) Grasp the handles or a bar using a narrow- or medium-close grip and pull down to your upper chest. Don't sway backward, but try to concentrate on using the lats to do the movement. (2) Draw the shoulders down and back and stick the chest out. Let the handles go upward again until your lats are fully stretched out.

BENT-OVER BARBELL ROWS

Purpose of Exercise: To thicken the upper back.

This exercise also helps widen the upper back and, to a lesser degree, adds density to the lower back.

Execution: (1) Standing with feet a few inches apart, grasp the bar with a wide, overhand grip. With your knees slightly bent, bend forward until your upper body is about parallel to the floor. Keep your back straight, head up, and let the bar hang at arm's length below you, almost touching the shinbone. (2) Using primarily the muscles of the back, lift the bar upward until it touches the upper abdominals, then lower it again, under control, back to the starting position; then immediately start your next rep. It is important to make the back work so as not to make this a biceps exercise. Think of the arms and hands as hooks, a way of transmitting the contraction of the lats to the bar. Don't bring the bar up to the chest area itself; bringing it only to the abdomen reduces the role of the arms. Make sure your first set of any rowing exercise is relatively light to let your back get warmed up. By the time you get to your last set, a little bit of cheating is all right to get you through it, but keep it to a minimum.

In Bent-Over Barbell Rows, you pull with the lats but don't lift with the lower back. Keep your upper body parallel to the floor all through the exercise. Notice how the bar is pulled up to the abdomen rather than up toward the chest.

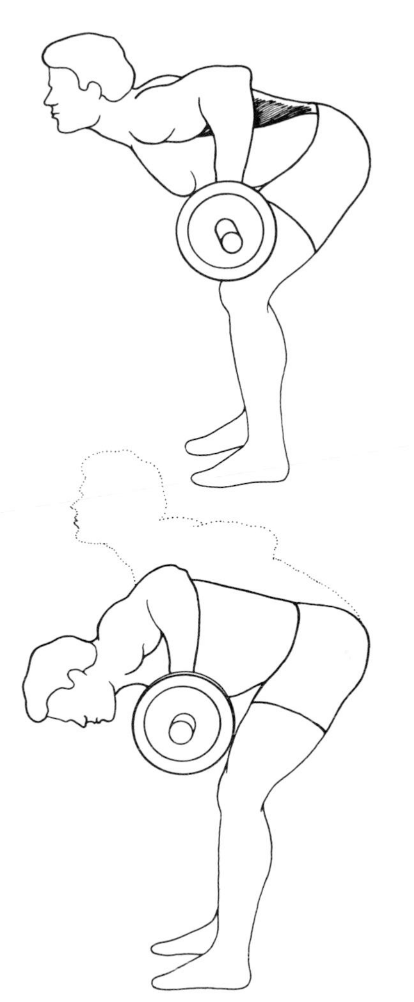

This drawing illustrates two major mistakes: If you don't hold your body steady when doing Bent-Over Barbell Rows, you involve the lower back muscles rather than isolating the lats. And if you lift the bar up toward the chest instead of the abdomen, you involve the arms, so that the biceps are doing a lot of the work you are trying to get the lats to do.

When you do Rows with an Olympic barbell set with its larger plates you need to stand on a block or a bench so that you can lower the bar all the way down without the plates touching the floor. With your head up, back straight, and knees flexed, you are in a position similar to an Olympic lifter about to clean a heavy barbell.

BENT-OVER DUMBBELL ROWS

Purpose of Exercise: To work each side of the upper back independently.

You can still work heavy and give your back a good workout using dumbbells, but by using them you force each side of the body to work up to its own capacity, rather than running the risk of having the stronger side help out the weaker one. This is a good weak point exercise for anyone lacking upper back symmetry.

Execution: (1) Grasp a dumbbell in each hand, bend your knees slightly, then bend forward from the waist, keeping your head up and your back straight. Let the weights hang at arm's length below the shoulders. (2) Simultaneously lift both weights up as far as possible to your sides, holding your upper body steady to avoid involving the lower back (the weights should come up to your sides, not your chest, in order to keep biceps involvement to a minimum). Then lower the weights again, slowly.

T-BAR ROWS

PURPOSE OF EXERCISE: To thicken the middle and outer back.

EXECUTION: (1) Standing on a block with your feet close together, knees slightly bent, bend down and grasp the handles of the T-Bar machine with an overhand grip. Straighten your legs slightly and lift up until your body is at about a 45-degree angle. Without changing this angle, lift the weight up until it touches your chest, (2) then lower it again to arm's length, keeping the weight off the floor.

Remember that this is an upper back exercise—you are not supposed to do much lifting with the lower back or legs. If you find you are not able to do this lift without swaying and lifting up with your back to an excessive degree, you are simply using too much weight and should take off a plate or two. However, a small amount of movement is inevitable. But be certain to keep your back straight or even slightly arched and never to bend over hunchback fashion, which could result in injury. By using a narrow grip, this exercise will work mostly the outer lats because you cannot get the range of motion to fully involve the inner back muscles. However, this limited range of motion means that you will eventually be able to lift more weight than when doing Barbell Rows, which makes this a good power movement.

ONE-ARM DUMBBELL ROWS

Purpose of Exercise: To independently work each side of the back.

Rowing one side at a time with a dumbbell has two unique advantages over Barbell Rows: It isolates the latissimus muscles on each side, and it allows you to lift the weight higher and therefore get a more complete contraction. Using heavy weight in this exercise is less important than getting the fullest range of movement, which will help develop and define the center of the back.

Execution: (1) Taking a dumbbell in one hand, bend forward from the waist until your upper body is nearly parallel to the floor. Place your free hand on the bench for support. Begin with the weight hanging down at arm's length, feeling the fullest possible stretch. Turn your hand so that the palm faces toward your body. (2) Keeping your body steady, lift the weight up to your side, concentrating on doing the work with the back rather than the arm. Lower the weight, keeping it under control. Finish your repetitions with this arm, then repeat with the other arm.

Lee Priest

ONE-ARM CABLE ROWS

Purpose of Exercise: To develop the lower lats.

This is an especially good movement for tying in the lower lats to the waist.

Execution: (1) Using a floor-level pulley, take hold of a handle with one hand. If done standing, assume a balanced stance, the leg opposite the arm you will be using in the exercise forward, other leg back. (This can also be done while seated.) Begin with your arm fully extended in front of you; you may even want to twist your hand inward so that the thumb is lower than the little finger to create the fullest possible stretch. (2) Pull the handle back by your side as far as you can, twisting your hand outward so that the thumb ends up on the outside, feeling the back muscles contract. Release and extend your arm and twist your wrist back to the starting position. Complete your repetitions, then repeat the exercise using the other arm.

The secret to success doing One-Arm Cable Rows is range of motion. When you pull the cable, bring your elbow as far back as possible—which is a lot farther than you can go doing regular Cable Rows. Also, as you release and lower the weight again, make sure you stretch your arm and lats as far as possible.

SEATED CABLE ROWS

PURPOSE OF EXERCISE: To develop the thickness of the back and the lower lats. This movement also works the lower sections of the lats.

EXECUTION: (1) Take hold of the handles and sit with your feet braced against the crossbar or a wooden block, knees slightly bent. Extend your arms and bend forward slightly, feeling the lats stretch. You should be situated far enough away from the weight stack so that you can stretch like this without the weight touching the bottom.
(2) From this beginning position, pull the handles back toward your body and touch them to your abdomen, feeling the back muscles doing most of the work. Your back should arch, your chest stick out, and try to touch the shoulder blades together as you draw the weight toward you. Don't involve the lower back muscles by swaying forward and back. When the handles touch your abdomen you should be sitting upright, not leaning backward. Keeping the weight under control, release and let the handles go forward again, once more stretching out the lats.

SEATED CABLE ROWS (OPTIONAL)

Using separate handles as pictured here allows you to get your hands and elbows farther back, putting more of the stress on the center of your back.

MACHINE ROWS

Many gyms are equipped with a variety of specialized rowing machines. Some duplicate the effect of Seated Rows, while others allow you to do a rowing motion by pushing back with the elbows and not involving the contraction of the biceps. Each of these hits the back a little differently, and all are useful devices to include occasionally in your workouts to provide variety and to surprise the muscles.

BENT-ARM PULLOVERS WITH BARBELL

PURPOSE OF EXERCISE: To work the lower lats and the serratus. It also stretches the pectorals and helps widen the rib cage.

EXECUTION: (1) Lie on your back along a flat bench. Place a barbell (or an E-Z curl bar) on the floor behind your head. Reach back and grasp the bar.
(2) Keeping your arms bent, raise the bar and bring it just over your head to your chest. Lower the bar slowly back to the starting position without touching the floor, feeling the lats stretch out to their fullest. When using a heavy weight for this movement, I have someone sit on my knees to stabilize me so that I can put all my effort into lifting the bar.

Mark Erpelding

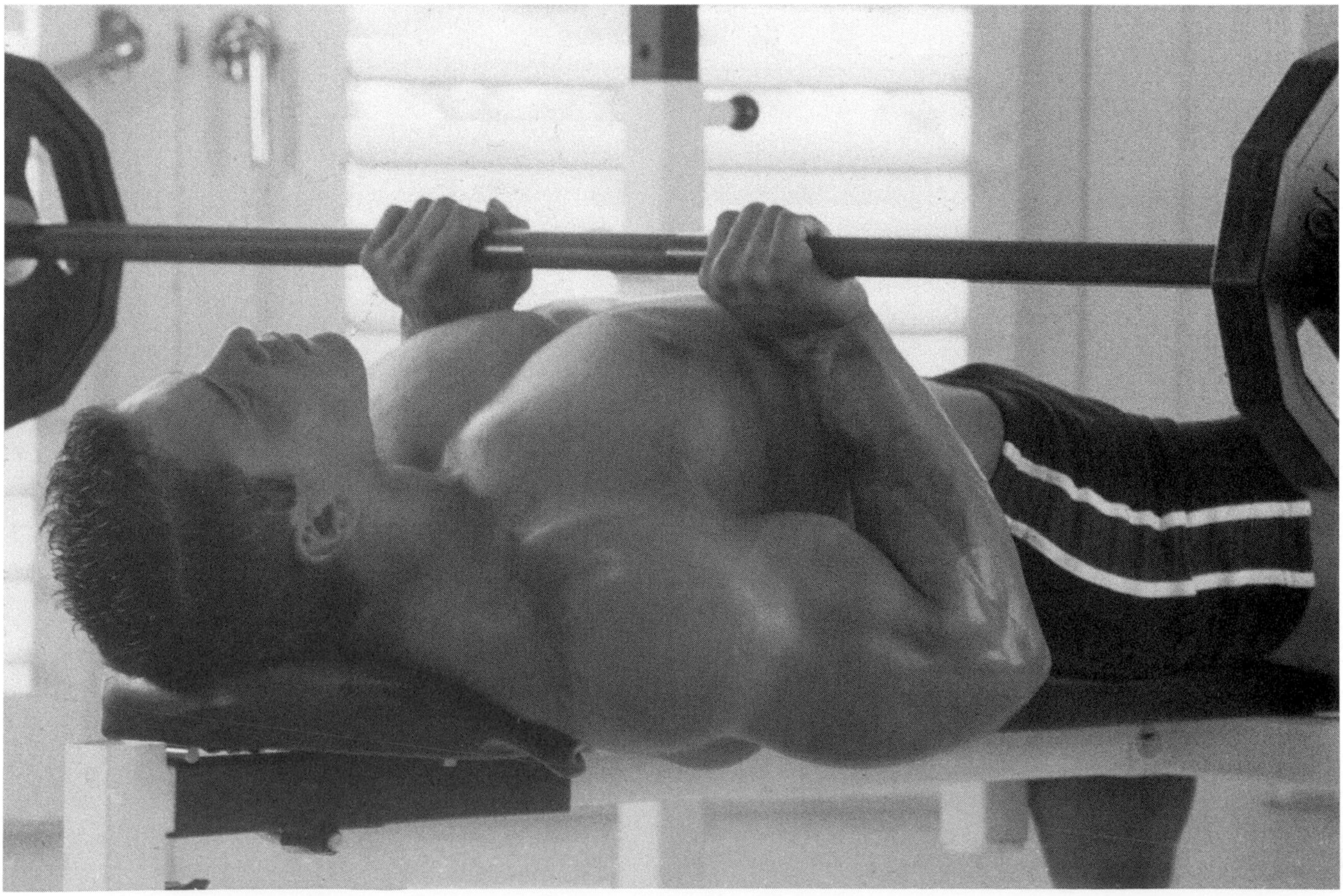

MACHINE PULLOVERS

The Pullover is actually a circular motion, and it is often difficult to work the muscles through a full range of motion using free weights (although advanced bodybuilders learn to do this purely by experience). Some pullover machines are valuable in that they allow you to work against variable resistance, and some also provide for training one arm at a time, giving you the opportunity for additional isolation. In fact, in my opinion, Pullover machines are among the most valuable exercise machines you will find in a gym.

EXECUTION: (1) Grasp the bar over your head, and (2) drive it down, feeling the lats contract. At the end of the movement the bar should be jammed against your abdomen.

DEADLIFTS

Purpose of Exercise: To work the lower back. Deadlifts are an overall power exercise that involves more muscles than any other exercise in your routine, including the lower back, upper back, and trapezius muscles, the buttocks, and the legs. A strong lower back is especially important when doing movements like Bent-Over Rows and T-Bar Rows, which put a lot of strain on this area.

Execution: (1) Place a barbell on the floor in front of you. Bend your knees, lean forward, and grasp the bar in a medium-wide grip, one hand in an overhand grip, the other in an underhand grip. Keep your back fairly straight to protect it from strain. If you curve your back you risk injury. (2) Begin the lift by driving with the legs. Straighten up until you are standing upright, then throw the chest out and shoulders back as if coming to attention. To lower the weight, bend the knees, lean forward from the waist, and touch the weight to the floor before beginning your next repetition.

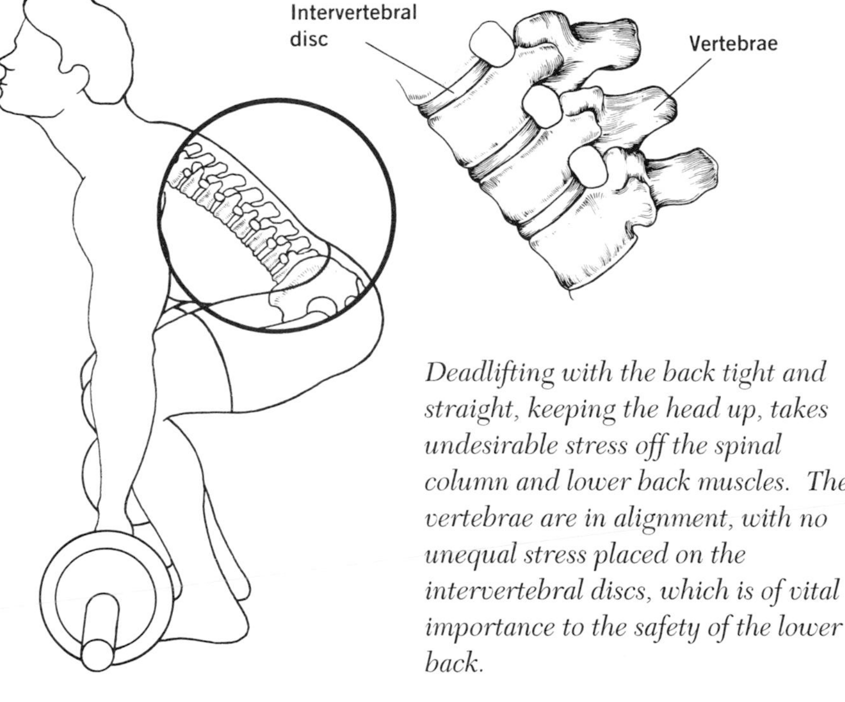

Deadlifting with the back tight and straight, keeping the head up, takes undesirable stress off the spinal column and lower back muscles. The vertebrae are in alignment, with no unequal stress placed on the intervertebral discs, which is of vital importance to the safety of the lower back.

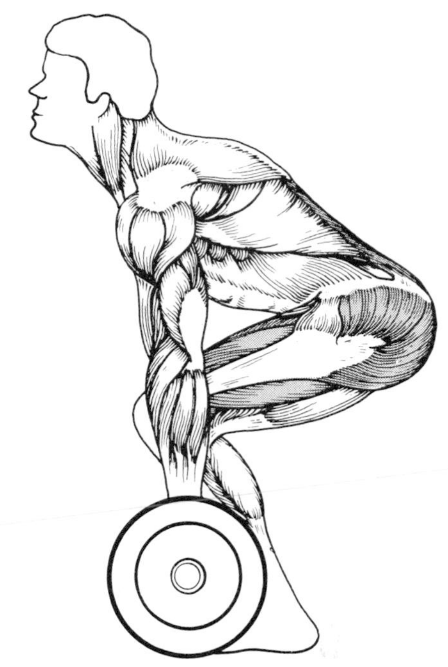

When you begin the Deadlift with your head up and back straight, you allow the glutei, leg muscles, and lower back to drive the bar upward with maximum force.

Deadlifting with the back in a rounded position with the head down places unequal pressure on the delicate intervertebral discs and lower back muscles. The discs are simultaneously compressed on one side and extended on the other. Keeping the head up and the back straight distributes the stress and reduces the chance of injury.

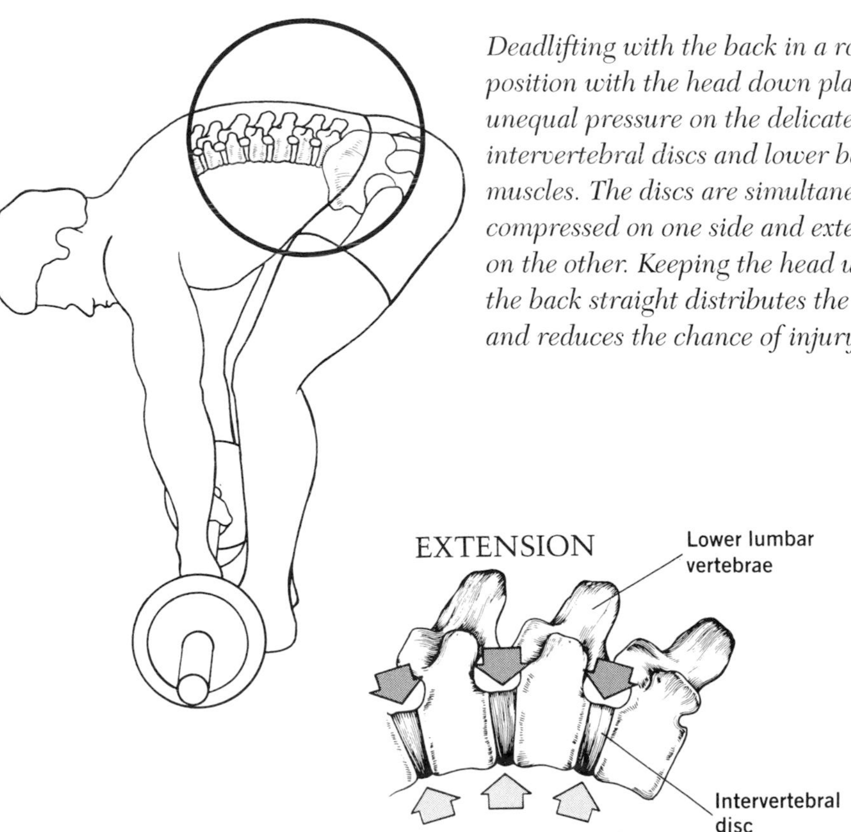

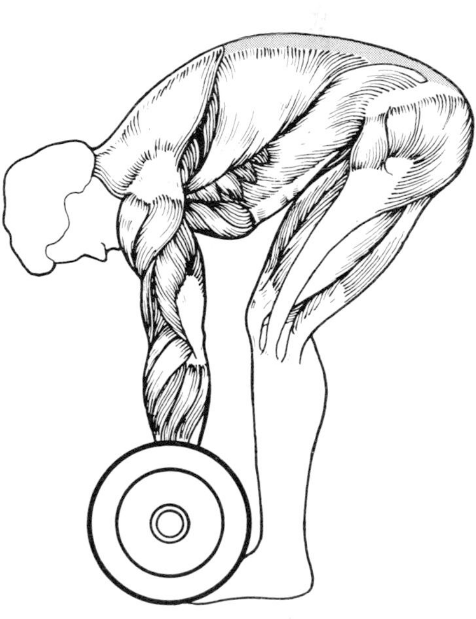

Starting a Deadlift with your back bent forward means that the lower back is going to have to do most of the initial work to get the bar moving. This is dangerous.

GOOD MORNINGS

PURPOSE OF EXERCISE: To work the lower back in isolation.

EXECUTION: (1) Standing with feet a few inches apart, hold a barbell across the back of your shoulders as for Squats (see page 497). (2) Keeping your legs locked and your back straight, bend forward from the waist, head up, until your torso is about parallel to the floor. Hold for a moment, then come back up to the starting position.

HYPEREXTENSIONS

PURPOSE OF EXERCISE: To develop the spinal erectors of the lower back.

EXECUTION: (1) Position yourself facedown across a hyperextension bench, with your heels hooked under the rear supports. Clasp your hands across your chest or behind your head and bend forward and down as far as possible, feeling the lower back muscles stretch. (2) From this position, come back up until your torso is just above parallel. To prevent hyperextension of your spine don't lift up any higher than this.

Flex Wheeler

The Arms

THE MUSCLES OF THE ARMS

There are three major muscle groups in the arms:

The **biceps brachii,** a two-headed muscle with point of origin under the deltoid and point of insertion below the elbow

Basic function: To lift and curl the arm, to pronate (twist downward) the wrist

The **triceps brachii,** a three-headed muscle that works in opposition to the biceps, also attaching under the deltoid and below the elbow.

Basic function: To straighten the arm and supinate (twist upward) the wrist

The **forearm,** involving a variety of muscles on the outside and inside of the lower arm that control the actions of hand and wrist

Basic function: The forearm flexor muscles curl the palm down and forward; the forearm extensor muscles curl the knuckles back and up.

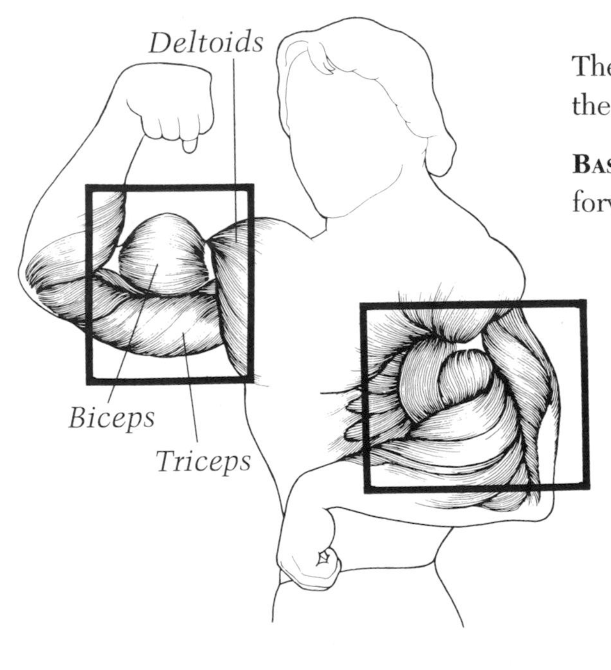

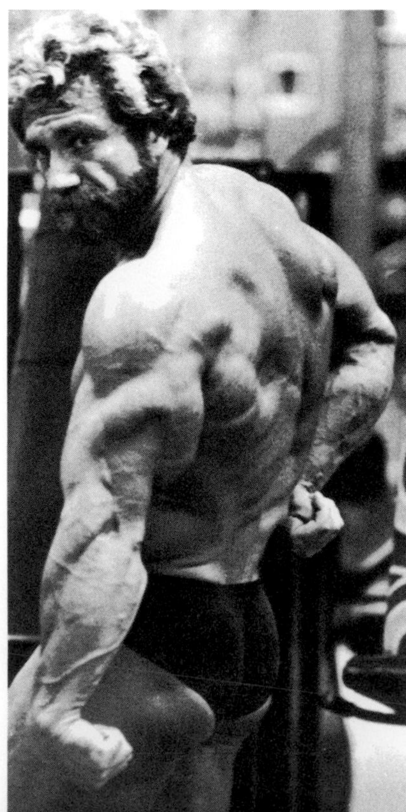

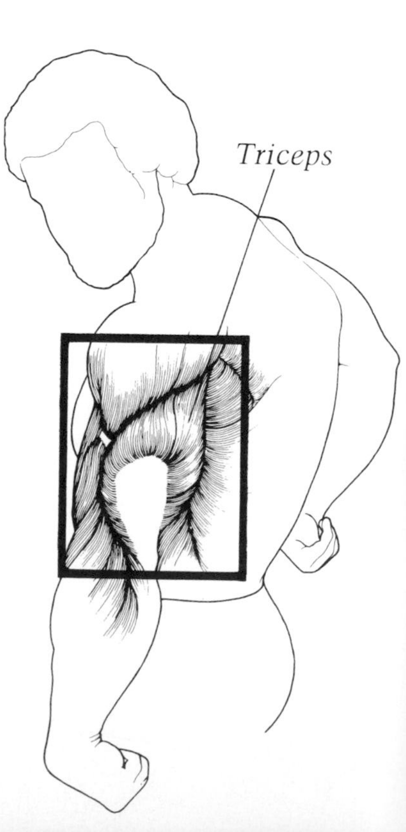

Lee Priest

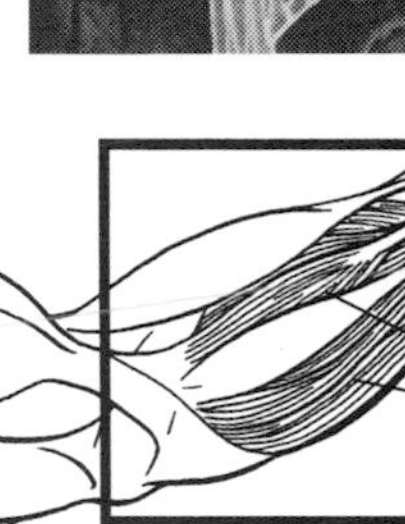

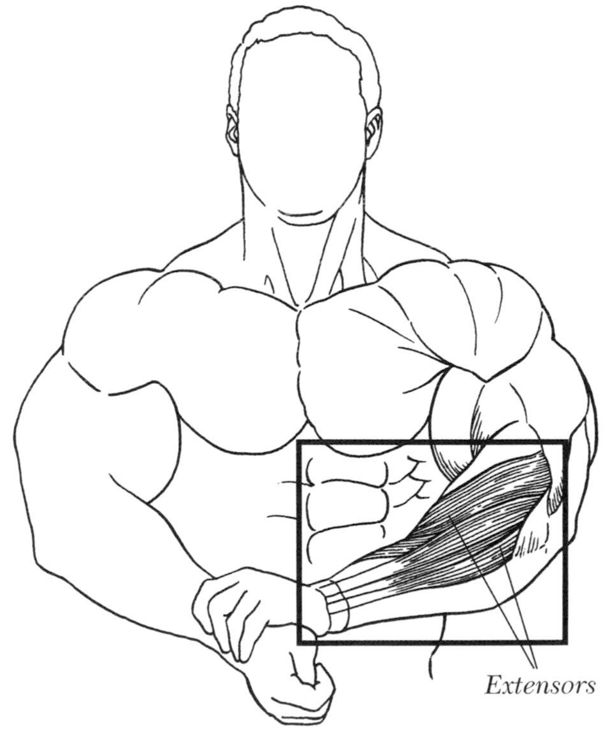

Kevin Levrone

Leroy Colbert

TRAINING THE ARMS

Along with the chest and back, bodybuilders have always considered massive arms the most impressive body part, an indicator of truly outstanding size and strength. When I began training I would study photographs of bodybuilders, and what drew my attention most was the huge biceps. Leroy Colbert, for example, could hit fantastic biceps poses. Reg Park, Bill Pearl, and Serge Nubret were all known for tremendous arm development. I would go through the magazines, page by page, looking for examples of outstanding biceps and vow that someday my arms would look like that, too.

Eventually I did become known for my huge, high-peaked biceps. My arms measured over 20 inches when I was still only nineteen years old, and continued to develop until, at their largest, they measured 22¼ inches pumped. There are few things as thrilling on a bodybuilding stage as true 19- or 20-inch arms.

There is one great advantage when it comes to training arms. Because muscles and big arms are so closely associated, it is not difficult to get yourself mentally into arm training. If you go into any serious gym around the country you will probably see young bodybuilders who are just beginning to show overall signs of competition potential, but who already have made great strides in arm development.

One of the reasons this happens is that bodybuilders, especially when starting out, train the arms according to the Priority Principle, whether they know it or not. They train arms first, with great concentration and energy. They flex and pose them all the time, measuring them constantly to see if they have made any progress, so naturally they grow. If they thought the same way about their other body parts, we no doubt would see a lot of them walking around with 20-inch calves as well as huge arms.

But developing top-quality arms for competition is more than just a matter of size. They need to look good in a lot of poses and from a number of different angles. This means that every part of the arm muscles, every contour and angle, must be fully brought out. This takes a lot of thought and planning. You don't develop championship-level arms simply by throwing around a heavy barbell doing Curls and blasting out some reps for triceps.

Me at nineteen

Front double-biceps pose

Back double-biceps pose

Two aspects of the biceps. In the right arm, a high peak, great shape, and clear definition and separation; in the left, the biceps provides the mass and separation that helps make the arm look huge.

For a front double-biceps pose, for example, you need high-peaked biceps, triceps that hang impressively below the arm, and a well-defined separation between biceps and triceps. For the same pose from the back, you need forearm development at the elbow, good development of the outside head of the biceps, and a clear, visible tie-in between the deltoid and the muscles of the upper arm.

Along with biceps and triceps development, you need to build and shape your forearms so that they are in proportion to the muscles of the upper arm. When you look at the arms of Flex Wheeler or Kevin Levrone—or in the past, Frank Zane, Dave Draper, Bill Pearl, Larry Scott, or Sergio Oliva—you see biceps, triceps, and forearms all developed in proportion to one another.

These various aspects of development do not come about by accident. You need to work at it, which means breaking the muscles of the arms down into separate categories and making sure that each gets its share of hard training.

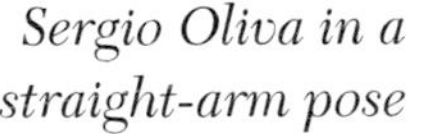
Sergio Oliva in a straight-arm pose

Side chest pose

Another straight-arm pose

Awesome arm development from Mike Matarazzo—full, high-peaked biceps, a balance between biceps and triceps development, and full, powerful arms.

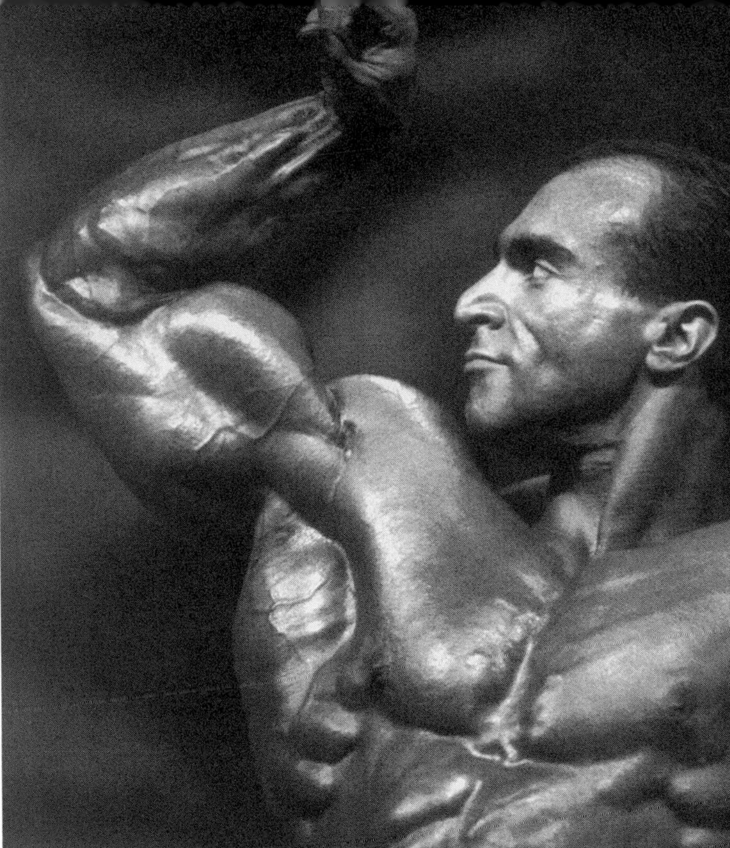

Nasser El Sonbaty

Larry Scott, the first Mr. Olympia, was one of the first modern bodybuilders with what I would call perfect arms.

Having big arms isn't enough. The shape of the biceps and triceps is also important, as are the proportions of the entire upper arm.

When it comes to total arm development, Mike Matarazzo is able to hold his own with just about anybody.

DEVELOPING PERFECT ARMS

The front double-biceps pose is one of the hardest to do well. Flex Wheeler carries it off because he has everything: proper proportion, good biceps, triceps, deltoids, and pecs, a full rib cage, sweeping lats, and a small waist.

Though we tend to think of giant, bulging biceps when we think of well-developed arms, in point of fact the triceps are the larger, more complex muscle group. The biceps have two heads, the triceps have three. The ideally proportioned arm is usually one-third biceps and two-thirds triceps.

Ronnie Coleman

Lee Priest proves that impressive muscularity—and tremendous arm development—is possible for competitors of all statures.

Nasser El Sonbaty and Jean-Pierre Fux don't rely solely on incredible mass when they step onstage to compete. They have complete physiques, including proper forearm proportion, outstanding biceps, triceps, deltoids, and pec development.

Albert Beckles displays one of the best peaked biceps in bodybuilding history.

Paul Dillett shows the importance of proportion in creating a championship physique. It isn't enough for a bodybuilder this big to build big arms. They have to be big in proportion to the rest of his body, as is the case here.

Achieving arm perfection means knowing which muscles to train, with which exercises, and what amount of effort to give to each. There are different ways of approaching arm training. You can train the whole arm in one workout, either finishing each muscle group before going on to the next or alternating sets for biceps and triceps, getting the whole arm pumped at one time. Or you can break up your training so that you train triceps one day, biceps the next, and forearms whenever it suits you.

As with other body parts, total development comes about only when you are able to shock the arms into responding, no matter how big they become. Employing variety, change, and as many of the Shocking Principles as possible will all help give you the kind of quality arms you are training for.

Lee Priest is a "giant killer" in the tradition of Danny Padilla and Franco Columbu, and this view of the outstanding development of his upper arms and forearms shows why.

Biceps Training

Biceps have always been one of my best body parts. When I was young, building up my biceps was especially important to me, so I worked very hard and soon they blew up like balloons.

However, as hard as I may have worked, I now realize that my outstanding biceps development is largely hereditary. My biceps are like Tom Platz's thighs—once subjected to the hard work to *make* them develop, they possessed the genetic potential to be among the best in the world.

Hard work and proper training technique will bring out the full potential of any muscle, but not everybody has the same degree of potential. Some bodybuilders have longer biceps, some shorter; some with a higher or lower peak; some that develop enormous thickness and others that do not. You can work on each of these aspects of your development, bring up weak points with intelligent planning, but it certainly helps if you have a predisposition to great shape and proportion in the first place.

Actually, there are many different-shaped biceps that can still be considered first-rate. Among the bodybuilders against whom I competed, Larry Scott was noted for long biceps, both thick and full at the same time. My own were noted for an extremely high peak. Franco Columbu's biceps were high, but short. Sergio Oliva had long biceps, but not particularly high. Boyer Coe had high, long biceps, but narrow. Despite these different arm structures, each of these bodybuilders won impressive titles. The same is true today—you will see bodybuilders with different proportions, different genetic gifts, but each can be a champion if he or she possesses a certain "package," a balancing set of characteristics.

The underlying bone structure and physical proportions have a lot to do with how the arm will ultimately look. Because Franco has short arms, it was not difficult for him to develop biceps that looked proportionately massive. But Lou Ferrigno, with his very long arms, needed 22-inch biceps just to have them look in proportion to his 260-pound body. If he had had 20-inch arms, even though they might be the biggest onstage, he would have looked proportionately underdeveloped.

Proportion and the relative strength of various other muscles can also make a difference in how the biceps are trained and developed. For example, when watching Franco Columbu and Ken Waller doing Barbell Curls, it seemed to me that because the front delts were so powerful, these muscles were taking over a lot of the lifting effort from the biceps. Therefore, they had to make a special effort to isolate the biceps, or else they would never have gotten the training they required. One way they did this was by using the "Arm Blaster" to lock their elbows in place while doing Curls. (You can see me using this apparatus on page 429.) Another was by doing a lot of biceps training using a preacher bench to further isolate the arm muscles.

If you have a similar problem but don't have this kind of specialized equipment, you can simply do your Curls standing with your back against a wall in order to minimize cheating.

Since my front delts were not so proportionately strong, I didn't have that problem. Therefore, I found doing regular Barbell Curls very beneficial. I did not have to make the special effort to isolate the biceps, which was just as well since I didn't know that much about the physiology of training in my early years.

Nonetheless, you can't use other muscles to help with the lift and expect to develop great biceps. You also need to find the right groove—doing any Curl movement through the longest range of motion. When you do a Curl, you must bring your hand directly up to your shoulder. If you change that line an inch to the inside or the outside, you are taking stress off the biceps and you won't get the same results.

Another mistake I see all the time—Sergio Oliva used to do this—is starting off a Curl movement with a Wrist Curl—bending the wrist back, then curling it up just before engaging the biceps. All this does is take stress away from the biceps by using forearm strength rather than biceps strength, and the result will be huge forearms and mediocre biceps.

But one Curl movement is not enough to work the entire biceps. The biceps not only lift and curl the arm, they also rotate the wrist. Lifting with a bar produces biceps mass, but it locks the wrists and keeps them from moving. So I always include a number of dumbbell exercises that let me twist the wrist to the outside as I lift the weight, giving me a more complete biceps contraction. Working with dumbbells, I'm able to get a better brachialis development at the elbow, and that creates a much sharper separation between the biceps and triceps in a rear double-biceps pose.

Biceps length is also important. Many people do Reverse Curls as a forearm exercise, but I have noticed this exercise also increases the apparent biceps length. The muscle should extend all the way down almost to the elbow and then swoop into a full and powerful-looking curve.

I also like to change my hand position as much as possible when doing Curls in order to completely stimulate all the different areas of the biceps. The Barbell Curl locks the hand, the Dumbbell Curl lets you rotate the hand, the Reverse Curl brings the hand up in a palm-down position, and lifting a dumbbell with the thumb on top, a kind of Hammer Curl, hits the brachialis directly and is necessary for complete biceps development. And I add variety to my biceps workouts by using different kinds of equipment—the Arm Blaster, a straight bar, an E-Z curl bar, a preacher bench, a prone bench, barbells, dumbbells, cables, and machines. Again, the major mistake I see in biceps training is lack of a full movement. There is probably no body part in which training for a full range of motion is so important. You will restrict the range of motion if you do things like lifting your elbows up or holding them too far back and therefore not getting a wide enough arc in the exercise.

This is an incorrect beginning position for Barbell Curls. The arms are bent and elbows back, which prevents the biceps from being fully extended and drastically shortens the range of motion. Since the arms never get stretched out using this technique, you never fully stress the lower part of the biceps.

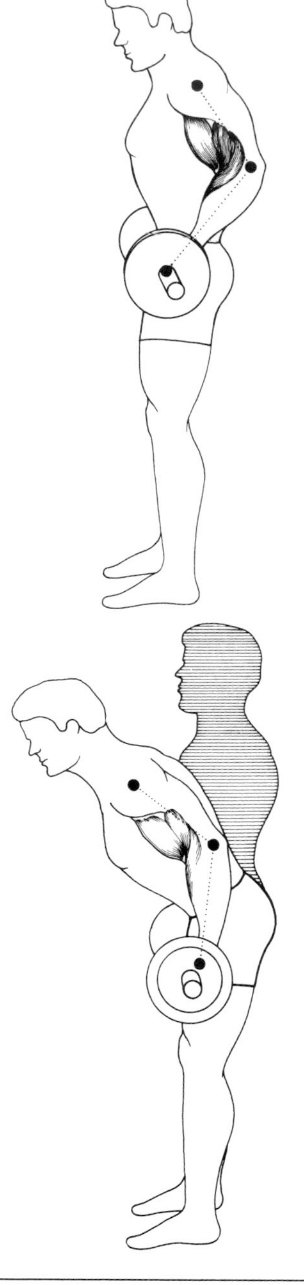

Starting the lift from a bent-over position is one of the most common mistakes made when doing Barbell Curls. If you begin the lift and straighten up at the same time, the lower back becomes involved. This produces extra momentum during the movement that causes you to swing the weight up instead of lifting it with an intense contraction of the biceps, so the lower part of the biceps never gets properly stimulated. For the correct approach to this exercise, see page 428.

Some bodybuilders don't want to lower the weight to full extension, with their arms locked out, because they can't lift as much weight that way. But they forget that it is this lower area of the range of motion that creates the real thickness in the lower biceps and makes the muscle appear to come right out of the forearm—an important look when you do poses with your arms extended. This part of the muscle also rolls up and helps create height when you flex.

You see bodybuilders locking out their arms on Curls, but then they ruin the movement by not doing a strict curling motion right from the beginning. Instead, they lift the weight up, using a little shoulders and some back, so the first few inches of the movement are wasted because the biceps are simply not involved.

Another mistake is to bring the weight all the way up and then neglect to flex and contract the muscle. When the weight is up at your chin, the bones and joints are taking most of the strain. To keep the muscle working, you have to really flex it hard or it remains soft because you are not keeping it under stress. You are never going to have full, hard, and thick biceps with which to impress judges if you get lazy at the top of your Curl movements.

CHEAT CURLS

Curls are one of the exercises where cheating can be used effectively. Curls are essentially a rotary movement, yet the resistance of the weight works vertically. In other words, you are lifting with a circular motion but gravity continues to pull the weight straight down. Sometimes during the movement you are lifting out, other times lifting up, but the resistance is always up and down. So you are not continuously lifting in direct opposition to the weight. This makes the exercise less effective in certain parts of the movement.

The designers of Curl machines state that their equipment, which acts with a rotary rather than linear motion, is better for doing Curls than barbells or dumbbells. However, you don't need a complicated machine to overcome this difficulty. Instead, you can do some of your Curls using a weight that is too heavy for a strict movement. So even though you are using your back and shoulders to help "force" the weight up, you are also forcing the biceps to work to the maximum at every point along the movement.

The barbell or dumbbell is harder to lift at the point where your forearms are parallel to the floor than at the beginning of a Curl when your arms are pointed more toward the floor. Doing Cheat Curls, you can use a weight that feels very heavy in the "easy" part of the movement and then cheat a little to get you past the "hard" part where the resistance is too great to overcome using strict technique.

Doing exhibitions for Reg Park in South Africa I would do 5 repetitions of Barbell Cheat Curls with 275 pounds. Handling this amount of weight does not help create great biceps shape or give the muscle a high peak, but it certainly is effective as a mass builder. However, Cheat Curls should be no more than 10 percent of your biceps program. You also need a variety of strict movements to develop the complete quality of the muscle.

BEGINNING PROGRAM

The Barbell Curl, done strictly for beginners, is the fundamental exercise for building mass in the biceps. The Barbell Curl remains in the program all the way through, from Beginning to Competition Training. This is the only way to continue to build and maintain maximum muscle mass and thickness. But I also recommend including Dumbbell Curls from the very start because this exercise allows you to supinate your wrist, which gives you a more complete contraction and helps develop the full shape of the muscles.

I also recommend One-Arm Curls almost from the beginning. When doing these, I hold on to something with one hand to steady myself, lean a little to the side to give myself a free range of motion, and concentrate totally on each biceps in turn—something you can't do when you are working both arms at the same time.

ADVANCED PROGRAM

When you get into Advanced Training, you continue trying to build additional mass, but you must also be concerned with creating separation and shaping the entire biceps structure. If your biceps lacks peak, work on height. If it's not thick enough, make it thick.

Incline Dumbbell Curls are the best exercise for developing the shape and quality of the biceps and getting an even greater stretch in the muscle. Along with this, the Concentration Curl can help add biceps height.

As you progress, you will begin to superset your exercises, creating more intensity by cutting down the time interval. I like the idea of supersetting biceps and triceps, which gives an enormous pump to your arms and makes you feel gigantic. Also, you can handle heavier weights for triceps when your biceps are pumped like a pillow, giving you a kind of cushion you can bounce off with each triceps repetition.

Supersetting different muscles is also valuable in preparing you for competition, when you will need to pump your whole body at the same time. If you aren't used to this, you will not be able to show yourself at your best when you step out onstage.

The closer you get to competition, the more you have to be certain that you do enough additional exercises to fully develop every aspect of the biceps. Besides the mass-building Barbell Curls, you need to do more Incline Curls, which help develop the lower part of the muscle. I often would go even further and actually lie on a flat bench to do Dumbbell Curls, stretching the biceps even more. You also need additional cable and dumbbell work which allows you to twist your wrist and more fully shape the muscle.

COMPETITION PROGRAM

At each level, you are required to do something extra, to continue to overload and demand more of the muscles. This principle is even more important when you are training your arms for competition. One good way of increasing the intensity of your training is by doing Alternate Dumbbell Curls instead of Barbell Curls. In this way you are able to isolate each biceps, and concentrate all your energy on each arm in turn. Because of the way this exercise is done—with one arm coming up as the other is going down—you are able to achieve a much stricter movement with very little cheating. You can increase intensity by going farther and locking in the elbows by doing Preacher Curls, which force you to work in a stricter manner while hitting the lower biceps to a greater degree.

The degree of time-intensive training you need for competition preparation is greater than ever before, involving trisets—three exercises in a row without any stopping to rest in between. This will be difficult at first, but as your conditioning increases you will find this accelerated program gives you a tremendous pump and allows you to do an enormous amount of training in a very short time.

Above all, you need to employ as many techniques as possible to shock the biceps into further development. I always liked, for example, to do Barbell Curls with a partner: I would do a set, hand the weight immediately to him to do his set, have him hand it back to me immediately for my next set, and so on until exhaustion.

For total competition development, I made sure I did a lot of single sets, supersets, and trisets with a large variety of exercises—a set of biceps once an hour every hour the day before a contest; cheating reps; partial reps; forced reps; negative reps; Curls to the inside, Curls to the outside—nothing left out, nothing left to chance.

I attacked my biceps for competition with the Stripping Method, but also with 21s, combining a lot of partial reps and full reps, and supersetting one biceps exercise with another as well as supersetting biceps with triceps, or biceps with whatever.

I also used a lot of visualization in biceps training. In my mind I saw my biceps as mountains, enormously huge, and I pictured myself lifting tremendous amounts of weight with these superhuman masses of muscle.

This kind of intense training will ensure that you build enough mass in the biceps; that you gain biceps length, thickness, and height; that you develop the inside and outside of the biceps and the separation between biceps and deltoids and between biceps and triceps—all of which you have to have if you want to build a championship physique.

WEAK POINT TRAINING

But even if you do everything I have just outlined, and more, you may still find that certain areas of the biceps are relatively less well developed than others.

In general, when you are trying to build up a weak area of the biceps, the best technique you can employ is one-arm dumbbell exercises. Doing an entire set with just one arm at a time allows for maximum concentration and intensity, and ensures that each arm works to its maximum. This keeps a stronger biceps from overshadowing the weaker, which can result in asymmetrical arm development. Also, be sure to twist the wrist during the movement for total biceps contraction.

However, I believe one major reason bodybuilders show weak points in the biceps is that they do the exercises incorrectly. You need to master proper technique—keeping the elbows steady, lowering the weight rather than dropping it, employing as many Shocking Principles as possible—and then you will be much less likely to have problems in this area.

For example, I see a lot of bodybuilders using their forearms when they do Curls, starting the motion with a kind of Wrist Curl which takes away from the effectiveness of the exercise. Or they will do a Curl and, at the top, instead of flexing their biceps—to maintain maximal tension—they will just throw the weight back toward their shoulders, leaving the biceps loose and not working at all. I recommend instead using the peak contraction principle—flexing the biceps as hard as possible when you get to the top of the Curl.

One-Arm Dumbbell Curl (Jay Cutler)

This photo shows my arms at their most massive, when I weighed 245 pounds and relied heavily on Barbell and Cheat Curls using very heavy poundage. Notice how thick and huge the unflexed arm looks.

But sometimes biceps development lags behind simply because they aren't being trained hard enough, the bodybuilder feeling that 5 sets of biceps is plenty and ending up with big but relatively shapeless masses of muscle where he should have beautifully sculpted biceps.

To correct specific weak points in the biceps, I recommend the following exercises:

For Mass

Heavy Barbell Curls and Cheat Curls. Muscle size comes from lifting heavy weights. If you can curl 110 pounds and you train up to the point where you can curl 130 pounds, your biceps are going to get bigger. Try using my visualization technique to imagine your biceps growing to superhuman size.

For Length and Thickness

Curls that concentrate on the lower third of the range of motion

Incline or Prone Curls to stretch the biceps to their maximum

Strict movements, like Preacher Curls or Curls with the Arm Blaster, to lock your elbows and allow you to get the fullest extension of the biceps

After completion of each set of my Dumbbell Curl exercise, rotate the wrists 180 degrees 5 or 6 times.

The longer and thicker your biceps, the better they will look when you hold your arm straight out, and the bigger and higher they will be when you curl and flex your arm in a biceps shot.

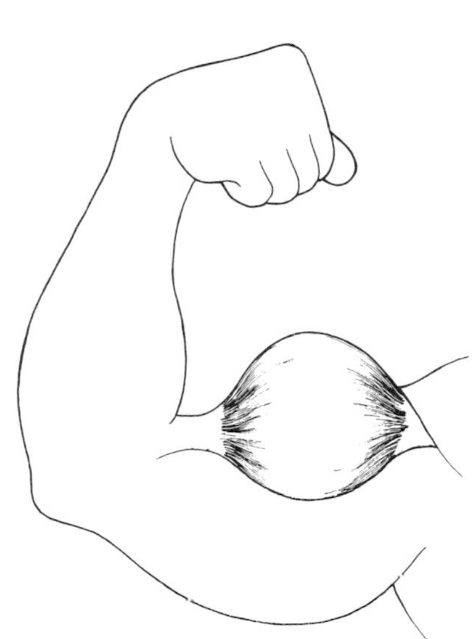

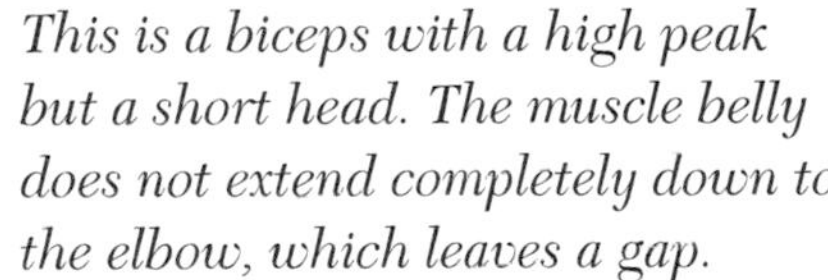

This is a biceps with a high peak but a short head. The muscle belly does not extend completely down to the elbow, which leaves a gap.

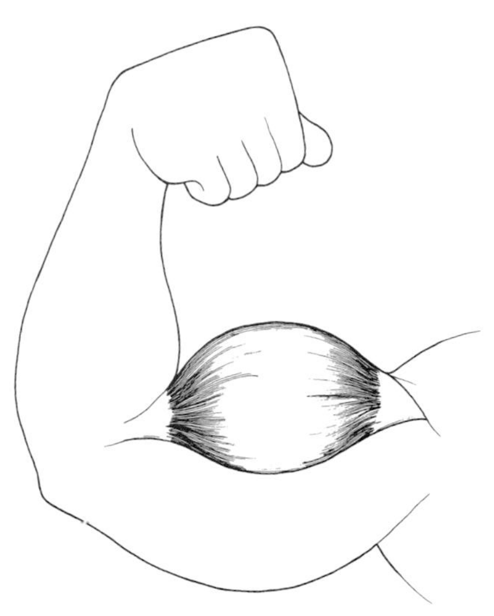

This biceps has a long head, but it lacks height.

Many bodybuilders don't realize that the function of the biceps is to twist the wrist as well as lift and curl. This is why I always started a curling movement as shown in pictures 1 and 2.

1

2

The hand positions in pictures 3 and 4 are good if you want to eliminate wrist rotation while doing Dumbbell Curls.

3

4

Thickness in the biceps is important, but height is a quality that is often overlooked. I have always worked hard on developing peaks, and I feel that I won a lot of competitions because of my high biceps.

For Height

Concentration Curls with a dumbbell or cable

Dumbbell movements emphasizing a twist of the wrist (turning the thumb outward) as you raise the weight, making certain you concentrate on the top third of the range of motion

Use the peak contraction principle—flexing the biceps as hard as possible at the top of the movement—and do a series of contractions and relaxation.

Keep going until you get a tremendous pump.

Include burns in your workout—finishing off by bringing up the weight and fully contracting the biceps, then bringing the weight down a third of the way, then back up to another full contraction. Do 3 or 4 reps of this movement and then put the weight down and pose and flex your biceps.

For Biceps Mass and Outer Thickness

Curls done inward toward the center of the body, such as Close-Grip Barbell Curls or Close-Grip Preacher Bench Curls

Concentration Curls that bring the weight into your chest

Well-developed outer biceps allow you to hit a number of poses effectively. For example, one of my favorite biceps poses is where I simply flex my arm and show the judges the outer biceps. But to get this kind of development you need to work the biceps.from all angles.

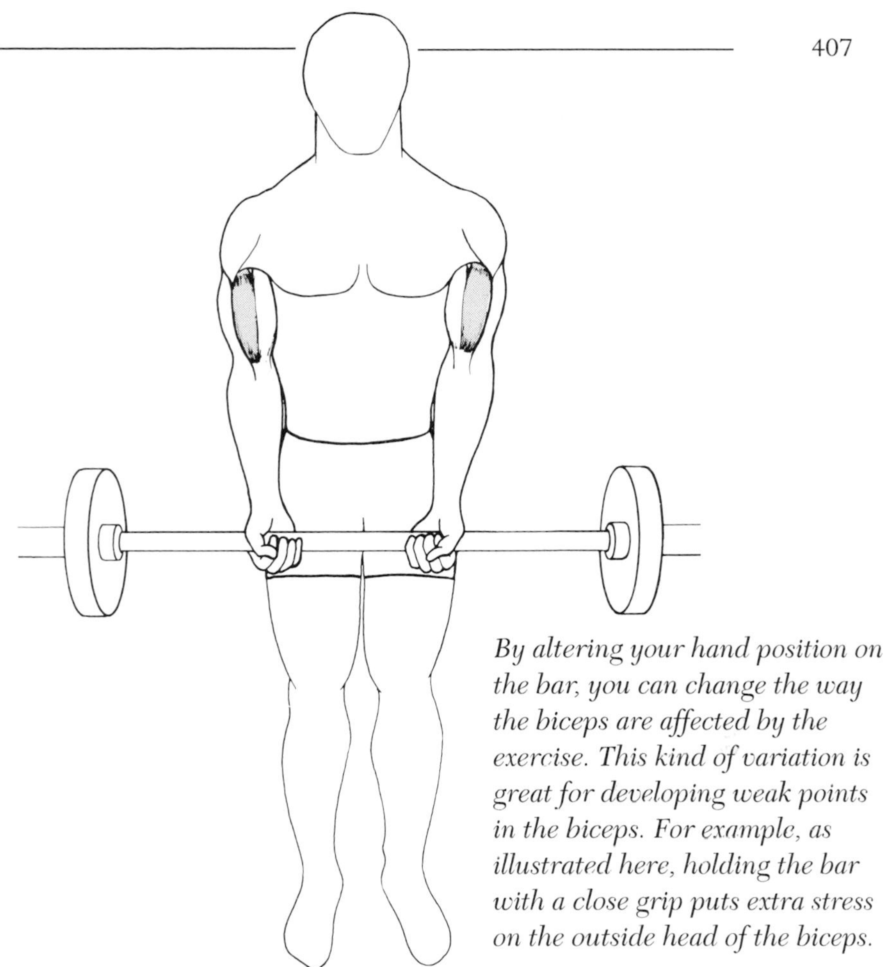

By altering your hand position on the bar, you can change the way the biceps are affected by the exercise. This kind of variation is great for developing weak points in the biceps. For example, as illustrated here, holding the bar with a close grip puts extra stress on the outside head of the biceps.

In order to make back poses like this twisting three-quarters back shot work, you have to have good outer biceps and brachialis development (at the elbow) in order to separate the biceps and triceps.

Vince Taylor

David Hughes

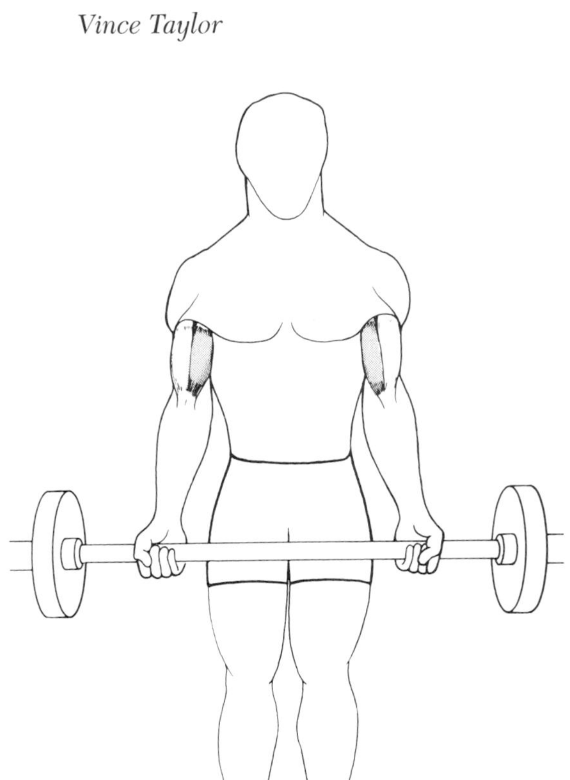

If your weak point is the inner region of the biceps, you can put more stress on this area by holding your hands in a wide grip for Barbell Curls.

Lee Priest

Flex Wheeler

Robby Robinson's arms are one of the best examples of biceps definition and separation. Looking at Robby in this photo is like examining an anatomy chart.

For Biceps Mass and Inner Thickness

Hold dumbbells in a "hammer" position—palm turned toward the inside rather than facing upward. You can feel how this changes the stress on the biceps.

Standing Barbell Curls

Barbell Preacher Curls done with a wide grip

Seated or Standing Dumbbell Curls

Incline Dumbbell Curls

Standing Alternate Dumbbell Curls in which your arms are kept wide, angling away from the body. If you curl out and downward and turn wrists slightly outward, dropping your thumbs slightly, you will feel the exercise much more specifically in the inner biceps.

For Separation and Definition

High set training, supersets, and trisets. Try to use as many different biceps exercises as possible, especially dumbbell movements that allow you to train at the greatest variety of angles and lots of one-arm movements to create maximum isolation.

Reverse Curls, to develop brachio radialis and biceps that look so good when you do a rear double-biceps shot. Remember to keep your elbows steady as a pivot point and your wrists steady throughout the movement.

Serge Nubret has full, thick triceps, so his arms still look massive even when he is standing relaxed.

Triceps Training

The triceps is a larger muscle mass than the biceps, and it needs training from more angles. Like the biceps, the triceps have to look good from any view. But unlike the biceps, the triceps need to make your arm look big, massive, and impressive when your arms are not flexed as well. When somebody says, "Wow, look at the size of that guy's arms!" you can be sure it is the triceps that are creating that effect. They are visible 90 percent of the time you are onstage, whether you are standing relaxed or hitting poses.

Bill Pearl, Serge Nubret, Sergio Oliva, Albert Beckles, Freddy Ortiz, Casey Viator, Jusup Wilkosz, and Frank Zane are all good examples of bodybuilders who have great triceps. The triceps need to be developed in such a way that they look good when you do a side triceps shot, a front or rear biceps shot, or pose with your arms raised overhead or held straight out (a pose Larry Scott, Dave Draper, and I were noted for and which requires outstanding triceps). Imagine doing a rear lat shot and how effective good triceps can be from that angle. Or a most-muscular pose, with the triceps sticking out right from the elbow and continuing on to the rear deltoid. Or a front abdominal shot where your hands are behind your head.

While it is possible to hide weak biceps to some extent, weak triceps are obvious in almost any pose. When the judges look at you standing relaxed in round one they will know immediately if you have good triceps or not. Sergio Oliva, for example, could just stand there, his triceps looking huge and powerful, and make an impression on the judges, even though his biceps were not that outstanding.

However, just as with other body parts, there is a difference between big triceps and good triceps. Every part of this relatively complex muscle needs to be fully developed. When your arms hang, the triceps need to be evident all the way from the elbow to the rear deltoid. When they are flexed, each of the heads must be fully shaped, separated, and distinct.

BEGINNING AND ADVANCED PROGRAMS

The first step in training triceps is to build up the mass and strength of the muscle structure. This means doing the basic triceps press and extension movements, gradually adding more and more weight until the area begins to respond. Different kinds of presses and extensions are designed to develop specific areas of the triceps. But there are also techniques you can use to maximize your triceps training. Remember that anytime you straighten your arm against resistance—whether you are specifically doing triceps training or not—you will involve the triceps muscles.

In most cases, muscle mass and strength are enhanced by employing a cheating technique, but you don't need to cheat in order to put extra stress on the triceps. With all the effort you expend doing power training with Bench Presses, Dumbbell Presses, and Shoulder Presses, you are already putting an enormous strain on the triceps area.

Even though the triceps are involved in a wide range of different exercises, it is also necessary, especially as you become more advanced, to isolate the heads and put the stress on each part directly to make certain you get full development of the muscle structure. For this, I recommend a number of different Triceps Extension movements, using barbells, dumbbells, and cables, each of which tends to hit a different area of the triceps.

Bill Pearl is the king of this particular triceps pose, which is a great way of showing the development of the upper triceps.

Proportions and bone structure of individual bodybuilders will make it easier for some to develop good triceps. When doing Triceps Pressdowns, for example, it is easy for some to isolate the triceps, while others with different proportions and muscle attachments will find themselves involving the pectorals or even the lats instead of just the triceps. You see this a lot when some bodybuilders try to do Triceps Pressdowns and end up with a good chest pump. In a case like this, learning to totally isolate the triceps becomes extremely important, and can be accomplished by doing One-Arm Triceps Extensions or Barbell Triceps Extensions.

Lying Triceps Extensions work the muscle from the elbow to the rear deltoid, and are also great for developing the triceps for straight-arm poses. One-Arm Triceps Extensions help develop the triceps so that they look good when you are doing biceps shots, with the fullness of the triceps offsetting the peak of the biceps. Lying Dumbbell Extensions work the outer head of the triceps to a greater degree, giving you the shape and thickness you need for total triceps development.

Your hand position makes a difference in how an exercise affects the triceps. If you hold your hand so that the thumb is up, palm facing the inside, you work the outside of the triceps, to a slightly greater degree, as when doing Triceps Pressdowns holding on to a rope rather than pressing down on a bar or performing Dumbbell Kickbacks. If you turn your hand so that the palm is facedown, as in a Triceps Pressdown, you put more stress on the inner part of the triceps. If you twist your wrist, thumbs in and down, which is easiest when doing One-Arm Cable Triceps Pressdowns, you really hit the muscle a little bit differently.

Advanced training also involves supersetting, hitting the muscle with one exercise after another to develop size, strength, shape, and endurance. You need to work the upper and lower long, lateral, and medial heads. Adding on exercises is important only if you pursue them with the kind of intensity that forces the muscles to continue to grow, no matter how advanced you become.

COMPETITION PROGRAM

Until you have seen a top-rated bodybuilder in shape for competition hitting a triceps shot, you probably have no idea what the muscle structure is supposed to look like. It is, in fact, almost like a horseshoe that curves up from the elbow, separated clearly from the deltoids above it and the biceps on the other side of the arm. In a bodybuilder, this muscle can be awesome.

The Competition Program, which will help you achieve this kind of look in your own physique, uses additional exercises besides those you have already learned, and a lot of time-intensive supersets to create the maximum training intensity.

Exercises like Cable Pressdowns, Kickbacks, Close-Grip Presses, and Dips tend to fully work the triceps. Almost any triceps exercise will help develop the lower part of the muscle if you work only the lower range of motion. Take hold of the weight and bend your elbows, stretching the triceps as fully as possible. Then start to straighten out your arms, but stop after going through only about a third of the range of motion. Go back and forth just through this partial range and you effectively work the lower area.

For upper triceps, completely lock out your arms on any triceps exercise and hold this contraction for 3 or 4 seconds, tensing the muscle isometrically. Following your set, pose and tense the muscle while your training partner does his set and you will get even more response from the upper triceps.

Remember, too, that the triceps rotates the wrist in opposition to the biceps. Just as you twisted the wrist outward in biceps exercises, you should do some triceps exercises in which you twist the wrist in the opposite direction. This will give you complete contraction of the triceps muscle. Behind-the-Neck Dumbbell Extensions and One-Arm Cable Pressdowns are exercises for this purpose.

Lee Haney displays the ultimate in triceps mass. He doesn't have to squeeze his arm in against his lats to make the triceps appear huge; all he has to do is extend the arm downward and flex.

WEAK POINT TRAINING

If you have a real problem with the triceps, I recommend training them according to the Priority Principle, working them first, when you are fresh. I did this myself years ago when I realized that my biceps had developed out of proportion to my triceps. I began to concentrate on this area, using the Priority Principle, and soon they began to respond so I had an Olympia-quality arm rather than just Olympia-quality biceps.

I also found that supersetting triceps exercises, going right from one to the other, was another way of getting extra triceps development. I would first do a few sets to pump up the biceps, which creates a "cushioning" effect, and then really blast the triceps. After the superset I would continue to flex and pose the triceps, never giving them any relief.

If triceps are an especially weak point for you, I recommend changing your program so that you train them by themselves from time to time, allowing you to concentrate only on the back of the arms to totally shock and stimulate the triceps. To overcome specific weak points, I recommend the following exercises:

For Mass

Use a heavy weight in each exercise:

- Close-Grip Barbell Presses
- Weighted Dips
- Dips Behind the Back

Dorian Yates

For Mass and Upper Triceps

Cable Pressdowns and One-Arm Cable Pressdowns (regular and reverse grip)
Kickbacks
Dips

Do all triceps exercises strictly so that you really flex them totally, concentrating on locking out on each movement. Use the peak contraction principle, holding the full contraction for a few moments at the top of each repetition.

Nasser El Sonbaty

Chris Dickerson is not known for having huge arms, but his triceps—particularly his upper triceps—are so well developed that his arms look really massive in this pose. Notice also the kind of superb separation between triceps and deltoid that helped Chris win the 1982 Mr. Olympia title.

For Mass and Lower Triceps

Weighted Dips

Dips Behind the Back—doing partial reps in which you go all the way down, but come up only about three-quarters of the way (and not locking out) to keep the lower area of the triceps under stress the whole time (the more your arm is bent, the more your lower triceps takes up the stress)

Here Shawn Ray demonstrates two different and effective ways to display outstanding triceps development.

Forearm Training

Forearms should be taken just as seriously as any other body part if you want to develop a truly quality physique. They are involved in nearly every exercise for the upper body, either by helping you grip a piece of equipment or by being a part of all pushing and pulling actions. So they get a lot of incidental training even when you are not specifically doing forearm exercises. In fact, anytime you flex the elbows or wrists, you put stress on the forearm muscles.

Good forearm development is necessary to create a championship physique, but forearm strength is just as important. Strong forearms allow you to train with heavier weights and, in exercises such as Chins and Cable Rows, in which the hand and wrist are generally the "weak link," give you the capacity to train hard and put more stress on other muscles.

As with other muscles, genetic structure is a factor in determining the potential size and strength of the forearms. The reason some forearm muscles seem to extend all the way to the hand, with almost no tendon intervening, is that that person has an extremely long "muscle belly"—the

Ronnie Coleman's arm development is a perfect example of how inner biceps development helps create the necessary separation between the biceps and triceps, as well as between the biceps and forearms.

actual contractile part of the muscle-tendon structure. Muscle size is affected by the length of the muscle belly because mass is a product of *volume*—that is, three dimensions rather than just one. So having two inches more length in the forearm actually translates into a lot of extra potential when you consider what the increase in cubic measurement can be. Many bodybuilders constructed like this claim they do not need to do forearm training but get adequate results with exercises like heavy Barbell Curls. However, when I trained with Casey Viator, who had incredible forearm development, I saw him doing Barbell Wrist Curls with 155 pounds and Reverse Curls with 135 pounds. Sergio Oliva did endless sets of Reverse Curls on a preacher bench to get that enormous upper forearm development. Dave Draper did a lot of forearm training. So, even if you are genetically gifted with good forearms, this doesn't mean you don't have to train them.

It is also possible to have high forearms—that is, to have a relatively short muscle belly and a long tendon, limiting the cubic volume of the muscle mass. Most bodybuilders, myself included, are somewhere in between, with neither the full forearm structure of a Sergio Oliva nor impossibly high forearms. With this kind of forearm, it is possible to build the muscles up to where they are proportionate to the upper arm, but you have to train them hard to do so.

Casey Viator demonstrates a basic forearm pose.

BEGINNING PROGRAM

Forearm training should be included as a part of your regular workout schedule right from the beginning, but these workouts will differ somewhat from those for other body parts. Because forearms are involved in so

These poses by Lee Labrada require great forearm development to balance the mass and separation of the upper arm.

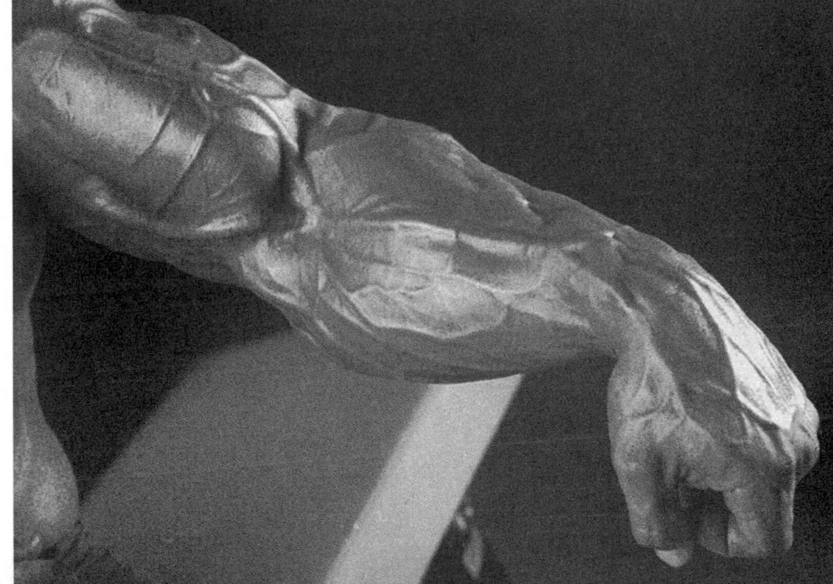

many other exercises, you will not need very many forearm exercises to start with—Barbell Wrist Curls and Reverse Wrist Curls will suffice. I do not recommend doing as many sets for forearms as for legs, back, or other body parts, but I have found that doing sets of relatively high reps gives the best results.

One mistake many bodybuilders make with forearm training is that they don't use enough weight. Forearms are somewhat like calves in that they are accustomed to continual use and heavy stress. So you need to use a fairly heavy weight in order to really stimulate the muscles.

Strict technique is also necessary to totally isolate the forearms and not let the biceps do the work. This is done by laying your forearms firmly on a bench, elbows close together and locked in between your knees.

It may seem to some that concentrating on forearms right from the beginning is not that important, but I disagree—forearm and grip strength are so essential to being able to train hard and heavy that you need to develop the forearms right from day one. And since forearm growth comes slowly to some people, the sooner you get started working on it the better.

ADVANCED PROGRAM

In the Advanced Training Program I have added One-Arm Wrist Curls to isolate and increase the intensity on each forearm, and constructed the workout so that you superset Wrist Curls and Reverse Wrist Curls, giving you a total forearm pump.

Of course, just the fact that you are training the rest of the body so much more intensely at this point will in itself force the arms to work harder. Your total workout will tend to exhaust forearms so that, once you get to training them specifically, it will take a great deal of concentration and dedication to work these tired and worn-out muscles.

Remember that forearm size, more than almost any other part, depends on genetics. If you have a short forearm muscle belly and therefore have trouble gaining the kind of size you'd like to have, begin thinking about extra forearm work early. Because forearms gain in size slowly, you need time to make the changes you are looking for.

But you might be surprised just how quickly you can develop forearms if you really make the effort. Often, the reason bodybuilders have problems developing forearms is simply that they don't train them hard enough. They tack forearm training onto the end of their workout and do a few halfhearted sets. Believe me, if you want any body part to develop to its maximum you have to take it seriously. Forearm training is no less important than training the chest or biceps—if you truly want to become a champion.

COMPETITION PROGRAM

Once you begin training for competition, I recommend that you make sure you have hit every one of the fourteen muscles by adding Preacher Bench Reverse Curls and Behind-the-Back Wrist Curls to your forearm program.

When you do Reverse Curls for the upper part of the forearms, use a straight bar rather than an E-Z curl bar. As you lift the bar in an upward arc from the area of your thighs, you curl the wrists back and fully involve the upper forearms. Incidentally, many bodybuilders lean back as they do Reverse Curls, but you should actually lean slightly forward. This further isolates the arms, puts continuous stress on the forearms, and gives you a much stricter movement.

Reverse Curls also work well on certain kinds of curl machines and a preacher bench. But no matter which way you do this exercise, always remember to get a full range of movement—all the way down, all the way up, and keep it slow and under control. Remember, too, that your wrists and forearms will also be affected by heavy Barbell Curls and Cheat Curls, Triceps Extensions, and a number of other exercises throughout all the various levels of training.

I recommend doing forearm training at the end of your workout. If you try doing other upper body exercises when your wrists and forearms are already fatigued, you will severely limit your ability to train intensely.

One good method for totally stimulating your forearms is after you do your Wrist Curls—when you are too tired to do any more reps—simply let the bar hang in your fingers and then flex your fingers by opening and closing your hands and getting to those last few available muscle fibers.

POSING THE FOREARMS

There are two different kinds of forearm poses: direct, in which you are deliberately calling attention to these muscles; and indirect, in which you are primarily posing other body parts but the forearms play a part nonetheless. Often when you hit a pose, people watching don't specifically notice forearm development, but they would certainly notice if it wasn't there.

Since forearms are a third of the total arm, without proper forearm development the whole arm looks out of proportion. In a front double-biceps pose, the forearm must look full enough to balance off the development of the biceps. From the rear, in a back double-biceps, the muscularity of the forearm is part of the total effect.

Impressive forearms help you in every pose from side chest to most-muscular and are extremely important when you have your arms ex-

Dave Draper showing a direct forearm pose

tended, as in the classic javelin-thrower pose in which one arm is flexed, the other extended.

Certain poses are virtually impossible to carry off without exceptional forearm development. One that comes to mind is Sergio Oliva's famous pose where he lifts both hands overhead, flexes his forearms, and flares out his fantastic lats. In spite of Sergio's enormous back, if he didn't have such large and powerful forearms this pose would be much less impressive.

Some bodybuilders have such well-developed forearms that they can turn non-forearm poses into forearm showcases. Casey Viator is one of these. When he stands onstage and simply lifts his arms out to either side, it is impossible not to notice these huge forearms sticking out below the massive upper arms.

Another pose in which good forearms are absolutely essential is one Dave Draper and I both liked so much, in which the arms are held straight out, parallel to the floor. It takes both fully developed biceps and forearms to do this pose effectively.

Larry Scott was another bodybuilder who was able to pose his forearms to great advantage. When he won the very first Mr. Olympia contest in 1965, he had a thickness and muscularity that very few bodybuilders had ever attained. But he had also spent a lot of time in detail training, so his forearm development matched the rest of his physique, making many of his other poses that much more effective.

Flex Wheeler

Here I demonstrate a pose in which the back and biceps are featured but well-developed forearms are necessary to make the pose complete.

Sergio Oliva

Larry Scott

WEAK POINT TRAINING

Many bodybuilders end up with a weakness in forearm development simply because they don't train forearms right from the beginning. Another reason for forearms lagging behind, aside from the obvious one of bone structure, is failing to execute the exercises correctly and in a strict enough manner. The more you isolate the forearms and force them to do the movements without any help from the upper arms, the more they will respond. This means being very, very strict in your execution.

It is also important to work the forearms through a long range of motion. You need to lower the weight as far as possible, getting the maximum stretch, then come all the way back up to get a total contraction of the muscles. Working through only three-quarters of the range of motion is not that beneficial because you already use this part of the muscle in a variety of other exercises.

If you want to drastically increase your forearm development, you can use the Priority Principle in a special way: train forearms by themselves when you are rested and strong, or train your forearms on leg days when your arms are rested. You can also keep a barbell or dumbbells at home and do a couple of sets of Wrist Curls and Reverse Wrist Curls as often as you like, even once an hour every hour.

Many bodybuilders forget that you can use the Shocking Principle to help develop your forearms, just as you can other body parts. Every shock method that works with Curls will also work for Wrist Curls—forced reps, supersets, the Stripping Method, partial reps, and so on.

An important technique for bringing up lagging forearms is one-arm training. Forearms that are used to working together to curl a barbell will often be shocked into accelerated development when you force them to lift and control a weight on their own. Dumbbell Wrist Curls and Dumbbell Reverse Wrist curls are two of the primary exercises for accomplishing this. Additionally, doing cable work one arm at a time not only forces each forearm to work independently, but to work against a different kind of resistance as well. For this kind of movement, I recommend One-Arm Cable Reverse Curls.

It is also necessary to pose and flex your forearms as often as possible—not just when you are training them, but between sets of arms, chest, back, and shoulders as well. Your forearms will have to be flexed every time you hit any kind of pose in competition, so you might as well get them used to it. And the effort of contracting them like this will also accelerate their development.

To sum up, the exercises I recommend for forearm weak point training are:

Here is a pose by Dave Draper in which inner forearm development is extremely important.

For Upper Forearms/Wrist Extensor Muscles

- Reverse Curls with a barbell, dumbbells, and on a preacher bench
- One-Arm Cable Reverse Curls
- Hammer Curls
- Reverse Wrist Curls

For Inner Forearms/Wrist Flexor Muscles

- One-Arm Wrist Curls
- Barbell Wrist Curls
- Behind-the-Back Wrist Curls

In this side chest shot, Shawn Ray shows the importance of good upper forearm development as well as long forearm muscle that inserts all the way to the wrist.

Arm Exercises—Biceps

STANDING BARBELL CURLS

Purpose of Exercise: To develop the overall size of the biceps.

This is the most basic and popular of biceps exercises.

Execution: (1) Stand with feet shoulder-width apart and grasp the bar with an underhand grip, hands about shoulder width apart. Let the bar hang down at arm's length in front of you. (2) Curl the bar out and up in a wide arc and bring it up as high as you can, with your elbows close to the body and stationary. Keep the arc wide and long, rather than bringing the bar straight up and making the movement too easy. Fully flex at the top. Lower the weight again, following the same arc and resisting the weight all the way down until your arms are fully extended. A small amount of body movement in this exercise is acceptable because it is a mass-building movement, but this is to be kept to a minimum unless you are doing deliberate Cheat Curls. Bending forward and leaning back cut down on your range of motion.

To build maximum mass and work the total surface of the biceps, do Barbell Curls with your hands shoulder width apart. Notice how this puts the shoulders, arms, and hands in a straight line.

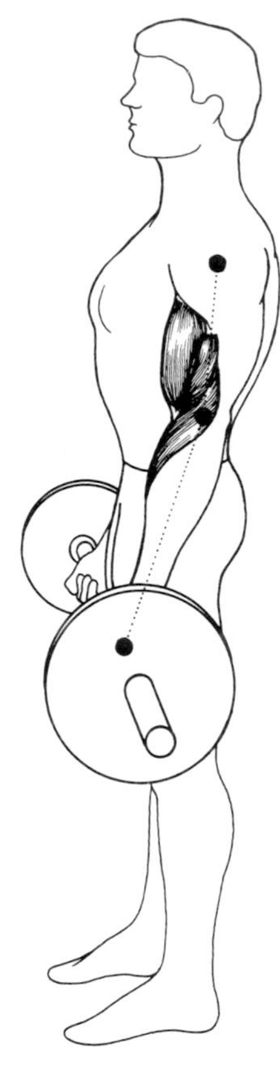

The correct beginning position for Barbell Curls: standing upright, elbows at sides, arms fully extended to stretch out the biceps

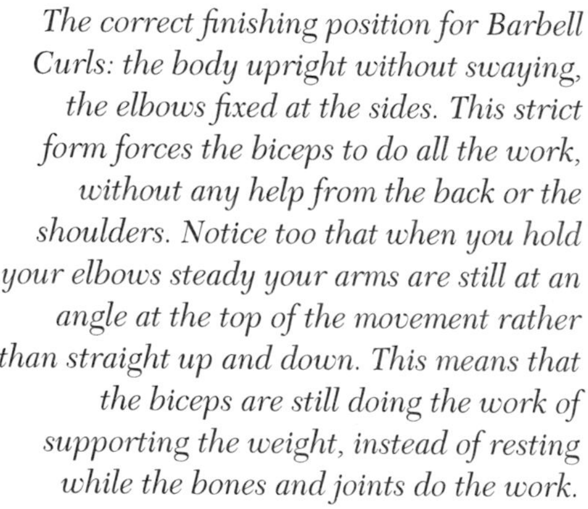

The correct finishing position for Barbell Curls: the body upright without swaying, the elbows fixed at the sides. This strict form forces the biceps to do all the work, without any help from the back or the shoulders. Notice too that when you hold your elbows steady your arms are still at an angle at the top of the movement rather than straight up and down. This means that the biceps are still doing the work of supporting the weight, instead of resting while the bones and joints do the work.

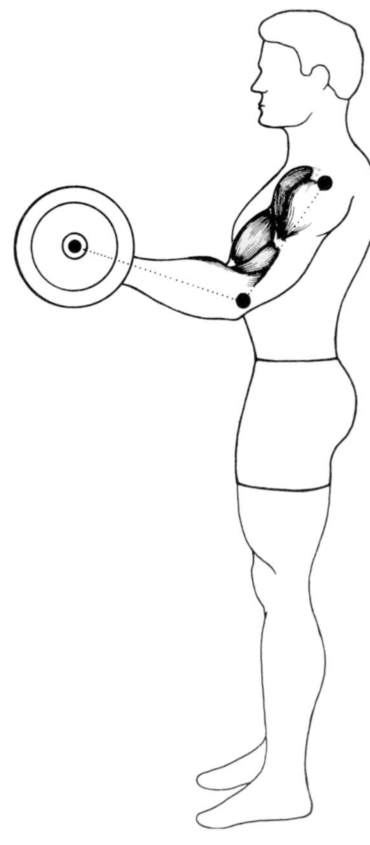

Notice what happens when you lift the elbows during the Barbell Curl. Instead of isolating and really working the biceps, you are involving the front deltoids, which defeats the purpose of the exercise.

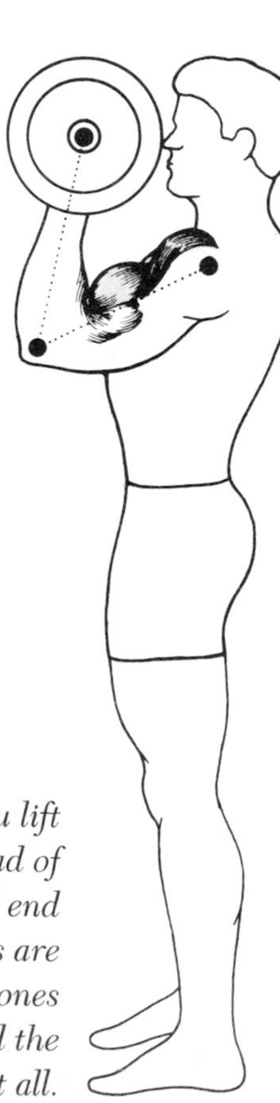

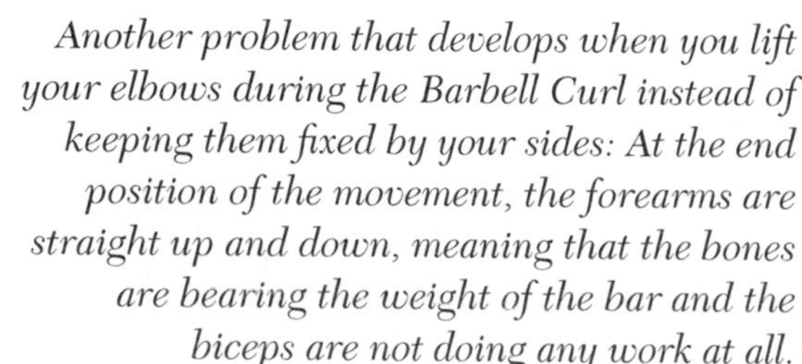

Another problem that develops when you lift your elbows during the Barbell Curl instead of keeping them fixed by your sides: At the end position of the movement, the forearms are straight up and down, meaning that the bones are bearing the weight of the bar and the biceps are not doing any work at all.

ARM BLASTER CURLS (OPTIONAL)

Doing Curls with an Arm Blaster—a piece of equipment that, unfortunately, you don't see very often today—is a very strict way of working the biceps that minimizes cheating. By using the Arm Blaster, you get the same kind of effect as with a preacher bench—no elbow movement at all and strict isolation of the biceps.

CHEAT CURLS

Purpose of Exercise: To develop extra mass and power in the biceps.

Execution: Stand and hold the bar as for Barbell Curls, but use enough weight so that it becomes difficult to do more than just a few strict repetitions. At this point, you begin to swing the weight up, using your back and shoulders to help your arms. The trick is to keep your biceps working as hard as they can, and cheat only enough to keep the set going. Keep the elbows stationary at the waist. I like to combine Barbell Curls and Cheat Curls, doing a normal set of Curls and, when my arms are too tired to do any more strict repetitions, loading on extra weight and doing some Cheat Curls to really blast the biceps.

PREACHER CURLS

Purpose of Exercise: To develop the biceps especially the lower end.

This is especially good for anyone who has space between the lower biceps and the elbow joint, to help fill in and shape this area.

Execution: Preacher Curls are an even stricter movement than regular Barbell Curls. (1) Position yourself with your chest against the bench, your arms extending over it. This puts the arms at an angle, which transfers additional stress to the lower area of the muscle. Take hold of a barbell with an underhand grip. (2) Holding your body steady, curl the bar all the way up and then lower it again to full extension, resisting the weight on the way down. You can use an E-Z curl bar for this movement, or even use the bench for One-Arm Dumbbell Curls. Don't lean back as you lift the bar, and deliberately flex the muscle extra hard as you come to the top of the movement, where there is little actual stress on the biceps muscles.

Preacher Curls can also be done with an E-Z curl bar.

Doing Preacher Curls with dumbbells forces each arm to work independently.

Robby Robinson

Doing this exercise with the dumbbells held closer together works the outer biceps to a slightly greater degree . . .

. . . and doing it with the dumbbells apart works the inner biceps more strongly.

3-PART CURLS (21S)

Purpose of Exercise: To develop and shape the entire biceps area.

This exercise, a combination of partial- and full-range movements, is a great test of endurance. Because of the combination of 3 sets of 7 repetitions each, this exercise is also known as 21s.

Execution: (1) From a seated or standing position, take a dumbbell in each hand, holding the weights at arm's length down at your sides. (2) Curl the weights upward but stop halfway, when your forearms are about parallel to the floor, then lower them again to the starting position. Do 7 repetitions of this movement. Then, without stopping, (3) curl the weights all the way up but stop halfway down and do 7 repetitions of this partial movement. At this point, even though exhaustion will be setting in, finish off the set by doing 7 full-range Dumbbell Curls. I like to do this exercise in front of a mirror so that I can really be sure of lifting in exactly the proper range.

INCLINE DUMBBELL CURLS

Purpose of Exercise: To stretch the biceps and for overall biceps development.

This exercise develops mass and biceps peak at the same time. If you do the movement to the front, it is a general biceps exercise. If you do it to the outside, it becomes a specialized exercise that emphasizes the inner part of the biceps.

Execution: (1) Sit back on an incline bench holding a dumbbell in each hand. (2) Keeping your elbows well forward throughout the movement, curl the weights forward and up to shoulder level. Lower the weights again, fully under control, and pause at the bottom to keep from using momentum to swing the weights up on the next repetition. I find I get the best results with this exercise by pronating and supinating my wrists during the movement—turning the wrists so that the palms face each other at the bottom, then twisting the weights as I lift so that the palms turn upward, then outward, with the little finger higher than the thumb at the top.

Dumbbell Curls to the outside help build the inner biceps and are an important part of weak point training.

SEATED DUMBBELL CURLS

Purpose of Exercise: To build, shape, and define the biceps.

Doing a standard curl with dumbbells rather than a barbell means you will use slightly less weight, but the arms are left free to move through their natural range of motion and you can achieve an even greater degree of contraction. As with Barbell Curls, you can cheat a little with this exercise, but keep it to a minimum.

Execution: (1) Sit on the end of a flat bench, or against the back support of an incline bench adjusted to an upright position, a dumbbell in each hand held straight down at arm's length, palms turned toward your body. (2) Holding your elbows steady as unmoving pivot points, curl the weights forward and up, twisting your palms forward as you lift so that the thumbs turn to the outside and the palms are facing up. Lift the weights as high as you can and then give an extra flex of the biceps to achieve maximum contraction. Lower the dumbbells down through the same arc, resisting the weight all the way down, until your arms are fully extended, the biceps stretched as far as possible. Twisting the wrists as you lift and lower the dumbbells causes a fuller contraction of the biceps and develops the inner biceps and separation between biceps and triceps. You can also do this exercise standing instead of seated, which will allow you to use a little more weight, although the movement will not be as strict.

HAMMER CURLS (OPTIONAL)

This is done the same way as regular Dumbbell Curls except the palms face inward and stay that way throughout the movement. This way you train the forearms as well as the biceps.

ALTERNATE DUMBBELL CURLS

Purpose of Exercise: To isolate the biceps of each arm.

This is a variation of a Dumbbell Curl in which you curl the dumbbells alternately, first one arm and then the other, to give you that extra bit of isolation, allowing you to concentrate your energy on one arm at a time and to minimize cheating.

Execution: Stand upright, a dumbbell in each hand hanging at arm's length. Curl one weight forward and up, holding your elbow steady at your waist and twisting your wrist slightly, bringing the thumb down and little finger up, to get maximum biceps contraction. Curl the weight as

high as you can, then bring it back down under control through the same arc, simultaneously curling the other weight up so that both dumbbells are in motion and twisting the wrist of the other hand as you bring it up. Continue these alternate Curls until you have done the required repetitions with both arms. Make sure you fully extend and contract the arm to get the fullest possible range of motion.

Using the Arm Blaster you get the strictness of a Preacher Curl, with the elbows fixed solidly in place, which is especially good for training the lower biceps.

You can do Alternate Dumbbell Curls in a sitting position as well.

CONCENTRATION CURLS

PURPOSE OF EXERCISE: To create maximum height in the biceps, especially the outside of the biceps.

I like to do this exercise at the end of my biceps training because it is one of the best means of peaking the muscle. This is a very strict movement, but it is for height, not definition, so use as much weight as you can handle. The name Concentration Curl is significant: You really need to concentrate on the biceps contraction and on being strict to make this exercise effective.

EXECUTION: (1) In a standing position, bend over slightly and take a dumbbell in one hand. Rest your free arm on your knee or other stationary object to stabilize yourself. (2) Curl the weight up to the deltoid and without moving the upper arm or the elbow and make certain you don't allow your elbow to rest against your thigh. As you lift, twist the wrist so that the little finger ends up higher than the thumb. Tense the muscle fully at the top of the Curl, then lower the weight slowly, resisting it all the way down to full extension. At the top of the Curl, the biceps are taking the full stress of the weight. Don't curl the weight to the chest—it should be curled to the shoulder.

LYING DUMBBELL CURLS

Purpose of Exercise: To build the entire biceps throughout a maximal range of motion.

This is an exercise I learned from Reg Park, and it is particularly effective because it gives you a great biceps stretch and helps lengthen the muscle. Also, due to the angle, the biceps must contract fully to offset the pull of gravity.

Execution: Use an exercise bench and, if necessary, place it on blocks to raise it higher off the ground. (1) Lie on your back on the bench, a dumbbell in each hand, your knees bent and feet flat on the bench. Let the dumbbells hang down (but not touching the floor) and turn your palms forward. (2) With your elbows steady, curl the weights up toward the shoulders, keeping the movement very strict. Then lower the dumbbells back toward the floor, resisting the weight all the way down.

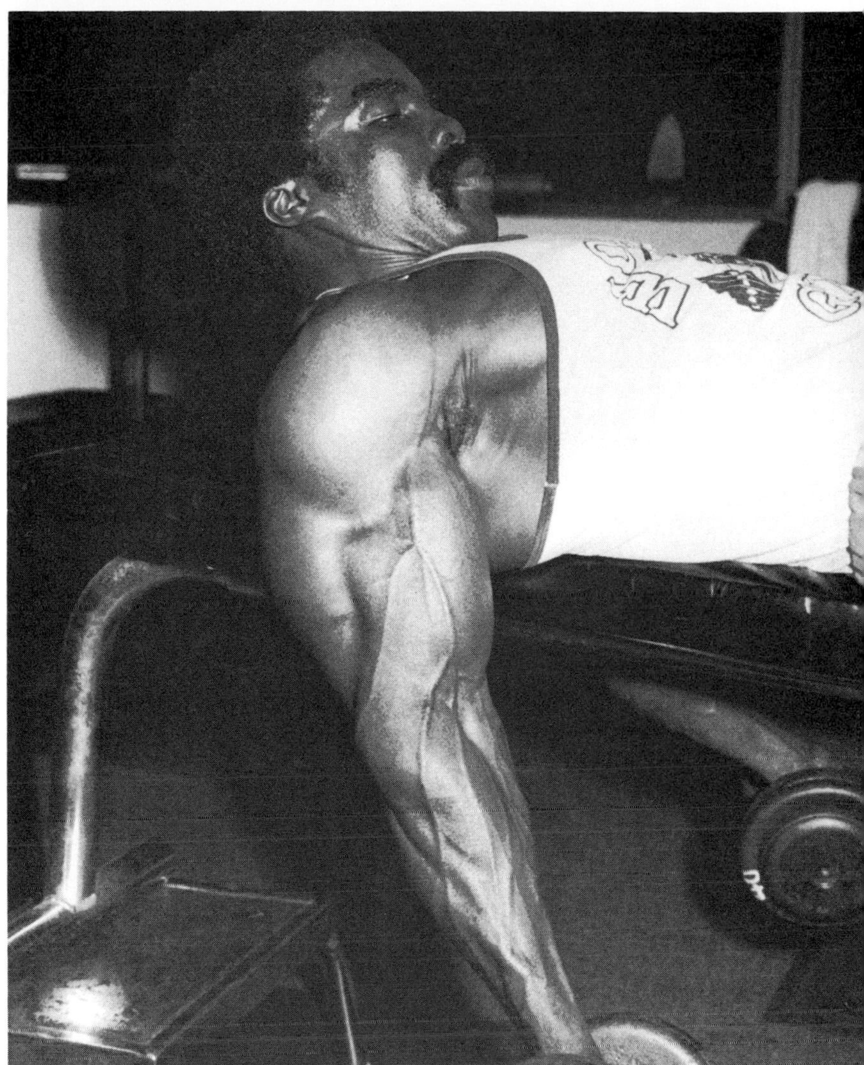

TWO-HAND CABLE CURLS

Purpose of Exercise: To develop and shape the biceps, particularly the height of the biceps peak.

Execution: Attach a bar to a floor-level cable and pulley. (1) Grasp the bar with an underhand grip, hands about shoulder width apart. Keeping your elbows fixed at your sides, extend your arms out and down until your biceps are fully stretched. (2) Curl the bar upward, not letting your elbows move, to a position just under your chin. Contract your biceps as hard as possible on top, then lower the bar slowly back down until your arms are fully extended, biceps stretched. This is not generally considered a mass exercise, so the key to doing it properly is a slow, smooth, controlled motion.

Lee Priest

CABLE CURLS WITH PREACHER BENCH (OPTIONAL)

EXECUTION: To do this movement with a preacher bench, (1) sit down and place your arms over the bench to hold them steady as you (2) curl the weight up and slowly lower it again, resisting the weight all the way down.

Preacher Cable Curls combine the strictness of the preacher bench with the strictness that comes from the steady resistance provided by a cable.

Doing Preacher Curls with a cable gives the biceps resistance even on the top. (With dumbbells or barbells, the resistance is mostly on the bottom.) Therefore, doing the exercise with a cable helps you to add peak contraction to your workout.

REVERSE CURLS

Purpose of Exercise: To develop the biceps.

This exercise is also good for forearm development.

Execution: (1) Standing with your feet shoulder-width apart, grasp a barbell with an overhand grip and hold it down in front of you at arm's length. (2) Keeping your elbows steady, curl the weight out and up to a position about even with your chin. Lower the weight through the same arc, resisting all the way down. Gripping the bar this way, you put the biceps in a position of mechanical disadvantage, so you will not be able to curl as much weight. The reverse grip makes the top of the forearm work very hard. Reverse Curls for the biceps rather than the forearms do not begin with any kind of Reverse Wrist Curl. Keep the wrists steady as you curl the weight up. Notice that the thumb is kept on top of the bar.

REVERSE PREACHER BENCH CURLS

Purpose of Exercise: To develop the biceps and the top of the forearm.

Using a preacher bench, the movement is done very strictly.

Execution: (1) Grasp a bar with an overhand grip, hands about shoulder width apart. (2) Lean across a preacher bench and extend your arms fully. Let your arms hang toward the floor, then curl the weight up, with the wrists as well, keeping the elbows firmly anchored. Curl the weight as far as possible, then lower it again, keeping it under control and resisting all the way down. Keep your body steady throughout the movement and avoid rocking back and forth.

BICEPS MACHINES

A lot of equipment companies make Curl machines designed to allow you to subject your biceps to full-range rotary resistance. One advantage of these machines is that they allow you to do heavy forced negatives, your workout partner pressing down on the weight as you resist during the downward part of the movement. Another is that you can often get a longer range of motion, giving you more stretch and total contraction. However, machines lock you into one narrow movement path, which will not allow for a really full development of the biceps. Use machines as a method of getting more variety in your workouts in addition to, but not instead of, free-weight Curls.

Flex Wheeler

MACHINE CURLS

Purpose of Exercise: To work the biceps through the longest range of motion possible.

When you do Curls on a machine, the movement becomes extremely strict and you are able to contract against resistance over the longest range of motion possible, from the point of full extension to that of a full peak contraction. Because of this, Machine Curls are a shaping, finishing exercise rather than one designed to build mass.

There are a wide variety of Curl machines found in gyms. With some, the resistance is provided by loading the machine with weight plates, while others use a cable attached to a weight stack. With many machines you grasp a bar and curl both arms simultaneously. With others, like the one pictured here, the two sides of the machine work independently, so you can either curl your arms simultaneously or, as shown here, use the machine to do Alternate Curls.

Execution: When doing Curls on any machine, position yourself with your elbows on the pad and grasp the bar or the handles with an underhand grip. (1) For two-handed Curls, contract the biceps and curl both arms as far as possible, feeling a full peak contraction at the top, then extend downward under full control to a point of full extension. (2) For Alternate Curls, contract one arm to a point of peak contraction, extend it downward under full control to a point of full extension, then do the same with the other arm, and continue to alternate the two arms until your set is complete.

Arm Exercises—Triceps

TRICEPS CABLE PRESSDOWNS (OR LAT MACHINE PRESSDOWNS)

Purpose of Exercise: To work the triceps through a full range of motion.

Execution: (1) Hook a short bar to an overhead cable and pulley, stand close to the bar and grasp it with an overhand grip, hands about 10 inches apart. Keep your elbows locked in close to your body and stationary. Keep your whole body steady—don't lean forward to press down with your body weight. (2) Press the bar down as far as possible, locking out your arms and feeling the triceps contract fully. Release and let the bar come up as far as possible without moving your elbows. For variety, you can vary your grip, the type of bar you use, how close you stand to the bar, or the width between your hands; or you can do a three-quarter movement, going from all the way up to three-quarters of the way down in order to work the lower triceps more directly.

Jusup Wilkosz

Arm Blaster Pressdowns . . . I frequently did Pressdowns using an Arm Blaster to keep the elbows from moving and to create a superstrict movement.

Mike Matarazzo

When doing Pressdowns with an incline board, you force the triceps to work at an unfamiliar angle, and you can't cheat.

Changing from an overhand to a reverse grip will change the feel—and muscle recruitment.

ONE-ARM CABLE REVERSE PRESSDOWNS

Purpose of Exercise: To isolate the triceps and develop the horseshoe shape of the muscle.

This exercise is especially good for contest or weak point training because by using a cable you can work each arm separately in isolation.

Execution: (1) Using an overhead cable and pulley, take hold of the handle with a reverse grip, palm up. (2) Keeping your elbow fixed and unmoving, straighten your arm until it is locked out and extended straight down. Flex the triceps in this position for extra contraction. Still not moving the elbow, let your hand come up as far as possible until the forearm approaches the biceps, feeling a complete stretch in the triceps. Finish your repetitions, then repeat with the other arm.

SEATED TRICEPS PRESSES

Purpose of Exercise: To hit all three triceps heads, especially the long head.

Execution: Grasp a barbell with an overhand grip, hands close together. (1) Sit on a bench and raise the bar straight up overhead, arms locked out. (2) Keeping your elbows stationary and close to your head, lower the weight down in an arc behind your head until your triceps are as stretched as possible. Only the forearms should move in this exercise. From this position, using only your triceps, press the weight back up overhead to full extension. Lock your arms out and flex your triceps. You might prefer doing this exercise using an E-Z curl bar or on an incline bench.

STANDING TRICEPS PRESSES

PURPOSE OF EXERCISE: To develop the full sweep of the triceps.

Doing this movement gives your triceps a full look to complement the biceps when doing a double-biceps pose. Performing Triceps Presses standing instead of seated allows you to do a cheating movement and thus use more weight. This exercise can also be done with a cable and rope through a floor-level pulley, which puts greater emphasis on the long head of the triceps.

EXECUTION: (1) Grip a straight or E-Z curl bar with an overhand grip, hands about 10 inches apart. Stand upright and hold the bar extended straight overhead. (2) Keeping your elbows stationary and close to your head, lower the weight down behind your head as far as possible, then press it back up to the starting position through a semicircular arc.

Chris Cormier

LYING TRICEPS EXTENSIONS

PURPOSE OF EXERCISE: To work the triceps all the way from the elbow down to the lats.

EXECUTION: (1) Lie along a bench, your head just off the end with knees bent and feet flat on the bench. Take hold of a barbell (preferably an E-Z curl bar) with an overhand grip, hands about 10 inches apart. (2) Press the weight up until your arms are locked out, but not straight up over your face. Instead, the weight should be back behind the top of your head, with your triceps doing the work of holding it there. Keeping your elbows stationary, lower the weight down past your forehead, then press it back up to the starting position, stopping short of the vertical to keep the triceps under constant tension. Keep control of the weight at all times in this movement to avoid banging yourself on the head with the bar. When you can't do another rep, you can still force the triceps to keep working by repping out with some Close-Grip Presses.

This photograph shows the arms perpendicular to the body at finish position; for maximum contraction they should be at a forty-five degree angle. (Roland Kickinger)

If you keep your head up as you do a Lying Triceps Extension, you will not be able to lower the bar far enough to stretch the triceps completely.

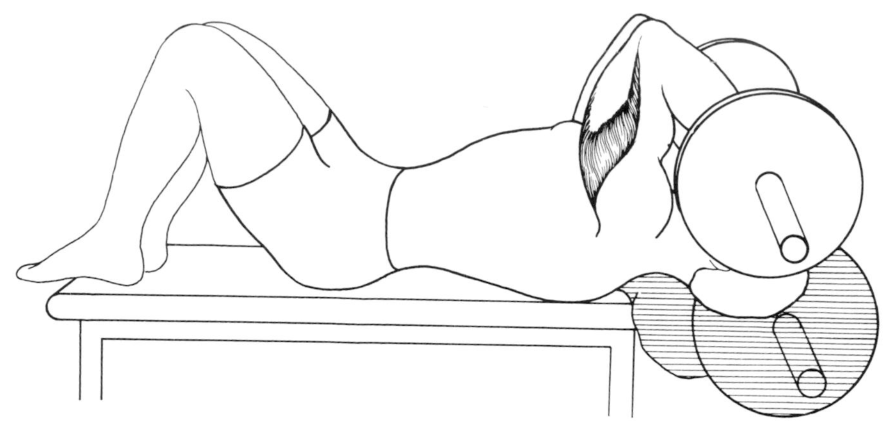

Letting your head drop slightly over the end of the bench gives you room to lower the bar far enough to get full extension of the triceps.

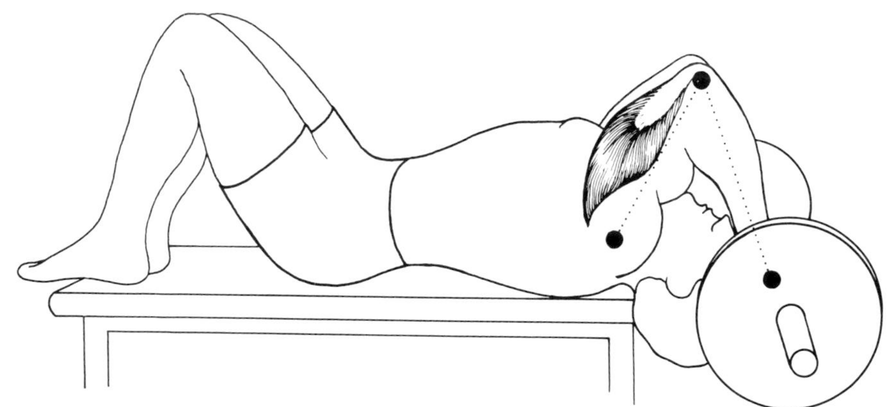

A common mistake when doing Lying Triceps Extensions is to lift the weight up so that you hold it straight overhead, which means the bones and joints are doing the work rather than the triceps. This illustration shows the right way to do it—positioning yourself so that your arms are still at an angle when you lock out. This angle ensures that the triceps can't rest on top but still have to fight gravity to support the weight.

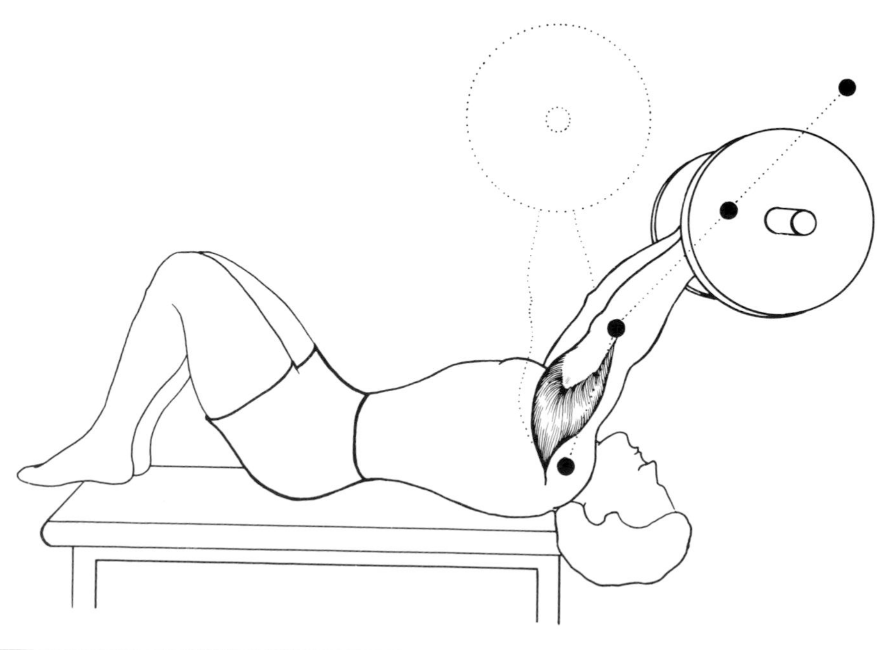

Close-Grip Presses—
starting position

Close-Grip Presses—
ending

Mike Francois

LYING DUMBBELL EXTENSIONS

Purpose of Exercise: To work the triceps.

Execution: (1) Lie on a bench, head even with the end, knees bent, feet flat on the bench. Hold one dumbbell in each hand overhead, arms straight, palms facing each other. (2) Hold your elbows stationary and lower the dumbbells down on either side of your head until your triceps are fully stretched and the weights almost touch your shoulders. Press them back up through a sweeping arc, but lock your elbows out before your arms are pointed straight up overhead and flex your triceps.

LYING CROSS FACE TRICEPS EXTENSIONS (OPTIONAL)

Lying Dumbbell Extensions also can be done with one dumbbell at a time by bringing the dumbbell across your body to the opposite shoulder. When you finish your reps with one arm, repeat with the opposite one. Changing the angle changes the feel in your triceps.

DUMBBELL KICKBACKS

Purpose of Exercise: To develop the triceps, especially the upper area.

Execution: (1) Stand with knees bent, one foot in front of the other, putting one hand on a low bench for balance. Take a dumbbell in the opposite hand, bend your arm and raise your elbow back and up to about shoulder height, elbow close to your side and letting the dumbbell hang

straight down below it. (2) Keeping your elbow stationary, press the weight back until your forearm is about parallel to the floor. Hold here for a moment and give the triceps an extra flex, then slowly come back to the starting position. For added triceps development, twist your hand slightly as you lift the weight, bringing the thumb up, and twist back the other way as you come down. Finish your set, then repeat the movement using the other arm. Make sure that only your forearm moves in this exercise, not the upper arm. This exercise can also be done with cable pulleys.

ONE-ARM TRICEPS EXTENSIONS

PURPOSE OF EXERCISE: To work the entire triceps and separate the three triceps heads.

EXECUTION: (1) Sitting on a bench, take a dumbbell in one hand and hold it extended overhead. (2) Keeping your elbow stationary and close to your head, lower the dumbbell down in an arc behind your head (not behind the shoulder) as far as you can. Feel the triceps stretch to their fullest, then press the weight back up to the starting position. It is essential to do this as strictly as possible. Looking in the mirror helps you check your form. Finish your set, then repeat the movement with the other arm. Be sure to go back and forth from one hand to the other without stopping to rest in between.

VARIATION: Various machines allow you to do Triceps Extensions with one arm at a time or both together, and many give the opportunity to work the full range of motion of the triceps under constant resistance. Use these machines for variety in your workout or to allow your training partner to help you with forced reps and forced negatives when you feel like working extra heavy.

One-Arm Triceps Extensions can also be done standing up—just balance yourself by holding on to something with your free hand.

DIPS

Purpose of Exercise: To develop the thickness of the triceps, especially around the elbow.

Dips are often thought of as a chest exercise, but they can be done in such a way as to hit the triceps really hard as well.

Execution: (1) Taking hold of the parallel bars, raise yourself up and lock out your arms. (2) As you bend your elbows and lower yourself between the bars, try to stay as upright as possible—the more you lean back, the more you work the triceps; the more you bend forward, the more you work the pectorals. From the bottom of the movement, press yourself back up until your arms are locked out, then give an extra flex of the triceps to increase the contraction. You can also increase the effort involved in this exercise by using a weight hooked around your waist and by coming up only about three-quarters of the way rather than locking out the movement and taking the tension off the triceps.

Jusup Wilkosz

Darrem Charles

DIPS BEHIND BACK

PURPOSE OF EXERCISE: To develop the thickness of the triceps.

This movement is also known as Bench Dips, or Reverse Push-Ups.

EXECUTION: (1) Place a bench or bar behind your back and hold on to the bench at its edge, hands about shoulder width apart. Place your heels on a bar or another bench, preferably at a level higher than the bench you are holding on to. Bending your elbows, lower your body as far as you can toward the floor. (2) Then push back up, locking out your arms to work the upper triceps. To work the lower triceps, stop just short of locking out. If your own body weight is not enough, try doing the movement by having a training partner place a plate on your lap.

FIXED BAR TRICEPS EXTENSIONS

Purpose of Exercise: To fully stretch and develop the triceps.

Using this movement, you can completely stretch the triceps more safely than with any other exercise.

Execution: (1) Using a fixed horizontal bar positioned at about waist height, grasp the bar with an overhand grip, hands about shoulder width apart. Lock your arms out to support your weight, then move your feet back until you are in a semi-Push-Up position above the bar. (2) Bend your arms and lower your body so that your head comes down below and under the bar as far as possible. When you feel the maximum stretch in your triceps, press forward with your arms and raise yourself back to the starting position, arms locked out.

Lee Priest

Arm Exercises—Forearms

BARBELL WRIST CURLS

Purpose of Exercise: To develop the inside (flexor muscles) of the forearms.

Heavy Barbell Curls make the forearms work very hard, but Wrist Curls allow you to more fully isolate these muscles.

Execution: (1) Take hold of a barbell with an underhand grip, hands close together. Straddle a bench with your forearms resting on the bench but with your wrists and hands hanging over the end, elbows and wrists the same distance apart. Lock your knees in against your elbows to stabilize them. (2) Bend your wrists and lower the weight toward the floor. When you can't lower the bar any farther, carefully open your fingers a little bit and let the weight roll down out of the palms of your hands. Roll the weight back up into your hands, contract the forearms, and lift the weight as high as you can without letting your forearms come up off the bench. Forearms, like calves, need a lot of stimulation to grow, so don't be afraid to make them really burn.

DUMBBELL ONE-ARM WRIST CURLS

PURPOSE OF EXERCISE: To isolate and develop the forearms.

This is a variation of Wrist Curls that allows you to isolate one forearm at a time.

EXECUTION: (1) Take hold of a dumbbell and sit on a bench. Lean forward and place your forearm on your thigh so that your wrist and the weight extend out over the knee, with your palm and the inside of your forearm facing upward. Bend forward, reach over with your free hand, and take hold of the elbow of the working arm to stabilize it. Bend your wrist and lower the weight as far as possible toward the floor, opening your fingers slightly to let the dumbbell roll down out of your palm. (2) Close your fingers again and, keeping the effort in your wrist, rather than the biceps, curl the weight up as high as you can. Finish your repetitions, then repeat using the other wrist.

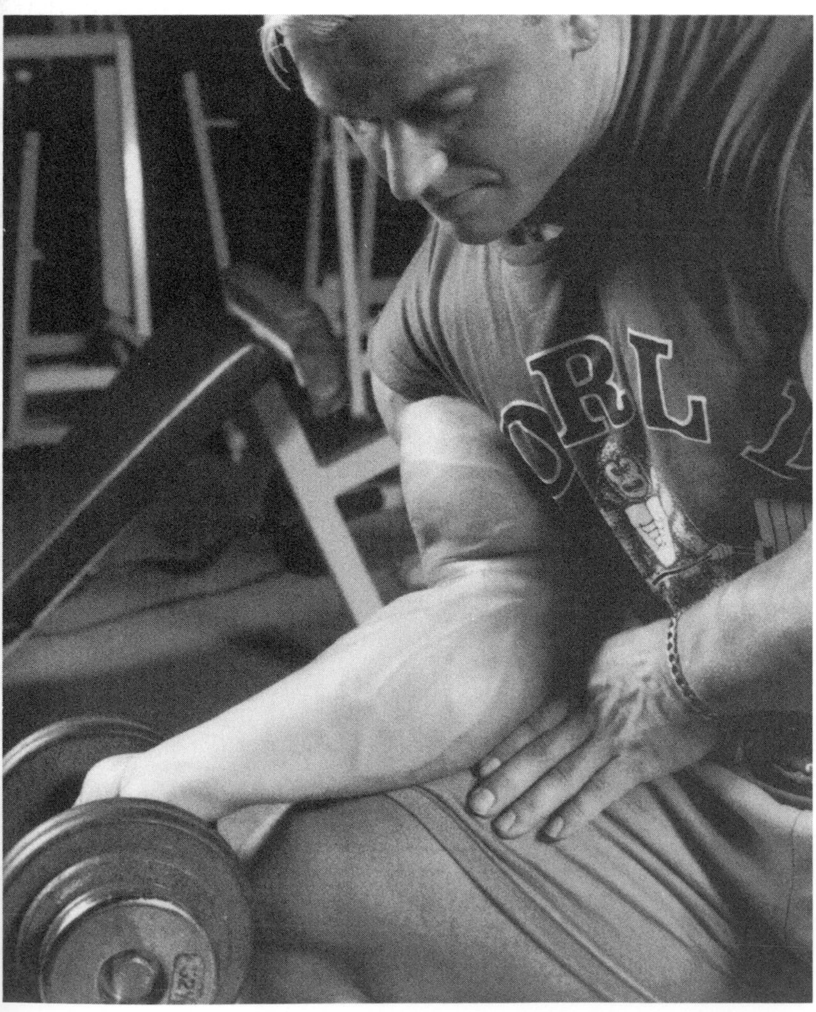

BEHIND-THE-BACK WRIST CURLS

PURPOSE OF EXERCISE: To develop the flexor muscles of the forearm. This is a real power exercise for the forearm flexors, and you can go for the heaviest possible weight.

EXECUTION: (1) Back up to a barbell rack and grasp a bar. Lift it off the rack and hold it down at arm's length behind you, hands about shoulder width apart, palms facing toward the rear. (2) Keeping your arms steady, open your fingers and let the bar roll down out of your palms. Close your fingers, roll the bar back up into your hands, and then lift it up and back behind you as far as possible, flexing your forearms. Make sure only the wrist moves in this exercise.

REVERSE WRIST CURLS WITH BARBELL

Purpose of Exercise: To develop the outside (extensor muscles) of the forearms.

Execution: (1) Grasp a barbell with an overhand grip, hands about 10 inches apart. Lay your forearms on top of your thighs or across a preacher bench so that they are parallel to the floor and your wrists and hands are free and unsupported. Bend your wrists forward and lower the bar as far as you can. (2) Then bring the wrists back up and lift the bar as far as possible, trying not to let the forearms move during the exercise.

REVERSE BARBELL WRIST CURLS WITH PREACHER BENCH (OPTIONAL)

This movement can also be done with your forearms on top of your thighs.

REVERSE WRIST CURLS WITH DUMBBELLS

Reverse Curls work the forearm extensors. Using dumbbells, you ensure that each side of the body will work up to its own capacity, with no help from the other.

REVERSE BARBELL CURLS

PURPOSE OF EXERCISE: To develop the biceps, the forearm extensors, and the brachio radialis.

EXECUTION: (1) Grasp a barbell with an overhand grip, hands about shoulder width apart. Let the bar hang down at arm's length in front of you. (2) Keeping your elbows fixed in position at your sides, curl the bar upward, beginning the movement with a curling motion of the wrist. (3) Bring the bar up to a position just under the chin, contract the biceps as fully as possible on top, then lower the weight slowly back down to the starting position.

REVERSE PREACHER BENCH BARBELL CURLS

PURPOSE OF EXERCISE: To develop the biceps and forearm extensors.

EXECUTION: (1) Position yourself with your arms extended over a preacher bench. Grasp a barbell with an overhand grip, hands about shoulder width apart. Let the bar hang so that your arms are fully extended. (2) Curl the bar upward, beginning the movement with a curling motion of the wrist, and bring it up as far as possible toward your chin. Your position on the bench should be such that, at the top of the movement, your forearms have not come up completely to a perpendicular angle. From the top of the movement, lower the weight slowly back down to the starting position.

REVERSE CURLS MACHINE

Purpose of Exercise: To develop the forearm extensors.

This movement works the forearm muscles all the way to their origin at the elbow. In addition to flexing the wrist, you lift the forearm. Although machines are designed with limited functions, a little thought and imagination will allow you to get the maximum benefit from their use. By reversing your grip on a Curl machine, you can perform very strict Reverse Curls.

Execution: (1) Grasp the handle on a Curl machine in an overhand grip. Place your elbows firmly on the pad. (2) Starting at full extension, lift the handle up and toward your head as far as it will go. Lower the weight again slowly and under control until you have returned to a position of full extension.

ONE-ARM CABLE REVERSE CURLS

Purpose of Exercise: To isolate and develop the forearm extensors.

Using one arm at a time with cables, you get constant, full-range-of-motion resistance that doesn't vary with position as much as when you use dumbbells. This makes this exercise an excellent specialized one for overcoming weak points in the forearm extensors, especially if one arm is bigger than the other.

Execution: (1) Using a floor-level pulley, grasp a handle with one hand, using a palms-down grip. (2) Concentrating on keeping your elbow completely still as a pivot point, curl the back of your hand up as far as possible toward your shoulder. At the top of the movement, lower your hand again, resisting all the way down. Finish your set with one arm, then repeat with the other.

The Thighs

THE MUSCLES OF THE UPPER LEG

The **quadriceps** are the muscles at the front of the thigh which act as extensors of the leg. The four muscles involved are the rectus femoris, the vastus intermedius (these two muscles making up the central V-shape delineation of the middle front thigh), the vastus medialis of the inner thigh, and the vastus lateralis of the outer thigh.

Basic function: To extend and straighten the leg

The **biceps femoris** and associated muscles—the thigh flexors at the rear of the leg

Basic function: To curl the leg back

Other important muscles of the upper leg include the tensor fasciae latae, coming down from the hip to the outer thigh; and the sartorius, the longest muscle in the body, which weaves diagonally across the front of the thigh.

THE IMPORTANCE OF THIGH TRAINING

The muscles of the upper leg are the largest and most powerful in the entire body. There are few movements in sports that do not involve intense leg effort. A baseball player, golfer, discus thrower, shot-putter, and boxer

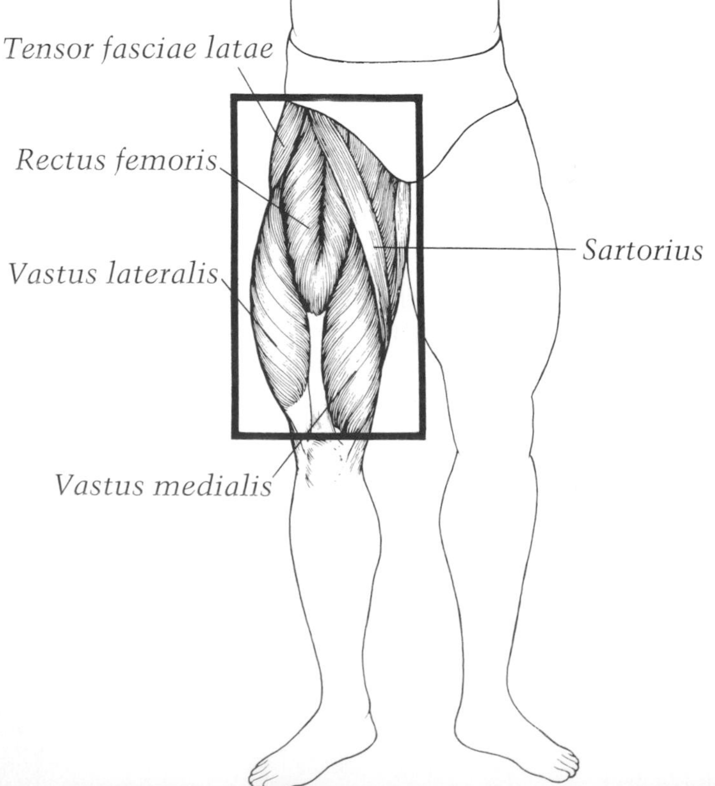

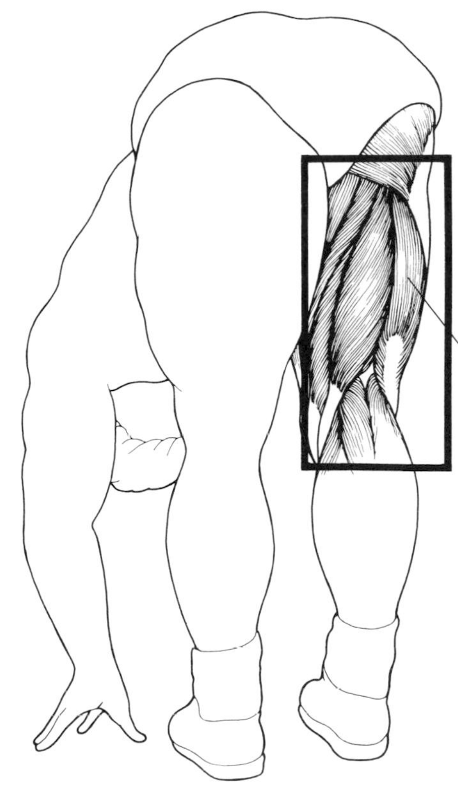
Biceps femoris

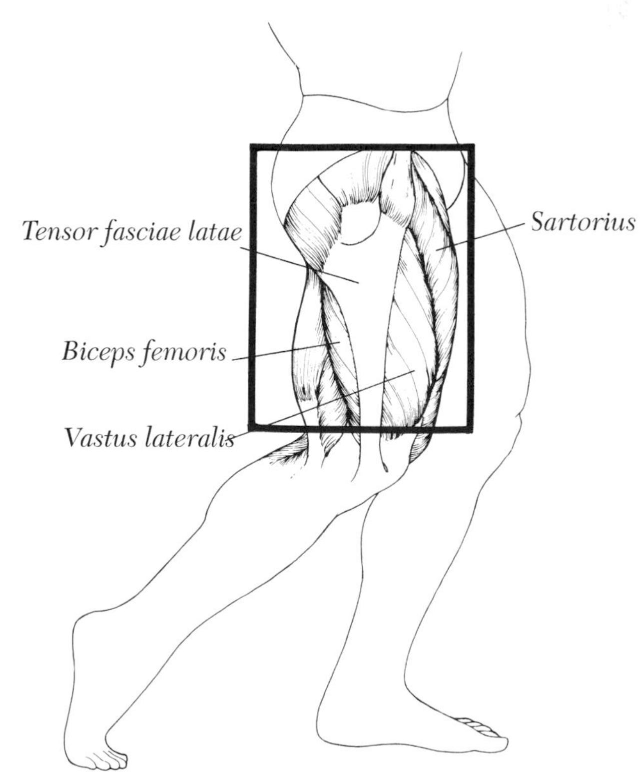
Tensor fasciae latae
Sartorius
Biceps femoris
Vastus lateralis

Milos Sarcev's leg development is the result of a lot of hard training and use of the Priority Principle.

all begin their respective movements with a powerful leg drive. In weightlifting, most power moves like Power Cleans, Clean and Press, and Deadlifts involve a lot of leg effort, as do the lifts used in Olympic weightlifting competition.

However, there is no sport in which thigh development is as important as in bodybuilding. While contest judges have the shoulders, chest, arms, back, and abs to occupy their attention above a bodybuilder's waist, when they look at the lower body the single most compelling visual element is the thighs—the quadriceps and the hamstrings. Thighs are the most massive muscle group in the body and proportionately constitute almost half of your physique.

Can you imagine a Sergio Oliva with weak thighs? Or a Nasser El Sonbaty with skinny legs? What is the point of building your arms up to 21 inches or bigger if you display them on top of a physique with thighs that hardly measure any larger?

When I was playing soccer and skiing as a teenager in Austria, the coaches urged us to do exercises like Squats, Lunges, and Calf Raises to strengthen our legs. This early training eventually led to my falling in love with the sport of bodybuilding. We were lucky in those days to have coaches who understood the need for leg strength and how to train for it. Nowadays, whenever I talk to athletic coaches around the world, virtually all of them agree that great leg strength is the foundation of athletic excellence and that weight training is the best way to develop that strength.

But the legs have another quality besides great strength—they are capable of great endurance. Capable of moving up to a ton of weight, the legs are also designed to carry you long distances without tiring. A person in good condition can walk for weeks through rugged terrain and run for 100 miles. No other muscles of the body can deliver this dual quality of great strength and great endurance.

This is why training the legs for bodybuilding is so demanding. It isn't enough just to subject the legs to heavy overload. You have to use heavy weights and sufficient volume of training that you stress the fibers involved and exhaust the endurance capacity of the leg muscles. Doing 5 sets of Barbell Curls for the biceps can be demanding, but doing 5 sets of Heavy Squats with 400 or 500 pounds on your shoulders is more like running a mini-marathon, with that kind of total exhaustion squeezed in 8 or 9 minutes of concentrated effort.

Like many young bodybuilders, I had a tendency to train my upper body harder than my thighs. Luckily, I realized in time how important this muscle group is to a championship physique, and I began to indulge in superhuman Squats and other thigh exercises to build up this muscle mass.

An exception to the tendency of young bodybuilders to overlook leg training was Tom Platz. Tom actually had the *opposite* problem. He got heavily into leg training, then found himself with Olympia-level legs that outclassed his upper body. Since then, he has made great strides in creating a totally proportioned body, but his unbelievable leg development has set new standards for bodybuilders to strive for.

THE DEMANDS OF LEG TRAINING

Because upper leg training is so strenuous and demanding, a lot of bodybuilders find their leg development lagging behind simply because they don't put an all-out effort into it. They look in the mirror and are disap-

When Lee Priest hits a leg shot you can clearly see that the quadriceps is composed of four separate muscles—along with the adductor muscles at the inside of the leg.

pointed in how their legs look, but they don't realize the kind of total concentration of effort it takes to make those huge muscles respond.

For many years, I did only 5 sets of Squats when I really should have been doing 8 sets. I did not include enough Front Squats and, I now realize, I did not put enough weight on the Leg Press machine.

Once I realized my mistakes and corrected them, my thighs began to grow thick and massive. I accepted the fact that leg workouts simply have to be brutal to be effective. This involves a mental effort almost as much as a physical one. It's easy to be intimidated by 400 or 500 pounds on a Squat bar (or even 200 or 300 when you are a beginner). It is difficult to gear yourself up to loading up the Leg Press machine and grinding out rep after rep, set after set.

Normal workouts are hard enough, but if thighs happen to be a weak point in your physique, you have to be prepared to push yourself even more. That means forcing yourself to break down any inhibition or barrier, blasting your thighs to create total development.

Many bodybuilders have trouble going to total failure in leg training. After all, going to exhaustion with 400 pounds across the back of your neck can be scary. This is why having a training partner to spot you is especially important for leg training. When you have forced out all the reps you can for your Squats, stand there holding the weight for a moment, then try for one more rep. Push your body to its limit. But make sure somebody is standing by to spot you when you do this. Also, when doing Leg Presses try to push yourself to this same degree, forcing the legs to exhaustion just the way you would any other body part.

If you want to build gigantic thighs and shapely glutes, you must always ask yourself this question: Is it true that I really cannot do another rep? In my experience, whenever I challenged anyone this way, he usually could force out one more.

However, as important as hard and heavy training is for thigh and glute development, don't make the mistake of confusing sheer effort with effective effort. As in any bodybuilding training, you have to use the correct technique if you want the maximum results. Besides going for maximum intensity in all of your thigh exercises, pay close attention to how the movement is supposed to be executed and try to master the technique involved. That way, your efforts will not be wasted and your thigh development will never lag behind.

Of course, your own physical proportions may dictate variations in your training. Certain bodybuilders with short legs, like Casey Viator, Mike Mentzer, and Franco Columbu, find Squats easy and rewarding. Their physical proportions give a mechanical and leverage advantage that makes it easier to execute Squats properly using very heavy weight. A taller bodybuilder like myself usually finds that the lower back becomes much more involved in this exercise than would be true for a shorter man. But I always did a lot of work on my lower back, so it was strong enough to enable me to squat with very heavy weight in spite of my proportions. In fact, I have often thought that Squats were my best lower back exercise. Doing Front Squats—a movement in which you must keep your back straight—in addition to regular Squats, is the best way of getting the most out of your leg workouts when you have proportions like mine.

Incidentally, by trial and error I found that I was able to stay in a much better groove doing Squats by putting a low block under my heels. You can try this yourself to see if this improves your balance and the feel of the exercise. Just be careful not to use too high a block, which throws you too far onto your toes and tends to make you fall forward. Another variation that can prove useful is doing Squats on a Smith machine, where the bar slides along a fixed track and you don't have to worry about the weight sliding off your shoulders.

My ultimate model for leg development has to be Tom Platz. Tom not only worked as hard as any bodybuilder in the gym—to the point where he didn't believe he had really done anything until the pain started—but he also executed all of the exercises to perfection. You see bodybuilders all the time doing Squats by sticking out their rear ends, bending over too far, spreading their legs way out to the side—but not Tom. His form was perfect, his efforts all-out intense, and his mental concentration complete. So it is obviously more than just genes that produced his fantastic leg development.

The thighs are the most massive muscle group in the body. There are a number of exercises that produce thigh shape and separation, but for building mass there is no substitute for heavy Squats.

BUILDING THE QUADRICEPS

For great thighs you need mass, shape, and separation between each of the important quadriceps muscles: the rectus femoris, vastus intermedius, vastus medialis, and vastus lateralis. You need to develop the overall mass of your thighs to bring them up to where they are proportionate with your upper body. Great size comes about only by lifting heavy weight, especially with exercises like Squats and Leg Presses.

But modern bodybuilders need more than just size to win contests. They need to develop legs that show as much quality as quantity:

1. Full development and shape of each of the separate muscles of the quadriceps; a full and satisfying sweep of muscle on the outside of the thigh from hip to knee; the central V-shaped delineation of the middle front thigh; fullness and thickness where the quadriceps insert into the knee; and a fully developed and defined leg biceps.

2. Clear and evident definition in the thigh area, with striations and cross striations standing out as if revealed in an anatomy chart.

3. Full, rounded development of the thigh as seen from the side, almost as if you were looking at a pair of parentheses (), with a distinct separation between the front of the thigh and the leg biceps.

Nobody has achieved more fullness and thickness of the quadriceps than Tom Platz, especially in the lower area where the thigh muscles insert into the knee.

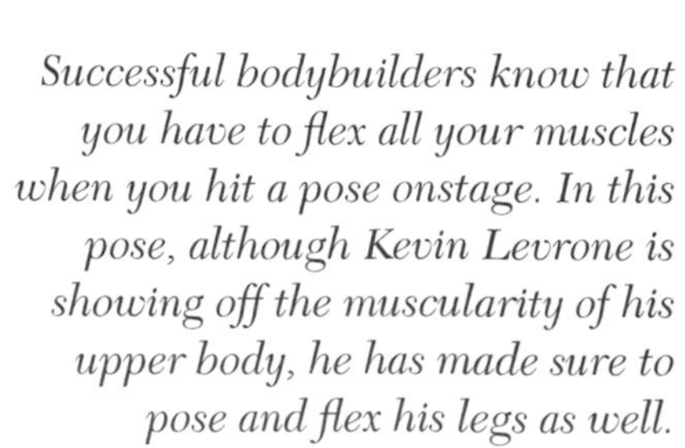

Successful bodybuilders know that you have to flex all your muscles when you hit a pose onstage. In this pose, although Kevin Levrone is showing off the muscularity of his upper body, he has made sure to pose and flex his legs as well.

Bodybuilders try to develop a split between the thigh and the leg biceps—the split on Flex Wheeler's leg is so prominent that it looks as if it were achieved by the slash of a sword!

Lee Priest is a great fan of the legendary Tom Platz and has done his best to create a development of the upper leg that, like his idol, is so massive it doesn't look as if it quite belongs on a human being.

Another bodybuilder whose quads are both massive and highly detailed is Flex Wheeler.

The basic mass-building exercise for quadriceps and gluteals is Squats—an exercise you will find in every program from Beginning to Competition and one which every great bodybuilder has learned to rely on. Squats have a complicated mechanical effect on the body.

As you begin the Squat, the thighs bear most of the effort; the farther down you go, the more the stress is transferred to the hamstrings; at the bottom of the movement, the buttocks take up a larger proportion of the strain. However, as I explained earlier, Squats may be more or less effective depending on an individual's particular proportions. Sometimes exercises like Front Squats are also needed to more directly work the quadriceps and lessen the involvement of the lower back muscles.

Heavy Leg Presses also contribute to building massive thighs and glutes. Leg Extensions, which isolate the quadriceps themselves, are not considered a mass-building movement.

Good muscle separation and definition obviously cannot be achieved unless you diet to severely reduce your body fat. But it takes more than just diet—you also need to work your thighs with exercises like Leg Extensions, Lunges, and Leg Curls. Including Hack Squats in your workouts also helps give you ultimate hardness and definition. (Incidentally, Squats and Lunges actually work the hamstrings to some degree, too—along with the exercises described in the next section.)

THE HAMSTRINGS

Even though many bodybuilders a few years ago had well-developed upper legs in both the front and the back, there wasn't all that much emphasis put on the leg biceps in competition. Now they have become enormously important thanks to bodybuilders like Tom Platz, Sergio Oliva, and Robby Robinson, who are great examples of how much this area can be developed.

Like triceps, the leg biceps play a major part in a wide variety of poses. When you do a side chest or triceps shot, the sweep of the leg biceps is very evident. In any back shot, powerful and defined rear delts, traps, and lats will not compensate for underdeveloped leg biceps. Seen from the back, development of the distinct heads of the leg biceps, along with ripped and developed calves, is needed to create a balance to muscularity of the back, shoulders, and arms displayed in poses like a rear double-biceps or rear lat spread. Also, we are seeing more and more examples of striated and even cross-striated leg biceps, something that almost didn't exist ten or fifteen years ago. And, just as in auto racing or virtually any other sport, as soon as somebody achieves something new, everybody else dives in and pursues the same achievement. So, fabulously muscular, striated, and vascular leg biceps are likely to be the norm rather than the exception in the future.

Shown here at the 1974 Mr. Olympia, even though I am standing relaxed, I am consciously keeping my hamstrings tight and flexed. I was very glad that I had made an extra effort that year to really work this area hard.

The more developed the leg biceps are, the more your legs are going to meet in the middle and touch each other, even though your legs are held some distance apart. A properly developed leg biceps leaves a distinct line separating the back of the leg from the front of the thigh when seen from the side, and is a sure indication of a bodybuilder who has really succeeded in achieving quality leg training.

The primary exercises for developing the hamstrings are Leg Curls. These can be done lying down (usually using both legs at the same time) or standing (getting extra isolation using one leg at a time). But this muscle also comes into play in Squats and Lunges, especially as you work through the lower half of the range of motion.

To get a full stretch in the leg biceps, I recommend doing Straight-Leg Deadlifts and Good Mornings, exercises that are primarily for the lower back, but which also help develop the back of the thighs and glutes.

Don't forget that leg biceps also respond extremely well to various

Shocking Principles like the Stripping Method, partial and forced reps, and supersetting. The more you can shock this important muscle, the more development you can expect to see.

BEGINNING AND ADVANCED PROGRAMS

In the Beginning Program, I have included just basic exercises designed to work each important area of the leg: Squats, Lunges, and Leg Curls. The first two exercises work well in combination to build up the size and strength of the frontal thighs and glutes, and the last is the most direct way of developing the back of the thighs.

But don't make the mistake of believing that these exercises are merely for beginners simply because they are included in the Beginning Program. No matter how advanced you become, these exercises are still vital to building and maintaining great thighs. Except for very specialized training in which you are working only on certain weak points, you will always need to rely on these basic movements.

In Advanced Training you need to do Squats in different ways. Front Squats, for example, force you to keep your back straight, which works the muscles differently. In Hack Squats you go all the way down, which works the lower thighs and helps separate the quadriceps from the leg biceps. The various kinds of Squats attack the leg from different directions; exercises for leg biceps, such as Straight-Leg Deadlifts, allow you to continue to escalate the intensity of effort you impose on these muscles.

Because leg training is so demanding, conditioning is an important factor. In the beginning, you will find the few leg exercises included to be difficult enough. But after a while, when you have become stronger and more conditioned, the total efforts of the Advanced and Competition Programs, as difficult as they are, will be well within your increased capabilities.

COMPETITION PROGRAM

Once you begin to train for competition, you have to be conscious of many more aspects of leg development—full muscle shape, greater striations, cross striations, complete muscle separation, the mass of the thighs developed in proportion to the rest of the body. To achieve this you need to demand even more from your leg training, making already difficult workouts almost impossible by using every one of the Shocking Principles you can.

Supersetting leg training, for example, can really deplete you. The thighs are the biggest muscles in the body and when you start doing two or more sets without resting you can easily drive yourself to total exhaustion unless you are in great condition. You can superset within the same muscle—Squats and Leg Extensions, for example—or back to front with

Lunges and Leg Curls. But all of this intensity is for a purpose: to do everything possible to develop every part of the thigh.

At this level, you need to be extremely honest with yourself, looking at your thighs and accurately assessing where your development is merely adequate, outstanding, or simply unsatisfactory. The key to winning is to detect weak points early on and begin to correct them as soon as possible rather than waiting until it may be too late.

The Competition Program is designed to teach you total control over your own development. You will need to understand your own body structure more completely, and to fully comprehend which movements are designed to emphasize the various areas of the legs—the upper or lower thighs, the inside or outside, the insertion, origin, or thickness of the leg biceps. You will need to learn to feel precisely where Squats, Front Squats, Leg Presses, and Hack Squats are having their effect, and how to alter your program to include a greater proportion of those exercises that work best for you. Knowing all this enables you to achieve the comprehensive development that it takes to win titles.

Remember, all the exercises detailed in these programs are important. Even if you vary the program, it is not a good idea to leave out the fundamental exercises entirely. Squats may build mass and Leg Extensions create shape and definition, but the combination of these two movements, plus the other important exercises, is what gives you total quality development.

The Competition Program is not so much a matter of doing more or different exercises as of increasing the "time intensity" of the training with a lot of supersets. For competition, it is extremely important that the thighs be super-defined, with tremendous muscle separation. I have found that the way to achieve that look is by doing a lot of supersets: Leg Extensions and Squats, Front Squats and Leg Curls, Hack Squats and Leg Curls. Using these methods, which will intensify the burn so greatly that your desire for success will be tested on each and every set, is the best way to achieve your goals.

I wouldn't use the Stripping Method in thigh training all the time, but it really works well when you are preparing for competition. Years ago when I was looking for extra thigh definition, I experimented on a sliding Hack Squat machine—I put on enough weight to allow me to just do 6 reps, took a little off, and did 6 more. Eventually I did 5 sets this way for a total of 30 reps, which gave me a tremendous burn in the quadriceps muscles. I also found this method worked great with Leg Extensions.

Since legs have a tremendous capacity for endurance, continuing your set with the Stripping Method helps you totally exhaust all the muscle fiber available. Some machines are very useful when you train this way because you can strip off weight quickly by just changing the pin, and can continue working your legs to total failure without fear of being unable to control the weight at the end. You can do the same thing with Squats by pulling plates off the bar, although you may find this the most grueling exercise you have ever done.

The biggest progress I made in thigh training was in 1971 when, in addition to sheer size, what I needed most was deeper definition and separation. So I began leg training with a superset of Leg Extensions followed by Squats. I hit the Leg Extensions hard, so I was very weak and tired when I got to the Squats. My thighs felt dead, and I found that I could hardly move 315 pounds. But I kept trying and soon was able to do Heavy Squats immediately after Leg Extensions, and my thighs responded tremendously to this new shock. Another superset that worked well for me was Front Squats immediately followed by Leg Curls.

For emphasizing the thigh muscles above the knee I've always relied on Hack Squats, especially for competition training. Hack Squats produce maximum hardness, definition, and separation. I discovered the merits of this exercise through Steve Reeves, who found it really beneficial when getting his legs into competition shape.

Tom Platz had a method of exhausting the endurance capacity of the legs as well as blasting the muscles. When he was doing Leg Extensions, for example, he would do as many full reps as he could. Then, as he began to tire and couldn't do full-range movements anymore, he continued the set, moving the weight just as far as he could—three-quarter reps, half reps, quarter reps. Finally, he ended up lying back on the machine, totally spent, but you could see his legs still contracting, moving the weight only inches at a time. He didn't stop until his quadriceps were so literally exhausted that he couldn't move the weight even a fraction of an inch. This was how he used partial reps, a method in which Tom cut down on the range of motion rather than lightening up on the weight.

Platz demanded more of his legs, which is why he got so much more than other people. For example, he would do as many as 35 reps of Squats with 315 on the bar, another 25 reps after less than 60 seconds' rest, several sets of total-exhaustion Leg Extensions and Leg Curls, Hack Squats and Leg Presses, brutal calf work—and then go out and ride his bicycle for 20 miles to finish off his leg workout.

These are just some of the methods the champions have used to develop their thighs. Developing really top-quality legs is a matter of hard work, good knowledge of technique, and application of all the Shocking Principles to create the maximum level of training intensity—for example, forced negatives with Leg Extension, Leg Curls, Hack Squats, or Machine Squats, all of which are done on machines, allowing the techniques to be done in safety; or Staggered Sets with an exercise like Squats, doing 8, 10, or even more sets over the course of a workout; or pre-fatiguing the quadriceps with Leg Extensions and immediately trying to do Squats with your thigh muscles screaming in pain. Pushing the legs to their ultimate development requires a mixture of courage, technique, and imagination.

The one basic need shared by all bodybuilders is, of course, simply the

To build big muscles, you need to train with heavy weight. At one point, simply to put an extra inch on my thighs, I concentrated on doing Squats with 500 pounds for reps.

I was perfectly happy this day to flex for photographer John Balik's camera, but I always welcome any excuse to flex during a workout. After every set, I like to stand in front of the mirror and tense the muscles I'm training. Flexing them as hard as I can brings out maximum definition, especially in the thighs.

Muscle-bound? Look at Tom Platz's incredible flexibility.

development of mass in the upper leg. I remember when I had pretty good overall development, but simply lacked size. To build up the mass I needed, I included a lot of very Heavy Squats in my leg routine, especially Half Squats. Half Squats let you use an enormous amount of weight, really make the legs work intensely, but with no real danger of injury to the knees. Whenever you are trying to build mass, you need to train according to basic power principles—fewer reps and sets, more rest between sets, but with increased poundage, Full Squats, Half Squats, and Front Squats done with a barbell or on a machine are the principal power exercises. You can also do Leg Presses on a machine as a power exercise by using very heavy weight.

FLEXING AND STRETCHING

Whenever you see body builders cramping up from fatigue in a contest, it is usually the leg muscles that go first. These are huge, strong muscles and it takes a lot of practice to develop the kind of endurance needed to pose the legs for hour after hour.

Hard posing practice and flexing the legs constantly during your workout help create maximum muscle separation and the cross striations that modern bodybuilders are now achieving. However, the more you contract these large muscles, the more they tend to shorten up, so it is equally important to lengthen them again with stretching movements. Virtually all the top champions use a lot of stretching in order to develop their fantastic legs. Again, using Tom Platz as an example, he would spend 15 minutes stretching before doing a leg workout, and then stretch again after he finished.

But you can also stretch during a workout by including the right exercises—for example, doing Straight-Leg Deadlifts or Good Mornings to stretch the leg biceps right after you do your Leg Curls, being sure to go all the way down when doing Squats and Hack Squats, and bringing your knees all the way to your chest when doing Leg Presses.

When I first began competing, my legs were considered a weak point, but a lot of hard work, training my thighs according to the Priority Principle and every Shock Principle I could learn or invent, made the difference, so by the early 1970s my thigh development was no longer a problem.

WEAK POINT TRAINING

Because the leg muscles are so large and complex, almost any bodybuilder is going to discover some weak points at some stage in his career. It is necessary to analyze what the problem is and to understand what exercises and techniques can be used to correct it.

In general, I recommend training legs according to the Priority Principle. Leg training is so demanding that, if you want to get the most out of it, you had better train them when you are fresh and strong. It is also important to have a good workout partner to push you to your limits and to be there when you need spotting.

For specific problem areas I recommend the following leg exercises:

Lower Thigh Development

Since the lower thigh works hardest when the knee is fully bent, I recommend the following exercises with a three-quarter movement in which you go all the way down but come up only about three-quarters of the way.

- Squats, Hack Squats, and Leg Presses
- Leg Extensions, concentrating on letting the legs go all the way back and stretching out the thigh to the point where the lower thigh is working the hardest

Outer Thigh Development

- Front Squats
- Hack Squats
- Any Squat or Leg Press with toes pointed straight and the feet close together
- Abductor machines and movements

Inner Thigh Development

- Lots of Lunges—a very valuable inside thigh exercise
- Straight-Leg Deadlifts
- Any Squat or Press movement with the toes turned outward with a relatively wide foot stance
- Adductor machines and movements

Front Sweep of Thighs

- Hack Squats with a block under the heels to further stress the quadriceps
- Sissy Squats

In developing the thighs, it is helpful to vary your foot position when doing various thigh movements:

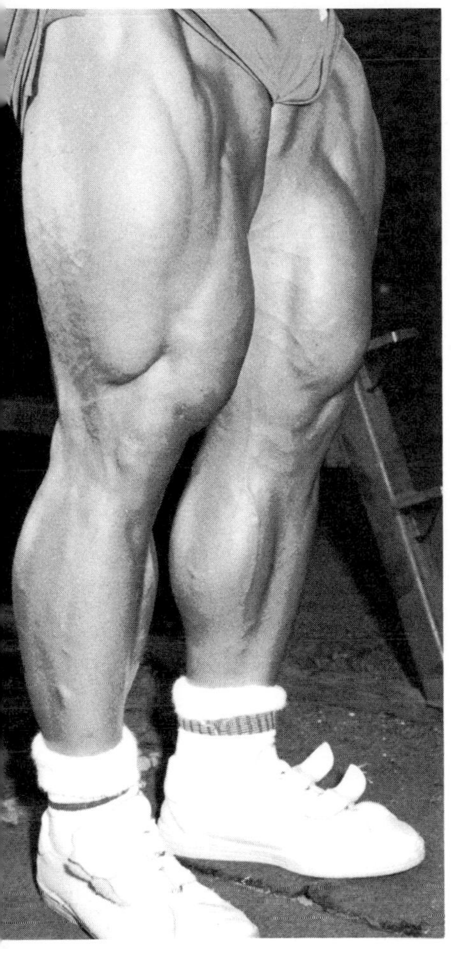

For Overall Development

Feet shoulder-width apart
Toes pointed slightly out

For Outer Thigh (vastus lateralis) Emphasis

Feet close together
Toes pointed straight ahead

For Inner Thigh (adductors) and Front Thigh (vastus medialis) Emphasis

Feet relatively wide apart
Toes pointed out at a wide angle

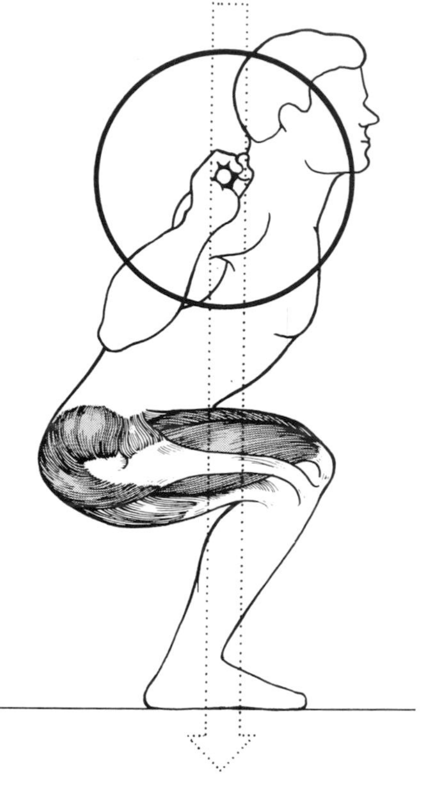

To get the most out of Squats, the bar should remain directly over your feet. As you bend your knees coming down, make sure your head is up and your back straight. This takes the lower back out of the movement and puts the stress on the leg and glute muscles where it belongs.

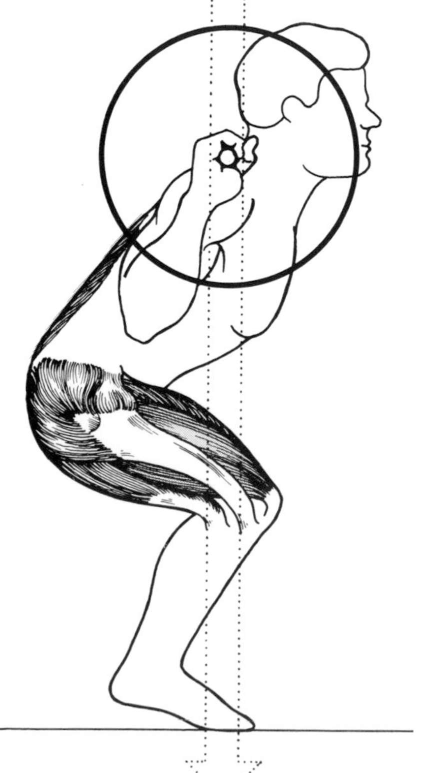

Allowing your head to lean forward, as shown here, puts additional stress on the lower back and less on the thighs, where you really want it. Bodybuilders with long legs tend to have this problem more than those with short legs.

Leg Exercises

SQUATS

Purpose of Exercise: To build mass and strength in the legs, especially the thighs. Full Squats are one of the traditional mass-building exercises for the entire lower body but are primarily for developing all four heads of the quadriceps.

Execution: (1) With the barbell on a rack, step under it so that it rests across the back of your shoulders, hold on to the bar to balance it, raise up to lift it off the rack, and step away. The movement can be done with your feet flat on the floor or your heels resting on a low block for support. (2) Keeping your head up and back straight, bend your knees and lower yourself until your thighs are just lower than parallel to the floor. From this point, push yourself back up to the starting position.

It is important to go below parallel in this movement, especially when you are just learning the exercise, so that you develop strength along the entire range of motion. If you don't go low enough in the beginning, you could injure yourself later when using heavier weight. Foot position to some extent determines which area of the thighs you work the most while doing Squats: A wider stance works the inside of the thighs to a greater degree, while a narrower stance tends to work the outside more; toes turned out hits the inside of the thighs. The basic stance for greatest power is usually feet shoulder-width apart, with toes turned just slightly out.

HEAVY SQUATS

Your Squat technique will vary a lot depending on your physical proportions. Because of my height, whenever I do Heavy Squats I am forced to bend forward quite far, bringing my lower back very strongly into the exercise. Ideally, you should do Squats with your back as straight as possible. Bodybuilders like Franco Columbu and Tom Platz can do this easily with the rear end and bar in about the same line when coming down with the weight, instead of the way I do it, bar way forward and rear end stuck out toward the back. I always include a lot of Front Squats in my routine in order to make certain I emphasize the quadriceps.

Tom Platz

HALF SQUATS

Purpose of Exercise: To develop extra mass and power in the thighs.

Execution: This exercise is done the same way as regular Squats except you go only halfway down, which will enable you to use more weight.

MACHINE SQUATS

Purpose of Exercise: To develop the quadriceps. When you do Squats on a machine, you can work the thighs intensely while putting less strain on other areas such as the knees and lower back. There are a number of machines designed to approximate the Squat movement. They use a variety of techniques to create resistance, including weights, friction, and even air compression. Personally, I have always preferred doing Machine Squats on a Smith machine.

Execution: (1) Place your shoulders under the bar and come up to a standing position. Position your feet to obtain the desired effects from the exercise (see page 495). (2) Bend your knees and squat down until your thighs are lower than parallel, then press back up to the starting position.

Turning your toes out helps develop the inside of the thighs. Balancing a barbell in this position could be difficult, but the machine makes it easy. Standing with your feet moved forward helps isolate the quadriceps, especially the lower area near the knee, and minimizes strain to the lower back since you don't need to bend forward at all.

Machine Squat—toes out

Machine Squat—feet forward

Wrapping the knees when you do Heavy Squats raises the hydrostatic pressure within the joint and helps to prevent joint or ligament injury.

FRONT SQUATS

PURPOSE OF EXERCISE: To work the legs, with special emphasis on the thighs. Front Squats develop the outside sweep of the quadriceps.

EXECUTION: (1) Step up to the rack, bring your arms up under the bar, keeping the elbows high, cross your arms and grasp the bar with your hands to control it. Then lift the weight off the rack. Step back and separate your feet for balance (I find this exercise easier to do if I rest my heels on a low block to improve balance). (2) Bend your knees and, keeping your head up and your back straight, lower yourself until your thighs are below parallel to the floor. Push yourself back up to the starting position. Do this exercise slowly and strictly, making sure you keep your back straight. If possible, do all Squats in front of a mirror so you can check that you are keeping your back straight.

Front Half Squats are done in the same manner as Front Squats except you go only halfway down.

SISSY SQUATS

Purpose of Exercise: To isolate the lower quadriceps. Although this movement is called a Squat it is very close to a Leg Extension in the way it affects the legs. You will feel a lot of stress right down to where the quadriceps insert into the knee.

Execution: (1) Stand upright, feet a few inches apart, holding on to a bench or something else for support. (2) Bend your knees, raise up on your toes, and slowly lower yourself toward the floor, letting your pelvis and knees go forward while your head and shoulders tilt backward. (3) Continue down as low as possible, until your buttocks practically touch your heels. Stretch the thigh muscles and hold for a moment, then straighten your legs and come back up into a standing position. Flex your thigh muscles hard at the top of the movement for maximum cuts and development.

LEG PRESSES

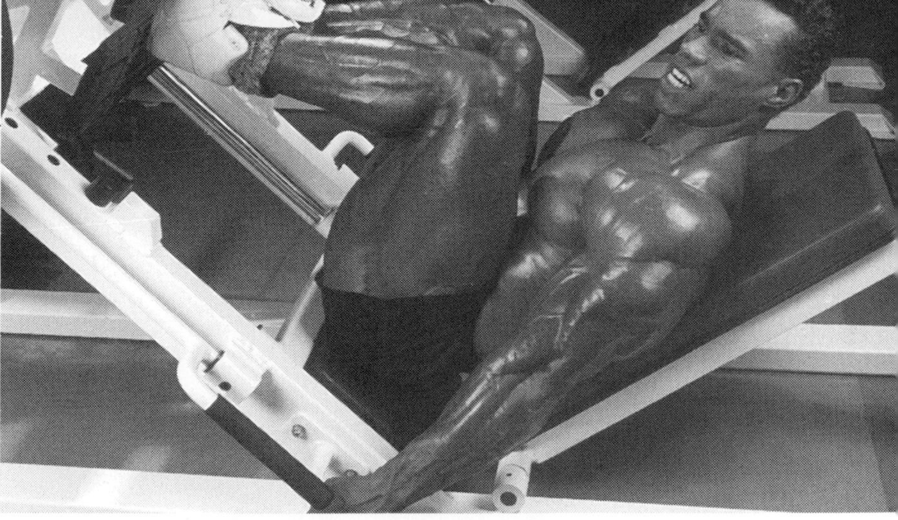

Purpose of Exercise: To build the mass of the thighs. If Squats have a disadvantage, it's the pressure they put on the lower back. Doing Leg Presses is a way around this that allows you to work the legs with very heavy weight.

Execution: (1) Using a Leg Press machine, position yourself under the machine and place your feet together against the crosspiece. Bend your knees and lower the weight as far as possible, bringing your knees toward your shoulders. (2) Press the weight back up again until your legs are fully extended. Don't get in the habit of pushing on your knees to help your legs press upward, or of crossing your arms across your chest and limiting your range of motion.

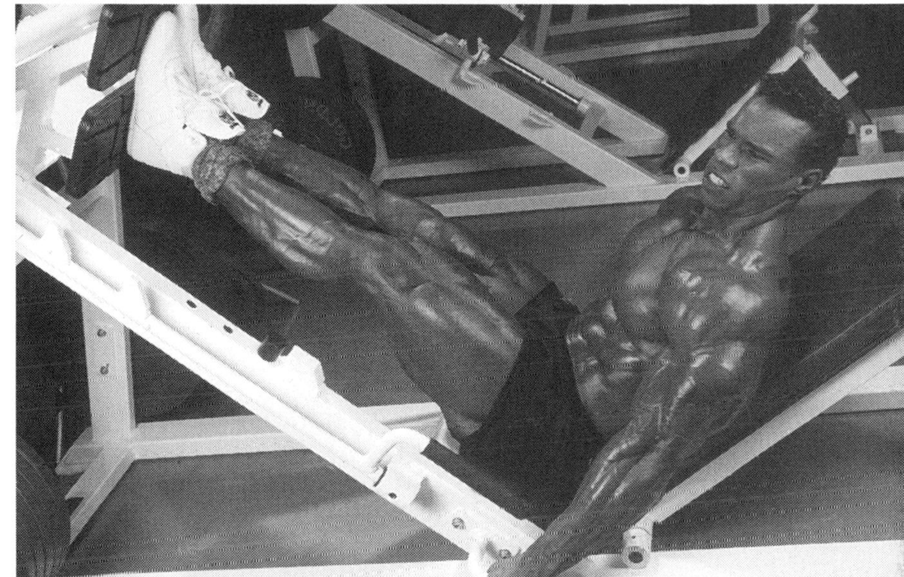

Kevin Levrone

LEG PRESS VARIATIONS

There are a number of other machines on which you can do the Leg Press movement. Some of these move along an angled track, others along a horizontal. No matter which type of machine is used, the exercise should be done in a similar manner, with the knees coming back as closely as possible to the shoulders.

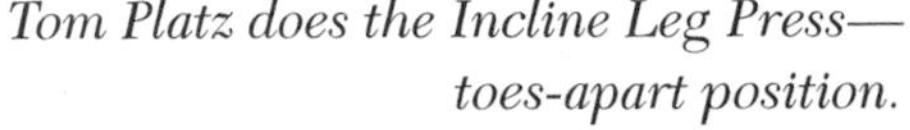

Tom Platz does the Incline Leg Press—toes-apart position.

HACK SQUATS

PURPOSE OF EXERCISE: To develop the lower area of the thigh. Hack Squats are a good movement for working the lower range of the pressing motion.

EXECUTION: (1) Depending on the design of the machine you use, either hook your shoulders under the padded bars or take hold of the handles. Your feet should be together, toes pointed slightly out. (2) Press downward with your legs and lift the mechanism, stopping when your legs are fully extended. This keeps constant tension on the legs. Bend your knees and lower yourself all the way down. Your legs should end up bent at a much more acute angle than when you do Squats. In all your repetitions, keep working this lower range of motion by going all the way down. (3) For some of your last repetitions, lower yourself in the normal way, but as you press back up, arch your back and bring your hips away from the machine without locking your legs out. This will emphasize the separation between the leg biceps and the quadriceps, which makes the thighs look huge when you do a side chest shot.

Lee Priest

LUNGES

Purpose of Exercise: To develop the front of the thighs and glutes.

Execution: (1) Holding a barbell across the back of your shoulders, stand upright with your feet together. (2) Keeping your head up, back straight, and chest thrust out, take a step forward, bend your knees, and bring your trailing knee almost to the floor. The step should be long enough so that the trailing leg is almost straight. Push yourself back up to the starting position with one strong and decisive movement, bringing your feet together, then step forward with the other foot and repeat the movement. You can do all your repetitions with one leg, then switch and repeat with the other, or you can alternate legs throughout the set.

LEG EXTENSIONS

Purpose of Exercise: To define and shape the front of the thigh. Leg Extensions are great for getting really deep definition in the thighs without losing size, and especially for developing the area around the knees.

Execution: (1) Using one of the various Leg Extension machines, sit in the seat and hook your feet under the padded bar. (2) Extend your legs out to the maximum, making sure you remain sitting flat on the machine (don't let yourself lift off and cheat up the weight). Extend your legs as far as possible until they are locked out to achieve maximum contraction of the quadriceps, then lower the weight slowly until your feet are no farther back than the knees and the thighs are fully stretched out. To make sure you always extend your legs fully enough, have your training partner hold out a hand on a level where your feet will kick it at the top of the extension.

LEG CURLS

Purpose of Exercise: To develop the hamstrings (rear of thigh).

Execution: (1) Lie facedown on a Leg Curl machine and hook your heels under the lever mechanism. Your legs should be stretched out straight. (2) Keeping flat on the bench, curl your legs up as far as possible, until the leg biceps are fully contracted. Release and lower the weight slowly back to the starting position. Hold on to the handles or the bench itself to keep yourself from lifting up off the bench. This exercise should be done strictly and through the fullest range of motion possible. I have found that supporting myself on my elbows helps keep the lower part of my body more firmly on the bench.

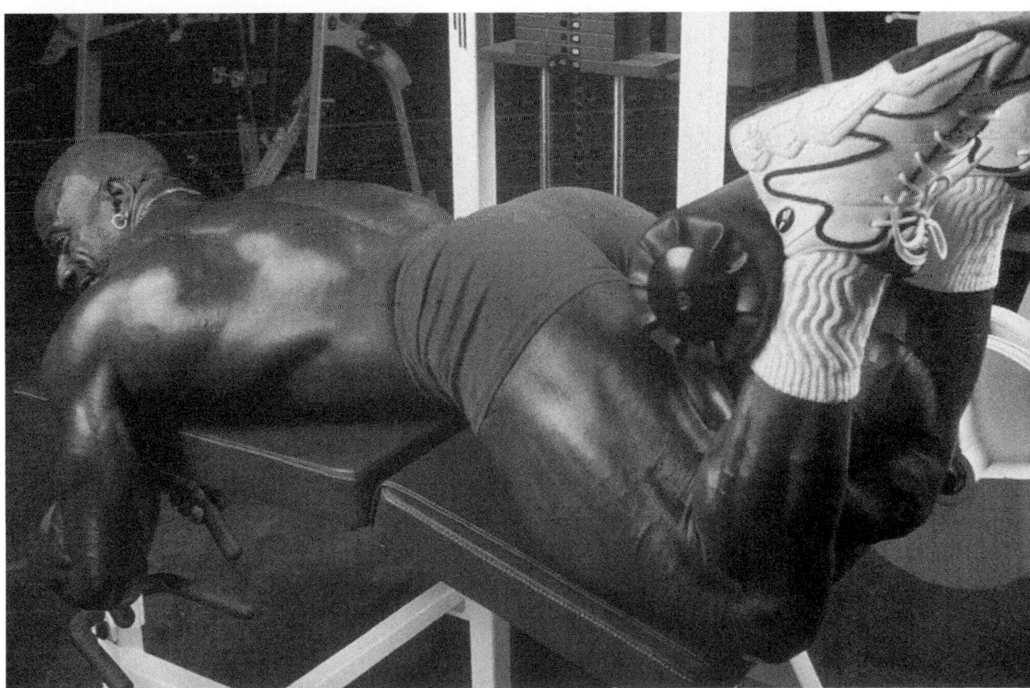

Willie Stallings

STANDING LEG CURLS

Purpose of Exercise: To develop the leg biceps. Using a Standing Curl machine, you can train one leg at a time and further isolate the leg biceps.

Execution: (1) Stand against the machine and hook one leg behind the lever mechanism. (2) Hold yourself steady and curl the leg up as high as possible. Release and lower the weight back to the starting position. Do your set with one leg, then repeat the exercise using the other leg. Be certain to keep the movement slow and strict.

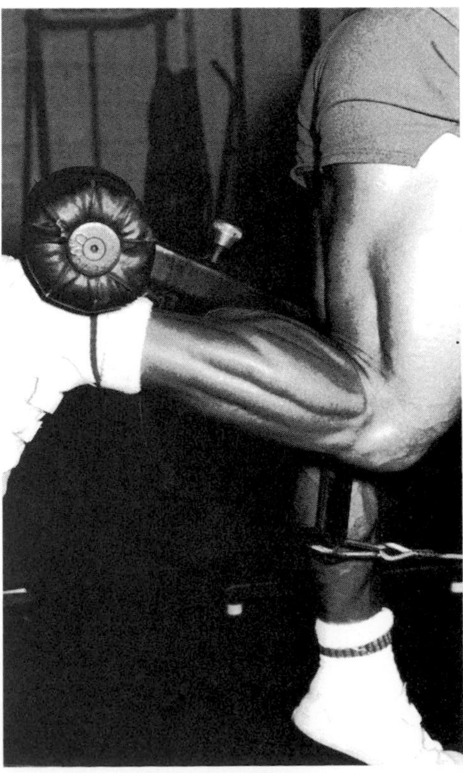

STRAIGHT-LEG DEADLIFTS

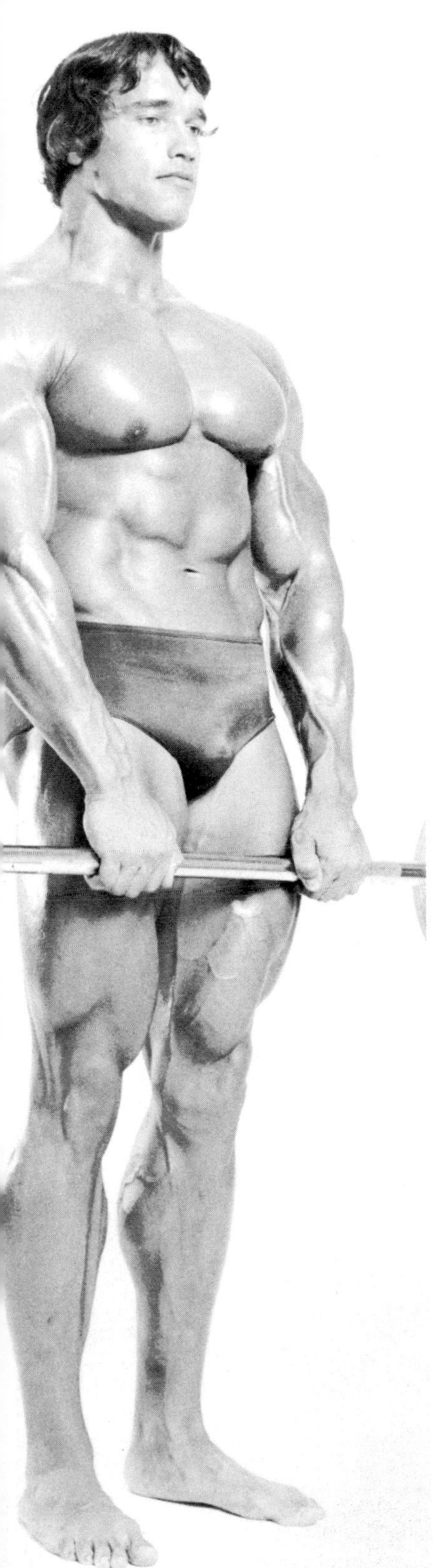

Purpose of Exercise: To work the hamstrings. Also works glutes and lower back.

Execution: (1) Take hold of a barbell as for Deadlifts and come up to a standing position. (2) Keep your legs nearly locked and bend forward from the waist, your back straight, until your torso is about parallel to the floor, the bar hanging at arm's length below you. Straighten up again, pull your shoulders back, and arch your spine to get the spinal erectors of the lower back to contract completely. Without your legs to help you as in regular Deadlifts, you will use much less weight doing this exercise. If you use Olympic weights, it is best to stand on a block or a bench so that you can lower the weight to the maximum extent without the large end plates touching the floor as long as your back doesn't begin to round.

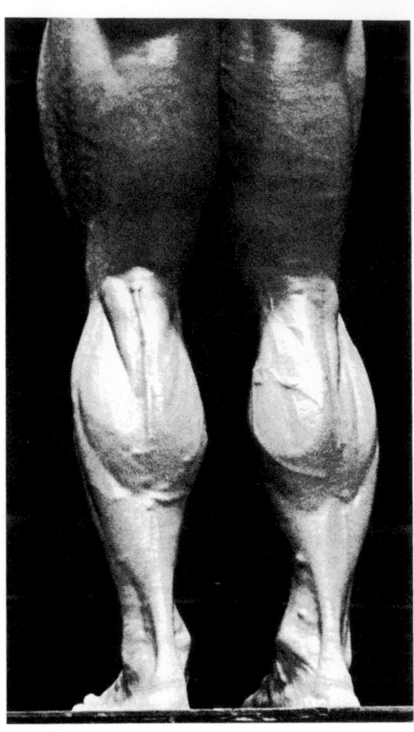

The Calves

THE MUSCLES OF THE CALF

The **soleus**, which is the larger and deeper of the two calf muscles and originates from both the fibula and the tibia

Basic function: To flex the foot

The **gastrocnemius,** which has two heads, one originating from the lateral aspect and the other from the medial of the lower femur. Both heads join to overlay the soleus and join with it to insert into the Achilles tendon, which inserts into the heel bone.

Basic function: To flex the foot

The **tibialis anterior,** which runs up the front of the lower leg alongside the shinbone

Basic function: To flex the foot

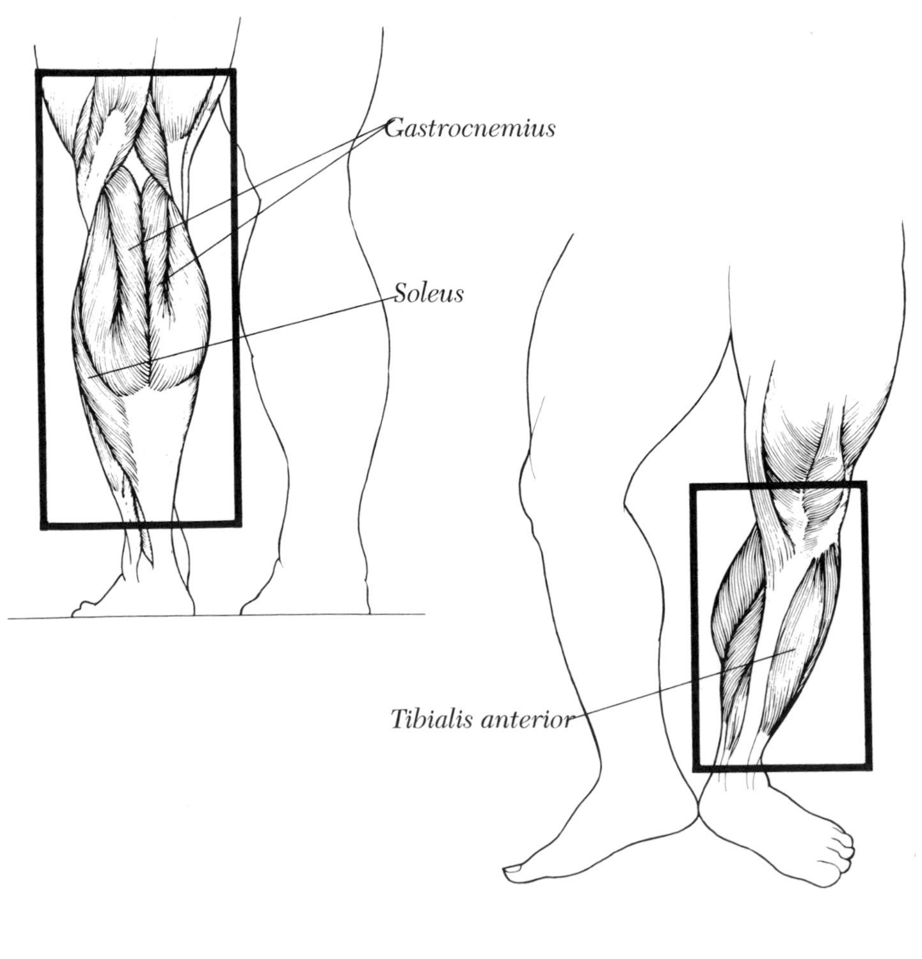

Check out Kevin Levrone, Dorian Yates, Shawn Ray, and Chris Cormier in the 1995 Mr. Olympia. As great as their backs, shoulders, traps, and arms are, if nothing happened when they flexed their calves, the entire effect would be ruined.

TRAINING THE CALVES

Calves, like the deltoids and abdominals, are a very aesthetic body part. A good pair of calves look good on the beach or tennis court as well as onstage. But more than that, outstanding calf development has historically been associated with the ideal male physique. Huge deltoids, washboard abs, and powerful calves were the qualities the Greek sculptors fashioned in their classical images of warriors and athletes.

Ideally, your calf development should about equal the development of your biceps. If your calves are smaller than your arms, then you need to give them extra attention. (One exception to this is Chris Dickerson, the only bodybuilder whose calves have always been naturally larger than his arms.)

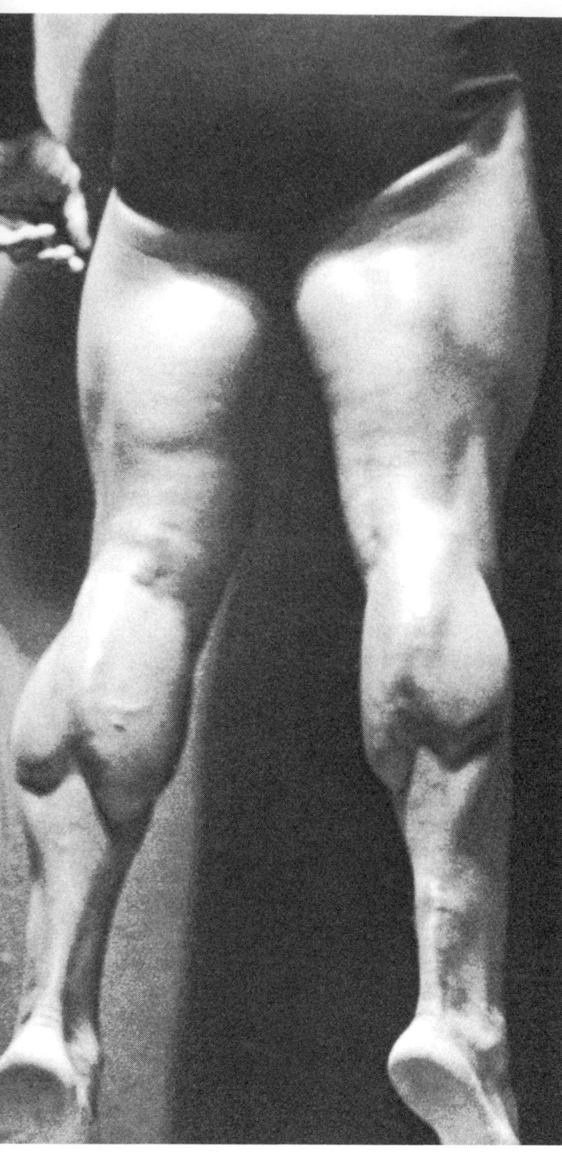

Reg Park

Calves are considered the most difficult muscle group in the body to develop. But calves respond to training just like any other muscle—you just have to be aware that they need to be trained at many different angles and with extremely heavy weight.

Think about what happens when you walk and run: You turn your foot and ankle first one way, then the other; you push off, stop suddenly, turn and change direction, you climb upward, walk downhill. And with each different movement you make, the calf muscles bear your weight, raising you up on your toes, lowering you down onto your heels, helping you twist your feet in different directions.

Until I trained with Reg Park, I had trouble getting my calves as big as I wanted them. I was doing Calf Raises with 500 or 600 pounds, but he was using 1,000! He pointed out to me that each of my calves individually was comfortable supporting my 250 pounds of body weight, so 500 pounds of resistance was actually a "normal" amount for them to deal with. So by training with the weight I was using, I was hardly making any impression on my calves at all!

The primary mass builder for calves is Standing Calf Raises, and here extra weight is really important. This exercise, along with Donkey Calf Raises, works both the gastrocnemius and soleus muscles of the calf. Seated Calf Raises better target the soleus.

Many bodybuilders do their calf training as an afterthought. Before or after their regular workout they give them 10 minutes or so, far less than they would for any other body part. And then they complain when their calves do not respond.

I believe in treating the calves just like every other body part. Since the calves are designed for constant work and rapid recuperation, I train them 30 to 45 minutes a day. I also use a wide variety of exercises; not just some sets of Standing and Seated Calf Raises, but enough movements to work every area of the calf muscles—upper and lower, inside and outside.

The calves are tough and used to a lot of hard work, so the best way to make them grow is to constantly shock them, using every high-intensity training principle possible. For example, when doing Donkey Calf Raises, I frequently started off with three 220-pound bodybuilders sitting on my back. I would continue the set until I could not do another rep, then have one of them slide off so that I could continue until my calves were screaming in agony. Finally, I would finish off the set using only my own body weight and feeling as if my calves were going to explode.

Another shock method involves doing partial reps. About one out of four of my calf workouts involved doing half and quarter movements with extremely heavy weights, which put an enormous demand on the calf muscles. Actually, you can use virtually all of the Shocking Principles described in this book to develop your calves—Staggered Sets, Rest/Pause, forced reps, 21s, supersets, running the rack, and so on. The more you shock the calves, the more you subject them to unexpected stimulation, the more calf development you will see as a result.

A young bodybuilder once came over to me while I was doing Standing Calf Raises and told me how much he admired my calf development. "You can have calves just as good," I told him, "if you are willing to pay the price." He looked puzzled and asked me what I meant. "Calves like this will cost you five hundred hours," I said. "Anything less and you won't get the results."

If you analyze that 500-hour figure you get: 500 hours equals more than 660 forty-five minute calf workouts; 660 divided by 4 workouts a week equals about 165 weeks, or over three years! So, unless you are genetically gifted like a Chris Dickerson and were born with magnificent calves, building them up takes a minimum of three years of brutal training.

Even with that effort, calves may not turn out to be your best body part. But I doubt there are many bodybuilders with enough physical talent to build up the rest of their bodies who will not find their calves responding well to the regimen I prescribe.

STRETCHING THE CALVES

To get a full contraction of a muscle, first you have to get a full extension. With the calves this means going all the way down when you do full-range movements, lowering your heels as far as possible before coming up all the way onto your toes to get a contraction.

Tom Platz carries this to the ultimate by having a partner sit on the end of a Seated Calf Raise machine to force his heels lower and lower and stretch his calves to the extreme (something other bodybuilders ought to approach with great caution if they try to copy him). What Tom is doing is using a principle that I discovered for myself many years ago: The longer the range of movement and the fuller the extension and contraction of muscle, the more it will develop. This is especially valuable in calf training, since our normal use of the calf when we walk and run involves mostly the mid-range function.

I like to use a block for Standing Calf Raises just high enough so that my heels touch the floor at the bottom of the movement. This way I know I have lowered my heels enough to get maximum stretch from my calf muscles.

BEGINNING PROGRAM

When you begin to train calves, you will probably not be able to use the amount of weight I have been talking about. The untrained calf muscle is very disproportionate in its "strength curve." Your calf muscles have carried your body weight throughout your whole life, but you rarely require them to function at the extreme ends of their range of motion—at full extension or full contraction.

Therefore, when you start doing Calf Raises you will probably find you are enormously strong in the mid-range, but very weak at the extremes. So what you have to do the first few months of training is bring up the strength of your calves at full contraction and full extension so that you acquire some balance throughout the strength curve. At this point, you can begin to pile on the weight and develop the entire range of motion of the muscles.

Still, you will find that the mid-range is disproportionately strong—due to mechanical and leverage factors—and this is why I recommend doing partial- as well as full-range movements right from the beginning. In this way, you can use enormous amounts of weight to fully stress the muscle at its strongest angles.

To get you started, I have limited the calf training in the Beginning Program to 4 sets, 15 reps each of Standing Calf Raises 3 times a week. Concentrate on these to begin with and learn to do them correctly:

1. Get a full range of motion, full stretch at the bottom, up on your toes for a full contraction at the top.

2. Use a block high enough so that your heels can drop all the way down.

3. Use a strict movement, keeping your knees straight enough so that you are lifting the weight only with the calves, not by pressing with your legs.

4. Use a "normal" foot position—that is, with your feet pointed straight ahead, so that your entire calf is worked proportionately.

5. Do not rush through your calf training to get to something else, or simply tack on some sets for calves at the end of your workout—work your calves with as much energy and concentration as any other body part.

ADVANCED AND COMPETITION PROGRAMS

For Advanced and Competition Training, I recommend working calves 6 times a week. I have heard theories that this amount of frequency represents "overtraining," but when I look at the bodybuilders who have the best calves, I usually find they are the ones who train them more frequently.

In Advanced Training, I have included both Donkey Calf Raises and Seated Calf Raises along with the mass-building Standing Calf Raises. The Seated Raises are designed to work the soleus muscle, extending your calf lower toward your ankle, and the Donkey Raises allow you to do strict repetitions against resistance centered at the hips rather than the shoulders.

Donkey Calf Raises create a kind of deep development unlike any other calf exercise. You feel different after Donkeys—not just a pump but the feeling that you have worked the muscle right down to the bone. Another thing I like about this exercise is that the bent-over position increases the amount of stretch you can get, which gives you the longest possible range of motion.

Once you advance to the Competition Program, there will be two new exercises to learn: Front Calf Raises to develop the tibialis anterior, and One-Leg Calf Raises to further isolate the calf muscles of each leg. But beyond the exercises themselves, you'll begin to work on shaping the entire area of the calves by varying the position of your toes during the exercises.

As I said earlier, most bodybuilders whose calves refuse to grow are simply not training them hard enough or with enough weight. By the time you reach the level of Competition Training, the program will include anywhere from 9 to 15 sets of calf training, and if you do this much work correctly, with the right amount of intensity and the proper amount of weight, your calves will simply be forced to develop and grow. But there is something else you can do to help ensure this response from your calf muscles: Learn to vary your program to continually surprise and stimulate the calves.

In the late 1960s and early 1970s, I began changing my calf training around constantly. I would come into the gym one day and do Donkey Calf Raises, 5 sets of 10; Standing Calf Raises, 5 sets of 10; Seated Calf Raises, 5 sets of 10; Calf Raises on a pressing machine, 5 sets of 10; One-Leg Calf Raises, 5 sets of 10 to bring up my weaker left calf (which measured only 19½ inches, while the other was 20 inches cold). The next training day I might begin with Seated Calf Raises and then do Standing or Donkey Raises afterward, the idea being to force the calves to work in unfamiliar and unexpected ways as often as possible. Sometimes I would do 20 repetitions instead of 10, or do more sets of an exercise than just 5—maybe 40 sets total for calves one day with only 10 sets of full-range movements and the rest partial-range exercises.

In addition, I would employ every one of the Shocking Principles I could, from the Stripping Method to forced reps. I would always stretch after every single exercise, keeping the muscles working all the time and forcing them to work through the longest possible range of motion.

Doing Calf Raises with as much as 1,000 pounds might seem like an unobtainable goal if you are up to lifting only 450 pounds. But the way to reach that goal, like most other things, is by stages, a little at a time. Try increasing weight at the rate of 50 pounds per month. This gives your tendons and ligaments time to adapt and grown stronger along with your calf muscles.

Another good idea is to choose a weight that is 50 or 100 pounds higher than you can comfortably use in your regular sets and, at the end of your calf workout, try to do just 3 or 4 reps with the increased resistance. This accustoms other parts of your body—like the back, legs, and Achilles tendon—to deal with that amount of weight; but it also trains your mind to cope with the extra weight so that you will not be intimidated by it when you are ready to move up in poundage again.

Sometimes, when you are training calves for the special requirements of competition, you may find that using slightly lighter weight is actually a good idea. Working lighter, with perhaps a few additional sets, and paying extra attention to contracting the muscles through the fullest range of motion can help finish off and fully shape the calves. Ken Waller, who at one time probably had the biggest calves in the world, likes to use heavy weights for Standing Calf Raises, but feels he got much better development by using lighter weights (300 pounds) for Seated Calf Raises. This, of course, is not the way to build calf size in the first place, but it does show how an individual can learn to use what is best for him once he gets up to this level of development.

Advanced Training involves hitting the calves from every angle—toes-in and toes-out foot position as well as the normal standing and seated movements—to develop both the soleus and gastrocnemius, and not neglecting the tibialis anterior at the front of the lower leg.

Give your body every advantage by being careful with technique and wearing shoes that give you strong support. Give your mind every advantage by learning to psych yourself up and increase your motivation—by hanging a photo of a great set of calves on the calf machine, for example.

Another training technique I liked to use in calf training was supersets. For example, I would begin with a set of Seated Calf Raises, then go immediately to the Leg Press machine and do another set of Calf Raises, both movements working the lower area of the calves. I also occasionally did Staggered Sets—perhaps a set of Chins for the back then a set of Standing Calf Raises. A few back exercises later I would again do another set for calves. So by the time I was finished with the overall workout, I had already done about 8 sets for calves and I could finish off my calf training with a big head start. This is great when you find yourself getting tired of calf training and not giving it all the effort you should.

WEAK POINT TRAINING

You might find your calves are growing, but not proportionately; certain areas are lagging behind. The answer in calf training is the same as with any other body part—you choose specific exercises to help correct the imbalance:

Lower Calves

Do additional sets of Seated Calf Raises to develop the soleus muscle of the lower calf—that V look in which the muscle descends down to the Achilles tendon.

Bend the knees slightly when doing Standing Calf Raises to bring the lower calves into the movement. This works especially well if you do partial movements at the extreme bottom of the range of motion—your heels almost touching the floor.

Upper Calves

Standing Calf Raises with special emphasis on the top part of the range of motion, especially when you hold yourself in a full contracted position at the top of the movement

Emphasis on the Inside of the Calves

Do sets of every one of the calf exercises with toes turned outward.

Emphasis on the Outside of the Calves

Calf Raises with toes turned inward

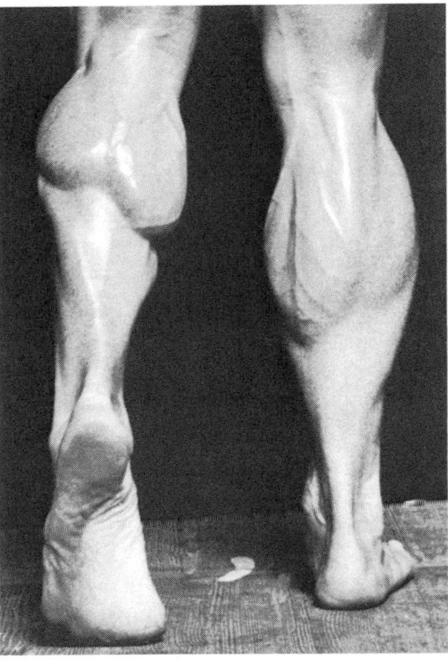

Ken Waller's calves are superior to many other top bodybuilders' because he has such good lower calf development. The gastrocnemius, which underlies the more defined soleus muscle, is full and pronounced all the way down to the ankle.

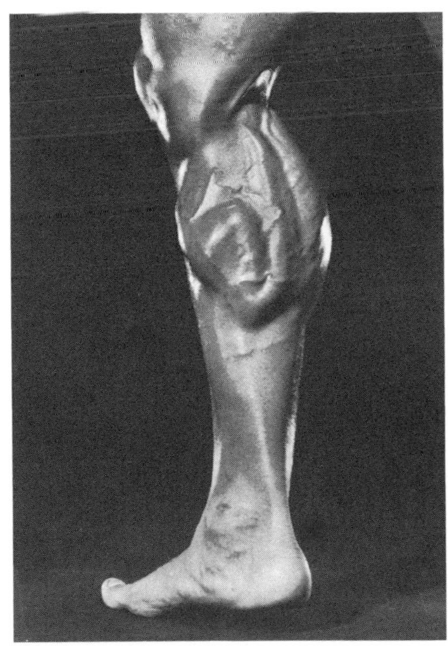

For calves like mine you have to be willing to pay the price: at least 500 hours of intense, concentrated, and sometimes painful calf training.

One Calf Too Small

Add on two extra sets of One-Leg Calf Raises for the smaller calf. Your two sets could be Standing Calf Raises on one leg while holding a dumbbell in your hand, and to bring up the lower calf, Seated Calf Raises performed one-legged. In fact, most calf exercises can be adapted to a one-leg movement. Just be sure to use enough weight to really stimulate the muscle you want to bring up.

Front of the Calves

Developing the tibialis anterior creates a split that makes your calves look extra wide from the front. Doing Front Calf Raises can make the calves look an inch bigger. This exercise helps to separate the outside from the inside and creates a wide look that sheer calf size alone cannot accomplish. Therefore, this muscle needs the same attention that the others get—a full 4 sets of intense training and plenty of stretching.

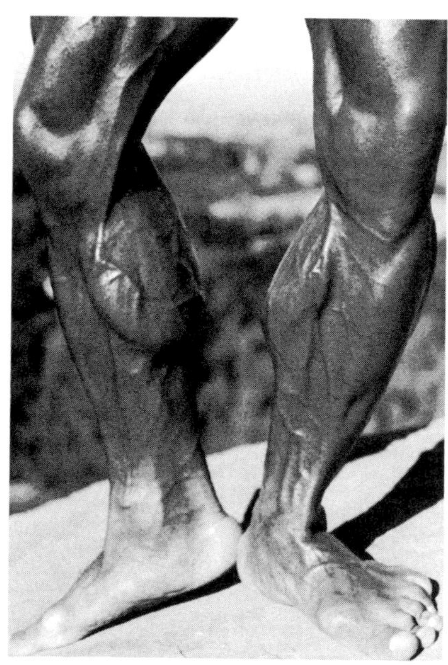

Chris Dickerson's calves are so remarkable that they look big even when viewed from the front.

The toes-out position helps to develop the inside of the calf muscles.

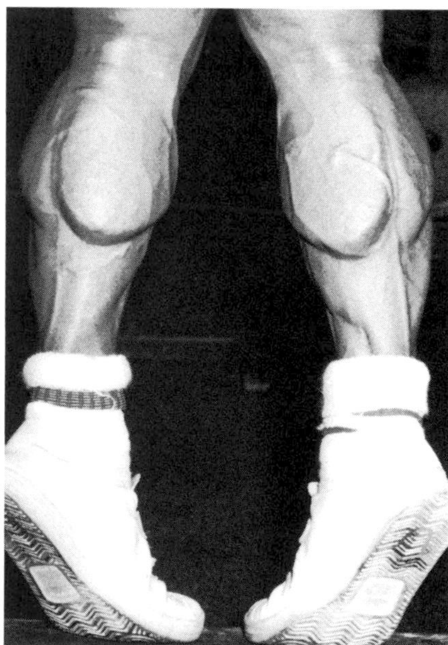

The toes-in position is used to add emphasis to the outside of the calf muscles.

In the beginning my calves were a real weak point, so I did most of my early posing shots with my calves in the water!

One reason that bodybuilders with weak calves tend not to develop them is that they can cover them up in the gym by wearing long pants, so they can forget about them. I used to do this myself, but once I realized my mistake I began to make really fantastic progress in calf training.

When I was young and growing fast, getting up to 230 and then 240 pounds, I was very proud of my flaring back and powerful arms. So I loved to train wearing a tank top or no shirt at all. I would see the reflection of my muscles in the mirror and this would inspire me to train even harder so as to build greater and greater mass and quality. But one day it occurred to me that I wasn't treating the calves as seriously as the other muscles. So I made up my mind to rectify this situation.

The first thing I did was to cut off the bottoms of my training pants. Now my calves were exposed for me and everyone else to see. If they were underdeveloped—and they were—there was no hiding the fact. And the only way I could change the situation was to train my calves so hard and so intensely that the back of my legs would come to resemble huge boulders.

At first, this was embarrassing. The other bodybuilders in the gym could see my weakness and they constantly made comments. But the plan eventually paid off. No longer able to ignore my calves, I was determined to build them into one of my best body parts. Psychologically, it was a brutal way to accomplish this, but it worked, and that is what I really cared about. Within one year my calves grew tremendously, and the comments I got in the gym were complimentary rather than critical.

If calves are your problem, use the Priority Principle to really attack them. Put calf training first in your workout, when your psychological and physical energy is at the highest. Another thing you can do is work on your calves even when you aren't in the gym. For example, when you are walking, make an effort to go all the way up onto your toes to make the calves work through a longer range of motion. If you are on a beach, do the same thing in the sand. After a half hour of walking in the sand, digging in with your toes, you will feel a fantastic burn in your calf muscles.

This photo is a great example of how effective using the Priority Principle and zeroing in on your weak points can be. When I stepped onstage at a competition two years after I first began trying so hard to bring up my calves, and I turned my back to the audience, my calves were so huge that I got an ovation even before I flexed them.

POSING THE CALVES

In every pose you do onstage, you need to flex the calves. Bodybuilders usually learn to pose from the ground up—set the feet, flex the calves and legs, then the upper body. But most bodybuilders don't spend time learning to flex and pose the calves by themselves. The ability to do this comes in handy when you are standing relaxed in round one and you want to hit your calves, fanning them out to impress the judges.

To learn to do this, I recommend posing and flexing the calves be-

Even when you are doing side poses, calf development plays an important part. When you are doing a side chest shot, for instance, and concentrating on your upper body, a good judge will also take your calves into consideration.

You can create a stronger visual impression if you can keep your calves flexed while "standing relaxed" in the first round of competition. But you must practice flexing or you will lack the endurance to stand this way for more than a few minutes. I've seen a lot of competitors develop leg cramps because they failed to work hard enough at this.

tween each set of calf training, developing the connection between the mind and muscle so that you gain absolute control over how the calf looks. This also makes the muscle harder and more developed, since the flexing is itself a kind of isometric exercise.

Remember, you will want to be able to show off your calf muscles in poses in which your feet are flat on the floor as well as when you are up on your toes, so you should practice flexing in order to get the kind of muscle control you need to accomplish this. While leaning against a machine or a wall, go up on your toes as far as possible, to get maximum contraction of the calf muscle.

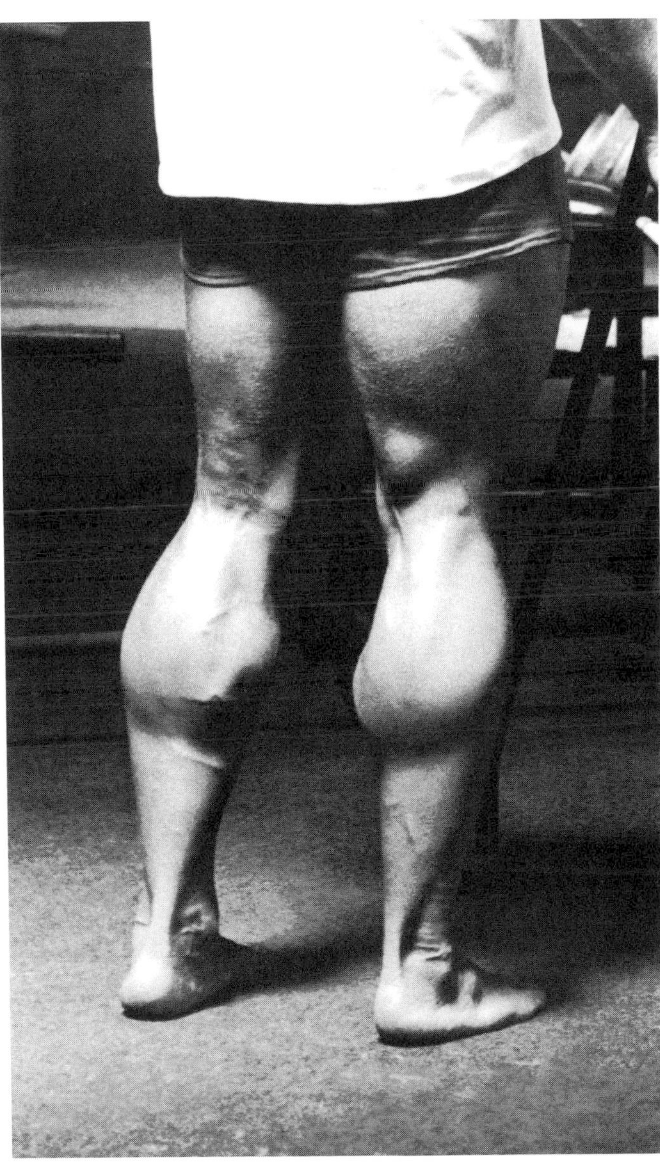

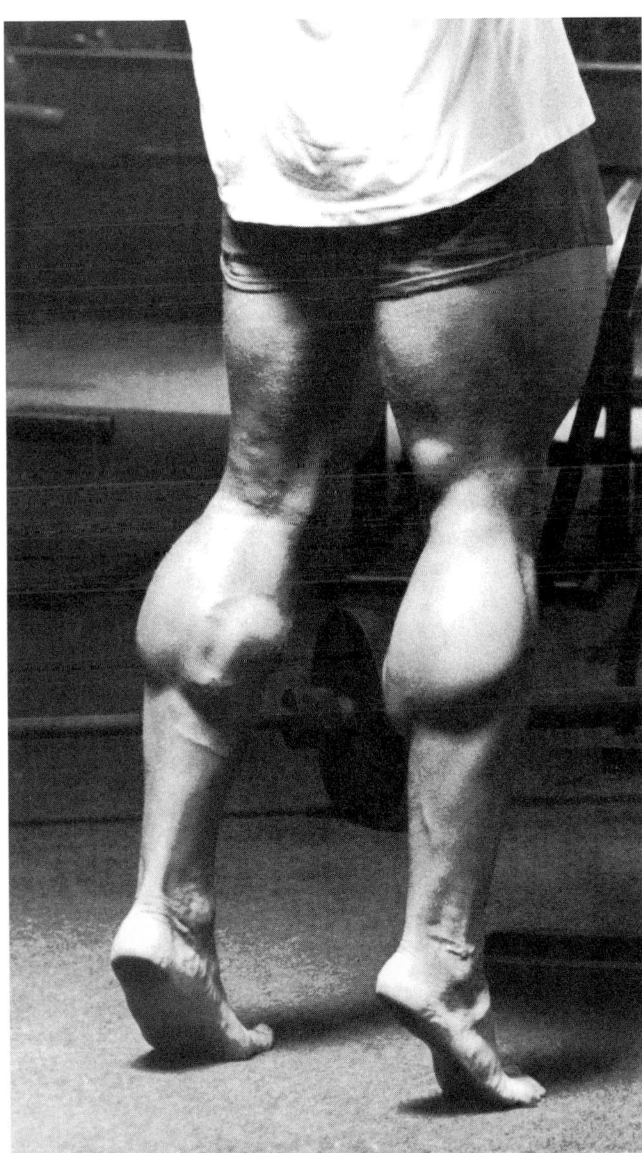

Calf Exercises

STANDING CALF RAISES

Purpose of Exercise: To develop the overall mass of the calves.

Execution: (1) Stand with your toes on the block of a standing Calf Raise machine, your heels extended out into space. Hook your shoulders under the pads and straighten your legs, lifting the weight clear of the support. Lower your heels as far as possible toward the floor, keeping your knees slightly bent throughout the movement in order to work the lower area of the calves as well as the upper, and feeling the calf muscles stretch to the maximum. I like a block that is high enough so that I get a full stretch when I lower my heels. (2) From the bottom of the movement, come up on your toes as far as possible. The weight should be heavy enough to exercise the calves, but not so heavy that you cannot come all the way up for most of your repetitions.

When you are too tired to do complete repetitions, finish off the set with a series of partial movements to increase the intensity of the exercise.

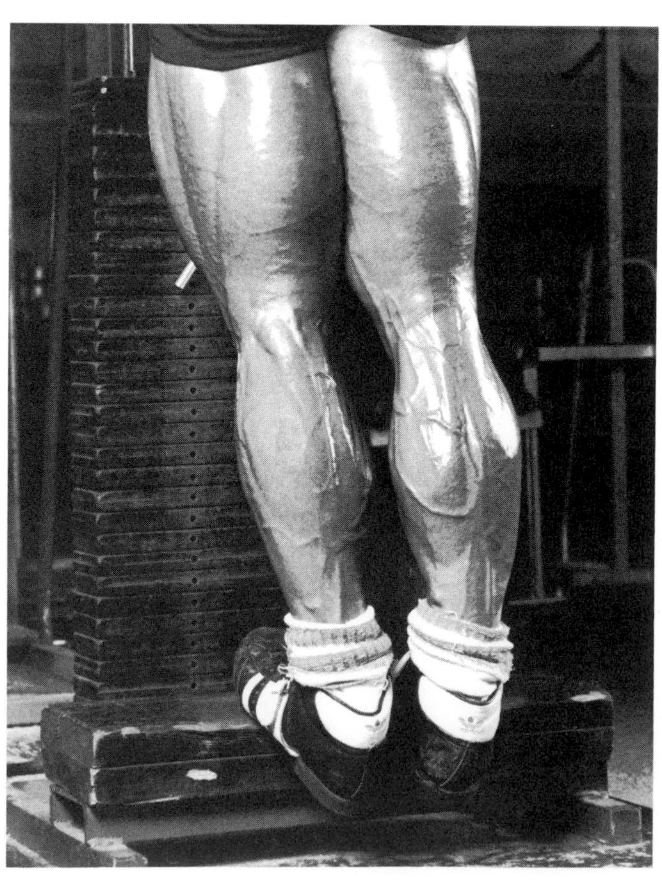

Here's what happened one time when I couldn't load up enough weight on the Standing Calf Raise, though I wouldn't recommend it for you.

The normal position, with toes straight ahead, is best for overall calf development.

CALF RAISES ON LEG PRESS MACHINE

PURPOSE OF EXERCISE: To develop the calves.

EXECUTION: (1) Using one of the various types of Leg Press machines (I prefer the Vertical Leg Press for Calf Raises), position yourself as if to do a Leg Press, but push against the foot pads only with your toes, leaving your heels unsupported. Straighten your legs and press the weight up until your knees are almost locked out. With your knees just slightly bent, keep your heels pressed upward but let your toes come back toward you, feeling the fullest possible stretch in the calf muscles. (2) When you can't stretch any farther, press the weight upward with your toes as far as you possibly can to fully contract your calf muscles. You can't cheat at all when you do Calf Raises on a machine. Lying with your back braced against the pad, you can totally isolate the calves to give them a really intense workout. Make sure the safety bars are in place in case your toes slip.

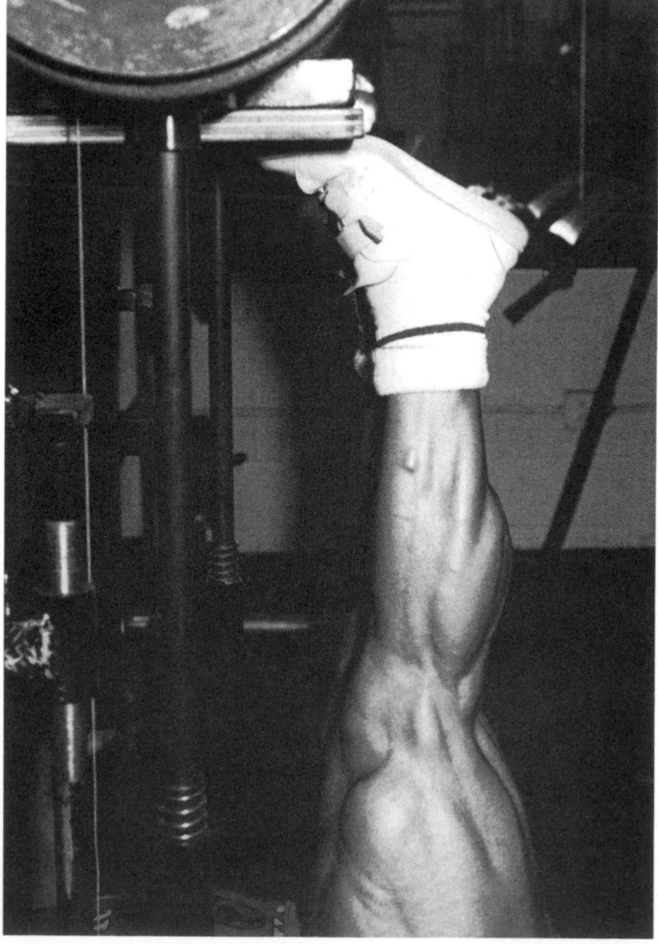

Tom Platz

SEATED CALF RAISES

PURPOSE OF EXERCISE: To develop the lower and outer areas of the calves.

EXECUTION: (1) Sit on the machine and place your toes on the bottom crosspiece, hooking your knees under the crossbar. Slowly lower your heels as far toward the ground as possible, (2) then press back up on your toes until your calves are fully contracted. Try not to rock back and forth too much, but keep the calves working with a steady, rhythmic motion.

DONKEY CALF RAISES

Purpose of Exercise: To develop the thickness of the back of the calves.

Donkey Calf Raises are one of my favorite exercises, and really make your calves look huge when viewed from the side.

Execution: (1) Place your toes on a block, bend forward from the waist, and lean on a bench or a table for support or use a Donkey Calf machine. Your toes should be directly below your hips. Have a training partner add resistance by seating himself across your hips, as far back as possible to keep pressure off the lower back. (2) With your toes pointed straight ahead, lower your heels as far as possible, then come back up on your toes until your calves are fully contracted. If you try to cheat on this movement you end up bouncing your training partner around, so have him call this to your attention if it happens.

You can use a variation of the Stripping Method doing Donkey Calf Raises. I would frequently start with as many as three men on my back. As I got tired, I would do a few sets with just two guys, then finish off with just one. Talk about getting a burn!

ONE-LEG CALF RAISES

Purpose of Exercise: To isolate each set of calf muscles. Doing Calf Raises one leg at a time is essential when one calf is larger than the other and you need to bring up the size of the smaller one.

Execution: (1) Stand with the toes of one leg on a block and the other leg suspended in midair behind you. Lower your heel as far as you can, (2) then come back up on your toes. Finish your set, then repeat with the other leg. If one of your calves is smaller or weaker than the other, give it some extra sets to help achieve the necessary symmetry. One-Leg Calf Raises can also be done on a Leg Press machine.

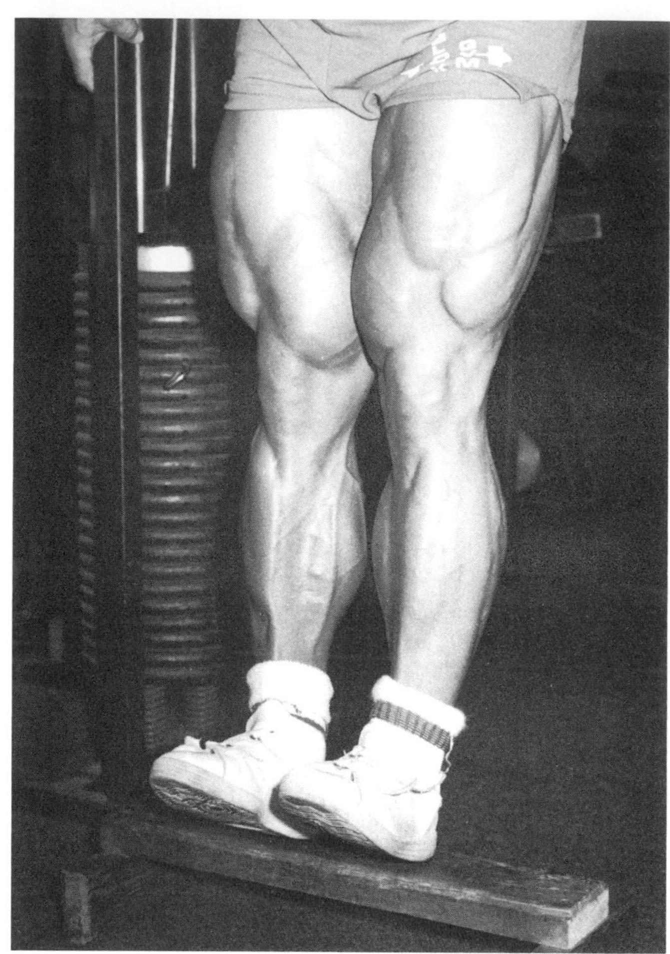

REVERSE CALF RAISES

PURPOSE OF EXERCISE: To develop the front of the lower leg. Many bodybuilders with good calves forget about developing the muscles at the front of the lower leg, primarily the tibialis anterior, which separates the inside calf from the outside calf and makes the leg seem much bigger.

EXECUTION: (1) Stand with your heels on a block, lower your toes as far as you can, (2) then lift them up, feeling the muscles at the front of the lower leg contract as fully as possible. Do about 20 or 30 repetitions with your own body weight. As a variation, you can hook your toes under a light weight to provide extra resistance.

The Abdomen

THE MUSCLES OF THE ABDOMEN

The **rectus abdominis,** a long muscle extending along the length of the ventral aspect of the abdomen. It originates in the area of the pubis and inserts into the cartilage of the fifth, sixth, and seventh ribs.

Basic function: To flex the spinal column and to draw the sternum toward the pelvis

The **external obliques** (obliquus externus abdominis), muscles at each side of the torso attached to the lower eight ribs and inserting at the side of the pelvis

Basic function: To flex and rotate the spinal column

The **intercostals,** two thin planes of muscular and tendon fibers occupying the spaces between the ribs

Basic Function: To lift the ribs and draw them together

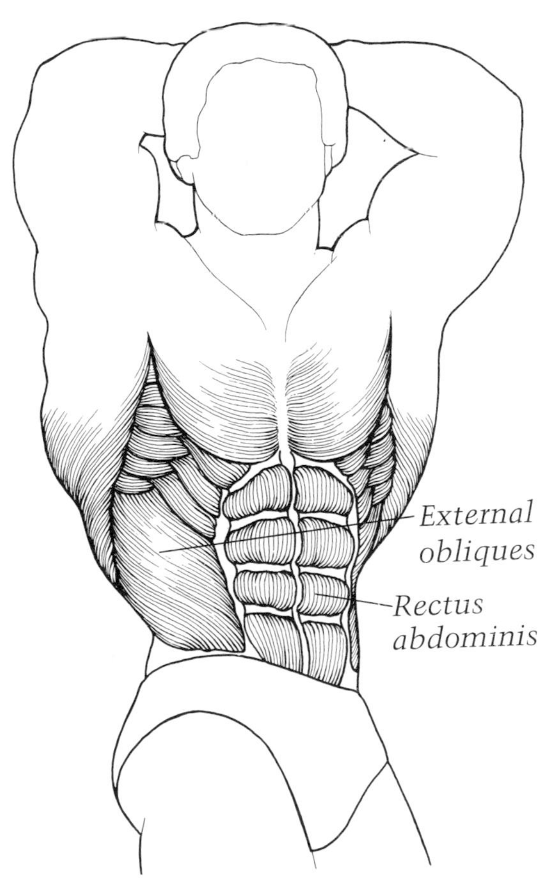

Mohamed Makkawy

Mike Francois, Flex Wheeler, and Chris Cormier demonstrate the IFBB mandatory abdominal pose: hands behind the head, abs flexed, and one leg extended.

Well-defined abdominals are important, but so is having a small waist, which makes poses like this twist biceps shot so much more effective.

TRAINING THE ABDOMINALS

Strong abdominals are essential to maximizing performance in almost all sports. In bodybuilding, the abdominals play an extremely important role when it comes to the visible impression your physique makes on an observer. The abs are, in fact, the *visual* center of the body. If you superimpose an X on the body with the terminal points being the shoulders and the feet, the two lines cross at the abdominals, and this is where the eyes are inevitably drawn. Men carry a disproportionate number of fat cells in the abdominal area compared to women (who can often be relatively fat and still have abs showing), so well-defined abs are one sign of being in top condition—lean, hard, and strong.

A bodybuilder is likely to score points in a contest if he has wide shoulders and flaring lats that taper down to a firm, narrow waist. A small waist

In a posedown, when you can hit any shot you want, it makes sense not to try to hit the same pose as other competitors who have advantages as a result of superior development of certain body parts or greater mass. (Nasser El Sonbaty, Vince Taylor, Milos Sarcev, and John Sherman)

tends to make both your chest and your thighs appear larger, more impressive, and more aesthetic.

The traditional V-shaped torso is as important as sheer mass when it comes to creating a quality, championship physique. I have often seen contests in which good bodybuilders came in a few pounds overweight in order to appear bigger but found the extra weight they were carrying at the waist spoiled the visual effect. When I got into bodybuilding, there were a few bodybuilders who made up for lack of overall size by the outstanding development of their abs—competitors like Pierre Vandensteen and Vince Gironda, for example. But in modern bodybuilding *every* would-be champion, no matter his body type, has to have well-developed abs in order to be competitive, from the really massive bodybuilders (Dorian Yates, Nasser El Sonbaty, Paul Dillett) to mid-size (Flex Wheeler) to smaller (Shawn Ray) to short (Lee Priest).

If my waist had been small and hard, and with defined abs and obliques, when I came to compete in the United States in 1968, I might not have finished second to Frank Zane. But along the same lines, if Frank had gone to the 1982 Olympia in London in the kind of shape he achieved in 1979 when he beat Mike Mentzer for that title, he might well have defeated Chris Dickerson instead of having to settle for second. Frank had actually gained mass for this competition, but in doing so appeared on-

The posedown at the 1980 Mr. Olympia contest demonstrates very clearly that top bodybuilders have to have great abs to stay in competition. As the biggest man, it was essential for me to have abs that would stand up to the likes of Mike Mentzer, Frank Zane, and Chris Dickerson.

Shawn Ray

stage without the washboard abs that make him at his best so tremendously impressive. Lack of abdominal development, or failure to display the abs properly, can be very costly in competition. Boyer Coe had great success in competition in the 1960s and 1970s, but he was one of the few top bodybuilders who couldn't boast of a well-developed "six-pack." Boyer's lack of ab development was genetic and not due to incorrect or lax training. But the sport has become so competitive that there is no longer any such thing as a champion bodybuilder without excellent abs at almost any level of competition.

When Bill Pearl won his first contests in the early 1950s, outstanding abdominal development was not considered essential. However, by the time he had won his NABBA Mr. Universe titles, even though his body weight had actually increased, Pearl's abdominals were fantastic.

Nowadays, the bigger men in the sport often have problems because their abdominals have become *too massive*, and they get too thick in the middle and at the sides of their torso. Often this happens as the result of doing very heavy exercises like Squats, for example, that call for a lot of involvement on the part of the abdominals and the obliques as stabilizers. Because of this, you almost never see these bodybuilders using weights to train their abs or their obliques. But the fact that you put so much stress on the muscles of the waist whenever you train heavy means that no bodybuilder—even the smaller ones—needs to train abs using any kind of extra resistance (though many will just before a contest). Of course, there are some abdominal exercises that involve more effort because more of your body weight is involved and we'll discuss those in detail.

SPOT REDUCTION

Since most of the top bodybuilders today, regardless of stature, are massively developed for their body size, the most important goal of abdominal training has become *definition*. This involves two things—training and developing the abdominals and reducing body fat sufficiently to reveal the muscularity underneath.

When I got into bodybuilding most competitors believed in something called spot reduction, and there are a lot of people who still think this is possible. Spot reduction refers to training a specific muscle in order to burn off fat in that particular area. According to this idea, to develop abdominal definition, you do a lot of ab training, lots of high reps, and burn away the fat that is obscuring the development of the abdominal muscles.

Unfortunately, this doesn't work. When the body is in caloric deficit and begins metabolizing fat for energy, it doesn't go to an area where the muscles are doing a lot of work in order to get additional energy resources. The body has a genetically programmed pattern by which it determines from what adipose cells to access stored fat energy. Exercise does burn calories, of course, but the abdominals are such relatively small muscles that no matter how much ab training you do you won't metabolize nearly the energy you would by simply going for a walk for the same amount of time.

But this is not to say that training a given area like the abs doesn't increase definition. As I said, the abdominals get a hard workout when you do heavy exercises, but what they don't get is *quality training*—that is, isolation, full-range-of-movement exercises. Movements that do this bring out the full shape and separation of the abdominals instead of just making them bigger. So although training the abs like this doesn't do a lot to reduce the fat around the waistline, it does create very well defined muscles that are revealed once you are able to reduce your body fat sufficiently by means of diet and aerobic exercise.

AB-SPECIFIC EXERCISES

When the abdominal muscles contract, a very simple thing happens: They pull the rib cage and the pelvis toward each other in a short, "crunching" motion. No matter what kind of abdominal exercise you do, if it is *really* a primary ab movement this is what happens. In the past, before the physiology of abdominal training was well understood, bodybuilders used to do a lot of "conventional" abdominal exercises such as Sit-Ups and Leg Raises. Unfortunately, those are not primary abdominal exercises but instead work the iliopsoas muscles—the hip flexors. The hip flexors arise from the lower back, go across the top of the pelvis, and attach to the upper thigh. When you raise your leg, you use the hip flexors. When you hook your feet under a support and lift your torso up in a conventional Sit-Up, you are also using the iliopsoas muscles.

Try this experiment: Stand up, hold on to something for support, and lift one leg up in front of you while putting one hand on your abdominals. You'll feel a pull at the top of the thigh but it will also be obvious that the abdominals are not involved in lifting the leg. The abdominals attach to the pelvis, not the leg, so they have nothing to do with raising the leg up in the air.

The same thing is true of a Sit-Up or Slant-Board Sit-Up. This exercise is really the reverse of a Leg Raise. Instead of keeping the torso steady and lifting the leg, you are keeping the legs steady and lifting the torso—and the same muscles are being used, the hip flexors. When you do any of these exercises, the primary role of the abdominals is as *stabilizers*. They keep the torso locked and steady. But this is directly opposite of what you want to achieve in your ab-specific training because the role of the abs, as I have pointed out, is simply to *draw the rib cage and pelvis together*—to crunch them together in a very short movement which involves the back curling forward. The back doesn't bend much doing a Sit-Up, while it curls a lot doing a Crunch. That is the secret to full-range, quality isolation training of the abdominals.

ALL KINDS OF CRUNCHES

All ab-specific exercises are some kind of crunch. You can crunch your rib cage down toward your pelvis (the Crunch), your pelvis up toward your rib cage (Reverse Crunch), and the rib cage and pelvis toward each other (Leg Tucks). You can do Reverse Crunches on a flat bench, a decline bench, or hanging from a bar. But in all of these cases, the same fundamentals of exercise physiology hold true: The abs are contracting full range (through their limited range of motion), the pelvis and rib cage are coming together, and the spine is rounding forward during the movement.

This photograph was taken just a week before the 1980 Mr. Olympia contest; you can see how prominent and well defined my abdominal muscles were.

OBLIQUE EXERCISES

The obliques, located at the side of the torso, are primarily stabilizers. There aren't a lot of movements you do in the gym or in daily life that call for a lot of bending from side to side. Therefore, the obliques (like the stabilizer muscles of the lower back) tire fairly quickly from a lot of full-range repetitions and are relatively slow to recover.

There was a time when bodybuilders did a lot of oblique exercises, some of them using substantial amounts of weight. You rarely see successful bodybuilders doing those exercises today because the obliques, like any other muscle, get bigger when you train them with weight, and massive obliques tend to make the waist thicker and take away from the aesthetics of an outstanding V taper.

Of course, the obliques get an isometric workout whenever you do heavy training such as Squats or Shoulder Presses, but since they are only acting as stabilizers and not working through a full range of motion these exercises usually don't cause them to grow to the degree that you'd get from doing Side Bends, for example, holding on to heavy dumbbells. So bodybuilders who train obliques at all tend to stick to nonresistance movements, such as Twists or Side Bends, using no weight, which tighten the muscles without causing them to become too big.

SERRATUS AND INTERCOSTALS

These muscles, located at the side of the upper torso, are crowd pleasers as the abdominals are. When you do a pose such as the Arms Overhead Abdominals and Thighs, and work the torso side to side to show definition in this area, it can really add to the impression you make on the judges.

Again, these muscles are worked with a kind of crunching movement, only this involves squeezing the shoulder and elbow down and in, and bending the torso to the side. Try this and you'll see how easy it is to feel the muscles flexing in this area. These are also muscles that become developed as a result of your overall training program, but you can do specific definition training for serratus and intercostals by adding a twist to various Crunches as you perform them.

BEGINNING PROGRAM

Many bodybuilders who are just starting out get excited about training the chest and arms and tend to ignore the abdominals. Then, later, when they begin to think about competition, they find they have to go on extreme abdominal programs in order to try to catch up in this area. So I recommend training abs right from the beginning, just as you do other body parts. This way, they will develop along with the rest of the body and you will never be forced to play catch-up.

I recommend training abs in every workout. In the Beginning Program, I recommend alternating each day between 5 sets of Crunches and 5 sets of Reverse Crunches. Both exercises work the abdominals as a whole, but the Crunches tend to work the upper abdominals to a greater degree, while the Reverse Crunches put a greater amount of stress on the lower area.

Another practice I recommend for beginners is to start immediately working on your stomach "vacuum"—simply blow out all your breath, suck in your stomach as far as possible, then try to hold this for 15 or 20 seconds.

Holding in your stomach and tensing your abs as you go about your daily business is also a good way of firming and strengthening them and making yourself more conscious of how to control this important area of the body. You should begin to notice right away whether your abs are likely to be a weak point in your physique so that you can take appropriate action when you move on to Advanced Training.

ADVANCED PROGRAM

Once you have started to develop your abdominals, you can begin to train each of the particular areas that contribute to a firm and well-defined waist. This involves doing more sets and a wider variety of exercises like Twisting Crunches, Leg Tucks, and different kinds of Reverse Crunches, as well as Twists.

In Level II, I recommend beginning your workout with a warm-up session of Roman Chairs, one of my favorite crunching movements. For obliques, in addition to twisting movements, you will find exercises like Side Bends and Twists.

COMPETITION PROGRAM

When you are getting ready for competition, your aim should be to sculpt and define your total abdominal area rather than to build more size and strength. To intensify your workout, begin with 10 minutes of Roman Chairs. I always got good results starting out with Roman Chairs, as did many of my contemporaries such as Franco Columbu, Zabo Koszewski, and Ken Waller. Roman Chairs help get you warmed up and are a continuous-tension exercise that keeps the abdominals working for the entire period.

Serge Nubret

The end product of Competition Training is total quality, and each of these exercises is designed to develop and shape a particular area of your waistline. To develop abdominals that will really impress the contest judges, you have to do exercises for the upper and lower abs, the obliques, serratus and intercostals, as well as develop the lower back doing Hyperextensions and other exercises for this area from the back training program. You should demand enormous effort from these areas in order to totally blast them into submission. Keep going, never stop for a second, and you will get the results you need.

WEAK POINT TRAINING

It is just as possible to have a weak point in your abdominals as in any other body part. To help you overcome this, I have included in the abdominal training program exercises designed to work all the specific areas with which you will be concerned. Although most abdominal exercises tend to work several areas of the torso at the same time, certain movements are

Shawn Ray

Milos Sarcev

When you have really outstanding abdominal development, your abs look defined whether you are standing relaxed, semi-flexed, or are hitting an all-out abdominal pose, as Serge Nubret, Shawn Ray, Milos Sarcev, and I demonstrate.

best for each specific area, such as upper or lower abs, obliques or serratus and intercostals. However, be aware that the lack of visual development of the abs is frequently caused by one of two things:

- not enough dieting, so there is a layer of fat over the abs
- not enough isolation, full-range-of-motion, quality training

You don't train abs for quality by contracting them against heavy resistance, by doing hip-flexor rather than abdominal exercises, or with fast, short choppy movements. The best abdominal training involves slow, controlled, full-range-of-motion exercises, and holding at the point of full contraction to achieve a full peak contraction.

Abdominal Exercises

ROMAN CHAIRS

Purpose of Exercise: Emphasizes upper abs.

Execution: (1) Sit on the Roman Chair bench, hook your feet under the support, and fold your arms in front of you. (2) Keeping your stomach tucked in, lower yourself back to approximately a 70-degree angle, but not all the way back so your torso is parallel to the floor. Raise and curl your torso forward as far as possible, feeling the abdominals crunch together in a full contraction.

I like to rest the front of the Roman Chair bench on a block of some sort to create an incline and increase the intensity of the exercise. You can introduce variable resistance into this exercise by starting out with the front of the bench raised and then, when you are getting tired, lower it to the floor and continue with your set.

CRUNCHES

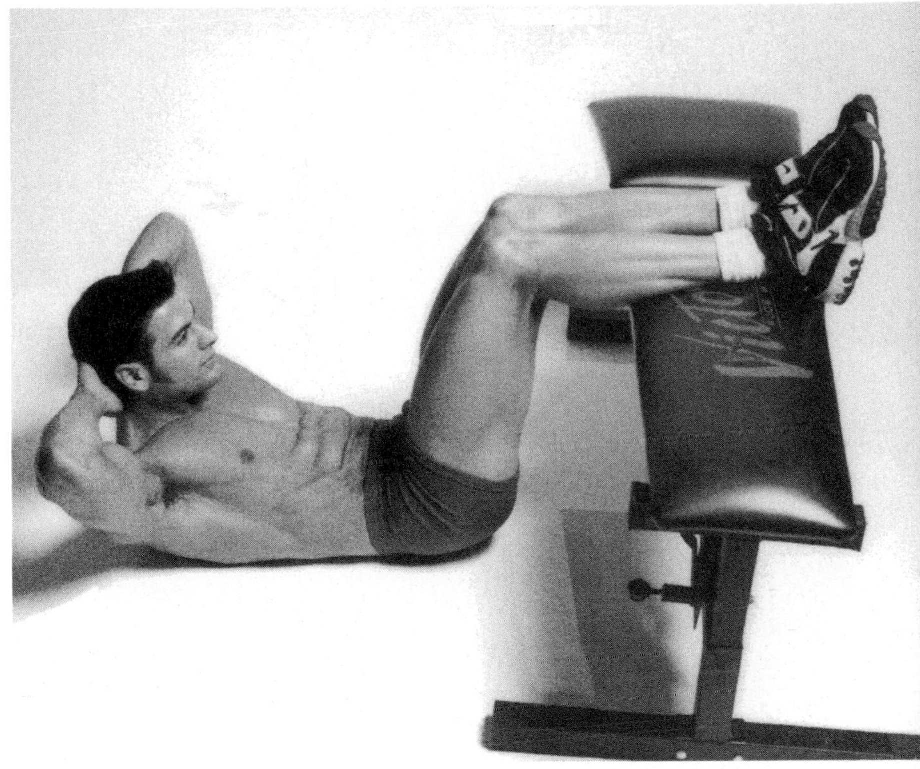

Purpose of Exercise: Emphasizes upper abs.

Execution: (1) Lie on your back on the floor, your legs across a bench in front of you. You can put your hands behind your neck or keep them in front of you, whichever you prefer. (2) Curl your shoulders and trunk upward toward your knees, rounding your back. Don't try to lift your entire back up off the floor, just roll forward and crunch your rib cage toward your pelvis. At the top of the movement, deliberately give an extra squeeze of the abs to achieve total contraction, then release and lower your shoulders back to the starting position. This is not a movement you do quickly. Do each rep deliberately and under control.

You can vary the angle of stress on your abdominals by raising your foot position. Instead of putting your legs across a bench, try lying on the floor and placing the soles of your feet against a wall at whatever height feels most comfortable.

TWISTING CRUNCHES

T. J. Hoban

Purpose of Exercise: For upper abs and obliques.

Execution: (1) Lie on your back on the floor, your legs across a bench in front of you. (2) You can put your hands behind your neck and curl your trunk up toward your knees, rounding your back. As you do this, twist your torso so that your right elbow comes across toward your left knee. Release and lower your torso back to the starting position. Repeat, this time twisting in the opposite direction, bringing your left elbow toward your right knee. Continue to alternate, twisting in one direction and then the other throughout your set.

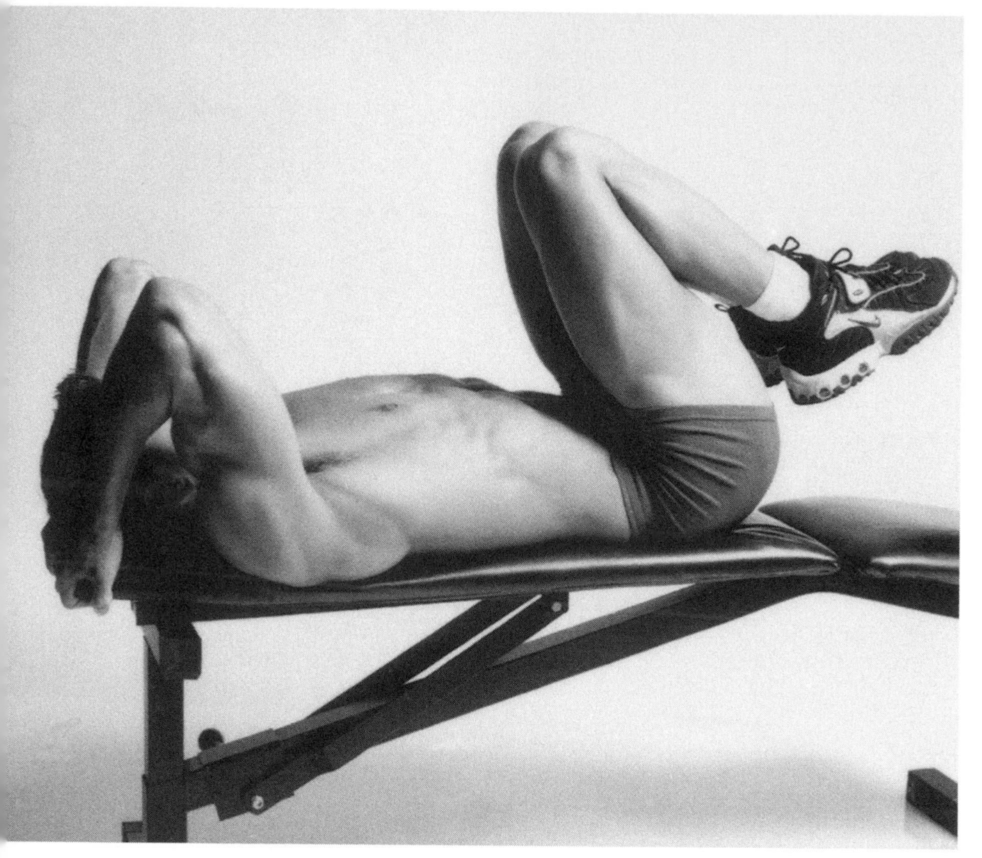

REVERSE CRUNCHES

PURPOSE OF EXERCISE: Emphasizes lower abs.

EXECUTION: This exercise is best done lying on a Bench Press bench that has a rack at one end. (1) Lie on your back on the bench and reach up behind you to hold the rack for support. Bend your knees and bring them up as far toward your face as you can without lifting your pelvis off the bench. (2) From this starting position, bring your knees up as close to your face as you can, rounding your back, with the glutes coming up off the bench and crunching up toward the rib cage. Hold for a moment at the top and deliberately squeeze the ab muscles for full contraction. Slowly lower your knees until your rear end comes to rest on the bench again. (Don't lower your legs any farther than this. You aren't doing Leg Raises.) Again, do this movement deliberately and under control rather than doing a lot of quick reps.

HANGING REVERSE CRUNCHES

Purpose of Exercise: Emphasizes lower abs.

Execution: This is another version of Reverse Crunches, only you do it hanging by your hands from a bar or resting on your forearms on a Hanging Leg Raise bench instead of lying on a bench. (1) Get into the hanging position and bring your knees up to the level of your abdomen. (2) From this starting position, raise your knees up as far as possible toward your head, rounding your back and rolling yourself upward into a ball. At the top of the movement, hold and crunch the ab muscles together for full contraction, then lower your knees to the starting position with the knees pulled up. Again, don't lower your legs beyond this starting point.

A lot of people and most bodybuilders (because of the mass of their legs) can't really do Hanging Reverse Crunches. An easier variation is to lie head upward on a slantboard. This gives you more resistance than Reverse Crunches on a flat bench, but you can dial in the amount of resistance you want by the angle at which you set the slantboard.

VERTICAL BENCH CRUNCHES

PURPOSE OF EXERCISE: Emphasizes lower abs.

EXECUTION: This is a variation of Hanging Reverse Crunches. (1) Instead of hanging from a bar, position yourself on a vertical bench that allows you to support yourself on your elbows and forearms and bring your knees up to the level of your abdomen. (2) From this starting position, raise your knees up as far as possible toward your head, rounding your back and rolling yourself upward into a ball. At the top of the movement, hold and crunch the ab muscles together for full contraction, then lower your knees to the starting position with the knees pulled up. Again, don't lower your legs beyond this starting point.

CABLE CRUNCHES

PURPOSE OF EXERCISE: For upper and lower abs.

EXECUTION: This is an exercise you used to see much more in the "old days" than you do today, but it's an effective one. (1) Attach a rope to an overhead pulley. Kneel down and grasp the rope with both hands. (2) Holding the rope in front of your forehead, bend and curl downward, rounding your back, bringing your head to your knees and feeling the abdominals crunch together. Hold the peak contraction at the bottom, then release and come back up to the starting position. Make sure the effort involved is made with the abs. Don't pull down with the arms.

MACHINE CRUNCHES

Purpose of Exercise: For upper and lower abs.

Execution: A great many bodybuilders feel that machines are unnecessary when it comes to ab training. But others swear by some of the ab training equipment currently available. Charles Glass, for example, often has his clients use a Nautilus Crunch machine. In all cases, however, concentrate on feeling the rib cage and the pelvis squeeze together as the abdominals contract. If you can't achieve this feeling, the piece of equipment you are using may not be suited to your individual needs.

Milos Sarcev

SEATED LEG TUCKS

PURPOSE OF EXERCISE: For upper and lower abs.

EXECUTION: In all ab exercises the rib cage contracts toward the pelvis or the pelvis toward the rib cage—in this exercise, both of these things happen.
(1) Sit crosswise on a bench, holding on to the sides for support. Raise your legs slightly and bend your knees and lean backward at about a 45-degree angle.
(2) Using a scissors movement (this exercise is sometimes called Scissors Crunches), curl your upper body toward your pelvis, rounding your back, and simultaneously lift your knees up toward your head. Feel the crunch as your rib cage and pelvis squeeze together. From this position, lower your torso and knees back to the starting position.

SEATED TWISTS

Purpose of Exercise: To tighten the obliques.

Execution: (1) Sit on the end of a bench, feet flat on the floor and comfortably apart. Place a broom handle or light bar across the back of your shoulders and hold it. (2) Keeping your head stationary, and making sure your pelvis doesn't shift on the bench, deliberately turn your upper body and shoulders in one direction as far as you can. Hold at the extreme rotated position, then turn your torso and shoulders back in the other direction as far as you can, keeping the movement fully under control rather than swinging. Because this exercise contracts the oblique muscles but uses no additional resistance, it keeps them tight but doesn't add any extra bulk that might thicken your waist.

BENT-OVER TWISTS

Purpose of Exercise: To tighten the obliques.

Execution: (1) Standing with your feet apart, place a broom handle or light bar across the back of your shoulders, hold it, and bend forward from the waist as far as is comfortable. (2) Keeping your head stationary, and blocking your pelvis from rotating, deliberately turn your upper body and shoulders in one direction as far as you can. Hold at the extreme rotated position, then turn your torso and shoulders back in the other direction as far as you can, keeping the movement fully under control rather than swinging.

LEG RAISES

Leg Raises are a traditional abdominal exercise that has fallen out of favor with exercise physiologists. The reason is that the abdominals don't attach to the legs, so raising and lowering your legs works them only indirectly, as stabilizers. The muscles that raise and lower the legs are the iliopsoas muscles (hip flexors) that run from the lower back across the top of the pelvis and attach to the upper leg.

Nonetheless, I have gotten good results doing Leg Raises, as have many other champions, so I feel this encyclopedia would be incomplete if they were not included. I am a big believer in science and exercise physiology, but when it comes to bodybuilding the bottom line is always what works for you, regardless of what the "experts" might think.

FLAT BENCH LEG RAISES

PURPOSE OF EXERCISE: Emphasizes lower abs.

EXECUTION: (1) Lie on your back on a flat bench, your rear end just at the end of the bench, put your hands under your glutes for support, and extend your legs out straight. (2) Keeping your legs straight, raise them as high as you can, pause, then lower them until they are slightly below the level of the bench.

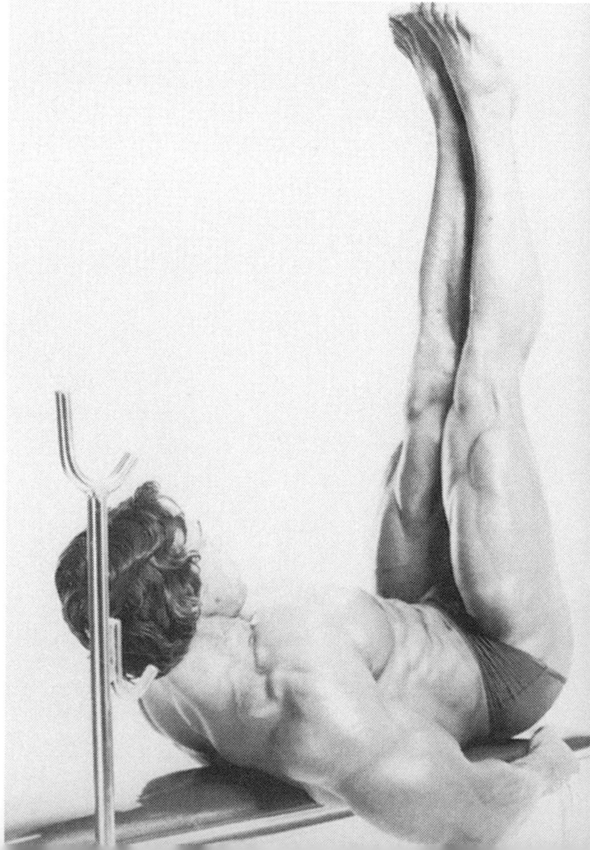

BENT-KNEE FLAT BENCH LEG RAISES

PURPOSE OF EXERCISE: Emphasizes lower abs

EXECUTION: Lie on a bench in the same position as with Flat Bench Leg Raises. Bend your knees, then raise your legs as far as possible, pause at the top, then lower your legs again, keeping them bent throughout the entire range of motion.

BENT-KNEE INCLINE BOARD LEG RAISES

PURPOSE OF EXERCISE: Emphasizes lower abs.

EXECUTION: (1) Lie on your back on an incline board, head higher than your feet. Reach back and take hold of the top of the board or some other support. (2) With your *knees bent,* raise your legs as high as you can, then lower them slowly, stopping just as your rear end touches the board. Exhale as you lift and inhale as you lower your legs. Bending your knees makes the movement a little easier and helps to increase your range of motion.

B. J. Quinn

BENT-KNEE VERTICAL BENCH LEG RAISES

PURPOSE OF EXERCISE: Emphasizes lower abs.

EXECUTION: (1) Support yourself on your arms on a vertical bench. (2) Holding your upper body steady, bend your knees and raise them up as high as you can, flexing your abs through the full range of the motion. Keeping your legs bent, lower them again to the starting position.

VARIATION: Any variation of an exercise forces the muscles to respond in new and different ways. When working the abdominals with Vertical Bench Leg Raises, try doing the movement using each leg alternately instead of simultaneously.

HANGING LEG RAISES

PURPOSE OF EXERCISE: Emphasizes lower abs.

EXECUTION: (1) Grasp an overhead bar and hang at arm's length. (2) Keeping your legs fairly straight, raise them as high as you can, hold for a moment, then lower them under control back to the starting position. Keeping your legs straight adds to the resistance in this exercise, which makes the movement more difficult.

Milos Sarcev

Mike O'Hearn

TWISTING HANGING LEG RAISES

Purpose of Exercise: For the obliques and detail at the side of the torso.

Execution: Start as in Hanging Leg Raises, hanging at arm's length from the bar and keeping your legs fairly straight. Next, raise your legs as high as you can slightly to the side while twisting the torso to involve the obliques, serratus, and intercostal muscles. Hold for a moment, then lower them under control to the starting position.

ADDITIONAL LEG-RAISE EXERCISES

In addition to the basic abdominal exercises, there are a number of leg-raise movements I have always liked and that I believe help firm and tighten areas like the hips, the lower back, and the buttocks. These are exercises that can be done for very high reps and that are just as easy to do in a hotel when you are traveling as when you are home or at the gym.

One benefit of these movements is the way they work the lower body from every angle—front, back, and rear. They are also useful for a wide range of people, from competitive bodybuilders to serious athletes, weekend athletes, and men and women simply trying to stay fit and in good shape.

SIDE LEG RAISES

Purpose of Exercise: For the obliques and intercostals.

This exercise works the entire side of the torso and can really help give your waist a narrow look from the front.

Execution: (1) Lie on your side, supporting yourself on your elbow with your lower leg bent under for support. (2) Keeping the upper leg straight, raise it slowly as high as it will go, then lower it again, but stop short of letting it touch the floor. Finish your reps with this leg, then turn onto your other side and repeat the movement. Don't move your hips at all during this movement.

BENT-KNEE SIDE LEG RAISES

Purpose of Exercise: For the obliques and intercostals.

Execution: Lie on your side, supporting yourself on your elbow with your lower leg bent under for support. Bend the knee of your upper leg and raise it slowly toward your chest as high as you can, then lower it again, stopping short of touching the floor. Finish your reps with this, then turn and work the opposite leg.

FRONT KICKS

Purpose of Exercise: For the obliques and intercostals.

Execution: This exercise begins in exactly the same position as Side Leg Raises. Here, though, you slowly move your upper leg forward as far as you can, keeping it straight throughout the movement. Finish your reps, and turn and work the opposite leg.

BENCH KICKBACKS

Purpose of Exercise: For the glutes.

Execution: (1) Kneel with one leg on the end of a bench. Grip the bench with arms locked for support. (2) Kick one leg back as high as you can, then bring it back down, not letting it quite touch the bench. Concentrate throughout the movement on flexing and contracting the buttocks. Complete your repetitions then repeat using the other leg. (This can be done kneeling on the floor, but it's slightly more difficult.)

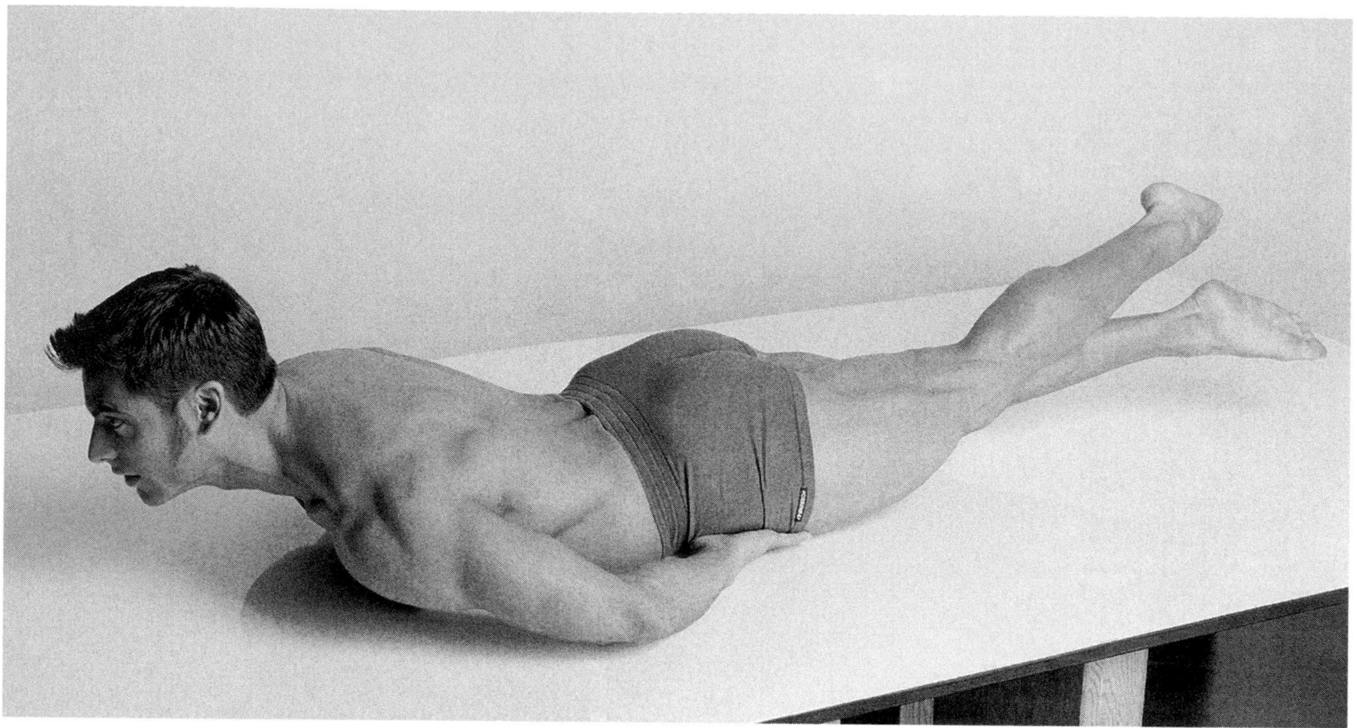

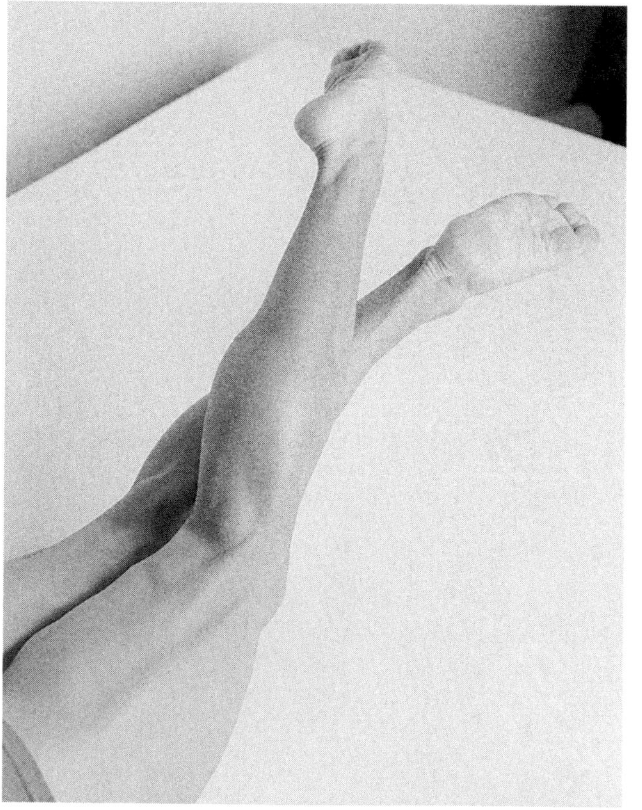

REAR LEG SCISSORS

Purpose of Exercise: For the glutes.

Execution: (1) Lie on your stomach, hands under your thighs. Raise your legs off the floor as far as possible. (2) Move your feet apart a short distance, then bring them together and cross one over the other. (3) Move them apart and then cross them again with the opposite leg on top. Repeat, alternating legs continuously until you have completed your repetitions. Throughout the exercise, concentrate on feeling the contraction of the buttocks.

VACUUMS

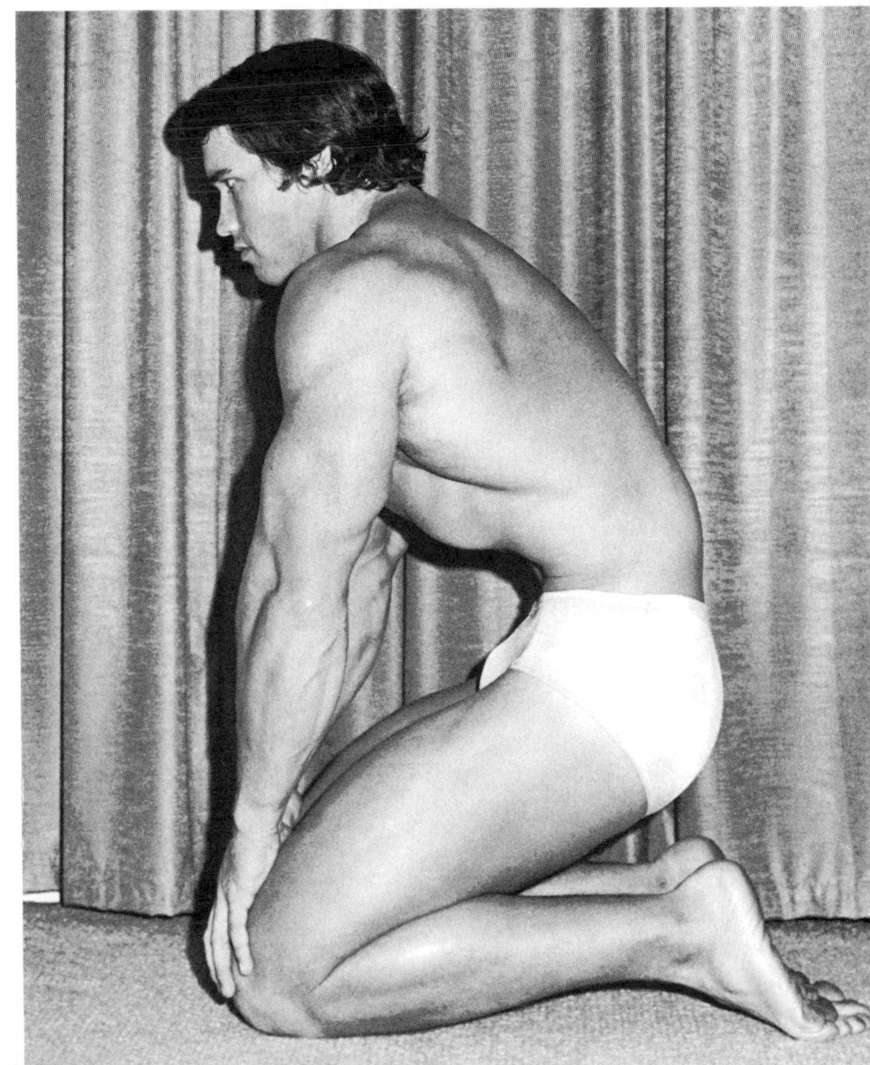

Being able to control your abdominal muscles to the point where you can hit and hold a full vacuum is becoming a lost art in bodybuilding. This is unfortunate, since a vacuum pose is not only impressive onstage, creating a much smaller waistline and exaggerating the size and fullness of the chest and rib cage, but also helps to develop abdominal definition and gives you the total control of the abdominal muscles that helps you avoid letting your abs bulge the moment you relax and stop concentrating on them.

Bodybuilders often forget under the pressure of competition that they are being watched the whole time they are onstage—even when they are standing at the back of the stage waiting for a comparison call-out. You should never give the judges the impression that you are tired, and keeping your abs from bulging and protruding is one way to assure you make the proper impression.

Nowadays, bodybuilders frequently have trouble hitting a vacuum because their abs get so massive—but the primary reason is that *they don't practice hitting vacuums*. This is not something you can master in an hour. You have to practice on a regular basis, just as you do any other kind of posing, for a period of weeks or months until you develop full control over these muscles.

To practice vacuums, get down on your hands and knees, blow out all your breath, and suck in your abdominals as much as you can. Hold this for 20 to 30 seconds, relax for a few moments, and then try it again two or three times.

The next step is to practice your vacuum in a kneeling position. Kneel upright with your hands on your knees and try to hold the vacuum as long as you can.

Doing a seated vacuum is more difficult still. But once you can hold a vacuum in a seated position without any problem, you will be able to practice holding a vacuum while standing and doing a variety of poses.

BOOK FOUR

Competition

CHAPTER 1

Posing

POSING IS VITALLY important because, after years of hard training, working out for hours a day in the gym, and dieting with great discipline for ten to twelve weeks, *you can win or lose a show with the same body!* It isn't just your physique that is being evaluated; it's your physique as you are able to present it to the judges.

Presentation can be all important. I remember seeing some paintings in a storage area at an auction house—hundreds of them, from Andy Warhol to Roy Lichtenstein. A number were shown to me, one after another, unframed and under poor lighting. Under those conditions it was hard to appreciate what great works they were. Later, when they were appropriately framed and displayed in an aesthetic setting, with excellent lighting, the effect was totally different. You could instantly see why these works were so respected and revered. In the same way that a fabulous jewel is set off by a beautiful setting, these paintings could be fully appreciated only because somebody went to a lot of trouble and did a lot of preparation to present them in the most effective way—*and that's what you have to do with your physique to compete in a bodybuilding contest.*

The key to presentation in bodybuilding, as well as in other sports, is painstaking and careful preparation. Skaters need to prepare in order to skate well in competition. Divers need preparation in order to succeed in a meet. And bodybuilders need preparation to ensure their performance will represent their best efforts in a bodybuilding contest—their "performance," of course, being their ability to show off their physiques to maximum advantage in front of the judges.

One time I did TV commentary for the Arnold Classic World Bodybuilding Championships. I watched one bodybuilder walk out and do his routine and I said to my commentating partner, "No way, this guy isn't going to do anything in this contest." As I watched his posing on the monitor backstage I was amazed to see muscles suddenly popping out everywhere. "Where did that muscularity come from?" I said. "I've changed my mind about this competitor completely!"

I've seen the opposite happen as well. When I first saw the gigantic Paul Dillett backstage in Columbus I was very impressed. But out onstage it was obvious that Dillett was not able to pose his massive physique to its best advantage. When I mentioned this to Joe Weider, he told me that Dillett had started competing late in his twenties, had qualified as a pro in only his second contest, and simply had not had time to develop the skills onstage to match his awesome body. "Remember," Joe pointed out, "when Frank Zane won his first Mr. Olympia title he'd already been competing for something like fifteen years. The kind of control and polish Frank was famous for took a lot of years to learn, and it's virtually impossible to perform at that level without a lot of experience."

This point is very important. Training involves one set of skills. Posing involves another set of skills completely. You have to practice posing for endless hours to learn those skills, and you also have to compete in a lot of contests in order to be able to use those skills under the pressure of competition. Of course, many beginners don't realize how much there is to learn when it comes to posing. Posing can seem much simpler to master than it really is. For example:

- You have to master each of the individual compulsory poses.
- You have to practice these poses until you have established total control over each of the muscles involved.
- You need to devote many, many hours to practicing so you can hold your poses for long periods of time without feeling undue fatigue, having your muscles start to shake, or developing muscle cramps.
- You have to create an individual posing routine that best displays the qualities of your physique.
- You have to practice your routine until you can do all the transitions between poses with perfect smoothness.
- You have to actually use these skills onstage because only experience teaches you to pose correctly when under pressure at an actual contest.
- In addition to working on the poses themselves, you need to work on your *facial expressions.* Part of the impression you make on the judges depends on them.

Hitting and holding your poses correctly in front of the judges is essential. But you also have to realize that you are posing *all the time you're onstage,* not just when you are out front hitting shots. I can't count the number of times I've seen a bodybuilder who looked good when he was posing go to the back of the stage and suddenly start to slump down, to let his stomach stick out and in the process totally destroy the good image he had created.

In one Mr. Olympia contest Franco and I were standing at the back of the stage and we could see another competitor standing nearby with his stomach stuck so far out he looked pregnant. "Too bad," I said to Franco, "he doesn't look like he usually does. He looks like a whole other bodybuilder." "No," Franco replied, "he looks like he *swallowed* a whole other bodybuilder!"

Again, it doesn't matter what kind of physique you have if you can't display it properly. A very well-known bodybuilder came up to me in the dressing room backstage at the Arnold Classic, hit a pose, and asked me what I thought. "You look great," I told him. "If I had your physique, I'd win the show." He went off and started telling everyone I had said he was going to win. But that wasn't the case. I meant if *I* had his physique I could win, but I knew his posing skills weren't that great so I doubted that *he* would be able to show himself off to his best advantage. And I was correct—he didn't do nearly as well in the competition as he would have if he had been a better poser.

In addition to being able to pose, you have to pay careful attention to your overall appearance. The judges are not just looking at your muscles and your cuts, they are looking at the total *you*—everything from how you stand, move, and pose, to your skin tone, haircut, and posing trunks, to your overall demeanor. This is where facial expression becomes so important. Do you look confident, like a winner? Or anxious, like a loser? When you hit your poses and are contracting your muscles as hard as you can, is your face all screwed up, are you grimacing like a gargoyle—or have you learned to pose "from the neck down" so that your body is flexed but your face is relaxed?

Think about how a singer uses facial expressions to help sell the emotion of a song. Or somebody doing a skating exhibition. Or an actor. When you are onstage, you are not only an athlete but a performer as well. Bodybuilding is a sport, but it is also theater. You not only have to *be* good, you also have to make sure the judges take notice. The point is not to *fake* the facial expression, but to really believe in yourself and to let that belief show to everybody in the audience.

THE HISTORY OF POSING

Bodybuilding started out as "physical culture" contests, and in the 1920s and 1930s competitors in these events demonstrated their athletic ability in a variety of ways—everything from gymnastics and weightlifting to boxing. In the early days of actual physique competition, bodybuilders didn't do complete posing routines to music as they do today, but instead contracted and flexed each of the major muscles and muscle groups, hit stomach vacuums, and sometimes made their muscles writhe as if there were snakes under the skin as a demonstration of total muscle control.

Early bodybuilding contests still featured athletic demonstrations like hand-balancing, a feat for which John Grimek, the second Mr. America, was particularly noted. Former Mr. USA and *Muscle & Fitness* writer Armand Tanny, a veteran of the Muscle Beach days, recalls that Grimek was such a good athlete he could fascinate audiences for hours with his gymnastic and hand-balancing feats. It was amazing to see how athletic, coordinated, and flexible Grimek and other heavily muscled bodybuilders were back then. Can you imagine the competitors in the Mr. Olympia trying to do the same thing today?

THE ART OF POSING

Posing involves learning the basic poses, individualizing them to suit your physique, and then putting together your best poses in an individual posing routine. Top bodybuilders all have poses for which they are famous, poses that allow them to compete effectively against their opponents. Some bodybuilders like to do certain basic poses to show off the fact that they have the best development of certain body parts. Others avoid these poses because they can't compete directly in displaying basic muscle development, but instead develop creative variations that display other qualities such as shape, symmetry, and proportion.

When I was first learning to pose, I took a hard look at myself to determine what suited me best. I had to be a realist. It would have been very foolish for me to attempt Steve Reeves's style of posing, the arms overhead kind of thing. Reeves had broad shoulders, a flat chest, and narrow waist, and overhead poses suited him very well. But they wouldn't have looked good for me, John Grimek, or Reg Park, since all of us had a more boxy look to our physiques. Along the same lines, when it comes to developing your own posing style, if you are a fan of bodybuilders like Dorian Yates, Flex Wheeler, Shawn Ray, or anyone else, be sure you have the same kind of physique before blindly trying to copy their poses.

Posing can be a tool for drawing attention to your strengths and away from your weaknesses. Different poses for the same body part tend to emphasize different qualities of the entire body. For example, certain back poses will draw attention to mass and others to symmetry; one might display your triceps most effectively, another your delts. By using the proper pose, you could force the judges to notice outstanding calves, or camouflage the fact that your calves are not as good as they should be.

One should choose poses that are creative on two levels: making them as aesthetic and dramatic as possible, almost like a form of dance; and manipulating the focus of attention of the judges so that they notice what you want them to and ignore what you'd prefer they ignore. This is not easy to learn, and it takes time. But it is a valuable and virtually essential skill for any bodybuilder desiring to become a true champion.

LEARNING BY OBSERVING

One of the best ways of learning what's involved in becoming an effective competitor is to train with a bodybuilder who has contest experience. Not only will you pick up vital training information, but you will also have a chance to share his knowledge of posing, diet, and contest preparation.

Another strategy is to attend as many bodybuilding competitions as possible. I learned more about what goes on in a competition by watching other people compete than I ever did when I was in the show and preoccupied with my own performance. Standing aside and watching can be invaluable. You can see what is happening onstage much better from the audience than you can when you are standing up there yourself. You can detect mistakes and learn how to avoid them. You need to watch everything that goes on: what takes place in each of the rounds, how the contest is conducted, and what sort of instructions the bodybuilders are given onstage. You can study the competitors and try to understand why one is doing something right and another isn't. You see if one competitor is using too much oil, one is too smooth, and how effective different styles of posing and presentation can be. Once you have a clear idea of what works and what doesn't, you can begin to plan your own presentation. I recommend taking some notes so that you don't forget what you've observed.

I have used the same approach in making films. When I was hired to act in *Stay Hungry* in the 1970s, Bob Rafelson, the director, sent me out to observe films and television shows being made all over Hollywood. This helped me to learn the vocabulary and techniques of the business. The more I learned about moviemaking, the more effective I was when it was my turn to be in front of the camera.

Later, when I starred in *Conan the Barbarian,* I was supposed to be a master sword fighter, so I not only had to spend months learning how to swing a big, heavy sword (that was no lightweight prop, by the way, but the real thing) but I had to understand how to *move* like a highly skilled fencer—much the way that Kevin Costner had to *look* as if he were a pro golfer in *Tin Cup,* no matter his actual ability at the sport. So I not only took lessons three times a week and practiced fencing, I studied the world of sword fighting as well—going to tournaments and kendo schools, and watching samurai films. I observed how swordsmen moved, their sense of

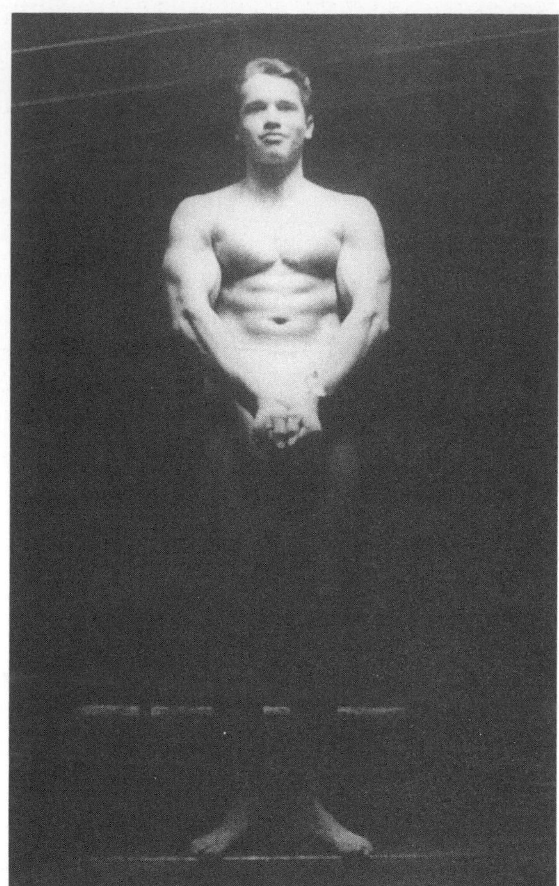
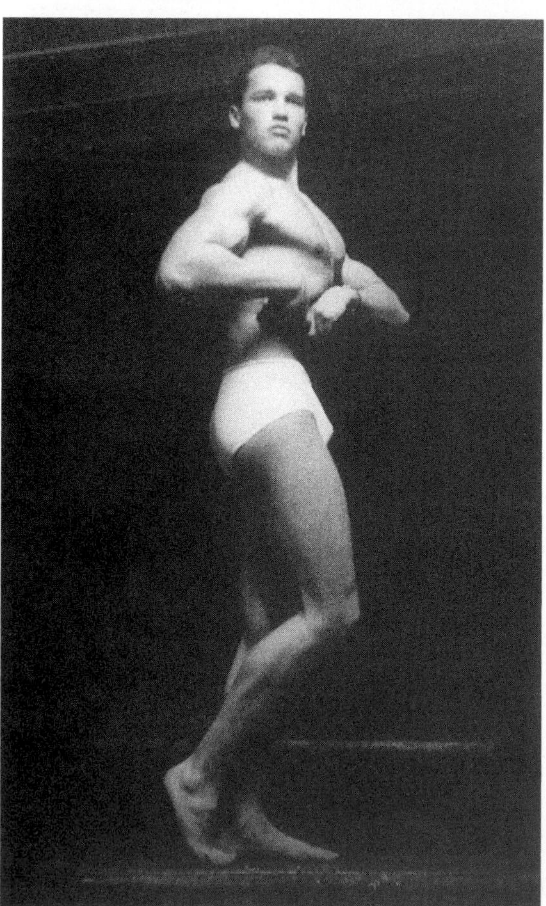
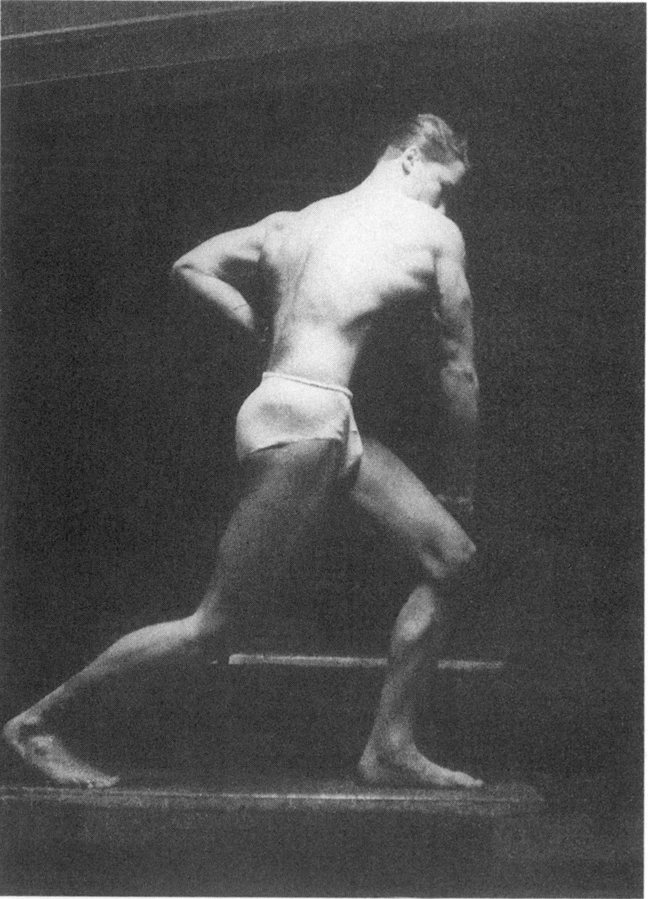

Here's a portrait of a bodybuilder as a young man. These photos of me at sixteen were taken by a friend of mine in the weightlifting club in Graz where I began my training.

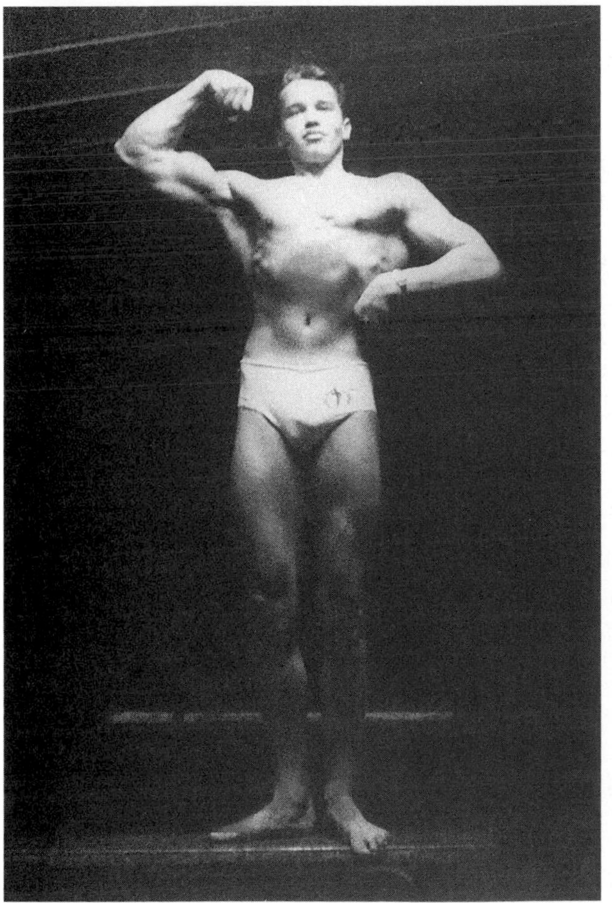

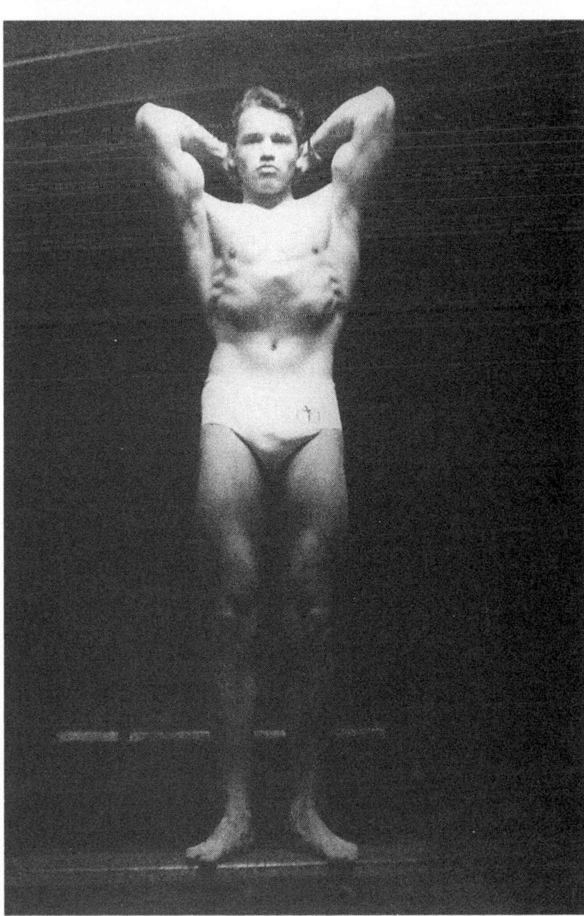

balance, their posture, the position of their feet, how they made the transition from one position to another. In other words, I did much the same thing learning to wield a sword as I did when I was learning to pose—I watched, I observed, I studied, and I practiced.

HOW IFBB CONTESTS ARE CONDUCTED

When a bodybuilder does a posing exhibition, he just goes out onstage and does his routine. But to learn how to pose effectively in a contest, you need to understand something about how bodybuilding competitions are organized and conducted.

The International Federation of Bodybuilders sanctions international amateur competition and all authorized professional events. In amateur events, competitors are divided into weight classes:

bantamweight
lightweight
middleweight
light heavyweight
heavyweight
super heavyweight

In professional contests, there are no weight classes. All competitors are put in one class, regardless of size. In the past, height was used rather than weight to determine which competitor was placed in which class. However, over time it was realized that using weight classes created a much more closely matched group of competitors, with much greater similarity of development, than did separating them by height.

Until 1980, IFBB pro events were conducted in two weight classes, with 200 pounds being the dividing line, and the winners of each class would compete against each other in a posedown for the overall title. However, for an event as important as the Mr. Olympia, this meant the judges would have all the time they needed to compare competitors in each class but only a few minutes to determine which of the class winners should take the coveted Mr. Olympia title. Having all the competitors, regardless of size, compete in one class may seem to put the smaller bodybuilders at a greater disadvantage, but this is not necessarily the case. When the judges compare bodybuilders of different sizes over an extended period of time, they are better able to look at the actual quality of the various physiques onstage, to examine them in detail and to notice any superiority of development displayed by the smaller competitors. On the other hand, when bodybuilders of different sizes compete in different classes and the overall winner is chosen in a brief posedown, the judges have to make their decision much more quickly, and the larger bodybuilder, who can make a greater impression in a short time, has a clear advantage.

IFBB contests today are divided into two parts and four rounds. The first part is the *prejudging.* Prejudging is clinical and technical, highly interesting to bodybuilding fans, but not that entertaining for those who don't know what they're looking at. Prejudging consists of two rounds:

Round One: Standing Relaxed

The first round involves bodybuilders being judged as they stand, hands at their sides, facing forward, to the back, and to both sides. In spite of this kind of posing being called standing relaxed, the competitors are usually

"Standing relaxed"—front view. Notice that these competitors, although not hitting a pose, have every muscle flexed and under control. (Bertil Fox, Albert Beckles, and Johnny Fuller)

"Standing relaxed"—side view (Johnny Fuller, Jusup Wilkosz, and Roy Callender)

tensing all their muscles very hard indeed. This round is usually referred to as a symmetry round. Indeed, when you are standing in this position the overall shape of the body (called symmetry in bodybuilding), as well as its shape and proportion, is what you are most easily able to observe. Judges also look at things like grooming, skin tone, tan, and whether the trunks fit well and are of an appropriate color. Actually, the first round is often referred to as overall assessment, and this is more accurate than symmetry. The judges are supposed to look at everything in every round, not just symmetry or muscularity. What makes the rounds different is the way in which the body is posed and presented, which tends to reveal one aspect of the physique more than the others.

Round Two: Compulsory Poses

In round two, the bodybuilders go through a series of compulsory poses designed to show the judges their specific strengths and weaknesses. These poses are:

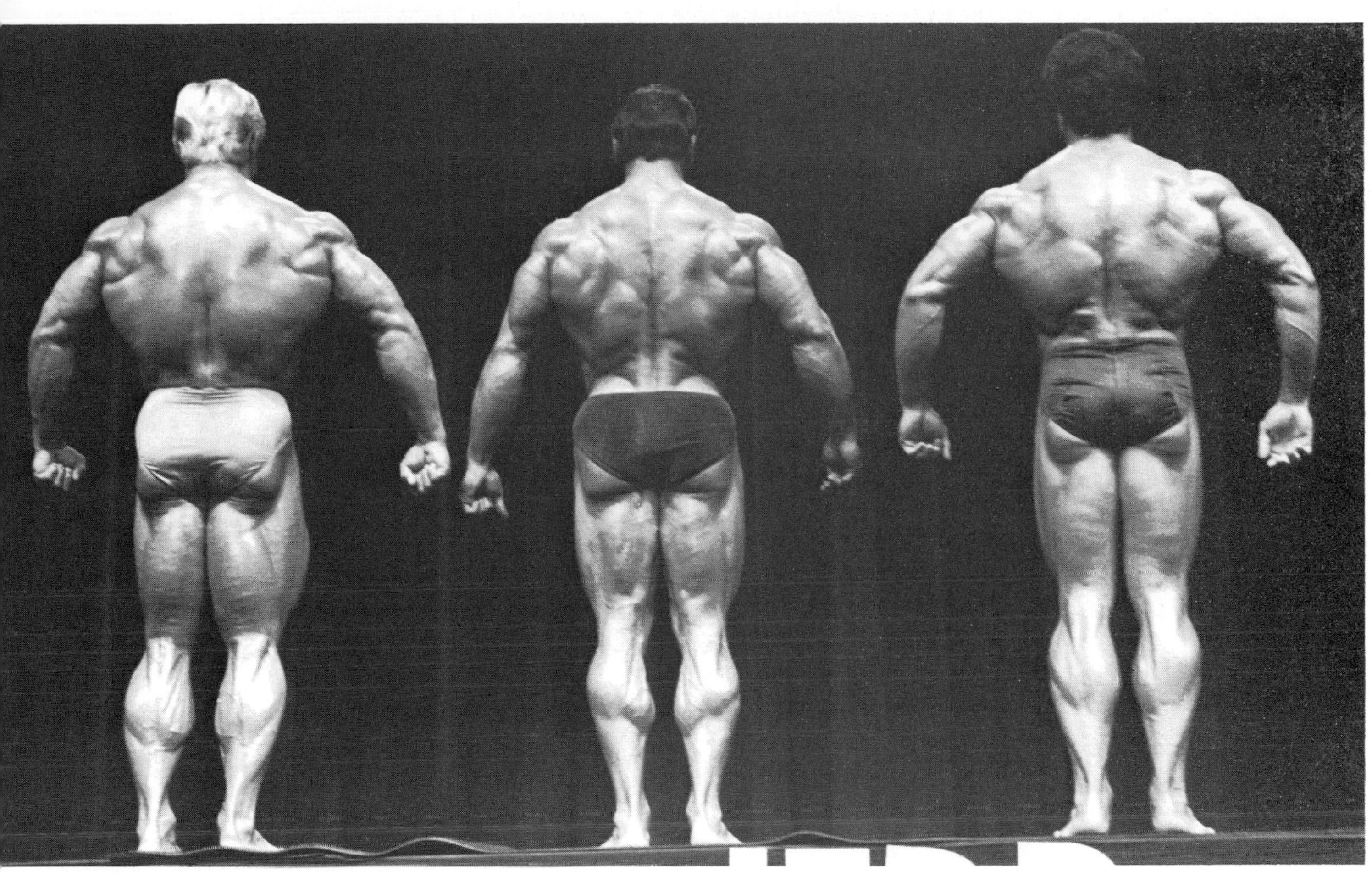

"Standing relaxed"—back view. Each of the contestants has his leg biceps, calves, and lower back totally flexed, even though this is a relaxed back-view pose. (Tom Platz, Casey Viator, and Samir Bannout)

front double biceps
front lat spread
side chest
back double biceps
rear lat spread
side triceps
hands over head abdominals and thighs

(Women bodybuilders do the same poses, with the exception of the lat spreads, which were deleted some years ago by an official who thought they looked unfeminine, and have not at this point been put back in.) The compulsory poses are not designed to be pretty or to make the body look aesthetic. They are intended to give the judges a cold, clinical look at the body, to highlight strengths and expose weaknesses. And because this is the round that tends to give the judges a lasting impression of your physique, it can be the most important in the show. So practicing the compulsory poses, over and over, sometimes until your muscles start cramping, is absolutely necessary to doing your best in an IFBB contest.

Front double biceps

Front lat spread (Samir Bannout)

Side chest shot

Rear double biceps

Rear lat spread (Chris Dickerson)

Side triceps (Chris Dickerson)

Abdominal pose with hands behind head and leg extended (Tom Platz)

The second part of the contest is the finals, or the "night show," since it is usually (but not always) held in the evening; prejudging usually takes place in the morning or the afternoon. The finals consist of:

Round Three: Free Posing

In this round you do your own posing routine to your own choice of music. You hit the poses that are the most flattering, in the way that best shows off your body, while at the same time not appearing to be avoiding showing off any body parts (which will inevitably draw the judges' attention to just what you're trying to hide). In your own posing routine, you can hit *any* pose you want—twisting shots, kneeling and lunging poses,

Milos Sarcev has developed a number of aesthetic poses designed to show off his physique to his best advantage onstage.

hard-core muscle or beautiful aesthetic poses. In some amateur contests there is a time limit for your posing routine, perhaps only a minute, while the pros can take as long as they like. *Always* check before any contest on what the rules are, especially when it comes to free posing. In round two, you do the poses the judges want to see, the way they want to see them. But in round three, you have the opportunity to say to the judges, "We've looked at my physique your way; now let me show it to you the way I want you to see it." Here is where you can let your personality and creativity shine through. You can come across as powerful, confident, energetic, and imaginative—or dull, predictable, and boring. It's all up to you.

Round Four: Posedown

At the end of the contest, the bodybuilders who are in the lead (usually the top six) give the judges a final look at themselves in a posedown round, where they free-pose together onstage, hitting comparison shots, sometimes elbowing each other out of the way, trying to earn one extra point from each of the judges. You don't really have the opportunity to go through your own posing routine during this round, but you should try to do your best poses and avoid close comparison with other competitors who may be better in certain body parts. For example, at the 1981 Mr. Olympia, I remember one competitor in the posedown rushing across the stage, eager to stand next to Tom Platz and hit leg shots. Why would you want to hit leg shots with the guy who has the most awesome legs in the

This picture of Boyer Coe, myself, and Chris Dickerson from the 1980 Mr. Olympia was taken at the beginning of the posedown when the six finalists go through the compulsories together, giving the judges a chance to make direct comparisons.

Kevin Levrone, Dorian Yates, and Shawn Ray in a side-triceps pose comparison at the 1994 Mr. Olympia.

The most dramatic part of the posedown comes when the finalists are free to pose any way they want, to show their strong points, expose their opponents' weaknesses, and try to dominate the stage. At the 1982 Olympia in London, Frank Zane, Samir Bannout, Chris Dickerson, Albert Beckles, Tom Platz, and Casey Viator contended fiercely in this exciting and important round.

sport? That bodybuilder must have been delusional or self-destructive to think he was doing anything more than telling the judges, Look, my legs aren't as good as Tom's, are they?

SCORING

Scoring in the IFBB is done round by round, with each judge placing the competitors in order from first on down (usually with the high and low score thrown out, as in the Olympics) and the final score being the total earned by each bodybuilder in all the rounds taken together. The IFBB has used different scoring systems in the past (for example, a points system), and many different systems have been used by different organizations throughout the history of the sport, but the current procedures have been in place in the IFBB for quite a while.

NPC CONTESTS

The national affiliate of the IFBB in America is the National Physique Committee of the U.S. The NPC is the official sanctioning body for amateur bodybuilding competition in the United States. Although NPC contests use the same weight classes as IFBB amateur shows, they are conducted differently from those sanctioned by the international federation:

1. During prejudging the bodybuilders each come out and do a one-minute free-posing routine, with no music. They are then brought out all together for comparison posing.
2. The judges can call for any pose they choose, including most-muscular poses or just say, "Show me your best leg shot." Also, while the maximum number of competitors brought out to be compared in the IFBB is usually three, in the NPC the judges can compare as many or few bodybuilders at a time as they choose.
3. The competitors return and do their posing routines at the evening show, this time to music, but this round is not scored. *All* the scoring in NPC contests is done during prejudging. Also, since free posing is done twice—once without music and once with music—NPC competitors frequently prepare two different posing routines, one for prejudging and the other (usually more theatrical) for the night show.
4. NPC judges use a system of placing, but the individual rounds in prejudging are not scored separately. The judges watch the different rounds, take notes, and then at the end of prejudging write down the placings as they see them.

1998 NPC USA Bodybuilding & Fitness Championships

July 10–11, 1998

BANTAMWEIGHT MEN

NUMBER	CONTESTANT	JUDGE 1	2	3	4	5	6	7	8	9	SCORE	PLACE
5	Randy Leppala	1	1	1	1	1	1	1	1	4	5	1
18	Ronald Nurse	3	3	3	3	3	2	3	2	3	15	2
14	Steve Gaver	2	2	6	4	2	3	2	5	5	16	3
10	Jonathan Hunt	4	4	4	5	5	4	5	4	1	21	4
1	Thomas Armstrong Jr.	5	5	2	2	6	6	4	3	6	23	5
11	Clifton Torres	6	6	5	6	4	5	6	6	2	28	6
15	Gary Passmore	7	7	7	8	9	8	7	7	7	36	7
16	Lance Harano	9	8	8	10	7	7	8	8	9	41	8
3	Jim King	10	9	10	7	8	9	11	9	8	45	9
7	Michael King	8	11	9	9	10	10	10	10	11	49	10
4	Steve Kluger	11	10	11	11	12	11	9	11	12	55	11
9	Paul Sake	12	12	12	12	11	12	12	12	10	60	12
12	John Ligsay Jr.	13	13	13	13	13	14	13	13	14	65	13
6	Paul Anloague	14	15	16	14	14	13	14	16	15	72	14
13	Anthony Lattimore	16	14	15	16	15	15	15	14	13	74	15
2	Matthew Alloy	15	17	14	15	16	16	16	15	16	78	16
17	Dusty Bush	18	16	17	18	17	17	17	17	17	85	17
8	Michael Smith	17	18	18	17	18	18	18	18	18	90	18

Judge's score eliminates 2 high & 2 low

JUDGES FOR THIS CLASS

Judge 1	Dick Fudge	FL
Judge 2	Fred Mullins	FL
Judge 3	Daniel Campbell	CA
Judge 4	Pat Sporer	FL
Judge 5	Ernest Bea	IN
Judge 6	Larry Pepe	CA
Judge 7	Pete Fancher	FL
Judge 8	Linda Wood-Hoyt	NY
Judge 9	Dave Sauer	CA

1998 NPC USA Bodybuilding & Fitness Championships

July 10–11, 1998

MIDDLEWEIGHT MEN

NUMBER	CONTESTANT	JUDGE 1	2	3	4	5	6	7	8	9	SCORE	PLACE
31	Richard Longwith	1	1	1	1	3	3	3	2	2	9	1
36	Stephen Cantone	3	4	2	3	2	1	2	1	1	10	2
37	Kevin Creeden	2	2	5	5	1	2	4	3	3	14	3
32	Paul Smith	4	3	3	4	5	4	1	4	4	19	4
46	Steve Williams	5	5	4	2	4	5	5	5	5	24	5
30	Ron Norman	6	6	6	6	6	6	6	6	6	30	6
33	Steve Dufrene	7	9	11	7	7	7	9	9	9	41	7
42	Craig Santiago	9	8	8	9	8	8	7	7	10	41	8
48	Tito Raymond	8	7	7	8	11	12	10	10	8	44	9
39	Kris Dim	10	10	12	10	10	11	8	8	11	51	10
45	Garrette Townsend	11	11	9	12	9	16	11	11	7	53	11
29	Mark Dugdale	12	12	10	11	12	10	12	12	12	59	12
35	Patrick Matsuda	13	13	14	13	13	13	13	13	13	65	13
43	Tommy Potenza	15	14	15	16	15	14	14	15	15	74	14
41	Jason Coates	14	15	13	14	14	19	15	17	17	75	15
47	Mike Cox	16	16	17	15	16	17	16	14	14	79	16
49	Randy Samuels	17	17	16	17	17	15	17	16	16	83	17
40	Bryant Zamora	19	18	18	18	18	9	19	18	18	90	18
34	Nino Siciliano	18	19	19	19	19	20	18	19	19	95	19
44	Arnold Watkins	20	20	20	20	20	18	20	20	20	100	20

Judge's score eliminates 2 high & 2 low

JUDGES FOR THIS CLASS

Judge	1	Kevin Wagner	TX
Judge	2	Matt Crane	NY
Judge	3	Peter Potter	FL
Judge	4	Bob Pentz	NC
Judge	5	John Kemper	NJ
Judge	6	Clark Sanchez	NM
Judge	7	Michael Stoole	CA
Judge	8	Ted Williamson	CA
Judge	9	Don Hollis	MS

1998 NPC USA Bodybuilding & Fitness Championships

July 10–11, 1998

LIGHT HEAVYWEIGHT MEN

NUMBER	CONTESTANT	JUDGE 1	2	3	4	5	6	7	8	9	SCORE	PLACE
62	Troy Alves	1	1	1	1	1	2	2	2	3	7	1
57	Robert Lopez	5	2	2	2	2	1	1	1	2	9	2
54	Parenthesis Devers	3	3	3	3	3	3	3	3	1	15	3
50	Joe Hubbard	4	4	4	5	4	5	5	5	5	23	4
56	James Restivo	2	6	6	6	6	6	4	4	4	26	5
51	Andre Scott	6	5	5	4	5	4	6	6	6	27	6
59	Michael Cruthird	7	7	7	8	7	7	7	7	8	35	7
61	Charles Ray Arde	8	9	9	7	8	8	9	9	7	42	8
55	Darryl Holsey	9	8	8	10	10	9	10	8	10	46	9
52	Rommy Abdallah	10	10	10	9	9	10	8	10	9	48	10
53	Leonardo Pita	12	11	11	11	11	11	15	11	16	56	11
58	Samuel Jordan	15	13	13	12	12	13	13	15	11	64	12
63	Jon Vorves	11	14	12	13	14	15	11	13	13	65	13
60	Charles Lawson	16	16	16	16	13	12	14	12	12	71	14
64	Eric Dixon	13	15	14	15	15	16	12	14	14	72	15
65	David Coleman	14	12	15	14	16	14	16	16	15	74	16

Judge's score eliminates 2 high & 2 low

JUDGES FOR THIS CLASS

Judge	1	Art Bedway	PA
Judge	2	John Tuman	CA
Judge	3	Ty Fielder	GA
Judge	4	Ken Taylor	SC
Judge	5	John Kemper	NJ
Judge	6	Matt Crane	NY
Judge	7	Steve Weinberger	NY
Judge	8	Al Johnson	LA
Judge	9	Steve O'Brien	CA

1998 NPC USA Bodybuilding & Fitness Championships

July 10–11, 1998

HEAVYWEIGHT MEN

NUMBER	CONTESTANT	JUDGE 1	2	3	4	5	6	7	8	9	SCORE	PLACE
70	Jason Arntz	2	1	1	2	1	1	1	1	2	6	1
74	Tevita Aholelei	1	2	2	3	2	2	2	2	3	10	2
69	Garrett Downing	3	3	3	1	3	3	3	3	1	15	3
76	Rodney Davis	4	4	4	4	4	4	4	4	4	20	4
73	John King	5	5	5	5	9	5	9	7	5	27	5
75	Joseph Carlton Jr.	6	6	6	6	5	6	5	5	6	29	6
78	Darrell Terrell	7	7	7	7	7	7	8	6	7	35	7
77	William Matlock	8	8	9	9	8	8	7	8	9	41	8
72	Rusty Jeffers	9	10	10	8	10	9	10	9	8	47	9
67	Shilbert Ferguson	10	9	8	10	6	10	6	10	10	47	10
80	Joseph Patterson Jr.	11	14	11	11	12	14	12	12	11	58	11
68	Hans Hopstaken	13	11	13	12	13	13	13	13	14	65	12
79	Dan Fine	15	13	12	13	14	11	14	14	13	67	13
71	Joel Cutulle	12	12	14	14	15	12	15	15	12	67	14
66	Christopher Bennett	14	15	15	15	11	15	11	11	15	70	15

Judge's score eliminates 2 high & 2 low

JUDGES FOR THIS CLASS

Judge	1	Peter Potter	FL
Judge	2	John Tuman	CA
Judge	3	Ty Fielder	GA
Judge	4	Debbie Albert	PA
Judge	5	Mike Katz	CT
Judge	6	Jim Rockell	NY
Judge	7	Steve Weinberger	NY
Judge	8	Jerry Mastrangelo	CT
Judge	9	Sandi Ranalli	CA

1998 NPC USA Bodybuilding & Fitness Championships

July 10–11, 1998

SUPER HEAVYWEIGHT MEN

NUMBER	CONTESTANT	JUDGE 1	2	3	4	5	6	7	8	9	SCORE	PLACE
93	Dennis James	2	1	1	1	2	1	2	2	2	8	1
94	Melvin Anthony	1	2	2	2	1	2	1	3	1	8	2
91	Orville Burke	3	3	3	3	3	3	3	1	3	15	3
83	Aaron Maddron	4	4	4	4	4	4	4	4	4	20	4
87	Dan Freeman	6	5	6	5	5	5	5	6	6	27	5
89	David Nelson	5	6	5	6	6	6	6	5	5	28	6
85	Erik Fromm	7	8	8	8	7	8	7	10	7	38	7
81	Justin Brooks	9	7	7	10	9	7	9	7	8	40	8
90	Leo Ingram	10	10	9	7	8	9	8	8	9	43	9
95	Leon Parker	8	9	10	9	10	10	10	9	10	48	10
92	Jack Wadsworth	12	14	11	11	11	12	14	11	14	60	11
88	William Harse	11	12	14	12	13	13	11	13	12	62	12
84	Kevin Sosamon	13	11	13	13	14	11	13	12	13	64	13
82	Brad Hollibaugh	14	13	12	14	12	14	12	14	11	65	14

Judge's score eliminates 2 high & 2 low

JUDGES FOR THIS CLASS

Judge	1	Ted Williamson	CA
Judge	2	Art Bedway	PA
Judge	3	Jeff Taylor	CA
Judge	4	Debbie Albert	PA
Judge	5	Mike Katz	CT
Judge	6	Ken Taylor	SC
Judge	7	Jim Rockell	NY
Judge	8	Jerry Mastrangelo	CT
Judge	9	Steve O'Brien	CA

It's never too soon to begin practicing posing. Do what Lee Priest demonstrates here: Between sets, flex the muscles you are training, hit a pose, and study yourself in the mirror.

OVERALL WINNERS

In most amateur contests, after the weight-class winners are announced there is a posedown among the winners of each class to determine the overall winner. This means that, having won a weight class, you can't relax and begin to celebrate. You have another posedown to deal with. While the bigger bodybuilders tend to win these overall titles, it is by no means a sure thing. Middleweights and even lightweights have been known to take the overall. Furthermore, since the overall winner is selected in just a few minutes onstage, it is essential that you pump yourself up to the highest energy levels for this challenge, especially since overall winners in amateur contests frequently win the privilege of turning pro!

One exception to this procedure is the IFBB World Amateur Championships—until 1976 known as the Mr. Universe contest. There is no overall winner selected at the World Championships. In the past, each class winner was eligible to turn pro and was immediately qualified for the Mr. Olympia contest. However, this resulted in too many bodybuilders at the Mr. Olympia who simply weren't competitive, so more recently the IFBB has been holding a posedown for the class to select one competitor from the Universe to be invited to enter the Mr. Olympia. Even then, the winner's national federation still has to recommend him to the pro division of the IFBB before he is invited to compete at the Mr. Olympia.

ENDURANCE

Another thing to remember is that you might end up being onstage for quite a while during a contest. The more comparisons you are brought out for and the more posing you do, the more endurance you need in order to get through the show without experiencing undue fatigue or even cramping up. How do you achieve this endurance? By practicing all the poses over and over for a period of weeks or months. Again, keep in mind that you are doing a kind of posing even when you stand in the lineup onstage waiting to be called out for a comparison. Even at the back of the stage you are still visible to the judges, and if you let your body sag, your abs stick out, or appear to be tired or discouraged, this is bound to influence how the officials are going to score you.

PRACTICING POSING

As important as it is to competitive bodybuilding, it is never too soon to practice posing. You should begin the first day you walk into the gym. Study photos of other bodybuilders, go to contests and watch how the competitors pose, and try to emulate them. Begin by doing your poses in front of a mirror until you think you have a feel for them. Then try doing them without a mirror while a friend watches you.

Between sets, flex the muscles you are training, hit some poses, and study yourself in the mirror. This will condition you to hard, sustained contractions of the muscles and also help you to analyze the current state of your development.

Remember the need for *endurance!* The judges will often have you holding poses for minutes at a time; you might have to stay flexed for hours during a strenuous prejudging. So in your posing practice, don't just hit poses for a few seconds and then relax. Hold them until it hurts, then hold

Posing in front of the mirror helps you to analyze faults in your posing techniques. Here I am getting critical advice from Robby Robinson, Ken Waller, Franco Columbu, and Ed Corney. This kind of criticism is sometimes painful but really helps.

Checking out my triceps after doing twenty-five sets of triceps training

I liked to do this straight-arm triceps pose after my chest or triceps training, to bring out the muscles I had just trained while they were still pumped and hard.

Even at age twenty I knew instinctively to spend time flexing and posing my biceps after a session of arm training.

Holding the muscles flexed for a few minutes after a workout helps condition you to the hard discipline needed for competition posing.

Franco Columbu posing between sets

them some more—now is the time to go to failure, to get muscle cramps, to suffer so that your posing in competition will be smooth, competent, and powerful. Keep at it for at least an hour a day, maybe even more as you get closer to a contest. You will be glad you did once you find yourself standing onstage.

Another thing to remember is that bodybuilders under pressure tend to pose faster than they would in practice. So I recommend that you count slowly to three, four, or five, and to use this as a measure of how long to hold your pose. This way you will avoid rushing when you get caught up in the excitement of an actual contest.

One of the most important qualities to develop in your posing is confidence. Whether you are standing relaxed onstage, going through the compulsories, or doing your own routine, you need to appear confident, to radiate energy and competence. But to do this requires a lot of practice so that you can hit each shot perfectly and continue to pose over and over again without showing signs of strain and fatigue. And remember to practice posing from the neck down, but keeping your face relaxed and showing a confident expression.

My training partners and I always hit poses together—had sort of mini-posedowns in the gym—so that we could compare and analyze what we had achieved and what areas we still needed to work on. If you are less experienced, it helps to train with somebody who knows a lot more than

The best way to learn to pose is to work with someone with experience. Here, Jean Pierre Fux and Nasser El Sonbaty check out Fux's form in the mirror.

Casual posedowns are great practice for competition.

As you can see by Don Long's and Flex Wheeler's expressions, gym posedowns are also lots of fun.

Here are Ed Corney, Denny Gable, Brian Abede, and I watching a mini-posedown between Robby Robinson and Ken Waller. Competing in the gym in this way will teach you timing and how to quickly counter a competitor's pose with one that makes you look better.

you do. When I went to visit Reg Park in South Africa when I was eighteen, we would get together in the gym every day and pretend we were having a posedown. At that point, he was much better and more experienced than I was, and working with him every day on posing after working out, standing under a skylight, and hitting poses, I learned an incredible amount. He would do a pose and say, "If I'm hitting this shot, you should be hitting that one." In *Pumping Iron,* you can see me doing the same thing with Franco and other bodybuilders.

In addition to your regular, concentrated practice, I recommend that from time to time you just run through your poses very quickly, not really hitting them with full strength, but just familiarizing yourself with the feeling of going from one to the other quickly and without hesitation, smoothing out the transitions and teaching your body how to get from one pose to another without stumbling or awkwardness.

It may be called a relaxed pose, but as you can see in this photo you still have to flex everything, and you need a lot of practice to be able to stand in this position for long periods of time.

Standing relaxed from the side—thighs flexed, abs tight, arms hanging loose

PRACTICING FOR ROUND ONE

Round one is called standing relaxed, but it is anything but that. It is also called a symmetry round, as if all the judges are supposed to be looking at is the shape and proportion of your physique, but that is also incorrect (although a lot of judges don't understand this). Every round in the contest is a physique round and the judges should be looking at *everything* they can see all the time.

To practice for this round, stand straight up, feet together, your hands at your sides. In all posing, you start from the ground up, so begin by flexing your thighs. Some bodybuilders bend their knees slightly to help flare out the thighs, but sometimes this can make you look too squat, so look in the mirror and see if you look better with your knees locked or slightly bent. Tuck your butt in slightly, pulling up with the abdominals, which tilts the pelvis slightly and helps keep the abs tight and defined. Extend your

Although a head judge might call you on this, I found it possible to attract the attention of the judges in round one by hitting this variation of the relaxed pose every once in a while—a slight twist of the waist, arms and chest flexed hard, and up on my toes to show my calves.

Today's bodybuilders tend to flex a lot more doing the "standing relaxed" poses than was allowed when I was competing in the Mr. Olympia.

Flex Wheeler shows the advantage of being in extremely good shape for a contest. Even before he has hit a specific pose his definition and muscularity are clearly evident.

spine upward, keeping it as long as possible. Stretch the spine; don't lift the shoulders. This allows you to stand tall and expands the chest. Flare your lats slightly, enough to push your arms out to the side, but not so much that it appears you are doing a lat pose. Tense your arms, make sure your abs are flexed, and keep your face relaxed.

In theory, the proper way to pose for round one is to hit this pose to the front, turn 90 degrees to the right and keep hitting it, turn to the back, to the other side, and then again to the front—keeping that same standing-relaxed pose the whole time. In practice, when they turn to the side, competitors tend to straighten the arm nearest the judges, flexing the triceps, and twisting in their direction as well. This makes no sense at all in a round designed to show the judges your overall shape and proportion. But as long as the head judge allows it, competitors will try to get away with whatever they can. However, the better your symmetry, the less I would advise your flexing and twisting to hide it.

The only way to condition yourself for standing with all of your muscles tensed for long periods of time is to do it. Stand with your thighs and abs tensed, your lats flared, your pecs massive. Don't be too obviously posed, but let your arms hang almost naturally at your sides. Use a clock or a stopwatch and practice standing like this for one minute, then turn and stand for one minute facing each of the other three directions. Flex the calves, especially when your back is facing where the judges would be, and don't forget the leg biceps, the buttocks, the lower back, and the lats; keep the waist pulled in, be conscious of the whole body. A few minutes of this will exhaust you, but you need to keep at it until you can stand like this for half an hour or more without shaking, sweating, cramping, or looking too strained and anxious. It is best to practice this with a training partner watching to see that you keep everything flexed and warning you when you start to let down.

PRACTICING FOR ROUND TWO

The first thing to do in mastering round two compulsories is simply to study the basic poses and learn to do them competently. After you can hold each pose for one minute by itself, try hitting all seven poses without stopping.

Front double biceps. Stand to the front. Flex your thighs and tuck in your butt as in the standing-relaxed pose. Lift your arms up into a double-biceps position, flaring your lats as you do so. Supinate your wrists (turn your hands in toward you) to get a maximum biceps peak. To finish off the pose, push your elbows just slightly forward to bring out the chest and make sure your abs are tight. When doing front double biceps, hit the thighs hard and don't relax them as long as you are holding that pose, and be sure to keep your abdominals flexed the whole time as well.

Having huge lats and arms makes the front double biceps an effective pose for Nasser El Sonbaty, but this pose is made even more impressive by his tight waistline and V-shaped torso.

Robby Robinson is one of the few bodybuilders who can successfully execute a stomach vacuum while doing a front double-biceps pose.

The front double biceps is one of the most difficult poses, because it tends to emphasize any weaknesses. In the second round of compulsory poses you are not supposed to do anything to disguise your development or proportions. However, there are certain conventional variations the judges will accept that bodybuilders can use to show their individual physiques off to best advantage. It is, for example, common for bodybuilders to try and minimize their waistlines doing this pose—although when you have the symmetry of a Flex Wheeler or Ronnie Coleman, genetics has pretty much accomplished this already.

It may be called the front double-biceps pose, but more than the biceps are involved—you need to flex every muscle, from the calves and thighs to the abs, muscles of the torso, and the pecs.

There are a number of ways of doing a side-chest pose. Here I am demonstrating the pose as it is usually done.

When Lee Priest does a side-chest pose, he also flexes hard to show off the muscularity of his deltoids, upper and lower arms, as well as the intercostals at the side of the torso.

Extending the arms and holding a stomach vacuum when doing a side-chest pose lets you show off your upper pecs much more than a regular chest pose. It can be used in combination with the regular chest pose—hit this one, hold it a moment, then bring your elbow back into the conventional compulsory pose.

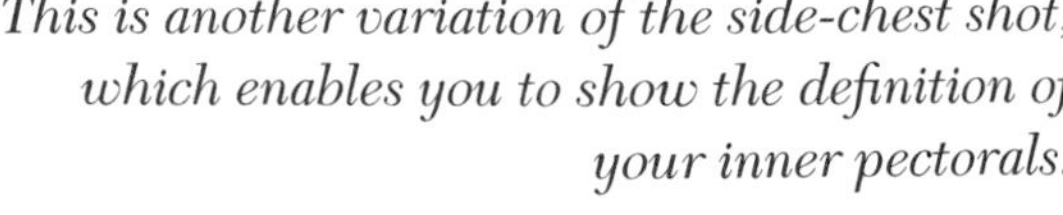

This is another variation of the side-chest shot, which enables you to show the definition of your inner pectorals.

Hitting a side-chest comparison shot, Kevin Levrone, Dorian Yates, Nasser El Sonbaty, and Shawn Ray are able to look relaxed and confident while flexing virtually every muscle in their bodies as hard as possible. You can do this only if you've devoted many hours to practicing posing.

Front lat spread. Pose your legs as in the front double biceps. Put your hands on your hips, grabbing your obliques, bring your elbows forward and flare your lats, keeping your chest high. Many bodybuilders forget how important the chest muscles are in a front lat spread. As you spread your lats, lift the chest high and bring the shoulders forward to accentuate the pectorals.

Side chest (to either side). Stand to the side and go up on your big toe on either leg to flex the calf (the higher you are on your toe, the more the calf flexes naturally). Curl your arm by your side, palm facing up, bring your other hand across your chest and hold the top of your wrist. Pull your elbow as far back as you can. Suck in your stomach and keep your chest high. Twist slightly to show more of your chest to the judges. Try standing on the leg closest to the judges, bending the rear leg and flexing the calf, or standing on the rear leg and flexing the calf of the front leg, and decide which is the best way for you.

Back double biceps. Turn to the back. Put one leg slightly behind you, go up on your toe to flex your calf. Raise your arms up into the double-biceps position, flaring your lats at the same time. Keeping your lats flexed, press your elbows back against them, which brings out the muscularity in the back. Supinate your biceps to get maximum peak. Turn your head to the side to bring out the asymmetry of the traps. Pull your elbows back and arch your back somewhat—the judges are looking up at you, don't forget, and you need to bend backward slightly for them to get a good view.

Rear lat spread. Put one leg slightly behind you, go up on your toe to flex your calf. Put your hands at your sides, grabbing hold of your obliques. Bring your elbows forward and slowly open up your lats, letting the judges watch the process as these muscles unfold. Flare out your lats and round your back slightly to show maximum lat width. Turn your head to the side to bring out the asymmetry of the traps.

Although they are hitting the same pose, it's obvious Kevin Levrone, Dorian Yates, and Nasser El Sonbaty do not have identical proportions, shape, or muscular development. For example, Dorian's chest appears higher and more striated, while Nasser displays a totally awesome abdominal development.

By putting his fists in tight to his obliques, you can see how Nasser El Sonbaty makes his extreme V-shape appear even more tapered than it is.

When I did a front lat spread, I pressed in at the waist to make it look smaller and flared out my lats to get as much of a V-shape as possible. Notice how I managed to bring out pectoral striations at the same time.

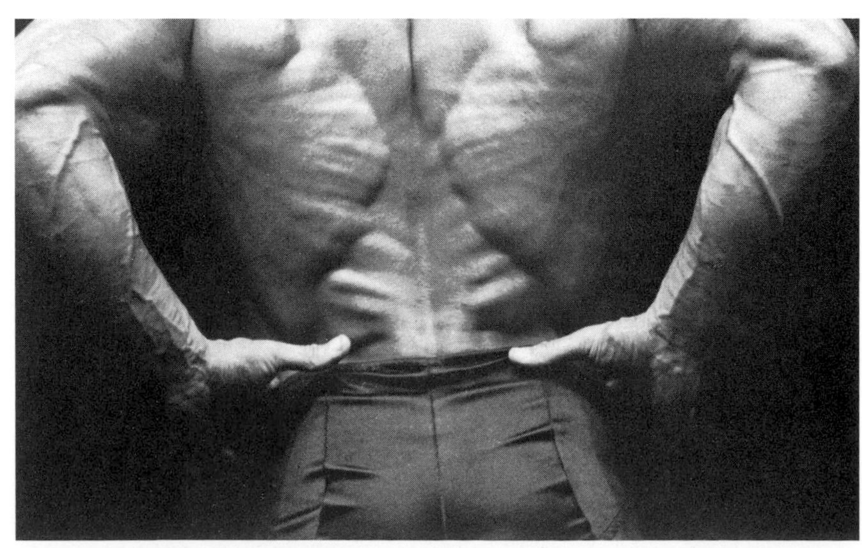

Samir Bannout starting a rear lat spread. Talk about being in fantastic shape! See how far back he starts to press in his thumbs.

Shawn Ray

The side-triceps pose can be done with the arm slightly bent, as demonstrated by Shawn Ray; with the arm straight and body turned more to the front or to the side, as we see with Ronnie Coleman and Nasser El Sonbaty. Looking in the mirror or posing for photos will help you to see which variation of the pose is best for you.

Nasser El Sonbaty

The hands-overhead abdominal pose is one of the most exhausting. Achim Albrecht, Nasser El Sonbaty, and Vince Taylor show the degree to which you have to work your abs, bending your torso to one side and the other while flexing and posing your legs at the same time, to impress the judges with your quadriceps development.

Although he carries a lot of mass, Nasser El Sonbaty still displays a streamlined and cut midsection. Here, he shows a perfect execution of the hands-overhead abdominal pose.

Side triceps (to either side). Stand to the side and go up on your toe on the leg nearest the judges to flex the calf. Straighten your arm and move it toward the back. Reach around behind you with your other hand and grab your wrist. Flex your triceps, and turn your body slightly one way and the other to show your arm to all the judges. For a triceps pose, you can again choose which leg should be used to support you.

Abdominals and thighs. Stand to the front. Put one leg out in front and flex the quadriceps. Put your hands behind your head and crunch forward, contracting your abdominals as much as possible. Lean your torso to either side, working and showing off the abs to their best advantage. During your pose you can switch legs, bringing the back one forward and flexing the quad. Some bodybuilders do a stomach vacuum first and then crunch forward to blast their abs. With an overhead abdominal pose, when you are fully into the pose, cough to get the last of the air out of your lungs and bring out the abdominals fully.

Frank Zane practically owned this vacuum pose. It showed off the serratus in the best possible way; it showed the biceps in a favorable position; it displayed maximum symmetry and allowed him to dwarf other bodybuilders onstage doing shots like a most-muscular. Bill Pearl was also a master of this shot, but if you don't have this type of body, it's not for you.

PERSONALIZING YOUR POSES

There isn't supposed to be much variation in the mandatory poses, but in reality there are always variations you can introduce that make the poses suit your physique. For example, I used to notice that when Bill Pearl and Sergio Oliva did a double-biceps pose they did it with their legs straight on. They were both huge, with great legs, so they could afford to do that. Someone with a body like Frank Zane's would never have done a straight-on double-biceps pose but would always add a little twist. By doing this, Frank took what is a power pose for the other guys and turned it into a ballet-like, aesthetic pose for himself. Since my waist was never as small as somebody like the incredible Sergio Oliva, when you see photos of me doing a front double biceps you'll usually see me twisting from the waist slightly to increase the V taper of my torso.

For your own practice, study posing photos of the champions and try to duplicate them. Study yourself in the mirror, have someone take photographs of you, or, if you can arrange it, make a videotape of yourself posing. It is also important to pose in front of other people—your training partner, other bodybuilders at the gym, anyone who can watch you and spot weaknesses in your presentation.

PRACTICING FOR ROUND THREE

The idea of free posing is to present the best elements of your physique to the judges. In your early competitions, you will not yet have the total development you are training for, so there will be poses you will want to

Steve Reeves was one of the few bodybuilders to ever master this pose. You need long legs, a very symmetrical body, a V-shaped torso with a small waist, wide shoulders, and an almost flat chest (which helps to show off your lats). It also helps to have a square, flat-chested frame like that of Frank Zane, Don Howorth, or Jim Haislip, for example. A bodybuilder like Sergio Oliva would do an overhead shot like this very differently.

avoid until you can really bring them off. Find the poses that make you look your best and base your routine on them.

The basis for the third-round free-posing routine is the compulsories from round two. In doing these poses, remember the rule I gave earlier: Pose from the ground up. Plant your feet, flex your calves, thighs, and abs, and then hit the upper body. Take inventory of each body part and make certain nothing is ignored.

As time goes on and your body improves, you can go beyond the compulsories and begin to add more poses in order to show this new development. For example, you don't need 20-inch arms to be able to do a front double-biceps pose—which is good, because you will need to do this pose during the compulsories. However, until your arms are really outstanding you should avoid a pose with your arms straight out, which will emphasize their relative lack of development. But once your arms have improved, you might choose to add a movement like one Sergio Oliva used to do, where you stand with your arms straight out and then bring them into a double-biceps, which will call attention to their size and development. If your lats are particularly outstanding it makes sense to learn three or four new ways to show them off, or if you have great abs, by all means find a way to display this strength. On the other hand, if you are especially weak in an area, work like hell in the gym to correct the imbalance, but in the meantime, try not to pose in such a way as to call attention to that particular body part.

Anytime you pose, make sure that all the judges have an equal chance of seeing you, the ones at the side as well as those directly in front. It is a lot easier to remember to turn slightly when doing the compulsories; during your free posing, with so much going on, it takes a little more effort.

Remember, free posing is drama: Keep a smile or relaxed expression on your face. All your tensing and flexing should be done from the neck down. This projects confidence. In some poses look out at the audience; in others, look at the muscle. Keep your routine varied and interesting.

Nowadays, a lot more creativity is displayed onstage than when I got into bodybuilding. Nevertheless, I recommend to all beginners that they concentrate on doing a few poses well rather than a lot of them less competently. Start out with eight or ten and become the master of them. Once you can do your routine without a hitch—and you should practice it constantly, three or four times a day for at least three months before a competition—you can begin to expand and develop it.

Have photos taken of your posing routine and study these pictures to determine what you are doing right and in which areas you still need work. If a pose doesn't look right, don't use it until it does.

Your posing routine should be just that—a routine, not a series of poses. You have to work on the transition between poses as well as the poses themselves. Next time you see the movie *Pumping Iron,* watch for the scene in which Franco and I are taking a ballet class. That was for

Kevin Levrone demonstrates how even intermediate poses, as you are going from one standard pose to another, can make your body look aesthetic and muscular.

Milos Sarcev, in the tradition of legends like Steve Reeves and Frank Zane, takes advantage of his outstanding aesthetics to create poses that show off his muscularity and proportion—but that are simply beautiful as well.

You can't call this a triceps pose, an abdominal pose, or a chest pose. It is an in-between pose used while going from, for example, a side chest to a twisting double biceps, which allows me to flex the abs and triceps, show the small waist, and then go on to the next pose. This is the kind of pose you have to play around with to see if it suits you or not.

real; we took ballet in California and some classes in New York as well as at a studio owned by actress Joanne Woodward. Both Franco and I were expert at doing poses that suited our physiques, but we knew we could improve the transitions between poses and the overall style and gracefulness of our movements onstage. Just because you are going through a transition rather than hitting a pose, it doesn't mean the judges can't see you. I even went a step beyond—standing and moving in such a way as to maximize the effect of my physique even when I was backstage! The other competitors are always checking you out, and if they see you looking great, you can sometimes defeat them before they ever set foot onstage.

Your type of muscle structure should determine the speed and style of your posing. If you are a Frank Zane or Flex Wheeler type, slow it down and concentrate on grace and rhythm, keeping your execution smooth like a classical symphony. With my build, I have always adopted the philoso-

This twisting double-biceps pose maximizes the size of the arms while minimizing the waist.

The twisting one-arm biceps shot creates an aesthetic effect and makes your waist look small. With this pose you can show off the inside of one arm and the outside of the other simultaneously. However, if you don't have good height on your biceps, you would do better to avoid this pose. (Incidentally, keep the thumb inside the fist of your raised arm or it will stick out and cause a distraction.)

This biceps shot, with the arm behind the head, introduces an aesthetic twist that really makes it a beautiful pose. But it won't work unless you keep your thighs and calves tensed for the duration of the pose.

Another variation of the biceps shot: raised arm, wrist (not hand) into the waist to make the forearm look shorter and smaller, torso twisted slightly, and legs flexed really hard.

This arms-extended pose shows the judges just how huge my arms—forearms, biceps, and triceps—really are.

I used a number of conventional twisting back poses in my routines, which showed the development and muscularity of my back, minimized my waist size, and displayed my arms to their best advantage.

Shawn Ray demonstrates that there are other impressive ways to show off back development than just the standard compulsory back poses.

Aaron Baker is certainly not lacking in mass, but he believes in showing off his physique to its best advantage by hitting a lot of aesthetic and interesting variations of the standard poses.

Kevin Levrone has always understood that it takes more than a great physique and being in terrific shape to impress the judges. He approaches his posing routines with a confidence and energy that communicate "I deserve to win this contest."

If it's hard to believe that Ronnie Coleman won the World Amateur Championships title two years after getting into competition bodybuilding, this look at his outstanding back development and definition should put any doubts to rest.

This three-quarters back shot is not done by many bodybuilders. By opening up my hands instead of clenching my fists I emphasize symmetry as much as muscularity. In all twisting shots, the leg away from the judges should be to the front, making the pelvis twist against the torso so that your waist looks smaller.

In the tradition of the great Frank Zane, Darrem Charles is able to defeat bodybuilders far more massive because of his unbelievably aesthetic shape, symmetry, and proportion.

Flex Wheeler

Aaron Baker doing a lunging most-muscular and Flex Wheeler executing a kneeling twisting back pose. Lunging and kneeling poses allow for interesting and creative variations of basic poses, and have been a part of bodybuilding since the very beginnings of the sport.

Aaron Baker

Shawn Ray's creative approach to posing is one reason why he has so often been able to defeat bodybuilders outweighing him by 30 pounds, 40 pounds, or even more. Here he demonstrates how kneeling poses can be used to show off the front of the physique and the back as well.

The great champions have taken the trouble to develop poses that are uniquely suited to their individual physiques. Flex Wheeler likes to remind the judges that, although he has one of the most aesthetic physiques of all time, he is by no means lacking in muscularity and definition.

Before I did a most-muscular pose, I b down, took hold of my wrist, and rea pumped up the biceps. This was a gr crowd pleaser, combining movement wit display of the outside of the bice

Lee Priest is a short man without short-man proportions. His physique is so well balanced and symmetrical that he looks as good in most poses as do competitors who may be nearly a foot taller.

Franco Columbu was the master of the most-muscular pose and was able to do at least eight effective variations. This was one of his favorites, almost in standing-relaxed pose, but displaying the development of his arms, forearms, deltoids, chest, abdominals, and legs—with the promise of even more awesome muscularity to come.

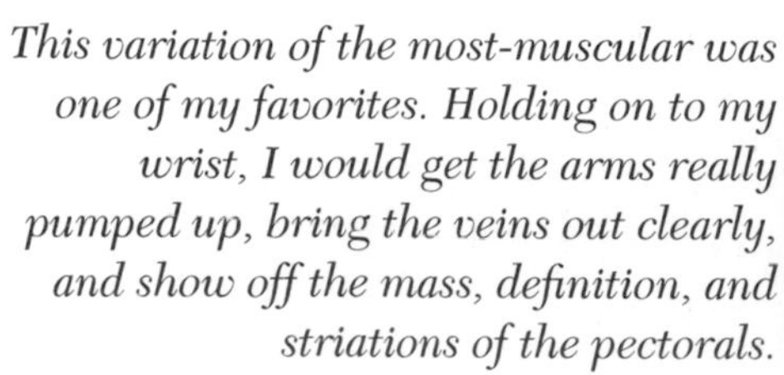

This variation of the most-muscular was one of my favorites. Holding on to my wrist, I would get the arms really pumped up, bring the veins out clearly, and show off the mass, definition, and striations of the pectorals.

I always used the conventional most-muscular pose in my routine because it allowed me to show off both my mass and outstanding definition. Bending forward like this, the pose also called attention to trapezius development.

Kevin Levrone doing two variations of the most-muscular pose.

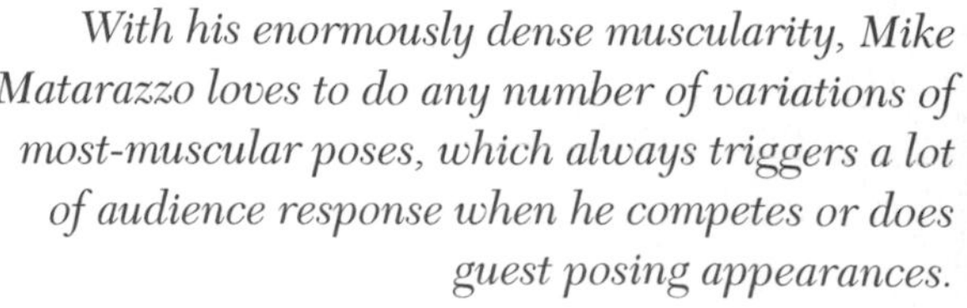

With his enormously dense muscularity, Mike Matarazzo loves to do any number of variations of most-muscular poses, which always triggers a lot of audience response when he competes or does guest posing appearances.

1

2

3

4

5

Ed Corney is considered one of the great posers of all time, not just because of his mastery of each individual pose, but also because he considered each transition *between poses to be as important as the poses themselves. Corney developed a free-posing routine that was both beautiful and dynamic and that was carefully constructed to emphasize his strong points and draw attention away from his less impressive body parts.*

6

7

8

12

13

14

9

10

11

15

16

17

18

19

20

24

25

21

22

23

26

27

phy "If you have a big gun, shoot it!" and I have gone in for a more dramatic style, faster and more dynamic, relying on my ability to blow minds with my size and muscularity.

Another thing every bodybuilder has to learn is how to pace himself when he poses. With the pressure and excitement of a contest, adrenaline floods your body, and you may have a tendency to rush your posing. Even an experienced bodybuilder like Mike Mentzer found himself doing this in the 1979 Mr. Olympia in his posedown with Frank Zane. Mike kept hitting his poses faster and faster, while Frank posed calmly and deliberately. This made Frank look much more confident and in control and ultimately contributed to his victory.

I always attempted to pace my poses evenly, timing each one by counting slowly to three. My attitude was, if a pose was worth looking at, it was worth holding long enough to give everybody a good look—and this also allowed magazine photographers time to get the shots they needed.

If your method is to jiggle around a bit before settling into your pose, that's okay as long as you are getting approval from your audience. This is where experience before crowds becomes invaluable. Be alert to the reactions of the audience; the feedback they give you can be extremely helpful. Remember, a gym mirror can tell you only so much.

Take special care in setting up the pose that will knock the audience out of their seats. You see this a lot in good back shots: The bodybuilder scrunches his shoulder blades together, fists on hips, and holds this comparatively poor pose for about five seconds. Then he finally, slowly, spreads out the lats and leaves the audience gasping.

Good posing is a performing art, and like all performing arts, it is most often a matter of good timing. You should leave the stage at the high point, when anything else would be anticlimactic. By having your routine build up to a crescendo and saving the major wallops for last, your audience will be entertained and excited by your performance.

Good posing is like a symphony: The faster movements contrast with the slower ones; the dynamics should constantly change. There are quick, dramatic movements, to be followed by slow, graceful ones. There is rhythm and there is emotion. And it is here that you will find the highest level of achievement in bodybuilding.

Many bodybuilders today are looking for help in *choreographing* a routine. Some turn to other bodybuilders who specialize in this sort of thing. Others turn to outsiders, like professional dance choreographers. Videos on "how to pose" are available. The higher the level at which you are competing, the more important having a suitable, impressive, well-crafted routine becomes. Often, this makes the difference between winning and losing.

But using the wrong kind of choreography can be a disaster. In 1981, Chris Dickerson hired a dancer to help him develop a routine. The normally very dignified Chris ended up onstage doing some kind of break-dance moves, including a poor execution of a Michael Jackson moon walk. The following year, being very bright and able to learn from his mistakes, Chris went back to a style that suited him better, did a very dramatic posing routine in London to an operatic selection, and ended up winning the Mr. Olympia title.

One prominent bodybuilder advised in his seminars that bodybuilders should never make any overdramatic moves. He said you should go from a back pose to a side pose, for example, not from a back pose immediately to a front pose. There are certainly times when you should follow this advice, but there are others in which an unexpected move is effective—like Dorian Yates's dramatic most-muscular shot, in which he contracts his upper body, thrusts out his leg, and appears to be some mythical monster suddenly manifesting himself onstage.

THE WAY JUDGING USED TO BE

Bodybuilding contests have not always been conducted as they are today. Once, in addition to demonstrating athletic ability, bodybuilders had to talk—to answer questions and demonstrate their ability to think and express themselves. Judges didn't always sit at a table and write down their scores. In some formats, the judges would go off together to discuss and debate the qualities of the various bodybuilders in the contest.

I had a very interesting experience when I was competing in the Mr. Olympia contest in New York in 1969. Head judge Leroy Colbert took Sergio Oliva and me off the stage and into a back room, like a judge bringing the opposing sides into his chambers. He gathered the other judges around us in a circle and told us the contest was so close he wanted the judges to have a better look at our physiques without any showmanship or presentation to distract them. "Let's just see the body," he told us, and started calling out poses. That particular year, using that format, Sergio won because he was more cut than I was. But the next year our positions were reversed—I was more cut and he was not as cut as he had been—so this unusual method of judging worked to my advantage this time.

Of course, that is not the way judging is done today, but judging methods change over time and the point is to show up at a contest in your best shape and be able to respond and adapt to whatever way the sanctioning organization has decided to conduct the event.

CHOOSING POSING MUSIC (FOR ROUND THREE)

In the early days of the sport, bodybuilders did not pose to specific pieces of music in competition and posing exhibitions. Often music was played, but it was simply meant to provide background. The individual posing routines were not geared to the mood, style, or rhythm of the music.

In the 1950s, Reg Park was one of the first bodybuilders to pose to specific music, a piece called "The Legend of the Glass Mountains." His wife was a ballet dancer, so he was familiar both with music and the idea of combining music with movement onstage as they do in dance. And, of course, once other bodybuilders saw how well this worked, soon everyone was doing it.

When I got into bodybuilding I knew nothing about music so I sought out experts to recommend different types of music I might be able to use in my routine. Eventually, because I have a big, dramatic kind of body, I settled on a big, dramatic kind of sound—the theme from *Exodus.* On the other hand, Mr. Olympia Chris Dickerson, who was also an opera singer, posed to very theatrical operatic themes. In fact, after *Titanic* became such a big hit, a number of bodybuilders began using music from the movie soundtrack to back up their routines.

But be careful not to use music that is *too* popular at the moment, or you risk subjecting the judges to the third rendition of the same piece. There was a time when every other bodybuilder seemed to be posing to "Chariots of Fire" or "Eye of the Tiger."

And it's very important that you choose music that is *appropriate,* something that works for *you,* not just something that is popular. It wouldn't make sense for aesthetic Flex Wheeler to use the same kind of music as granite-hard Dorian Yates. I used to see smaller, less muscular bodybuilders trying to pose to the same music I did. I appreciate that they were fans, but the effect was ridiculous for two reasons: (1) The music was way too dramatic for the physiques they were displaying onstage; and (2) it doesn't make sense to use any music that is too closely identified with a well-known champion.

Length of music is important because when you pose for longer periods of time you risk boring the judges. I kept my routine to around two minutes, hitting about twenty to twenty-two poses, showing the judges the superiority of my development and then getting off the stage, keeping it short and sweet. Posing for longer periods is risky, but it can be done. When Franco Columbu won the 1981 Mr. Olympia contest, his free-posing routine was a full 4 minutes 15 seconds—longer than any other competitor's! He just kept making the drama build, impressing the judges, and then, when they thought they had seen everything, surprising them with something new and even more interesting. As a result, he got superior scores from the judges right across the board.

Sergio Oliva, on the other hand, never bothered with this kind of presentation. He came out, posed for a minute or two, hitting maybe fourteen poses, and let his awesome physique speak for itself.

How Do You Go About Choosing Music for Your Own Routine?

- Listen to a lot of different music, not just the kind you find most entertaining—classical music, opera, pop music, rap, everything.
- Consider whether the music makes you *feel* the way your posing does.
- Try posing to different selections and see whether or not the music and your posing style seem to go together.
- Take this a step further by taping your posing and watching the video while listening to the music. Do the two seem to go together? Get some other opinions by asking your friends what they think.

Remember, you don't have to use music exactly the way it was recorded. You can have different sections of a piece or even parts of different musical selections edited together. Nowadays, a lot of bodybuilders are going to sound-mixing studios to create posing tapes that contain a lot of varied elements, giving a very theatrical feel to their individual presentation. When this is done well, it can be great. For example, Vince Taylor wowed audiences when he introduced a posing routine in which he played a mechanical *Terminator* character. It worked because Vince is such a good poser and obviously worked very hard on developing both the tape and his routine. But when some other bodybuilders try the same thing, without the same skill or quality of audio production, it can just look silly—which is certainly not the kind of impression you want to make on the judges. Remember, as entertaining as posing can be, the point of free posing is to convince the judges what a good physique you have.

By the way, in addition to finding the right music, having it edited, and practicing posing to it, it's important to take the simple precaution of *bringing more than one cassette to the contest.* You need at least two copies, one to use for practice and another to give the music director backstage. But I would recommend that you bring three copies. You need a backup in case your contest cassette is lost or if the tape machine accidentally "eats" it. Having extra cassettes is cheap insurance considering how devastating it can be to find yourself ready to go onstage with no music.

To sum up, make sure your selection of music meets with these criteria:

1. It should be the right length, long enough to allow you to create an impressive routine but not so long that the judges and the audience begin to get bored. In amateur competition the length of posing routines is often limited (check with the sanctioning organization or promoter in advance to be sure), but on the professional level you can pose for as long as you want.

2. The music you choose should have the right pace and rhythm to go with the kind of routine you want to perform. You don't want the music to force you to pose faster or slower than you would prefer or force you to conform to an uncomfortable rhythm.
3. As we discussed, the mood and feel of the music should complement your posing style. A posing routine backed up by classical music should be very different from one done to rock 'n' roll.
4. If there are lyrics or sound effects in the piece, they should not distract from your posing.
5. The music should be appropriate to your individual physique. A smaller, more aesthetic bodybuilder takes risks when he poses to grandiose, fate-and-doom music better suited to a massive, Herculean physique.

THE BOREDOM FACTOR

In some contests as many as thirty different bodybuilders pose. This can be difficult to sit through, even if you are as big a fan of bodybuilding as I am. But I see some events where I'm almost ready to fall asleep after only three or four posing routines. The problem is that way too many bodybuilders go about their routines in a very boring way.

Many try to be dramatic in ways that just don't work. For example, the music starts and we listen for a while before the competitor slowly walks out from the wings to the center of the stage. What's that all about? What a waste of time! It's better to just get out there, start the music, and begin hitting shots. It's a bodybuilding contest, and it's all about impressing everybody with the presentation of your physique. When your name is announced, you should come out and show us what you've got. We don't need to watch you walking across the stage.

PRACTICING FOR ROUND FOUR

In round four, you stand onstage with the other top competitors, go briefly through some compulsory poses, and then are free to hit any poses you want while the judges watch you and make their final determinations. You don't go through one set routine; you are in direct competition with the other bodybuilders for the attention of the judges. They have only a minute or so to make up their minds, so you need to make a quick and decisive impression.

During this short, intense bout of posing competition your most formidable opponents are right onstage next to you, which gives you a tremendous opportunity to convince the judges that you are the one who

This series of six photos shows "defensive posing" on my part. In this contest, after I hit a front-lat pose Franco followed suit, and he had about the best lats in the world.

So as not to look bad next to his lat spread, I immediately went to a biceps shot, allowing me to use my height to tower over him. To counter, Franco hit a one-arm biceps shot and flexed his abs. And, although my abs were sharp, I was not ready to go into a direct comparison with Franco.

ought to be declared the winner. But to use posing to gain that end, you need to use your *mind.* Posing at the highest level is almost more mental than physical, a kind of three-dimensional chess game.

By the time the posedown occurs, everyone is tired—you have been posing all day in the prejudging and done your posing routine under the pressures of the evening show. It is very easy to let down at this point. I have seen bodybuilders in the middle of a posedown begin to hesitate, lose track of what they were doing, and then have to quickly hit any random pose so as not to make complete fools of themselves. Fatigue, both mental and physical, becomes the enemy at this stage. The only way to avoid burning out before the posedown is finished is to prepare for it thoroughly, to practice this kind of free posing over and over. Only constant conditioning will prepare you for the rigors of this phase of the competition.

When preparing for a contest I always made it a point to know who I would be posing against and planed accordingly. I would look at tapes of my opponents' posing routines when possible and study each one to see how they put each sequence of poses together. I would look for inconsistencies indicating an opponent who was not sure of his routine, one who might be looking for something better. A consistent routine, on the other hand, would always indicate to me that a given opponent was satisfied, so

My turn to counter: To avoid direct comparison of our abdominals, I moved into a twisting three-quarter back pose to show my arms and the definition of my shoulders and back.

I would take what he considered to be his best poses and improve on them. To me, it was always as if I were challenging my opponent to a duel—knowing that a great competitor will always rise to the challenge. Then I would wheel in the heavy artillery, throwing in a lot of big muscle, make a flank attack with a changed routine, and completely screw up the opposition. Too many bodybuilders in the posedown just hit their best shots and pay little attention to the other competitors. The only time this works is when you are clearly the most superior bodybuilder onstage—and as competitive as the sport is these days, this is something that rarely happens.

You have to pose *smart* as well as hard. I already used the example of the bodybuilder who thought he could match quad shots with Tom Platz. Definitely not smart! In 1975 at the Mr. Olympia contest in South Africa, I was onstage with Franco Columbu. He hit a lat spread that was awesome. Now, I was confident of my own lat development, but I also knew I had size on my side. So while he hit his lats, I did a front double biceps, emphasizing how much bigger I was than Franco, trying to make him look small. I then went quickly into a most-muscular pose (to demonstrate I was as muscular as my opponent) and followed with a twisting back shot (demonstrating how impressive my own back was). I was able to do all

Franco's next move was to turn around and do a back double-biceps pose. Since I was confident that my own back was thick, muscular, and highly defined, I hit the same shot and let the judges see how good I was.

three of these poses because I knew that Franco takes a lot of time bringing out his lats. And by changing poses (without appearing to rush) I was able to draw the judges' attention away from what Franco was doing.

In another instance, Franco did a kneeling shot. Being so much taller and wanting to keep trying to dominate the comparisons, I immediately did a pose that brought me down to the same level. The point of this is that it takes observation, creativity, and intelligence to adjust your posing to that of the competitors sharing the stage with you in the final posedown.

Being able to exercise this kind of strategy takes a lot of time and experience to learn, and most beginners shouldn't worry about such things but instead ought to concentrate on showing off their physiques as competently as possible. But this is the kind of "smart" posing you'll need to learn in the future if you want to be truly a master of competition posing.

It's also important to realize that bodybuilders, like boxers, have to learn to pace themselves during a competition. You work as hard as you have to, but not harder. If the opposition grows weak, you lessen your own intensity so that you stay just ahead of him. When you see him hit a good pose, you hit an equal or better one. If he strikes a mediocre pose, you can warm up one of your leftovers to keep pace. You shouldn't unload all of

Franco and I hitting a most-muscular, each of us confident in his ability to look better than the other.

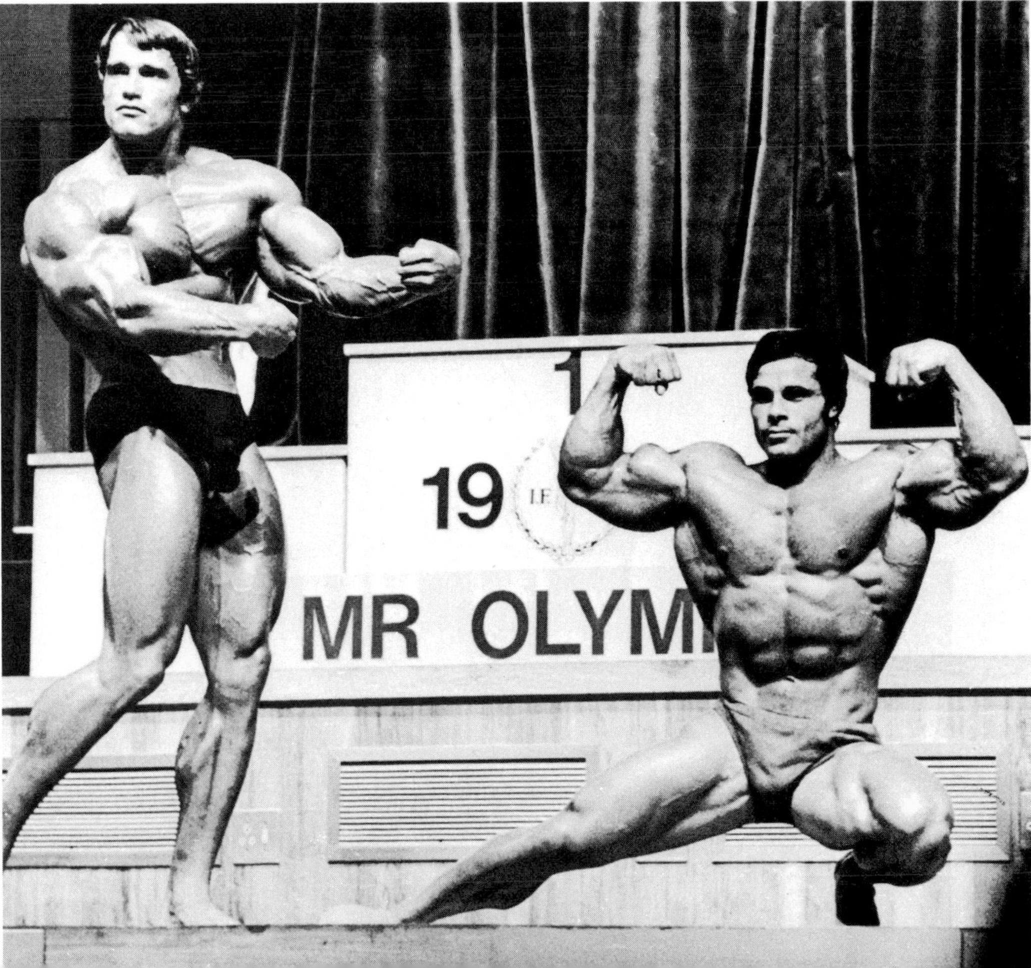

Franco also used the trick of doing kneeling shots when I tried to dominate him with height. This way the fact that he was much shorter than I did not cost him points with the judges.

By 1972 the posedown had become an institution. Notice that neither Serge Nubret, on the left, nor I was willing to go directly up against Sergio Oliva's formidable lat spread. Instead, we did back double-biceps poses.

your best poses in a row; save them for the end and then pull the cork, giving the judges all your favorites and leaving your foe in shambles.

And as I've cautioned before, be very careful how you approach a confrontation. When Sergio Oliva and I went head-to-head in the 1970 Mr. Olympia, he seemed to completely forget I was standing next to him and paid attention only to his own posing. I was hitting three or four shots to his one, doing counterposes to what he was doing, trying to make myself look good and call attention to Sergio's weaknesses. His body was as good as mine that night onstage, but I won primarily because of how I conducted myself in the posedown.

The posedown helps the judges make their final decision, but it can also be the most enjoyable part of the contest for the audience. It is like watching Roman gladiators in hand-to-hand combat, only without the swords and tridents. When the top bodybuilders in the world begin to duel on a championship stage, the decibel reading in the auditorium goes right off the scale—and the more enthusiastic the cheering of the audience, the more inspired the bodybuilders become.

Many people don't realize it, but the posedown as we know it today came about because of a battle between Sergio Oliva and me at the 1970 Olympia in Columbus. Until that time the judges brought out the finalists and simply asked them to do certain set poses for direct comparison. That evening we were doing a double-biceps shot—one of my best poses—and

Sergio looked over at me and I suppose he began to feel outclassed. Suddenly, he turned one arm down into a triceps pose as if to say, The perfection of the arm is to have both triceps and biceps! I knew enough not to follow him. Instead, I switched to a side-chest pose, and then he hit the same shot. We kept this up, with the audience going crazy, and nobody could stop us for fifteen minutes. The M.C. realized how exciting it was and just let us go.

The important thing to remember is that improvisation requires an absolute command of each pose, an ability to move from one to another smoothly and gracefully. The only way to acquire this kind of skill—so that you appear just as competent and graceful during the posedown as you do performing your own routine—is by hard and constant practice.

Always remember the reason for the posedown—it's your chance to garner a few extra and maybe essential points. The judges are looking for the winner, the bodybuilder to whom they will each give a final placing, so it is important to act like a winner, to stand there confidently with a smile on your face, as if the whole thing was a piece of cake. The idea of competition, after all, is to try to win.

Tactics are all-important in a posedown. When the six top guys are standing out there together, nobody wants to be the first to hit a pose. If a

In a posedown, you go with your strengths. At the 1973 Mr. Olympia, Serge Nubret relied on his enormous chest, Franco Columbu on his amazing lats, and I on my superior definition with a variation of a most-muscular shot.

Doing your best in a posedown is often a matter of mastering defensive posing. You have to pay attention to what the other bodybuilders are doing onstage. Never hit the same pose as another competitor unless you are sure you look better doing it than he does. Unless you are another super-massive bodybuilder, you wouldn't trade mass shots with somebody as thick as Dorian Yates. Instead, when he poses his legs, do an upper body pose; if he poses from the front, turn and show the judges your back. On the other hand, if he does a pose in which you feel you definitely look better, jump in quickly and give the judges a chance to make the comparison. Here, Kevin Levrone, Dorian Yates, and Flex Wheeler show you just how it's done.

double biceps is called and you hit it first, the judges will look at you and then look at the others as they each hit the same shot. By the time the last competitor hits the pose you will be fading somewhat—you are always at your best when you hit the pose fresh—and you will suffer by comparison.

I sometimes did things like pretend that I was hitting the pose, making an upward move with my arms to make the others believe I was doing the pose so that they would go ahead and hit it. This way, when I actually flexed for the pose, I was the last and I had the judges' complete attention.

Another tactic is to move over in line next to the competitor you most want to beat or who you think is your toughest rival and let the judges compare you directly—making sure you hit shots that really make you look superior. I have sometimes done things like hit a biceps shot and pointed to the biceps, daring my opponents to hit the same shot.

Boxers trying to get in shape for a long fight frequently use several sparring partners in a row—two rounds with one, two rounds with the next, and then two more rounds with another fresh and rested opponent. Being that tired and boxing someone full of energy is much more difficult than going up against an opponent who is as tired as you are. To adapt this same technique to your posedown practice, try posing against a friend or training partner for five full minutes, then bring in somebody else and continue to pose against him. He'll be fresh and energetic, you'll be tired, but bodybuilding is much like other sports in that the real champions are the ones who can keep going and perform well even though they are fighting off exhaustion. And the only way to develop that capacity is by long, hard hours of practice.

COMMON POSING MISTAKES

To sum up, here are some of what I think are the most common mistakes made in posing:

- Not practicing enough or doing enough preparation.
- Failing to learn to do the poses correctly.
- Tensing up the face while posing.
- Looking worried or tired instead of energetic and confident.
- Flexing so hard the whole body shakes and quivers with the effort.
- Making a poor choice of poses for the individual posing routine.
- Choosing inappropriate music.
- Using too much or too little oil.
- Losing balance while posing.
- Doing poor transitions between posing.
- Letting yourself relax while standing at the back of the stage, forgetting the judges are still looking at you.

One important factor I haven't mentioned is something you do *before* you get onstage and that involves what you have to eat prior to a competition to make your muscles full, hard, and shapely so that they "pop" when you

The top champions have mastered the art of hitting the pose last, often to the frustration of the head judge. Although the pose called for is a back double biceps, Shawn Ray, Nasser El Sonbaty, and Dorian Yates are doing all sorts of preliminary moves before eventually executing the standard compulsory pose. But notice that even at this point each bodybuilder is still showing off aspects of his back development that are bound to impress the judges.

After my chest workout I would always hit the side-chest pose ten times from each side to really bring out the definition of the deltoids, inner and outer pectorals, and biceps. With Franco looking on, I knew he would tell me if I did the pose incorrectly.

pose. This "carbing-up" process is something we'll go into in more detail in the nutrition section starting on page 701.

CONTROLLING YOUR EMOTIONS

Another mistake that can make your posing less than it ought to be is to let yourself get too emotional. A big difference between acting and sports is that actors generally have to psych themselves up to do a scene, while athletes—subject to the pressures and stress of competition—have to psych themselves down, to keep their emotions under control. This doesn't mean you approach a contest without enthusiasm or intensity. Far from it. But a really competitive person will feel so much excitement and emotion that he can easily begin making bad decisions if those emotions are not controlled.

This need to control emotion exists in most sports. Archers and target shooters learn to quiet their minds and control their breathing. Boxers and martial artists are constantly warned not to let themselves get angry during a bout. Even football players have been described as playing with "controlled rage," the operative word here being "controlled." If your emotions get out of control, so does your performance.

Incidentally, one of the all-time greats at emotional control was Frank Zane. Few people seeing him onstage would ever guess how emotional he really is. He was always able to keep his cool and not get too caught up by the reactions of the audience. And although Dorian Yates often appeared to the audience as if he were unemotional and carved out of granite, he would never have won so many Mr. Olympia titles without being driven by a very intense, and emotional, desire for victory.

POSING AS EXERCISE

You will never be able to really refine every single muscle in the body just by training. Workouts tend to hit just the big muscle groups. But for the serratus, intercostals, and obliques, for extra chest, deltoids, thigh and biceps definition, the finishing touches are supplied by posing. And when I say posing I mean up *to four hours a day* in the weeks before a competition!

A basic physique is developed by training, but posing adds sharpness and quality. I have noticed time after time that many bodybuilders seem to be in their best shape a day or two after the competition. This is due, I am sure, to all the flexing and posing they had to do during the contest.

A bodybuilder who trains but never poses is like an uncut diamond—the quality is there potentially, but it cannot be seen. Just as the diamond cutter brings out the brilliance of the stone as he reveals first one facet and

After my biceps workout I would flex the biceps as hard as I could and hold the pose for a minute or so, which gave them extra height and hardness. At the same time, I tensed the chest and legs and held in the abdomen, just the way I would do the pose onstage.

Posing for Joe always ended up giving me a terrific workout, which helped increase my endurance, muscle control, and definition.

87

Photo sessions force you to pose hard and long under hot lights. This picture of Joe and me was taken at Jimmy Caruso's studio just before the 1975 Mr. Olympia.

then another, the bodybuilder sharpens and completes his physique by long, hard hours of posing practice. I learned this firsthand when I used to go over to Joe Weider's office and he would say, "Arnold, take off your shirt and let me see you pose." This annoyed me because I would start sweating; I just wasn't ready for this kind of exertion. But he would keep me posing for hours, forcing me to flex the serratus and keep the abdominals tense, until I was exhausted. He almost drove me out of my mind, but I would be so sore the next day that I soon realized the posing had actually been a terrific workout for parts of my body that my normal workouts apparently didn't touch.

I also made it a practice to have as many photo sessions as possible during the week before a contest. Standing under the lights, with the photographer making me hit pose after pose and holding them for long periods while he adjusted his camera and strobes ("Flex your legs," "Flex your abs," "Hold it!") was enormously tiring, and yet the next day I looked even better because of it. When I was working on *The Jayne Mansfield Story* I had to spend a full day posing in front of the cameras. I looked good in the studio, but the next day, after the hours and hours of flexing and going through my posing routine for the movie, I was in really top shape.

One of the reasons that posing (which is, after all, isometric contraction of the muscles) helps so much is that it works muscle areas that training frequently misses. You may stand in front of a mirror and flex your thighs, pectorals, or deltoids, but how often do you consider what lies in between these larger muscle groups? What posing does is tie those areas together and give the physique a truly finished look, the kind of polish that makes the difference between a good bodybuilder and a true champion. It exercises and stimulates all those in-between areas, the tie-ins, the minor but essential areas of the muscle structure.

So be certain, as your contest approaches, that you really hit the posing hard, not just to condition yourself for posing in prejudging, but to give you the ultimate definition and muscle separation that diet and training alone won't provide. It is really impossible for me to exaggerate how much time and effort it takes to be really prepared—in terms of doing the poses correctly, in regard to creating a smooth and graceful posing routine, and to what degree you can finish off and detail your physique by hours and hours of posing practice.

POSING FOR PHOTOGRAPHS

In many respects, preparing for a photo session is much the same as getting ready for a contest: You need to master the individual poses, choose the proper posing trunks, and get a good tan. However, the bodybuilder is dependent to a great deal on the skill of the photographer. Everyone will not have the benefit, as I had, of being photographed in my early career

Albert Busek lines up a photograph so that the nineteen-year-old Arnold looks huge in the foreground, dominating the "tiny" Alps in the background.

Here are two Albert Busek photos in which the camera angle is low so that the scenery in the background does not overpower my physique. This is how you can appear bigger than a mountain!

For this photo, Albert Busek and I took a boat far out on a lake so that the shoreline became distant and unobtrusive. We chose a time of day when the sun would be at about a 45-degree angle, to minimize harsh shadows.

by an Art Zeller, Jimmy Caruso, John Balik, or Albert Busek. Or of working today with Chris Lund, Ralph Dehaan, Bill Dobbins, Mike Neveux, or Robert Reiff. A top pro photographer will help you adjust your poses, make sure you are flexing properly from head to toe, and position you properly for the light. But if you are being shot by somebody not as experienced, *you* have to be sure that you keep all of these factors in mind if you want the best possible photographs.

The background is extremely important as to how a bodybuilder appears in a photograph. For example, when you pose with a huge building, a large bridge, or anything else big or confusing behind you, your body will tend to be dwarfed by the background and look smaller, unless the photographer is very careful in his choice of lenses and his composition. By studying many photographs I discovered that a neutral background, like the sea or sky, usually works the best for physique photography. Also, having huge mountains far in the distance can make you appear enormous.

Getting the right angle is also important. If the camera is pointing down, the body will look small. But if it is at waist level or below, and shooting upward, the physique looks that much taller and more massive.

This is a John Balik photo taken at "Muscle Rock," where so many great bodybuilders have been photographed. Again, the hills behind me are soft and distant and remain in the background.

The neutrality of the sky and beach make a good backdrop that does not compete for attention with my physique. The buildings in the background look small and insignificant. Notice, also, the lack of harsh shadows, since John Balik set up this session for late in the afternoon.

A foggy day at the beach, the fog providing a neutral background that really makes the body stand out. These shots would have been even more dramatic in color, since flat lighting allows for maximum color saturation.

If you shoot at the proper angle and the right time of day, the ocean can make a dramatic background. But when you stand in the bright sun like this, you need a deep tan to keep the light from washing out all your definition.

This is an example of how not to do it. Even though the photographer tried to leave the background out of focus, it is still so busy that it distracts from the figure in the foreground. The huge mountain also makes me look shorter and smaller than if I had been photographed against the sky.

Another example of a background that is too big, close, intrusive, and busy.

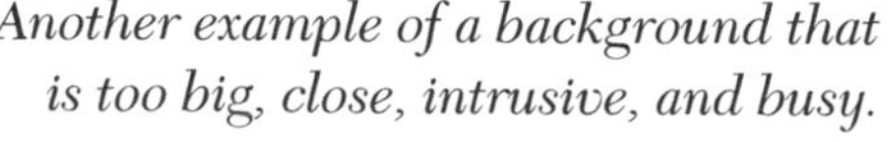

In this photo I am posing in the niche of a building to make myself look like a statue.

For outdoor shots, time of day is also vital. Around noon, the sun is straight overhead, which creates harsh and unflattering shadows. Your photos will look better if you do your photo sessions when the sun is close to a 45-degree angle, before nine or ten in the morning or later than three or four in the afternoon, depending on the time of year. Overcast days are generally better for color shots than black-and-white. A good photographer will often use fill-in flash or a reflector to get rid of the shadows under the eyes that can occur even when you are shooting at the right time of day.

The way your physique comes out on film is dependent to a large degree on the lens used. The longer the lens, the less distortion. With a wide-angle lens, you introduce curvature into the picture that can create an

Russ Warner liked to shoot against a white background, which made the body look huge and massive.

A black background, like this one used by Jimmy Caruso, is much more dramatic, making the body look harder and more defined.

unpleasant effect. In 35mm photography, unless you are looking for a special effect, never use a lens shorter than 50mm, and even then the photographer must be careful. You are much better being photographed with a 90mm or 135mm lens (or their equivalents in other formats), which makes distortion virtually impossible.

Sometimes, bodybuilders pose with props or in unusual locations, like Steve Reeves holding a discus or me holding the sword used in *Conan the Barbarian.* In doing this, care must be taken that the photo really works, that the props, buildings, or whatever is in the picture makes the physique look better rather than distracting from it.

Shooting in a studio is an art that requires an experienced professional. I have had young bodybuilders send me photos that were apparently done by studio photographers, but looked terrible—the poses were so awkward that it was evident the photographer had little knowledge of physique photography. There are many different approaches to studio physique photography. Russ Warner, for example, always liked to shoot against a white background. With the right lighting, this can make you look huge. However, the most dramatic results are achieved by using a black background—a favorite technique of veteran shooter Jimmy Caruso—which makes the muscles look even harder and more defined.

CHAPTER 2

Total Preparation

IT IS REALLY unfortunate to see a bodybuilder with a great physique, who has obviously paid his dues in the gym, posing beautifully onstage and then ruining the total effect because he has overlooked some detail of his presentation. The higher the level you reach in bodybuilding, the more competitive it becomes. And when a judge is comparing you to an equally good bodybuilder and having trouble deciding to whom to award the higher score, some minor aspect of your appearance may make the dif-

ference, such as your posing trunks, skin tone, skin color, haircut, or cleanliness.

Obviously, you can't win a contest purely on the basis of presentation. Bodybuilding, after all, is primarily about development of the body. But the overall impression you make on the judges is made up of more than just your muscles and conditioning, and anything that detracts from that appearance can cost you when the final scores are tallied.

POSING TRUNKS

It is important to choose the right posing trunks well before competition. If you wait until just a few days before the event you are taking a chance. You may have to search quite a while to find the ones you want, to order a pair through the mail, or even to have them specially tailored for you. Evaluate the color and texture of a particular pair of posing trunks, and have photos taken wearing them so you are absolutely sure they suit you in every way.

In the past, there was much more variation in the styles of posing trunks you'd see onstage than there is today. For example, bigger and more Herculean bodybuilders, such as Reg Park and I, wore trunks cut fuller than did leaner competitors such as Frank Zane. Today, virtually all the top bodybuilders wear very narrow-cut posing trunks, even the more massive physique competitors like Dorian Yates and Nasser El Sonbaty.

But even if trunks tend to be more of the same general style, there is still a big difference in how they are cut and how they fit. Some ride higher on the hips, some lower. Some are cut fuller in the back and others show more glute. So it is still important to be sure that the trunks you choose fit you well and show off your physique to your best advantage. For example, if you have powerful obliques, trunks that cut right across the bottom of these muscles are likely to make you look fat, as if there is fat hanging over them, while lower-cut trunks reveal the full extent of your muscular development in the area and make the entire waistline look extremely impressive.

hen I was an active competitor, bodybuilders wore a wide riety of differently styled posing suits—some wider or inner, with higher or lower waists, cut higher or lower on the les. Modern bodybuilders like Nasser El Sonbaty, Dorian tes, and Shawn Ray, on the other hand, wear suits that are uch more alike, even when their physiques are considerably fferent. However, there are still some differences, so be reful that the style and color of the suit you choose shows ur physique off to best advantage.

Frank Zane

Franco Columbu

Lou Ferrigno (left) and I, both of us having large, massive frames, looked much better in higher-cut posing trunks. Serge Nubret (center), on the other hand, with his narrow waist, could wear trunks cut much lower at the waist and higher at the leg.

The top of my posing trunks came to just about an inch below my obliques. Any higher, and they would have made the obliques look fat. Lower, and the cut would not have suited my body type.

Do you have long legs or short? Is your waistline long or short? Do you have a very small waist or are you somewhat thicker in the middle? Do you have a powerful, Herculean physique or one that is more slender and Apollonian? You need to take all these questions into account and choose the type of trunks that are appropriate to your individual physique.

I remember doing television commentary at a contest and seeing a competitor with a good physique, but who had high lats, high chest, and a very long waist. Unfortunately, he had chosen to wear very small, low-cut trunks, and this just exaggerated the length of his torso and made him look out of proportion. If he had chosen trunks that came up an inch or so higher they would have suited him much better and improved his appearance onstage.

Steve Reeves, for example, who is considered one of the most aesthetic bodybuilders of all time, had a very long waist and very narrow hips. He wore fuller posing trunks to bring his body into proportion. If he had worn narrower, lower-cut trunks they would have detracted considerably from the aesthetic impression he was able to make.

It is also important to choose the right color. There is no hard and fast rule on this, but depending on your build and skin tone one color trunks can make you look great while another might easily detract from your overall appearance. Deciding what color trunks are best for you is largely a matter of trial and error.

Try different colors, look at yourself in front of a mirror, have some photos taken, or ask the advice of friends. When you compete, look at photos of yourself taken onstage to see if you like the effect of the trunks you've chosen. Ask the judges for their opinion.

I always subscribed to the Reg Park theory of wearing dark brown trunks because I felt they didn't distract from the physique in the way colored trunks, or even black ones, might have done. Bill Pearl wore very theatrical trunks, powder blue and sparkling, through most of his career, and he could do that. But I noticed in his last few contests he wore darker ones, so perhaps he came to believe the same thing. Of course, I've seen bodybuilders who looked great in bright red trunks, but for others a bright red color makes their skin seem too red and ruddy, taking away from the quality of their tan. Again, you need to find out what works best for you.

Once you have determined the cut and color of the posing trunks you want to use, try to obtain several pairs so that you can put on fresh trunks after a long prejudging session and look your best for the evening show. It is also good to have extra trunks so that you can change for backstage photos or a picture-taking session the day after a competition. I always liked to have a variety of different-color trunks available, too, for photos taken against various colored backgrounds or outdoors.

A good tan helps to keep your definition from disappearing under the bright stage lights. These bodybuilders take the communal approach to catch a few rays.

TANNING

Look at photos of contests from the early days of bodybuilding and you'll see a lot of competitors standing onstage with virtually no tan. This is definitely not a good idea. When a light-skinned bodybuilder stands under the bright lights onstage the illumination tends to wash him out and makes it difficult for the judges to see his definition and development.

A good tan will keep this from happening. The skin tans to protect itself from the dangerous ultraviolet rays of the sun. When the skin is exposed to these rays, the melanin (skin pigment) which has remained from your last tan, but has faded, becomes dark again; this is why you can seem to tan after just one day in the sun but, in fact, your body has produced no new pigment to protect you. True tanning, during which new melanin is produced, takes considerably longer, a week to ten days, so it doesn't pay to stay out in the sun for long hours at a time trying to rush a tan.

It is best to tan in stages, twenty minutes to a half hour a day in the beginning, depending on your skin type, where you live, the time of year, and the altitude (the higher up you are, the stronger the ultraviolet rays). If you are fair-skinned and burn easily, you must take extra caution. But remember, even the darkest skin can be burned and damaged by the sun if the exposure is long enough. Experts advise us not to sunbathe between the hours of 10 A.M. and 2 P.M., when the rays of the sun are most intense (and can therefore do the most damage to the skin), but that is exactly the time when most people prefer to lie out in the sun. So let me just pass on the warning that excessive exposure to the sun tends to cause wrinkles and gives the skin a leathery look and that the sun's ultraviolet rays can cause skin cancer. Tanning, then, must be approached with a certain degree of moderation and care.

If you want to spend more time in the sun—a day at the beach, for example—and you have fair skin, I would recommend using some kind of sunscreen to cut down your overall exposure. As I said, you can only tan a little at a time; too much sun will simply cause you to burn and peel, and the damage that can be done to both health and appearance by overexposure to ultraviolet rays is all too well documented.

A lot of bodybuilders complain that they don't have the time or the patience to lie around in the sun for hours. But there are other ways. Franco and I used to go down to the weight pit in Venice (now christened the new "Muscle Beach") so we could work out and get some sun at the same time. World Gym there has an outdoor deck where you can train and tan simultaneously, and a number of gyms around the country have decks or rooftop facilities that allow you to do the same thing. When we worked laying bricks, Franco and I would take off our shirts in order to work on our tans as well. You don't always have to be doing only one thing at a time.

Even in Los Angeles, we don't always have enough sun to maintain a good tan. There are often a lot of clouds and fog along the coast. Some L.A. bodybuilders spend a lot of time in places like Palm Springs to soak up the desert sun. When I first came to California, we discovered you could go up in the mountains above the Malibu area and often be high enough to be in the sun looking down on the clouds below. This is where "Muscle Rock" is, where we used to go to do outdoor physique photography.

Tanning, by the way, is not just for fair-skinned bodybuilders. Most darker-skinned bodybuilders like African-Americans or Latinos find that spending at least some time tanning changes the skin texture and depth of tone and adds to their appearance onstage.

One aesthetic consideration is that you don't want your face to be darker than the rest of your body. But your face, and your nose in particular, tends to absorb a lot more sun. So take care to protect your face by wearing a hat or using a sunscreen to prevent your nose and forehead from getting burned.

TANNING PARLORS AND SUNLAMPS

Indoor tanning parlors have proliferated all over the country. You lie on a bed that is, in effect, a giant sunlamp, and you get your exposure in short, calculated doses. People generally consider tanning beds to be safer than exposure to the sun, but it is important to realize that any rays that can tan

Where I lived in Europe the sun wasn't intense enough for me to get a dark tan, whereas Dennis Tinerino had the advantage of a much hotter climate. As a result, he looks tan and defined, while I look white and appear smoother than I really was.

This photo was taken in Palm Springs in 1974. See how much more attractive, hard, and defined the physique looks with a dark tan.

you can also burn and damage your skin, so the same cautions apply to using suntan parlors as to lying out in the sun. Start slowly. Give your skin the time it needs to tan, and try to avoid burning and peeling, which not only make you look bad but also force you to start all over. Home sunlamps present the same dangers. Many people have burned themselves badly, even damaging their eyes, by remaining too long under a sunlamp.

ARTIFICIAL TANS

Using artificial coloring agents to deepen skin tone has become almost universal in bodybuilding. No matter how good your tan, a skin dye or bronzer can make it better. That's why hotels frequently despair when playing host to a group of bodybuilders. Their laundry rooms fill up with sheets and pillowcases covered with rubbed-off skin dye.

The use of artificial tans allows a bodybuilder with only a base tan to look as if he'd spent the summer in the tropics, and allows bodybuilders who are very fair-skinned and don't tan well at all to compete equally against those who are more blessed with melanin. This also has a health benefit, since the use of these coloring agents means that the competitors don't have to spend as much time in the sun as they once did. However, for fair-skinned bodybuilders, it's a mistake to try to get your *entire* tan from a bottle. Artificial tanning agents over totally pale skin tend to look very unnatural. The bodybuilding physique itself, with its exaggerated muscle development, looks very strange to many people in the first place. If you combine that with an odd unnatural-looking skin color, the final effect is very strange indeed. So I recommend that you get as good a tan as possible first and then increase its depth with the use of artificial agents.

The most often used coloring products are based on a product called Dy-O-Derm, a skin-dyeing product developed for individuals with severe skin problems. One of the more popular products based on Dy-O-Derm is Pro-Tan, available in gyms and by mail order. Another version of this type of dye, giving a slightly more bronze look, is Tan Now. These and other similar dyeing products are advertised in most of the physique magazines.

Skin dyes like these actually bind to the skin cells themselves and won't come off until the cells do—which takes about twenty-one days. After a few days you'll begin to see the color gradually flaking off, which gives an odd appearance unless you reapply some color. The best procedure for applying these products is to (1) shower and scrub off as much dead skin as possible, (2) apply a coat of the color, wearing rubber gloves to keep the palms of the hands from staining, (3) allow to dry for several hours, and (4) shower again to wash off the stain that has not actually bonded to the skin. This process should be done gradually over a period of days. Do not try to get a deep tan with only one application.

There are other types of artificial tan products that are more like a traditional bronzer than a dye. This type of coloring is easier to apply and fades fairly quickly, but doesn't give the same solid, deep look that the skin dyes do. Skin bronzers are available at most drug and cosmetic stores, and there is a version called Competition Tan by Jan Tana that is specially formulated for bodybuilders. Most bodybuilders don't use a bronzer by itself. Instead, they create a base color by tanning and applying a skin dye, and then use the bronzer-type coloring on top of this to create a finished look and to cover areas where the stain may have begun to flake off.

Applying color correctly is very important since it has a tremendous effect on your overall appearance. Some bodybuilders show up looking yellow onstage or so dark it looks as if they were covered with shoe polish. Others apply the coloring too late, or when they are perspiring, so that rivers of color run down their body onstage, spoiling the effect they are trying to create. Too much color on the face also creates a very strange and unattractive look, as does getting stain on the hands and feet, or too much on the knees and elbows. Remember, you spend years learning to train and months following a strict diet; it's worth some time and effort to learn to get your color correct or else you end up ruining all your other efforts.

Putting color on at the last minute can also be very dangerous. I remember one contest in which Lou Ferrigno applied a bronzer just before he went onstage, and with the oil on his skin and the amount he was sweating, the artificial tan ended up running down his body and totally spoiling his appearance. In some cases you can apply color at the last minute, but it takes a lot of experience and know-how to do it right. Which look would you rather have—being a little paler onstage than you'd like or having little streams of color running all down your body?

POSING OIL

Bodybuilders use oil onstage to highlight the shape of the body and bring out the full definition of the muscles. Intense lights have a tendency to flatten you out, and a light coat of oil along with a good tan allows the judges to fully appreciate your development. When you see a competitor standing onstage without enough oil you can immediately see that he looks flatter, less muscular, and much less interesting.

You need help to oil yourself completely—somebody to put oil on your back and tell you whether you have achieved an even application. In your early contests, you can generally find another competitor who will oil your back if you oil his. However, when you get into higher-level competition, you can never be sure that a rival won't play a trick on you. For example, at the 1975 Mr. Olympia contest in South Africa, I was oiled up and ready to go onstage and somebody said to me, "Only going to pose half your body, huh?" But I didn't get it until Ed Corney told me that only half of my back was oiled. I remember quite clearly who put the oil on me, but I won't mention any names. I'd been in enough contests so that I should have known not to trust any other competitor in that situation, but to double-check for myself in order to be sure.

Oil, like color, is often best applied in stages. When your skin is dry, especially if it is hot backstage, the first coat is likely to sink in fairly quickly. After a few minutes, add another coat and you'll begin to see the kind of effect you are seeking. Be careful of putting on last-minute color and oil one right after another, since this is almost guaranteed to make the color run.

You need to experiment to find the kind of oil that looks best for you. A product like baby oil is great for photo shoots, where the light is totally controlled, but generally makes you too shiny onstage. I've seen bodybuilders use everything from olive oil to Pam spray to oil up before a show, as well as various kinds of body oils and creams. Use experimentation and experience to see what works best for you. Just keep in mind that too much oil is as bad as too little. Having the lights glaring off your body as if you were a mirror is not going to gain you any advantage with the judges.

HAIRSTYLE

Hairstyles vary in bodybuilding just as they do in the rest of society. In the 1960s and 1970s there were bodybuilders who went with the then-current fashion of long hair. In the 1990s suddenly you saw a number of bodybuilders standing onstage with shaved heads. Neither extreme, in my opinion, is a particularly good idea for competition bodybuilders.

Now, let me make it clear that I understand how you wear your hair is part of *you*—part of your personality and self-expression. Fashions change and that includes fashions in hairstyles. I look at photos of extreme skiers with their spiked, multi-colored hair, guys who are really out there and who are really terrific athletes, but it's important to realize that *they are not judged in their sport on their appearance.* In the same regard, who cares how long a runner's hair is or whether a long jumper has a tattoo or words shaved into the side of his head? But the look, the visual element, is an essential part of bodybuilding, as it is, for example, in figure skating. Figure skaters also have to be extremely careful of what kind of appearance they present to the judges.

In bodybuilding, if your hair is long and shaggy, it not only comes down over your neck and obscures your traps, but also makes your head look bigger—and your body correspondingly smaller. The Afro haircut of the 1970s always seemed to me to do the same thing, making the head

Hair today, gone tomorrow. Bodybuilders long ago learned that shorter hair tends to make the body look more massive, but Shawn Ray illustrates the degree to which many bodybuilders during the nineties took this idea to its ultimate conclusion.

look bigger and the shoulders and upper body smaller in comparison. Compare photos of Robby Robinson as he looked in the 1970s with long hair with his appearance in the 1980s, wearing his hair shorter, and you'll see the difference.

As I said, bodybuilders appear so strange to people that anything that adds to that strangeness can be detrimental, making them look more like pro wrestlers than physique competitors. This includes dyeing the hair, shaving it off, or anything else you can do with hair. Of course, Tom Platz and later Lee Priest opted for a semi-long, slicked-back total blond look, which most of their fans approved of. Some bodybuilders look good with shaved heads. But I've seen competitors at the Arnold Classic in Columbus whose strange tastes in hair styling, or the lack of it, did not do them any good with the judges. The idea is to present yourself onstage in a way that works best for you. You should avoid copying someone you admire or following a particular fashion unless the look you arrive at suits your particular physique and overall appearance.

How, then, do you decide about hairstyle? Study your haircut in the mirror, look at photos, and decide whether you would present a better appearance with longer or shorter hair, or hair cut in a different style. Think about it—is having your name shaved into the side of your head really going to help you win contests? Is wearing a ponytail or a Mohawk going to add to or detract from the overall impression you make on the judges? The bottom line to all of this is simple: Is what I am doing with my appearance, color, haircut, or trunks going to help me win this contest or not?

Also, don't shy away from getting help from professionals. In my movies, I rely a great deal on hairstylists to help me create the character I'm playing. In *Commando* and *Predator,* playing tough soldiers, I wore my hair in a kind of macho brush cut. For *Twins,* director Ivan Reitman wanted to soften my look, so he had my hair lightened, which he felt suited the character. So by all means try working with a hairstylist, maybe wear your hair a number of different ways over time, until you find the style that suits you best.

BODY HAIR

Another means bodybuilders use to improve their appearance is to shave off their body hair prior to a contest. This gives the skin a much smoother and cleaner appearance, and makes the muscles more visible. The simplest way to do this is just with a regular safety razor, carefully going over the chest, arms, and legs, anywhere you want to get rid of hair. It feels funny to be shaved like this, and it takes getting used to. For one thing, it always made me feel smaller and lighter, and that can be a psychological disadvantage going into a contest until you get used to it.

Therefore, I don't recommend that you shave just before a contest. Instead, try shaving a couple of weeks prior to the competition and then giving yourself periodic touch-ups. This way, if you should cut yourself or irritate your skin, there will be plenty of time for your skin to heal and return to normal. Franco Columbu always had an odd approach to removing body hair: He didn't like to shave, so some time before any contest he would begin pulling out body hair with his fingers! By the time he was ready to shave, there was very little hair left. This is not a method I would generally recommend, to say the least.

DRESSING FOR SUCCESS

In the past few years, there has been a press conference held in association with the Mr. Olympia contest and all the competitors attended wearing suits and ties. I think this is a very good idea. In the early days of bodybuilding, the stars of the sport didn't go around wearing multicolored baggy, obnoxious "clown pants" as they have been called. John Grimek, Steve Reeves, Reg Park, Bill Pearl, Larry Scott, and others knew how to dress. They wore suits, casual pants, and sports shirts and generally managed to look like solid citizens rather than gym rats. Sergio Oliva had short-sleeve shirts specially tailored with a V cut into the sleeve to accommodate his gigantic arms.

Bodybuilding contests are won and lost onstage, of course, but making a good impression on the judges and other bodybuilding officials can certainly help when things get close. And since bodybuilders make a good part of their living doing seminars and guest appearances, being respected and well thought of certainly isn't going to hurt. You don't have to go around in a tuxedo all the time, but check out what kind of nice-looking, classy sweats somebody like Michael Jordan wears. Be aware that how you dress and comport yourself can convey the impression for the entire weekend that you are a winner, the kind of person who is a good representative for the sport of bodybuilding.

FINISHING TOUCHES

Really good bodybuilders leave nothing to chance onstage. Many wear something on their feet backstage so that when they come out to pose, their soles will not be dirty. Others bring several changes of posing trunks and change whenever their trunks become soiled with coloring, sweat, or oil.

One simple factor often overlooked in terms of hair, and other aspects of personal appearance as well, is basic hygiene. Steve Reeves, the first really famous modern bodybuilding champion, was known for his immaculate personal hygiene—his hair was always clean and cut well, his fingernails immaculate, his grooming impeccable. Go backstage at many contests and you'll see competitors who need to learn this lesson and who throw away success for lack of nothing more than personal grooming and cleanliness.

CHAPTER 3

Competition Strategy and Tactics

TACTICS IN BODYBUILDING involve everything we've talked about so far—learning to pose, practicing your posing, choosing the right music, the right color and style of posing trunks, and working on getting a great tan. Tactics are also about what you do the day before the contest, and the morning of the contest, everything that will guarantee you are able to make your best showing onstage.

Strategy, on the other hand, is how you plan and conduct your overall bodybuilding career, including when to compete and in which contests, and how to handle things like publicity and public relations.

The ultimate goal for serious bodybuilders is, of course, getting into competition. Some bodybuilders like to jump right in and get their feet wet. The possibility of making a poor showing in a contest doesn't discourage them. They just chalk it up to experience. Others prefer to bide their time and not compete until they have a chance of finishing with a high placing. They plan their strategy like a good boxing manager who brings his fighters along slowly, making sure they don't get into contests in which they are overmatched.

I started at a young age, was a fast developer, and was able to begin competing fairly early, moving up quickly to the level of Junior Mr. Europe, Best Built Man in Europe, Mr. Europe, and even Mr. Universe. There have been other bodybuilders who achieved early success. In the 1970s, Casey Viator was one of these, winning the AAU Mr. America title in 1971 at age nineteen. Australia's Lee Priest was able to qualify as a professional in his early twenties. A few bodybuilders have waited until they were considerably older, but then rose quickly. Canadian Paul Dillett was able to qualify as a

This was the shape I was in when I entered my first bodybuilding contest.

pro after only his second contest. Police officer and pro bodybuilder Ronnie Coleman, who didn't even start training for bodybuilding until his late twenties, won the World Amateur Bodybuilding Championships just two years after making up his mind to be a physique competitor.

How quickly you develop is a matter of genetics and how young you start training. But what kind of athletic training you had before becoming a bodybuilder is also a factor. Ronnie Coleman had done some kind of weight training ever since he was a teenager and had also done some serious powerlifting. So he wasn't really starting from scratch when he decided to get into bodybuilding. Franco Columbu, who also started bodybuilding late, was a powerlifter. Some athletes walk into a bodybuilding gym after years of playing football or doing some other sport that calls for being strong and for which you train for additional strength. For these individuals, building muscle is seldom a problem; their challenge is to create physiques that are aesthetic as well as muscular.

It is also a fact that most bodybuilders will never make it up to the pro ranks, many of them will not even win national shows, just as most basketball players don't make it to the NBA and most football players to the NFL. But to a dedicated athlete competition on any level can be exciting. All that counts is that the competitors be more or less evenly matched and then fight it out to see who will win. As long as you're competing at the highest level you're capable of (whatever that is) the stakes are always the same—as they say on television, the thrill of victory and the agony of defeat.

THE ROLE OF EXPERIENCE

Whenever you decide to compete, you have to start somewhere. And it is only by competing that you gain the experience necessary to compete successfully. Bodybuilding involves two different kinds of activities—training in the gym and competing onstage. Being good at one doesn't automatically mean you are good at the other. Even if you've worked very hard on your posing, practicing posing in front of a mirror is not the same as posing onstage, under pressure, in front of the judges and the audience.

Some bodybuilders have a more intuitive sense of how to behave onstage, but everyone needs *experience* in order to perfect their stage presentation. For example, we've already seen how much experience Frank Zane had before he became Mr. Olympia. That's why, at the 1979 Mr. Olympia, during the final posedown between Frank Zane and Mike Mentzer, Frank's stage presence and experience were immediately obvious, while it was equally obvious that Mike, who had previously been in only a handful of shows, was struggling to keep his presentation together under such intense pressure.

As a matter of fact, it seemed to me as I watched that Mentzer quickly became too fatigued to hold his waist in. As a result, he lost control of his abs and let them bulge out too much. Boxers know that sparring is much less tiring than actually fighting in the ring. In bodybuilding as well, the tension and stress of posing onstage make you tire much more quickly than happens when you are just practicing.

We've already seen an example of the problems that arise from lack of experience in the career of gargantuan Paul Dillett. As I've already pointed out, Dillett waited a long time before entering his first contest, the IFBB North American Championships. He finished second, won the same show the following year, and became a pro with the experience of only two contests behind him. However, his subsequent problems with posing and stage presentation were most probably the result of his lack of contest experience.

HOW OFTEN TO COMPETE

So experience is obviously important, and I recommend getting into competition relatively quickly. But it is impossible to prepare for competition and make the same kinds of gains as you would if you were training with full intensity and not dieting. When you're training to compete, you have to focus on details, bringing out small muscles, separation. And it's obvious that you can't make maximum gains while you are restricting your food intake. This is a dilemma that bodybuilders, especially young amateurs, have to deal with. Which is more important, gaining contest experience or continuing to focus on maximum development? This is where strategy comes in, deciding at what point to start competing and then deciding how often you can compete and still make gains. There are no hard and fast rules about this. It's always a judgment call. You'll need to set your own priorities, experiment, and see what works for you.

GETTING YOUR FEET WET

Knowing when and where you are going to compete really focuses your energies. Just the possibility of standing onstage looking bad and making a fool of yourself because you didn't train or diet hard enough should be enough to motivate you to do those few extra sets and reps, and to stay with the discipline of a strict diet. No matter how hard you train, the reality of having a fixed competition date ahead of you is bound to raise your intensity a few extra notches.

When it comes to competing, you have to start somewhere. So don't be surprised if, the first time you step out onstage, you go completely blank. I've seen young bodybuilders come out forgetting to take off their glasses or still wearing the slippers they put on to keep their feet clean backstage. With inexperienced competitors, when the judge says "quarter turn to the right" they may go right, left, or just stand there looking confused. And hitting the compulsory poses correctly in the gym or at home in front of a mirror is very different from doing the same thing onstage in full view of the judges and audience. You hit a front double biceps and forget to flex your legs. The judge calls for a back lat spread and for a moment you can't remember how that pose is done. You get tired so much faster than you expected you're afraid you won't make it through prejudging. And if your prep hasn't been perfect, you are likely to start cramping from the effort.

Under the lights, whether or not you have adequately prepared as we discussed in the previous chapter becomes very evident—whether your tan is right or not, or if you've put on the right amount of oil. Those posing trunks looked fine backstage, but how do they look out there in the middle of competition? Did you get skin dye all over them? Or too much on your elbows and hands? And this is the time when how well you've practiced your posing is revealed. Are you shaking with nervousness? Are you hitting the poses with grace and authority? Can you remember the routine all the way through?

Of course, experience really benefits you only if you learn from it. So it's important that you are honest with yourself about what you did right or wrong in any contest. I also have always felt that you can learn more from a contest, win or lose, if you talk to the judges and get some feedback as to what you were doing right or not doing right. For example, even though I won in 1972 against Sergio Oliva, one of the judges came up to me and said, "I voted for you, but I almost didn't because when you turned around and did a back pose, you leaned back so far it created a crease in the lower back that looked like fat." But in those days, the judges could get up and walk around you, and when he did this he could see I was not fat. But I took the hint and didn't lean back so much in my next contest. In the same way, every bodybuilder should make sure he learns from every competition in every way he can. Learning from experience means you don't have to continue to make the same mistakes over and over.

ADVANCED COMPETITION

Once you have gained some experience and have proved yourself a good enough bodybuilder to win small contests, you now have to begin to choose competitions on the basis of what they mean to your career.

I have been asked a number of times by amateurs who've won titles that qualify them to compete in the Mr. Olympia whether or not they should go to the show or wait until later. Certainly, you can't expect to go from the amateurs into the Olympia and do very well. In fact, there has been a time when a Mr. Universe winner has gone on right away to the Mr. O. and finished dead last! On the other hand, you really have nothing to lose since nobody is expecting anything from you. You can go into the contest for the experience without caring too much where you place, in the same way that it really helped Tiger Woods to have competed as an amateur in the U.S. Open, and gotten used to the pressure, once he finally decided to turn pro.

On the other hand, Franco Columbu is a good example of somebody who was able to get into high-level bodybuilding competition very quickly and to be successful. Franco decided to go into bodybuilding after competing before only in powerlifting. He did bodybuilding training intensely for a year, entered the Mr. Italy contest, and won by a point. Then he went to the Mr. Europe contest and won that. A year later he competed against Chuck Sipes at the Mr. Universe and won that. Of course, Franco already had a tremendous physique before he started bodybuilding and was immensely strong—doing 10 sets of 25 Chin-Ups, for example—so he was hardly starting from scratch.

However, while you should think twice about jumping into competition, you also have to be careful not to stay out of shows you really should enter. For example, Tom Platz finished third in the 1981 Olympia and impressed a lot of people. The next pro contest on the schedule was the Professional Mr. Universe in Australia, but instead of entering it he decided to spend his time doing seminars and exhibitions. Subsequently, the Pro Universe was won by Dennis Tinerino, whom Tom had defeated handily at the Olympia. If Tom had gone into that contest, he most probably would have won another international title and furthered the momentum of his career.

Lou Ferrigno made a smart move entering the Mr. Universe contest twice (and winning). But in 1974, a year he could probably have won the Professional Mr. Universe contest, he entered the Mr. Olympia instead and lost. There is nothing wrong with losing a competition, but if you have a choice of two contests it makes sense to enter the one you can win. At whatever level you're competing, realizing that certain contests may be over your head and choosing one that you have a better chance of winning is no disgrace—just good sense.

This is where strategy comes in—deciding where to compete, when to compete, and being aware whom you will be competing against, or whether to enter only one contest or two in a row. In amateur competition in the United States, bodybuilders want to win the Nationals because all of the class winners are eligible to turn pro, while at the USA only the overall winner becomes a professional. But the USA takes place several months before the Nationals. So if a competitor waits and takes his chances at the Nationals and loses, there are no other opportunities to win a national event and turn pro that year. Entering the USA and then going on to the Nationals gives a bodybuilder two chances to win a national title, but training and dieting for the USA and then having a relatively short time to try to get in shape again for the Nationals can be a difficult task. Again, it's a judgment call and each bodybuilder has to plan his own strategy based on his own feelings and individual priorities.

Of course, being eligible to turn pro and doing well in pro competition are two different things. I remember how difficult it was for even highly talented bodybuilders like Mike Christian and Shawn Ray to make the transition; it took something like two years for both to adjust to the higher standards and greater pressures of the pro ranks. In his first year as a pro Lee Haney lost the Swiss Grand Prix in Zurich to a bodybuilder who weighed only about 169 pounds! This transition is not as difficult for everyone—Dorian Yates certainly managed to take the pro ranks by storm—but it tends to happen more often than not.

With this in mind, a bodybuilder who wins a pro qualifier should be very careful about what professional contest to enter. There are professional Grand Prix events that are a good way to get your feet wet. The Ironman Invitational is another good introductory pro contest. The next step up would be something like the Night of Champions, held each year in New York. If you do well in shows like this you are likely to earn an invitation to the Arnold Classic, and this will give you an idea of how well you can do against Mr. Olympia–level competitors. If you are successful in the Night of Champions or the Arnold Classic, this indicates you may be ready for the ultimate challenge of the Mr. Olympia.

Momentum is important in any sports career, and bodybuilding is no exception. Winning can become a habit if you handle your career properly. But remember, you can't win if you're too afraid to lose. Being scared of losing makes you think like a loser; it inhibits you and robs you of energy. Make a reasonable decision as to what you ought to do, and then go for it without reservation; give it your all, and let the chips fall where they may. In my career, I didn't lose very often, but I did lose. That's what sport is all about. All you can do is your best, and if that isn't enough, that's just the way it goes.

Olympic decathlon champion Bruce Jenner once told me that he was so concerned about losing prior to the 1976 Olympics that his performance suffered badly. But then the simple thought occurred to him that if you lose, you don't die. You just lose, you're unhappy, and then you get on with it. If you have an all-out, positive attitude, confidence in your own ability, and massive enthusiasm, you can handle losing; it ceases to be anything you have to worry about. Which means you can concentrate on winning, which is the name of the game.

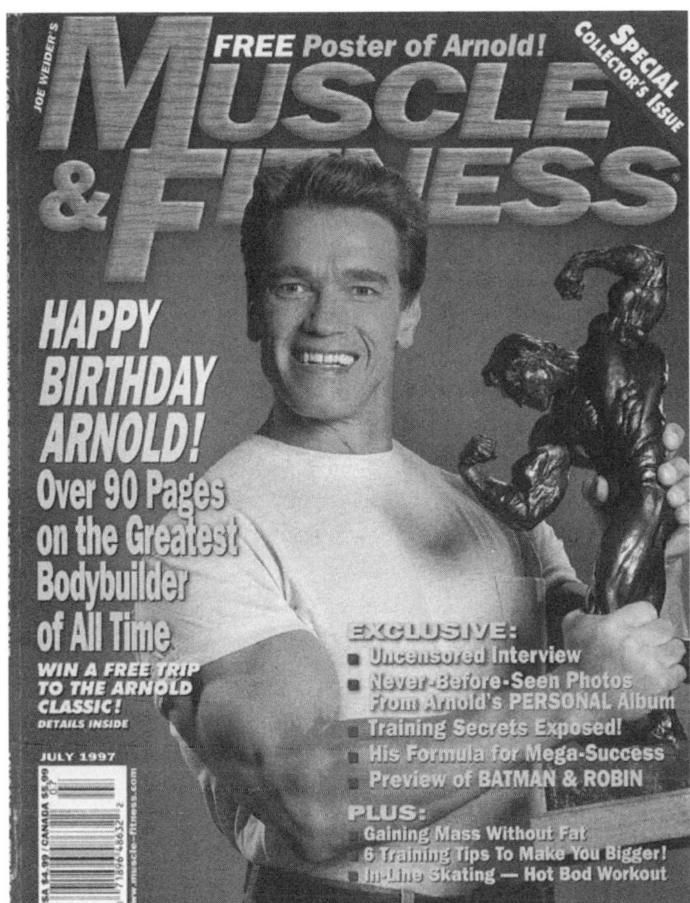

PUBLICITY

"I can't possibly win that contest," bodybuilders are all too likely to complain. "I just haven't gotten enough publicity in the magazines." Getting the right kind of publicity is a great asset to a successful bodybuilding career. And the easiest way to garner publicity is to win contests! But there are other ways as well. Simply being available for pictures and interviews is very important. Some bodybuilders fly in on Thursday for a contest and are out of there Sunday morning, with no time given to working with the magazine photographers. Some bodybuilders go to photo shoots and immediately start to complain that they're too tired, they're being worked too hard, while others are dying for the chance to do the photos they've been chosen for. That can make a big difference when the photographers decide whom to shoot next time. A lot of bodybuilders schedule shoots or interviews and don't show up. That is extremely destructive to a bodybuilding career.

Reporters for the magazines will call your hotel room at contests or try to talk to you backstage. Sometimes this can be distracting, but if you can possibly find the time and energy to talk to them, do it. After all, staff writers get paid whether or not they interview you, so getting the interview on tape is more beneficial to you than it is to them.

Many bodybuilders simply wait around for the magazines to come to them, but I always took the initiative and sent articles on my training methods, stories about my feelings and ideas about bodybuilding and life in general to various publications. I never worried about getting paid for articles or a cover shot. I figured that the more the judges and people got to know and like me, to understand who I was and what I was about, the better chance I had for a successful career.

Publicity can ensure that you are noticed for call-outs at a contest. But it can be a double-edged sword as well. If a magazine starts hyping you too much before a contest, the judges and audience are likely to be expecting to see King Kong step out onstage. So be careful of too much hyperbole when it comes to magazine coverage. And remember, when Dorian Yates showed up at the Night of Champions and took the title, nobody really had any expectations about him at all. He hadn't gotten much publicity. He let his physique do the talking and that's all that was needed.

Of course, seeing is a complex process, and if the judges don't really know much about how you look it is easy for them to overlook your best qualities on a crowded bodybuilding stage. Publicity helps the judges become familiar with the particular qualities of your physique. They don't have to study you for long periods onstage to know that you have, for example, good lats or fantastic calves. They already know this, so they just check you over quickly, confirm their expectations, and then go on to examine others and see if they measure up to you.

Some people seem to generate more publicity than others without really trying. When I was training and running a gym in Munich, I did a picture story for a magazine in which I walked around the city in my posing trunks during a snowstorm and was photographed window-shopping, in front of the train station, and so on. This was clearly manufactured publicity, the kind Hollywood was once famous for—a publicity stunt. But it was done for *Stern* magazine, with a readership of millions, and this was my way of bringing bodybuilding to the general public. To get into this kind of magazine, you need to so something highly unusual. Publicity in bodybuilding magazines is quite a different matter.

When I went to London for the Mr. Universe contest I had no need for such stunts. I was young, huge, and relatively unknown—the European contender who came out of nowhere. I just seemed to attract attention and publicity without even trying. I've seen a lot of other bodybuilders who simply have a flair for publicity. They are "promotable," and the magazines and audiences love to hear about them. Franco was always like that, and so was Frank Zane, even though he seemed quiet and reserved. Shawn Ray and Flex Wheeler have done as many magazine layouts as anybody, but so did Mike Matarazzo. In spite of not having the same kind of winning record, he was extremely popular with the fans and made himself available for shoots. Dennis Newman, before his career was interrupted by illness, was on his way to becoming the new Steve Reeves—big, muscular, aesthetic, and good-looking. A magazine publisher's dream.

Publicity is also a great way to gain an edge in a contest, but is even more important when it comes to capitalizing on victory. It used to be that the winner of the Mr. America contest would be featured all the following year in Bob Hoffman's magazines with personality profiles and training instructions. This helped to indelibly impress the winner's name on the public's consciousness. Nowadays, winners of the major amateur contests and pro shows are usually sought out by Joe Weider's magazines as well as the other physique publications. Not every bodybuilder is prepared to take advantage of this opportunity. There have been some champions from Europe I have had to beg to fly over to the United States for interviews and photo shoots.

When you *don't* win a contest, publicity is still important. You want to keep yourself in the public eye following a show as much as you can. After all, more money is made in things like guest posing and seminars than in contest winnings. Disappointed bodybuilders who finish second or third, and think they should have won, are only cutting their own throats by disappearing and not making themselves available for publicity. Of course, publicity is just one factor in a bodybuilding career, although it is an important one. Publicity won't win you a contest, but it could help in a close decision. And if you are contemplating going on to a professional career, publicity is a great help when it comes to booking seminars and exhibitions or selling mail-order products.

Just keep in mind that the magazines need interesting bodybuilders to feature in their pages. So if you are good, if you do well in contests and make yourself available, you'll get publicity. The trick, then, is to live up to the publicity you get, and that can be even more difficult than getting the coverage in the first place!

POLITICS AND PUBLIC RELATIONS

Some bodybuilders who are disappointed by poor showings in contests feel that somehow "politics" are to blame—that certain competitors are taking advantage of relationships with judges or officials to place higher than they deserve. On the one hand, this kind of feeling is totally understandable: When you are a bodybuilder, it is you—your own body—that is being judged, and when you don't do well the blow to your ego can be tremendous. Not only that: By the time a bodybuilder is ready for a competition he has undergone months of strenuous training and diet and then is put under the additional strain of the contest itself, at a time when he is most vulnerable emotionally. Nonetheless, as understandable as this view is, the idea that politics are what get you ahead in bodybuilding, or that friendly relations between the individuals involved in the bodybuilding world is somehow bad, is just not true.

Politics are simply the way human beings get together and regulate their behavior and the behavior of the institutions in which they are involved. Without political interaction, nothing gets done. Politics are a fact of life. And judges, contest officials, and bodybuilding federation administrators are just as human as anybody else, so there are bound to be certain political considerations in any contest, no matter how honest and ethical the officials involved may be.

I have been a promoter as well as a competitor, and I can tell you that the accusations of wrongdoing that come about when certain bodybuilders do badly in contests and have to salve their egos usually have little or no basis in truth. Bodybuilding is not perfect, but the judging in the sport is remarkably accurate. I can certainly attest firsthand to the integrity of the contests I put on with Jim Lorimer in Columbus. Nor have I seen more than an occasional problem in all the contests I have entered or been present at as a spectator. Bodybuilding is the same as any other sport: The best man should win, without regard to any outside factors. And all of us should strive to see that this rule is enforced no matter what.

Nonetheless, a lot of political considerations do play a part in bodybuilding, falling under the heading of what I would simply call public relations. Judging a bodybuilding contest is a subjective, imperfect process. Remember, in most of the famous victories in bodybuilding history (including the battles between Sergio Oliva and me) the margin of winning was frequently no more than a point or two. And when it comes down to a close decision, especially one in which the bodybuilders involved are so evenly matched that it becomes extremely difficult for a judge to decide who is the better man on strictly objective grounds, what he thinks of the competitors is likely to play a large, if only subconscious, part in determining the final outcome.

Maintaining good relations with bodybuilding judges is not a way of getting extra points; it is a way of ensuring that you won't lose points because of any unconscious hostility on the part of one judge or another. It's simply a way of making sure that you get all the points coming to you. Unfortunately, many bodybuilders seem to go out of their way to damage their careers by their behavior toward the judges. Competitors have been known to throw their trophies around backstage or even come out onstage and insult the judges in public. I once saw a competitor get very upset about the judging and say all kinds of things onstage. An hour later he had cooled off and regretted his outburst. He sent letters of apology and tried to make up for his behavior. In the next Mr. America contest he lost, and I believe he lost partially for that reason. So it pays to keep control of your temper, to behave like a sportsman, and not to attack the judges in public.

Certainly, gentlemen like John Grimek, Steve Reeves, Bill Pearl, Reg Park, Larry Scott, Frank Zane, and Lee Haney would never have behaved that way.

LEARNING TO PEAK FOR COMPETITION

A good bodybuilder plans his competition strategy the way a successful general conducts a military campaign. You need to choose the right time and place to do battle, to be certain that your army (your physique) is well trained and ready. You need to be confident of your battle tactics, know when to attack, when to withdraw, and how to conserve ammunition (energy) so that it lasts until the end of the conflict.

But many bodybuilders with fantastic physiques, who have a thorough grasp of preparation, posing, and everything else, come up short because their strategy fails in one significant area: They are not at their absolute best on the day of the competition.

A bodybuilding contest is about who is the best *bodybuilder on that particular stage on that particular day.* Who is potentially the best, or who is best most of the time, should have nothing to do with it. You may be great the day before the contest or the day after, but unless you can time your preparation so that you peak on the very day of the competition you are going to be constantly disappointed.

Peaking for a competition is a matter of experience and careful timing. Each individual has to find out exactly how to manipulate his own diet and training to be able to come into a contest in absolutely top shape. However, there are certain general techniques that are very useful. Until 1970, I came into contests just a little off—peaking a bit too early, getting into my best shape a few days after the competition. But then, quite by accident, I discovered how to come in just right the day of the show.

In the 1970 NABBA Mr. Universe contest in London, I was again a little off—too smooth—but I was the best one there, so I won. The next day I went to Columbus for the Mr. World contest. I had lost to Sergio in the Olympia the year before, and I was determined to avenge myself in this contest.

When I arrived in Columbus, only a day after the London show, I was cut, hard, and in the best shape of my life, and I began to wonder why. I realized it was more because I had competed such a short time before and then posed for photographs afterward. The effort of all this posing left me in better shape than I was before the contest. Competition, in other words, turned out to be a great way to get in shape *for* competition.

I beat Sergio for Mr. World in Columbus and then got ready to compete again the next week at the Mr. Olympia contest. I felt too light and skinny, too depleted from two contests right in a row, so many hours of posing after so much dieting, so I ate a little carrot cake every day, had four or five good meals, and trained a little less. By the time of the competition I found I had all of the definition I had had at the Mr. World, and all of the size I had had at the NABBA Mr. Universe!

This taught me a lesson: If I got so much better a week after a competition, why not aim for getting into contest shape *a full week before the contest?* Spend that pre-contest Saturday posing like crazy all day, hitting all sorts of shots, just as if I were performing in the contest. Then have photos taken all day Sunday, which means a lot more posing, and from Monday to Wednesday train well (minimum of fifteen sets per body part), eat well, but not excessively, and rest on Thursday and Friday, except for continued posing practice.

Most young bodybuilders do it quite differently. They diet right up until a day or two before the contest (or even until Saturday morning, in the worst cases), and then stuff themselves full of carbohydrates just before the competition. I know from experience this doesn't work. One explanation is that muscle size depends not only on the quantity of muscle

These "before and after" photos were taken about eighteen days apart, two or three months before a competition. I marked the earlier photos to pinpoint weak areas I wanted to improve. Biceps before . . .

. . . and after

Thighs before . . . *. . . and after*

Triceps before . . . *. . . and after*

tissue present, but also on carbohydrate energy stored in the muscles in the form of glycogen (see Contest Diet Strategies, page 748). When the glycogen is depleted, the muscles get flat. It takes at least three full days for your body to completely restock its glycogen supply once it is exhausted (or longer: The time varies somewhat with the individual!). So dieting hard right up to the contest leaves you too little time to replenish the glycogen, and eating excessive carbohydrate simply raises your blood sugar level precipitately and leads to excess water retention. How many times have you heard a bodybuilder complain about coming into a contest both flat and puffy? This may well be one explanation, and it's also why my improvisational approach to contest preparation paid off.

Any last-minute experimentation before an important contest can be a disaster. The day before a contest, after months of discipline and preparation, what you need most is patience—and few bodybuilders have it. So they try to do something extra and get totally screwed up. This can even happen with experienced bodybuilders. At the 1981 Olympia, one competitor tried a special liquid "sensitizer" to help him tan and ended up with burned and peeling skin; another who had been in competition fifteen years suddenly decided to try a diuretic, which he had never used before, and got terrible cramps during prejudging.

I believe in simply sticking to the essentials. The more special requirements you have, the more that can go wrong and upset you. Sergio used to show up at a contest with his posing trunks under his clothes. He would just undress, oil up, and be ready to go. The only extra thing he brought along was a long white butcher's coat he wore backstage while pumping up.

For other bodybuilders a more complex approach seems to work better. Frank Zane, for example, always paid close attention to every single detail. He checked out his dressing room to make sure it was suitable and provided enough space. He had everything he needed, including somebody to help him pump up and oil up. Frequently, that someone was his wife, Christine, who was a great asset to him throughout his career. Zane even went so far in the 1979 Olympia as to have his own trailer parked outside the auditorium, giving him a place to pump up in total privacy, which helped to psych out his opposition. In similar circumstances, I have arranged to have dumbbells available in a separate room so that I could pump up in privacy.

WATER

Another concern bodybuilders have is holding water—that is, retaining water under the skin, which destroys definition. To prevent this from happening, many competitors begin to severely restrict their water intake days (or even weeks) before the show. They avoid sodium. They take large amounts of potassium. And many resort to the use of diuretics.

The problem with this approach is that muscles are more than 75 percent water, so dehydrating yourself will only flatten out your muscles and make you smooth. The best way to increase water retention is to dehydrate yourself because when the body senses you aren't taking in enough water it holds on tightly to what it has. Excess sodium is normally washed out of the body with the water you excrete, so restricting this cycle simply means any sodium in your body will be retained, resulting in even more water retention. If you don't take in enough sodium you risk ruining your electrolyte balance, which can cause muscle cramping. Large amounts of potassium, especially when your sodium is low, can lead to problems like upset stomach or worse. And diuretics, which pull more water out of the body, just create a worse condition of dehydration.

What should you do instead? First, allow yourself a normal intake of sodium. Don't salt your food, but don't avoid natural sodium either. Then, drink plenty of water right up until Friday night before a Saturday contest. Any excess water will cycle out of your body, taking excess sodium with it. That evening, simply cut your water intake in half. Some time will pass before your system realizes that water intake has been restricted and you will continue to eliminate water at the same rate, losing far more than you are taking in. The next morning, before prejudging, make sure you keep drinking to prevent dehydration. But between this semi-restriction of fluids, plus your increased carbohydrate ingestion (which pulls water into the cells when it is stored as muscle glycogen), you should find that there is little subcutaneous water in evidence.

Afraid to try this? Think of what goes on in modern bodybuilding contests. During prejudging expediters backstage are standing by with water bottles, and competitors frequently go to the rear of the stage and drink water by the liter. Do they think there is some special mechanism in the body that somehow knows that prejudging has started and therefore will process the water differently? If not, why not drink the water *before* prejudging starts rather than waiting until you're out there in full view of the judges and audience? If water is okay during prejudging, it's okay before, so control your subcutaneous water rather than trying to dehydrate and you'll be that much harder, more muscular, and less likely to feel weak or to cramp.

While low-sodium water is acceptable, distilled water is not. Distilled water is good for batteries—and cigar humidors—but it's lack of necessary minerals is not good for the human body, especially one about to undergo the stress of the bodybuilding contest.

THE DAY OF THE CONTEST

On the day of the contest, you don't want any surprises. Every detail counts. For example, how are the lights set up onstage? As a producer, I know there are areas onstage with strong light and others where the light is weaker. Therefore, it pays to check out the stage lighting so you know where to stand and where not to stand during the contest. The angle at which the light hits you is also important. If the angle is steep, you have to be very careful not to bend forward too far when you do your poses or all

Doing a set of towel pulls for the lats

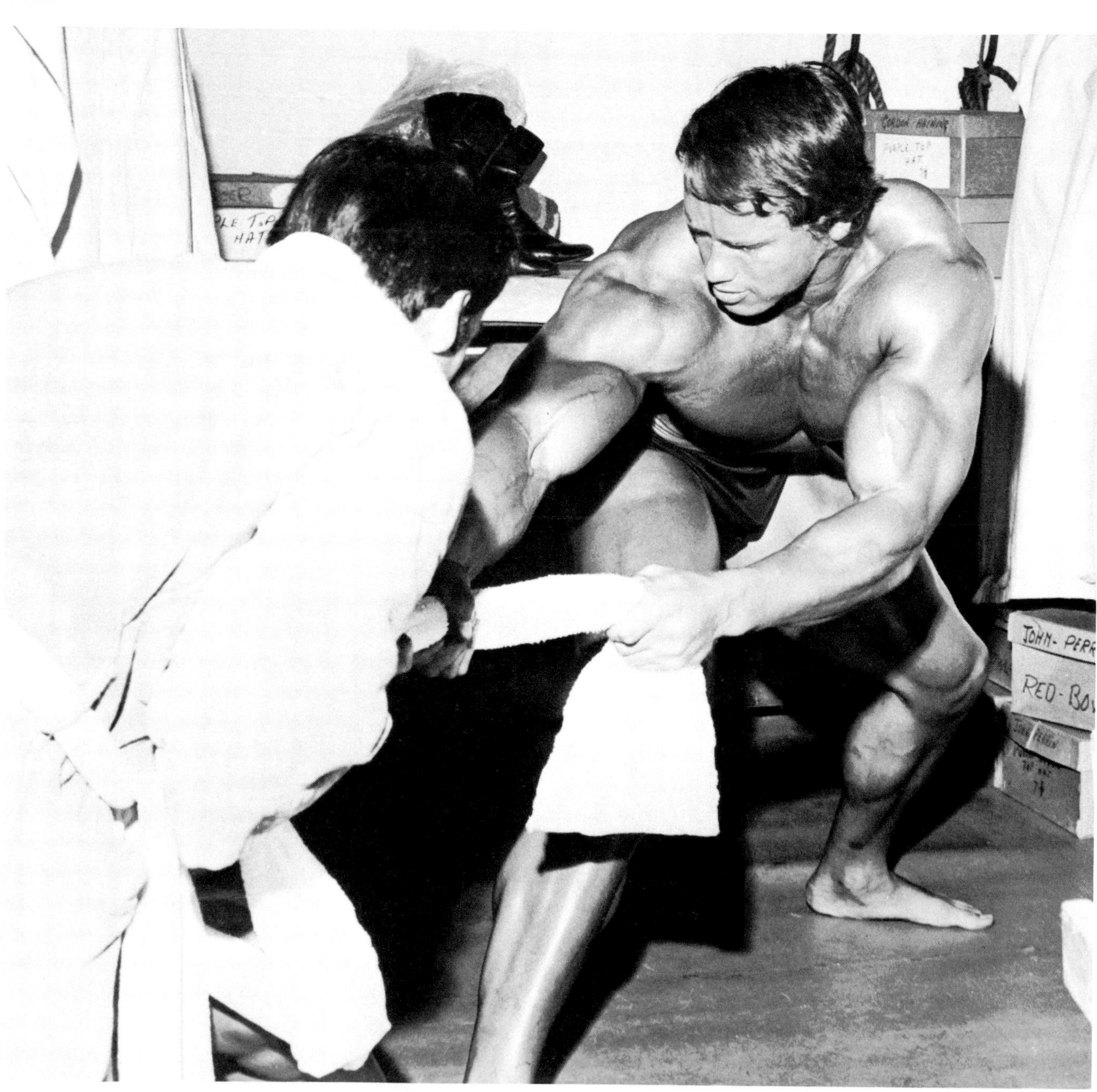

you will do is create a giant shadow over your body. Also, when you are doing your own posing, be aware of the areas of the stage that are *not* lit. I've seen bodybuilders constantly jump down off the platform and come to the front of the stage, where there was little or no light, so that the judges couldn't see them clearly and photographers couldn't take their pictures.

Learn what you can about the judges. After you have been in a few contests, you will begin to understand what different judges are looking for. Some prefer size, while others give more points for definition or symmetry. You can't change your physique for the contest, but you can alter your posing routine somewhat if you know what the judges like.

It is also a good idea to introduce yourself to the master of ceremonies and make sure he has enough information to be able to give you a good introduction. I know that when I have acted as the M.C. at bodybuilding events, I was always willing to cooperate when a bodybuilder asked me to say something specific in introducing him. This can have an influence on both the judges and the audience.

You should also know exactly how you are going to spend your day. On the morning of the contest, I would generally have a good breakfast—eggs, potatoes, cottage cheese, orange juice—but not an excessive amount. Generally, prejudging starts around one o'clock, so I would have the morning to walk around and prepare my mind for the competition ahead. For those bodybuilders who have to make an earlier prejudging, nine o'clock for example, I would recommend getting up very early, maybe five o'clock, and having an early meal, so that the body has time to wake up.

I remember seeing bodybuilders who made good use of the time between breakfast and the start of the contest. They would find someplace to lie in the sun (when contests are held at hotels, there is usually a pool area available to lie in the sun). This tended to bring out the veins and dry out the skin, although whenever you sweat in the sun you need to drink water to keep your fluid levels up or your body will dehydrate and start to hold excessive water.

Try to avoid letting negative thoughts and feelings dominate your mind. During the IFBB Mr. Universe contest documented in the *Pumping Iron* movie, I remember Mike Katz walking around a few hours before prejudging talking about what he would do when he lost the competition and complaining how everything was wrong and that a certain competitor should not have been allowed in the contest. As a lifelong competitive athlete and former professional football player, Mike should have remembered the degree to which negative thoughts can set you up for losing, becoming in effect a self-fulfilling prophecy.

We used to spend the time leading up to a contest differently than most seem to do now. A camaraderie existed then that has now largely disappeared. I remember checking into adjoining rooms at a hotel in New York with Zabo Koszewski, Franco Columbu, and Eddie Giuliani, all well known in bodybuilding at the time, and there was protein powder all over the place, liver pills under the pillows, and Tan-in-a-Minute all over the sheets and towels. We had a lot of fun, painting each other with color, going out to eat together, and sharing a taxi to the auditorium. This was a lot more pleasurable than the hiding out in the dressing room, don't-let-anyone-see-you kind of thing that goes on today. Maybe it's the fact that there is so much more money involved that accounts for the change, but bodybuilders certainly don't relate to each other as well as we used to.

Pumping up before the contest is also an important part of your strategy. I learned a trick from my old friend Wag Bennett in England, something the old-time bodybuilders used to do: The day before the contest, do one set to failure each hour for each of your weak points for a minimum of fourteen hours—one set only, not multiple sets that will overly fatigue and deplete the muscles. This pumping can theoretically increase the size of that muscle from 1/2 inch to a full inch the day of the contest. Maybe it stimulates glycogen retention, or just brings more fluid to the area, I don't know, but I do know it worked for me. At the NABBA Mr. Universe contest in

Franco eating pizza during prejudging to keep his energy level up

London in 1967, I was able to pump up my calves during the last twenty-four hours before the contest from 17 1/2 inches to well over 18 inches.

The advantage of pumping up the day before is that you don't need to pump that body part excessively during the contest itself. It is my experience that too much of a pump can destroy your definition. Of course, this depends on your body type. If you are naturally fairly smooth, when you pump up too much you will just look bloated onstage. This is all the more reason to come into the contest with a lower body weight to retain your definition, provided you get down to that weight early enough and keep it stable for a period of time. I believe the longer you keep your body weight at a given level, the more mature and finished your muscle structure will appear. Dropping down five pounds a week or so before the contest will not allow you to get hard and cut, and all the pumping in the world won't improve it.

And, after all, you may be out onstage for forty-five minutes or more in some contests, and the pump you got backstage is hardly going to last that whole time. So while pumping up is recommended, you can have too much of a good thing. For example, Sergio Oliva was famous for pumping up at a furious pace for a full two hours before a contest. His pump-up routine was more exhausting than many bodybuilders' workouts in the gym! This was obviously counterproductive, depleting the glycogen in the muscles, flattening them out and creating an unnecessary amount of fatigue. But since I was competing against him, I was certainly not going to be the one to tell him this—even if he had been willing to listen!

In my own case, I would start a half hour before the prejudging with some stretching and posing, going through my routine a few times. Then I would pump only the areas that I thought were weak—shoulders, for example, which were never as outstanding as my pectorals—or do a set of lats. I would do a set, then some more posing, then another pumping set. This way I would not burn myself out. After all, prejudging can start at one o'clock and go until three o'clock, and no quick pump you get backstage at the beginning is going to last all that time. One thing you should never do in a competition is to pump your thighs because this will destroy the definition in that area and you will not be able to get the proper effect when you flex them.

This process is as much about warming up as it is about pumping. So at the beginning of this preparation I would keep my training suit on until I began to feel hot and started to sweat. Then I would take off the top, keeping a T-shirt on. Gradually, off would come the long pants, then the T-shirt, and I would be stripped down to posing trunks just in time to oil up and go right out onstage.

The last thing I did before going out onstage was to put on a small amount of oil. Then before each round I pumped up a little more and put on more oil if I needed it. Again, this backstage preparation is about staying pumped over a period of time, not some kind of intense, peak effort.

You should pace yourself, continuing to flex enough offstage to keep your body hard and throwing in a pumping set now and then to keep your muscles full.

The effort of being onstage during prejudging is a depleting one, and you have to keep your body supplied during this time with what it needs to keep "popping" when you pose. You should drink water to keep from dehydrating. During contests Franco and I would usually eat some homemade, low-sugar carrot cake to provide carbohydrate energy. Some bodybuilders sip wine (and some stronger spirits, which I don't recommend if you want to keep your strength up and your wits about you). This is the kind of thing you experiment with in low-level shows in the earlier part of your career. Avoid any radical new tactics backstage in important contests. Experimenting at this point is very dangerous and usually just a sign of tension and nerves.

During prejudging I rarely paid attention to what the other bodybuilders were doing. I just concentrated on what I was going to do and didn't really take their presence into consideration until the posedown.

Between prejudging and the evening show, I generally walked around; ate a little something; thought through what I had done right or wrong; planned what I was going to do in the evening show; talked to people who had watched the prejudging to get an honest evaluation of my performance; decided who among my opponents was a threat, who was not, and what tactics I could use to get the upper hand in the posedown. Above all, onstage or off, I always acted like the winner. I enjoyed the evening show and my chance to perform for the audience.

Admittedly, under the pressure of competition it is hard to keep in mind everything you ought to be doing at all times. No matter how experienced you are, it helps to have somebody with you at a contest to act as a coach. Franco and I frequently helped each other in this way. In 1980 he came to Australia to help me win the Mr. Olympia, and in 1981 I returned the favor in Columbus, advising him on contest strategy and helping him to focus his energy on winning. Of course, not everyone is lucky enough to have a Mr. Olympia around as a contest coach, but you can usually find a friend or training partner to go to shows with you and cheer on your efforts to win.

Finally, I always kept a journal handy to write down everything I did and how I felt right up to and during the contest: Did I start to get cramps, and why? Did the audience respond more to one kind of pose than another? Anything that could help me do better in the next competition. I know that Franco and Frank Zane did the same thing, and so do many other bodybuilders. After all, there are only so many variables you can keep in your head, and when you want to be a champion you can't afford to leave anything to chance.

You have to be aware of everything. At the 1981 Olympia, I told Franco not to lean too far forward because of the heavy shadows cast by the overhead lights onstage.

PSYCHOLOGICAL WARFARE

There is always a psychological element in any sports competition. Athletic performance at the highest levels requires a tremendous degree of self-confidence and concentration, and anything that interferes with either will seriously threaten the athlete's chances of winning.

Psyching out your opponents, or gamesmanship, is common to all sports. Before his fight with Sonny Liston in the 1960s, Muhammad Ali appeared at the weigh-in screaming and hysterical, apparently totally out of his mind, and really shook up the then heavyweight champion. I know of a swimmer who admits to suddenly checking his suit just before the gun sounds to start the race, knowing that one or two of his opponents will begin to wonder if their own suits are in order and look down to check just as the starting pistol fires—breaking their concentration and causing them to hesitate a fraction of a second as the race starts.

None of this is cheating. Cheating is when you break the rules, not when you take advantage of an opponent's psychological weakness. When you think about it, anyone who wishes to claim the title of champion should be the master of his own mind as well as of his sport. If he isn't, and

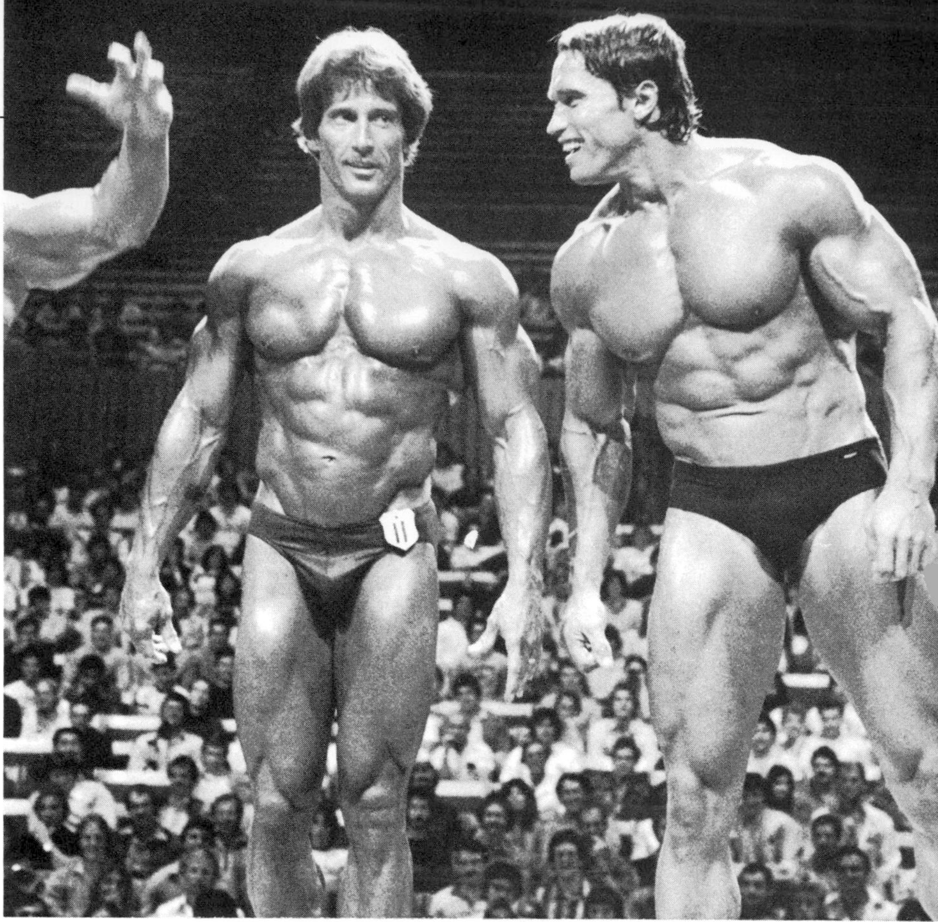

The gentle art of psychological warfare: At one point during the 1980 Olympia I leaned over and told Frank Zane a joke . . .

. . . and, sure enough, he was laughing so hard that his concentration for his next pose was gone.

your psyching him out throws him, then he has no business complaining.

One of the most famous examples of psyching out in bodybuilding occurred during the 1975 IFBB Mr. Universe contest in South Africa (documented in *Pumping Iron*). Ken Waller, the ultimate winner, more as a joke than anything else, made away with Mike Katz's T-shirt—nothing that would actually prevent him from competing, but just one more thing that Mike had to deal with in a situation in which the pressures were already almost overwhelming. Although the movie exaggerated how seriously Mike actually took this prank, I believe he did waste a certain amount of time and concentration looking for his T-shirt—and when you are in a competition on this level, you can't afford to waste anything.

I have to confess to having used similar tactics myself on occasion. In the 1980 Olympia I was standing onstage next to Frank Zane and started telling him jokes. Soon he was laughing so hard he could hardly hit his poses. In another contest I repeated to Serge Nubret that one of the judges had remarked that he looked too small and probably should have been in the lighter weight category. "That's what I was afraid of," he told me, and from that moment on he was obsessed with this idea, kept asking me how he looked, and his posing was thrown way off because he was reluctant to do certain shots that he felt he was too light to bring off. In close contests like those between Serge and me, psychological factors can be decisive.

Franco had a direct way of psyching out his opponents before a contest. He would arrange for somebody to telephone him when one of his competitors was training in World Gym. Franco would hasten to the gym, do a few warm-up sets, then take off his training suit and run around the gym in just a pair of shorts. Most bodybuilders like to keep themselves covered when they're getting ready for a contest, but Franco acted as if he were totally unconcerned about his competition and was eager to show off what good shape he was in. I saw Chris Dickerson practically run out of the gym once when Franco pulled this stunt and then challenged Chris to take off his shirt too. So you can see how far in advance of a competition psychological warfare can begin.

At the 1981 Olympia, Franco saw to it that he had a lot of media coverage. With Italian television there to film him and other photographers taking all sorts of shots of him as if he were already the winner, the other competitors were made to feel like also-rans. I used to do the same thing myself. I would get photographers to spend a lot of time just photographing *me* onstage, letting the other competitors see that I was getting all the attention. When the next competitor came out to pose, they'd turn away. I'd have them come backstage and shoot photos of my posing, ignoring the other bodybuilders and telling me how fantastic I was looking. The other guys stood around thinking What am I, chopped liver?

Nobody is immune to being pysched out. In fact, I have to admit that I've been on the receiving end of this treatment as well as dishing it out.

In 1969, Sergio Oliva pulled a trick on me which taught me what psychological warfare is really all about. At that contest Sergio walked around the whole time before we went onstage with his shoulders pulled in, looking very narrow, and wearing a long butcher's coat. I remember thinking that his back didn't look very big. He went into a corner to put some oil on, and I still didn't get a good look. But then he lowered the boom: As he walked out into the light on his way to the stage he said, "Take a look at this!" and he flared his lats—and the way those lats came out, I swear to you, I have never seen anything like it since. It was his way of saying That's it, it's all over. And it was. I was destroyed. I looked over at Franco and he tried to tell me it was just the lighting, but I knew better.

During the posing Sergio kept calling me "baby." He was totally in control and at ease—"Hey, baby, take a look at this shot!"—and I just didn't have a chance. But keep in mind, he could accomplish this only because of the genuine quality of his physique. If a lesser bodybuilder had tried any of these things I would have just laughed at him.

And that is the most potent way of psyching out your opponents: by simply being good—by having a dynamite physique and knowing how to present it. Many bodybuilders make the mistake of staying onstage posing as long as they can. But this is risky because the audience is likely to get bored. "Always leave them laughing" is the show-business axiom that applies here. I would try to work the audience up to a fever pitch and then leave the stage. This always meant I would be called back for an encore, which had a devastating effect on the judges as well.

Psychological warfare can be very subtle, just as it can be blatant and brutal. At the 1979 Olympia, as all the contestants were milling around waiting to be weighed, none of them willing to be the first to strip down and show the others his body, Frank Zane slipped in quietly, took off his sweats, and was weighed and gone before anyone else realized what was going on. Someone had also arranged that a motel billboard near the airport carried a big welcome for "Frank Zane, Mr. Olympia," a definite psychological jolt for the arriving competitors.

If your personality is such that you prefer not to get involved in efforts like this, just be aware that you are likely to be the target of psyching at some time. Being aware of this is half the battle in keeping these maneuvers from upsetting you and throwing you off your stride.

REPRESENTING THE SPORT

Until now I have touched on the things that allow a bodybuilder to best represent himself, onstage and off—thing like how to pose, how to dress, how to comport himself and to gain favorable publicity. Now I'd like to touch on another aspect of bodybuilding that is too often lacking among today's competitors—how to represent the sport.

When I got into bodybuilding, I admired champions like John Grimek, Reg Park, and Bill Pearl not only because of their fine physiques but also because of what kind of men they were. These were individuals to be looked up to. Bodybuilders like these, as well as others like Steve Reeves and Larry Scott, were terrific ambassadors for the sport of bodybuilding. The way they looked, dressed, talked, and conducted themselves reflected extremely well on the entire sport.

They didn't just take from bodybuilding, they put something back in. And this is something I have always tried to do and which I urge others to do. When you get to a certain level everything you do reflects on the whole of bodybuilding. You are no longer just a bodybuilder, training for yourself; you are in a position to promote bodybuilding or to detract from its image depending on what you say and what you do. When I go to Atlanta to promote the Inner-City Games, the mayor always includes Lee Haney among the famous professional athletes he invites to the ceremonies because Lee has been very active in civic affairs since retiring from competition. It speaks well for the sport to have Lee standing side by side with nationally celebrated football and basketball players, as well as athletes from the Olympics and a variety of other sports.

In addition to having a big impact on the public perception of bodybuilding, you as a champion are in a position to influence the future of the sport—by being a judge or official, writing magazine articles, or becoming as I have a promoter of bodybuilding events and using your experience to create the best possible contests with the best possible atmosphere. You should never forget you are in a position to make a difference.

To paraphrase a relative of my wife, Maria, don't always ask what the sport can do for you, but sometimes stop and think what you might do for the sport. If you do, there will be a lot of young and future bodybuilders who will be very much in your debt.

BOOK FIVE

Health, Nutrition, and Diet

CHAPTER 1

Nutrition and Diet

TRAINING STIMULATES MUSCLE growth. But for your training to work, your body needs a sufficient amount of energy and enough raw materials to get the full benefit from your exercise program. Providing that energy and those raw materials is the role of *nutrition.*

Nutrition involves learning how to stay lean, mean, and muscular. It means knowing how much of what kind of food to eat for the best possible result. It means learning the basic nutrients and determining how much of each you need. Good nutrition is also concerned with protein, vitamin, mineral, and other supplements. It not only helps you get bigger and stronger, but keeps you healthier as well as supports your immune system so that you don't miss training sessions due to problems like colds. The benefits of good nutrition also include everything from enhancing your recovery from heavy workouts to giving you good skin to producing optimum function of the liver and other internal organs.

Because of this, *the basic principles of nutrition are as valuable to a bodybuilder as the basic principles of training.* Nutrition is as absolutely essential to building a strong, healthy, great-looking body as your workouts. Exercise creates a demand for nutrients; how much of what kind of nutrients you provide is a major factor in producing the kind of results you want.

At the Arnold Classic every year, I interview the competitors as they come offstage. One of my favorite questions is, "What do you feel was the most important factor that helped you get in such tremendous shape for this contest?" More often than not, champions like Shawn Ray, Nasser El Sonbaty, and Flex Wheeler (or the winners of the Ms. International or Arnold Fitness contest) do not answer this question by talking about, say, doing heavier Bench Presses or adding more rest days to their programs or working more on isolation movements. No, in most cases (especially in recent years), they refer to better nutrition, to the increased use of supplements, or to a more effective diet that allowed them to gain muscle, lose fat, and be able to train with maximum energy right up until the contest.

I believe that advances in nutrition and supplements are the major reason we see so many first-rate competitors in the sport nowadays. Training has been improved over the years, not revolutionized. But increased knowledge of nutrition is the reason we see more and more first-rate competitors entering contests these days. Needless to say, better nutrition will not create a champion without a lot of hard and dedicated training. But along with hard training and a good mental attitude, nutritional knowledge and excellence is the third factor that most determines success in bodybuilding. In the past, bodybuilders approached diet and nutrition on an instinctive, seat-of-the-pants basis. So, at first, they were able to build size, but not get really ripped. When bodybuilders came along who were able to get totally cut-up—like Harold Poole or the late Vince Gironda—they tended to be smaller. They hadn't yet learned the difficult trick of staying big and getting ripped at the same time.

In my own early years, I ate well and grew to a tremendous size. But I found that sheer bulk would not take me to the heights I wanted. So, about the time I came to live in California, I began a serious study of diet and nutrition in an attempt to develop a physique that had *everything*—size, shape, proportion—ripped to shreds! To be a top champion, I reasoned, means you have to push your body to its limit. And the body will not be able to respond to the maximum unless it has enough vital nutrients on hand at the right place and the right time.

The fundamentals of nutrition are relatively simple. Learning to apply them to your own training, understanding the individual needs of your own body, how it responds to various kinds of weight-loss or weight-gain diets, is something else again. Like in many other aspects of training, ultimately you are forced to fall back on the Instinctive Principle.

First, you must learn the fundamentals, isolating the variables that play such an important part in the production of energy and the building and maintenance of muscle tissue. Moving beyond the fundamentals, understanding nutrition is more than just knowing what the various nutrients are and how the body uses them; you have to learn to apply this information to your own needs and your own individual body type.

In this chapter, we'll see exactly what the various important nutrients are, what they're made of, and what they do. Later, we will look at how to put together a nutritional program for muscle-building, weight control, or competition preparation.

THE SPECIAL REQUIREMENTS OF BODYBUILDING

Bodybuilders are virtually unique in the demands they place upon their bodies. They require simultaneously maximum muscle mass and minimum body fat, which is an extremely difficult state to attain. Athletes like gymnasts, boxers, and wrestlers, who need to become very lean, follow a training regimen that burns up so many calories that they rarely have to diet to reduce body fat. Nor do they usually attempt, as competition bodybuilders must, to get down to a relative body fat of about 8 to 11 percent for men and 7 to 9 percent for women (many tests report much lower percentages than this, but extremely low readings in the 3 to 5 percent range are most probably in error). Most strength athletes such as football players work to maximize the size and strength of the muscles with only minor attention to reducing body fat.

Bodybuilders have little margin for error. They have to eat enough to grow, then be able to reduce body fat without sacrificing muscle mass. They can use aerobic exercise to burn up extra calories, but not to the point where their gym workouts suffer. They need to control calories, but get sufficient protein to build and maintain their muscle tissue. Nutrition is a complex and ever-expanding science, and nutritionists are giving us new information almost daily. However, certain basic principles of nutrition are well established, and mastering these fundamentals is essential for the bodybuilder who wants to achieve his total genetic potential for growth and physical development.

THE BASIC NUTRIENTS

There are three basic nutrients known as *macronutrients:*

1. *Protein,* composed of various amino acids, provides the building blocks for muscle tissue. It is also a component of all organs, and is involved in the structure of skin, bones, and tendons as well as being involved in many bodily functions (all enzymes are proteins).
2. *Carbohydrates,* fuel for energy, is composed of a variety of less complex or more complex sugar and starch molecules.
3. *Fats* (or oils), the nutrient that contains the most densely packed energy stores.

Water is also an essential nutrient. It constitutes 72 percent of muscles and most bodybuilders drink liters of it a day. In addition, nutritional supplementation can include a number of other substances such as herbs and hormones, which will be dealt with at length in a later section.

Other nutrients, called *micronutrients,* include:

vitamins—essential chemicals that facilitate various biochemical reactions
minerals—essential for a number of vital body functions, including muscular contraction
essential amino acids—parts of proteins that we obtain in foods
essential fatty acids—obtained from plants or fish oils

PROTEIN

Protein is used by the body to build, repair, and maintain muscle tissue. As we'll see, in this area bodybuilders have been way ahead of most nutritional experts in recognizing that building muscle (in fact, hard training of all sorts) requires a *lot* more protein intake than had been formerly realized.

The body cannot use the protein you ingest for muscle-building unless all of the necessary amino acids are present. However, the body itself can produce only some of these amino acids. The others, called the *essential amino acids,* have to be obtained from the foods you eat.

Protein is made up of carbon, hydrogen, and oxygen (as are the other macronutrients) and one more element none of the other nutrients have—nitrogen. If you ever hear somebody talking about being in positive nitrogen balance or negative nitrogen balance what they are referring to is whether they are in an anabolic state—able to build muscle—or in a catabolic one—losing muscle.

Some foods contain what is called *complete protein*—that is, they provide *all* the amino acids necessary to produce usable protein. Examples of these foods are milk, eggs, meat, fish, and various vegetable products, such as soybeans. But even these foods contain differing amounts of usable protein per weight. That is, even though a food might contain, say, 10 grams of protein, your body is able to use only a certain percentage of it—for example, only 7 or 8.5 grams.

Following is a chart that shows on the left what percentage protein makes up of various foods commonly used as protein sources and on the right what percentage of that protein your body is actually able to use for building muscle:

Food	% Protein by Weight	% Net Protein Utilization
Eggs	12	94
Milk	4	82
Fish	18–25	80
Cheese	22–36	70
Brown rice	8	70
Meat and fowl	19–31	68
Soybean flour	42	61

(Whey, a milk derivative, which is a refined product, has even more net protein than eggs.)

This chart tells us, for example, that an egg contains only 12 percent protein by weight. Yet because of the specific balance of amino acids present in that protein, 94 percent of it can be used by your body. In contrast, 42 percent of soybean flour is protein, but the makeup of that protein is such that your body is able to use only 61 percent of it. *So there is a big difference between how much protein a food contains and how much of that protein you can actually use to build muscle.*

Eggs are such a good source of quality protein that they are used as a basis of comparison in rating the protein quality of other foods, with eggs given an arbitrary value of a "perfect" 100.

Food	Protein Rating
Eggs (whole)	100
Fish	70
Lean beef	69
Cow's milk	60
Brown rice	57
White rice	56
Soybeans	47
Whole-grain wheat	44
Peanuts	43
Dry beans	34
White potato	34

Incidentally, notice that I have given you the value of *whole* eggs. It is fashionable to eat only egg whites nowadays because the yolk contains some fat and the egg white does not. However, I never do this. The yolk actually contains as much protein as the egg white, as well as the majority of the vitamins and minerals. If you feel the need to limit the fat in your diet, I recommend you do so by eliminating other foods, not by throwing away what is in many ways the best part of the egg. (The egg yolk does contain cholesterol, so if you have problems with cholesterol you should check with your doctor regarding your diet.)

Going back to the list, you can see that foods like rice, potatoes, and beans give you considerably less *usable* protein than eggs or fish. The reason is they have some, but too few, of the essential amino acids that are required for complete protein. You can, however, combine two or more sources of this low-quality (incomplete) protein to obtain high-quality, complete protein. That is, one food lacks certain aminos that are supplied by the other food, so in combination they give you what you need. Having incomplete protein is like trying to play a baseball game with eighteen players, five of whom are pitchers and three catchers. It doesn't matter that there are eighteen players because the two teams are incomplete.

This need to assemble a complete "team" of amino acids means that adding just a small amount of the right food to your eating plan can make a big difference. To continue the baseball analogy, suppose you have seventy-two players ready to play baseball, but none of them can play first base. Then suppose you recruit just nine additional players—all first basemen. Now instead of seventy-two athletes standing around able to do nothing, you suddenly have nine complete baseball teams ready to take the field. That's the same thing that happens when you have a lot of incomplete sets of amino acids and add just a few of the ones that are necessary to allow the body to build additional muscle mass.

Combining incomplete protein in this way is useful because it usually involves eating foods that are relatively low in fat, and thus contain fewer calories than many common complete protein sources. When you are trying to build maximum muscle mass with as little body fat as possible, this can be a great advantage. (You can also get protein without fat by using protein supplements, which we'll deal with in detail a little later.)

As I said, since each of the sources of incomplete protein lacks certain essential amino acids, you need to be very *specific* in your food combinations in order to end up with complete protein. *In Diet for a Small Planet* by Frances Moore Lappé (Ballantine Books, 1974), the following combinations are recommended:

Grains plus Seeds

Breads with added seed meals
Breads with sesame or sunflower seed spread
Rice with sesame seeds

Grains plus Milk Products

Cereal with milk (and now you know why this is an often recommended breakfast food!)
Pasta with milk or cheese (Aha . . . Parmesan cheese on spaghetti)
Bread with milk or cheese (a traditional lunch in many parts of Europe)

Grains plus Legumes

Rice and beans (which is a fundamental part of diets all over the world, especially in countries where animal protein is scarce)
Wheat bread and baked beans
Corn soy or wheat-soy bread
Legume soup with bread

You could consult a nutritional guide to find out exactly which of the eight essential amino acids are missing in any particular food, but this is actually unnecessary. If you simply remember the food groups as listed here, you will be able to combine your foods correctly to maximize usable protein.

Of course, all the knowledge about the nature of protein and what foods to eat in order to get protein means very little if you don't know *how much* protein you are supposed to eat—and that is something we'll discuss in detail in the next chapter.

Protein Supplements

Training for muscle mass requires more than just hard work, it requires protein, as much as 1 gram per pound body weight per day for some individuals, but as you may discover, obtaining enough protein without consuming too much fat is often a problem. A solution to this problem comes in the form of protein supplements. Not only are protein supplements a cost-effective means of increasing protein intake without significantly increasing dietary fat, they are also convenient, which is important since meal frequency is such a critical aspect of bodybuilding nutrition.

The variety of protein supplements available at your local health food store is staggering, and unlike years past, today's supplements taste more like desserts than high-protein, low-fat bodybuilding foods. But many of today's protein supplements are more than just protein in a can or envelope; they are nutrient-dense supplements containing vitamins and minerals as well as macronutrients such as protein and carbohydrate. Finding supplements that fit your nutrient requirement as well as your taste can be a valuable asset in your nutritional plan.

Considering the huge selection of supplements that are now available, there are several factors that may help you choose one. First, make sure you read the label. Some protein supplements contain various amounts of carbohydrate, and although carbohydrate enhances the conversion of dietary protein to muscle protein, excessive carbohydrate also adds extra calories, making burning fat more difficult. Consequently, counting the carbohydrates included in your protein supplement is important if you are to maintain an accurate account of your macronutrient intake.

Second, pure protein supplements that are not consumed with a meal or added carbohydrate are not metabolized efficiently. Research indicates that for protein to be utilized more for protein synthesis than for energy production, it must be consumed with additional calories, especially those from carbohydrate. This may be no big deal if you are on a low-carbohydrate diet and expect a greater portion of your dietary protein to be used for energy, but if your goal is to get the most bang for your protein buck, make sure you include carbohydrate with your protein supplement (if it doesn't already contain carbohydrate) or consume your protein supplement as a part of a meal.

Third, there are three different types of proteins typically used in protein supplements. Milk proteins (whey, milk protein concentrate, and caseinate), egg, and soy protein. All are considered high-quality protein, and although there is little scientific evidence that suggests one protein source is better for muscle growth than another, protein supplements that are derived from milk or egg have gained the greatest acceptance among bodybuilders. But soy protein has benefits that milk and egg proteins don't. Soy protein has recently gained attention in the medical community because of research that shows soy protein can lower serum cholesterol in some individuals. So for individuals who have problems with their cholesterol, soy protein may be the best choice.

And, finally, remember that protein supplements are not designed to be the sole source of dietary protein. A balanced whole-food diet is an important aspect of a healthy diet as well as a bodybuilding diet.

CARBOHYDRATES

Carbohydrates are the body's primary and most easily available source of energy. All carbohydrates are sugars, molecules containing carbon, hydrogen, and oxygen synthesized by plants through the process of photosynthesis (using the energy of the sun) or by animals through the process of glycogen synthesis. But when I say sugar I don't mean the table sugar that you put in your coffee or on your morning cereal. There are a wide variety of different carbohydrates, as we'll see. Following are the basic categories of carbohydrates:

Monosaccharides

Glucose (blood sugar)
Fructose (fruit sugar)
Galactose (a kind of milk sugar)

Oligosaccharides

Sucrose (table sugar)
Lactose (milk sugar)
Maltose (malt sugar)

Polysaccharides

Plant polysaccharides (starch and cellulose)
Animal polysaccharides (glycogen)

How quickly carbohydrates are metabolized is measured by something called a glycemic index. A high glycemic index (large increase of serum glucose) means the carbohydrates are metabolized quickly; a low index (relatively small increase of serum glucose) means they are metabolized more slowly or differently. The glycemic index has replaced the terms we used when I was competing—simple and complex carbs. What we called simple carbs are now categorized as those with a high glycemic index (fruits, processed sugar), and complex carbs are characterized by a low glycemic index (starches, cellulose). Carbs with a low glycemic index provide their energy over a period of time, and therefore have a kind of time-release effect.

By the way, you often have to look up foods in a guide to be certain of their glycemic index. Ice cream, because of the fat it contains, has a relatively low glycemic index. The kind of rice you get in a Chinese restaurant, the kind that sticks together so well, has a surprisingly high glycemic index (unlike brown rice or wild rice).

As explained, carbohydrates are the easiest form of food for the body to convert into energy. Once ingested, they are turned into *glucose*, which circulates in the bloodstream and fuels muscular contraction, and *glycogen*, which is stored in the muscles and the liver for future use. Adequate supplies of carbohydrates are essential for the serious bodybuilder for a number of reasons:

1. Carbohydrates are a primary form of energy. The carbohydrates stored in the muscles as glycogen are what allow you to do heavy and intense weight training.

2. Muscle size is increased when the body stores glycogen and water in the individual muscle cells.

3. Carbohydrates in the body have a "protein-sparing" effect, keeping the body from burning up excessive protein for energy. More about this important aspect of carbs later.

4. The carbohydrate glucose is the main source of energy that fuels the functioning of the brain, and deprivation can have severe effects on mood, personality, and mental ability.

The reason that carbohydrates are so important as fuel for intense training is that most exercise like this is *anaerobic*—that is, it takes place in short, intense bursts and outruns the ability of the body to supply enough oxygen to sustain the effort. But the structure of carbohydrates is such that they can continue to fuel exercise for short periods in the *absence* of oxygen. So when you do a hard set of weight training or run a 100-meter sprint, the source of your energy for those efforts is primarily carbohydrates.

Carbohydrate Supplements

Intense training creates a demand in the body for glycogen (carbohydrate) replacement as well as for amino acids. It is important to have enough carbohydrates in your system after training because otherwise the body may start to use amino acids for energy instead. The "window" for carbohydrate replenishment—that is, the period during which the body is in very high demand for this nutrient—is much shorter than it is for protein. In fact, your best results occur when you are able to get the necessary carbohydrates into your body within about 20 minutes of finishing training.

This need for immediate glycogen replacement is why many bodybuilders use a carbohydrate supplement after workouts as well as a protein supplement. This is especially valuable if you follow up weight training with a session of cardiovascular training. If you try to work on a treadmill, stepper, or exercise bike too soon after your workout, and your body is carbohydrate-deprived, you will find yourself lacking in energy and you can be sure your body is metabolizing more amino acids to supply energy than would otherwise be necessary.

DIETARY FATS

Fats are the most energy-dense of the three macronutrients. Fats are made up of the same elements as carbohydrates—carbon, hydrogen, and oxygen—but the way the atoms are linked together is different. (Oils, by the way, are simply fats that are liquid rather than solid at room temperature.) Fats, which can be found in both plants and animals, are insoluble in water. They are grouped in three categories: *simple fats* (triglycerides), *compound fats* (phospholipids, glucolipids, lipoproteins), and *derived fats* (cholesterol).

Fats in the body serve three basic functions: (1) They provide the major source of *stored* energy (body fat); (2) they serve to cushion and protect the major organs; and (3) they act as an insulator, preserving body heat and protecting against excessive cold.

Fat is the most calorie-dense of any nutrient. A pound of fat contains about 4,000 calories, as opposed to 1,800 calories stored in a pound of protein or carbohydrate.

When you exercise, assuming you stay within your aerobic capacity (don't get out of breath), the body uses fats and carbohydrates for energy on about a 50-50 basis. But the longer you continue steady exercise, the higher the percentage of fat used. After working three hours or so, the body may derive as much as 80 percent of its energy from fat.

Fat molecules differ biochemically in their composition, being either *saturated, unsaturated,* or *polyunsaturated.* These terms simply refer to the number of hydrogen atoms that attach to the molecule. To use an analogy, consider a ball of string. Saturated fat is like a length of string in a badly tangled mess. Unsaturated is like string with only a few tangles. And polyunsaturated is like neatly coiled string without the sign of a tangle. The more saturated (tangled) the fat, the more it is likely to remain in the body and clog the arteries, adding to the risk of heart disease.

In addition to other factors, diets high in saturated fat tend to raise the cholesterol level of the blood. Therefore, health experts recommend that about two-thirds of your fat intake be polyunsaturated fats.

Saturated fats are found in foods such as:

Beef
Lamb
Pork
Chicken
Shellfish
Egg yolks
Cream
Milk
Cheese
Butter
Chocolate
Lard
Vegetable shortening

Unsaturated fats are found in:

Avocados
Cashews
Olives and olive oil
Peanuts, peanut oil, peanut butter

Polyunsaturated fats are found in:

Almonds
Cottonseed oil
Margarine (usually)
Pecans
Sunflower oil
Corn oil
Fish
Mayonnaise
Safflower oil
Soybean oil
Walnuts

Essential Fatty Acids

Fats are an absolutely necessary nutrient in a healthy diet. But bodybuilders today often go on such low-fat diets that they develop dietary fat deficiencies. However, foods and supplements are available that supply these "good" fats in the necessary amounts. Some examples are:

Fish oil. Instead of low-fat fish, try salmon, trout, or mackerel. Fish fats cannot readily be made in the body, but are needed by organs (especially the brain). You can also take fish oils in supplement form.

Polyunsaturated vegetable oils. Two valuable oils are linoleic and linolenic acids. Supermarket oils, such as corn, sunflower, and safflower oils, cannot provide linoleic acid. Soybean oil is the only supermarket oil that contains linolenic acid. Flaxseed oil, which can also be found in walnuts and pumpkin seeds, is the ideal source of linolenic acid.

MCTs (medium-chain triglycerides). Obtained from coconut oil, MCTs have an unjustified reputation in the world of bodybuilding. It is commonly believed that MCTs cannot be deposited into fat cells, but research has shown this to be incorrect. Although MCTs are rapidly available to the bloodstream, they don't give an athlete more strength, size, speed, or endurance. MCTs are pretty much just fat calories, so I don't recommend them.

Monounsaturated fats. These are the most benign of fats in that they don't affect your cholesterol or prostaglandins (regulators of hormone action) like some of the polyunsaturated fats. Monounsaturated fats are found in olive oil and macadamia nuts.

Fatty acid supplements. Various supplements in health food stores contain essential fatty acids derived from fish oils and other sources.

WATER

Water, a major component of the body, is often overlooked as a vital nutrient. It acts as a means of transportation for the various chemicals in the system and is the medium in which the various biochemical reactions among the basic nutrients take place.

The body is made up of 40 to 60 percent water. You may recall that muscle is composed of 72 percent water by weight, whereas fat weight is only 20 to 25 percent water. This means that diets or activities that result in excessive fluid loss have a significant effect on muscle size. Furthermore, without sufficient intake of water, you become dehydrated. Your body begins to retain water to protect itself, and much of this water is stored subcutaneously, which smooths out muscular definition dramatically.

Retained water becomes contaminated because your kidneys can't filter out contaminants properly when you're dehydrated. The liver is then called upon to help process these waste products, which interferes with one of its main functions, breaking down body fat. So without sufficient water in your body you're likely to end up water-logged, bloated, and obese—which is disastrous for a bodybuilder working for maximum definition.

This also leads to problems with sodium. When you're dehydrated, sodium can't be adequately flushed from the body, causing further water retention, and any additional sodium ingested in your diet simply aggravates the problem.

For anyone involved in intense exercise, the need for water is at least eight 12-ounce glasses per day. Some bodybuilders drink even more than this. And water in solution doesn't count. You need pure water, not juice, soft drinks, coffee, tea, or some other substitute.

VITAMINS

Vitamins are organic substances that the body needs in minute amounts and that we ingest with our foods. Vitamins do not supply energy, nor do they contribute substantially to the mass of the body; rather, they act as catalysts, substances that help to trigger other reactions in the body.

The two basic categories of vitamins are water-soluble and fat-soluble. Water-soluble vitamins are not stored in the body, and any excess amounts are flushed out in the urine. Fat-soluble vitamins are dissolved and stored in the fatty tissues of the body. It is necessary to take in water-soluble vitamins on a daily basis, but fat-soluble vitamins can be ingested less often.

Water-Soluble Vitamins

B_1 (thiamin)
B_2 (riboflavin)
B_3 (niacin, nicotinic acid, nicotinamide)
B_5 (pantothenic acid)
B_6 (pyridoxine)
B_{12} (cyanocobalamin)
Biotin
Folate (folic acid, folacin)
Vitamin C (ascorbic acid)
Vitamin A (retinol)

Fat-Soluble Vitamins

Vitamin A
Vitamin D
Vitamin E
Vitamin K

Vitamin B_1 (Thiamin)

Use in the Body: Helps release energy from carbohydrates during metabolism. Important for health of nerves and muscles, including heart. Helps prevent fatigue and irritability.

Sources in Diet: Pork, whole grains, dried beans and peas, sunflower seeds, nuts.

Symptoms of Deficiency: Beriberi (nerve changes, sometimes edema, heart failure).

Symptoms of Overdose: None known.

RDA: 1.5 mg

Vitamin B_2 (Riboflavin)

Use in the Body: Helps the body to metabolize carbohydrates, fat, and protein to release energy. As an antioxidant, riboflavin protects cells from oxidative damage. Supports good vision and is needed for healthy hair, skin, and nails. Necessary for normal cell growth.

Sources in Diet: Liver and other organ meats, poultry, brewer's yeast, fish, dried peas, beans, nuts, sunflower seeds, cheese, eggs, yogurt, milk, whole grains, green leafy vegetables, nori seaweed.

Symptoms of Deficiency: Skin lesions.

Symptoms of Overdose: None known.

RDA: 1.7 mg

Vitamin B_3 (Niacin, Nicotinic Acid, Nicotinamide)

Use in the Body: Energy metabolism. Important for healthy skin and digestive tract tissue. Stimulates circulation. (Caution: If nicotinic acid is taken by itself, it may cause flushing.)

Sources in Diet: Liver and other organ meats, veal, pork, poultry, fish, nuts, brewer's yeast, dried beans, dried fruit, green leafy vegetables, whole grains, milk, eggs.

Symptoms of Deficiency: Pellagra (sensitivity to light; fatigue; loss of appetite; skin eruptions; and sore, red tongue).

Symptoms of Overdose: Flushing of face, neck, and hands; liver damage.

RDA: 19 mg

VITAMIN B_5 (PANTOTHENIC ACID)

USE IN THE BODY: Pantothenic acid is an active part of coenzyme A (CoA), important in energy production and utilization. It supports adrenal glands to increase production of hormones to counteract stress. Important for healthy skin and nerves.

SOURCES IN DIET: Nuts, beans, seeds, dark green leafy vegetables, poultry, dried fruit, milk. Highest source: royal jelly (from honeybees).

SYMPTOMS OF DEFICIENCY: Fatigue, sleep disturbance, nausea.

SYMPTOMS OF OVERDOSE: None known.

RDA: 6 mg

VITAMIN B_6 (PYRIDOXINE)

USE IN THE BODY: Helps body protein to build body tissue and in metabolism of fat. Facilitates release of glycogen from liver and muscles. Helps in red blood cell production, fluid-balance regulation.

SOURCES IN DIET: Sunflower seeds, beans, poultry, liver, eggs, nuts, green leafy vegetables, bananas, dried fruit.

SYMPTOMS OF DEFICIENCY: Nervous and muscular disorders.

SYMPTOMS OF OVERDOSE: Unstable gait, numb feet, poor hand coordination, abnormal brain function.

RDA: 2 mg

VITAMIN B_{12} (CYANOCOBALAMIN)

USE IN THE BODY: Important in formation of red blood cells and building genetic material. Stimulates growth in children. Helps functioning of nervous system, and in metabolizing protein and fat in body.

SOURCES IN DIET: Animal protein foods, including meat, fish, shellfish, poultry, milk, yogurt, eggs.

SYMPTOMS OF DEFICIENCY: Pernicious anemia (weight loss, weakness, pale skin), confusion, moodiness, memory loss, depression.

SYMPTOMS OF OVERDOSE: None known.

RDA: 2 mcg

BIOTIN

USE IN THE BODY: Energy metabolism.

Sources in Diet: Egg yolks, liver, sardines, whole soy flour.

Symptoms of Deficiency: Dermatitis, depression, muscular pain.

Symptoms of Overdose: None known.

RDA: 30 to 100 mcg

Folate (Folic Acid, Folacin)

Use in the Body: Helps form red blood cells. Assists in breakdown and utilization of protein. Essential during pregnancy for its importance in cell division. In its active form (the so-called methyl-containing form) folate stabilizes proteins, nucleic acids, and membranes of cells as well as supporting brain function.

Sources in Diet: Dark green leafy vegetables, nuts, beans, whole-grain products, fruit, fruit juices, liver, egg yolks.

Symptoms of Deficiency: Anemia, gastrointestinal disturbances.

Symptoms of Overdose: Masks vitamin B_{12} deficiency.

RDA: 200 mcg

Vitamin C (Ascorbic Acid)

Use in the Body: Essential for connective tissue found in skin, cartilage, bones, and teeth. Helps heal wounds. Antioxidant. Stimulates immune system. Aids in absorption of iron.

Sources in Diet: Citrus fruits, berries, melons, dark green vegetables, cauliflower, tomatoes, green and red peppers, cabbage, potatoes.

Symptoms of Deficiency: Scurvy (bleeding gums, weakness), delayed wound healing, impaired immune response.

Symptoms of Overdose: Gastrointestinal upsets, confounded results from certain lab tests.

RDA: 60 mg

Vitamin A (Retinol)

Use in the Body: Tissue maintenance. Healthy skin, hair, and mucous membranes. Helps us see in dim light. Essential for normal growth and reproduction.

Sources in Diet: Liver; deep yellow, orange, and dark green vegetables and fruits (including carrots, broccoli, spinach, cantaloupe, sweet potatoes); cheese; milk; fortified margarine.

Symptoms of Deficiency: Night blindness; dry, scaling skin; poor immune response. Serum (blood) values of vitamin A should be between 0.15 and 0.6 µg/ml.

Symptoms of Overdose: Damage to the liver, kidney, and bone; headache; irritability; vomiting; hair loss; blurred vision; yellow skin.

RDA: 1,000 mcg (3,333 IU)

Vitamin D_3 (Cholecalciferol)

Use in the Body: Helps regulate calcium metabolism and bone calcification. Called the sunshine vitamin because it is manufactured in human skin when in contact with ultraviolet light. Wintertime, clouds, and smog reduce its production in the body.

Sources in Diet: Fortified and full-fat dairy products, tuna, salmon, cod liver oil.

Symptoms of Deficiency: Rickets in children, bone softening in adults.

Symptoms of Overdose: Gastrointestinal upset; cerebral, cardiovascular, and kidney damage; lethargy.

RDA: 10 mcg

Vitamin E (D-alpha-tocopherol)

Use in the Body: Antioxidant to prevent cell membrane damage.

Sources in Diet: Vegetable oils and their products, nuts, seeds, fish, wheat germ, whole-grain products, green leafy vegetables.

Symptoms of Deficiency: In humans, diseases of the pancreas and liver as well as various forms of chronic diarrhea. Anemia.

Symptoms of Overdose: Perhaps fatal in premature infants given intravenous solution. There are no known symptoms of oral overdose.

RDA: 10 mg (alpha-tocopherol equivalents)

Vitamin K (Phylloquinone)

Use in the Body: Necessary for normal blood clotting.

Sources in Diet: Dark green leafy vegetables; cabbage; polar bear liver (actually, fatal amounts).

Symptoms of Deficiency: Severe bleeding on injury; internal hemorrhaging.

Symptoms of Overdose: Liver damage, anemia (from synthetic forms).

RDA: 80 mcg

MINERALS

Minerals are inorganic substances that contain elements the body needs in relatively small amounts. There are twenty-two metallic elements in the body, which make up about 4 percent of total body weight.

Minerals are found abundantly in the soil and water of the planet, and eventually are taken in by the root systems of plants. We obtain minerals by eating the plants or the animals that eat the plants. If you eat a variety of meats and vegetables in your diet, you can usually depend on getting sufficient minerals.

Then minerals in the body play a part in a variety of metabolic processes, and contribute to the synthesis of such chemical compounds as glycogen, protein, and fats. Following is a basic guide to the most important minerals the body needs in substantial amounts:

Calcium: Essential for strength of bones and teeth. Found in milk products; vegetables such as kale, turnip greens, and mustard greens; tofu; and seafood such as sardines, clams, and oysters. Lack of calcium can cause muscular cramping and, in the long term, osteoporosis. *RDA:* 1200 mg for males eleven to twenty-four; 800 mg for males over twenty-five

Phosphorus: A component of every cell, including DNA, RNA, and ATP. Found in whole-grain cereals, egg yolks, fish, milk, meat, poultry, legumes, nuts. Essential in the regulation of body pH (acidity/alkalinity). *RDA:* 1200 mg for males eleven to twenty-four; 800 mg for males over twenty-five

Magnesium: Present throughout the body, an activator of enzymes involving most processes in the body. Found in green vegetables, legumes, whole-grain cereals, nuts, meat, milk, chocolate. *RDA:* 400 mg for males fifteen to eighteen; 350 mg for males nineteen and older

Sodium: Regulates body fluid levels, involved in activating muscular contraction. Sodium is available in common table salt and in most foods except fruit, particularly animal foods, seafood, milk, and eggs. Excess sodium tends to increase water retention and is associated with elevated blood sugar levels. Lack of sodium can cause muscular weakness and cramping. *RDA:* 1,100 to 3,300 mg

Chlorine: A component of digestive fluids and functions in combination with sodium. Found in table salt, meat, seafood, eggs, milk. *RDA:* 1,700 to 5,100 mg

Potassium: Involved in protein and carbohydrate metabolism, functions inside cell (in combination with sodium outside) to control fluid osmosis. Found in meat, milk, cereals, vegetables, fruits, legumes. Excess potassium supplements can cause vomiting. Potassium deficiency can result in muscular weakness. *RDA:* 1,875 to 5,625 mg

Sulfur: Needed for synthesis of essential metabolites. Found in protein foods such as meat, seafood, milk, eggs, poultry, cheese, legumes. No RDA recommendation.

Other minerals are important to the body, but at levels of only a trace amount per day. These are:

Iron	Fluoride
Zinc	Molybdenum
Copper	Cobalt
Iodine	Selenium
Manganese	Chromium

There are other minerals known to be essential, but for which no recommended daily amount has been established:

Tin
Nickel
Vanadium
Silicon

Vitamin and Mineral Supplements

Many experts feel that we don't get an adequate amount of vitamins and minerals in our daily food intake. They cite a number of causes, including the manner in which food is grown or raised, how it is processed, the additives used to help preserve it, and the complexity of the distribution system. Whether this is true or not, it is a fact that intense exercise increases our need for *all* types of nutrients. And taking vitamin and mineral supplements is, if nothing else, an easy form of insurance against any sort of nutritional deprivation.

In my own career, I came to rely on supplements more and more as I became more experienced at bodybuilding. I was never any kind of superexpert on supplements, and in the 1960s and 1970s it wasn't as easy to get advice about supplements as it is today. I asked various experts I came in contact with to suggest types and amounts of supplements, and then would experiment and see if taking these recommended supplements seemed to add to my energy, strength, endurance, or ability to recover from hard training. As with everything else, I was always less interested in theory than whether something actually worked for me.

Nowadays, things are much simpler. Not only are all the supplements available in any health food store, but you can also get supplements in daily packs, with just the right amount of each vitamin and mineral in the correct balance (often the effectiveness of supplements depends on the proportion of each taken at any given time).

One caution about mega-dosing. In terms of their role in the body, vitamins and minerals need to be present in only relatively small amounts to do their job. Research has indicated that supplements can be very beneficial in preventing a number of diseases, but these again don't need to be taken in huge amounts. For example, the claims made for huge doses of vitamin C in preventing colds or even cancer—doses in the 3- to 6-gram range—have never really been substantiated, although vitamin C has been shown to lessen the severity of colds, which is valuable in itself.

In general, taking mega-doses of water-soluble vitamins just makes your urine extremely expensive, but large amounts of fat-soluble vitamins are stored in the body and can build up to toxic levels. However, taking certain prescription drugs can lead to vitamin deficiencies, and large doses of vitamins can also interfere with the actions of various drugs. For this reason, you should be very cautious about taking large doses of vitamin or mineral supplements without medical consultation and advice. Again, I recommend that you try *basic reasonable amounts first* and then experiment carefully to see what suits you best. Franco used to add certain supplements to his program each month, write down what he felt the effects to be, then change and try different ones the next month, keeping track of the results in a nutritional journal. This takes time, but eventually he became an expert, not just on what worked best for him, but on supplements in general. Franco believes as I do that getting expert advice is a good place to start, but for best results you need careful, methodical trial-and-error experience to find out what works best for your body and your metabolism.

Incidentally, according to the late Dr. Linus Pauling, as well as most other nutrition experts, it makes no difference whether the supplements you take are natural or synthetic (made in a laboratory). Your body simply can't tell the difference.

THE ENERGY CONTENT OF FOOD

The amount of energy contained in any given amount of food is measured in *calories*. A calorie is a measurement of heat, which makes sense because energy production for muscular contraction in the cell is a form of oxidation. It is slow oxidation, of course, but simply another form of the rapid oxidation we know as *fire*. Calories, then, are a measurement of the amount of heat given off by the "slow burning" of energy in the muscle cells.

All of the macronutrients—protein, carbohydrate, and fat—contain energy, and therefore calories. But they differ in the amount of calories they have. For example,

- 1 gram of protein or 1 gram of carbohydrate = *4 calories*
- 1 gram of fat = *9 calories*

This makes it obvious why those trying to lose body fat try to minimize the fat in their diets—and why backpackers hiking for days across mountains carry food very rich in fat. Fat is more than twice as dense in calories (and therefore "fattening") as either protein or carbohydrate.

One thing to remember when thinking about fat and calories is that all fats, regardless of type, contain the same amount of food energy. Whether you are talking about olive oil, animal fat, butter, lard, or fats and oils in any other form, they all contain the same amount of energy—9 calories per gram.

METABOLIC RATE

Your body metabolizes (oxidizes) calories in two basic ways: in basal metabolism (the energy it takes to maintain basic life functions) and in physical activity. Interestingly, muscle tissue determines the caloric requirements of the human body. This is significant for two reasons:

1. The more muscle you have, the more calories you consume at rest.
2. The more muscle effort you put out, the more calories are consumed in the process.

Actually, your resting metabolic rate (RMR) is calculated on the basis of your lean body mass, which is basically the amount of muscle you have, not counting the mass from fat. The leaner your body mass, the higher your RMR. For those who want to get technical, the formula to calculate this is:

RMR = lean body mass (pounds) $\div$ 2.205 $\times$ 30.4

By this reckoning, a person with a lean body mass of 150 pounds would have an RMR of about 2,100 calories, and a 250-pound individual would burn up about 3,500 calories during the day (not counting any additional exercise). There are other factors that influence metabolic rate—age, gender, body type, thyroid function, to name a few—but essentially the smaller you are, the less you have to eat to maintain your body weight; the bigger you are, the more you have to eat to maintain your body weight. We will talk about this more in the next chapter when we deal with the subject of diet and weight control.

EXERCISE AND ENERGY EXPENDITURE

Any athlete can tell you that the number of calories you burn when exercising depends on the kind of activity you are engaged in. The harder you exercise and the more work you do, the more calories you metabolize. Whether you are moving your own body (running) or lifting a barbell, the more you do it and the harder you do it, the more energy it takes. Following are some examples to give a rough illustration of how this works:

Activity	Calories Burned per Hour
Sleeping	72
Sitting	72–84
Walking (3.5 mph)	336–420
Calisthenics	300–360
Swimming (basic)	360
Cycling (10 mph)	360–420
Jogging (5 mph)	600
Skiing (moderate to steep)	480–720
Running (7.5 mph)	900

Incidentally, notice something about the relationship between walking, jogging, and running. When you go on foot, you burn up about 100 calories per mile (depending, again, on your overall body weight and lean body mass). It doesn't really matter whether you walk or run. You metabolize the same amount of energy for the same distance because you have done about the same amount of work. The difference, of course, is that you burn off the energy much *faster* when you run than when you walk.

The energy expenditure of bodybuilding is largely determined by how intense the training is. When you lift heavy weights for relatively few reps and take long rest periods between sets, you burn relatively few calories. When you train continuously, going from one set to another, one exercise to another, with very little rest, you burn considerable calories over the one and a half or two hours of your workout. When you train on a split schedule, with two workouts a day, you burn up that much more energy, which is why I always trained in this fashion to get cut-up and ready for a contest. Exactly how many calories are consumed in this kind of workout is hard to say. But an expert once estimated that Franco Columbu and I each burned up close to 2,000 calories total in our two daily competition workouts—that is, about 500 calories an hour, about the same as if we had been running at a good pace during all that time.

"FALSE" ENERGY

Bodybuilders and other athletes are always looking for an edge, some way of taking their performance past established limits. However, as they say, there is no such thing as a free lunch. When you subject your body to various kinds of artificial stimulation, you may get short-term results, but there is an inevitable letdown and your overall performance ability is damaged over time. Dr. Lawrence Golding has compiled a partial list of those drugs and hormones that fall into this category:

Adrenaline
Alcohol
Alkalis
Amphetamines
Caffeine
Cocaine
Coramine (nikethamide)
Lecithin
Metrazol (pentylenetetrazol)
Noradrenaline
Sulfa drugs

Obviously, there is nothing wrong with a couple of cups of coffee before training, but a handful of caffeine pills is just going to make you climb walls and possibly injure yourself during your training. Aspirin can reduce soreness, but also seems to interfere with nervous system stimulation of the muscles. As to most of the others, those who think that substances like alcohol, amphetamines, adrenaline, marijuana, or cocaine are going to help them develop outstanding physiques, much less become champions, are living in a fantasy world. To develop the optimum physique, you need to be in an optimum state of health, and to achieve that state "just saying no to drugs" is absolutely essential.

NUTRITIONAL MINIMUMS

Certain nutritional minimums have to be met or else the body is going to suffer from some sort of deprivation. Of course, the harder you exercise, the more stress you are under, and the harsher an environment you live in, the greater your nutritional needs are likely to be.

There is some disagreement over what actually constitutes nutritional minimums for both athletes and nonathletes, but the following guidelines represent a reasonable approach. In terms of the macronutrients, these are:

Protein. The generally recommended amount of protein in the average diet is *1 gram per kilo (2.2 pounds) of body weight.* A few experts believe wrongly that even hard-training bodybuilders do not require any more protein than this—that, in fact, the need for protein in the diet is highly overrated. However, the majority of bodybuilders prefer to take in larger amounts of protein, recommending at least *1 gram per pound of body weight.*

Some bodybuilders take in much larger amounts of protein than this. However, as we will see in the next chapter, the goal of a bodybuilder is to build maximum muscle while keeping body fat to a minimum. And since protein, like all food categories, contains calories, eating too much protein can often mean you are taking in more calories than you can digest and get or stay lean, so this has to be taken into consideration when developing an eating program.

Carbohydrates. The need for carbohydrates in the diet varies a great deal depending on your level of activity. The body requires about *60 grams of carbohydrates* simply to carry on the basic processes of the nervous system (the brain, for example, is fueled almost entirely by carbohydrates).

Carbohydrates, as we've discussed, are also an important fuel for muscular activity. So if your diet is too low in carbohydrates, your workouts will suffer, and this too needs to be taken into consideration when planning what and how much of various foods you can eat.

When it comes to carbohydrates, the amount you choose to eat is largely governed by whether you are trying to gain, lose, or maintain weight, as we'll see in the following chapter on weight control. But there is a way to ensure that you are not taking in too little, and thus putting your body into a state of carbohydrate deprivation. This state is called ketosis. What it is and how to avoid it is discussed in detail on page 728.

In nutritional terms, your best bet is to include some of each type of carbohydrate in your daily diet. As we've discussed, some carbohydrates can metabolize very quickly. Fruits contain high glycemic carbohydrates, so they are good for providing short-term energy, as well as being loaded with essential vitamins. Low glycemic carbohydrates, which take a much longer time for the body to process, turn into energy and provide long-term, time-release energy and nutrition with minimum calories. Green and yellow vegetables are also excellent carbohydrate sources.

How fast carbs metabolize is also important because of the action of insulin. Insulin is released by the body to break down carbohydrate sugars (diabetes is a disease of insulin deficiency, which is why diabetics need to take insulin shots). When a lot of high glycemic carbs are introduced into the body in large amounts, the body has to provide a lot of insulin to deal with it. This is called an insulin spike. This insulin rapidly processes the carbohydrate, your blood sugar levels drop quickly, your energy levels drop as well, and you end up getting hungry again fairly soon. Eating higher glycemic carbohydrates, or eating faster-absorbing carbs in smaller amounts or in combination with protein, fat, or low glycemic carbs, tends to smooth out this process, so the body releases only moderate amounts of insulin and your blood sugar levels tend to stay more constant, meaning you don't lose energy and start to feel hungry nearly as quickly.

Of course, many people who have been told to avoid excess carbs ask me why I praise carbohydrates as an excellent source of nutrition and energy. First of all, I am not recommending "excess" anything. Carbohydrates are an essential part of a good nutritious eating plan, but only in balance and proportion to the other basic foods. But it is also true that people often confuse nutritious carbohydrate foods with those containing processed sugar—cakes, candy, soft drinks, or processed foods with sugar added. The problem with these fast foods is that they provide virtually empty calories, adding tremendously to your caloric intake and very little in the way of nutrition. This simply is not the case when you eat foods like fruit, vegetables, rice, or potatoes.

Fats. Getting enough fats is seldom a problem in the American diet. Eggs, red meats, dairy products, and oils are all very high in fat. It is common to see diets that contain as much as 50 percent fats. For health reasons, the normal recommendation is to keep fats below 30 percent, and there seems to be no benefit to health (and some problems resulting) when you drop your fat intake below the 20 percent mark. (See the next section, Balanced Diet.)

BALANCED DIET

The body works best when you ingest foods in certain combinations. The required dietary balance is pretty much the same for the bodybuilder as for anyone else. The currently recommended balance, according to the McGovern Select Committee on Nutrition and Human Needs, is approximately: *protein, 12 percent; carbohydrates, 58 percent; and fats, 30 percent.*

In my own career, I usually found myself eating a diet balanced quite differently: protein, 40 percent; carbohydrates, 40 percent; and fats, 20 percent. It should be remembered, however, that I was 240 pounds and training very hard. My 40 percent of carbohydrates represented more actual food than the average person's 58 percent, so I was certainly getting all of the nutrients my body needed.

However, there are bodybuilders who go much too far in their pursuit of protein, eating as much as 70 percent protein in their diets. Others believe protein is not that important, and eat as little as 10 or 12 percent. I believe that neither of these approaches is likely to be very successful.

Other bodybuilders eat only a few foods for months on end—tuna, chicken, fruit, and salads, for example. This may help them to cut down on body fat, but it also prevents them from taking all the nutrients they need for maximum energy and growth. Cutting way down on any of the general food groups leaves you open to developing vitamin and mineral deficiencies. Eating a disproportionate amount of fruit, as some fad diets have recommended, makes it difficult to obtain sufficient protein and a wide enough variety of vitamins and minerals. Vegetarian and super-high-carbohydrate diets might not provide enough protein for a bodybuilder attempting to build maximum muscle mass. Diets too high in protein can put an unhealthy strain on your kidneys and liver, cause your body to lose calcium, and make you fat.

I remember a big eater like Ken Waller downing three high-protein portions at each meal in the 1970s because he believed his body could use all of this at one time. The result was that his system was overwhelmed by all this protein and transformed what it couldn't use into stored body fat. As a result Ken usually had to lose a lot of excess weight prior to a contest in order to get in shape.

THE IMPORTANCE OF GLYCOGEN

Glycogen is the form in which carbohydrate is stored in the liver and in muscles to be used as fuel for exercise. The trained muscle increases its ability to store glycogen, and since glycogen is found together with water (2.7 grams of water for each gram of glycogen), this extra bulk in the muscles causes them to swell up and appear larger. This is why bodybuilders carb up at the end of a contest diet before they go onstage. Muscles full of glycogen are big, round, and full; muscles deprived of glycogen are small and flat.

KETOSIS

Ketosis is the result of carbohydrate deprivation. Your body requires adequate amounts of carbohydrates in order to properly metabolize body fat. As the saying goes, "fat is burned in the furnace of carbohydrate." When there is not enough carbohydrate in the body for this process to take place (usually as a result of an overly strict weight-loss diet), the body has to take emergency measures. The primary symptom of ketosis is ketonemia, the appearance of ketone bodies in the blood. Ketone bodies are the product of the incomplete burning of fats. These ketones can be used in place of glycogen for energy production, and they can also be used as energy to fuel brain and nervous system function (which otherwise rely entirely on glycogen).

The problem is that ketone bodies are not nearly as efficient in fueling exercise as glycogen. In a prolonged state of ketosis, you tend to be sluggish, your mental processes suffer, and your body gradually becomes dehydrated. Worse, in the absence of carbohydrates your body begins to metabolize larger and larger amounts of amino acids (protein) for additional energy. This is obviously highly counterproductive for anyone trying to build and maintain a solid foundation of muscle mass.

There are other disadvantages to the ketosis diet as well, which we'll examine in more detail in the next chapter. In the meantime, take it from me: *Any* kind of serious deprivation is detrimental to your health, training intensity, and ability to build maximum muscle mass.

EATING AND TRAINING

Many young bodybuilders ask me for advice about what and when they should eat in relation to their training program. The muscles require an ample supply of blood during training, since a lot of the pump you experience is from blood swelling up your muscles. But if the digestive system is also using excess amounts of blood to digest a big meal, there won't be enough to go around and your muscles will suffer for it. When you eat too heavily before training, you are setting up a conflict in the body, a demand for excess blood in too many places at once. This is why parents are right when they tell children not to go swimming right after a big meal; lack of adequate blood supply to the muscles used in swimming can lead to problems like severe cramps.

Training with a full stomach can be a very unpleasant experience. You feel bloated, sluggish, and slow, and a really hard set can make you feel nauseated.

The body metabolizes food at different rates. It takes from 2 to 6 hours for the stomach to empty its contents. Foods rich in carbohydrates digest first, followed by protein foods; fatty foods are the last to leave.

When you wake up in the morning and haven't eaten anything for 8 to 12 hours, your body is depleted of carbohydrates. Since carbohydrates are needed to produce the glycogen the muscles need for intense contraction, it makes sense to eat a high-carbohydrate breakfast before going to the gym to train in the morning.

A light meal of fruit, fruit juice, or toast can be eaten before you train and will give you energy without slowing you down. However, a breakfast that includes eggs, meat, or cheese—all high in both protein and fats—will take longer to digest, so you would do better not to eat foods like these before you train.

It is not a good idea to eat a big meal immediately after a workout either. You put your body under great stress when you train and you need to give your system time to return to normal, for the blood to leave the muscles and the stress reaction to diminish. A protein or protein/carb supplement drink after a workout supplies needed nutrition to satisfy the demands created by training in a form that is easy on your digestive system. By the time you shower, get dressed, and leave the gym your system will return to a more normal state and you can sit down to a nutritious balanced meal of "real food."

HOW OFTEN TO EAT

There is a myth that your digestive system needs to "rest," that you shouldn't eat too often because it somehow overwhelms your ability to digest food efficiently. Actually, the opposite is true. In the early days of human evolution people often grazed during the day—that is, they ate periodically whenever they found the appropriate plants or fruit, or happened upon an opportunity to get some animal protein.

Your body handles a lot of small meals better than a few big ones. Three meals a day is good, 4 meals a day is better. Bodybuilders frequently eat every 2 to 3 hours, which means at least 5 meals a day (a little bit extreme for most people). Eating fairly often is a good strategy when it comes to weight control, assuming your total calories for the day remain under control, since you rarely get extremely hungry eating this way and the body has little reason to store a lot of your food intake as body fat—which we will deal with in greater depth in the next chapter.

CHAPTER 2

Weight Control: Gaining Muscle, Losing Fat

THE PURPOSE OF diet in bodybuilding is to help you gain muscle and lose fat. A lot of popular diets are concerned with losing overall body weight, but many of them result in losing a substantial amount of muscle tissue as well as stored body fat. Even some bodybuilders fall prey to the temptation to half-starve themselves in an attempt to achieve maximum muscularity. But most successful bodybuilders have learned the strategies outlined in this chapter for building muscle mass, keeping body fat to a minimum, and maintaining energy levels even during times when they are restricting calories.

In the following pages we will first examine what some of the goals and problems are when it comes to dieting for weight control, then go on to give specific programs for achieving your personal dietary goals.

BODY COMPOSITION

The bodybuilding diet is very different from many popular diets. For bodybuilders, what is important is not weight but *body composition*—that is, the amount and proportion of

1. lean body mass (muscle, bone, connective tissue)
2. body fat
3. water

When young bodybuilders start out, their main concern usually is to *get big.* But as they become more experienced, they realize that their goal ought to be *control* of their body composition, to change one kind of body into another kind of body, rather than just trying to add (or lose) body weight without regard to whether the alteration involves lean body mass (muscle) or not. In my opinion, the sooner you realize the importance of *building muscle mass* rather than just putting on bulk the better off you'll be. Bulking up by getting fat just gives you that much extra weight to work off later, and it promotes some very bad habits that you'll eventually have to break.

In this chapter we will look at how to get the necessary control of your body composition by watching what to eat, how much to eat, and how much effect exercise has on your diet program, as well as look at other variables such as body type and age.

For those who are bodybuilding for other purposes than competition—whether for better athletic performance, health and strength, or any other reason—the type of diet that bodybuilders have developed by trial-and-error experiment over the years has been shown to be the most effective and efficient way to control body composition. The body doesn't really like to do two contradictory things simultaneously, namely, to (1) gain muscle and (2) lose fat. Achieving this is very difficult. But bodybuilders all over the world routinely make changes to their body weight and body composition that are incredible by normal, everyday standards. How they manage to do this is the subject of both this chapter and the one on competition dieting that follows.

INFLUENCES ON BODY COMPOSITION

Whatever your body composition happens to be at any given point is the result of a number of factors:

Genetics. What is your body type? Are you a naturally skinny ectomorph, a muscular mesomorph, or a heavier endomorph?

Metabolism. Do you burn off everything you eat, or the opposite? This is another genetic factor. Some people can't seem to gain much weight no matter what they do, while others complain they can get fat just by *looking* at food.

Calorie consumption. Are you a big eater? How many calories do you eat in the course of the day? If you take in more food energy than you need—whether in the form of protein, carbs, or fat—your body will tend to store the excess as body fat.

Quality of diet. Do you "eat clean"? Are the calories you are consuming in the form of quality food, including lean protein sources, a variety of nutrient-rich carbohydrates that include vegetables, fruits, and starches? Are you eating a diet relatively low in fat? Or do your eating habits include a lot of fast food, highly processed packaged foods, food items calorically dense in fat and sugar?

Type of exercise. Are you doing serious bodybuilding training, the kind of weight training that encourages your body to turn your daily food intake into lean muscle tissue? If so, are your workouts sufficiently intense and consistent?

Amount of exercise. How many calories do you consume with daily exercise? Are you doing enough aerobic exercise to help burn off any excess calories and/or force the body to turn stored body fat into fuel for your workouts?

DIET AND BODY TYPES

We've already talked about the differences in body types (see page 162). When it comes to eating for controlling body composition:

Ectomorphs have fast metabolisms and bodies that tend to turn food into energy easily and quickly. They need to eat high protein and to increase their overall caloric intake as well. Needing more calories, they often benefit from having more fat in their diets than the other two body types.

Mesomorphs, whose bodies easily turn food into muscle, also require high protein for muscle maintenance, but they can eat a relatively normal number of calories, or just a little lower number, and burn off fat effectively.

Endomorphs, with their slower metabolisms and greater number of fat cells, have a strong tendency to turn ingested food into stored body fat. They have to eat enough protein, but otherwise have to keep their caloric intake to a minimum. This means making sure that no more than 20 percent of their calories come in the form of fat.

About 20 percent of endomorphs have lower-than-average thyroid output, which compounds the problem. However, although they always have to work harder at keeping lean, they tend to build muscle relatively easily compared to ectomorphs, and they can eventually lose a lot of excess body fat by diet and exercise.

AGE AND BODY FAT

Many teenagers, especially the ectomorphic and ecto-mesomorphic ones, have such fast metabolisms that they can seemingly eat anything, even high-fat and sugar junk food, without getting fat. These are the ones who benefit from "weight gainer" products.

However, even these individuals will likely see some change in their bodies as they get older. In fact, studies have shown that the adult metabolism tends to slow down by about 10 calories per day per year after the age of thirty. This may not seem like much, but it does account for why many individuals of forty and older find themselves gaining weight even though they have made no change in their exercise and diet habits.

This slowing of the metabolism with age is not an insurmountable obstacle. It just means watching your diet a little more closely, and doing an extra 10 minutes a day or so of cardiovascular training. However, one factor that contributes to a slowing metabolism with age is slow, gradual loss of muscle tissue. So if you continue to train hard and keep your muscles big and strong, this tendency to get fatter as you get older will be much less of a problem for you.

CALORIE CONSUMPTION

No matter what your body type, you will lose body fat if your energy expenditure is consistently greater than your energy intake—if you burn off more calories than you consume. In other words,

(A) your RMR (resting metabolic rate) + calories consumed in activity = calories expended
(B) food eaten during the day = calories consumed

So, when A is consistently larger than B, *you lose body fat.* And when B is consistently larger than A, *you gain body fat.*

A friend of mind who is an avid cross-country hiker once told me, "When I go backpacking in the Sierras for days at a time, across rugged terrain with a sixty-pound pack on my back, it is *impossible* to carry enough food to maintain my body weight." That's why various kinds of trail mix you buy in sporting goods stores are so high in fat (although some still seem to think these products are diet food). In many cases, hikers have to have caches of food waiting for them along the trail to replenish their provisions, so demanding is this kind of activity in terms of energy expenditure.

The more active you are—the more you walk, run, ride a bicycle, ski, swim, play sports—the more calories you burn and the more easily you are going to be able to control your fat weight. This is why most serious bodybuilders increase their overall level of activity over that involved in their gym training by doing some kind of cardiovascular or aerobic exercise, using a treadmill, exercise bicycle, stair stepper, or other exercise device.

QUALITY OF DIET

But *what you eat* is also important, along with how much. The more you restrict your calories, the more certain you have to be that you are getting the most nutritional density possible—the most bang for your buck. A bodybuilder who consumes 3,000 calories a day of mostly lean protein and a variety of vegetable, fruit, and starch carbohydrate sources is going to be able to train more intensely and build more muscle than somebody whose 3,000-calorie intake consists mostly of good, processed fast foods, high in fat and sugar, all adding up to too many empty calories devoid of much nutritional value.

"Eating clean" is what the bodybuilding diet is all about. "You are what you eat," is the old saying. And if you eat junk your body will become—well, you get the point.

CREATING "DEMAND"

When you eat, you take food energy into your body. All of those food calories—whether from protein, carbs, or fat—will make you fat if your body doesn't use that energy for some specific purpose.

What your body *does* with the food you eat depends a lot on what kind of demand you create by the amount and type of training you do. For example, aerobic training tends to burn a lot of calories, and therefore depletes your body of *glycogen*—which is the primary source of energy for physical activity. As a consequence, when you eat carbohydrate after an endurance training session, the body turns that carbohydrate into replacement glycogen as quickly as it can, and little of that carbohydrate is likely to be diverted to become stored body fat.

On the other hand, intense weight training—working your muscles against heavy resistance—creates a major demand for replacement *protein.* Protein eaten soon after a workout, or on the same day as an intense gym workout, will be used by the body to rebuild muscle tissue at a much higher rate than on days when you are not doing that kind of training. Again, when the body is in this high state of demand, it is unlikely that nonexcessive amounts of ingested protein will be stored as body fat to any great degree.

So, in general terms, *when your goal is to direct protein into your muscles, you need to train with weights. When your goal is to burn off excess energy, you need to do increased amounts of aerobic training.*

HOW MUCH AEROBICS?

Everyone should do some cardiovascular training because it's good for your heart, lungs, and circulatory system. I do some kind of aerobic training for *at least 30 minutes a day, 4 or 5 days a week.*

Slow gainers, individuals who are ectomorphic, who are slender and have trouble gaining weight, should probably not do much more than this.

Aerobic exercise burns energy, and hard gainers need to conserve energy in order to achieve maximum muscle growth.

Those trying to lose body fat, especially if they tend toward being endomorphic and have trouble getting lean, can benefit from more aerobic training—say, *45 minutes to an hour, 4 or 5 days a week.*

However, if you are not used to doing much cardiovascular training, start out slowly and give your body a chance to get used to it, especially if you do any kind of weight-bearing exercise like running or using a treadmill. You won't make much progress if your program is interrupted because you become too sore or develop some kind of stress injury.

Also, try to avoid doing your cardiovascular training too soon before your gym workouts. Some people feel doing aerobics first is a good warm-up, but this kind of exercise will fatigue your body and make it hard to train as intensely as you're capable of.

EATING TO GAIN MUSCLE

As we've discussed, many bodybuilders, young ones in particular, start out relatively underweight, in a "Hey, skinny, your ribs are showing" state. For them, gaining muscle will involve:

1. stimulating muscular growth by heavy, intense, consistent bodybuilding training.

2. eating a sufficient amount of protein to fill the demand for amino acids created by the training.

3. increasing overall caloric intake to a sufficient degree to support the demands of intense exercise, but not so much as to create an unwanted gain in body fat.

4. keeping your aerobic training to a healthy minimum, no more than 30 minutes a day, 4 or 5 days a week, as we discussed.

To give you a head start when it comes to planning your weight-gain diet, I have outlined a sample diet plan you can follow, or use as a guide in developing your own. Since I don't think you ought to suddenly introduce such large quantities of food into your system that your body may not be able to handle them, the program is constructed on three levels, to be followed in this order:

1. Begin eating according to Level I, and continue on this level until you stop gaining weight, then go on to Level II.

2. If after 3 weeks you are not gaining weight on the Level I diet, go on to Level II.

3. Once eating on the Level II diet, continue on it as long as you continue to gain weight. When the weight gains cease, go on to Level III.

4. If after 3 weeks on Level II you don't experience any weight gain, go on to Level III.

Stuffing a lot of calories into your body at one time is not a good idea, as we learned in the last chapter. The digestive system simply can't handle this volume of food. So, to eat a lot more, you have to eat more often. This is why I recommend eating more than 3 meals a day in order to spread your caloric intake out. It would be better to eat 4 meals, and to supplement your food intake with high-protein drinks—drinks that contain large amounts of easily digested amino acids (which we'll look at in more detail later). This is exactly what I did when I was fifteen years old and desperate to gain weight, and I found that drinking protein drinks not only satisfied my extra need for calories and amino acids, but also cost a lot less than other protein foods.

MUSCLE-GAIN MENU PLAN

We talked about the need for sufficient protein to support muscle growth and how slow gainers also need an overall increase in calories to support their very fast metabolic rates. However, while this kind of eating plan is primarily for those who tend toward the ectomorphic, I want to caution again that just because you tend to be very lean *doesn't mean that eating a lot of junk food and empty calories is good for you.* Train hard and eat more, fine. But try to eat clean, to eat nutritious meals. After all, you can't gain muscle if you lack energy and don't have the nutrients you need in your system.

Of course, those who are already heavy eaters may be surprised at the following muscle-gain recommendations, but ectomorphs are generally very lean, not only because many have fast metabolisms, but also because *they tend not to be big eaters in the first place.* However, if you are an ectomorphic type yet find that the Level I diet or even that of Level II is actually less than you normally eat, obviously you are going to have to increase your food intake even further and go right on to a higher level. Adjust caloric intake up or down to suit your individual needs. Just make sure that the food you eat is wholesome and nutritious.

If you eat according to the menu plans detailed here and supplement your meals with the recommended protein drinks, you will be getting more than enough protein and shouldn't give it another thought. For ectomorphs, who have a great deal of problems adding body weight, the key is hard training and a lot more calories, not any lack of protein. To demonstrate this, I have included the approximate protein content of each of the suggested meals.

LEVEL I

Breakfast

2 eggs, preferably poached, but any style okay
¼ pound meat, fish, or fowl
8 ounces whole milk
1 slice whole-grain toast with butter

(protein = approx. 52 grams)

Lunch

¼ pound meat, fish, fowl, or cheese
1 or 2 slices whole-grain bread
8 ounces whole milk or fresh juice

(protein = approx. 43 grams)

Dinner

½ pound meat, fish, or fowl
Baked potato with butter or sour cream
Large raw salad
8 ounces whole milk

(protein = approx. 48 grams)

LEVEL II

Breakfast

3 eggs, poached or any style
¼ pound meat, fish, fowl, or cheese
8 ounces whole milk
1 or 2 slices whole-grain toast with butter

(protein = approx. 61 grams)

Lunch

½ pound meat, fish, fowl, or cheese (or any combination)
2 slices whole-grain bread with butter or mayonnaise
8 ounces whole milk
1 piece fresh fruit

(protein = approx. 71 grams)

Dinner

½ pound meat, fish, fowl, or cheese (or any combination)
Baked or boiled white or sweet potato
Large raw salad

(protein = approx. 59 grams)

LEVEL III

Breakfast

4 eggs, poached or any style
8 ounces whole milk
1 or 2 slices whole-grain bread with butter
1 piece fresh fruit

You may substitute hot oatmeal, bran cereal, or other cooked cereal for the fruit and bread, but sweeten only with fructose. Use half-and-half or cream if higher caloric intake is desired.

(protein = approx. 72 grams)

Lunch

½ pound meat, fish, fowl, or cheese
1 or 2 slices whole-grain bread with butter or mayonnaise
8 to 16 ounces whole milk
1 piece fresh fruit (with cottage cheese if desired)

(protein = approx. 74 grams)

Dinner

½ to 1 pound meat, fish, fowl, or cheese (or any combination)
Baked or steamed potato, or baked or boiled beans
Lightly steamed fresh vegetable
Large raw salad
1 piece fresh fruit
8 ounces whole milk

(protein = approx. 112 grams)

HIGH-PROTEIN, HIGH-CALORIE DRINKS

We discussed the benefits of protein supplement drinks in the last chapter (see page 709). Actually, there are two very different kinds of drinks you can use to obtain additional protein:

1. protein drinks that have no added (or very few additional) calories except for those found in the protein itself.
2. weight-gainer drinks that are loaded with a lot of additional calories as well as those contained in the protein.

When you take the time to read the labels on these two different products (which we'll discuss in more detail later in the chapter) you can easily see the difference. A straightforward protein-supplement drink providing 27 grams of protein, mixed with water and sweetened artificially, contains 108 calories. On the other hand, a weight-gainer product I'm familiar with that has the same amount of protein but is also loaded with carbohydrates and contains some fat as well, when mixed with whole milk as recommended, contains a whooping *2,000* calories per serving! Obviously, you should make sure you know the difference when you decide to use such a product.

In my own career, before there were as many commercial protein drinks (or bars) available as there are now, I always preferred to create my own drinks, since that way I knew precisely what was in them and what kind of nutritional benefit I was getting.

I began mixing my own protein drinks right from the start, but when I was fifteen years old I didn't have access to the protein powder you can buy today. Instead, I put together a drink combining ingredients like skim milk powder, eggs, and honey poured into a thermos bottle, and took it with me to school or work. That way I could drink half of it around ten in the morning, between breakfast and lunch, and the other half around three o'clock. The habit of having a protein drink with me proved even more valuable when I was in the army and couldn't always depend on getting three good meals a day. Sometimes my container of protein drink was the only dependable supply of protein to get me through the day.

As I learned more about nutrition, I developed protein-drink formulas that were even more effective and nutritious than those I concocted in Austria. But the purpose remained the same: to super-saturate the body with protein, making the necessary amino acids available for maximum muscle-building, and to supply the necessary calories to fuel training and growth.

The best protein powders are those that derive their amino acids from milk and egg sources—whey in particular is becoming popular at the moment. Most of these do not mix easily with juice or milk, so use a blender if you have one. Always check the label of any protein powder you are considering purchasing. For example, a typical milk-and-egg protein powder has a nutritional content something like the following:

Serving size: 1 ounce (about ⅛ cup)
Calories: 110
Protein per serving: 26 grams
Carbohydrate per serving: 0 grams
Fat per serving: 0 grams

Each of the drinks here is made in sufficient quantity for 3 servings a day, preferably to be drunk between breakfast and lunch, between lunch and dinner, and an hour or so before you go to bed. However, because protein takes a long time to digest, be sure to have the protein drink at least 1½ hours before a workout.

LEVEL I

(protein = approx. 50 grams)

20 ounces milk or juice
4 ounces cream (or 1 ounce safflower oil and 3 ounces water)*
2 eggs
2 teaspoons lecithin granules
¼ cup good-quality milk-and-egg protein powder
Flavoring

In a blender, place the milk, cream, eggs, and lecithin; blend for an instant. Wait several minutes for the lecithin granules to dissolve, then add the protein powder and blend until mixed. For flavor, use your imagination: a very ripe banana, vanilla extract, any other fruit or flavoring. To make the drink sweeter, add a tablespoon or less of fructose—do not use high sucrose foods like ice cream or chocolate syrup.

*For those with a slower metabolism, substitute safflower oil and water for the cream. If additional calories are not a problem, try alternating cream one day with oil and water the next.

LEVEL II

(protein = approx. 72 grams)

16 ounces milk or juice
6 ounces cream (or 2 ounces safflower oil and 5 ounces water)
4 eggs
4 teaspoons lecithin granules
½ cup milk-and-egg protein powder
Flavoring

In a blender, place the milk, cream, eggs, and lecithin; blend for an instant. Wait several minutes for the lecithin granules to dissolve completely, then add the protein and blend until mixed. Flavor as in Level I drink, except that you can use as much as 2 tablespoons of fructose for sweetness.

LEVEL III

(protein = approx. 98 grams)

16 ounces milk or juice
8 ounces cream (or 3 ounces safflower oil and 6 ounces water)
6 eggs
6 teaspoons lecithin granules
¾ cup milk-and-egg protein powder
Flavoring

In a blender, place the milk, cream, eggs, and lecithin; blend for an instant. Wait several minutes for lecithin granules to completely dissolve, then add the protein and blend until mixed. Flavor as desired.

If you find your weight gain is not as large as you would like, even at Level III, here is an even more potent drink you can add to your diet (protein = approx. 96 grams).

12 ounces milk or juice
12 ounces cream (or 4 ounces safflower oil and 8 ounces water)
6 eggs
6 teaspoons lecithin granules
¾ cup milk-and-egg protein powder
Flavoring

In a blender, place the milk, cream, eggs, and lecithin; blend for an instant. Wait several minutes for lecithin granules to completely dissolve, then add the protein and blend until mixed. Flavor as desired.

While vitamin and mineral supplements are not specifically fundamental to gaining weight, making sure you have no nutrient deficiencies is essential to making optimum progress in bodybuilding, whether your short-term goals are weight gain or weight loss.

HOW TO LOSE FAT

Fasting would seem to be the quickest way to lose fat. But for every pound you lose, 60 percent is muscle and only 40 percent is fat. This is not acceptable to somebody trying to build a solid structure of lean body mass. You actually lose more muscle than fat.

In bodybuilding terms, losing fat weight involves maintaining your protein levels while cutting back on all other caloric intake. You increase the caloric deficit by adding more aerobic exercise to your program and thus burning up more energy.

It is hard to say how many calories you need to eat in order to lose weight—because of so many variables, such as body type, body weight, level of exercise, and natural metabolism—except that you need to put your body into caloric deficit, to burn off more energy than you take in from your food. This is often mostly a matter of trial and error. For example, if you write down what foods you are eating and find they add up to 3,000 calories a day, and you are maintaining your body weight with this amount, you can try cutting back to 2,500 or 2,000 calories a day in order to create a caloric deficit and lose body fat. You can also increase your level of physical activity to burn off additional energy. If you have a very slow metabolism, you might have to cut back further to 1,600 or 1,800 calories. As I said, this is a matter to a great degree of personal experience and experiment. But the rule is simple: To lose fat, you have to cut back on calories, increase exercise, or both.

However, I can tell you the *maximum* amount you can diet if you are trying to lose *absolutely as much fat as possible*—without sacrificing muscle tissue. This is the formula:

1. Continue to eat a sufficient amount of protein (at least 1 gram of protein for each pound of body weight) on days in which you are training—the demand is somewhat less on your rest days.

2. Eat low fat—about 20 percent of your total daily caloric intake. (But research shows supplementing your diet with 6 grams—6 one-gram capsules—of fish oil each day lowers body fat and increases muscle mass with no change in diet.)

3. Reduce your carbohydrates as far as possible without going into a state of ketosis (see page 728).

4. Try to do 45 minutes to an hour of aerobic training, 4 or 5 times a week, as we discussed earlier.

If you continue to eat enough protein, and you are not in a ketonic state (and therefore are not using an excessive amount of amino acids for energy), and your fat intake is reasonably low, *you are then dieting as hard as you can without suffering from nutritional or caloric deprivation.* Remember, the amount of carbs you need to stay out of ketosis will vary depending on how much exercise (weight training plus aerobics) you are doing. So if you are planning to diet hard, you need to be prepared to check whether you are in ketosis on a regular basis.

Incidentally, remember that carbohydrate is in no way bad for you or particularly fattening. As long as it is nutritional it is not ingested in the form of empty calories. The reason you cut way back on ingestion of carbs when you are dieting is to keep your overall caloric intake (except for protein) to a minimum.

KETOSIS

Ketosis is caused by eating too little carbohydrate. Though this condition should be avoided (see page 728), a lot of bodybuilders like the ketosis diet anyway. Since it lets you eat both a lot of protein and fat, being in ketosis tends to reduce your feelings of hunger. Carbohydrate deprivation also causes dehydration, and it is easy to confuse the loss of water weight with loss of body fat.

When you are limiting your carbohydrate intake, you can test for ketosis by obtaining some Ketostix at virtually any pharmacy. When these test strips are passed through your urine they turn red to purple if you are in ketosis; the color indicates the depth of your detogenic state. As long as the test strips show no indication of ketosis, you are not depriving yourself of carbohydrates. As soon as you see *any* sign of a color change you will know that your body lacks the glycogen it requires and that you need to increase your carbohydrate intake. This is the bottom line: *Cut back your carbohydrates as far as you want as long as the Ketostix don't change color. When they do, increase your carbs.*

RECOMMENDED PROTEIN SOURCES

There are many possible sources of low-calorie protein, but following are what most bodybuilders tend to rely on:

Fish (particularly canned tuna packed in water, not oil). A few types of fish are high in fat. Shellfish is low in fat, but high in cholesterol. (By the way, as we saw in the last chapter, fatty fish like salmon and trout are actually beneficial to eat occasionally because of their oils.)
Fowl (chicken, turkey). Remove skin, which is high in fat; some fowl, such as duck, are higher in fat.
Eggs. Egg whites are lower in calories, but whole eggs have more protein and are much more nutritious.
Nonfat milk (instead of low-fat). Nonfat milk is 50 percent protein and 50 percent carbohydrate, whereas about 2 percent of low-fat milk is fat.
Milk-and-egg or whey protein powder

The following protein sources tend to be higher in fat, but are a good nutritious source of amino acids:

Beef. Stick to lean cuts; a regular 3-ounce sirloin steak gives you about 330 calories, with 20 grams protein, 27 grams fat; by comparison, a very lean cut of the same size might contain 220 calories, with 24 grams protein and only 13 grams fat.
Pork. Lean cuts only; avoid pork foods like sausage and bacon.
Lamb. Lamb chops are higher in fat than pork chops.
Cheese. Some cheeses are higher in fat than others; if you are a cheese lover, check a food guide for lower-fat kinds.
Whole milk (and other dairy products like butter, cream, and sour cream)

RECOMMENDED CARBOHYDRATE SOURCES

Vegetables (green vegetables especially—broccoli, asparagus, Brussels sprouts, peas, etc.; whenever possible, eat vegetables either raw or lightly steamed)
Beans (not out of a can, too high in sugar). Beans are not a complete protein, so they need to be eaten in combination with meat, rice, or some other complementary food.
Salads. Go easy on the dressing.
Fruits (fresh, not canned)
Whole wheat or rye bread
Baked potatoes. A medium potato contains only about 100 calories; pass up the butter or sour cream.
Rice (not white processed rice or Minute Rice)

To keep your calories low, keep your food relatively plain. Avoid butter, sour cream, and such oily condiments as ketchup and mayonnaise. Bake, broil, or steam your food—don't fry (which adds calories) or boil (which destroys nutrients). Go light on salad dressings: A tablespoon of oil contains 100 calories, the same as a pat of butter. Cut down on your use of salt.

A SUMMARY OF FAT-LOSS DIET RULES

1. As recommended, give yourself time to lose the fat—if you are losing more than 2 pounds a week you are probably losing muscle as well as fat.

2. Lower your caloric intake until you begin to notice weight loss. Stay at this level as long as you continue to lose weight. If a diet is successful, don't make it more severe.

3. Don't diet any more extremely than the maximum recommended here—at least 1 gram of protein per pound of body weight, low fat, and reduce carbs as much as possible without going into ketosis.

4. Metabolize additional calories with aerobic exercise. If this is new to you, start out slowly and build up, but ultimately 45 to 60 minutes, 4 or 5 days a week, of fast walking, jogging, or bike riding, in the gym on exercise devices or outdoors on your own, will make a big difference in attaining your weight-loss goals.

5. Take vitamin and mineral supplements to ensure that you are getting adequate nutrition.

6. Eat fresh food whenever you can. This gives you maximum nutrition with a minimum of calories. Canned, frozen, or otherwise processed foods are less nutritious and are generally loaded with sugar, salt, and chemical additives.

7. Learn to keep count of calories. Otherwise, it is easy to think you are eating less than you really are.

READING LABELS

I would like to recommend that everyone get in the habit of reading labels. A quick glance at a product can be misleading. There is an effort to standardize such terms as "low fat" or "low sugar" or "lite," but advertisers often use those phrases to mean pretty much whatever they want.

Nutritional labels themselves nowadays are pretty specific. For example, I'm holding a can of tuna packed in water. Obviously, I don't want tuna packed in oil because oil is 100 calories per tablespoon, which makes the oil as calorically rich as the tuna itself. I see it has zero carbs. That makes sense. It is fish protein, and there are no carbs in that. How much protein?

Twelve grams per 2-ounce serving. Okay, so how much fat? The fat content is 2 grams per serving. Not too bad, that is only 18 calories from fat and 80 calories total. The sodium content is 250 milligrams, which is of no concern to us now but will be in the next chapter when we talk about competition dieting.

All right, suppose I decide to have some pasta with my tuna as a change from eating it with rice. Let's see, here's a package of dried fettucini. Well, it's got 8 grams of protein per serving and 39 grams of carbohydrate. Good, it's not pure carbs but has protein, too. Total fat is 2.5 grams, again pretty low. If I stick to the serving size (and the only way to be sure of doing that is by using a diet scale!) the pasta is only 210 calories, with just 25 calories from fat.

What I've just done is put together a 290-calorie meal, with 20 grams of protein and not a whole lot of fat. A nice, healthy meal. Of course, if I put butter on my pasta, well, that's another 100 or 200 calories, almost all from fat. How about spaghetti sauce? The label says ½ cup serving gives me 80 more calories, not too much fat and 2 more grams of protein. Hey, 370 calories and 22 grams of fat, complex carbs from the pasta, that's a pretty good meal for a weight-control diet.

Now, do I have to be a nutrition expert to do all this? Nope. I just read the labels. Just as I read the label of a prepackaged, all-in-one, pop-in-the-oven pasta and cheese product the other day that had only 8 grams of protein, was a total of 750 calories, and 40 percent of that was from fat! Sure, I know most bodybuilders would avoid eating a packaged meal like this, but other food products out there can easily fool you; they seem to be low in calories and fat but aren't. They may say "reduced fat" on the front label, they may claim to be "lower in calories" (than what?), but check carefully on the nutritional label and see what's really in them.

By the way, many foods don't come with labels. The fast-food cheeseburger and large fries that keep tempting you. The thick-crust pizza. However, the nutritional content of many of these foods *is* available nowadays, posted in the restaurant that serves them, but there are also books and food guides, sold in bookstores and most health food stores, that give you the nutritional and caloric breakdown of most popular foods. I recommend that you get one of these, but if you do, be prepared for a shock. Like the people mentioned earlier who think trail mix is a diet food, you may learn to your surprise that those "healthy" breakfast cereals you like so much, or the "high-fiber" bran muffins that taste so good, or the "reduced-calorie" salad dressing you have come to rely on have a lot more calories than you bargained on and are chock-full of what have often been jokingly referred to as the "three basic food groups" of the fast-food industry—fat, sugar, and salt.

CHAPTER 3

Contest Diet Strategies

BODYBUILDING IS THE most effective way to train, shape, develop, and define the muscles of the body ever devised. And although it is extremely beneficial for getting stronger and healthier, looking better, and improving your ability at athletic performance from baseball to golf and skiing to football, *it is also a sport*—in fact, one of the most demanding, difficult, and disciplined of any sport in existence.

We've discussed aspects of bodybuilding competition such as posing extensively in Book Four. However, to maintain maximum muscularity and minimum body fat, with as little subcutaneous fluid obscuring your definition, once you have achieved it, the proper nutritional and dieting strategies are absolutely essential for competition success. Contest dieting is about *total control* of your physique and the methods involved are the subject of this chapter. We will consider such topics as:

1. Controlling your body weight *off-season* to give your contest diet a better chance to work.
2. Measuring all your food intake—protein, carbs, fat, and calories—to make your diet as complete as possible, and learning to keep careful track of your dietary progress in a diet diary.
3. When to eat, how often to eat, and how to avoid the pitfalls of nutritional and caloric deprivation as well as metabolic slowdown.
4. How to measure the changes in your body composition using the scale, calipers, and other body-fat percentage testing methods.
5. How to create a complete diet strategy from 12 weeks before the contest to carbing up the few days before, controlling your subcutaneous fluid levels, and peaking the day of the contest.

GETTING IN SHAPE TO GET IN SHAPE

When you begin a contest diet, you have to start somewhere. And how heavy you are at the beginning of your diet can make a big difference in how successful you are. It may seem obvious, but a lot of bodybuilders don't understand this simple idea—the leaner you are able to stay off-season, the easier it is to diet for a contest. Some bodybuilders like to gain a lot of weight off-season. They call this bulking up, and believe that it not only makes them stronger—so they can train heavier and harder—but also accelerates the muscle-building process. And, from a psychological point of view, a lot of bodybuilders just like to feel big, and walking around in the gym off-season, or in a T-shirt around town, who cares if you are not exactly ripped?

Certainly, you are stronger when you bulk up, if only because an increase in volume in your arms and legs gives them a mechanical advantage, making them better levers. And you definitely want to be sure you are getting enough protein and other nutrients in order to facilitate your muscle-building. But there is a price to be paid for gaining a lot of weight between contests—you have to diet that excess weight away before you compete. And the more body fat you put on, the longer it is going to take to get rid of it and the more muscle you are likely to sacrifice while doing it.

I had this experience many times myself. In the 1960s, when I was younger and enjoyed the ego boost of feeling gigantic, I would let myself gain a lot of weight between contests. Looking at photos of myself back then I can see that I was much smoother after dieting for competition than I was a few years later when I learned to control my weight between competitions. Remember, it isn't how big you look or feel off-season that counts, it's *how you look onstage during the competition.*

Of course, many bodybuilders who compete at, say, 230 pounds, but who walk around off-season at 280 pounds or more, would argue that they are not fat, just smooth. True, a man carrying that amount of solid muscle can put on a great deal of fat without *seeming* to be fat in the normal sense of the word. The hardness of a body like that obscures the excess body weight. But that fat is there nonetheless and has to be gotten rid of in order to come into a contest muscular, ripped, and defined.

Additionally, as we discussed, the longer you have to diet and the more weight you have to lose, the more muscle you are likely to lose in the process. It's not impossible to lose a lot of weight and still get in great shape—obviously, Dorian Yates had a great career but was also famous for getting very heavy off-season—but it's a lot harder. And as far as I'm concerned, competition bodybuilding is hard enough as it is. Contest dieting has become much more scientific than it was when I got into bodybuilding. In the months prior to a contest, I found that cutting out sweets and desserts, bread and butter, and wine with dinner, in combination with intense twice-a-day training, got me hard and defined with relative ease. But what was considered hard and defined twenty years ago would probably not be adequate in today's intensely competitive bodybuilding environment.

In fact, the standards for contest dieting changed considerably from the time I started in bodybuilding until the time I retired. The longer I competed in bodybuilding the more I learned about getting in great contest shape, and the more all of us were learning about how to achieve this in the most effective and efficient way possible. Of course, at one point the pendulum swung too far. Whereas competitors in the 1960s tended to be way too smooth at contests, in the 1970s a lot of bodybuilders showed up so depleted and emaciated that they were often described as looking "near death." I remember seeing bodybuilders who walked around the gym huge and not fat at 240 pounds standing onstage at a depleted and stringy 195 pounds, looking like their own grandfathers.

WRITING IT ALL DOWN

Contest dieting involves a "high-power" version of the dieting we talked about in the last chapter, including eating high protein (sometimes very high protein) to maintain maximum muscle mass, reducing your fat and carbohydrate calories as much as possible, and doing a sufficient amount of aerobic exercise to burn off any excess calories.

But keeping track of all this, making sure you are getting the right amounts of each of the important nutrients, means:

1. Creating a detailed, specific diet plan, writing it down, and keeping careful track of what and how much you eat every day in a diet diary.
2. Using a food scale, measuring cups and spoons to ascertain the calories and grams of protein, carbs, and fat in whatever you eat. (And being *extra* careful when it comes to reading labels.)
3. Eating every 2 or 3 hours.
4. Preparing meals in advance if necessary and carrying them with you in plastic containers so that you can eat on a regular basis every 2 or 3 hours.
5. Taking sufficient amounts of *all* the necessary supplements whenever necessary, including protein, vitamins, minerals, essential fatty acids, and some additional supplements we'll discuss.
6. Drinking a lot of water, at least 4 or 5 liters a day.

I can't emphasize enough how important it is to write down your diet program and keep track of exactly what and how much you are eating on a daily basis. In some studies in which individuals' food intake was monitored, the subjects didn't keep exact track of how much they were eating.

At the end of the day, when they were asked to estimate their caloric intake, it was amazing how far off most of them were. Some thought they ate much more than they really did, and others much less.

When you try to diet without a written program, and without writing down your food intake and its caloric value, the same thing tends to happen. Your sense of how much you are eating can be way over or way under, neither one of which makes sense if you are trying to diet for a contest. Is it tedious and time-consuming to weigh out all your food, control portions, and write down everything you eat and how many calories you are ingesting? You bet. But it's necessary in order to maximize the efficiency and effectiveness of your bodybuilding competition diet.

EATING, EATING, AND EATING

How often to eat can be as important as *what you eat*. In the last chapter we discussed the benefits of eating more than three meals a day. But for competition dieting, you should eat even more often. In fact, many competition bodybuilders complain about how difficult it is to constantly interrupt their daily activities to stop and eat. You wake up, you eat. You go to the gym and train, then eat. You go to a photo shoot. Halfway through, you stop and eat.

Prior to a competition, bodybuilders travel with plastic containers of food. They trail the aroma of tuna wherever they go. They sit down with friends in restaurants, order water, and munch on their tuna, skinless chicken, turkey, rice, baked potatoes, and sweet potatoes. Of course, all of this food is carefully measured; bodybuilders frequently fill containers the night before and label when they are to be eaten, and the total caloric value of all the food is taken into consideration.

Does this sound like a lot of trouble? It is. But this kind of *control* is basic to the ability of today's competition bodybuilders to get in shape on a predictable schedule, peaking right on time and looking great onstage. Somebody once said that bodybuilding ain't rocket science, but sometimes it starts to feel as if it is.

DEPRIVATION

When you diet strictly for a long period, especially when you are training hard, it is easy to deprive your body of essential levels of nutrients. The reason I advise staying (just) out of ketosis is to avoid carbohydrate deprivation. The reason for taking generous amounts of supplements is to avoid carbohydrate deprivation. The high-protein diet ensures that your muscles will never be deprived of the amino acids they require, but you still need fuel for those muscles and that's why you have to keep pouring on those carbs.

Many bodybuilders diet so strictly and restrict their fat intake to such a degree that they experience deprivation when it comes to the essential fatty acids required by the body. First of all, you don't need to get down to a 10 percent fat intake in order to get ripped for a contest. A diet consisting of 20 percent fat is strict enough. Second, you can ensure against taking in too little fat by using essential fatty acid supplements, as described in the last chapter.

METABOLIC SLOWDOWN

The body is a homeostatic organism. It tries to keep itself the same, to keep everything in balance. So when you cut back on your caloric intake, your metabolism will eventually slow down in response, which is detrimental to your dieting efforts.

Hard training, both in the gym and doing aerobic exercise, helps to keep the metabolic rate stimulated. But another way is by varying your caloric intake over time. Suppose you normally eat 3,200 calories and have gone on a 2,000-calorie diet. As your body begins to notice caloric restriction, it will slow down accordingly. But you don't need to actually eat as few as 2,000 calories every day—you can *average* 2,000 calories. You do this by increasing calories for a day or so (say, 2,600), dropping them way down (1,600 calories) for a few days, then bringing them back up to 2,000 calories. Additionally, every week or so you can add a day of caloric intake at your previous level (3,200 calories) to further stimulate your metabolic rate (and reward your hard work with a treat of some sort).

You can sit down with a pencil and paper and calculate exactly how to achieve the average you are looking for, but by dieting this way you will be ensuring that your metabolism is functioning at the highest possible level and therefore *burning more calories* in spite of your reduced-calorie diet.

MEASURING BODY CHANGES

There are a number of ways of keeping careful track of the changes in your body composition:

The scale. As you lose considerable fat, even if you gain some muscle mass in the process (which gets less likely as your diet progresses) you will lose weight.

The tape measure. Is your waistline shrinking? Then you know your diet is working.

Body fat measurement. There are a number of ways of doing this: underwater weighing, calipers, electrical impedance. If you have this done, remember that the specific percentage you get is not necessarily exact. But with multiple measurement (using the same method, with the same equipment) the *direction* of change is what is significant.

The mirror. This is bodybuilding, and the bottom line, after all, is *how you look.*

Certainly, weighing yourself on a regular basis is a fundamental way of gauging how well your diet is working. But hard as it may be to do, the best idea is not to weigh yourself too often, not more than once or twice a week. As I said, the body doesn't lose weight on a regular, continuous basis, so you need to check your weight only at intervals wide enough so that you see real progress when it occurs.

In addition to using the scale, I always preferred to look at *results.* You show your physique to the judges, not how much you weigh. So the mirror is a primary gauge of how far along you are toward getting into contest shape. To use the mirror properly, the best idea is to always look in the same mirror in the same light—one particular mirror in one area of the gym, for example. This cuts down on the variables involved so any changes you observe are likely to be due to diet, not environment or lighting conditions.

There are other ways of ascertaining how much your body is changing. For example, when I was preparing for the 1980 Mr. Olympia contest in Australia I had Franco shoot photos of me once a week so that I could see what effect my training and dieting were having.

Those pictures told me all I needed to know. If I thought the results were coming too slowly, I made changes in my program. If I liked what I saw, I kept doing the same thing.

Dieting, like training, should be done intelligently. Check your results as you go along and make any changes you think are necessary to further your progress. Since your metabolism can vary from season to season, year to year, and since one individual varies so much from the next, no arbitrary number is going to be a sufficient guide for you when it comes to designing a diet.

GETTING STARTED: 12 WEEKS OUT

Most bodybuilders diet for competition for about 12 weeks. This length of time allows the average bodybuilder to lose from 20 to 25 pounds without sacrificing any appreciable amount of muscle mass. It is *very difficult* to go on an extreme diet without losing muscle mass, so your best strategy is to get yourself to a body weight prior to your diet that will allow you to get into top shape in 12 weeks, losing no more than 2 to 2.5 pounds per week.

Of course, a few rare individuals actually *lose* weight between contests and have to work to gain weight as a show approaches. Frank Zane was such an individual. He was usually much lighter off-season than he was at competition time. Franco has always been like that as well—while I was looking for ways to eliminate body fat, he was laughing at me and eating pasta.

However, even bodybuilders like Franco still have to lose body fat to get ripped for a contest. This is just not as apparent because they are also eating enough to allow themselves to gain muscle during this pre-contest period. So even for this type of physique, dieting to lose fat is still necessary.

TESTING FOR KETOSIS

Even though ketosis is not itself a desirable state, it can be used to your advantage when you are trying to establish a competition diet involving the minimum amounts of various foods. As I mentioned, you can test for ketosis by using Ketostix, which are available at most drugstores. When there are ketone bodies in your system, the test sticks will turn purple when they come in contact with your urine.

To help guide you in determining the minimum amount of carbohydrates you should have in your diet, gradually cut down on carbs and test occasionally for ketosis. When you finally see the sticks start to turn purple, *immediately* increase the amount of carbs in your diet until the ketone reaction ceases. At this point, you will be near ketosis, but not in it. You will be eating just enough carbohydrates to avoid a state of carbohydrate deprivation.

Repeat this test occasionally to make sure you are not slipping into ketosis. Keep in mind that the harder you train, the more carbohydrates you will need to keep you out of ketosis. And there is no way to get in shape, no matter how strictly you diet, without very hard training.

AVOIDING TOO MUCH AEROBICS

During my competition career most bodybuilders did some cardiovascular training, but nothing like the amount of aerobics today's champions include in their pre-contest programs. However, some experts feel that aerobic activity in general is counterproductive to maintaining maximum muscle mass and the best amount for bodybuilders to do is *none.* But modern competitors don't believe this, and engage in cardio to help them lose body fat, so the question is how they should go about it.

Too much aerobics also encourages the body to metabolize lean body mass—muscle—to create additional energy. The body can actually cannibalize muscle tissue, especially white fiber "power" muscle, in order to fuel aerobic exercise.

Finally, there is the problem of systemic fatigue. A lot of aerobic exercise makes you tired. When you are tired, you don't have the energy to do hard and heavy workouts. You may not feel fatigued, but the physical systems which allow for recuperation and replenishment of both muscle and energy can't keep up with demand when you do too much cardiovascular training.

We looked at the basics of aerobic training in the last chapter. But when it comes to cardio for pre-contest dieting, you have to be much more precise and careful to make it work for and not against you. For example, I recommend that cardio should be:

1. Done no more than 45 to 60 minutes a day (not necessarily in one session—aerobics in two or more sessions works great), 4 or 5 times a week. Plan your diet carefully so no more than this is necessary.

2. Not done immediately before working out with weights. That will just fatigue you and cut down on the intensity of your workouts.

3. Not done immediately after a workout. Your body is depleted at this point and needs to rest and recuperate, at least for a short time—although doing your aerobics at another time entirely is a good idea. In fact, I recommend taking in some glycogen replacement (carbo meal, supplement drink) after your gym workout and before you do any aerobic training.

DRUGS

One problem in modern society is that everybody today is too often looking for quick and easy answers. Corporations have to show profits very quickly or their stock falls, no matter the harm this might do to long-term success and growth. If a television show doesn't get good ratings in a few weeks, it is taken off the air. Movies are judged by opening-day box-office receipts. In a world that has no patience to wait for results, it's no wonder that athletes are encouraged to try to take shortcuts rather than dedicate themselves to a long-term regimen of discipline and hard work.

This is why any discussion of serious athletics nowadays has to include a mention of performance-enhancing drugs. The media is full of stories of athletes from a variety of sports failing drug tests. *Sports Illustrated* ran an article which stated that usage of various drugs including steroids, growth hormone, diuretics, and various illegal stimulants is rampant in sports across the board. Drug use, both in and out of sports, is unfortunately a continuing problem in modern society.

Certainly, as somebody who is in a position to influence young people, I want to make my position very clear. I am absolutely against the use of these dangerous and illegal substances. All the major sports federations and organizations have prohibited the use of these drugs and most have instituted testing to identify athletes who are using them. I applaud their efforts wholeheartedly. I only wish the physique magazines would take the same adamant position. Some profess to be against the use of drugs and then write articles explaining what they are and how to use them. This is shameful, in my opinion.

Using drugs is obviously dangerous to your health. We know there are tremendous side effects to many of these substances and in some cases—and I am not exaggerating—their use can even result in death. Drug use has also had a devastating effect on the image of sports, with the public no longer seeing athletes as representing the kind of ideals of discipline and dedication promulgated by the international Olympic movement. Drug use calls into question the kind of message we send to our kids, who so often view athletes as the ultimate role models and heroes. When I was growing up, I was taught that the harder you worked in sports, and the more you developed discipline and your skills, the better chance you had to become a champion. Do we want to instruct our youth today that the champion is the one with access to the best chemistry?

But if you follow the programs described in this book, you can build your physique without resorting to the use of anabolic drugs—depending on how much you are willing to dedicate yourself to this effort. To build a championship physique you have to have a championship desire, the will to train with intensity and consistency and not let anything else get in your way, and you have to take the trouble to learn how to train most effectively, not just try to lift heavy weights or throw the weights around with no attention to technique. It takes tremendous sustaining power to build your body to its genetic maximum, and that isn't easy. Without will, desire, and vision, nothing great is ever accomplished. But if you are willing to do what it takes, you will get the best results you are capable of, and that's all any of us can expect or hope for.

DRUGS AND SPORTS

As I mentioned above, there has been widespread drug use in a variety of sports for some considerable period of time. Steroids have been used in bodybuilding since before they were illegal and before bodybuilders knew any better, but competitors failing the drug testing at the IFBB World Amateur Championships in the recent past demonstrates that some competitors are willing to risk being suspended from the sport.

We are all familiar with Ben Johnson's disqualification from the 100-meter dash at the Olympics in South Korea. The many other suspensions and disqualifications of Olympic and other athletes have often been less publicized, but they have been numerous nonetheless.

There is limited drug testing in professional team sports. A number of pro football players, for example, have tested positive to anabolic drugs (as well as various "recreational" substances) and been suspended as a result. Three players in Canadian football were suspended in 1997 due to steroid use. Arena football, still in its infancy, has announced one of the strictest drug policies of any organized sport.

In cycling, the Tour de France made international news in 1998 when it expelled the Italian Festina team for drug use, after which the coach of the team was taken into police custody. In swimming, a Chinese swimmer was discovered to be carrying human growth hormone by Australian customs officials. Some months earlier two doctors were charged with supplying steroids to underage East German athletes, and the head coach of Germany's swim team subsequently was stripped of his accreditation. In fact, in February of 1998 the BBC reported that around 10,000 male and female Olympic athletes, some as young as ten years old, had been systematically doped in East Germany in the 1970s and 1980s. Russian swimmers have also been suspended in recent years for steroid use.

Winter sports are not immune to this epidemic. Two Australian bobsledders also failed a doping test and were barred from the Games. In 1997, the Romanian Athletics Federation banned a European cross-country skiing champion for two years for failing a doping test.

At the 1998 Goodwill Games, two athletes—a U.S. sprinter and shot-putter—were suspended from competition after testing positive for prohibited substances. Official figures show that 0.9 percent of NCAA student athletes tested were ruled ineligible, compared to 0.1 percent in 1995. Surprisingly, although drug failures were high in football (2.2 percent), they were actually higher in men's water polo (2.8 percent). A South African javelin thrower was suspended for testing positive for banned substances in 1995. In 1996, an English cricketer was suspended for use of prohibited substances.

In rugby, two players from the team that won the Australian grand final received suspensions after testing positive for steroids, and a third was found to have used another banned substance, ephedrine. There have also been accusations and/or suspensions due to failing drug tests in sports ranging from bicycle racing and mountain bike racing to boxing. In 1995, heavyweight Oliver McCall was suspended by the WBC for refusing to take a drug test after a bout.

I could go on with this list, but I think the point is made. The use of prohibited, performance-enhancing substances is epidemic and not restricted to bodybuilding. Some athletes are wrongly looking for shortcuts to immediate victory and turn to illegal drugs. This is a problem that all sports have to deal with, and how well we cope with the prevalance of drug use in sports will have a great impact on the future of organized athletics and the health and safety of the athletes involved.

SIDE EFFECTS OF STEROID USE

Anabolic/androgenic steroids have a wide-ranging effect on a number of important physical functions. The possible medical complications associated with steroid use include:

Altering of liver function. A great deal of stress is placed on the liver when you introduce steroids into your body. With prolonged use of high dosages, especially with oral steroids, there can be progressive cholestasis and jaundice, hemorrhaging, and even the possibility of liver cancer. There have been fatalities among patients subjected to this kind of therapy.

Altering of cardiovascular function. The use of steroids can lead to changes in the clotting mechanism of the blood, in the metabolism of glucose, and in triglyceride and cholesterol levels in the blood. The use of oral steroids can lead to hyperinsulinism, reduced glucose levels, and to a reduction in both oral and intravenous glucose tolerance, associated with a marked insulin resistance. Steroids raise the risk of cardiovascular disease.

Increases in nervous tension and/or blood pressure. This can lead to hypertension, as well as radical changes in the body's fluid/electrolyte balance.

Depression of normal testosterone production. The body has mechanisms that monitor the amount of testosterone in the system and alert the endocrine system to increase or decrease in hormone production. When steroids are taken, the body registers the increase as excessive and tends to lower or shut down the production of testosterone. This can lead to changes in libido and many other physiological and psychological functions related to hormone levels, such as increased aggression, depression, or an increase in body fat.

Androgenic effects. Some of these include increased facial and body hair; increased sebaceous secretions (oily skin), which can cause acne; priapism, thinning of scalp hair; prostate hypertrophy; and premature epiphyseal closure (stunted growth).

In addition to the above effects, the following short-term effects are seen frequently:

Muscle cramps and spasms
Increased or decreased feelings of aggression
Headaches
Nose bleeds
Dizziness, faintness, drowsiness, or lethargy
Skin rash or local reactions at the site of injection
Sore nipples
Gynecomastia (development of breastlike tissue in males)
Alteration of thyroid function

Gastrointestinal disorders with use of the oral steroids, including loss of appetite, burning of the tongue, gagging, vomiting, diarrhea, constipation, intestinal irritation, and a bloated feeling in 1 to 2 percent of those taking oral steroids

Absolute contraindications to steroid use are pregnancy or the presence of prostate or male breast cancer.

Steroids and Teenagers

Teenagers should never take anabolic steroids in an attempt to build up the size and strength of their muscle structure. During the teenage years, young males are already in their most anabolic state, with testosterone flooding the system. Adding synthetic anabolics at this point is totally unnecessary and dangerous.

Additionally, steroids tend to close over the ends of growing bones. A teenager who has not yet achieved his total growth may find that steroids prevent him from growing to his full height, and this effect is totally irreversible.

Steroids and Women

Women have only about one one-hundreth the amount of testosterone in their bodies as do men, so even relatively small doses of anabolic steroids can have significant androgenic (masculinizing) effects on their bodies. These include such things as development of facial hair, deepening of the voice, change in facial features, reduction of breast tissue, and enlargement of the clitoris. These changes are generally permanent and remain even after use of the drugs are discontinued.

Because of their sensitivity to male hormones, side effects from their use in women tend to be dose related, rather than time-related as occurs with men.

DIURETICS

Achieving maximum muscular definition onstage involves having a minimum of water stored under the skin. Subcutaneous water smoothes out the physique and generally costs a competitive bodybuilder points.

Proper preparation, diet, and "carbing-up" prior to a contest is effective in directing the fluid in the body into the muscles rather than having it stored under the skin. But for some time now some bodybuilders have resorted to the use of diuretics, substances designed to purge the body of excess water.

Unfortunately, diuretics can have a negative effect on the appearance of the physique. Loss of too much fluid flattens out the muscles and reduces muscularity. When the body becomes excessively dehydrated, it tends to hold water under the skin in response, which is the opposite of the desired effect. Also, excess loss of fluid upsets the electrolyte balance in the body, leading to muscular weakness and cramping.

While using diuretics can be debilitating, it can also be dangerous—even lethal. A couple of bodybuilders have had to be treated backstage at contests by medical personnel because of diuretic use. Some have had to be transported to the hospital. In one infamous case, a champion pro bodybuilder actually died as a result of using diuretics to try and get super hard and defined.

Because of the dangers of diuretic use, the IFBB and the NPC began testing for diuretics at the1996 Mr. Olympia contest and have continued to do so at all major competitions.

GROWTH HORMONE

Some bodybuilders have also experimented with human growth hormone (hGH), often in combination with insulin, in order to try to maximize muscle size and minimize body fat. Side effects of growth hormone can include such things as unregulated bone growth, particularly around the face, and severe damage to the heart. Increasingly during the 1990s bodybuilders began appearing onstage with thick waistlines and distended bellies, which most experts have attributed to the use of hGH.

In addition to other medical considerations, there has been an association observed between high levels of growth hormone and prostate cancer. If there is a definite causal link operating here, we are liable to see a number of bodybuilders suffering from cancer of the prostate in the not too distant future.

DRUG TESTING AND BODYBUILDING

The use of various anabolic drugs has long been contrary to the rules of the IFBB. And, as I said above, the IFBB began testing for diuretics in 1996, but not for steroids. As part of the recognition of bodybuilding by the International Olympic Committee, the IFBB has committed itself to following Olympic doping rules to the letter as of 1999, at least as far as amateur competition is concerned. This involves testing the top three finishers in each class, as well as other competitors randomly selected. The various national federations affiliated with the IFBB will be obligated to follow the same regulations regarding doping tests.

While the IFBB has not yet established testing for professional bodybuilders, a spokesperson for the federation has confirmed that they plan to implement the same drug testing procedures for the professionals that they have established for amateurs, perhaps as early as the year 2000.

Personally speaking, I have been trying for more than ten years to convince the IFBB to use the latest state-of-the-art technology to test both amateurs and professionals for any and all anabolic/androgenic agents. I believe that, in the end, drug testing will not only save bodybuilding, but lives as well. I simply hope that my dream and my wish will come true before it's too late for the sport I have loved for so many years. My goal is to reduce drug use so that once again the sport is about body-building, not body-destroying.

SUPER-SUPPLEMENTATION

Nowadays, there are a number of legal, cutting-edge supplements that were not known about or available when I was competing in the Mr. Olympia contest. Use of these supplements is controversial, and there is a lot of debate as to how effective some of them really are. Following is a list of some of the most important of these and what we know about them as of this writing.

Hormone Precursors

These are drugs that were illegal before the Dietary Supplement Health and Education Act of 1994 (DSHEA). They are considered precursor hormones since the body converts them to male (and in some cases female) hormones. Although considered dietary supplements under DSHEA, these products are banned by certain sports agencies such as the National Football League and the International Olympic Committee. Great caution should be exercised when considering these products since once converted to male hormones, they can have the same range of effects on your health and well-being as do anabolic steroids. To put it bluntly, if you are considering using any of these, I recommend getting medical advice before you begin.

Hormone precursors should not be taken by males in their teens or early twenties; females of any age; nor should they be taken by adults who suffer from high blood pressure or heart or prostate disease. Remember, there is very little scientific evidence available regarding the safety or efficacy of these products. The following products are considered hormone precursors: DHEA, pregnenolone, 4-androstenedione, 4-norandrostenedione, 4-androstenediol, 4-norandrostenediol, 5-androstenediol, 5-norandrostenediol.

DHEA (dehydroepiandrosterone), the first of the legal adrenal steroid hormones (the adrenal glands are attached on the top of each kidney) to be considered a dietary supplement. Although useful as an antioxidant, its use as a testosterone booster is dubious, as DHEA is not a direct precursor, and generates various estrogenic-like compounds for the small amount of testosterone finally converted.

Androstenedione. Another adrenal hormone that is a direct precursor to testosterone. Androstenedione is more effective in women than men, as they generate more liver enzymes necessary for the conversion to testosterone.

Norandrostenedione. This is the same hormone precursor that pregnant women secrete to make the naturally occurring anabolic nandrolone, which is similar to testosterone, but not as masculinizing.

4-AD (4-androstene-3beta, 17beta-diol). Another adrenal hormone that directly converts into testosterone, but using a more plentiful and efficient enzyme, so the conversion is better. However, in its unconverted state, 4-AD has more masculinizing effects than testosterone.

Nor-4-AD. This is a 4-AD variant that mimics the effects of norandrostenedione, but has a greater conversion to nandrolone because of its better enzymatic pathway. Of all the adrenal hormones, this is the most anabolic and least masculinizing.

Herbs

Though supplements of herbal and other natural origin are generally regarded as safer than pharmaceuticals, you should still exercise caution. Do not exceed recommended doses and do not use untested combinations of supplements.

Boswellia serrata. This extract contains boswellic acids, which have a proven anti-inflammatory effect and are effective in the treatment of joint injuries. (Another natural anti-inflammatory agent is capsaisin, extract from *Capsicum annum.*)

Citrus aurantium. Commonly called bitter orange, *Citrus aurantium* is used for regulation of the lipid level in the blood, lowering the blood sugar in diabetics, blood purification, functional disorders of liver and gallbladder, stimulation of the brain, heart, and circulation. It can help with sleep disorders, kidney and bladder diseases, and imbalances of mineral metabolism. It is also helpful in dealing with neuralgia and muscular pain, rheumatic discomforts, bruises, and phlebitis.

Echinacea purpurea. This root extract from the purple coneflower has a nonspecific immunostimulant action. It improves your ability to resist various infections, including viral infections. It can help you cope with cold and flu season.

Eleutherococcus senticosus (also called Siberian ginseng). Siberian ginseng has strong immunomodulating properties; it improves the ability of the organism to resist different forms of stress. It has profound positive effects on cardiovascular and nervous systems.

Ephedra sinica. Commonly known as Ma Huang. Ma Huang contains ephedrine, which has effects similar to those of epinephrine (adrenaline), but is milder and longer lasting. It acts mainly on the cardiovascular system, stimulates blood vessels, increases blood pressure, and relaxes smooth muscles to prevent spasms. Side effects reported with the use of ephedra products (even at low dosages) are insomnia, motor restlessness, irritability, headaches, nausea, vomiting, disturbances of urination, and tachycardia. In higher dosage, ephedra can cause a drastic increase in blood pressure, cardiac arrhythmia, and development of dependency. Because of the possibilities of the mentioned side effects, ephedra preparations should be used very cautiously and for short-term periods only.

Garcinia cambogea. Its fruits contain hydroxycitrate, which affects the carbohydrate and lipid metabolism. Hydroxycitrate inhibits fatty acid and cholesterol biosynthesis and has the ability to suppress appetite and reduce weight gain. It is used to prevent and control obesity.

Gotu kola (Centella asiatica). Gotu kola, also known as Indian Pennywort, improves mental activities: memory, attention, and concentration; actually it is one of the few herbs with proven memory improvement effect. It also strengthens the cardiovascular system and blood circulation.

Green tea (Camellia sinensis, unfermented). Green tea contains caffeine and antioxidants; it promotes digestion and kidney function, improves respiratory functions, increases blood circulation, and is a tonic for the cardiovascular system.

Guarana (Paullinia cupana). Guarana has stimulant properties due to a high content of caffeine and related alkaloids, such as theophylline and theobromine, and thus can help increase stamina for physical endurance. It also has an appetite-depressant action. Frequent use can result in caffeine dependency, lead to dysfunctions of the central nervous system, and cause blood sugar imbalances that may lead to hypoglycemia. Therefore, moderate use is highly recommended.

Kava (Piper methysticum). Kava is often used to relieve nervous anxiety, stress, and restlessness. Kava contains kava-pyrones, which may potentiate other substances acting on the central nervous system, such as alcohol, barbiturates, and psychopharmacological agents. Therefore, users of kava should never use these interfering substances. There are no known side effects for short-term, low-dosage users. However, extended usage may result in serious nervous disturbances; a temporary yellow discoloration of skin, hair, and nails; and, in rare cases, allergic skin reactions.

Kelp (Fucus vesiculosus, Laminaria). Kelp is brown marine algae and an excellent source of iodine. Used to improve thyroid function. It is also the source of alginic acid, which contains ingredients that help to rebuild joints and tendons.

Panax ginseng. This root extract is traditionally used as a tonic. It works as an adaptogen, or "biological response modifier." It improves the ability of the organism to adapt to changing external and internal disturbances, improves nonspecific resistance to stress.

St. John's wort (Hypericum perforatum). This herb is often used internally to calm psychological disturbances, depressive moods, anxiety and/or nervous unrest. External uses include treatment and post-therapy of acute and contused injuries, myalgia, and first-degree burns.

Tribulus terrestris. This is derived from an herbal plant commonly known as puncture vine. *Tribulus terrestris* extract is considered by many to be a safe alternative to anabolic steroids. It reportedly stimulates immune response and production of several hormones. Originally, it was used for treatment of infertility and other reproduction disorders.

Valeriana officinalis. Preparations from the Valerian root are used in cases of restlessness and sleeping disorders based on nervous conditions.

Yohimbine (Corynanthe yohimbe). Yohimbine is contained in the bark of the yohimbé tree. It is a stimulant that works by increasing your natural stimulant noradrenaline. It has both thermogenic and fat-mobilizing properties. Since it increases blood pressure, yohimbine should be used with caution.

Active Metabolites

Arginine. This amino acid and component of proteins is sometimes used as a supplement to increase growth hormone levels.

Branched-chain amino acids. (BCAAs) Leucine, isoleucine, and valine are essential amino acids that are used by bodybuilders as energy sources for muscles and as anabolic agents.

Caffeine. This stimulant, usually used in coffee, or as a supplement, improves athletic performance. Overdose causes many negative side effects; insomnia, disturbances of heart rhythm, and gastric disturbances are common. Large doses and stress may lead to dysfunctions of the central nervous system.

Chrysin. This is a plant flavone found to have anti-estrogen activity. It inhibits the transformation of androstenedione and testosterone to estrogen and therefore may alter steroid hormone metabolism.

CLA (conjugated linoleic acid). A modified version of the essential linoleic acid, CLA is known for its antioxidant and anti-carcinogenic properties. CLA appears to be hypocholesterolemic and anti-atherogenic. Additionally, it may work as an anti-catabolic by interfering with the production of certain prostaglandins and lymphokines. It is believed to reduce body fat and promote lean muscle. Thus, CLA is viewed as a potential regulator of body-fat accumulation and retention.

Creatine monohydrate. This amino acid derivative participates in energy production in cells. Over 90 percent of the creatine in the human body is localized in muscle, much of it in the form of creatine phosphate. Its concentration is especially high when a large amount of chemical energy is converted into mechanical energy. Creatine phosphate serves as a store of energy in muscle, and it provides a reserve of high energy phosphates that can be rapidly mobilized to maintain the intracellular level of ATP (the main source of energy for all cells). Creatine monohydrate is regarded as a necessity by most bodybuilders. Creatine monohydrate is the most cost-effective dietary supplement in terms of muscle size and strength gains. It can not only increase power and strength, but it may also support protein synthesis. Since creatine supplementation affects water and electrolyte balance, extra caution should be taken to consume a balanced diet with plenty of minerals (especially potassium) as well as to drink a lot of water. There is no preferred creatine supplement, but it is believed that creatine works best when it is consumed with simple carbohydrates. This can be accomplished by mixing powdered creatine with grape juice. Some bodybuilders use creatine mixed with water thirty minutes before meals or are using creatine supplements, which contain carbohydrates.

Essential fatty acids. This group includes linolenic acid, linoleic acid, arachidonic acid, fish-oil acids, and derivatives. These substances are essential for the optimum functioning of all cells in the body. Deficiencies of these compounds affect all of the body's functions. Supplies of essential fatty acid improve athletic performance, post-exercise recovery, immune resistance, and endurance. Specifically, among these compounds DHA and EPA are of importance for bodybuilders. Docosahexaenoic acid (DHA), present in fish oil and some marine algae, is essential for nervous system function, including visual functions. Eicosapentaenoic acid (EPA), also a component of fish oil, is needed for cardiovascular system function.

Forskolin (synonym Colforsin). This is another herbal compound (isolated from *Coelus forskohli*), an activator of the enzyme adenylate cyclase, which is an important part of intracellular regulatory system. In particular, it participates in adaptation of myocardial and skeletal muscle cells to intensive exercise.

Glucosamine and chondroitin. These are nutrients that improve joint health. Since bodybuilders place a great deal of stress on their joints, these products are becoming popular as a preventive measure for joint damage.

Glutamine. Glutamine is an amino acid important for optimal muscle protein metabolism. During stress glutamine is released from skeletal muscle to support immune functions. The flow of glutamine out of muscles makes protein synthesis more difficult and can lead to muscle protein degradation. Supplementing with glutamine between meals is believed to improve muscle growth and overall health. Glutamine is most effective when consumed on an empty stomach or mixed with a low-fat protein shake.

Glycerol. A trivalent alcohol (not intoxicating) that breaks down to glucose and ketones in the body. It is used for its fluid-drawing abilities. Glycerol in the blood pulls excess fluids from the skin, so it can be used in the place of a diuretic.

Guar gum. This dietary fiber is made out of the endosperm of guar plant seed and has been shown to reduce blood cholesterol and control food cravings.

HMB. Beta-hydroxy-beta-methylbutyrate is a metabolite of the amino acid leucine. Research suggests that this nutrient reduces protein breakdown associated with heavy exercise and stress. HMB can be most effective when you are dieting. HMB can be used by itself or along with a protein shake.

L-carnitine. Once considered a vitamin and today a semi-essential metabolite, carnitine is a normal component of muscle tissue, although it is sometimes produced in the body in inadequate supply. Its function is to transport fatty acids inside mitochondria (parts of cells) where oxidation of fatty acids takes place. For bodybuilders, supplementation with L-carnitine may be needed because of the intensity of their exercise. It is beneficial for cardiac muscle; it improves cardiac performance and thus improves exercise performance. Another important effect is the ability to improve the lipid profile of blood and tissues.

Lipoic acid. Once considered a lipid soluble vitamin, lipoic acid is now considered a semi-essential fatty acid. It participates in the synthesis of prostaglandins (thus related to inflammatory reactions and immunoregulation). Its importance for bodybuilders is in improving the energy yield from food, and its strong antioxidant activity.

Ornithine. This is used, like arginine, to increase growth hormone levels. Ornithine is not a component of proteins.

Pectin. This dietary fiber slows the transit of carbohydrates from the stomach, preventing the rapid increase of blood sugar. As a "soft" fiber it reduces the pressure of feces in the colon and stimulates the expulsion of the feces.

Polyphenols. The most common sources of polyphenols are pine bark extracts and grape seed extracts. Polyphenols are a group of chemical compounds that occur naturally in plants: vegetables, fruits, flowers, seeds, nuts, and barks. Botanists have described more than 8,000 different polyphenols. The most important and widely distributed group of polyphenols are flavonoids, which include flavones, flavonols, isoflavonoids, anthocyanidins, etc. Food polyphenols exhibit health benefits as powerful antioxidants. They support cardiovascular functions, improve general metabolism, and prevent oxidative damage to the body.

Pyruvic acid. Pyruvate improves the energy production from food and is itself a source of energy. Also helps increase endurance.

Vanadium (in form of vanadyl sulfate). Vanadium is a trace mineral required by humans in only very small amounts. It participates in a wide spectrum of biochemical pathways. Vanadium products have become popular as a result of research that proposed their use for certain forms of insulin resistance (Type-II diabetes). However, this research was never intended to promote vanadium as a dietary supplement. The safety of these supplements has yet to be determined, so caution is advised.

THE LAST WEEK

No matter how intelligently you diet, it's a fact that strict dieting depletes you. Your muscle cells shrink. You lose muscle glycogen. Your energy stores are empty. At the end of the diet you really don't look big, strong, energetic, and healthy, which is how you want to look standing onstage in front of the judges. The way to avoid this is simply to stop dieting a week before the contest and give your body a chance to rest, recuperate, and replenish itself.

However, most bodybuilders make the mistake of dieting right up until a few days before the show. They begin eating at the last minute, in particular trying to carb up by forcing as much carbohydrate into their bodies as possible. But it is often a case of "too little, too late." There just isn't enough time for the process of physical restoration to take place.

This is one reason so many bodybuilders find they look much *better* a day or two after the competition, especially after a good, fat-and-carb-loaded meal or two. Their poor, depleted physiques have finally been given enough raw materials to start repairing and replenishing themselves!

I never dieted this way. When I was preparing for a contest, I would finish my diet a full week (and sometimes more) before the show, and then gradually increase my food intake and give my muscles and glycogen stores plenty of time to recover from the depleting effect of the diet. It is possible to get this effect in less time, but not in a day or two. The body doesn't work that way. These processes need a certain time to take place. Therefore, I recommend that bodybuilders think about ending their contest diets no later than the Monday or Tuesday before a Saturday contest, and certainly no later than Wednesday morning (which is cutting it very close).

"DEPLETION"

A few years ago it became fashionable for bodybuilders to go on a zero-carb diet for a day or two before beginning the carbing-up process just before the contest. This generally does not produce beneficial results and can be very detrimental. Who is not already extremely depleted after 10 or 12 weeks of dieting? What good does it do to further deplete the body just at the point where you should be giving it the food it needs to replenish itself?

The idea behind pre-contest depletion is that the shock of this extra deprivation will cause the body to absorb more carbohydrates during the carbing-up process. But (1) this isn't necessary and (2) even if it worked there isn't nearly enough time for the body to absorb all the carbohydrates it can handle.

CARBING-UP

The process of carbing-up involves increasing your carbohydrate intake just prior to a contest in order to supply more glycogen to the muscles and make them bigger. Actually, it involves eating more fat as well. After all the time you've spent dieting, the body is hardly going to start making body fat immediately when it finally starts getting a more normal amount of food. This process is necessary because the size of your muscles is very much affected by the amount of glycogen (stored carbohydrate) and water they contain.

It takes at least three days for glycogen-starved muscles to sufficiently replenish themselves, but taking slightly longer makes the process occur more easily. And since the body can absorb only a certain amount at any one time, you need to ingest your carbohydrates in a number of small meals—which you have been doing anyway—rather than a few really big ones in order to give your body time to convert it into stored glycogen in the muscles. Therefore, for a Saturday contest, you must be sure your body has an adequate supply of carbohydrates starting no later than Wednesday. If you wait until the last minute, you will simply overload your body with carbohydrates that it can't metabolize. This will send your blood sugar rate skyrocketing, which will tend to cause your body to retain a lot of water—and yet your muscles will still be flat.

In the early days of my career, I didn't know much about this glycogen-storage mechanism, but, as I've indicated, I did find out by trial and error that I ended up looking much better if I got down to contest weight a week before the competition and then spent the next week training, posing, and eating. What I was doing was giving my body the carbohydrates it needed to create new glycogen supplies and the time to get it done. However, even though I have explained this many times in seminars and articles, I still see bodybuilders dieting right up until the day before a contest and then stuffing themselves full of carbs at the last minute.

LOSING WATER

Another problem that bodybuilders are always concerned about is holding water—meaning subcutaneous fluid, which makes you look smooth and puffy. Samir Bannout was known for being almost paranoid about his body holding too much water. One solution bodybuilders have chosen to deal with water is the use of diuretics. But this creates a number of difficulties. For one, muscles themselves are more than 75 percent water, so losing too much water simply causes your muscles to shrink. Another is that diuretics flush out electrolytes from the body—the minerals which are essential for optimum contraction of the muscles. After using diuretics, many bodybuilders feel weak as well as look small, and are subject to cramping, sometimes severe, and sometimes when they are onstage trying to pose.

In one case, a well-known pro bodybuilder overdosed on diuretics, was not diagnosed or treated properly when he began to experience difficulties, and eventually died. As a result, as of this writing the IFBB is conducting testing for diuretics at the major championships. This has evidently had an effect because very few competitors have failed these tests.

What do you do about the problem of holding water? To begin with, look at what the body does with water. The more you drink, the more your body flushes out the excess in your urine. In this process excess minerals like sodium are also removed from the body. If, on the other hand, you restrict your water intake the body immediately begins to retain as much fluid as possible to guard against dehydration. So the more you drink, the less water you retain; the less you drink the more water you retain.

Therefore, the proper approach is to continue drinking water right up to the night before a contest, rather than beginning to restrict fluids days before. That evening, try cutting your water intake in half—not restricting it totally. Your body will continue to flush water out at about the same rate for several hours, and by taking less in you will ensure that no excess fluid is held subcutaneously. The morning of the contest, continue to drink water at a moderate level to prevent dehydration. This should take care of any problem.

By the way, although many of the pros (who should know better) continue to dehydrate too much before a contest, it is almost comical to see them standing onstage in prejudging and being handed liter after liter of water to drink. What is the principle—it's not okay to drink water before a contest, but once you get onstage somehow the body will process it differently and not cause you to retain water? If these bodybuilders would drink enough before a contest, they wouldn't need all that water once they hit the stage.

There is more water in your body than any other element. Muscle is mostly water. Fat, on the other hand, contains very little water. When your body turns carbohydrates into stored glycogen, the glycogen binds with water—almost three times as much water as glycogen, which represents quite a bit of mass. So getting rid of water the wrong way will simply mean that you cause your muscles to shrink, which is not a good way to set about winning a championship.

Sodium

Some years ago bodybuilders began to develop a deep fear of ingesting sodium before a contest. It's true that excess sodium can lead to increased water retention (which is why individuals with blood pressure problems have to watch their sodium intake). But this doesn't happen if you are fully hydrated and the body is flushing excess sodium out of your system along with excess water. So the bodybuilders who were experiencing problems with sodium were evidently highly dehydrated in the first place, so the body was retaining water and excess sodium as well.

I've heard some very strange stories about sodium. Bodybuilders have been known to restrict their sodium for *weeks* before a contest. They try to avoid food that contains even normal and healthy amounts of sodium. They drink distilled water, which is not really good for you. And as a result they end up weak, more depleted than necessary, with chemical imbalances in the body and painful, debilitating cramps.

Instead, bodybuilders should simply avoid foods with excessive amounts of sodium (potato chips, fast-food chicken) and drink enough fluid to avoid dehydration. Nothing else is necessary when it comes to "controlling" sodium intake.

Summing Up on Water Retention

1. Avoid foods that contain excess amounts of sodium.

2. Limit your fluid intake only starting the night before a contest. You don't have to cut out fluids entirely; just cut down somewhat on the amount.

3. Keep your blood sugar level steady. Don't let yourself get too hungry, and don't stuff yourself right before a contest. Too much food raises your blood sugar level and makes your body retain water.

4. Let your body sweat normally through exercise. Training gets rid of a lot of water. So does aerobic exercise like running and bicycle riding. Posing is an especially good way to squeeze water out of the body and harden you up.

5. Don't develop an overreliance on the steam room or sauna to lose water. You can lose water this way, but you also tend to deplete the body if you overdo it. Remember, sweat is not just water; you also sweat away a lot of minerals. Taking a multi-mineral supplement after a hard workout should be part of your overall supplementation program.

6. Before you take any drug or chemical, check to see what its side effects are. Just before the 1980 Mr. Olympia I took a cortisone shot for a shoulder injury. I didn't know that this would cause me to retain excess water. I was so puffy that I had to pose all day before the contest and most of the night in order to get my body hard again.

7. Include as many outdoor workouts in your training as you can, to let the sun help bake any excess water out of your system. But make sure you drink lots of fluid to replace what you have sweated away.

TRAINING, POSING, AND DIET

In part because of the effects of their diet, some bodybuilders start to lighten up on the weight training in the weeks prior to the show, to do more isolation training and additional aerobics. But your muscles are big because of heavy weight training, and if you don't keep stimulating them with intense iron pumping they won't stay as big and as hard.

It's true that strict dieting tends to take away some of your strength and endurance, but I recommend that you continue doing at least *some* heavy sets for each body part right up to the Tuesday or Wednesday before a Saturday contest. A few heavy sets will keep your muscles solid and dense, and they won't make too many demands on your depleted glycogen stores.

In the last 2 or 3 days before the show, when you are no longer working with weights, the posing and flexing I recommended earlier will keep your muscles hard and defined. You can practice your posing routine, but you should also stand in front of the mirror and squeeze and flex all the major muscles as hard as you can. Again, this keeps the muscles hard and won't burn up the glycogen you are getting into your system with the carbing-up process.

THE NIGHT BEFORE

Bodybuilders often get very anxious the night before a contest. As the joke goes, they can get so desperate you could talk them into trying almost anything. (However, it is a myth that one Mr. Universe hopeful was talked into taking a whole bag of M&Ms the night before—in suppository form—hoping to bring out his "veins.")

As President George Bush often said, sometimes you have to "stay the course." You have a plan, so stick with it. Cut back your water as recommended, keep eating small meals, and do some posing—but don't panic and do something stupid. This is a time when mental focus is important. Do what you have to do, then lie back and relax. Watch some television. Take it easy. Remember that the other competitors are worried too—and that excessive stress tends to cause the body to hold subcutaneous fluid.

THE MORNING OF THE CONTEST

I once sat with a pro bodybuilder at breakfast on Saturday morning, a few hours before prejudging was scheduled to begin, and watched him eat a plate piled high with enough food for three people. He had about three huge helpings of home-fried potatoes, and he explained this was to help him carb up. He was also putting table salt all over his food.

Later, onstage, this bodybuilder looked smooth and bloated, and he was sweating rivers under the theater lights. I kept thinking to myself, This guy is a pro. How can he have gotten this far in bodybuilding knowing so little about diet?

The morning of the show, you should continue doing what you've already been doing. Eat. Not huge meals, but several small ones (depending on whether prejudging is in the morning or the afternoon). Drink water, although you should probably take in only about half of your "normal" amount. Don't put table salt on your food, but don't avoid foods that have normal sodium. And while you can practice your posing routine, a lot of flexing and posing will just fatigue you for the demands of prejudging coming up.

BETWEEN PREJUDGING AND THE NIGHT SHOW

In some contests, the evening finals is just a performance and in some the posing is judged, but either way you want to look as good as you can in front of the nighttime audience. So after prejudging you need to eat, not to stuff yourself, to continue to drink fluids, and to rest to give yourself a chance to recuperate after the demands of the prejudging posing.

Some bodybuilders tend to overindulge after prejudging, either because of the stress of competing or, in some cases, because they are disappointed by how they did, get discouraged, and start pigging out. I remember that Mike Mentzer, who had looked really fantastic during prejudging at the 1979 Mr. Olympia, showed up at the finals with an obviously bulging abdomen. There was speculation that he had been drinking a large number of Cokes during the intervening time and become bloated as a result. I don't know for sure if this was the cause, but Mike did *something* between the shows to make himself look worse. And it probably cost him the Mr. Olympia title. So the lesson here is to avoid doing *anything* odd or extreme after prejudging that would interfere with your appearance in the evening finals.

AFTER THE CONTEST

Whoever coined the phrase "pig out" might have been talking about the way some bodybuilders react once the contest is over and they feel they are no longer bound by the restrictions of diet. In some cases the "feeding frenzy" can be so extreme that even bodybuilders who *didn't* compete get caught up in it, experience a kind of "contact high," and start shoveling down food as if *they* were the ones who had been on an extreme diet for 12 weeks.

This kind of behavior is understandable, but sometimes it is not advisable. Sure, after so much dieting a good meal not only won't hurt you, but it's probably good for you as well. Your body can absorb the extra calories without much trouble—as long as you keep it within reason. But you should keep in mind that the next few days are an ideal time for you to shoot physique photos, so smoothing out your body by undisciplined eating can be a problem. Joe Weider always told bodybuilders, "Your work isn't over when the contest ends. Doing well in competition gives you the opportunity to shoot for the physique magazines, and that means you need to try and stay in shape for up to another week."

Not everybody has opportunities to shoot for *Muscle & Fitness, Flex, Iron Man,* or *Muscle Mag International,* but if you do you should take advantage of them. If not, you can certainly find *somebody* to do some physique pictures—maybe outdoors in a park or by a pool—which will at least give you a good record of what you looked like at that particular contest. But there is another reason for not totally overindulging in the food department—you've spent so long getting your body to look so terrific, why not maintain your eating discipline and enjoy it for a while? Not only that, the more you control your body weight off-season, the easier your next contest diet is going to be.

CHAPTER 4

Injuries and How to Treat Them

To become successful at bodybuilding, you must constantly try to push beyond your physical limits. But there is always a chance that you will exceed the ability of your physical structure to endure the strain. This can result in injury.

Some injuries are so slight and so common that we barely take notice of them. Others are more serious and require the attention of a physician. Progress for a bodybuilder is dependent on good physical health, and an injury can lead to a serious setback. Therefore, it is important to understand the types of injuries that might occur, how to prevent them, how to work around them, and what can be done to treat and rehabilitate them.

The body is a highly complex physical and biochemical mechanism which is subject to a variety of injuries, and each individual is more susceptible to certain types of injury. Injuries usually occur at the weakest place along a given structure: in the muscle, at the muscle/tendon juncture; along a tendon, at the tendon/bone attachment; in a ligament, at a joint; and so on. Sometimes injuries occur over a period of time because of overuse, sometimes because of an acute episode, such as mishandling a very heavy weight.

In dealing with the subject of injuries, it is important to be technically and medically accurate. The medical concepts and vocabulary may be dif-

---

The authors would like to give special thanks to orthopedic surgeon Barry L. Burton, M.D., of Los Angeles and Inglewood, California, for his invaluable contributions to this chapter on training injuries and their treatment.

ficult for the layman to absorb, but it is important that the dedicated bodybuilder have access to the information he needs to help prevent, treat, and avoid recurrence of physical injuries. Therefore, I have divided this section into two basic parts:

Technical information—a clinical examination of how the muscle/tendon and the joint/ligament structures of the body can incur injury, and what can be done to prevent and rehabilitate the various kinds of strains and sprains that can accompany intense physical training.

Practical information—a specific look, body part by body part, at those injuries which are most likely to affect the competition bodybuilder and how to deal with them.

Technical Information

MUSCLE AND TENDON

Tendons connect skeletal (voluntary) muscle to bone. Tendinous connective tissue is found at both ends of a muscle (tendons of origin and tendons of insertion).

Injuries to the muscle or tendon can occur in several ways. One way is by direct trauma, such as a blow from a blunt or sharp object, causing a contusion (bruise) or a laceration (cut).

Another way is from strain caused by overworking these structures or by a single violent episode, such as a sudden stretching force applied to a muscle that is in the act of vigorous contraction when the force applied is stronger than the structure's ability to withstand tearing. The tear may be complete or partial and can occur at the link between muscles and tendons, in the tendon, or where the tendon attaches to bone.

Sometimes a small piece of bone is pulled off and left attached to the end of the tendon. This is known as an avulsion fracture. In a sense, the muscle or tendon is overpowered by the amount of resistance it is working against, and the area of the least resistance is the site of injury. The degree of injury, whether mild or severe, depends on the force of the contraction and the amount of resistance. A few fibers may be torn or the entire structure may be disrupted.

In most cases the strain is mild—simply an overstretching of the muscles, with no appreciable tearing. This would result in pain and discomfort with movement, and a subsequent muscle spasm. In more severe injuries with actual tearing of some fibers, symptoms are increased. Pain and discomfort are more severe and there is swelling and limitation of movement.

Initial Treatment

Initial treatment for all these injuries is rest; the injured area must be protected against further injury. Working through or working out the injury can make it only worse.

For a mild strain, rest and avoid the activity that caused the injury. This may be the only treatment necessary until the extremity has recovered.

In a more severe injury to the leg, for example, crutches may be required for complete or partial limitation of weight on the injured extremity, or bed rest may be required for elevation of the leg, compression (pressure) dressing, splinting, and application of ice packs. If the injury occurs in a non-weight-bearing extremity the same logical thinking should follow.

In very severe muscle and tendon injuries, with complete rupture of any of the components, the integrity of these components must be restored and surgical repair may be required. Even in these severe cases, the first-aid principles are the same as just described: rest (to promote healing), elevation (to aid blood flow out of the injured area), ice packs (to cause vasoconstriction—a decrease in the diameter of the blood vessels—and reduce hemorrhaging), compression (again, to reduce hemorrhaging and swelling), and immobilization (to prevent further injury).

Spasms and Cramps

Muscle spasm, a sudden, often violent contraction of muscle, is another sign of strain. It is a protective reflex that, in a sense, is guarding that area against further motion until there has been time for recovery. The spasm may last for an extended period of time, causing a great deal of pain, or it can be of shorter duration, such as the muscle cramping that is the result of overuse and fatigue. Rest and protection against further injury may be all that is required.

Tendinitis

Overuse may result in tenosynovitis, an inflammatory condition of the synovium which lines a tendon sheath and surrounds the tendon. One of the most common examples is bicepital tenosynovitis, which involves the tendon of the long head of the biceps brachii, in the bicepital groove of the shoulder. The early symptom is shoulder pain, which may be present only with motion as the tendon passes back and forth in its sheath, or may be constant and occur even at rest.

In the early stages, treatment is the same as for muscle strain: rest, moist heat, and protection against further injury. In the very acute stage, injection of corticosteroid may also be required. In advanced stages, the complications are serious and surgery may be required.

Pain

Pain when you're training is a warning sign that an area has been injured. By letting the pain be your guide, you can practice preventive medicine. First avoid the activity that caused the pain and allow the area involved to recover. After an adequate period of rest you can gradually resume the activity.

Once you have regained full range of motion of the injured extremity and there is no associated pain, you have healed enough to increase the resistance to that movement on a gradual, progressive basis.

If you begin to feel pain, you have gone too far. Healing takes place by degrees over a period of time, and pain is an indicator of how far along you are. To progress too much too soon and not stay within the boundaries described—freedom from pain—risks reinjury, more severe injury, and chronic injury.

Bodybuilders often become frustrated with prolonged or even short recuperation periods because of the resultant loss of conditioning, the setbacks, the "shrinking" (muscular atrophy and loss of muscle volume), and the mental and emotional anguish of not being able to train. However, the ability to deal competently with injury and to have the discipline to allow healing to take place is essential to a successful bodybuilding career. To do otherwise could further delay or completely prevent you from achieving your goals.

Therapy

If there is no bleeding or swelling, moist heat should be applied in some form of hot pack rather than a heat lamp, which just tends to warm the skin. A steam bath, Jacuzzi, and even nice hot bath are all good therapy. There is no evidence that soaking in Epsom salts has any positive benefits, and the various commercial preparations advertised as soothing muscle soreness only stimulate the surface of the skin and have no real therapeutic value.

In cases where muscle strain has been severe enough to cause actual rupture of fibers, with the associated bleeding and swelling of tissues, heat should not be used, since it would promote vasodilation (an increase in the diameter of the blood vessels), which would increase blood supply to the part involved and induce swelling. Here, ice packs should be used to promote vasoconstriction, reducing the flow of blood to the area. Compression, elevation, and immobilization are all recommended treatments in the event of swelling.

Bleeding into tissues can be localized, as in a bruise or contusion, collected in a local pool (hematoma), or extravasate and, with seepage, discolor a large part of an extremity distant from the site of injury (ecchymosis).

The common black-and-blue mark is a local hemorrhage into the skin and subcutaneous tissue from rupture of minor vessels (capillaries), probably the result of a direct blow. Most bodybuilders just take such common bumps and bruises for granted. However, ice packs and compression can be used to reduce the swelling.

Gravity can work for as well as against you. Elevating the swollen extremity allows gravity to escalate the return of blood to the heart through the venous system and helps to reduce swelling. Think of it as having water run downhill rather than having to pump it uphill. Compression in the form of a pressure dressing is also useful in limiting the amount of bleeding into the tissues of an injured extremity.

Also, be aware that self-treatment of minor muscle pulls is fine, but for more serious injuries you should seek medical treatment. A severe injury left untreated can get worse and cause you an extended setback. However, not every doctor is experienced in sports medicine or in dealing with the particular needs and abilities of athletes. In the event you need medical help, seek out the services of a doctor or, more specifically, an orthopedist qualified to help you with your particular problem.

Injury Prevention

"An ounce of prevention is worth a pound of cure" should be the rule of every bodybuilder. There is a fine line between overuse and chronic strain due to heavy workouts. Intense workouts are bound to lead to occasional residual muscular soreness or soreness of the muscle/tendon complex. This kind of overuse is not exactly an injury, and most bodybuilders take it as a sign that they have trained hard enough. However, if you are so sore that you can hardly move and the intensity of your subsequent workouts is diminished, you have probably gone too far.

Muscles that are tight, tired, and sore are more vulnerable to injury. If you insist on working out even under these conditions, there is a good chance that you will pull or tear some part of the muscle/tendon complex. The best preventive under these circumstances is gradual stretching, warm-ups, or, when the condition is severe, light workouts. Stretching involves the entire muscle/tendon complex, lengthening it so that the chance of an exercise movement's suddenly stretching these structures past their limits and causing damage is reduced. Warming up pumps blood and oxygen to the area and literally raises the temperature of the muscles involved, allowing them to contract with greater force.

The best way to avoid training injuries is by taking care to stretch and warm up before working out and by observing proper technique when training with heavy weights. Remember, the stronger you are, the more strain you are able to put on your muscles and tendons, but often the muscles gain strength at a faster rate than the tendons, thus creating an imbalance that can cause problems. You must allow yourself to progress at a reasonable rate, and not attempt to train too intensely or with too much weight without proper preparation.

JOINTS AND LIGAMENTS

Movement occurs at a joint where two bones come together. The articulating parts of the joint, the parts that come in contact with each other, are composed of hyaline cartilage, a very smooth, gristle-like substance. It allows for the smooth gliding or motion of one part of the joint on the other.

Chondromalacia is a condition involving the softening or fraying of his smooth joint surface. This is often the first step in a long chain of events leading to degenerative arthritis—the degeneration of the bone and cartilage of a joint—which is a very painful and chronically disabling condition. Degenerative joint disease may also be initiated by chondral (cartilage) and osteochondral (bone and cartilage) fractures.

The joint capsule, a thick, fibrous envelope enclosing the joint, is intimately associated with the ligaments. Ligaments are tough, fibrous bands which connect two bones. They help to stabilize the joint and prevent abnormal joint motion, while allowing motion to proceed in the normal functional direction.

The capsule and ligaments are the passive stabilizers of the joint, as opposed to the muscle/tendon group, which has an active stabilizing effect. In addition to its motor function, the muscle/tendon group on one side of a joint can actively stabilize the joint when it combines with the muscle/tendon group on the other side to prevent motion. You can think of this as something like two tug-of-war teams so equal in strength that no matter how hard they try, they stay right where they are, as if glued to the ground.

Injuries to the Capsule and Ligaments

Injuries can involve the capsule and ligaments as well as the osteocartilaginous (bone and cartilage) structures of the joint. Injuries to a ligament can occur from a direct blow by a blunt object, resulting in a contusion (bruise), or by a sharp object, resulting in a laceration (cut).

Ligamentous injury can also occur from overstress, resulting in damage to the substance of the ligament or to the site of its attachment. Injury to a ligament in this manner is commonly called a sprain. It is a stretch injury to a passive, restraining structure. A strain, on the other hand, occurs in the active structure, the muscle/tendon complex.

Often a violent external force causes the joint to move in an abnormal direction, stressing the ligament or ligaments beyond their ability to withstand tearing. The area of least resistance becomes the site of injury.

A ligament stretched too far will tear. The tear may be partial or complete. It can occur anywhere within the ligament or at the site of bony attachment, in which case a small piece of bone may be pulled off and left attached to the end of the ligament. An avulsion fracture of bone occurs, and treatment is often the same as for a severe sprain.

Whether the injury is mild or severe depends upon the amount of force applied and the inherent strength of the structures involved. Only a few ligament fibers may be torn, or the ligament may be partially or completely disrupted. Usually, if you experience little pain and few symptoms, the damage is minor; if pain, swelling, and discomfort are more noticeable, the injury is more severe.

Treatment

In cases of mild sprain, where only a few fibers of a ligament have been torn, there may be little hemorrhage (bleeding) and swelling and only slight loss of joint function. Here treatment depends on the degree of pain and swelling, and many of the same general principles discussed in the treatment of strains apply.

Treatment may include one or more of the following: rest and limitation of the appropriate activities, elevation of the injured extremity, compression (pressure) dressing, application of ice packs, and splinting. Certainly, you should avoid any training movements that cause any discomfort to the injured area. This is another case where trying to work through an injury simply makes it worse.

In a more severe sprain (partial ligament tear), there is more extensive tearing of the ligament fibers, more bleeding and swelling, more pain with motion, and more loss of joint function. Here the joint definitely should be protected to permit proper healing.

For example, suppose you have sustained a moderately severe ankle sprain in which there is significant bleeding into the tissues, swelling (edema) of the ankle and foot, throbbing pain when the foot is "dependent" (below heart level, so gravity is working against you), pain with motion and with weight bearing, and limitation of joint motion. In this case, treatment by a doctor is recommended to be certain there are no broken bones and no clinically detectable instability (complete ligament rupture). The latter is often a difficult diagnosis, and stress X-rays—X-rays taken while the joint is subjected to a specific stress—may be warranted to rule out complete ligamentous rupture.

The ankle joint should be protected to allow for proper healing. Remember, we are talking about partial tears. In other words, part of the ligament still remains in continuity, and therefore there is no wide retraction, or gapping, of the torn portion. Rest the injured area. Since the ankle is part of a weight-bearing extremity, that means no walking on the leg involved.

Crutches can help you get around, but their use should be kept to a minimum since part of the treatment involves elevation of the injured area. A bulky compression (pressure) dressing helps to limit the amount of bleeding and swelling. Application of ice packs to the injured area for 48 hours or so is useful since this promotes vasoconstriction, which decreases blood flow to the area. Immobilization by splint or cast provides the most protection since it prevents motion, decreases pain, and allows for optimum healing. When the swelling goes down you can apply heat. Heat applied immediately, however, can increase swelling, so it is recommended that heat treatment and warm soaks be delayed until recovery is well under way and range-of-motion exercises are being undertaken. Also, keep in mind that these are first-aid treatments only, and in any severe injury further treatment should be carried out by an orthopedic surgeon.

When the torn ends of the ligaments are no longer in good apposition (touching or contacting) and a wide gap exists, reapposition is important. This allows ligament end to heal to ligament end, rather than having a large interposed scar formation, an elongated, lax ligament, chronic instability, and ultimately degenerative joint disease (degenerative arthritis).

Joint Dislocation

Joint dislocation and subluxation (partial dislocation) are conditions in which the opposing surfaces or articulating ends of the bones constituting a joint are no longer in normal relationship to one another. Instead, they are displaced, in the chronic condition because of ligamentous and capsular laxity (lack of tension) and in the acute condition because of tearing.

In severe sprain with ligament rupture, the joint subluxates—that is, moves in an abnormal direction. This may be only momentary and relocation may occur spontaneously. If the force is violent enough, the entire joint may be disrupted and there may be complete dislocation.

Practical Information

Every effort has been made to be certain that the preceding material is medically and clinically accurate. However, since a medical education is not one of the prerequisites to a career in competition bodybuilding, and since the anatomy of the various parts of the body can be extremely complex, the following section deals with how you can go about applying this knowledge to your own injuries and competitive goals.

THE CALVES

The calf muscles, especially when you include very heavy Calf Raises in your workout, are subject to overstress and tearing. With too much weight, the muscle/tendon structure can tear at its weakest point—either at the point of insertion or the point of origin of the tendon, at a tendon/muscle juncture, or within the body of the muscle itself.

One very good way to help prevent this kind of strain is by stretching the calves thoroughly before doing Calf Raises and in between each set and the next. In addition, be certain to use lighter weights to warm up in your first few sets before using heavier resistance.

Calf injury can also result from overuse. Constant overtraining may lead to progressively greater pain and soreness which will be alleviated only by resting the area.

This pain and soreness may be localized or may extend all the way down to the Achilles tendon. In cases of minor strain, stop training calves right away and rest the area until the pain goes away. If there is any swelling, the basic treatment is that described earlier, including ice, elevation, and compression. In more serious injuries, it is recommended that you consult a physician.

THE KNEE

In bodybuilding, injuries to the knee usually occur as the result of doing exercises like Heavy Squats, in which the knee is subjected to heavy stress while in a bent position. The injury may be to the ligamentous structures, to the patella (kneecap), to the internal structures of the knee, or to the muscles and tendon that attach to the knee.

The patella is covered by a layer of tendinous material that is part of the tendon structure by which the quadriceps attach below the knee and allow the leg to extend. Overstressing the knee may result in some degree of tearing anywhere within this area.

In knee sprains, some damage is done to the ligamentous structure of the knee joint itself. This most often happens when it is at its weakest, most acute angle, as in a full Squat. Also any twisting motion, especially in lifting a heavy weight, could result in knee sprain.

The meniscus is the cartilaginous structure inside the knee, and any twisting of the joint in an exercise like a full Squat could result in a tearing of the meniscus, which might then require orthopedic surgery.

To avoid overstressing the knee, it is important to engage in a full warm-up before putting it under any great stress. You should also be very much aware of the need to concentrate on proper exercise technique—for example, in a Squat, you should go down fully under control, no "bouncing" at the bottom, and stop when you are just below parallel. There is no need to go all the way down to the bottom, but half Squats will keep you from strengthening the lower range of motion of the movement.

Wrapping the knees or using an elastic brace will help support the area during very heavy lifts.

Treatment for knee injuries involves the normal prescription of rest, ice, etc., for mild strain or sprain and a physician's care for more serious injuries. Except for other conditions that are not directly injury-related, cortisone injections are not normally indicated for knee injuries.

For bodybuilders with knee problems who need to work around the injury prior to a contest, sometimes it is possible to do Squats on a Smith machine, positioning your feet well forward to isolate the quadriceps and take stress off the knee. If knee problems are too severe for this method, I recommend using Leg Extensions—partial range if necessary, or high-rep, low-weight movements—but not when excessive pain is present.

THE UPPER LEG

The vastus medialis is the long muscle of the quadriceps that attaches at the inside of the knee. When you fully extend the leg and lock it out, stress is placed specifically at this attachment and strain can occur. This may be felt in the area of the knee, but is actually an upper-leg problem.

Injuries to the back of the leg often occur because the leg biceps have not been stretched enough. Along with stretching exercises to lengthen the muscle/tendon structure, you can include Straight-Leg Deadlifts in your routine, which have a stretching effect.

THE GROIN

Groin pulls can occur when the area is overstretched during movements such as Lunges, and are among the most difficult problems to overcome because the area is in constant use, always being stretched whenever you are active. The basic treatment usually involves a lot of absolute rest to allow the injury to heal itself.

LOWER ABDOMEN

Males have a congenital weakness in the lower abdominal area. Sometimes when abdominal pressure is raised too high, a tear in the abdominal wall can occur. This can happen during any heavy lift in which you hold your breath.

A tear in the abdominal wall is called a hernia, and it may allow parts of the viscera to extrude through the opening. Serious cases may require surgery.

One way to help prevent hernias is to gradually expel your breath during heavy lifts. This keeps the abdominal pressure high enough to help stabilize you during the movement, but not so high that it can injure the abdominal wall.

It is also possible to strain the abdominal muscles and tendons, just as you can any other muscle/tendon structure, and treatment for strains in this area is the same as for any other muscle strain.

LOWER BACK

It is possible to strain the spinal erectors or other lower-back muscles by overstressing the area, especially when you do a movement that hyperextends the lower back, like Deadlifts, or bench exercises such as Bench Presses or Leg Raises, in which the lower back is lifted clear of the bench and hyperextended. A certain amount of curvature of the lower back is normal, but bending it too far under stress can cause problems.

When you strain the lower back, you may feel pain radiating down into the hips or upward toward the middle back. Sometimes these muscles will go into spasm to prevent further injury.

You can also have a sprain in the lower back when there is an injury to the ligaments in the area. It may often be difficult for you to tell whether you have incurred a strain or sprain, but in any event, the treatment is virtually identical.

Another lower-back injury you can incur is a ruptured disc. The discs are situated in between the vertebrae, and when they rupture, the pulpy material inside the disc can extrude and press upon adjacent nerves. You may feel pain anywhere along the back or even down into the legs, but it is this specific pressure which causes the pain, and treatment involves alleviating that pressure.

One specific type of nerve problem is sciatica. The sciatic nerve is the largest nerve of the body, extending from the back all the way down the leg, and when pressure is put on this nerve the pain is severe and disabling.

Lower-back problems can also be caused by abdominal work, such as Straight-Leg Sit-Ups and Straight-Leg Raises, which both put a lot of stress on the lower back. Bodybuilders who have been able to do heavy Deadlifts or Good Mornings with no difficulty have sometimes been surprised to find themselves incurring back injuries while doing abdominal training.

UPPER BACK

Any of the upper-back muscles may be subjected to strain—the trapezius, levator scapulae (the muscle that arises from the upper four cervical transverse processes and is inserted into the superior angle on the scapula), teres major (a muscle that arises on the dorsal surface of the scapula and is inserted into the humerus, it adducts the arm and rotates it inward), latissimus dorsi (a large, flat, triangular muscle covering the lumbar region and lower part of the chest; often called "widest of the back"), and so on. Neck strains, for example, are fairly common. Often it is difficult to say which particular muscle has been overstressed. You may feel pain when you turn your head, lift your shoulder, or bend your back. Frank Zane, for example, strained an upper-back muscle simply by tensing the area to stabilize himself while he did Preacher Bench Curls.

Often you will both contract these muscles and pull on them at the same time, which may lead to overstress and some degree of muscle tear. If the injury is not too severe, it is not necessary to know precisely which muscle is affected. Simply rest the area and use the appropriate treatment.

THE SHOULDERS

Shoulder injuries are relatively common among bodybuilders. Heavy Bench Presses, Dumbbell Presses, and Shoulder Presses put a particularly high degree of stress on the shoulders.

Heavy stress can cause partial tearing of the rotator cuff (the tendons of the rotator muscles for the internal and external rotators). It is also possible to overstress any part of the three heads of the deltoids or their tendons of insertion or origin.

Another possible problem in the shoulder area is subdeltoid bursitis. A bursa is a closed cavity in the connective tissue between a tendon and an adjacent bone that move relative to one another. It provides a lubricated surface so that the tendon can glide directly over the periosteum of a bone. Bursitis is an inflammatory condition in which a bursa is not able to do its job and movement in the area causes pain and difficulty. Frank Zane suffered from shoulder bursitis and was able to overcome it with extensive vitamin supplementation, treatment by a chiropractor, and light training until it healed.

Bicepital tendinitis is another common shoulder problem in which the biceps tendon working back and forth gets inflamed because of stress and friction. Medications such as cortisone are frequently indicated in treatment of shoulder injuries such as this.

In the event of shoulder injury, it is sometimes possible to do shoulder exercises at different angles—Bent-Over Laterals instead of Front Presses, for example, to work the rear head instead of the front—or to simply use the Flushing Method and hold heavy dumbbells out to the side, which will keep the deltoids toned and firm prior to a contest.

THE PECTORALS

Strains in the chest muscles most often occur where the pectorals insert into the humerus (upper arm). Since many bodybuilders like to bench as heavy as they can, this strain is often associated with overstress due to handling too heavy a weight, as well as failing to warm up properly.

Poor technique also accounts for a high proportion of chest injuries. Dropping the weight down too quickly while doing a Bench Press can cause a very heavy and sudden jerk to the whole pectoral structure. Similarly, dropping the weights too quickly when executing Dumbbell Flys can also overstress the pectorals, especially if the muscles are tight and have not been warmed up and stretched before the workout.

THE BICEPS

Biceps tears can occur at either end of the muscle—the origin, at the scapula, or the insertion into the radius—or anywhere along the muscle itself. Stress to the biceps can be acute or cumulative.

The biceps, relatively small muscles, are easily overtrained because they are involved in a wide range of exercises. Besides the exercises for biceps and back training, any kind of pulling motion—from Seated Rows to Wide-Grip Chins—works the biceps. This makes it difficult to work around a biceps injury, since the muscles are needed for so many different movements. Nonetheless, the only way a biceps strain will get better is through rest.

In cases of very severe injury, where there is a complete tear of the biceps, surgery would probably be necessary to repair the structure.

THE TRICEPS

Triceps are subject to the same sorts of strains as the biceps and other muscles. Another common triceps injury is olecranon bursitis (the olecranon is the point of the elbow). When you do extension movements like Triceps Extensions, you pull on the insertion of the triceps, at the elbow. This overlies a bursa, which can become irritated when a lot of stress is put on the area and produces a burning sensation.

Triceps can also be strained by overtraining or by sudden stress due to poor training technique. In cases of a complete tear of the triceps, surgery would be required to repair the structure.

THE ELBOWS

The elbows are subjected to constant stress whenever you do pressing movements. In addition to the acute problems that can result from overstressing the joint by using heavy weights or sloppy technique, a certain amount of cumulative damage occurs over months and years of heavy training, sometimes resulting in degenerative arthritis.

This kind of degenerative problem can occur in other joints such as the shoulder or knees and is difficult to detect in the early stages since it can come on too slowly to be immediately noticeable. Gradually increasing degrees of pain can be one symptom; an increasing limitation of range of motion is another. Either of these indicates some damage to the internal structure of the elbow which, if left untreated, may eventually become irreversible. In case of sudden strain of the elbow area, the same principles of treatment apply: rest, ice, elevation, and compression.

To stabilize the elbow joint for very heavy lifts, you can wrap the area or use an elastic brace.

THE FOREARMS

Since in most exercises you rely on your wrists and forearms to help you grip the weight, you are frequently both contracting and stretching these muscles at the same time. This can often lead to muscle or tendon strain.

Pulling or curl motions with your palms turned forward, such as Chins, Power Cleans, or Reverse Curls, put the forearms in a position of leverage disadvantage in which they are weaker and can be more easily strained. Often the injury is to the origin of the forearm extensor muscles, near the elbow; this is also known as tennis elbow. However, this kind of movement can lead to muscle strain anywhere along the muscles at the top of the forearm.

Because of the frequency of forearm injuries from doing Reverse Curls, Dr. Franco Columbu recommends avoiding this movement and instead using only Reverse Wrist Curls to build the top of the forearms.

Forearm injuries can become chronic because you need to grip hard during so many different exercises. Therefore, it is difficult to rest the forearm muscles once they have been strained.

In addition to resting the forearms to treat strain, I have found that acupuncture can help to speed up healing.

TRAINING AROUND INJURIES

While it is absolutely necessary to rest an injured area in order for it to heal, bodybuilders training for competition cannot simply stop every time they experience a minor strain or sprain. They need to find a way to continue training, yet avoid making an injury worse.

There is no one clear-cut way of doing this. It takes experience to find which movements aggravate a condition and which do not. Training for the 1980 Olympia, I injured my shoulder shortly before the contest. I was unable to do conventional Shoulder Presses without experiencing pain. However, I found I could do Presses using a narrow grip with my palms facing, so I was able to continue training shoulders without making the injury worse. There is also the isometric-like Flushing Method with dumbbells I mentioned earlier.

One bodybuilder who had strained a forearm so he could not do Barbell Curls or Machine Curls found by trial and error that he could do Hammer Curls with dumbbells, with his forearms turned at a certain angle. This allowed him to train without pain while the injury was healing. You can sometimes work around a forearm or biceps injury by doing E-Z Bar Curls to change the position of your hands.

Triceps injuries make most kinds of Presses and Triceps Extensions difficult. One exercise that is often still possible despite triceps strain is Dumbbell Kickbacks because there is very little stress on the triceps until the very end of the movement.

Often, in the case of mild strain, you can still train the injured area if you take a lot of extra time to warm up and stretch before you work against any significant degree of resistance.

Sometimes it is possible to train around an injury, and sometimes it isn't. Certainly, in the event of a very serious injury it is probably impossible to continue your workouts as before.

Just remember, a contest is only a contest. A career is much more. And trying to train through an injury and making it worse can lead to permanent and disabling problems which will remain with you the rest of your life.

COLD-WEATHER TRAINING

Training in cold weather necessitates taking certain additional precautions to avoid injury. In cold temperatures it takes longer for the body to warm up, so you need to delegate more time to warm-up and stretching before your workout. Additionally, it is a good idea to dress warmly in the gym so that your muscles don't cool off between sets.

A Quick Summary

Most injuries in bodybuilding are strains, overstressing or overstretching muscles and/or tendons. Proper warm-up, pre-stretching, and proper lifting technique help to prevent strain. Once a strain occurs, you need to rest the area. Other aids to healing may include the use of ice to keep down swelling, elevation to promote venous return of blood, and compression. Later in the healing process, heat can be used, including ultrasound.

In cases of light or moderate strain, it is often unnecessary to pinpoint exactly where in a complex structure the strain has occurred. You can feel which general area is involved, you can tell which movements aggravate the damage, so you can avoid working that area.

Strain can occur in areas that you are not actually working but simply contracting for leverage.

Most joint injuries that occur in bodybuilders are a result of years of wear and tear on the body. These problems build up slowly. Younger bodybuilders train very hard and don't notice any problems, but in later years they can pay the price of this physical abuse. Younger bodybuilders have greater recuperative powers and can bounce back from injuries faster than older bodybuilders. As you grow older and continue to train, there are things you can't get away with, training methods that would not have resulted in injury in your youth but will once you are older and your body has suffered from years of strain. This may involve a change in training style which may work fine, since you probably have the size that young bodybuilders are still trying to achieve.

The old saying "an ounce of prevention is worth a pound of cure" isn't quite true when it comes to nutrition. Here, sometimes prevention and cure are almost the same thing. Here are five of the most common problems that bodybuilders face, and a few measures that may just help you keep these things from holding you back.

MUSCLE STIFFNESS, SORENESS, OR INJURY

Bodybuilders will do almost anything to quickly increase muscle mass. What too many bodybuilders forget is that the process of increasing muscle mass is the result of microdamage of the muscle fiber. So, the process can, if one tries to increase muscle mass too quickly, result in soreness, muscle injuries, or even re-injury if one tries to speed up post-injury muscle recovery. Nutritional supplements can help to both prevent and heal soreness and injury. Supplementation with proteins, protein hydrolyzates, biologically active peptides, and amino acids can contribute to muscle-building. Polyphenols can improve circulation to speed healing. See page 764 for sources of these nutritional supplements.

PAIN OR PROBLEMS WITH YOUR JOINTS

Joint injuries are very common in bodybuilders. Under the stress of exercise, your joints—shoulders, elbows, knees, ankles, etc.—cannot respond as quickly or in the same way as your muscles. They cannot quickly adapt to changes that occur in the surrounding tissue as you rapidly build strength and bulk. Several nutritional supplements have recently appeared on the market that are very effective in protecting connective tissue and that can accelerate joint recovery. These agents include glucosamine, acetyl-glucosamine, chondroitin, collagens, and essential fatty acids.

PUMPING UP YOUR DIET

Whether you're getting ready for competition or just starting a new, tougher training regimen, your body is suddenly having to adjust to an increased level of exercise. When you start to feel that your standard diet isn't enough to get you up and running, there are a number of nutritional supplements that can help your body adjust to your increased exercise level. What you're looking for is a tonic. Among the most widely used tonics are ephedra, Siberian ginseng (Eleutherococcus), yohimbine, EPA, and caffeine-containing herbs.

WHAT TO WATCH OUT FOR: DEHYDRATION

In the process of intense exercising, bodybuilders encounter the risk of severe dehydration. Any time you dramatically change your exercise regimen, your body's water management may have trouble adjusting. Drink often. Remember that rehydration can be more efficient with the help of specific nutritional supplements to restore the minerals that you have lost. Also, remember that you must drink enough water to flush out damaged tissue in order to build new tissue.

WHAT'S GOING ON WITH MY IMMUNE SYSTEM?

The immune system's primary food is glutamine. Intensive training puts a high level of stress on the body, and as soon as you begin exercising you begin to exhaust your body's supply of glutamine. One of the natural results of increasing the level of your exercise regimen is that you may find yourself becoming more susceptible to illness. Several natural substances (mainly of plant origin) will help your body resist infections or at least cope with them more efficiently. Needless to say, the first thing that you should supplement is glutamine. Among the substances and preparations that can help you are echinacea, ginseng, amino acid glutamine, vitamin C, and polyphenols.

THE FINAL TOUCH

The body is not the only thing that exercise stresses. The mind reacts just as dramatically as the body does to the stress of physical exertion. One of the most important—though not easily measured—qualities of an athlete is the right mental attitude toward both training and competition. There are several supplements that can help, including *Ginkgo biloba*, polyphenols, and phosphatidyl serine (an essential fatty acid DHA). These aid you in maintaining mental acuity.

I N D E X

PHOTO CREDITS

Al Bello/All Sport: 59, 61

Charles Atlas Ltd.: 10

John Balik: 35, 36, 77, 120, 166 top right, 251, 263, 268 right, 269, 270 left, 286 top left, bottom left, 320, 321 right, 375 top, 404 top, 430, 433, 434, 435, 443, 445, 446, 479, 492, 495, 498 bottom, 499, 500, 502, 503, 504, 505 bottom, 507, 510, 512 top, 520 middle and right, 526, 528, 529, 531, 532, 533, 536, 555 top, 575, 576 bottom, 578, 580, 581 bottom, 600 right, 604 left and bottom, 613 top, 614 right, 618 left, 627–631, 646, 648, 654, 686

J. Bester: 345

Raheo Blair: 164 right

Albert Busek: 28 bottom, 30 bottom, 78, 79, 80, 112, 231 bottom, 255 left, 290, 297, 319 top, 327, 332, 333, 342 top, 363 bottom, 376 bottom, 377, 379, 384 bottom, 390 left, 391 top right, 392 bottom, 407 top, 423 top left and right, 431 bottom, 432, 437 bottom, 450, 466, 488, 491, 501, 521, 523, 524 right, 525, 527 right, 530, 544, 591 bottom, 592 bottom, 596 left, 614 left, 641, 642, 652, 653, 655, 656 right top and bottom, 657, 666

© 1991 Carolco: 237 bottom right

Jimmy Caruso: 1, 18 bottom, 19 right, 20 left, 20 top right, 26, 31, 32 right, 33 left, 41, 118, 166 bottom right, 250, 255 right, 257 top, 261, 268 left, 299, 315, 323, 347, 362 top, 388 middle, 389, 391 bottom, 407 bottom, 410, 412 bottom, 483, 519, 524 left, 534 bottom, 538, 543 right, 576 top, 577, 596 right, 597 top, 600 left, 601 bottom right, 615, 623, 624 right, 638, 639, 640, 650, 658 right, 662

Anita Columbu: 346

Courtesy Franco Columbu: 593

Benno Dahman: 18 top, 27 left, 28 top, 95, 320, 356

Ralph DeHaan: 257 bottom right, 279, 283, 296, 336, 403, 419, 448, 449, 509

Magda De Velasco: 21 bottom

Bill Dobbins: 151, 152, 153, 154, 155, 156, 157, 158, 159, 160, 161, 266, 319 bottom, 331, 364, 365, 366, 367, 368, 417, 456, 468, 470, 471 472, 474, 475, 476, 477, 485, 486 right, 508, 545, 546, 547, 548, 549, 550, 558, 559, 560

Robert Gardner: 123, 126, 128, 129, 130, 131, 267 bottom, 275, 281, 289, 324, 328, 357, 358, 370, 372, 382, 405, 409, 426, 438, 439, 441 bottom, 442, 455, 460, 461, 462, 463, 464, 465, 469, 473, 478, 493, 511, 551, 553, 554, 555 bottom, 562, 610

Irv Gelb: 287, 341, 408 top, 467, 556 top left and right

George Greenwood: 21 top, 22, 23, 24, 25 bottom

Ed Hankey: 690

Kevin Horton: 316

Robert Kennedy: 16 right, 514

Tony Lanza: 110, 253

Lon: 16 left

Chris Lund: 37, 125, 145, 165 top left, 166 left, 167 top left, right, 184, 185, 186, 252, 256 left, 264, 273, 274, 280, 282, 291, 293, 295, 306 right, 314, 329, 330, 334, 335, 338, 348, 349 top, 351, 353, 362 bottom left and right, 385, 391 top left, 392 top, 393, 394, 395, 408 middle, bottom left, bottom right, 411, 414, 415, 416 left, 418, 425 bottom, 444, 452, 453, 459, 480, 481, 484, 486 left, 505 top and middle, 513, 534 top, 535, 542 right, 543 left, 579, 581 top, 594, 597 bottom, 598, 599, 601 top right, 602, 603, 604 top right, 605, 606, 609, 616, 617, 619 left, 622, 626 left and bottom right, 644, 645, 660, 670

Samantha Lund: 537, 542 right, 618 right, 619 right, 620, 621, 626 top right

Robert Nailon: 613 bottom

Michael Neveux: 254 right, 276, 277, 339, 419, 556 middle and bottom, 557, 573, 661 top

Nordlinger: 304 left, 350 left, 563, 692, 695, 696

Courtesy of Oak Productions: 239 top and bottom, 240, 570, 571

© 1984 Orion Pictures: 236 right

Robert Reiff: 241, 309, 337, 374, 378, 383, 457, 506

Stephen Renz: 574

Bob Ringham: 238 left

Courtesy Ronald Reagan Library: 238 right

© 1988 TriStar Pictures: 237 top

© 1985 20th Century Fox: 236 left

© 1987 20th Century Fox: 234 bottom

© 1976 United Artists: 234 top

© 1982 Universal City Studios: 235

© 1988 Universal City Studios: 237 bottom left

Russ Warner: 322, 658 left, 661 bottom

Joseph Weider archives: 4, 5, 6, 7, 8, 9, 11, 12, 13, 14, 15, 19 bottom left, 20 bottom right, 25 top right, 27 right, 33 right, 54, 111, 165 bottom left, right, 167 bottom left, 175, 247, 254 left, 256 right, 257 bottom left, 267 top, 298, 302 left, 304 right, 305, 306 left, 321 left, 349 bottom, 359, 386, 394, 412 top, 413, 422, 423, 425 top, 440, 454, 512 bottom, 520 left, 552, 591 top, 607, 608, 624 left, 637, 639, 675, 681

Douglas White: 109, 113, 259

Art Zeller: 29, 30 top, 32 left, 75, 76, 114, 115, 116, 117, 119, 121, 133, 143, 145, 227, 231 top, 232, 258, 270 right, 271, 272, 278, 284, 285, 286 right, 288, 294, 300, 301, 302 right, 303, 312, 325, 326, 340, 342 bottom, 343, 344, 350 right, 352, 361, 363 top, 369, 371, 373, 375 bottom, 376 top, 380, 384 top, 387, 388 top and bottom, 390 right, 404 bottom, 406, 423 bottom left, 429, 431 top, 436, 437 top, 441 top, 447, 451, 498 top, 527 left, 540, 542 left, 561, 588, 590, 592 top, 595, 601 left, 611, 612, 625, 643, 649, 656 left, 664

Drawings on page 100 by Lynn Marks and Ellen Cipriano; drawings on pages 252 and 385 by Stuart Weiss; all other drawings by Bruce Algra